Multidisciplinary Perspectives on International Student Experience in Canadian Higher Education

Vander Tavares
York University, Canada

A volume in the Advances in Higher Education
and Professional Development (AHEPD) Book
Series

Published in the United States of America by
IGI Global
Information Science Reference (an imprint of IGI Global)
701 E. Chocolate Avenue
Hershey PA, USA 17033
Tel: 717-533-8845
Fax: 717-533-8661
E-mail: cust@igi-global.com
Web site: http://www.igi-global.com

Library of Congress Cataloging-in-Publication Data

Names: Tavares, Vander, 1988- editor.
Title: Multidisciplinary perspectives on international student experience
  in Canadian higher education / Vander Tavares, editor.
Description: Hershey, PA : Information Science Reference, 2021. | Includes
  bibliographical references and index. | Summary: "This book explores the
  various factors, aspects, challenges, and successes that characterize
  the international student experience in Canadian higher education"--
  Provided by publisher.
Identifiers: LCCN 2020012989 (print) | LCCN 2020012990 (ebook) | ISBN
  9781799850304 (hardcover) | ISBN 9781799856894 (paperback) | ISBN
  9781799850311 (ebook)
Subjects: LCSH: Students, Foreign--Canada. | Graduate students,
  Foreign--Canada. | Academic achievement--Social aspects--Canada. |
  Education, Higher--Social aspects--Canada.
Classification: LCC LB2376.6.C3 M85 2021 (print) | LCC LB2376.6.C3
  (ebook) | DDC 370.1160971--dc23
LC record available at https://lccn.loc.gov/2020012989
LC ebook record available at https://lccn.loc.gov/2020012990

This book is published in the IGI Global book series Advances in Higher Education and Professional Development (AHEPD) (ISSN: 2327-6983; eISSN: 2327-6991)

British Cataloguing in Publication Data
A Cataloguing in Publication record for this book is available from the British Library.

For electronic access to this publication, please contact: eresources@igi-global.com.

Advances in Higher Education and Professional Development (AHEPD) Book Series

Jared Keengwe
University of North Dakota, USA

ISSN:2327-6983
EISSN:2327-6991

MISSION

As world economies continue to shift and change in response to global financial situations, job markets have begun to demand a more highly-skilled workforce. In many industries a college degree is the minimum requirement and further educational development is expected to advance. With these current trends in mind, the **Advances in Higher Education & Professional Development (AHEPD) Book Series** provides an outlet for researchers and academics to publish their research in these areas and to distribute these works to practitioners and other researchers.

AHEPD encompasses all research dealing with higher education pedagogy, development, and curriculum design, as well as all areas of professional development, regardless of focus.

COVERAGE

- Adult Education
- Assessment in Higher Education
- Career Training
- Coaching and Mentoring
- Continuing Professional Development
- Governance in Higher Education
- Higher Education Policy
- Pedagogy of Teaching Higher Education
- Vocational Education

IGI Global is currently accepting manuscripts for publication within this series. To submit a proposal for a volume in this series, please contact our Acquisition Editors at Acquisitions@igi-global.com or visit: http://www.igi-global.com/publish/.

Titles in this Series

For a list of additional titles in this series, please visit:
http://www.igi-global.com/book-series/advances-higher-education-professional-development/73681

People-Centered Approaches Toward the Internationalization of Higher Education
Gabrielle Malfatti (University of Missouri, USA)
Information Science Reference • © 2021 • 323pp • H/C (ISBN: 9781799837961) • US $195.00

Current and Prospective Applications of Virtual Reality in Higher Education
Dong Hwa Choi (Park University, USA) Amber Dailey-Hebert (Park University, USA) and Judi Simmons Estes
(Park University, USA)
Information Science Reference • © 2021 • 328pp • H/C (ISBN: 9781799849605) • US $185.00

Advancing Innovation and Sustainable Outcomes in International Graduate Education
Mohan Raj Gurubatham (HELP University, Malaysia) and Geoffrey Alan Williams (HELP University, Malaysia)
Information Science Reference • © 2021 • 325pp • H/C (ISBN: 9781799855149) • US $195.00

Using Narratives and Storytelling to Promote Cultural Diversity on College Campuses
T. Scott Bledsoe (Azusa Pacific University, USA) and Kimberly A. Setterlund (Azusa Pacific University, USA)
Information Science Reference • © 2021 • 260pp • H/C (ISBN: 9781799840695) • US $185.00

*Introducing Problem-Based Learning (PBL) for Creativity and Innovation in Chinese Universities Emerging
Research and Opportunities*
Chunfang Zhou (Aalborg University, Denmark)
Information Science Reference • © 2021 • 150pp • H/C (ISBN: 9781799835271) • US $145.00

Higher Education Response to Exponential Societal Shifts
Jerrid P. Freeman (Northeastern State University, USA) Cari L. Keller (Northeastern State University, USA) and
Renee L. Cambiano (Northeastern State University, USA)
Information Science Reference • © 2020 • 444pp • H/C (ISBN: 9781799824107) • US $195.00

Optimizing Higher Education Learning Through Activities and Assessments
Yukiko Inoue-Smith (University of Guam, Guam) and Troy McVey (University of Guam, Guam)
Information Science Reference • © 2020 • 406pp • H/C (ISBN: 9781799840367) • US $195.00

Integrating Social Justice Education in Teacher Preparation Programs
Courtney K. Clausen (Utah State University, USA) and Stephanie R. Logan (Springfield College, USA)
Information Science Reference • © 2020 • 340pp • H/C (ISBN: 9781799850984) • US $185.00

701 East Chocolate Avenue, Hershey, PA 17033, USA
Tel: 717-533-8845 x100 • Fax: 717-533-8661
E-Mail: cust@igi-global.com • www.igi-global.com

Sihui Wang, *University of Glasgow, UK*
Jing Xiaoli, *McGill University, Canada*
Cindy Xing, *Queen's University, Canada*
Wei Yang, *McGill University, Canada*
George Zhou, *University of Windsor, Canada*

Table of Contents

Preface xvii

Section 1
Socialisation and Identity-Related Experiences

Chapter 1
Understanding Intercultural Socialization and Identity Development of International Students
Through Duoethnography 1
    Glory Ovie, The King's University, Edmonton, Canada
    Lena Barrantes, University of Calgary, Canada

Chapter 2
Increasing Awareness: Cultural Food Experiences of International Students in Canada 21
    Daphne Lordly, Mount Saint Vincent University, Canada
    Jennifer Guy, Mount Saint Vincent University, Canada
    Yue Li, Mount Saint Vincent University, Canada

Chapter 3
Learning at Half Capacity: The Academic Acculturation Reality Experienced by Chinese
International Students 41
    Deyu (Cindy) Xing, Queen's University, Canada
    Benjamin Bolden, Queen's University, Canada

Section 2
Classroom-Based Experiences

Chapter 4
Connecting Best Practices for Teaching International Students With Student Satisfaction: A
Review of STEM and Non-STEM Student Perspectives 63
    Clayton Smith, University of Windsor, Canada
    George Zhou, University of Windsor, Canada
    Michael Potter, University of Windsor, Canada
    Deena Wang, University of Windsor, Canada
    Fabiana Menezes, University of Windsor, Canada
    Gagneet Kaur, University of Windsor, Canada

Chapter 5
Why Don't They Participate in Class? A Study of Chinese Students' Classroom Participation in
an International Master of Education Program 81
    George Zhou, University of Windsor, Canada
    Zongyong Yu, University of Windsor, Canada
    Glenn Rideout, University of Windsor, Canada
    Clayton Smith, University of Windsor, Canada

Chapter 6
Multilingual International Students From the Perspective of Faculty: Contributions, Challenges,
and Support 102
    Vander Tavares, York University, Canada

Chapter 7
Chinese Graduate Students at a Canadian University: Their Academic Challenges and Coping
Strategies 120
    Wei Yang, McGill University, Canada
    Xiaoli Jing, McGill University, Canada

Chapter 8
Chinese International Graduate Students' Perceptions of Classroom Assessment at a Canadian
University 137
    Yue Gu, University of Windsor, Canada

Section 3
Beyond the Classroom

Chapter 9
The Role of Two Extracurricular Programs in International Students' Informal Learning
Experiences in Atlantic Canada 156
    Junfang Fu, Mount Saint Vincent University, Canada

Chapter 10
Within Discipline and Within Culture Advanced Academic Writing for Asian International
Students 177
    Dawn Julie Andrews, Thompson Rivers University, Canada

Chapter 11
International Turkish Student Experience in Canadian Higher Education 200
    Aylin Çakıroğlu Çevik, TED University, Turkey

Section 4
Student Support and Development

Chapter 12
Teaching and Learning Professional Development for International Graduate Students: The Role
of Teaching and Learning Centres 221
    Lianne Fisher, Brock University, Canada

Chapter 13
Plagiarism and Information Literacy Workshops for International Students 240
    Guoying Liu, University of Windsor, Canada
    Zuochen Zhang, University of Windsor, Canada
    Clayton Smith, University of Windsor, Canada
    Shijing Xu, University of Windsor, Canada
    Karen Pillon, University of Windsor, Canada
    Haojun Guo, University of Windsor, Canada

Chapter 14
Effect of Provision and Utilization of Support Areas on International Students' Perceived
Academic Success: A Case Study of a Canadian Community College 265
    Taiwo O. Soetan, Red River College, Canada

Section 5
Student Satisfaction and Recruitment

Chapter 15
International Undergraduate Student Choice of Alberta for Post-Secondary Education 292
    Darren Howes, Medicine Hat College, Canada

Chapter 16
Beyond Recruitment: Career Navigation and Support of International Students in Canada 308
    Philipp N. Reichert, UBC Okanagan, Canada
    Rohene Bouajram, UBC Vancouver, Canada

Chapter 17
Internationalization Through NNES Student Recruitment: Anticipated Gains and Reported
Realities 328
    Anouchka Plumb, University of Windsor, Canada

Compilation of References 346

About the Contributors 394

Index 400

Detailed Table of Contents

Preface xvii

Section 1
Socialisation and Identity-Related Experiences

Chapter 1
Understanding Intercultural Socialization and Identity Development of International Students
Through Duoethnography 1
Glory Ovie, The King's University, Edmonton, Canada
Lena Barrantes, University of Calgary, Canada

This chapter looks at how two international PhD students (re)constructed and (re)negotiated their identities, and intercultural socialization through the sharing their personal stories and experiences. This chapter employed a duoethnography research methodology. Duoethnography is a collaborative research methodology in which two or more researchers engage in a dialogue on their disparate histories in a given phenomenon. The use of duoethnography allowed the researchers to revisit their lives as sites of research to determine how their different experiences and backgrounds informed the (re)construction and (re)negotiation of their identities in the face of multiple and competing identities and their subsequent participation in the new culture. Through this process, the researchers acted as the foil for the Other, challenging the Other to reflect in a deeper, more relational and authentic manner as they sought to achieve a balance between participating in a new way of life and maintaining their cultural and personal identities.

Chapter 2
Increasing Awareness: Cultural Food Experiences of International Students in Canada 21
Daphne Lordly, Mount Saint Vincent University, Canada
Jennifer Guy, Mount Saint Vincent University, Canada
Yue Li, Mount Saint Vincent University, Canada

The authors situate student food experience as a key source of tension for international students. Multicultural food learning activities (MFLAs) are positioned as spaces for cultural connection and knowledge exchange. Through a review of relevant literature, three themes emerge: 1) food, diet and culture, 2) acculturation and identity through social connections with food, and 3) the implications of lack of food on culture, identity, and well-being. Reflecting on the authors' personal applications of MFLAs within nutrition curricula and a student-led society supporting cultural integration, the implications of such a learning platform are illuminated. In response to emergent themes, the authors share observations and make recommendations for university-based programming and future research. The authors urge academic communities to consider the complexity and impact of student food experiences when contemplating the international student experience in Canada. Food learning and experience-based platforms are opportunities to support student culture and identity.

Chapter 3
Learning at Half Capacity: The Academic Acculturation Reality Experienced by Chinese
International Students 41
Deyu (Cindy) Xing, Queen's University, Canada
Benjamin Bolden, Queen's University, Canada

First, this chapter provides an overview of current research on international students' academic acculturation under the lens of self-determination theory in relation to international students' psychological needs of autonomy, competence, and relatedness. Next, the authors report on a recent study that explored academic acculturation experiences using musically enhanced narrative inquiry, a unique form of arts-based research that produces musical representations of the stories of six international student participants studying at a Canadian university. Lastly, the authors propose future directions for Canadian higher education stakeholders to become more supportive and inclusive of international students on Canadian university campuses.

Section 2
Classroom-Based Experiences

Chapter 4
Connecting Best Practices for Teaching International Students With Student Satisfaction: A
Review of STEM and Non-STEM Student Perspectives 63
Clayton Smith, University of Windsor, Canada
George Zhou, University of Windsor, Canada
Michael Potter, University of Windsor, Canada
Deena Wang, University of Windsor, Canada
Fabiana Menezes, University of Windsor, Canada
Gagneet Kaur, University of Windsor, Canada

This chapter explores promising teaching practices for teaching linguistically and culturally diverse international students by identifying the teaching practices that have high levels of international student satisfaction and student perceptions of learning for science, technology, engineering, mathematics (STEM) and non-STEM international students. Research was conducted by an international, student-learning community, with guidance from a faculty-led research team. Data was collected through a qualitative research design that included focus groups and individual interviews conducted at a mid-sized Canadian comprehensive university. A total of 28 students participated (14 STEM students and 14 non-STEM students). Researchers examined differences between STEM and non-STEM students on 22 promising teaching practices regarding student satisfaction and students' perceptions of learning. Recommendations for professional practice are discussed, along with potential areas for further research.

Chapter 5

Why Don't They Participate in Class? A Study of Chinese Students' Classroom Participation in
an International Master of Education Program...81

George Zhou, University of Windsor, Canada
Zongyong Yu, University of Windsor, Canada
Glenn Rideout, University of Windsor, Canada
Clayton Smith, University of Windsor, Canada

This study explores how Chinese international graduate students participate in Canadian classrooms,
what factors promote and inhibit their participation, and what approaches can help to improve their
participation. Eight student participants and two of their instructors were interviewed individually.
Data analysis revealed that all participants appreciated the significance of classroom participation for
their learning, but they were quieter than domestic students. Many factors were mentioned that possibly
influenced their participation including their English language ability, differing education context and
pedagogy between Canada and China, class environment, their personal work experience, part-time
job commitments, personal interest, and emotional state. It is critical for instructors to distinguish and
observe why their students participate less, then adjust their teaching practice in different situations to
improve the participation level.

Chapter 6

Multilingual International Students From the Perspective of Faculty: Contributions, Challenges,
and Support.. 102

Vander Tavares, York University, Canada

This chapter explores the experiences and perceptions of 14 faculty members toward multilingual
international students at River University—a large, research-focused university in Ontario. Data was
collected through an online survey and analysed thematically. Responses were categorised under
three broad categories with respect to faculty's (1) perceptions of multilingual international students'
contributions to River's academic community, (2) challenges surrounding faculty's interactions with
multilingual international students, and (3) strategies developed and implemented to support students'
academic success. Overall, findings were consistent with those in the current research literature, in
which language proficiency was identified by faculty as a major concern, and multilingual international
students were considered important for the enhancement of cultural and intellectual diversity, and for
the internationalisation of higher education.

Chapter 7

Chinese Graduate Students at a Canadian University: Their Academic Challenges and Coping
Strategies.. 120

Wei Yang, McGill University, Canada
Xiaoli Jing, McGill University, Canada

With the growing trend of globalization and internationalization of education, an increasing number of
Chinese students choose to pursue higher education in Canada. In order to explore Chinese international
students' academic challenges and coping strategies in Canadian universities, the authors conducted
semi-structured interviews with 16 students studying graduate programs in one Canadian university.
The findings reveal that Chinese graduate students encounter a number of academic challenges due to
their limited English language proficiency, and the different educational norms and practices between

China and Canada. By employing the theory of student agency as the theoretical framework, the study finds that Chinese graduate students possess the agency to cope with their academic challenges. The coping strategies can be grouped into two categories: the first category is to rely on students' personal improvement and the second category is to resort to external resources. The chapter concludes with implications for future research.

Chapter 8
Chinese International Graduate Students' Perceptions of Classroom Assessment at a Canadian
University 137
    Yue Gu, University of Windsor, Canada

The purpose of this chapter is to investigate Chinese international students' perceptions of classroom assessment in Canadian higher education. Data collection for the study took place in a Canadian university and was comprised of two parts: an online survey for the collection of quantitative data, and semi-structured interviews for the collection of qualitative data. Sixty-two participants (n=62) voluntarily finished the online questionnaire and ten interview participants took part in semi-structured interviews. The exploration into the participants illustrated that Chinese graduate students held positive perceptions of classroom assessment at the Canadian university where the study was conducted, in terms of congruence with planned learning, authenticity, student consultation, transparency, and diversity.

Section 3
Beyond the Classroom

Chapter 9
The Role of Two Extracurricular Programs in International Students' Informal Learning
Experiences in Atlantic Canada 156
    Junfang Fu, Mount Saint Vincent University, Canada

This chapter is composed with a strong empirical base on international students' experiences at Canadian higher education institutions. It focuses on international students' sociocultural adjustment, development in intercultural awareness and professional skills, and integration within the community. A qualitative methodology has been applied in the study of 10 international student participants from two extracurricular programs in Halifax, the city with the most higher education institutions in Atlantic Canada. The author holds a unique perspective on this subject for her triple identity as a former international student, program organizer, and practitioner in international education for over 10 years.

Chapter 10
Within Discipline and Within Culture Advanced Academic Writing for Asian International
Students 177
    Dawn Julie Andrews, Thompson Rivers University, Canada

The purpose of this chapter is to challenge the Western education system to better understand the needs of international students, particularly from Asian countries. Higher education has become a big business, and many schools have popped up to meet the demand. North America's traditional universities are now well and truly dependent upon international students to fund full programs, and universities have come to rely on international dollars. International students are looking to the West for high-quality education, but may arrive in the West unprepared to face the challenge of writing advanced academic essays.

Chapter 11

International Turkish Student Experience in Canadian Higher Education 200

Aylin Çakıroğlu Çevik, TED University, Turkey

This study explores and discusses the experience of students from Turkey in Canadian higher education. It is known that international student experience is a complex and multidimensional issue and is influenced by various fixed or unfixed factors that vary at individual and national levels. Drawing on Jones's classification of international student experience (i.e., academic, pastoral/living, social experience) and the factors affecting these types of experience (i.e., personal, familial, institutional, and national milieus), the qualitative research method, namely in-depth interview, was used to acquire detailed knowledge about the issue by using the purposive sampling technique. The findings of this study basically indicate that personal, institutional, and national dimensions have a strong effect on the experience of international Turkish students in Canadian higher education.

Section 4
Student Support and Development

Chapter 12

Teaching and Learning Professional Development for International Graduate Students: The Role of Teaching and Learning Centres 221

Lianne Fisher, Brock University, Canada

In this chapter, Bakhtin's metatheoretical framework of dialogism is offered as a frame in which to consider the work of Centres for Teaching and Learning (CTLs) on university campuses. Dialogism keeps front and centre the co-construction of student learning and teaching and the ways in which international graduate students' knowledges and experiences enhance and inform university teaching and learning. The chapter outlines CTL professional development activities that support the scholarship of international teaching assistants (ITAs). A discussion of the differences and tensions between learning a language and using language to learn is offered. CTLs are often seen as sites for instrumental and pragmatic instructional purposes, rather than the sites where ITAs are invited into the teaching and learning scholarly community; this later idea will be highlighted throughout.

Chapter 13

Plagiarism and Information Literacy Workshops for International Students 240

Guoying Liu, University of Windsor, Canada
Zuochen Zhang, University of Windsor, Canada
Clayton Smith, University of Windsor, Canada
Shijing Xu, University of Windsor, Canada
Karen Pillon, University of Windsor, Canada
Haojun Guo, University of Windsor, Canada

The population of international students has increased significantly at the University of Windsor in recent years, and the university takes a variety of actions to address several key issues of interest to international students, including academic integrity, English language development, and writing support. This chapter reports findings from a multi-year collaborative project that was designed to enhance international students' library and academic literacy, with a focus on the understanding of plagiarism and measures to prevent it. A number of workshops that involved students at different levels were delivered to students from the English language improvement, undergraduate, and graduate programs. Research data collected from these workshops indicate that students benefited from the workshops, although at different degrees because of various factors, such as academic discipline, English language proficiency, previous educational experience. Further research can be conducted to explore ways to optimize such programs to meet the needs of students, particularly international students.

Chapter 14

Effect of Provision and Utilization of Support Areas on International Students' Perceived Academic Success: A Case Study of a Canadian Community College 265
    Taiwo O. Soetan, Red River College, Canada

This study examined the effect the provision and utilization of different support areas had on the perceived academic success of international students at a large community college in Canada. The study considered the effect of the provision of support areas on one hand, and the utilization of these support areas on the other hand on the perceived academic success of international students. A quantitative study was conducted to measure the effect of the provision and utilization of support areas on international students' perceived academic success. A target sample size of 399 international students who were pursuing different academic programs at a large community college in Canada was recruited to participate in a hard copy, one-on-one survey in the winter semester of 2019. The Canadian government's strategy at both the federal and provincial/territorial levels of increasing international students' presence in Canada as a way of addressing the aging workforce and population challenge in Canada would be more successful with increased investments in these support areas.

Section 5
Student Satisfaction and Recruitment

Chapter 15

International Undergraduate Student Choice of Alberta for Post-Secondary Education 292
    Darren Howes, Medicine Hat College, Canada

In this chapter, the author provides an overview of the decision-making process that international students will go through when choosing a country, province, and ultimately, an institution for their international higher learning education. After conducting exploratory qualitative research from an Alberta perspective, it was determined that international students are influenced by (1) safety, (2) quality, (3) knowing someone locally, (4) jobs and strength of the economy, and (5) cost. Subsequently, the author will also consider the factors that would influence international students to enjoy or remain in a province after their studies. Having an understanding of the factors that influence international student choice can help the reader understand some of the marketing implications of recruiting international students to institutions and how international students end up studying in the Canadian post-secondary system.

Chapter 16

Beyond Recruitment: Career Navigation and Support of International Students in Canada 308
    Philipp N. Reichert, UBC Okanagan, Canada
    Rohene Bouajram, UBC Vancouver, Canada

In this chapter, the authors provide an overview of internationalization efforts and the impact of substantial immigration policy shifts to support, recruit, and retain international students in Canada. Consideration is given to how higher educational institutions, and other key stakeholders play a role in supporting career exploration as well as the factors that influence international students' ability to stay in Canada post-graduation. Future directions and research are explored to further highlight the importance of understanding the international student lifecycle in the Canadian context.

Chapter 17
Internationalization Through NNES Student Recruitment: Anticipated Gains and Reported
Realities..328
 Anouchka Plumb, University of Windsor, Canada

It can be difficult to decipher the extent to which Canadian university internationalization efforts have been corralled to actualize mostly through non-native English speaking (NNES) foreign student recruitment. Although international surveys often report that an overwhelming majority of foreign students endorse Canada as a study destination and are satisfied with their Canadian study experience, the voices of students who experience a different reality are often overlooked. This chapter begins with an overview of internationalization values. The author then reviews the ways in which neoliberal ideology reshapes higher education as a good and places NNES foreign students as consumers in competition. Next, the foreign student recruitment is aligned with the internationalization rationales of generating revenue and migrating skills to benefit Canada's national economy. The reported realities of NNES foreign students are shared, followed by questions to springboard dialogue on identifying and mitigating gaps for NNES foreign student university study on Canadian campuses.

Compilation of References 346

About the Contributors 394

Index...400

Preface

Most chapters in this collection begin by foregrounding the very trend which has given impetus to the consolidation of this volume. Over the last few years, record numbers of international students have contributed to diversifying and broadening the Canadian higher education landscape. Indeed, according to the Canadian Bureau for International Education, more than 498,000 international students studied in Canadian colleges and universities in 2019, a figure which indicates a 14.5% increase from 2018 (CBIE, 2020). With higher numbers come more opportunities, responsibilities, challenges, and needs—one of these being the need to improve and enhance education for international students as a distinct population, while recognising and celebrating the rich linguistic, cultural, and ethnic diversity within this growing group of students. This volume seeks to contribute to this goal by positioning the international student experience in Canada at the centre of its multidisciplinary exploration. Considering the prevailing discourse of deficit that has often accompanied international students (Friedenberg, 2009; Leask, 2009), the need to approach the international student experience in higher education from a more ethical and humanistic perspective remains. This work is intended to be part of that progress.

This volume brings together the experiences of international students at all levels of post-secondary studies in Canada. From the college or university lecture to the doctoral seminar, individual chapters reflect the multilingual voices of international students from both traditional and emerging national groups to the Canadian terrain, including Brazil, China, Costa Rica, India, Mexico, Nigeria, South Africa, Thailand, Turkey, and Vietnam. The accounts presented illustrate experiences characterised by challenge, resilience, agency, and success in all dimensions of human experience, some of which are more apparent than others: the academic, linguistic, social, cultural, psychological, and spiritual. At the same time, chapters also represent the experiences of practitioners in the field through contributions that advance best practices, reflections, and critiques of a practical, conceptual, or theoretical nature. In here, researchers, instructors, administrators, recruiters, librarians, educational and curriculum developers, and international students themselves come together to shape this volume as a collaborative site for dialogue.

Multidisciplinary Perspectives on International Student Experience in Canadian Higher Education is divided into five sections. The first section (Chapters 1-3), "Socialisation and Identity-Related Experiences," considers how the interaction of multiple factors may impact the experiences of identity development and enactment for international students in their host communities. The second section (4-8), "Classroom-Based Experiences," consists of five chapters that explore the international student experience primarily within the classroom, including but not limited to, student participation, learning styles and preferences, challenges and coping strategies. The third section (9-11), "Beyond the Classroom," focuses on socio-academic experiences which are connected to traditional learning, but that extend beyond the classroom setting. The fourth section (12-14), "Student Support and Development," examines which and how academic services, resources, and programs can enhance the international student experience. The fifth and final section (15-17), "Student Satisfaction and Recruitment," investigates, challenges, and proposes different approaches to the interaction between international student recruitment and Canadian higher education. The boundaries between these parts are not fixed, as several chapters address concerns in more than one area.

In Chapter 1, "Understanding Intercultural Socialization and Identity Development of International Students Through Duoethnography," Glory Ovie and Lena Barrantes draw on their own personal and professional experiences to explore the process of identity (re)development and intercultural socialisation of international doctoral students. Ovie and Barrantes engage in a critical and reflective dialogue through the research methodology of duo-ethnography, and revisit their lives as sites of research to determine how their different experiences and backgrounds informed the (re)construction and (re)negotiation of their identities in the face of multiple and competing identities; and their subsequent participation in the new culture. This exploration affords us the opportunity to understand in detail some of challenges and successes characterising the international doctoral student experiences of both authors. Additionally, this chapter illustrates some of the inextricable multidimensionality of the international student experience by bringing together insights and experiences in the academic, social, cultural, psychological, and religious-spiritual domains.

In Chapter 2, "Increasing Awareness: Cultural Food Experiences of International Students in Canada," Daphne Lordly, Jennifer Guy, and Yue Li discuss the role of multicultural food learning activities (MFLAs) for cultural connection and knowledge exchange in the international student experience in Canada. Departing from the understanding that experiences with food can be a key source of tension for international students, Lordly, Guy, and Li review the literature on food and the international student experience, and reflect on their own research and teaching to explore the following themes: first, food, diet and culture; second, acculturation and identity through social connections with food; and third, the implications of lack of food on culture, identity, and well-being. The focus of the chapter is on the authors' personal applications of MFLAs within nutrition curricula and a student-led society supporting cultural integration at a university in Halifax, and on the implications of these activities for instructors, local and international students. In closing, Lordly, Guy, and Li share observations and recommendations for university-based programming and future research as food learning and experience-based platforms are opportunities to support international student culture and identity.

In Chapter 3, "Learning at Half Capacity: The Academic Acculturation Reality Experienced by Chinese International Students," Cindy Xing and Benjamin Bolden employ musically-enhanced narrative inquiry to explore the psychological needs and acculturation experiences of Chinese students at a Canadian university. Since much research has indicated that the international student experience can be characterised by persistent challenge in the psychological domain, Xing and Bolden investigate this concern deeply and creatively by drawing first on the theoretical framework of Self-Determination Theory, which recognises that achieving personal well-being and a healthy state depends on the satisfaction of one's psychological needs for personal autonomy, competence, and relatedness in particular; and second on the arts as a methodological approach to researching and representing human experience. Through a combination of music and narrative, the authors illustrate the ways by which feelings of inferiority, isolation, and loneliness, often rooted in insufficient linguistic proficiency in English, can significantly impact the overall experience of international students studying in Canada. The authors conclude their chapter by presenting important recommendations for the host academic community aimed at improving and enhancing support for international students.

In Chapter 4, "Connecting Best Practices for Teaching International Students With Student Satisfaction: A Review of STEM and Non-STEM Student Perspectives," Clayton Smith, George Zhou, Michael Potter, Deena Wang, Fabiana Menezes, and Gagneet Kaur investigate which pedagogical practices lead to international student satisfaction with classroom-based learning. By exploring the experiences and perceptions of a linguistically and culturally diverse group of 28 students (14 in STEM and 14 in non-STEM) through a qualitative approach that included interviews and focus groups, Smith and colleagues identify high levels of satisfaction reported by international students toward the student-centred model of teaching and learning, in which the students report feeling invited to actively and interactively co-construct knowledge with their instructors and peers. Furthermore, Smith and colleagues examine the teaching practices the international students preferred and enjoyed the least, and conclude their comprehensive study with recommendations for professional practice as Canadian universities continue to see increasing enrollments of international students.

In Chapter 5, "Why Don't They Participate in Class? A Study of Chinese Students' Classroom Participation in an International Master of Education Program," George Zhou, Zongyong Yu, Glenn Rideout, and Clayton Smith explore the classroom participation of Chinese international students at a mid-sized university in Ontario. While research has often focused on the experiences of Chinese students at the undergraduate level, this chapter offers insight into Chinese students' classroom behaviour at the graduate level in the context of a Master of Education program. By exploring the experiences and perspectives of both the international students as well as their instructors, Zhou and colleagues identify several factors which influenced the students' level of participation in complex and interconnected ways. The factors identified were both individual and contextual in nature, including the students' English language ability, personal interest, work experience, emotional well-being, and differences between the Canadian and Chinese academic environments. In light of their findings, Zhou and colleagues provide specific suggestions for both students and instructors aimed at improving the classroom participation of Chinese international students at the graduate level.

In Chapter 6, "Multilingual International Students From the Perspective of Faculty: Contributions, Challenges, and Support," Vander Tavares adopts a survey-based case study approach to understand some of the faculty-international student experience at a large university in Ontario. This chapter focuses on three dimensions of this co-constructed experience: first, faculty's perspectives about the ways in which international students contribute to the target university; second, the kinds of challenges faculty experience in working with multilingual international students both inside and outside the classroom; and third, the support mechanisms faculty draw upon in order to contribute to international student success. Findings demonstrate that faculty consider international students' contributions to the target academic community important for the enhancement and visibility of the institution's multicultural and multilingual profile. Moreover, faculty identify academic English language skills and cultural differences as most challenging, and report modifying and implementing a number of teaching strategies, including simpler language and assessment, to support multilingual international students.

In Chapter 7, "Chinese Graduate Students at a Canadian University: Their Academic Challenges and Coping Strategies," Wei Yang and Xiaoli Jing investigate the Chinese international graduate student experience with a focus on the ways in which language proficiency and different educational norms can impact the students' achievement of success. Yang and Jing employ a theory of student agency as the theoretical foundation for the study and interview 16 Chinese students to understand what academic challenges the students have encountered and the coping mechanisms the students have developed and employed to help them progress through graduate studies. Some of the challenges Yang and Jing report are related to classroom participation, reading comprehension, writing skills, and a disconnect between course theory and the students' past work experiences, while their coping strategies include resorting to peers and friends for skill development and to self-led activities that help with personal growth and improvement. Yang and Jing conclude that the Chinese graduate students in the study possess not only the agentic orientation to address their academic challenges, but also the agentic possibility to impact their learning trajectories.

In Chapter 8, "Chinese International Graduate Students' Perceptions of Classroom Assessment at a Canadian University," Yue Gu shares the findings of her mixed-methods study which investigated how Chinese graduate international students perceived and experienced classroom assessment at a university in southern Ontario. Through a survey administered to 62 students and semi-structured interviews conducted with 10 students, Gu builds on previous research that considered student perceptions of classroom assessment based on five interrelated dimensions: congruence with planned learning, authenticity, student consultation, transparency, and diversity. Among many important findings, Gu highlights that the students in her study generally enjoyed the assessment methods employed by their instructors, and valued the experience of having assessments designed with some consideration given to the students' individual profiles and real life situations. This vein of research is critical to the success of Chinese international students as Western and Chinese pedagogies are traditionally very different in many respects. Gu finishes her chapter with recommendations for instructors and administrators as the multilingual international student population, especially the Chinese, continues to grow in Canada.

In Chapter 9, "The Role of Two Extracurricular Programs in International Students' Informal Learning Experiences in Atlantic Canada," Sophia (Junfang) Fu examines the informal socio-academic learning experiences of international students studying in Halifax, Nova Scotia. Fu works with 10 international undergraduate and graduate students from colleges and universities in Halifax to understand their linguistic, professional, and social needs, and how these may be met through participation in two extracurricular programs associated with Mount Saint Vincent University: the Interfaith Engagement Program (IEP) and the International Student Volunteer Program (ISVP). Through a focus-group as well as individual interviews with the students, Fu explores the students' motivations for studying in Nova Scotia, their challenges once in Halifax, and their experiences in the extracurricular programs. Considering the students' challenges with language, academics, networking, and relationship-building, Fu emphasises the important role informal learning through extracurricular activities can play in contributing to students' socio-academic adaptation and their development of linguistic, intercultural, and professional skills. Fu concludes her chapter by foregrounding the significance of extracurricular activities particularly for international students who wish to remain in Atlantic Canada post-graduation, but who may need further professional experience in order to gain employment in the region.

In Chapter 10, "Within Discipline and within Culture Advanced Academic Writing for Asian International Students," Dawn Andrews proposes recommendations in response to the concern of how and why Asian international graduate students struggle in advanced academic writing. Andrews begins by exploring how Canada's higher education system and the neoliberal model of higher education have impacted the internationalisation of pedagogy and curriculum. Within this critical exploration, Andrews highlights bachelor- versus master-level differences in curriculum and writing proficiency and then focuses on advanced writing core competencies at two interrelated levels: within the discipline and within the culture. By reviewing a number of empirical studies related to writing skills development in light of multilingual Asian international graduate students' experiences, Andrews identifies the core competencies which characterise advanced academic writing in North American universities and offers key strategies aimed at supporting Asian international graduate students' writing skills development that can contribute to student success in their academic programs and essentially also in the Canadian marketplace. These recommendations are important considering many international students increasingly report a desire to remain in Canada post-graduation but may possess insufficient academic preparation for professional success.

In Chapter 11, "International Turkish Student Experience in Canadian Higher Education," Aylin Çakıroğlu Çevik explores the academic, social, and cultural experiences of international students from Turkey at universities across Canada. Çevik draws on in-depth interviews to understand the experiences and perceptions of Turkish students at the undergraduate and graduate academic levels, foregrounding important differences between the two and their impact on the students' lived experiences. Some of Çevik's findings illustrate the ways in which finances, living arrangements, previous academic studies, employment, and course schedules result in distinct individual challenges for the students. Yet, Çevik also discusses how the Turkish students' positive experiences with and perceptions of Canada's higher education system and multicultural society play a significant role in their narratives of satisfaction and success as international students. In addition to contributing to our broader understanding of the international student experience in Canada, this chapter offers insight into Turkish international students in particular, a student population whose experiences remain underexplored in the Canadian scholarly literature.

In Chapter 12, "Teaching and Learning Professional Development for International Graduate Students: The Role of Teaching and Learning Centres," Lianne Fisher discusses the unique position of teaching and learning centres in supporting the academic and professional development of multilingual international graduate students who undertake teaching assistantships in their host universities. Fisher begins by proposing that the work of Centres for Teaching and Learning (CTLs) on university campuses may be seen through the lens of Bakhtin's dialogism, which considers knowledge, discourse, and meaning as co-constructed, dynamic, and context-specific. Departing from this theoretical understanding, Fisher outlines some of the professional development initiatives she has participated in and demonstrates the ways in which international graduate students can help enhance and inform university teaching and learning through the support of CTL-led workshops. Taking the form of a critical practitioner reflection, this chapter draws attention to the challenging experiences multilingual international students can encounter in their professional development when definitions of academic teaching and learning are unilateral and when the students' multiple knowledges, experiences, and skills are not viewed as resources and assets.

In Chapter 13, "Plagiarism and Information Literacy Workshops for International Students," Guoying Liu, Zuochen Zhang, Clayton Smith, Shijing Xu, Karen Pillon, and Haojun Guo present findings from a multi-year collaborative project at the University of Windsor which was designed to enhance international students' library and academic literacy, with a focus on the understanding of plagiarism and measures to prevent it. In their project, Liu and colleagues worked with multilingual undergraduate, graduate, as well as international students enrolled in the university's English language program through a series of workshops designed to introduce international students to the often complex conceptual and practical definitions of academic and library literacy, which includes citation, referencing, and paraphrasing skills, among others. Results from pre- and post-tests demonstrated that the workshops were helpful for students' multi-skill development, especially for their knowledge and skills related to how to locate scholarly information and where to start research through library resources. At the same time, Liu and colleagues stress that the development of academic and library literacy in international students needs to happen continuously throughout an international student's academic journey considering how foreign this academic expectation can be for some.

In Chapter 14, "Effect of Provision and Utilization of Support Areas on International Students' Perceived Academic Success: A Case Study of a Canadian Community College," Taiwo Soetan examines the impact of support programs on the perceived academic success of international students at a large community college in Canada. To do this, Taiwo conducts a quantitative study with 399 international students at the certificate, diploma, and post-graduate diploma academic levels. The support areas considered are conceptualised according to three dimensions of Bronfenbrenner's theory of human development: micro, meso, and macro. The findings from this study show that the support areas at the micro and macro levels were most strongly related to international students' perceived academic success at the community college. These two levels included areas such as family, faculty, and peer support; work permit, study permit, immigration, and health service supports, respectively. Based on this and other important findings, Taiwo proposes that the Canadian government's strategy to increase international students' presence in Canada as a way of addressing the aging workforce and population challenge could be more successful if more investments were made in these support areas.

In Chapter 15, "International Undergraduate Student Choice of Alberta for Post-Secondary Education," Darren Howes explores the decision-making process behind international students' choice to study abroad as well as some of the factors which can influence students' decision to study specifically in the province of Alberta. To do this, Howes works with international students and recruiting managers, through interviews and focus groups, at three higher education institutions in Alberta. The findings point to five areas which influenced the decisions of the international students participating in his research: safety, quality of education, knowing someone locally, jobs and strength of the economy, and lastly, the cost of living. Equally important, Howes examines the factors which can potentially impact international students' decision to remain in Alberta post-graduation. Building on the findings, this chapter offers insight for Canadian colleges and universities as they consider effective strategies to both attract and retain international students.

In Chapter 16, "Beyond Recruitment: Career Navigation and Support of International Students in Canada," Philipp Reichert and Rohene Bouajram draw on their research, professional, and personal experience to discuss internationalisation and international student recruitment in Canada. Reichert and Bouajram begin by situating the Canadian context within the global higher education landscape while foregrounding some of the key concerns characterising the experiences of international students, including students' needs and experiences entering the labour market in Canada. The focus of the chapter is on a critical discussion around international graduate student employability outcomes, career navigation, and the student-to-worker transition as a complex experience that deserves more attention within the scholarly community. Additionally, Reichert and Bouajram add to the growing discussion about the factors which can influence international students' choice to remain or leave Canada after gaining work experience. The authors conclude their chapter by stressing the importance of researching and understanding the professional experiences of international students in Canada in light of the many changes and challenges faced by institutions of higher education in the country and globally.

In Chapter 17, "Internationalization through NNES Student Recruitment: Anticipated Gains and Reported Realities," Anouchka Plumb analyses the multifaceted role played by recruitment of non-native English-speaking (NNES) foreign students within the current model of internationalisation of Canadian higher education. Although international student surveys often report that an overwhelming majority of foreign students endorse Canada as a study destination and are satisfied with their Canadian study experience, the voices of students who experience a different reality are often neglected. Plumb begins with an overview of internationalisation values and then reviews the ways in which neoliberal ideology can reshape higher education as a good while positioning NNES foreign students as consumers in competition. Plumb also critically explores how foreign student recruitment is aligned with the internationalisation rationales of generating revenue and migrating skills to benefit Canada's national economy. Based on the reported realities of NNES foreign students with whom she worked, Plumb concludes the chapter by identifying questions that can help springboard dialogue to uncover and mitigate gaps for NNES foreign student academic study on Canadian campuses.

This volume is of value to all those who wish to further understand, enhance, and support the experiences of international students in Canadian colleges and universities. Considering its scope and the diversity of topics, theories, and methodologies used, the information presented in *Multidisciplinary Perspectives on International Student Experience in Canadian Higher Education* will resonate with researchers and practitioners from many academic disciplines and institutional areas. Together, the chapters in this volume help depict the state-of-the-art of Canadian scholarship on international students and higher education. Additionally, what makes this work unique is its truly multidisciplinary nature wherein experiences beyond the traditional research areas of language and education arc addressed, thus reflecting a more holistic engagement with international students and their experiences in Canada. This volume becomes a timely contribution to Canadian scholarship as the academic community in the country is faced with much uncertainty in the midst of the global pandemic. Like this volume, these times challenge us to do better while keeping the student experience in the foreground.

As the Editor, I would like to take this opportunity to sincerely thank all chapter authors and peer reviewers for their incredible work and continuous support. Your hard work makes this volume a rigorous and creative contribution to the field. In particular, I would like to acknowledge the support of Aneta Hayes, Hannah Hou, Rosalind Latiner Raby, and Clayton Smith for their energetic support.

Vander Tavares
York University, Canada

REFERENCES

Canadian Bureau of International Education. (2020). *International students in Canada continue to grow in 2019*. Retrieved from https://cbie.ca/international-students-in-canada-continue-to-grow-in-2019/

Friedenberg, J. E. (2009). Treating international students' language as a resource rather than a deficit. In M. S. Andrade & N. W. Evans (Eds.), *International students: Strengthening a critical resource* (pp. 163–169). Rowman & Littlefield Education.

Leask, B. (2009). Using formal and informal curricula to improve interactions between home and international students. *Journal of Studies in International Education, 13*(2), 205–221. doi:10.1177/1028315308329786

Section 1

Socialisation and Identity–Related Experiences

Chapter 1
Understanding Intercultural Socialization and Identity Development of International Students Through Duoethnography

Glory Ovie
ⓘ https://orcid.org/0000-0001-8754-7778
The King's University, Edmonton, Canada

Lena Barrantes
ⓘ https://orcid.org/0000-0003-3242-226X
University of Calgary, Canada

ABSTRACT

This chapter looks at how two international PhD students (re)constructed and (re)negotiated their identities, and intercultural socialization through the sharing their personal stories and experiences. This chapter employed a duoethnography research methodology. Duoethnography is a collaborative research methodology in which two or more researchers engage in a dialogue on their disparate histories in a given phenomenon. The use of duoethnography allowed the researchers to revisit their lives as sites of research to determine how their different experiences and backgrounds informed the (re) construction and (re)negotiation of their identities in the face of multiple and competing identities and their subsequent participation in the new culture. Through this process, the researchers acted as the foil for the Other, challenging the Other to reflect in a deeper, more relational and authentic manner as they sought to achieve a balance between participating in a new way of life and maintaining their cultural and personal identities.

DOI: 10.4018/978-1-7998-5030-4.ch001

BACKGROUND

International students play major roles in the internationalization agenda of higher education institutions in developed nations. These students strengthen the connections between different countries, create opportunities for communication with people from all over the world and bring cultural richness. In addition, international students bring substantial revenues to host institutions and contribute significantly to their intellectual and cultural capital (Malcolm & Mendoza, 2014). Their worldview, diverse cultural perspectives and backgrounds add to the discourse on diversity and inclusion (Heyward, 2002). Furthermore, they enrich the social and cultural fabric of a university, strengthen international links, and diminish scholarly and cultural chauvinism (El-Khawas, 2003). However, these contributions and benefits international students bring come at a high cost. International students experience acculturative stress (Berry, 2006), adjustment problems and often have to establish new social networks after leaving their friends and family back home (Smith & Khawaja, 2011). They are thrust into new and complex intercultural contexts.

INTERCULTURAL SOCIALIZATION

Ștefan (2019) defined intercultural as a kinetic, dynamic dimension, which involves reciprocity, interdependence and the identification of some forms of dialogue. It is the recognition of values, ways of life, and symbolic representations that we develop (Ștefan, 2019). Socialization involves the voluntary actions of social integration that appear as a result of a person's relations with the environment and with self, in the presence of the "other" (Ștefan, 2019). The process of intercultural socialization is multidimensional as one preserves a certain part of one's cultural specificity, while at the same time being a part of some structures of the dominant or host society (Ștefan, 2019). International students struggle with intercultural socialization and developing new identities as they transition into host institutions. Their former identities may be modified, switched, removed, or even reproduced as they negotiate and make changes (Bartram, 2009; Malcolm & Mendoza, 2014). They deal with high levels of homesickness, acculturation, and peculiarities of the host culture including food and weather conditions (Yen & Stevens, 2004). They struggle with social-cultural behaviors such as: culture shock, discrimination, new social/cultural customs, loss of identity and mental health issues such as depression due to feelings of alienation (Malcolm & Mendoza, 2014).

Using duoethnography, this study explored the experiences of two international PhD students as they (re)constructed and (re)negotiated their identities, and intercultural socialization through the sharing of their personal stories and experiences, while studying in Canada. They examined, compared and reflected on their individual and the host country's cultures and how they adjusted (Sam, 2006). In their intercultural socialization journey, they learned to adapt, adjust and deal with discrimination, new social/cultural customs, loss of identity and mental health issues. And also to understand their values in comparison to the host country, create social supports, and become integrated to the new culture they now live in. They grew to respect and understand their host country's cultural specificity and see culture as multi-dimensional. For them, intercultural socialization meant developing a deep understanding and respect for all cultures, as they learned from one another and grew together (Spring Institute, 2020).

The dialogue in this study includes how the nature of intercultural socialization engagement influenced our identities, how we navigated and established participation and membership in different social spaces within and outside the university community, how we dealt with opportunities to confront and shape our identity beyond our understood cultural norms, and how we understood the meaning of our identities within the multiple/divided social worlds experienced. Through this process we acted as the foil for the Other, challenging the Other to reflect on their life in a deeper, more relational, and authentic manner (Norris & Sawyer, 2012). The learnings from this study can be useful to the international students' offices and faculty of graduate studies in creating policies that enhance the successful integration of international students into Canadian universities.

INTERCULTURAL IDENTITY

Intercultural identity, as understood by the integrative communication theory of cross-cultural adaptation, refers to the extensive and prolonged experiences of communication across cultural boundaries (Kim, 2017). These experiences revolve around a gradual psychological evolution from a largely monocultural identity to an intercultural way of relating to oneself and to others (Kim, 2017). The result of this psychological transformation is the individual's capacity to envision themselves engaged in globalized world where they creatively construct their path.

For our interpretation of intercultural identity, we use personal narratives as a source of evidence because they offer insights to capture our experiences (Burr, 1995). We embraced the poststructuralist ideas that knowledge, meaning and interpretations are constructed through social practices which are contextualized in the specific settings where they occur. We agree that cultural identity is socially constructed through discourse, either oral or visual representations, and through social practice (Burr, 1995). Intercultural identity is flexible to change, a process rather than a final product. In this way, we evoke Kim's (2008) idea of an open-ended intercultural identity; one that has an "adaptive and transformative self–other orientation" (p. 364). Our identity then is developed through constant and always changing processes of acculturation and deculturation.

To understand the transformation of our intercultural identity, we approached intercultural identity through the components of core, reinterpreted and transient as suggested by Kislev (2012). Core components are characterized by a lack of processing and adaptation which makes them more resistant to change. Reinterpreted components pertain to advanced processing and reinterpretation of elements from both cultures. In this case, they bridge the gap between the two cultures. Lastly, transient components result in the interchangeable values, norms and behaviors held by the individual's encounter with the new culture. These components are not internalized and can be discarded with relative ease (Kislev, 2012). International students in Canada construct their intercultural identity while engaged in an environment where distinct cultures coexist in society within the framework of a dominant majority culture and several minority cultures.

WHO WE ARE

We are from two different countries on two different continents. Lena is from Costa Rica and I, Glory, am from Nigeria. Both countries have different cultures with different value systems. Our drive and dream to acquire an international education from a first world country was the motivation to pursue our dream of a PhD. Together we experienced struggles between what we knew as truth from our past life histories and the new paradigms in our roles as immigrants (Ovie & Barrantes, 2019). Our words are witnesses of our stories that narrate the days when we left our homelands to start a life in Canada. Our dialogue often connects two worlds to find truth in experience (Ovie & Barrantes, 2019). We met in a seminar class, fourteen eager students from different parts of the world starting a new journey together, doing a PhD. Lena and I sat with trepidation on opposite ends of the classroom wondering what we had gotten ourselves into. We gradually became friends over time as we discussed the challenges we faced in adjusting to a new culture while creating a new path.

A DUOETHNOGRAPHY APPROACH

The conversational-narrative approach of duoethnography and its collaborative methodology allowed us, two researchers of different backgrounds and life histories, to provide multiple understandings of intercultural socialization and identity. We did this through narrative exposure and interrogation of our beliefs and experiences (Norris & Sawyer, 2012). One characteristic of duoethnography is to use ourselves, the researchers, as the site for inquiry into sociocultural socialization and inscription (Norris & Sawyer, 2012). We share our personal narratives as we invite our readers into a dialogue to recall and question their own stories.

Through an emic lens and full of vulnerability, we ventured to reconceptualize our perceptions of our home culture and the host culture. To contribute to the understanding of intercultural processes behind the common adaptive experiences of international students who are born and raised in their home country and have relocated to Canada. We explored our interpersonal experiences with and within systems and cultures (Norris, Sawyer, & Lund, 2011). In addition, we recognize the moral dilemma behind the fieldwork challenge of wanting to recognize ourselves as "honest ethnographers" (Madison, 2012). As we use our personal narratives as the source of evidence to understand our intercultural socialization process and intercultural identity renegotiation. We analyzed our experiences in relation to our identities as we interacted with the majority culture. We met weekly for one hour at the initial stage of writing for three months, then monthly for three months to review and make edits on the manuscripts. We both transcribed different sections of the dialogue and shared the transcripts with each other for further dialogue. We analyzed the data separately and met biweekly online to discuss and go over the themes. When the manuscript was ready, we met one more time to reread and review the final edits and followed up with questions via emails. In analyzing the themes, we reinterpreted components from both cultures as a basis for our integration while completing our studies.

In keeping with the tenets that outline the types of researcher dispositions, principles and foci, we focused on *currere*, dialogue and trust (Norris, Sawyer, & Lund, 2012) to chart our own duoethnographic course. Through *currere*, we explored ourselves as the curriculum through four steps: our regression to our pasts, our progression to our not-yet future, our analytical interpretations for the present, and our synthesis for the integration of the previous three. The polyvocal and dialogic tenet made our stories and disparate opinions and experiences explicit. Researcher trust is a central feature of a duoethnography because trust promotes duoethnographers' sharing, disclosing, and interrogating personal aspects of their histories (Sawyer, 2012). To share, disclose, and interrogate personal aspects of our histories, we created a safe place for storytelling (Norris, Sawyer, & Lund, 2012).

THE DIALOGUE

We divided our dialogue into two based on the driving topics for this inquiry: intercultural socialization and intercultural identity development. We used face-to-face dialogue to gather our narratives. This method was chosen since we live in the same city and our work revolved around our university campus. We met regularly to discuss our stories of how we established socialization by exploring our participation and membership in our regular social spaces and how we (re)constructed and (re)negotiated our identities. In the first section, we addressed socialization and in the second section we unpacked intercultural identity. We were careful to use the ethics of care's relational and situational core principles. We built a relationship that allowed authentic self-reflective collaboration where we worked together with honesty and trust (Ovie & Barrantes, 2019). We respected each other's complex identities and cultural understandings while also recognizing the limits. We acknowledged the complexity and subjectivity behind telling our stories from our own points of view by recognizing that there are different perspectives on these stories (Ovie & Barrantes, 2019).

CONVERSATION ONE: INTERCULTURAL SOCIALIZATION

The Nature of Our Intercultural Socialization Engagement within the University and the Community

Lena – After reflecting on this topic, I realized that for the last three and a half years, I have focused on my academic enrichment mostly. Hence, the nature of my socialization engagement has been in relation to my university life. In doing this, I limited my interactions outside the university, however, I must say that my on-campus life has been interculturally rich.

My whole life in Canada revolved around my PhD program. I even lived on campus! From the first day in my program, I attended all workshops and academic events available in the university. I found that the university had lots to offer. Even so, I tried to be involved outside campus by attending church, but I never got to have an active role. On campus, I took a community advisor (CA) role with the Resident Education Office. This role provided opportunities for institutional dialogue. My on-campus life reinforced my intercultural socialization as I was in contact with international and newcomer students and their families daily. During my time as a CA, I have learned more about other cultures than in my entire life. I grew up in a mono-cultural country where everyone looks the same and has similar beliefs. From my life on campus, I appreciate the opportunity to voluntarily socialize with people from different parts of the world with whom I share common appreciation for the host country and homesickness for our home countries. From learning from others and growing together, I have developed a deep understanding and respect for all cultures (Spring Institute, 2020). I also participated in different peer-mentoring programs, first as a mentee and then as a mentor. These experiences gave me a strong sense of worth through serving others. What about you Glory?

Glory – My process of intercultural socialization can be summarized as an understanding of the academic environment and creating social supports. A concern I faced was critiquing my research, my peers' and professors' research as well. This was jarring for me because I needed to be very critical of my research, my ideas, and to challenge the ideas of others. I found this challenging initially because I was yet to develop a voice for myself before I could critique someone else's work. I struggled with this until I talked with my research supervisor and my peers, and I discovered I was not the only one struggling with this. In their research, Evans and Stevenson (2010) discovered that international students in the UK faced the same dilemma. I felt I was not equipped. I had several meetings with my research supervisor and sought resources to develop this skill. Overtime, I have found my research voice and I have gotten better at critiquing.

Another form of intercultural socialization for me was creating social supports. I felt that it was important to form strong social supports for the success of my studies and for my wellbeing. Severiens and Wolff (2008) pointed out that those [students] who feel at home, feel connected with fellow students and teachers, who took part in extra-curricular activities, were more inclined to persist in their studies. It was important to me to develop a sense of community, of belonging and a strong social support, because I was single and living alone in a foreign country, my kids and family lived in different parts of the world. I was susceptible to the feelings of isolation, depression, and anxiety. I needed to feel at home and feel connected, without creating social integration and supports, it would have been more difficult to persist, and ultimately graduate (Severiens & Wolff, 2008).

I was proactive in creating social supports by choosing to live on the campus residence because I felt that living on campus would give me an opportunity to meet other students. López Turley and Wodtke (2010) explained that racial minorities could benefit from the campus living environment because of their tendency to be concerned about being academically integrated; their frequent interactions with faculty and their level of involvement in institutional activities (López Turley & Wodtke, 2010). I attended many social events on campus, from professional development events to meet-and-greets. I interacted with students, staff, and advisors; I volunteered and served on many occasions on different committees. I believe my experiences and integration on residence impacted me positively because I integrated quickly and effortlessly into my host country. Through these events and living on residence, I met other international students and formed strong bonds of friendships. Through living in my host country and the friendships I have formed, I have developed a deep understanding of the different rich cultural diversities and values we all have. My cultural perspectives, understanding and values have gone through a shift and my worldview has been broadened and richer.

Lena – That is interesting! I can see how our status, as single or married, has influenced our socialization processes. In my case, I think of the "why" question. Why was I so focused on my academic socialization? I think the main reason was my interest to prioritize my family's interest, complete my PhD and return home afterwards.

Glory – My socialization process was focused on succeeding in my academics and creating social connections. Being here alone intensified my feelings of isolation and depression, which triggered mental health issues for me.

Lena – When you talk about establishing social support what were you looking for?

Glory – I was looking for membership, belonging, and being a part of a community. These were important factors to my sense of who I was as it reduced my feelings of isolation and depression. As a PhD student, my meetings with my research supervisor were key to the success of my doctorate but they were not enough as social interactions. I believe we are created to be social beings and we thrive when we belong to a group and our identity is strengthened. Establishing strong social support and friendship was important because it reduced the stress and anxiety of doing a PhD, chat with others, connect socially and interact. Mason and Hickman (2019) and Samimy, Kim, Ah Lee, and Kasai (2011) noted that peer support and collaboration supported doctoral students' personal and professional development in facilitating their engagement with and participation in their academic and professional communities. In addition, forming social connections gave me the opportunity to share my research interests with fellow students because they were familiar with the doctoral education context.

Some Social, Cultural and Educational Conflicts Experienced

Lena – One conflict for me has been the different ways to interact and communicate at the institutional level. In my home country, face-to-face dialogue represent the most effective way to communicate ideas, schedule meetings and organize events. In contrast, here, most communication is through emails. This shift was uncomfortable in the beginning. I felt I was missing the supralinguistic elements of communication such as facial expressions, body language and intonation. With emails, I cannot confirm that my message is being received the way I intend it. Overtime I have learned to read emails carefully and to understand the power behind every single word. I also learned to read between the lines. It took time, but I have adapted to communicating through this means.

Glory – I can understand how hard it must have been for you to make the change from face-to-face dialogue to emails. It is never really the same when we communicate via emails.

My cultural issue was the food: I missed eating my cultural food. I learned to look for alternatives, however, where to get these alternatives was such a hassle for me. Eventually, a friend directed me to an African store; it has been great because it links me to my home country.

An educational conflict was learning to write a publishable academic paper, which is a requirement in a PhD program. This gave me many nights and days of anxiety, sleeplessness and stress; it was a big learning curve for me. I doubted my writing ability. I was not sure if I could make a positive contribution to academia. What will I write about? My experiences? Do I publish my master's thesis? What journals do I publish in? Where do I start? How do I go about this? I had many questions that led to self-doubt. Stoilescu and DoMcDougall (2010) explained that as novice researchers, PhD students lacked the experience or were not always trained for academic writing. Writing requires time, quality of reasoning, expertise, and energy (Stoilescu & DoMcDougall, 2010). I could not start writing academic articles from nothing. I needed to incorporate my previous experiences, expertise, ideas, questions, and big pictures into an article (Belcher, 2009; Boice, 1990). However, at the onset, I did not know this, and it was a daunting but good learning process for me. After reading Stoilescu and DoMcDougall's (2010) work, I realized that working as a research assistant might provide some opportunities to publish academic papers. In addition, my research supervisor provided many opportunities for me to review publications and serve as a reviewer. I now understand the process and I have published several papers and even worked as an editorial assistant.

Many international students dread the process of publishing. This might be due to a lack of understanding of the processes and the how to, eliminating this fear might be one way to make the process of acculturation easier for these students. I suggest that faculties prepare their students for publishing by creating workshops on the publishing processes, model what a good paper might look like and co-author with students. Doing these might provide some form of scaffolding and support for international students. Lena, did you experience educational conflict like I did?

Lena – An educational conflict I experienced was the idea that as a researcher, I was expected to include my positionality in my dissertation explicitly and write in the first person. Back home, doing research and publishing requires that you detach yourself from your research to maintain an outsider view to not contaminate your results. Different authors have suggested criteria and guidelines to determine objectivity in social research (Hernández, Fernández, & Baptista, 2010; López Morales, 1994; Sandín,

2000). I found a different perspective here, one that gives the researcher a voice and a commitment. I deeply reflected on my ontological, epistemological and methodological positionality and found appreciation for the messiness of qualitative research in my doctoral studies, as argued by Denzin and Lincoln (2011). I resonated with Denzin's (2011) position on ways of knowing, hence, qualitative researches, are partial, moral and political, and as such should not be confined to a narrow evidence-based understanding of social phenomena. Adjusting was hard, but now I value it and have developed a good sense of it. Indeed, my supervisor said in our last meeting, "I can really see you in your paper." For me, that was a significant compliment.

Mental Health or Diversity Issues, Cultural Shock and Resilient Strategies

Lena – I honestly do not remember any culture shock experience. As an English as a foreign language instructor in my country, I am familiar with the North American culture. Regarding mental health issues, right now, I am dealing with the Imposter Syndrome. It was during my first year here that I heard about it for the first time in my life. At that time, I never expected that it would happen to me. This experience is typically defined as feelings of fraudulence and some reported characteristics that relate to failure to internalize success, the tendency to be a perfectionist, the fear of failure and rejection of praise (Cheung, 2018). Unfortunately, it is a common collection of feelings for graduate students and women (Robinson-Walke, 2011; Szuchman, 2012). Self-doubt about my skills and knowledge is directly affecting my professional confidence. The more I read about educational research and my specialization, the more I self-doubt about my knowledge and skills. It is a paradox because it can get worse as I acquire more experience and knowledge. I have reached out for help within the university because I choose not to give up. I push myself to take risks on purpose. From where I come from, we are resilient. We fight, we do not sit back and cry in a corner, even if we want to. Therefore, my way to confront this phenomenon was to meet with a counsellor, which is a big deal because I would not have done this back in my home country. There is much stigma attached to mental health. However, because my host country is open to discussing mental health issues, I have been able to seek the help and support I needed.

Glory – I have had issues with my mental health and wellbeing as well. Just before my final oral defense, I was so overwhelmed with the whole PhD process… at this point… close to my final oral defense, I was exhausted, burnt-out, depressed, anxious, and stressed. I suffered an emotional and mental breakdown. I spoke to a close friend about my challenges and she suggested that I talk to a counsellor because my mental health and wellbeing were compromised. I booked a time to speak to a counsellor, doing this took a lot of courage because mental health issues or talking to a counsellor was not part of my culture. Talking to a counsellor conjured up feelings of embarrassment, discomfort, and shame (Dixon, 2019). In addition, I value my privacy and I view myself as a resilient person. However, I sought help, because I was under so much stress and pressure. I booked a time to speak to a counsellor. After a brief 20-minute consultation with an on-call counselor, and several questions asked about any suicidal tendencies, I was told that the soonest I could get an initial appointment for counselling was in three weeks… so close to my final exams. I was discouraged and left wondering if I had to be suicidal before I could begin counselling.

It took an enormous amount of courage and boldness to seek help and support. In my background, it is unusual to talk to counsellors, because of the fear of stigma. I found myself trapped on an extensive waitlist, forced to endure a long period without help (Champlin, 2019). I know my situation is not peculiar, other students are also experiencing long wait times as well. I understand that the university may be short staffed, but a wait time of three weeks is long. A student might be over the edge at that point. A 2015 study by the National Academy of Sciences found that increased waiting times for healthcare services of any kind were linked to worsened health outcomes and patient satisfaction. They suggested reducing wait times for mental health services is particularly critical, because the longer a patient waits, the greater the likelihood that the patient will miss the appointment. Aaron Krasnow, associate vice president and director of counseling services at Arizona State University, explained, "when you cross the threshold from identifying that you have a concern and then seeking help for it, you need, in that moment, an immediately responsive environment." "And when you don't get that, you will not be validated for the choice that you made for help-seeking (as cited by Champlin, 2019, p. 22). This remark captured my thoughts succinctly. I do hope that the university can add more resources and counsellors, increase training programs for faculty, students and staff, and add internet-based screenings and online mental health treatment.

Lena – That must have been pretty tough for you. Unfortunately, I had the same experience. The first time I reached out to a counsellor, I was in the middle of a personal crisis. As I said before, back home we are not used to reaching out for help. Which means that when we reach out for help, it is serious. I remember I requested to talk to someone that day. They told me that there were no slots available. They got my email address and promised to give me a call. I was very disappointed. It took them a couple of days to contact me. I would like to take this opportunity to share that when we, international women students, request help from a counsellor, it is an emergency and much needed.

Glory – It crippled my belief in the system. Because I do not look suicidal does not mean that I am not under intense mental health pressure. I may not be exhibiting the behaviors that indicate suicide, but the behaviors are there. We are just better at concealing them. As women and international students, we have become good at building resilience and in so doing we have built walls that prevent our emotions and struggles from showing. It took a lot of courage and boldness to request for a counsellor. I rely deeply on my social support system and my family. Understanding the process of getting help and getting the help I need should not be a difficult nor cumbersome process. My mental health has been bad, and it has been a journey understanding how to cope with it and the different strategies to use.

Lena – Yes, I agree. We are good at hiding these behaviors. I am glad I did not give up my counselling sessions. I have found that even reaching out for counselling requires resilience. We are not used to getting the help we need, and we are not used to talking to counsellors, I am glad I did not give up.

Glory – We worry about the stigma, and the implications.

Influences that Enabled Us to See Culture as Multi-Dimensional

Lena – I relate to the multidimensional element of culture with the conceptualization of individualism versus collectivism as worldviews. These two concepts are no longer polarized but represent the beginning of a later understanding of what Brewer and Chen (2007) suggested are complexities of individualism, relational collectivism, and group collectivism. They proposed that it is necessary to pay attention to people's manifestation of individualism and collectivism in their self-representations, beliefs, and values. I found that Canada is an individualist society. People grow up looking for their personal benefits and individual goals. In Latin America, we are a collective culture. In my workplace, back home, all decisions that affect the whole group, I would consult. I would first try to understand the goal of the whole group, not just my goals. We tend not to see ourselves and others as "individuals with unique attributes and differences but, rather, as embodiments of a common shared social category" (Brewer & Chen, 2007,

p. 135). However, here I feel that I have been impacted positively and learned not that collectivism is better than individualism, but I see them both effectively functioning. My collective perspective speaks for my deep connections with other international graduate student-colleagues, where I recognize a collective group, a community. We shared a common self-representation of being foreign, we hold the same aspirations to complete our academic dreams and forge a better future, and we value formal education.

Glory – Our community and bond as international students have developed into deep connections and support for each other.

Lena – Yes.

Glory – I see both individualism and collectivism as two different multi-dimensional approaches to life and society. In recent times there has been a big push on collaborations and teamwork in developed countries, I think the society is beginning to understand the importance and benefits of creating some form of collective community. In this regard, the culture is gradually changing. As a student who comes from a collective society, I understand the importance of collaborations and teamwork. I readily consider other people's views and opinions and it is easy for me to be collaborative. From my collective perspective, I look out for the greater good of my group, my behavior is guided by relationships, norms, obligations, and duties and the group is more important than I am (Prieto-Welch, 2016). This perspective is manifested in my studies, my work and my relationship with others. I think of myself in the context of "we" not "I." Looking out for "me" was never an individual consideration: "me" was always in the context of the collective good.

However, in the individualist dimensional approach, independence is highly valued, as are competition, autonomy, privacy, and individuation (Prieto-Welch, 2016). An individual's personal needs and rights informs decisions and behavior, and assertiveness is desired (Prieto-Welch, 2016). In the first year of my studies in Canada, I struggled to understand the concept of "me" as an individual in an individualist society. I found it hard to reconcile the fact that my "success is the focus of my personality, my ability, and my attitude" (Khoury, 2006, p. 5) not that of the collective group. This new understanding was to be reflected in my opinions, including my voice in my papers, the use of the word "I" and looking out for myself. The individualist dimensional approach has taught me to look out for myself, be more self-aware, and understand my strengths and potential. I have learned to be comfortable with using the word "I." I know when to allow the 'self" to dominate and when to allow for the greater good of my group.

In this first conversation, we focused on intercultural socialization and why it was important for us to create social supports and belong to a community. We realized that we had developed strong psychological and emotional well-being through volunteering and serving because it created a sense of value, membership and belonging through participation. We suggest that universities offer spaces and communicate to students about similar initiatives and opportunities available on and off campus for service. Universities can consider the potential benefits of peer socialization through mentoring, as this may help promote the positive adjustment of international students. Peer mentors may promote strong multidimensional connections inside and outside the university.

CONVERSATION TWO: INTERCULTURAL IDENTITY

The Flexible and Dynamic Nature of Identity's Influence on Our Intercultural Identity

Lena – When I think about who I am and what my identity is, I think about the interconnection of social categorizations that makes me an overlapping being (Ovie & Barrantes, 2019). I am a woman and Christian; I am still the same person, but every single part of my life has been transformed. I value aspects of my life history and others' histories that I never paid attention before. My identity today is rooted in the idea of lifelong learning where I am always adapting and transforming. I do not intend to say, "I have a PhD, I learned what I had to learn, and that is it"! No! I am an educator by profession, and the words of Groen and Kawalilak (2014) strongly resonated in my mind "we [educators] are all navigating a pathway of lifelong learning, and our learning journeys are interconnected with those who we work, learn and live with along the way" (p. 229). Having seen so much around me and living in a different world has made me adaptable. It has made me bold. I did not know I was that brave, that resilient. I see the professional and personal transformation in only four years that I have been here. When I think about the future, I do not know where I will be in 5 years, but what I predict, and hope is that I am going to be learning formally and informally from the people around me.

Glory – Identity maybe conceived as an ongoing negotiation between the individual and the social context (Hawkins, 2005). Over the course of my studies and lifetime, my identity has become fluid, evolved and transformed based on my roles and situations. My personality, my style, my relationships and my ambitions are in a state of constant flux, ever changing. I have (re)constructed my identity through the lenses of my different intersections. I am not only an international student, I am also a person of color, a woman, a mother, and an author. I have become apt at negotiating and separating the multiple dimensions of my identity in this new social and cultural context (Malcolm & Mendoza, 2014). These ongoing negotiations between my social context and myself would not have happened if I was still in my homogenous predominately black community in my home country. As an international student, I have developed a system of beliefs and behaviors that recognizes and respects the presence of all diverse groups and races (Kim, 2012). I acknowledge and value the individual differences in my educational and cultural contexts (Kim, 2012). Furthermore, I have developed a strong sense of SELF… self-perception, self-representation, and self-awareness with the ability to voice out my opinions.

The Differences between THEN "before Canada" and NOW "in Canada"

Lena – Honestly, before Canada, I was close-minded. Now, I adapt to different ways of doing things and thinking, and handle changes better. I can relate to people despite the many differences we share. I know that to complete my PhD program, I have to think and act adaptively showing, emotional tolerance, strength of mind and spiritual guidance. It requires that I be open to opportunities and take action. My adaptability journey included developing a strong will and a constant inner strive to adapt to the development of the subject and social events, which results in not only behavioral but also mental change (Arkatova, Danakin, & Shavyrina, 2015).

It has been hard to adapt to times, deadlines, and processes. There has been much waiting and waiting shapes you, especially when you are not good at it. Getting a PhD in another country requires waiting for processes to happen. I see the accomplishments little by little. To wait for steps to be complete has made me adaptable to my own feelings, to places I visit, the people I talk to and the activities I participate in because even though I am uncomfortable, I comply with them and use them as opportunities to grow. In Canada, I have grown stronger. On a different note, I hope that you would agree with me that we have learned to research for information and find resources for us and for everyone around us. Furthermore, this skill transfers to life.

Glory – Indeed, we have learned to research for information and become quite apt. My identity has been influenced in a different way. In my home country, which is a patriarchal, male-dominated society, there is systemic bias against women. Women are regarded as subordinates and we face multiple forms of oppression (Arthur, 2019). There are many social structures and gender specific roles that women are expected to occupy such as wife, mother, be submissive and not have opinions. I conformed as best as I could to these roles because I did not want to be ostracized. I was often reminded of "my place" and my limitations in the social hierarchy (Arthur, 2019). However, in Canada, I find that there are many possibilities to excel and I am empowered to succeed irrespective of my gender. I am treated with respect as a woman and as a person. My opinions matter and I can express them without fear of reprisal. In addition, I have built a strong self-efficacy and agency to reshape my life.

Additionally, the openness and collaborative educational nature of the university system have influenced my approach to life. I am more analytic, more self-reflective, and more self-aware. I see the world from a broader context, and I have a better understanding of people. Furthermore, I have acquired an agency of self with a strong identity of who I am and developed a strong voice to speak with open dialogue. I have developed professional identity and have enjoyed exposure to cross-cultural ideas, behaviors, values, and practices (Davis, Fedeli, & Coryell, 2019). I have had a deep transformation of self and mind through my intercultural experiences and learning (Jindal-Snape & Rientes, 2016).

Lena – I like what you said about being self-reflective because I have experienced transformation in the way I question and share my thoughts and others' thoughts as well. I started to appreciate the powerful benefits of collaborative dialogue. In addition, I recognize "languaging," as explained by Swain, Kinnear and Steinman (2011) as a form of shared cognition. Languaging acknowledges both processes of internalization and externalization behind our actions and solutions to problems; by establishing that while we speak, "we often achieve new or deeper understanding of complex phenomena and plan and organize for the future" (p. 41). I am sure that it was through collaborative dialogue in the form of languaging that I completed my thoughts and transformed them into further contemplation and later into intellectual thoughts. The way I consolidated my dissertation topic was through collaborative dialogue with fellow graduate students and supervisors. I also relate this transformation with a new more mindful way to use the language and understand the power behind each word I say. It was in Canada that I started questioning every word I said or heard. I do not know if it was the courses, the readings or the conversations, but my interaction with people has made me reflect and question every word I hear and every idea I want to share.

Glory – The PhD journey has changed my perspectives and perceptions, equipping me with the skills to investigate and constantly ask questions as well as investigate my sources.

Values, Traditions and Cultural Heritage Resistant to Change

Glory – I see how duoethnography has enabled us to delve deeper into the motivations and layered ideas. I realize that I see my identity embedded in the things I do, in my values, traditions and cultural heritage. My Christian faith and beliefs are important cultural dimensions of mine and have not changed.

My faith is a part of my identity and is a highly valuable resource for maintaining my personal strength (Mckenzie, Khenti, & Vidal, 2011). Upon moving to Canada, I decided to look for a church to attend to create connections, memberships, and belonging as well as strengthen my resilience.

One change I experienced has been the reframing of my ethnic identity in the context of my social experiences, by developing an attachment to my home country that was previously non-existent (Malcolm & Mendoza, 2014). I connected with people who look and talk like me, who understand the nuances and dynamics of being an immigrant. Iwamoto and Liu (2010) pointed out that the strong identification and connection with one's home ethnic group may be protective. I do agree with them, as I reflect on this, I see the importance of sharing my experiences with others like me, I could not have the same depth of conversation with someone who was not from a similar background. This affiliation with others from my home culture, who share my values, beliefs, and customs, decreased my social isolation (Pham & Saltmarsh, 2013). I drew upon their expert knowledge in order to make sense of my world (Prieto-Welch, 2016). I freely speak in my mother tongue, cook my cultural food, and attend the various cultural celebrations, which have continued to strengthen my bond and connections to my home culture. I have developed a stronger attachment and a deeper appreciation for my ethnic background and the cultural nuances (Malcolm & Mendoza, 2014).

Lena – I resonate with your idea of being a Christian, this was one aspect of my life that I was not willing to negotiate even though I identified differences between being a Christian here and being a Christian in my country. I noticed differences in the frequency of church attendance and prayer, the level of importance ascribed to religion in our lives and even the way we worship. Our worship is more festive and emotional.

Regarding my cultural heritage, I was not willing to negotiate the value I give to my first language, Spanish. I was afraid of the possibility of language attrition. As explained by Schmid (2011), changing the linguistic environment and language habits can end in either losing, changing or declining the use of the native language. I never stopped speaking Spanish. I know some immigrants may refrain from speaking their native language once they live in an English-speaking country so that their kids can improve their second language learning. Unfortunately, they end up forgetting their native language and not only that, their attitudes and processes of identity are compromised. In fact, López, Krogstand, and Flores (2018) reported that later-Latino-parents' generations who ensured the language lives of their children, tend to decline as their immigrant connections become more distant. My determination to value Spanish as an identity marker never changed, even though it resulted in some uncomfortable conversations.

Regarding values, to be punctual, to be responsible, to be polite, remain as strong as always. I have to recognize though that politeness looks different here. The Canadian culture has taught me a lesson on how to be polite.

Our Descriptions of Our Reinterpretation of Elements of Both Cultures

Lena – I have reinterpreted the idea of tolerance. For me, tolerance was a controversial concept back home. Because of my Christian background, to be tolerant sometimes meant giving up your values. If I tolerated certain behavior, that meant I was giving up my values or religion. However, here, I have seen how tolerance has protected me as an immigrant as I have never felt targeted. Now, I value tolerance profoundly, and I see it from a different perspective. Because it has been tolerance that has given me a safe place, where I am not asked about my religion, nationality, and I am selected for opportunities because of who I am. Moreover, this looks different in my country. We say and think we are tolerant because we respect human rights, but we are not. We openly judge and criticize opinions or behaviours that we do not agree with. Fortunately, there was this reinterpretation of the concept tolerance that I appreciate and value. Another reinterpretation is the idea of politeness, as I mentioned before. I relate and agree with respondents in the study by Packer and Lynch (2013) when they listed the characteristics of people in Canada. From my international student's etic notions of Canadian culture, my perspective is that politeness is not just to be nice when you feel like being nice. Being polite means being considerate of others even when you do not feel like it. Furthermore, this sometimes represents to hold your emotions and treat others with respect because everyone, all the time deserves to feel comfortable.

Glory – It is a mix of cultures for me. I take the best of my Nigerian heritage, blend with the best of the Canadian culture, both cultures allow me to have a richer culture. I have enjoyed deep and meaningful friendships with people of all races and skin color that I may not have had in my home country. Have I faced discrimination and racism? Yes, but I choose not to be defined by other people's ignorance. I worry more about my lower-social worth and my earning penalty as an immigrant "visible minority" woman of color. "Visible minority" is term I struggle with. Grant and Balkissoon (2019) indicated that many say the term is outdated due to population shifts and even discriminatory and generalizing may hurt some of the very people it was supposed to help by masking diverging outcomes. Being a minority implies more than just a racial representation but encompasses the systemic implications of being marginalized from people in positions of power and privilege (Waterfall & Maiter, 2003). I think it is time to change the term "visible minority."

Furthermore, substantial evidence is available to indicate that people and women of visible minority origins carry an earning penalty in the Canadian labor market that can be attributed to their non-white origin (Li, 2000). This was true in 2000 and is still true today. Women of color earn, based on median total income 79.7% of what men of color earn and 56.7% of what all men earn (Statistics Canada, 2016). Only 13.8% of women among the top 1% of earners in Canada were women of color (Richards, 2019), these numbers are worrisome. It is unfortunate to learn that Canada has a long history of maintaining discriminatory policies and practices towards Canadians deemed to be racially different based on skin color and other superficial features (Li, 2000). Unfortunately, these superficial features attributed to racial minorities are inseparable from unfavorable social features attributed to them (Li, 2000). For me, there are more important in things in life than skin color and superficial differences.

In our second conversation, we dismantled the development of our intercultural identity. We recognized that our faith, language heritage and connection to people from our same culture were and are resistant to change. We reinterpreted components of our identity that have helped us bridge the gap between both cultures like our lifelong learner self-perception, new sense of adaptability, and the value given to collaborative dialogue. Lastly, some transient components of our identity that are interchangeable with the new culture include our understanding of tolerance, politeness, openness to friendship with people from different cultures and our recognition of race as a marker. Our stories captured an ongoing identity evolution that kept surfacing in our day-to-day experiences where we manage to juggle our rooted beliefs with our current transformation.

CONCLUSION

Duoethnography promotes complex and inclusive social constructions and conceptualizations of experience (Sawyer & Norris, 2012). With this perspective in mind, we utilized duoethnography to examine our individual stories in relation to each other's. Although our stories are our intimate possessions (Breault, Hackler, & Bradley, 2012), we shared them with the hopes of inviting our readers to a dialogue in which they recall and question their own stories and allow emergent meanings and meaning making.

We hope that sharing our stories and experiences will give universities some insights into international students' intercultural socialization and identity reconstruction processes. These insights might enable universities create programs in collaboration with their wellness services and the international students' offices to encourage smooth adjustments for international students. Furthermore, universities could implement programs and activities that create safe and open spaces for discussions through peer mentoring programs or a buddy system. The peer mentoring program is critical to the transition process as it could create positive relationships, strengthen the bonding process and promote strong multidimensional connections inside and outside the university between international students and domestic students. The program could also serve as an avenue for seeking resources and advice for international students' adjustment needs. Lehto, Cai, Fu, and Chen (2014) and Shalka (2017) suggested that peer mentoring opportunities should be systematic and allow both mentors and international students to create and connect on personal development outcomes. Thus, enabling international students to become an integral part of the student body (Lehto, Cai, Fu, & Chen, 2014; Shalka, 2017). These types of personal relationships may serve to foster the kinds of deeper connections that more fully integrate international students into the fabric of their campuses (Shalka, 2017).

Additionally, universities could introduce volunteer opportunities that enhance the relationship between international and domestic students through service-learning programs, international students as guides of study-abroad trips in their home countries and other types of volunteer initiatives. Volunteer opportunities between international and domestic students produces benefits for both groups. For international students, it encourages membership and participation and could foster integration into campus and community life, thereby creating a "sense of common identity, knowledge accumulation and self-confidence in interactions" (Lehto, Cai, Fu, & Chen, 2014, p. 851) with domestic students and community. For domestic students, they could learn and understand the value of multicultural relationships, different multicultural dimensions and global competence.

REFERENCES

Arkatova, O. G., Danakin, N. S., & Shavyrina, I. (2015). Enhancing adaptability of foreign students. *Mediterranean Journal of Social Sciences*, *6*(6), 276–281.

Arthur, N. (2018). Intersectionality and international student identities in Transition. In N. Arthur (Ed.), *Counselling in cultural contexts: Identities and social justice* (pp. 271–292). International and Cultural Psychology. doi:10.1007/978-3-030-00090-5_12

Bartram, B. (2009). Student support in higher education: Understandings, implications and challenges. *Higher Education Quarterly*, *63*(3), 308–314. doi:10.1111/j.1468-2273.2008.00420.x

Belcher, W. L. (2009). *Writing your journal article in 12 weeks: A guide to academic success.* Sage.

Berry, J. W. (2006). Stress perspectives on acculturation. In D. L. Sam & J. W. Berry (Eds.), *The Cambridge handbook of acculturation psychology* (pp. 43–57). Cambridge University Press. doi:10.1017/CBO9780511489891.007

Boice, R. (2000). *Advice for the new faculty member.* Allyn and Bacon.

Breault, R., Hackler, R., & Bradley, R. (2012). Seeking rigor in the search for identity: A trioethnography. In J. Norris, R. Sawyer, & D. E. Lund (Eds.), *Duoethnography: Dialogic methods for social, health, and educational research* (pp. 115–136). Routledge.

Brewer, M., & Chen, Y. (2007). Where (who) are collectives in collectivism? Toward conceptual clarification of individualism and collectivism. *Psychological Review, 114*(1), 133–151. doi:10.1037/0033-295X.114.1.133 PMID:17227184

Bryant, D. (1995). Survival of the interventionist: The personal cost of immersion and social change. *The Interdisciplinary Journal of Study Abroad, 1,* 17–25.

Burr, V. (1995). *An introduction to social constructionism.* Routledge. doi:10.4324/9780203299968

Champlin, R. (2019, October 16). *When college students want mental health help but get stuck waiting in line.* Vice Media Group. https://www.vice.com/en_ca/article/evjqwz/college-mental-health-center-wait-times

Cheung, L. (2018). *Understanding imposter phenomenon in graduate students using achievement goal theory.* Unpublished manuscript, Graduate School of Education. Fordham University.

Dalton, J. C. (1999). The significance of international issues and responsibilities in the contemporary work of student affairs. *New Directions for Student Services, 86*(86), 3–11. doi:10.1002s.8601

Davis, B., Fedeli, M., & Coryell, J. E. (2019). International experiences to increase employability for education doctoral students. A comparative study. *New Directions for Adult and Continuing Education, 2019*(163), 147–161. doi:10.1002/ace.20348

Denzin, N. (2011). The politics of evidence. In N. K. Denzin & Y. S. Lincoln (Eds.), *The Sage handbook of qualitative research* (pp. 97–128). Sage.

Denzin, N., & Lincoln, Y. (2011). *The Sage handbook of qualitative research.* Sage.

Dixon, S. (2018). The relevance of spirituality to cultural identity reconstruction for African-Caribbean immigrant women. In N. Arthur (Ed.), *Counselling in cultural contexts: Identities and social justice* (pp. 249–270). Springer Nature. doi:10.1007/978-3-030-00090-5_11

Eaglestone, R. (2002). *Doing English: A guide for literature students.* Routledge. doi:10.4324/9780203025437

El-Khawas, E. (2003). The many dimensions of student diversity. In D. B. S. R. Komives (Ed.), *Students services: A handbook for the profession* (4th ed., pp. 45–62). Jossey-Bass.

Grant, T., & Balkissoon, D. (2019, February 6). *Visible minority: Is it time for Canada to scrap the term?* The Globe and Mail. https://www.theglobeandmail.com/canada/article-visible-minority-term-statscan/

Groen, J., & Kawalilak, C. (2014). *Pathways of adult learning: Professional and education narratives.* Canadian Scholars' Press.

Hawkins, M. R. (2005). Becoming a student: Identity work and academic literacies in early schooling. *TESOL Quarterly, 39*(1), 59–82. doi:10.2307/3588452

Hernández, R., Fernández, C., & Baptista, P. (2010). *Metodología de la investigación.* McGraw-Hill Interamericana.

Heyward, M. (2002). From international to intercultural: Redefining the international school for a globalized world. *Journal of Research in International Education, 1*(1), 9–32. doi:10.1177/147524090211002

Institute of Medicine. (2015). *Transforming health care scheduling and access: Getting to now.* The National Academies Press., doi:10.17226/20220

Iwamoto, D. K., & Liu, W. M. (2010). The impact of racial identity, ethnic identity, Asian values, and race related stress on Asian Americans and Asian International college students' psychological well-being. *Journal of Counseling Psychology, 57*(1), 79–91. doi:10.1037/a0017393 PMID:20396592

Khoury, H. A. (2006). *Measuring culture: The development of a multidimensional culture scale.* Graduate Theses and Dissertations. https://scholarcommons.usf.edu/etd/2584

Kim, E. (2012). An alternative theoretical model: Examining psychosocial identity development of international students in the United States. *College Student Journal, 46*(1), 99–113.

Kim, Y. Y. (2008). Intercultural personhood: Globalisation and a way of being. *International Journal of Intercultural Relations, 32*(4), 359–368. doi:10.1016/j.ijintrel.2008.04.005

Kim, Y. Y. (2017). Identity and intercultural communication. In Y. Y. Kim (Ed.), *The international encyclopedia of intercultural communication* (pp. 1–9)., doi:10.1002/9781118783665.ieicc0999

Kislev, E. (2012). Components of intercultural identity: Towards an effective integration policy. *Journal of Intercultural Education, 23*(3), 221–235. doi:10.1080/14675986.2012.699373

Lehto, X. Y., Cai, L. A., Fu, X., & Chen, Y. (2014). Intercultural interactions outside the classroom: Narratives on a US campus. *Journal of College Student Development, 55*(8), 837–853. doi:10.1353/csd.2014.0083

Lei, L. (2020). Returning "home"? Exploring the re-integration experiences of internationally educated Chinese academic returnees. *Emerging Perspectives: Interdisciplinary Graduate Research in Education and Psychology, 4*(1), 13–18.

Li, P. S. (2000). Cultural diversity in Canada: The social construction of racial differences. *Research and Statistics Division: Strategic Issues Series.*

López, H. (1994). *Métodos de investigación lingüística.* Ediciones Colegio de España.

López, M. H., Krogstand, J., & Flores, A. (2018). *Most Hispanic parents speak Spanish to their children, but this is less the case in later generations.* Pew Research Center.

López Turley, R., & Wodtke, G. (2010). College residence and academic performance: Who benefits from living on campus? *Urban Education*, *45*(4), 506–532. doi:10.1177/0042085910372351

Madison, D. S. (2012). *Critical ethnography: Method, ethics, and performance*. Sage.

Malcolm, Z. T., & Mendoza, P. (2014). Afro-Caribbean international students' ethnic identity development: Fluidity, intersectionality, agency, and performativity. *Journal of College Student Development*, *55*(6), 595–614. doi:10.1353/csd.2014.0053

Mason, A., & Hickman, J. (2019). Students supporting students on the PhD journey: An evaluation of a mentoring scheme for international doctoral students. *Innovations in Education and Teaching International*, *56*(1), 88–98. doi:10.1080/14703297.2017.1392889

McKenzie, K., Khenti, A., & Vidal, C. (2011). *Cognitive-behavioural therapy for English-speaking people of Caribbean origin: A manual for enhancing the effectiveness of CBT for English-speaking people of Caribbean origin in Canada*. Centre for Addiction and Mental Health.

Norris, J., Sawyer, R., & Lund, D. (2012). *Duoethnography*. Left Coast Press.

Oberg, A., & Wilson, T. (2002). Side by side: Being in research autobiographically. *Educational Insights*. Retrieved from http://ccfi.educ.ubc.ca/publi catio n/insig hts/v07n0 2/contextual explorations/ wilso n_oberg/

Ovie, G. R., & Barrantes, L. (2019). A dialogue of shared discoveries on immigration: A duoethnography of international students in Canada. *Interchange*, *50*(3), 273–291. doi:10.100710780-019-09364-2

Packer, S., & Lynch, D. (2013). Perceptions of people in Canada: Canadian-born vs. internationally born postsecondary students' perspectives. *TESL Canada Journal*, *31*(1), 59–85. doi:10.18806/tesl.v31i1.1167

Prieto-Welch, S. L. (2016). International Student Mental Health. *New Directions for Student Services*, *156*. Advance online publication. doi:10.1002s.20191

Richards, E. (2019). *Who are the working women in Canada's top 1%?* Analytical Studies Branch Research Paper Series. Statistics Canada.

Rise, J., Sheeran, P., & Hukkelberg, S. (2010). The role of self-identity in the theory of planned behavior: A meta-analysis. *Journal of Applied Social Psychology*, *40*(5), 1085–1105. doi:10.1111/j.1559-1816.2010.00611.x

Robinson-Walke, C. (2011). The imposter syndrome. *Nurse Leader*, *9*(4), 12–13. doi:10.1016/j.mnl.2011.05.003

Sam, D. (2006). Acculturation: Conceptual background and core components. In D. Sam & J. Berry (Eds.), *The Cambridge handbook of acculturation psychology* (pp. 11–26). Cambridge University., doi:10.1017/CBO9780511489891.005

Samimy, K., Kim, S., Ah Lee, J., & Kasai, M. (2011). A participative inquiry in a TESOL program: Development of three NNES graduate students' legitimate peripheral participation to fuller participation. *Modern Language Journal*, *95*(4), 558–574. doi:10.1111/j.1540-4781.2011.01247.x

Sandín, M. (2009). Criterios de validez en la investigación cualitativa: De la objetividad a la solidaridad. *Revista de Investigación Educacional*, *18*(1), 223–242.

Sawyer, R. D., & Norris, J. (2012). Why duoethnography: Thoughts on the dialogues. In J. Norris, R. Sawyer, & D. E. Lund (Eds.), *Duoethnography: Dialogic methods for social, health, and educational research* (pp. 289–306). Routledge. doi:10.1093/acprof:osobl/9780199757404.001.0001

Schmid, M. (2011). *Language attrition*. Cambridge University. doi:10.1017/CBO9780511852046

Shalka, T. (2017). The impact of mentorship on leadership development outcomes of international students. *Journal of Diversity in Higher Education*, *10*(2), 136–148. doi:10.1037/dhe0000016

Spring Institute. (2020). *What's the difference between multicultural, intercultural, and cross-cultural communication?* Retrieved from https://springinstitute.org/whats-difference-multicultural-intercultural-cross-cultural-communication/

Statistics Canada. (2016). *Visible minority (15), Income statistics (17), Generation status (4), Age (10) and Sex (3) for the population aged 15 years and over in private households of Canada, provinces and territories, census metropolitan areas and census agglomerations, 2016 census – 25% sample data.* Data Tables, 2016 Census.

Ștefan, M. (2019). The human being and socialization through culture. *Memoria Ethnologica*, *72/73*, 78–85.

Stoilescu, D., & McDougall, D. (2010). Starting to publish academic research as a doctoral student. *International Journal of Doctoral Studies*, *5*, 79–92. doi:10.28945/1333

Swain, M., Kinnear, P., & Steinman, L. (2015). *Sociocultural theory in second language education: An introduction through narratives*. Multilingual Matters. doi:10.21832/9781783093182

Szuchman, P. (2012). Imposter syndrome. *Women's Health (London, England)*, *9*(5), 128.

Tseng, W. C., & Newton, F. B. (2002). International students' strategies for well-being. *College Student Journal*, *36*(4), 591–597.

Van Dijk, T. A. (1994). Academic nationalism. *Discourse & Society*, *5*(3), 275–276. doi:10.1177/0957926594005003001

Waterfall, B., & Maiter, S. (2003). *Resisting colonization in the academy: From indigenous minoritized standpoints*. Paper presented at the Canadian Critical Race Conference, Vancouver, Canada.

Yen, W. J., & Stevens, P. (2004). Taiwanese students' perspectives on their educational experiences in the United States. *International Education Journal*, *5*(3), 294–307.

KEY TERMS AND DEFINITIONS

Dialogue: A conversation or talk between two or more persons in which news, ideas and issues are discussed.

Duoenthongraphy: A conversational-narrative and collaborative research approach between two researchers.

Intercultural Identity: A gradual psychological evolution of one's self-conception and self-perception within a distinct social and cultural group to an intercultural way of relating to oneself and others from different social and cultural groups.

Intercultural Socialization: The recognition of cultural values, ways of life, customs, behaviours, and actions that result from a person's social interaction through a relationship with the environment, with self and others.

Membership: The state of belonging to or being a part of a group or an organization.

Mental Health: Is related to mental and psychological well-being. It is the state of well-being in which every individual realizes his or her own potential.

Volunteer: A person who willingly and freely offers to help or undertake a task.

Chapter 2
Increasing Awareness:
Cultural Food Experiences of International Students in Canada

Daphne Lordly
Mount Saint Vincent University, Canada

Jennifer Guy
Mount Saint Vincent University, Canada

Yue Li
Mount Saint Vincent University, Canada

ABSTRACT

The authors situate student food experience as a key source of tension for international students. Multicultural food learning activities (MFLAs) are positioned as spaces for cultural connection and knowledge exchange. Through a review of relevant literature, three themes emerge: 1) food, diet and culture, 2) acculturation and identity through social connections with food, and 3) the implications of lack of food on culture, identity, and well-being. Reflecting on the authors' personal applications of MFLAs within nutrition curricula and a student-led society supporting cultural integration, the implications of such a learning platform are illuminated. In response to emergent themes, the authors share observations and make recommendations for university-based programming and future research. The authors urge academic communities to consider the complexity and impact of student food experiences when contemplating the international student experience in Canada. Food learning and experience-based platforms are opportunities to support student culture and identity.

DOI: 10.4018/978-1-7998-5030-4.ch002

BACKGROUND

Studying abroad has become common practice for students wishing to participate in higher education. International registrations at Canadian postsecondary programs have almost doubled between 2009 and 2015 (Institute of International Education, Inc., 2020; Statistics Canada, 2019). Canada, known as a multicultural country, adopted multiculturalism as an official policy in 1971 (Government of Canada, 2012). In 1988, *The Canadian Multicultural Act* was passed, which promotes a celebration of diversity and ensures respect and equal treatment nationwide (Uberoi, 2016). Nonetheless, international students in Canada have experienced tremendous hardships and challenges during their acculturation journey (Spencer-Oatey, Dauber, Jing, & Lifei, 2017; Xing & Bolden, 2019). Numerous acculturative stressors have been identified, such as language, discrimination, feelings of marginality and alienation, lowered mental health status and identity confusion (Smith & Khawaja, 2011; Sullivan & Kashubeck-West, 2015; Vasilopoulos, 2016). Such stressors are purported to negatively affect international students' overall well-being and their academic experience.

Perhaps not as well understood are the relationships that exist with food experiences, student culture and identity. For example, Brown, Edwards, and Hartwell (2010) identified food as an important component of a successful acculturation process among international students. Kang (2014) indicated the original culture of international students was linked through food. Amos and Lordly (2014) found that food served as both a source of comfort, but also elicited homesickness in international students. Montanari (2006) described food as "an extraordinary vehicle of self-representation and of cultural exchange—a means of establishing identity to be sure, but also the first way of entering into contact with a different culture" (p. 133). Almerico (2014) described food as an expression of identity.

Food, as experienced by international students, can both contribute to or detract from the student experience. Saccone (2015) revealed resistance to new food amongst international students could be linked to compromised health (Alyousif & Mathews, 2018) and academic performance (Smith & Khawaja, 2011). Food insecurity was identified as impacting both personal and academic well-being (Hanbazaza et al., 2017; Pereira, 2020). As a result, disrupted well-being emerged as a threat to positive acculturation.

Through a review of literature that identifies food-related issues students face, the authors intend to describe how food, culture and identity interact to influence the international student experience in Canadian higher education. Additionally, the authors introduce two examples of multicultural food learning activities (MFLAs) they have used to support cultural integration on campus. The chapter demonstrates how students' culture and identity are manifested socially through food. Acculturation within the host society involves not only exploring and learning about new foods, but also maintaining connections with familiar cultural foods and food experiences which support well-being. The objectives of the chapter are to: 1) identify food experience as a key source of tension for many transitioning students, 2) position multicultural food learning activities (MFLAs) as spaces for cultural connection and knowledge exchange, 3) offer recommendations for those seeking to improve food experiences in a multicultural context, and 4) suggest areas of future research.

INTRODUCTION

Mount Saint Vincent University (MSVU) is an urban campus in Halifax, Nova Scotia, Canada, promoting small class size and personalized learning. The university hosts approximately 4000 students from across Canada and from more than 50 countries (MSVU, 2020a). The rise in international students over the past ten years has seen the development of an on-campus International Education Centre (IEC) that is a source of academic, financial and cultural advice, as well as language studies for visiting students (MSVU, 2020b).

The three authors, situated at MSVU, bring a particular understanding of food and international student food experience to the chapter. Guy and Lordly are Canadian-born dietitians and MSVU professors. Lordly works with nutrition students and Guy with tourism and hospitality students. These authors have seen firsthand the struggles experienced by international students as they attempted to learn and fit into the academic setting and host country culture. A number of these barriers related to international students learning to live, work, and study in an atmosphere favouring Western culture and the English language. Whether intentionally or unintentionally formed, Guy witnessed how these Western dominated environments created a hierarchy that both marginalized and isolated international students (Johnstone & Lee, 2017; McGarvey, Brugha, Conroy, Clarke, & Byrne, 2015). Additionally, the authors observed the role food played in international students' well-being, and how maintaining connection to their home culture through food supported the students' cultural identity. On campus, whether it was an international breakfast hosted by the university that celebrated each culture, or an opportunity in the classroom for an international student to present and share a particular food, food mattered. Li, the third author, identifies as an international student who received her primary education in China and is now pursuing her master's to become a dietitian in Canada. Li struggled to acculturate which provided the rational to develop a student-led society that supports the integration approach to acculturation for international students at MSVU.

The authors recognize food and food experiences contribute to and/or mitigate the challenges international students face during their studies. Food and eating are seen as a biological function that can be perceived as routine for those with access. Access can be defined as the cultural capital to buy and secure food in addition to the nature of the food itself. "Food security means that an individual or a community has access to nutritious, safe, personally acceptable and culturally appropriate foods that are produced, procured and distributed in ways that are environmentally sound, socially just and sustainable" (FoodArch, 2020, para. 3). Food and eating are also seen as a social endeavour. Food can be eaten alone, with another or in groups. Culturally, food meanings may differ among people and groups. Food can cause illness or heal and can evoke a wide range of emotions. The authors believe understanding this complexity enables readers to appreciate the far-reaching impacts of food as part of cultural integration. Retaining aspects of one's unique cultural identity within a new culture is a significant part of this process (Berry, 1997; Cleveland & Xu, 2019; Smith & Khawaja, 2015).

CANADIAN FOOD EXPERIENCES—AN OVERVIEW

Using a review of literature, the authors illuminate experiences associated with food that international students may face when adjusting to life in Canada. These experiences are implicated in cultural and social connections that influence both international student identity and well-being. The articles were identified through an online search of Pub Med, Google Scholar, EBSCO and ProQuest, using key terms: food, international student, acculturation, culture, identity, and post-secondary/university. All selected articles were reviewed for relevance to the chapter objectives.

Food, Diet and Culture

Photo voice research conducted at MSVU about Saudi Arabian and Chinese students' Canadian food experiences revealed key themes that provided a snapshot of typical food issues international students contended with upon arriving in Canada (Amos & Lordly, 2014). Amos and Lordly (2014) noted that with access to Canadian fat and sugar-laden convenience foods, some students gained weight or developed a fear of weight gain. Mycek, Hardison-Moody, Bloom, Bowen, and Elliott (2020) also described weight issues within an immigrant and refugee population in the United States (US). The research shed light on the social and cultural differences happening within different countries. A good diet, perceptions of a healthy weight and even the construct of health itself, were shown to be socially constructed. A Nigerian student who saw herself as "chubby," but healthy in her home country interpreted her weight loss once arriving in the US as unhealthy (Mycek et al., 2020). Amos and Lordly (2014) noted a disconnect between the foods students would eat in their home countries, which were perceived as healthy, and those that students were exposed to in Canada, which were viewed as less healthy. This tension was noted by a student who commented about her Canadian food experience: "my digestion is not as good as in my country… the smell in my mouth is not good" (p. 61). Cranfield (2012) and McDonald and Kennedy (2004) also noted similar physical symptoms that resulted in negative perceptions and a fear of eating Canadian foods.

While students in Amos and Lordly's (2014) study were relieved that access to traditional foods in Halifax was good, they commented that the quality and taste of those foods were not the same as similar foods from their home country. This also held true for eating out. While the act of eating as a social event was valued, ethnic restaurants fell short in replicating the taste and quality of the traditional foods participants were accustomed to. Participants believed available traditional dishes were made to appeal to Western tastes. That said, students noted that the social benefits of food extended beyond eating out and into the home kitchen. Individual or shared food preparation in personal kitchens was seen as an opportunity to create authentic versions of the foods students enjoyed in their home countries. This time was also used to socialize: "Food preparation, cooking, and eating with other students provided a human connection for students living away from their families" (Amos & Lordly, 2014, p. 61).

While finding comfort in food was important, and also noted by Brown et al., (2010), Amos and Lordly (2014) observed a paradox. Cooking traditional foods mitigated loneliness and stress through connecting students emotionally to home, but at the same time resulted in a sense of isolation. To minimize the negative effects of such loneliness, some students went to the extreme of avoiding the consumption of traditional foods. Amos and Lordly (2014) found that some study participants were eager to try Canadian foods and appreciated the variety of new foods available to them. Cultural identity and food were an overarching theme that ran throughout the study findings. The students maintained a strong connection to their culture through their relationship to traditional foods. Food and student food experiences played key roles in the acculturation experience. Amos and Lordly (2014) concluded that "the reinforcement of acculturation and identity through food is highly dependent on the opportunities to source, cook, eat and share food with other international students" (p. 62).

Acculturation and Identity Through Social Connections With Food

More recently, Liu (2019) described food acculturation experiences of Chinese university students in Ottawa, Canada. Using participant observation and semi-structured interviews, Liu (2019) examined the roles that festivals and festival foods played in Chinese students' acculturation and identity formation. In Liu's (2019) examination of hybridization, which was a coming together of separate entities such as culture and ethnicity (Pieterse, 2006), Liu (2019) suggested that an increase in hybridity did not diminish participants' Chinese identity. Rather, identity was maintained through existing beliefs participants held about food choice and through celebrating traditional festivals. In the case of Liu's (2019) research, it was attending a three-day Asian food festival part of Ottawa city's Night Market. Opportunities to socialize through food not only increased a sense of belonging but also created opportunities to maintain ethnic awareness (Liu, 2019).

In Liu's (2019) work, there appeared to be less of an integration of Canadian foods into students' diets but rather students developed "a greater appreciation of other Chinese regional cuisines and Asian cuisines served" (p. 69) in the city. Some Chinese students exerted personal choice and chose culturally similar foods over Canada's versions of their familiar Chinese foods. While not a rejection of the Canadian food experience, attending Chinese festivals or markets and eating Chinese or Asian foods enabled participants to maintain a sense of their Chinese identity. It was interesting that there were changes in the home food experiences while in Canada through the integration of food choices representing a broader intake of regionally similar Asian foods, not an increased intake of Canadian style food. Liu (2019) concluded, "identity and acculturation are two distinct processes in consumer acculturation" (p. 69). This delineation was also noted by Cleveland, Laroche, Pons, and Kastoun (2009).

Liu's (2019) research indicated a "shared cultural belief about food, as well as the friendships strengthened through food consumption" (p. 70) might actually pose barriers for creating or expanding potential social relationships in multicultural settings. As such, it may be expected that students prefer to maintain their existing cultural groupings and friendships in order to support positive mental health. The international education process itself and interacting with those from a different culture have been shown to affect mental well-being (Hattangadi, Vogel, Carroll, & Côté, 2019; Xing & Bolden, 2019).

Khulud Alotaibi, a Muslim woman completing graduate nutrition studies at a Canadian University, shared her integration experience through autoethnographic research (Alotaibi & Lordly, 2016). Food for Alotaibi was an important component of her increasing understanding of Canadian culture and how she could be part of that culture. In preparing to come to Canada to study, Alotaibi imagined that "her friends would be Canadian, [her] food would be Canadian, [and] her lifestyle would be a Canadian lifestyle" (p. 17). However, during her early years in Canada, she "recognized that [her] imaginations were still imaginations" (p. 17). This spoke to the frustration initially experienced by Alotaibi who came and expected to integrate into the Canadian culture and lifestyle. Similarly to what participants in Liu's (2019) study experienced, Alotaibi preferred initially socializing with her own cultural group. This group felt comfortable and provided a sense of home and connection through food, language and music for Alotaibi.

To integrate into the society, Alotaibi opened her home to non-Muslims through food-related activities. Alotaibi noted, "sharing Saudi traditional food was a fundamental part in my attempt to connect with Canadians" (Alotaibi & Lordly, 2016, p. 18). These exchanges provided opportunities for the sharing of emotions, identity and respect bi-directionally amongst all who participated. Despite her strong motivation and intentions, it took almost three years for Alotaibi to feel integrated into Canadian society. Alotaibi's integration was partially facilitated by a relationship developed with a fellow Canadian student. Alotaibi noted, "Heather opened the door for me to discover Canadian culture in a way that suited my beliefs and comforts... she arranged an all-girl party for me to discover her culture in a comfortable atmosphere and to network with Canadian girls" (p. 19). As Alotaibi reflected on that experience, she noted, "sitting with Canadians and eating Canadian food… the feeling of success, to know that I am finally here, I am finally with Canadians was an exhilarating feeling, a pressure off my chest. I will be OK here" (p. 19).

The Implications of Lack of Food on Culture, Identity and Well-being

Research on international student food experiences also encompassed issues of food insecurity. Not having access to culturally appropriate food eroded international students' identity and important connections to their culture as well as jeopardized their immediate health needs (Hattangadi et al., 2019). Food banks are often housed on or near Canadian university campuses. Pereira (2020) examined the usage of food banks by international master's students at Guelph University in Canada. Pereira (2020) concluded that there was a negative relationship between food bank usage and well-being. Additionally, it was noted that even when using food banks, many users remained food insecure. It cannot be assumed that all international students have the financial capacity to choose the foods they prefer or that are culturally appropriate.

Meldrum and Willows (2006) examined the adequacy of funding for students receiving student loans at the University of Alberta in Canada. Not only did researchers conclude the available funding did not meet student needs, they also highlighted the challenging work students engaged in to access healthy and economical foods. This invisible work included activities such as finding transportation to buy food or buying quantities large enough to experience some cost savings. A key question to ask would be on a student's budget, what percentage of purchased food was culturally appropriate?

Hanbazaza et al. (2017) compared food insecurity status, including coping strategies, demographics and self-assessed health characteristics among domestic and international students using the University of Alberta food bank. One finding was that international students paid a higher tuition rate and that might leave less money for food. The researchers advocated for access to nutritious low cost campus food. Chapter authors suggest attention must be paid not only to food availability for international students but also the availability of culturally appropriate food that support physical and social well-being and the cultural connections that provide scaffolding for their cultural identity.

Hattangadi et al. (2019) described the lived experiences of food insecure students attending the University of Ontario Institute of Technology in Oshawa, Canada, as it related to mental health. The thematic findings from the study included the factors contributing to, the consequences of, and strategies to manage food insecurity. Notably, the lack of available culturally appropriate food was a stress for one participant. His comments about "feeling alienated and longing to belong to a community" (Hattangadi et al., 2019, p. 5) highlighted the strong sense of isolation that was cultivated by a lack of foods from the home culture. The connection to the importance of maintaining identity was made when the participant commented: "I feel I'm a little distant… They don't have much Asian foods in Oshawa… I kind of miss my cultural foods… like I'm away from my community… a community, it brings you together… I'm forcing to fit into [Canadian culture]… I want to be myself freely" (Hattangadi et al., 2019, p. 5).

It was important for this student to maintain a cultural identity and not be forced into something that did not provide emotional comfort or support. Students viewed being food insecure as a personal failure that carried with it "feelings of shame, frustration, aloneness… and a reduced capacity to engage in social activities" (Hattangadi et al., 2019, p. 5). Social activities provided an important connection to others. Students used various coping strategies to deal with the limited food choices that included skipping meals when on campus or "powering through" (Hattangadi et al., 2019, p. 6) the situation. Powering through was a mental trick that positioned the physical, emotional and social hardships as short term. A notable recommendation from the researchers was that "institutions can work with health professionals, including dietitians, to design programs that assist students in developing important skills, including cooking and budgeting" (Hattangadi et al., 2019, p. 8).

Outcomes

Three themes emerged from the review of literature: 1) food, diet and culture, 2) acculturation and identity through social connections with food, and 3) the implications of lack of food on culture, identity and well-being. As a result of the cultural shift in food intake, international students experienced many changes that included a deterioration of well-being, cultural and social affiliation and connection. Student identity articulated through the values, beliefs and traditions associated with culturally relevant foods are positive but at the same time created barriers to integration with other cultures. Food insecurity and lack of culturally appropriate foods were related to the loss of community and feelings of isolation. This loss of connection impacted well-being, identity and integration. Opportunities to support positive international student food experiences can be created by fellow host country students, faculty, and administrators.

MULTICULTURAL FOOD LEARNING ACTIVITIES (MFLAs)

MFLAs, a term coined by the chapter authors, are leisure activities where people from different cultural backgrounds engage in dialogue around the preparation, tasting, and/or sharing of familiar and unfamiliar foods and/or beverages. Literature showed that engaging in leisure activities supported social integration, which in turn reduced acculturative stress and mitigated barriers faced by international students (Firth, Maye, & Pearson, 2011; Lechasseur, 2014; Shan & Walter, 2015). The authors have applied MFLAs as an innovative approach to help international students overcome some of the language, cultural, and social barriers they face when transitioning into life, work and study in Canada. Guy introduced an MFLA in the form of a food lab experience (FLE) during a university level course at MSVU, NUTR 2261—The Cultural Competence of Dietetics in Canada, taught to international nutrition students on campus. Li, who was previously a NUTR 2261 student, implemented MFLAs as key activities within a student society. Below, Guy and Li engage in reflection (Brookfield, 2005) to describe their MFLA experiences and insights about how food acted as a bridge for those entering a new culture. The reflections highlight how food was used to create inclusive learning spaces for intercultural exchanges and social connections. Personal communications were used to illustrate observations. Food was placed at the core of supporting cultural identity, friendships, and well-being to demonstrate how MFLAs can provide an integration approach to the acculturation process.

Application of an MFLA in Course Curriculum: The Food Lab Experience (FLE)

The FLE offered students in NUTR 2261 an opportunity to prepare, share and taste recipes of their choice. Informed by her travels in South East Asia, Europe and North America, and completion of a Master's Degree in Lifelong Learning, Guy's pedagogical approach applies a variety of adult education methods. For example, Guy included a learning platform into curriculum allowing each student to be a learner as well as a teacher (Freire & Mecado, 1987). Common platforms for learning are activities or contents that offer learners a degree of familiarity along with unfamiliarity. By asking students to draw on what is familiar to them, Guy positioned students as valuable contributors to the learning experience (Knowles, 1980). While common platforms for learning have included topics such as art, crafts, stories, photographs, and music (Amos & Lordly, 2014; Brigham, 2011, Hoffman, 2012; Massing, Pente, & Kirova, 2016; Mcgregor, 2012; Song & Buchanan, 2019), Guy contends that selection of common platforms for learning depends on the context and the learners.

According to Guy, most people know something about preparing food. That is why in an international context, food is an appropriate medium for learning. During an FLE, Guy recalled a student from Turkey brought in an ibrik and coffee from her home to use when teaching the class how to make traditional Turkish coffee. When the coffee was ready, Guy was impressed to see the other students gather around the student from Turkey. Guy noticed how students listened attentively as the student told stories about the significance of this coffee to her culture, how and when it was consumed and the relevance of this process to her personally. When exploring food preferences and cultural identity in Spain, Cantarero, Espeitx, Gil Lacruz, and Martín (2013) found "people prefer to consume foods that are symbolically associated with their own culture, in order to reinforce their sense of belonging" (p. 881). According to Brown et al. (2010), allowing students to take the lead in their teaching and learning promoted an understanding of the world from other perspectives. Guy observed how giving each student the opportunity to lead as well as be led supported an inclusive environment. In addition, Guy noted how this self-directed and empowering teaching approach, with food at the centre, increased both student engagement and confidence (Brookfield, 2005; Freire, 2000; Knowles, 1980).

While student engagement and fun were essential components to her teaching, Guy's approach used during the FLE was also inspired by adult educator Paulo Freire (2000; 2005). Similar to the way Freire (2000) used photographs to broaden viewpoints and empower illiterate peasants living in Brazil, Guy used food to draw out alternative perspectives and lived experiences from the students. Engaging in discussions about food culture fostered multiple perspectives, which allowed students to maintain their own cultural heritage while learning about additional cultures. Reducing the emphasis on a Western dominated belief system supported an integration approach to the acculturation process (Berry, 2013; Ward & Geeraert, 2016). The following quote demonstrated a student's reaction:

This activity brought learning and enjoyment together. It is a great chance to learn about different cultures by their food as a skill to develop that adds to other skills a dietitian need. It was also a very joyful and peaceful environment. It is now a sweet memory that we can take with us as we leave in different directions in life of a time where we all were together cooking, eating, laughing, and learning. (Anonymous, personal communication, March 17, 2017)

According to Guy, showcasing a variety of foods, flavours, and ingredients in the FLE helped students share stories and memories not commonly discussed in a formal learning environment. Additionally, using a tangible item like food as a learning platform enabled students to shed a light onto intangible nuances that informed their cultural identity.

While Guy assumed all students would bring in recipes related to their heritage, a student from Saudi Arabia prepared a traditional Russian cake: Medovik; and a student from China brought in a recipe that she had found in a Canadian Living magazine. Guy realized MFLAs provided not only opportunities to share familiar foods but also to foster a supportive environment where students felt comfortable and empowered to try new foods from different cultures. Therefore, what was significant and meaningful to each person appeared unique to that individual. The fact that students were comfortable trying new recipes was worth noting. Whether it was a way to avoid being homesick, to impress the professor by cooking Canadian foods or simply to try something new, the students did not bring in recipes Guy assumed they would. This unintentional stereotyping, which Guy engaged in, reminded her that students did not live in a cultural vacuum—they travelled, they had life experiences, and they used social media that exposed them to foods to which they were not culturally connected. Not all students from China were going to want to cook stir-fry. The authors contend that Guy would never have discovered these subtle, yet essential, experiences of her students if it were not for the FLE.

Despite these experiences taking place in a contrived setting, during the FLE Guy noted the comfort of familiar ingredients engaged students in conversations that appeared to encourage relationship-building. Flavours, aromas, ingredients, and preparation techniques provided students with an aesthetic experience that ignited all of their senses. Students shared memories and stories that led to discussions about the significance of the food ingredients, as well as the relationship the recipes had to their families, friends and communities. While it was common for Guy to see international students form social connections with students from similar cultural backgrounds, the FLE was unique in the way it fostered social connections among students from different cultural heritages. The following testimonial demonstrated a sense of belonging and an appreciation for cultural diversity one student felt after participating in the FLE:

If someone asked me to draw a picture of this food lab experience, I would draw a rainbow. We were all different and colorful, but when we come together, we become more beautiful like a rainbow. (Anonymous, personal communication, March 17, 2017)

Guy's reflection also noted how the FLE allowed students to use physical interaction, rather than relying solely on oral communication, to develop their communication skills. Guy remembered how one student found a lime in the fridge and wondered what it was called. Showing objects and asking questions allowed Guy to see what the students needed to learn. During the FLE, to supplement their oral communication, students demonstrated cooking and food preparation techniques. According to Guy, communication barriers were less of an issue in FLE because students had the added advantage of using food as a means of communication. Formal and Western-dominated classroom settings that rely heavily on oral communication skills in English can exacerbate language barriers experienced by international students (Medved, Franco, Gao, & Yang, 2013; Vasilopoulos, 2016). During the FLE, drawing on alternate forms of non-verbal communication, by showing objects and demonstrating skills, appeared to improve communication and showed potential to support language acquisition.

Overtime, Guy's discussions with international students showed her how removing key aspects from one's identity such as food, can elicit feelings of discomfort, pressure to assimilate and acculturative stress. When working with multicultural groups, incorporating familiar and unfamiliar foods into activities, and providing individuals with the opportunity to teach and learn, showed potential to create inclusive learning spaces which supported cultural identity, social connections, and well-being.

Application of MFLAs Within the Inter-Cultural Food Bridging Society (ICFBS)

During Li's acculturation journey, she struggled with stressors such as language, cultural differences, marginalization, and discrimination. Evidence indicated that different acculturation modes could result in significant divergence to the adaptive level and life quality of newcomer individuals or groups (Samnani, Boekhorst, & Harrison, 2013; Sullivan & Kashubeck-West, 2015). Assimilation occurs when individuals lose their behaviours and attitudes related to their native culture, to adopt beliefs, values, attitudes, and behaviours of the host culture (Berray, 2019; Schluter, Tautolo, & Paterson, 2011). Feeling pressured to be accepted into the competitive Internship Education Program, along with a strong desire to make Canadian friends, Li decided to assimilate into Canadian culture hoping to be more successful academically and socially. She even gave herself an Anglophone name "Kate." However, Li could not help but feel the indifference, sometimes in a disrespectful way, expressed by many of her Canadian classmates. For example, she noticed, during group meetings, some domestic students ignored opinions from international students, or simply moved away from them when groups were formed. Additionally, there were times when Li experienced a sense of otherness, where Canadian students called themselves "us" and the international students were described as "them." Li struggled with identity confusion as she strived to "fit in" and felt unhappy and unworthy. Li wished she could achieve a balance between her culture, identity, and social integration in Canada.

As Li continued to explore different acculturation strategies, she added NUTR 2261—The Cultural Competence of Dietetics in Canada—to her course roster to gain a better understanding of Canadian systems, processes, and practices related to dietetics. This course introduced Li to MFLAs. As part of the course, the instructor, Guy, held a cooking experience, or the FLE, in the food lab. During this lab, the students prepared a dish of their choice, which they subsequently shared with each other. Li noted the experience was different than a usual classroom encounter as the students opened their hearts and shared personal stories in a positive atmosphere. These cultural exchanges promoted opportunities to develop authentic relationships with each other. Research showed that intercultural contact is key to reduce stereotyping and prejudice, and to improve intergroup knowledge, attitudes, and social distance between different cultural groups (Gareis & Jalayer, 2018). Li also began to notice the power food could have on international students' acculturation process and started to apply those learnings to her own life. Li saw food as a universal language that anyone could relate to. After experiencing some challenging times connecting with Canadians, Li built intercultural friendships through sharing traditional meals and remembering how meaningful it was to prepare a traditional hot pot meal for her Canadian friends. What stood out most for Li were the conversations that the style of cooking, the ingredients, and the various sauces inspired. Li also remembered being invited to a Canadian Thanksgiving Dinner and a wine night with bread and dip. All these sweet memories kept strengthening the friendship and connection between people and cultures.

Culture, or the values, beliefs, attitudes, and practices accepted by members of a group, is the social identity learned and passed within ethnic groups (Sucher, Kittler, & Nelms, 2016). While people with the same cultural identity share similar languages, behaviour patterns and value systems, food is connected to special symbolism in every culture. In North America, a whole turkey is shared among family and friends on Thanksgiving to celebrate the harvest. In China, an abundance of meals are cooked and enjoyed during Spring Festival to signify a whole year of affluence. Researchers found people preferred foods that originated from their own culture in a host country, as a way to fight cultural insecurity and to reinforce a sense of belonging (Amos & Lordly, 2014; Cantarero et al., 2013). Li reflected that the special dishes from people's culture and childhood tie to family heritages as well as feelings of warmth that comfort them in difficult times. The emotional connection people have with their food that is created as they grow becomes an indispensable component of their cultural identity. During acculturation, learning a new language and appropriate behavioural rules can be challenging but necessary. Food-related activities offer people flexibility to decide the extent to which they express their culture and identity based on their comfort level. As an international student, Li had to speak English with Canadians, but she was able to choose what she would like to eat in the host society.

Li started to feel better adjusted in her fourth year of university through the integration acculturation strategy. Rather than always relying on her Anglophone name, "Kate," Li began to refer to herself by her Chinese name, Yue. While drawing on food to build relationships and maintaining her cultural identity helped Li navigate her life in Canada as an international student, Li continued to witness many fellow international students struggling with similar issues that she once experienced. To support these students, Li and another fourth-year classmate, who wanted to help other students overcome acculturation hardships, decided to start an on-campus society—the Inter-Cultural Food Bridging Society (ICFBS). Understanding the diversity in dietary cultures was essential for the international students to enhance their learning and living experiences in Canada. The society aimed to draw on food and nutrition culture to create global citizens at MSVU and beyond, and provided opportunities for international students to make close contacts with Canadian food culture. Since its inception in 2017, over 100 members joined the ICFBS for learning and communicating through various MFLAs. The following quote illustrated the impact of MFLAs on ICFBS members:

The ICFBS uses communal meals and food to connect its members, spark conversations, increase knowledge, and create life-long friendships. It is truly a unique and diverse society on campus—and not just in terms of the yummy new food items they share and teach us about. (Anonymous, personal communication, September 11, 2018)

The MFLAs offered by the ICFBS attracted great attendance from international students. Some activities included: a coffee museum tour to learn about the Fair Trade concept and taste different types of coffees, a harvest workshop at an urban farm to see how food grew and was harvested, dining with seniors at a retirement home to try traditional Canadian meals, a local grocery store tour to understand Canadian food availability, and a local food and drink tour to experience the social role foods played in Canadian culture. Through the MFLAs hosted by the ICFBS, members were able to expand their understanding about North American food culture and traditions. Food, at the center of these activities, provided a platform for learning, networking and cultural exchange for students and faculty at MSVU.

During an ICFBS annual valley tour, guides presented students with local wine, firewood pizza and a cheese platter at a vineyard in Wolfville, Nova Scotia, Canada. Students with various cultural backgrounds gathered together, shared their stories about alcoholic beverages from their countries and what food would usually accompany the drinks. Chinese students shared traditions about consuming white wine (Baijiu) with deep fried peanuts, students from Russia mentioned how vodka goes with smoked salmon in their country, and Canadian students talked about pairing ice wine with apple crisp. This cultural exchange fostered inclusivity as the cultural identity of each student was retained and respected. Additionally, connections among students were observed as the group shared laughter and empathy around the dining table. Although MFLAs in ICFBS showed potential to promote intercultural connections, Li noticed a continued tendency for cultural groups to form.

Similar to her previous experience in the FLE, Li again saw food as a powerful medium for people to communicate, interact, and build friendships during the society's MFLAs. These activities not only enhanced the connections between international and domestic students but also fostered collaborations within the local community. All the participants shared their individual identities through a multicultural lens that removed the hierarchies favouring Western culture. Without academic competition and evaluation, the food experiences created an informal and relaxed environment for people to connect and presented an inclusive space for exchange within the usually highly stressful university life. Li noticed the ICFBS activities increased the confidence level and sense of pride in international students, especially when engaging in MFLAs that showcased different cultures of students from all over the world.

Outcomes

Similar to other MFLAs, the FLE provided inclusive opportunities for international students to maintain their cultural identity while learning about additional food cultures. This inclusive framework reduced the Western dominant hierarchy traditionally experienced by international students. Teaching each other how to prepare their own recipes helped students establish social connections across multiple cultures, rather than reinforce connections only with students who share similar cultural traditions. The FLE provided a good example of how MFLAs can highlight the important role food plays in each student's personal journey. The FLE positively influenced student well-being by supporting integration as an acculturation strategy. An unexpected outcome was how the FLE allowed students to show food ingredients and cooking techniques, rather than relying solely on oral communication.

MFLAs through ICFBS have shown the capacity to create positive spaces for students with various backgrounds to start conversations and build friendships through food. Moreover, these activities improved food-related knowledge and skills as well as level of confidence among international students that in turn supported their physical and mental health. Although Li noticed students tended to form groups with their cultural folks, more intercultural interactions during and after the society MFLAs were also observed. Since most of the activities were designed for international students to learn Canadian food cultures, Li wondered if they were less appealing to domestic students. Small attendance from domestic students often left international students with the sole responsibility to bridge cultural gaps in the academic setting.

SOLUTIONS AND RECOMMENDATIONS

The authors offer the following recommendations:

1. Reflecting on the findings of Mycek et al. (2020) who encouraged a broad look at dietary shifts rather than on one aspect, administrators, educators, and students should not assume that immigrants want to change their traditions. Therefore, diverse traditions might be acknowledged and welcomed for inclusion into new ways of eating to be established on and beyond Canadian campuses.
2. Liu (2019) noted the dilemma of cultural affiliations rather than integration associated with dietary intake. While a challenge, chapter authors believe this tension presented an opportunity for change. Interventions that address and understand the foundations of a cultural divide could result in programming that promotes cultural understanding and collaboration (Hattangadi et al., 2019; Xing & Bolden, 2019) where food and culture are used to bring people together rather than to separate them.
3. A hidden implication of the differential tuition structure for international students was the possibility of less money for food purchases which impacted overall international student well-being. Although not a long-term solution, food banks or food pantries should be established on all campuses as

an emergency food source (Hanbazaza et al., 2017). Food security strategies among international students could also include student engagement in community gardens, and culturally appropriate cooking and budgeting workshops that can address basic financial and food access needs (Hattangadi et al., 2019).

4. An aspect of food experiences that was integrated within all the themes was the social nature of food experiences. This applied to eating within similar cultures as well as eating among different cultures. Decision-making to improve international students' food experiences must take this into consideration. All events, both formal and informal, should include a component for social connection.

5. The FLE used a "hands-on" embodied approach to learning that encouraged discussion and strengthened social relationships. The experience mitigated language issues by not solely relying on verbal communication. Given language is a common tension related to the acculturation process (Medved et al., 2013), MFLAs provide support in this area. It is recommended that a FLE could be implemented in any discipline as a social endeavour. A university food lab or a community grocery store kitchen could be utilized for food preparation. It is expected that the overall benefits of the FLE would be experienced regardless of the discipline.

6. Including MLFA's as an element in any student society is encouraged. The food-centered activities elicited a flattening of cultural hierarchies, facilitated opportunities to make friends, as well as opportunities for cultural integration in a relaxed environment. The issue of the authenticity of friendships and how this impacts both well-being and integration remains an issue (Robinson, Somerville, & Walsworth, 2020). Having ongoing exposure to MFLAs provides opportunities to deepen friendships. The activities are baby steps toward eliminating the long lasting estrangement between the international and domestic communities on campus (Bennett, Volet, & Fozdar, 2013; Trice, 2004; 2007). The ICFBS intends to survey domestic students to see what activities they would most enjoy attending in order to be attractive to a wide variety of students.

7. MFLAs in the future will include elements such as budgeting, grocery store tours, cooking on a budget or cooking collectively, to address food insecurity. Champions must advocate for funds to support this important work. If universities promote multiculturalism and diverse learning environments, financial resources must be available to implement innovative programming. Additionally, support for access to culturally available foods for international students will be key.

FUTURE RESEARCH DIRECTIONS

This chapter extends current research on the role food plays on culture and identity. The authors coined the term MFLA and applied it as an innovative platform in which cultural knowledge, respect and understanding could be fostered. Chapter authors illuminated several food-related tensions and shared personal experiences that suggested further research is needed in a variety of areas. Research has shown that sharing of familiar cultural practices can support the acculturation process (Gallant & Tirone, 2017). In addition, participating in leisure activities and non-formal learning settings could improve social development of individuals navigating new cultures (Alotaibi & Lordly, 2016; Firth et al., 2011; Lechasseur, 2014; Shan & Walter, 2015). While observational data at MSVU has suggested the merits of MFLAs and food related programming on a post-secondary campus, future research is needed to confirm the effectiveness of such interventions.

The chapter authors note an interesting offshoot of participation in the ICFBS for society leaders. Using their experiences and successes, leaders experienced greater integration academically. Several submitted peer reviewed abstracts and spoke at conferences, others gained confidence to apply to the dietetic internship program and to graduate studies. While authors encourage food-related programming, there is potential to explore how leadership skills, academic success, and confidence are influenced by opportunities to run societies or other social enterprises on campus.

According to Berry (1997; 2013), there are four modes of the acculturation process: integration, separation, assimilation, and marginalization. The authors purport that depending on the context, international students can experience any one of Berry's four modes of the acculturation process, at any given time. The integration approach supports preservation of cultural identity along with the adoption of aspects of the culture in the host country. While MFLAs support an integration approach to acculturation, more research is needed to understand the nuanced ways in which such acculturation occurs, in particular the unique role food experiences play.

Given the numbers of food insecure students on campus, both domestic and international, this is an area warranting further investigation as being food insecure negatively affects the student experience (Hattangadi et al., 2019; Meldrum & Willows, 2006; Pereira, 2020). The complexity of this issue requires research on a number of fronts. The authors support Pereira's (2020) call that food insecurity needs to be addressed within a student's wider social environment such as employment, housing and well-being. Additionally, the barriers to achieving the destigmatization of campus food banks (Pereira, 2020), adequate student funding (Hattangadi et al., 2019) and the quality of food provided must be investigated (Farahbakhsh et al., 2017; Pereira, 2020).

Research has shown that international students are vulnerable and marginalized because of their culture and economic status. As such, additional research that focuses on the individual experiences of international students is required. It cannot be assumed that cultural affiliation means experiences are the same for all. Byrne, Brugha, and McGarvey (2019) noted that this type of categorization might be problematic as some cultures varied by and within region, themselves having a background that represents a melting pot of ethnicities. Personal stories can increase understandings of international students' food experiences and how those experiences influence their study journey overall (Spencer-Oatey et al., 2017). Pereira (2020) noted, "Giving international students the opportunity to talk about their experiences [is] important… this group is a minority… and are thus marginalized, and may not have opportunities to have their voices heard" (p. 113).

University experiences extend beyond academic learning to include intercultural competence (Wilson-Forsberg, Power, Kilgour, & Darling, 2018). It remains unclear on different approaches institutions should continue to inspire and how to foster deep engagement and authentic connections between international and domestic students. Robinson et al. (2020) suggested that despite the multicultural features of Canada's society, "meaningful close friendships" (p. 65) are not supported. Given such friendships can positively influence personal experience and acculturative trajectories, friendship building has shown to be an important research area. MFLAs have provided a platform to explore new learnings and cultural understanding. It will be interesting for future researchers to explore other approaches or environments that are used to recreate some of the successes experienced at MSVU.

CONCLUSION

In this chapter, the authors described how food, culture, and identity interacted to influence the international student experience in Canadian higher education. International student food experience was problematized and identified as a key source of tension for many transitioning students. Specifically, chapter authors explored relevant research that exposed issues related to overall well-being, relationships with food, food acculturation, relationships with domestic students, food availability, and food insecurity. Additionally, authors shared their firsthand experiences with MFLAs as spaces for cultural connection and knowledge exchange.

Culture, identity, social integration, well-being and food were overarching themes woven throughout the chapter. Most international students maintained or attempted to maintain connections with their traditional foods. Food and food experiences provided sites of learning and opportunities to improve relationships with others that could both enhance or detract from acculturation journeys. Personal relationships and relationships cultivated through MFLAs showed great promise for personal growth and increased cultural understanding among students and faculty of different cultures.

While international students demonstrate resiliency, academic communities including faculty, domestic students, and staff are encouraged to reflect on current practices and use the contents of this chapter as a catalyst to find ways to enhance international student experiences and increase cultural understanding in multicultural contexts. Food and positive food experiences provide platforms upon which to achieve such goals.

REFERENCES

Almerico, G. M. (2014). Food and identity: Food studies, cultural, and personal identity. *Journal of International Business and Cultural Studies*, 8(1).

Alotaibi, K., & Lordly, D. (2016). A Muslim woman's experience with integration into Canadian culture while completing her graduate nutrition degree: An autoethnographic account. *Journal of Critical Dietetics*, 3(2), 13–22.

Alyousif, Z., & Mathews, A. E. (2018). Impact of migration on diet, physical activity, and body weight among international students moving from the Gulf Countries to the United States. *Case Rep. J, 2*(7).

Amos, S., & Lordly, D. (2014). Picture this: A photovoice study of international students' food experience in Canada. *Canadian Journal of Dietetic Practice and Researc*, 75(2), 59–63. doi:10.3148/75.2.2014.59

Bennett, R. J., Volet, S. E., & Fozdar, F. E. (2013). "I'd say it's kind of unique in a way" The development of an intercultural student relationship. *Journal of Studies in International Education*, 17(5), 533–553. doi:10.1177/1028315312474937

Berray, M. (2019). A critical literacy review of the melting pot and salad bowl assimilation and integration theories. *Journal of Ethnic and Cultural Studies*, 6(1), 142–151. doi:10.29333/ejecs/217

Berry, J. W. (1997). Immigration, acculturation, and adaptation. *Applied Psychology*, 46(1), 5–34.

Berry, J. W. (2013). Integration as a mode of immigrant acculturation. *US immigration and education: Cultural and policy issues across the lifespan*, 41-58.

Brigham, S. (2011). Braided stories and bricolaged symbols: Critical reflection and transformative learning theory for teachers. *McGill Journal of Education*, *46*(1), 41–54. doi:10.7202/1005668ar

Brookfield, S. (2005). *The power of critical theory: Liberating adult learning and teaching* (1st ed.). Jossey-Bass.

Brown, L., Edwards, J., & Hartwell, H. (2010). A taste of the unfamiliar. Understanding the meanings attached to food by international postgraduate students in England. *Appetite*, *54*(1), 202–207. doi:10.1016/j.appet.2009.11.001

Byrne, E., Brugha, R., & McGarvey, A. (2019). 'A melting pot of cultures'–challenges in social adaptation and interactions amongst international medical students. *BMC Medical Education*, *19*(1), 86. doi:10.118612909-019-1514-1

Cantarero, L., Espeitx, E., Gil Lacruz, M., & Martín, P. (2013). Human food preferences and cultural identity: The case of Aragón Spain. *International Journal of Psychology*, *48*(5), 881–890. doi:10.1080/00207594.2012.692792

Cleveland, M., Laroche, M., Pons, F., & Kastoun, R. (2009). Acculturation and consumption: Textures of cultural adaptation. *International Journal of Intercultural Relations*, *33*(3), 196–212. doi:10.1016/j.ijintrel.2008.12.008

Cleveland, M., & Xu, C. (2019). Multifaceted acculturation in multiethnic settings. *Journal of Business Research*, *103*, 250–260. doi:10.1016/j.jbusres.2019.01.051

Cranfield, J. (2012). The changing landscape of the Canadian food market: Ethnicity and the market for ethnic food. *Canadian Journal of Agricultural Economics*, *61*(1), 1–13. doi:10.1111/cjag.12000

Farahbakhsh, J., Hanbazaza, M., Ball, G. D., Farmer, A. P., Maximova, K., & Willows, N. D. (2017). Food insecure student clients of a university-based food bank have compromised health, dietary intake and academic quality. *Nutrition & Dietetics: the Journal of the Dietitians Association of Australia*, *74*(1), 67–73. doi:10.1111/1747-0080.12307

Firth, C., Maye, D., & Pearson, D. (2011). Developing "community" in community gardens. *Local Environment*, *16*(6), 555–568. doi:10.1080/13549839.2011.586025

FoodArch. (2020, March 10). *Our approach: Food Security*. Retrieved from https://foodarc.ca/our-approach-food-security/

Freire, P. (2000). Pedagogy of the oppressed (30th anniversary ed.). New York: Continuum.

Freire, P. (2005). Teachers as cultural workers: Letters to those who dare teach (Expanded ed.). Boulder, CO: Westview Press.

Freire, P., & Macedo, D. P. (1987). *Literacy: Reading the word & the world*. Bergin & Garvey.

Gallant, K., & Tirone, S. (2017). A 'good life without bells and whistles': a case study of immigrants' wellbeing and leisure and its role in social sustainability in Truro, Nova Scotia. *Leisure/Loisir, 41*(3), 423-442.

Gareis, E., & Jalayer, A. (2018). Contact effects on intercultural friendship between east Asian students and American domestic students. In Y. Ma & M. A. Garcia-Murillo (Eds.), *Understanding international students from Asia in American Universities* (pp. 83–106). Springer International. doi:10.1007/978-3-319-60394-0_5

Government of Canada. (2012, October 19). *Canadian multiculturalism: An inclusive citizenship.* Retrieved from https://web.archive.org/web/20140312210113/http://www.cic.gc.ca/english/multiculturalism/citizenship.asp

Hanbazaza, M., Ball, G. D., Farmer, A. P., Maximova, K., Farahbakhsh, J., & Willows, N. D. (2017). A comparison of characteristics and food insecurity coping strategies between international and domestic postsecondary students using a food bank located on a university campus. *Canadian Journal of Dietetic Practice and Researc, 78*(4), 208–211. doi:10.3148/cjdpr-2017-012

Hattangadi, N., Vogel, E., Carroll, L. J., & Côté, P. (2019). "Everybody I know is always hungry… But nobody asks why": University students, food insecurity and mental health. *Sustainability, 11*(6), 1571. doi:10.3390u11061571

Hoffman, A. (2012). Performing our world: Affirming cultural diversity through music education. *Music Educators Journal, 98*(4), 61–65. doi:10.1177/0027432112443262

Institute of International Education, Inc. (2020, February 25). *Infographics and data.* Retrieved from https://www.iie.org/en/Research-and-Insights/Project-Atlas/Explore-Data/Canada

Johnstone, M., & Lee, E. (2017). Canada and the global rush for international students: Reifying a neo-imperial order of Western dominance in the knowledge economy era. *Critical Sociology, 43*(7-8), 1063–1078. doi:10.1177/0896920516654554

Kang, D. S. (2014). How international students build a positive relationship with a hosting country: Examination of strategic public, message and channel of national public relations. *International Journal of Intercultural Relations, 43*, 201–214. doi:10.1016/j.ijintrel.2014.08.006

Knowles, M. (1980). What is andragogy? In *The modern practice of adult education: From pedagogy to andragogy* (2nd ed., pp. 40–62). Cambridge Books.

Lechasseur, K. (2014). Critical Race Theory and the meaning of "Community" in district partnerships. *Equity & Excellence in Education, 47*(3), 305–320. doi:10.1080/10665684.2014.933069

Liu, S. (2019). *Festivals, Festival foods, and dietary acculturation: A journey of hybridization and Identity Formation for Chinese International Students in Ottawa* (Doctoral dissertation). Carleton University, Ontario, Canada.

Massing, C., Pente, P., & Kirova, A. (2016). Immigrant parent-child interactional dance duets during shared art-making experiences. *European Early Childhood Education Research Journal, 24*(1), 37–50. doi:10.1080/1350293X.2015.1120518

McDonald, J. T., & Kennedy, S. (2004). Insights into the 'healthy immigrant effect': Health status and health service use of immigrants to Canada. *Social Science & Medicine*, *59*(8), 1613–1627. doi:10.1016/j. socscimed.2004.02.004

McGarvey, A., Brugha, R., Conroy, R. M., Clarke, E., & Byrne, E. (2015). International students' experience of a western medical school: A mixed methods study exploring the early years in the context of cultural and social adjustment compared to students from the host country. *BMC Medical Education*, *15*(1), 111. doi:10.118612909-015-0394-2

Mcgregor, C. (2012). Art-informed pedagogy: Tools for social transformation. *International Journal of Lifelong Education*, *31*(3), 309–324. doi:10.1080/02601370.2012.683612

Medved, D., Franco, A., Gao, X., & Yang, F. (2013). *Challenges in teaching international students: Group separation, language barriers and culture differences*. Genombrottet, Lunds tekniska högskola.

Meldrum, L. A., & Willows, N. D. (2006). Food insecurity in university students receiving financial aid. *Canadian Journal of Dietetic Practice and Researc*, *67*(1), 43–46. doi:10.3148/67.1.2006.43

Montanari, M. (2006). *Food is Culture (Arts and traditions of the table)*. Columbia University Press.

Mount Saint Vincent University. (2020a, March 10). *About MSVU*. Retrieved from https://www.msvu.ca/en/home/aboutus/default.aspx

Mount Saint Vincent University. (2020b, March 10). *International*. Retrieved from https://www.msvu.ca/en/home/international/default.aspx

Mycek, M. K., Hardison-Moody, A., Bloom, J. D., Bowen, S., & Elliott, S. (2020). Learning to eat the "right" way: Examining nutrition socialization from the perspective of immigrants and refugees. *Food, Culture, & Society*, *23*(1), 46–65. doi:10.1080/15528014.2019.1700681

Pereira, R. (2020). *An analysis of the use of the on-campus food bank by international graduate students at the University of Guelph* (Unpublished doctoral dissertation). Guelph, Ontario, Canada.

Pieterse, J. (2006). Globalization as hybridization. In Media and Cultural Studies (pp. 658-680). Malden, MA: Blackwell.

Robinson, O., Somerville, K., & Walsworth, S. (2020). Understanding friendship formation between international and host-national students in a Canadian university. *Journal of International and Intercultural Communication*, *13*(1), 49–70. doi:10.1080/17513057.2019.1609067

Saccone, B. H. (2015). Food choices and eating patterns of international students in the United States: A phenomenological study. *International Public Health Journal*, *7*(4), 357.

Samnani, A. K., Boekhorst, J. A., & Harrison, J. A. (2013). The acculturation process: Antecedents, strategies, and outcomes. *Journal of Occupational and Organizational Psychology*, *86*(2), 166–183. doi:10.1111/joop.12012

Schluter, P., Tautolo, E., & Paterson, J. (2011). Acculturation of Pacific mothers in New Zealand over time: Findings from the Pacific Islands Families study. *BMC Public Health*, *11*(1), 307. doi:10.1186/1471-2458-11-307

Shan, H., & Walter, P. (2015). Growing everyday multiculturalism. *Adult Education Quarterly, 65*(1), 19–34. doi:10.1177/0741713614549231

Smith, R. A., & Khawaja, N. G. (2011). A review of the acculturation experiences of international students. *International Journal of Intercultural Relations, 35*(6), 699–713. doi:10.1016/j.ijintrel.2011.08.004

Song, H., & Buchanan, D. (2019). Engaging English learners and their families: The power of nonfiction text and the participatory approach. *Reading Matrix: An International Online Journal, 19*(1), 47.

Spencer-Oatey, H., Dauber, D., Jing, J., & Lifei, W. (2017). Chinese students' social integration into the university community: Hearing the students' voices. *Higher Education, 74*(5), 739–756. doi:10.100710734-016-0074-0

Statistics Canada. (2019, September 20). *International postsecondary students at school and at work*. Retrieved from https://www150.statcan.gc.ca/n1/en/pub/11-627-m/11-627-m2019070-eng.pdf?st=iDdtQogV

Sucher, K. P., Kittler, P. G., & Nelms, M. (2016). *Food and culture*. Nelson Education.

Sullivan, C., & Kashubeck-West, S. (2015). The interplay of international students' acculturative stress, social support, and acculturation modes. *Journal of International Students, 5*(1), 1–11.

Trice, A. G. (2004). Mixing it up: International graduate students' social interactions with American students. *Journal of College Student Development, 45*(6), 671–687. doi:10.1353/csd.2004.0074

Trice, A. G. (2007). Faculty Perspectives regarding graduate international students' isolation from host national students. *International Education Journal, 8*(1), 108–117.

Uberoi, V. (2016). Legislating multiculturalism and nationhood: the 1988 Canadian Multiculturalism Act. *Canadian Journal of Political Science/Revue canadienne de science politique, 49*(2), 267-287.

Vasilopoulos, G. (2016). A critical review of international students' adjustment research from a Deleuzian perspective. *Journal of International Students, 6*(1), 283–307.

Ward, C., & Geeraert, N. (2016). Advancing acculturation theory and research: The acculturation process in its ecological context. *Current Opinion in Psychology, 8*, 98–104.

Wilson-Forsberg, S. C., Power, P., Kilgour, V., & Darling, S. (2018). From class assignment to friendship: enhancing the intercultural competence of domestic and international students through experiential learning. *Comparative and International Education/Éducation Comparée et Internationale, 47*(1), 3.

Xing, D. C., & Bolden, B. (2019). Treading on a foreign land: A multiple case study of Chinese international students' academic acculturation experiences. *Student Success, 10*(3), 25–35. doi:10.5204sj.v10i3.1406

KEY TERMS AND DEFINITIONS

Acculturation: An adaptive process by which an individual or group learns and adjusts to the practices and values of a new environment with a different culture.

Assimilation: A strategy to acculturate where an individual or group from a minority culture fully adopts the practices and values of the dominant culture without retaining the practices and values of the original culture.

Cultural Identity: One's behaviour pattern, beliefs, and value system that are learned and passed within ethnic groups.

Dietitian: A regulated health professional who receives extensive training in food and nutrition from an accredited university and internship program, and is licensed after writing a national registration exam.

Food Lab Experience (FLE): An activity developed by one of the chapter authors, Guy, to mitigate the communication, relationship and learning challenges faced by international students while navigating the university settings. Participants prepare recipes of their choice and share food within in a post-secondary controlled food lab environment.

Food Security: The ability to source and afford enough and acceptable food to enjoy a healthy life.

Integration: A strategy to acculturate where an individual or group from a minority culture learns and adopts features a new culture without sacrificing the original cultural identity.

Intercultural Connection: Deep, authentic relationships between people from different cultures that go beyond shallow courtesy and politeness.

Multicultural Food Learning Activity (MFLA): A leisure learning activity in which people from different cultural backgrounds engage in dialogue around the preparation, tasting, and sharing of new and familiar foods and beverages.

Chapter 3
Learning at Half Capacity:
The Academic Acculturation Reality Experienced by Chinese International Students

Deyu (Cindy) Xing
Queen's University, Canada

Benjamin Bolden
Queen's University, Canada

ABSTRACT

First, this chapter provides an overview of current research on international students' academic acculturation under the lens of self-determination theory in relation to international students' psychological needs of autonomy, competence, and relatedness. Next, the authors report on a recent study that explored academic acculturation experiences using musically enhanced narrative inquiry, a unique form of arts-based research that produces musical representations of the stories of six international student participants studying at a Canadian university. Lastly, the authors propose future directions for Canadian higher education stakeholders to become more supportive and inclusive of international students on Canadian university campuses.

INTRODUCTION

International student mobility is among the most prominent twenty-first century phenomena that higher education systems experience all around the world (Beech, 2019; Knight, 2012). Many Canadian universities are increasing international student enrollment to cope with challenges presented by the internationalization of Canadian higher education and to enhance their fiscal revenue and global prestige (Zhang & Beck, 2014). However, with the student population in Canadian universities becoming increasingly diversified, acculturation problems faced by international students have become critical, requiring more attention from Canadian higher education policy makers (Du, 2019). Tailoring infrastructure and services

DOI: 10.4018/978-1-7998-5030-4.ch003

to better support international students' successful academic acculturation has become a vital task for many Canadian higher education stakeholders (Du, 2019).

In Canada, enrolment of post-secondary international students was 435,415 in 2018—a 17% jump from 2017 (Canadian Bureau for International Education, 2019). The potential benefits for both host institutions and international students are substantial (Elliot, Reid, & Baumfield, 2016). The surge in international student enrollment provides institutions with economic advantages, a more internationalized campus, and a more global institutional impact (Zhang & Beck, 2014). Meanwhile, international students can benefit from better educational opportunities, enriched personal growth, and more promising employment prospects (Elliot, Reid, & Baumfield, 2016). However, international students can also encounter significant challenges (Carter, 2016; Du, 2019).

Acculturating into a foreign academic setting as an international student is a stressful process (Smith & Khawaja, 2011). Helping students acculturate successfully into a new academic setting has a significant impact on their subsequent overseas learning experiences (Xing, Bolden, & Hogenkamp, 2019). Studies have consistently demonstrated that international students are psychologically vulnerable during their academic acculturation (e.g., Aubrey, 1991; Gao, 2019; Smith & Khawaja, 2011). International students encounter a range of academic acculturation stressors including language challenges, educational and social differences, discrimination, and practical stressors (Smith & Khawaja, 2011). The interaction of these stressors often leads to harsh international academic acculturation experiences for international students on Canadian university campuses (Du, 2019; Xing & Bolden, 2019). The challenges of academic acculturation not only contribute to mental health crises, but also raise concerns around equity and inclusion that tax university administrators and faculty (Choy & Alon, 2019; Tannock, 2018).

While many Canadian universities affirm their commitment to educational equity and inclusion, there exists an increasing concern that these institutions have been focusing on the economic benefits brought by international students without allocating adequate resources to support their successful academic acculturation (e.g., Gao, 2019; Houshmand, Spanierman, & Tafarodi, 2014; Zhang & Beck, 2014). For example, cultural competence training and multilingual counselling services have been identified by international students as important resources that could facilitate their academic acculturation, but were lacking in their host institutions (Kim, 2018; Xing & Bolden, 2019). Lee (2015) suggested that instead of attributing international students' adjustment issues to their lack of coping skills or inability to adapt, host institutions should examine the effectiveness of the services they provide. For instance, many support programs designed to help international students acculturate socially cannot reach international students with limited oral English communication capacity who need the most support because such support programs required a high command of oral English to fully engage and benefit (Xing, 2017). As Canadian universities continue to develop strategies to attract international students (Gopal, 2017), it is incumbent on those institutions to ensure relevant personnel—including administrators, faculty, instructors, and student services staff—have a comprehensive and in-depth understanding of the academic acculturation realities experienced by post-secondary international students in Canada. Canadian universities need to design support programs and facilitate international students' academic acculturation so that they are able to have the positive Canadian educational experiences the institutions advertise.

Skyrocketing international student enrollment in Canadian universities has been accompanied by a plethora of research studies published on international students in Canada (Du, 2019). However, many of the studies have made use of quantitative research methods, with relatively few qualitative studies that report the realities experienced by international students struggling to acculturate into their host institutions (Smith & Khawaja, 2011). The authors propose that the use of qualitative methods can provide an in-depth understanding to help Canadian higher education stakeholders identify how to meaningfully support international students' learning experiences.

In this chapter, the authors begin by identifying the theorctical framework of Self-Determination Theory (SDT) (Deci & Ryan, 2002) that served as a lens for our inquiry. The authors then provide an overview of current research that addresses international students' academic acculturation, organized in relation to the psychological needs of autonomy, competence, and relatedness that SDT recognizes. Next, the authors zoom in to describe our own research and share findings from a recent study that used a unique form of arts-based research—combining narrative inquiry and musical processes—to explore and represent in-depth understandings of the academic acculturation experiences of six international students at a Canadian university. The authors conclude by proposing future directions for Canadian higher education stakeholders to become more supportive and inclusive of international students on Canadian university campuses.

THEORETICAL FRAMEWORK

While current literature addressing international students' academic acculturation has increased considerably in the past decades and provides many suggestions regarding how to support international students' success, the literature still lacks a comprehensive theoretical framework to understand and describe international students' academic acculturation in higher education settings (Ho, 2017). SDT is a comprehensive macro-theory often employed by researchers to understand human behavior and individual psychological health (Teixeira, Carraca, Markland, Silva, & Ryan, 2012). It is a powerful framework for understanding human experience that has evolved from a humanistic perspective and been supported by numerous empirical studies (Deci & Ryan, 2002). Within the SDT framework, the psychological health and personal wellbeing of all individuals hinge on the satisfaction of one's psychological needs for personal autonomy, competence, and relatedness (Deci & Ryan, 2002). The need for autonomy is met when one feels that one's behavioral choices are self-determined (Deci & Ryan, 2002); the need for competence is met when one feels competent and confident in the choice tasks (Deci & Ryan, 2002); and the need for relatedness is satisfied when a sense of belonging is achieved or when an individual feels personally close to others in their surroundings (Deci & Ryan, 2002). To function in a healthy state and achieve personal wellbeing requires the satisfaction of these three psychological needs for all individuals (Deci & Ryan, 2002). Given that the academic acculturation of international students is a dynamic psychological adaptation process (Smith & Khawaja, 2011), and that SDT is a comprehensive theory for understanding individual psychological health, the authors believe SDT can serve as a valuable theoretical lens to understand and illustrate the complex psychological processes international university students experience during their academic acculturation (Xing & Bolden, 2019).

INTERNATIONAL STUDENTS' AUTONOMY IN ACADEMIC ACCULTURATION

With regard to autonomy, the literature offers plentiful evidence that being in a foreign country creates situations that undermine the capacity of acculturating international students to make choice decisions regarding both their academic and sociocultural activities (e.g., Elliot, Reid, & Baumfield, 2016; Li, 2015; Gao, 2019; Tannock, 2018). When newly arrived international students settle in a foreign environment, changes abound in their life routines. International students often feel that their behavior choices both inside and outside academic contexts become limited in the new environment, especially due to their unfamiliarity with local educational and cultural norms (Xing & Bolden, 2019). For example, if a student lacks familiarity with norms associated with their university library, they may not feel comfortable going there to access resources or study.

The degree of autonomy for international students' choices to engage with both academic and non-academic activities is often dependent on the student's linguistic capacity to navigate participation in those activities; inadequate linguistic capacity limits international students' learning and social engagement (e.g., Li, 2015; Xing & Bolden, 2019). International students with low language proficiency often feel "forced" to choose courses that de-emphasize skills like reading, class discussions, oral presentations, and essay writing (Li, 2015; Xing & Bolden, 2019). Socially, international students with limited language capacity often report that they are unable to enter the social circle of their host culture peers due to (a) their inability to understand their peers' language and (b) their discomfort with the lack of patience demonstrated by peers frustrated by slow and inefficient conversations (Li, 2015). As a result, acculturating international students often only befriend other international students from the same or similar cultural and linguistic backgrounds, feeling isolated or excluded from the host community (e.g., Gareis & Jalayer, 2018; Li, 2015; Xing & Bolden, 2019). In addition to the reduced behavioral choices for academic and social engagement, acculturating international students may also have limited choices available to them in their essential daily life tasks. For instance, they may have limited food choices due to communication difficulties with the cafeteria staff (Xing, 2017). In summary, when settling down in a new place to live and study, almost all tasks involve some sort of language communication. International students' capacity to be autonomous in every aspect of their lives during their academic acculturation is greatly impacted by their capacity to utilize the target language for the tasks with which they choose to engage. A lack of language proficiency narrows international students' behavioural choices, therefore is likely to undermine the satisfaction of international students' need for autonomy.

INTERNATIONAL STUDENTS' COMPETENCE IN ACADEMIC ACCULTURATION

It is evident from literature that international students' need for competence is significantly hindered during their academic acculturation process (Kim, 2018; Xing & Bolden, 2019). International students may suffer from acculturative stress when adapting to new learning and living norms (Smith & Khawaja, 2011). This stressful state manifests in both psychological and physical forms. Many studies have reported that acculturating international students experience physical fatigue and psychological pathologies (e.g., Chen, Liu, Zhao, & Yeung, 2015; Sawir, Marginson, Forbes-Mewett, Nyland, & Ramia, 2012). These can negatively impact international students' learning capacity, resulting in a lower academic performance compared to domestic students (e.g., Li, Chen, & Duanmu, 2010; Poyrazli & Kavanaugh, 2006).

Linguistic capacity is fundamentally linked to international students' sense of competence. First, being able to communicate freely with native speakers is a prime factor in international students' perceived communication competence (e.g., Telbis, Helgeson, & Kingsbury, 2014; Zimmermann, 1995). Frequent intercultural contact has been identified as facilitative for enhancing international students' self-confidence (Yang, Noels, & Saumure, 2006). International students who can effectively and comfortably communicate with the host community tend to perceive themselves as more competent and, therefore, feel more confident during their academic acculturation process than students who have inadequate language capacity (Rosenthal, Russell, & Thomson, 2006). Second, being unable to meet the language demands of their academic tasks negatively impacts international students' academic performance. As all academic tasks are expected to be accomplished in the language of instruction in the host institution, international students' capacity to demonstrate their learning is constrained by how proficient they are in articulating their learning in the target language (Li, Chen, & Duanmu, 2010; Xing & Bolden, 2019). As many international students study the target language in a setting that precludes much target language contact outside their language classrooms, they often struggle to meet the language demands of their academic learning tasks during their academic acculturation (Du, 2019; Xing & Bolden, 2019). Many university courses assess students' academic learning from not only exams, but also in-class participation and group projects that require a written report. Penalizing acculturating international students with a reduced grade or a grade of zero due to incapacity to actively participate in group discussions or report writing seems to be the norm in many university settings (Li, 2015). In addition, studies have shown that international students tend to have a lower GPA compared to domestic students (e.g., Li, Chen, & Duanmu, 2010). When GPA is used to measure students' learning, a lower grade compared to domestic students, due to the constraint of their language proficiency, is likely to further undermine acculturating international students' sense of competence, leaving them feeling inadequate or inferior to their host academic peers.

INTERNATIONAL STUDENTS' RELATEDNESS IN ACADEMIC ACCULTURATION

A prominent theme in the literature on international students' academic acculturation is the exclusion from mainstream academic and social communities experienced by international students. Integration into the host community has been identified in numerous studies as one of the most challenging aspects of acculturation (e.g., Du, 2019; Li, 2015; Meng, 2018; Yeh & Inose, 2003). Intercultural competence and linguistic capacity have been shown to greatly impact international students' capacity to forge new relationships in a new environment (e.g., Gareis & Jalayer, 2018; Xing, Bolden, & Hogenkamp, 2019). Cultures are constructed, developed, and practiced by a community of people through socialization and are reflected in every aspect of life, including everyday social interactions (Razfar & Gutiérrez, 2003). Not being able to find the appropriate social conversation topics has been reported as a common socializing challenge encountered by many international students, particularly international students with a cultural background that is distant from the host community (Yan & Berliner, 2011). For instance, social conversation starters in Chinese contexts often start with inquiries on food and meals, which can come across as odd to many English native speakers.

The inability to speak the host language fluently is identified as the primary inhibiter for international students in developing intercultural friendships (e.g., Gareis & Jalayer, 2018; Xing, Bolden, & Hogenkamp, 2019; Yan & Berliner, 2011). Cultural diversity is becoming more and more common in a globalized world, especially in countries such as the United States and Canada (Joshee, 2004). Often it is not the cultural differences that hinder students from developing intercultural relationships, but rather the lack of language capacity to facilitate efficient communication and understanding of the true meanings or intentions behind those differences (Xing, 2017). International students with high English proficiency, particularly oral English proficiency, were found to have more host culture friends and a higher sense of connectedness to English-speaking surroundings as compared to international students with limited oral English capacity (Rosenthal, Russell, & Thomson, 2006). International students with the linguistic capacity to communicate efficiently in the target language cannot only navigate the cultural differences in social interactions but can also turn those differences into conversation opportunities for engaging conversations that could lead to the formation of meaningful relationships. Thus, international students with inadequate target language communication capacity are more likely to experience acculturative psychological stress (Gareis & Jalayer, 2018). Given that most universities have an admission language requirement that is far lower than what is needed to successfully acculturate into the host language community (Xing & Bolden, 2019), it is not surprising that the literature often reports that international students encounter challenges in developing meaningful intercultural relationships with host country peers, leaving them feeling disconnected and isolated (Gareis & Jalayer, 2018; Li, 2015; Xing, et al., 2019).

CULTURAL AND LINGUISTIC DIFFERENCE

Although it is often reported that international students experience difficult academic acculturation processes, this is not always the case. The academic acculturation stress international students experience seems to be correlated with the degree of cultural and linguistic difference they encounter (Yan & Berliner, 2011). The more different the two cultures and the more distant two languages, the more stressful the adjustment is likely to be (Yan & Berliner, 2011). Asian international students, particularly Chinese, Korean, and Japanese, are more likely to encounter difficult challenges when acculturating into English-speaking surroundings, compared to students from European countries (Yan & Berliner, 2011). International students from a Western or European context tend to experience a more positive academic acculturation process because the cultures and languages are less distant compared to English speaking countries (Nilsson & Stålnacke, 2009; Sam, 2001). In a study on international students' self-reported life satisfaction at a Norwegian university, international students from Europe and North America overall reported a higher life satisfaction than students from Africa and Asia (Sam, 2001). International students from non-European countries, developing nations and East Asian countries tend to suffer the most acculturating stress (Yan & Berliner, 2011). International students coming from China, a non-European East Asian developing country, are prone to much more academic acculturation anxiety than students from other countries at English-speaking institutions (Yan & Berliner, 2011).

CHINESE INTERNATIONAL STUDENTS' ACADEMIC ACCULTURATION

Chinese international students are the biggest international student group worldwide and have been reported to show lower oral English communication capacity and encounter more acculturative and psychological problems as a group than other international students (Chen, Liu, Zhao, & Yeung, 2015; Li, Cheng, & Duanmu, 2010; Yan & Berliner, 2009). Han, Han Luo, Jacobs, and Jean- Baptiste (2013) reported that 45 percent of the Chinese international students at an American university showed symptoms of depression. The language barrier is typically the greatest obstacle faced by Chinese international students during their academic acculturation (Bertram, Poulakis, Elsasser, & Kumar, 2014; Poyrazli & Kavanaugh, 2006; Xing & Bolden, 2019; Yeh & Inose, 2003). The acculturation experiences of Chinese international students are often fraught with emotional pains and loneliness (Xing & Bolden, 2019; Yi, 2004; Zhang & Beck, 2014). Communication difficulties isolate Chinese international students from their local peers more than other international students due to their relatively lower oral English communication ability (Ippolito, 2007). Although many Chinese international students seek connection and friendship from students from the same or similar cultural background, they still feel excluded and disconnected from the larger social and educational surroundings in English speaking countries (Bertram, Poulakis, Elsasser, & Kumar, 2014). Given the rising number of Chinese international students worldwide and the often-reported harsh academic acculturation they experience, there is an ongoing need to further understand the academic acculturation processes of these international students (Meng, 2018).

In summary, acculturating international students often feel constrained in their academic and social choices and opportunities, incompetent in their learning and daily life tasks, and excluded from their host community peers. When all three basic human psychological needs are unmet, the psychological stress international students experience in a foreign country can be overwhelming (Chen, et al., 2015; Xing, et al., 2019). As a result, their learning capacity is impeded, which in return exacerbates their academic acculturation stress. It is then not surprising that many researchers have voiced concerns about the harsh academic acculturation processes that international students experience and have raised concerns about impending mental health crises on campus associated with increasingly more internationalized universities (e.g., Arthur, 2004; Chen et al., 2015).

PROMOTING UNDERSTANDING OF ACADEMIC ACCULTURATION IN CANADA

Canada prides itself on welcoming international students. "Recognizing that international students are vital to Canada's growth, Citizenship and Immigration Canada has set out to transform Canada's immigration system to one that is faster, more flexible, and tailored to students' needs—a major distinguishing factor from other countries" (Gopal, 2017, p. 231). Recent immigration policies and programs have been specifically created to make it easier for international students to study in Canada, making Canada one of the leading destinations for international students seeking higher education around the globe (Gopal, 2017). The number of international students enrolled in Canadian universities has been increasing continuously for the past decade (Du, 2019). The majority of international students in Canadian higher education are from Asian countries that have the most distant cultural and linguistic differences from Canada (Du, 2019), leaving many international students on Canadian campuses prone to suffering from a lack of autonomy, competence, and relatedness during their academic acculturation.

Therefore, what are the realities experienced by international students on Canadian university campuses, especially the groups most culturally and linguistically distant from the Canadian norm? With a growing body of international students in Canadian universities, there is a continuous demand to further understand the academic acculturation processes of international students in Canada (Xing & Bolden, 2019). In particular, when more and more international students coming from China continue to enter the Canadian higher education system, a more in-depth understanding of Chinese international students' academic acculturation experiences in Canadian universities is needed. Stakeholders need such information to build global campuses that support international students' successful acculturation into the host institution and thereby enable them to truly reap the benefit of Canadian higher education. Therefore, this study aimed to explore the academic acculturation experiences of Chinese international students studying in Canada. The authors designed the following study to address the following main research question: What are the academic acculturation realities experienced by Chinese international students with low oral English proficiency on Canadian campuses where English is the medium of instruction?

METHODOLOGY

In response to the need to open up richer understanding of students' academic acculturation experiences, the authors employed musically enhanced narrative inquiry (MENI) to explore the in-depth experiences of international students enrolled at a Canadian university. MENI is a unique arts-based research approach that combines traditional narrative inquiry methods with musical processes to promote empathic understanding—a fundamental aim of qualitative inquiry (Bolden, 2017; Bresler, 2006)— "resonance, an embodied state of mind that is cognitive and at the same time, affective and corporeal" (Bresler, 2006, p. 25).

As the name implies, MENI builds on narrative inquiry practices with the artistic utilization of sound and music. It involves exploring the meanings of the participants' spoken words and stories through musical processes (Bolden, 2008). The authors chose MENI as the most appropriate approach for this study for two main reasons. First, narrative inquiry is an effective methodology for understanding and representing human experiences (Creswell, 2007). Second, music is a common form of art accessible to a wide audience with the provocative power to represent and evoke emotion in storytelling across cultures and contexts to promote empathic understanding (Bolden, 2017). The opportunity for the audience to connect sound to meaning can provide a powerful mechanism for eliciting memory and emotions that could compel actions (Gallagher, 2016; Trainor). The personal academic acculturation experiences that this study sought to unpack consisted of emotionally complex stories. Musically enhanced research methods offered profound possibilities to foster deep understanding and connections among the participants, the researcher, and audiences (Bolden, 2017).

Research Site and Participants

The study site was a research-intensive comprehensive university in Ontario with a large number of international students, where English is the language of instruction. Because the study strived to gain an in-depth understanding of international students' academic experiences, the authors followed the suggestion of Creswell (2007) to recruit a small number of individuals in order to capture their detailed stories. The authors targeted Chinese international students for recruitment believing their cultural and linguistic backgrounds, distant from those of most Canadians, would likely cause the students to encounter significant challenges for academic acculturation. Six Chinese international students enrolled in different undergraduate programs were invited to share their personal and detailed stories. The participants for the study were four female and two males. All participants self-identified as having low English proficiency. Participants had been in Canada between four to eighteen months and were in various stages of academic acculturation.

Data Collection and Analysis

The authors held one preliminary and one follow-up interview with each participant in person. The interviews were semi-structured, meaning the authors followed an interview protocol but improvised probing questions in response to participants' answers (Charmaz, 2003). Each interview lasted for 45-60 minutes and was audio-recorded and transcribed. The analysis of the data was conducted in two parallel analysis procedures. First, in keeping with narrative inquiry methods, the authors analyzed the data through the process of re-storying (Creswell, 2007). The re-storying involved (1) transcribing interview conversations; (2) coding significant text segments from the interview transcripts using a general inductive analysis approach (Thomas, 2006); and (3) organizing the coded text into a sequence for re-storying that highlighted and illuminated the most important themes. Meanwhile, processes associated with the "musically enhanced" aspect of the narrative inquiry were carried out (Bolden, 2008). The authors worked with the audio data (recorded interviews) within digital audio software in order to closely and repeatedly listen to and consider the participants' words and stories. This process enabled confirmation and deeper understanding of existing themes from the transcript analysis and the identification of new emergent themes. When the most salient themes had been identified, the authors composed music to interpret and build understanding of the meanings conveyed within the participants' stories, and to highlight the themes. The authors then used digital music composition software to combine the composed music with the recordings of the participant voices, weaving the music in and around the students' stories of academic acculturation.

RESULTS

Working with the data acoustically and musically enabled the crafting of seven musical representations ranging from 30 seconds to 2 minutes in duration. These representations re-tell participants' stories in their own words and with their own voices, with the researcher-composed music serving as commentary to communicate nuances of the identified themes. For this book chapter, the authors share three of these musical representations. The pieces highlight the participants' academic acculturation experiences and our understanding of them as informed by the SDT framework. The authors have provided permanent links to the audio files so that readers may access the musical narrative representations while reading the narrative texts.

Restricted Choices – Undermined Autonomy

Please navigate to the following link to access the musical representation for the theme:
    https://cindyxing17.wixsite.com/menistories/single-post/2017/12/28/MENI-Theme--Helplessness-and-Resignation

Musical representation transcript

Kandy: When you are home surrounded by your family, you feel like you have someone to fall back on. When you are all alone, far away from home, everything seems heavier.

But I couldn't tell anyone those feelings, because I didn't want my parents to worry or be disappointed with me. I couldn't talk about these feelings with other Chinese students around me either, because I felt they felt the same way and it would get too depressing for everybody if we started talking about those things too much.

Later on, I thought about using the counselling service but then I thought to myself: "It's English. I can't even talk with people in simple English. How am I going to talk to the counsellor?" I mean, I want to go talk about my problem of talking to make myself feel better but then I would find myself not even able to talk about my problem of talking. How would you feel? Of course, worse. So I gave it up. So I gave it up.

So I had to keep all those feelings to myself, though I felt like the person in The Scream. The most I could do to was just torture my beddings in my room alone when it got too hard and I wanted to smash things to vent. I couldn't even smash those hard objects because I was afraid that the sound would attract attention. It was a really lame way to vent but also the only way.

When I was alone in my room, I would just sit there and think about those embarrassing and suffocating moments when I couldn't talk, and I just felt like I was not made to communicate in English with people. Then I started to close myself up. Do you understand that?

When describing their academic acculturation experiences, the participants frequently made reference to the lack of choice that they had in their academic and non-academic lives. Their options were severely limited by their lack of English communication capacity, resulting in a perceived inability to access opportunities available to domestic students, as demonstrated in the participants' quotes below.

I heard from my Chinese friends that I should try to stay away from social sciences courses. Because in those courses, there are lots of group projects, presentations, reading and report writing…Chinese students always get a much lower score than Canadian students because they cannot keep up or do the assignments as effectively. I really wanted to take this psychology course but after what I heard about the grades other Chinese student got in this course, I gave up.

When I went to the cafeteria for food, I could not make the staff understand what I wanted as my oral English was not good. I would always get the wrong food, so I just chose to say simple things that they could understand. As a result, I always end up eating food that I hate in the cafeteria. I really hated the food and it was so frustrating.

I had to spend my after school time reviewing lecture recordings and notes in the library while other students relaxed and partied. I really wanted to take a break from studying but I couldn't. It felt so suffocating. I could not understand the lectures like Canadian students and had to make up for it after class. For tasks that would take Canadian students only an hour to comprehend, I would need to spend four or even five hours.

When describing their social acculturation experiences, the words "lonely" and "excluded" were used at a high-frequency when describing their social acculturation experiences, even though they all expressed a strong desire to mingle and socialize with their domestic Canadian peers. Reduced academic and social communication options undermined the participants' sense of autonomy during their academic acculturation. As Kandy described, above, she was so frustrated by the lack of choices available to her that she was reduced to screaming silently alone in her dorm room.

Inferiority Syndrome – Reduced Competence

Please navigate to the following link to access the musical representation for the theme:

https://cindyxing17.wixsite.com/menistories/single-post/2017/06/10/MENI-Theme--Anxiety- and-Inferiority

Musical representation transcript

Kandy: I got very nervous and anxious when talking to professors and other students. Because I knew I was supposed to participate by speaking English, but I also knew that I was not able to express myself in English. Then I got so anxious that I could not even sit still in class. I did not know where to look when talking, and I would nervously tap my feet when sitting in class.

Lisa: I felt I was not good enough compared to other Canadian students or other international students with sufficient oral English capacity. I felt like Canadian students and I were not equal anymore when I could not express myself. When I could not say what I thought and how I felt, I felt weak among them. I think only when one can express oneself can one truly exercise the right to speak. And only when that person's voice is heard can people really have respect for them.

In addition to having limited autonomy during their academic acculturation, the participants also reported a significantly reduced sense of competence. Being limited by their English proficiency, the participants often failed to perform tasks that they needed to do and felt frustrated. Constant frustrations were salient in handling simple life or academic tasks, which eroded their confidence as independent and capable adults. This is shown through the following interview quotes.

When my friends and I arrived at the airport in Canada, it was late. So we booked a hotel to stay over the night before we take the bus to the university campus. But when we arrived at the hotel, none of us could communicate with the English-speaking hotel staff about our reservation. It was such a stressful and embarrassing experience right after I landed in Canada. I felt really inadequate and ashamed even because I had studied English for more than ten years and was very confident in my English communication capacity.

When we had group meetings in the dorm to discuss things relating to campus events, other Canadian students all actively participated and shared their thoughts. But when it came to my turn to speak, all I could muster was 'Ok. I think it is good." I really wanted to say more but I could not because my English was not good enough for me express my thoughts freely... I felt very stupid and frustrated...

When we have group project discussions in class, I was always just listening and not saying much because I found it really hard to make them understand my English. Then gradually, other students stopped asking for my opinion. My inability to engage in effective English conversations constrained at least half of my academic capacity...I think I am just as smart as the other Canadian students intellectually, but I just could not learn things as effectively as they did...And I started doubting myself.

In the cases featured above, participants judged themselves as inadequate against domestic Canadian students. Along with frequent frustrations in their academic acculturation experiences came feelings of anxiety and inferiority.

Silent Isolation – Lack of Relatedness

Please navigate to the following link to access the musical representation for the theme:
    https://cindyxing17.wixsite.com/menistories/single-post/2017/06/10/MENI-Theme--Loneliness-and-Isolation

Musical representation transcript

Kevin: When I was back in China, I was a very social person, making friends wherever I went. But in Canada I was forced to suppress my desire to talk because my limited spoken English would not allow me to talk. Sometimes, I really just wanted to talk to someone to make a friend or two, but after the general greeting of "Hello," I would just get stuck there, unable to say anything more. So, I could not make friends with Canadian students and I always felt alone. I had taken thousands of pictures of the fabulous landscape of Canada. But I had no one, but I had on one to share them with around me.

During the orientation week, when we had the group dinner together, the Canadian students were all chatting and laughing with each other at the table. But I just sat there, struggling to understand what they were saying. Occasionally, I could grasp a sentence or two, but by the time I had finished thinking about how to respond, they had already moved on to something new. Then I was not able to say anything. So, I just sat there, feeling like an outsider, an invisible person, among a big table of Canadian students. Although they seemed to be right beside me, within my reach, they were still a world apart from me. I thought to myself, sitting there, "What am I going to do with a life like this? How I am going to live a life like this?" Although Canada seemed so beautiful, it did not feel like a world where I should be. It did not feel like a world where I should be.

The theme of "silent isolation" was prominent amongst all the six interviewed students' stories. All participants described substantial challenges in communicating with their domestic Canadian peers that prevented them from developing sustained and meaningful relationships. All the participants came to Canada with a very positive outlook on forming intercultural friendships with Canadians and a strong desire to socialize with and integrate into the domestic student community. But, unfortunately, in the academic acculturation realities they experienced, they felt excluded from the host student community and only connected with student communities that had the same or similar cultural and linguistic backgrounds as a direct result of their lack of oral English communication capacity. In the quotes featured below, students described how their limited English capacity made them feel separated from the Canadian student community.

I really wanted to make some Canadian friends. They all seem really nice and friendly. Some of my Canadian classmates would even go out of their way to come to say "Hi" to me when they saw me on campus at the beginning of my studies. However, because I could not really talk with them much due to my limited spoken English; they stopped doing that gradually. I felt really lonely and started socializing with Chinese students here even though I really do not like dealing with the Chinese student community sometimes…lots of them are very competitive and snobby. But as I cannot really become friends with Canadian students, I had to stay in the Chinese student community to feel less lonely. Even though I had Chinese friends, I still felt that I did not belong to the place where I was at, a Canadian university.

Before I came to Canada, I imagined my university life to be very colorful and multicultural...just like what I had seen in the English soap operas where university students hang out together on campus in groups, laughing out loud and having fun. I thought I would be one of them. But in reality, after I came to Canada, I found it was even hard for Canadian students to understand my basic English conversations... I never hang out with them after class, or even in class as I sit together with other Chinese students in class too...that image I envisioned for my Canadian university life now only feels like a dream that will never come true.

At the beginning of my study here, other Canadian students would invite to parties and other social events with them. But I felt alone like an outsider at those events because I could not really understand what they talk about or say what I wanted to say; Canadian students speak English so fast that I barely could keep up and they often misunderstood what I said because of my accent or they would not be patient enough to really hear me out. It was really hard to fit in at those events when you cannot talk like a normal person. Then gradually they stopped inviting me to parties.

None of the international students interviewed was able to forge close relationships with any Canadian students around them, even though all felt that Canadian students were friendly to them. Their need for relatedness in a foreign country was clearly unsatisfied.

DISCUSSION

The authors recognize that it is crucial to address the validity and trustworthiness concerns of this musically enhanced narrative inquiry as participant words were transformed through the music composition processes to create musical narrative representations, in which inherent manipulations happen. The authors acknowledge overtly that composing music to participants' words could potentially change their meanings. The musical representations could be argued to be more of a representation of the composer than participants as the author filtered the stories told by participants. Further, even though the authors intentionally employed repeating interpretive tendencies of sound to highlight the meanings identified in the reported themes, audiences could still interpret them differently based on their contexts (Gallagher, 2016). "Perception is in the ear of the beholder" (Xing, Bolden, & Hogenkamp, 2019, p. 43). However, the goal of employing music and sounds in this study was not triangulation or making truth claims of our participants' stories (Wargo, 2018). Narrative inquiry and sounded studies are not meant for pursuing "truths," but for enhancing readers' possibilities of understanding (Bolden, 2017; Gershon & Van Deventer, 2013) and achieving the fundamental aim of qualitative inquiry: promoting empathic understanding (Bresler, 2006).

Validity, the believability of a research study knowledge claim, is not "inherent in the claim but is a characteristic given to a claim by the ones to whom the claim is addressed. Thus any knowledge claim is not intrinsically valid; rather, its validity is a function of intersubjective judgment" (Polkinghorne, 2007, p. 474). Whether a knowledge claim made by the researcher is plausible or not is a judgement made by the audience based on the evidence provided by the researcher (Torrance, 2013). Thus the validity of a study can be assured if the knowledge claim made is supported with relevant and sufficient evidence for the audience to make a reasonable judgement (Barone & Eisner, 2012). The authors hope that the evidence, the participant words and stories, reported in this study are sufficient to support the knowledge claims we made in the findings section about participants' academic acculturation experiences.

Additionally, our findings resonate with a great deal of literature on Chinese international students' academic acculturation experiences in English-speaking countries (e.g., Chen et al., 2015; Choy & Alon, 2019; Meng, 2018; Yan & Berliner, 2011; Zhang & Beck, 2014). From previous literature, it was plausible to expect that Chinese international students with limited English language communication capacity would experience a stressful academic acculturation process in English-speaking countries. However, the magnitude and intensity of the psychological stress and reactions described by our participants were not expected. Even though the small sample size in this study used does not generalize to all Chinese international students (the academic acculturation process could be influenced by a host of personal factors such as family background and personality traits), the magnitude of psychological stress reported in this study does suggest that some international students on Canadian campuses clearly need more effective support to make Canadian higher education truly inclusive and equitable to all students. The authors believe that this study makes a unique contribution to the understanding of academic acculturation of international students in Canada by bringing the audience a little bit closer to what the academic acculturation stress felt like for our participants by utilizing the evocative power of music and sound.

RECOMMENDATIONS

Our research identified that the participants' academic acculturation in Canada was particularly stressful due to their undermined sense of autonomy, reduced sense of competence, and lack of relatedness to the Canadian community. This finding is significant for policy makers and senior management in Canadian higher educational institutions. When Canadian universities invest in recruitment efforts to attract more international students in the global higher education market, adequate infrastructure and support services have to be built simultaneously or preceding recruitment (Ma, 2018). Our research indicates higher education institutions should pay particular attention to the design of programs to support international students' basic psychological need for autonomy, competence, and relatedness. Student services offered to acculturating international students such as academic support and personal counselling could, ideally, be provided by staff who are culturally and linguistically diverse. Faculty and staff training programs on how to accommodate acculturating international students' learning needs would also be beneficial. Course design that better supports acculturating international students' sense of autonomy and competence should also be explored. For instance, group project and oral presentations can pose significant hurdles for international students. Alternative means of assessing student learning could be used to allow acculturating international students to demonstrate their achievement in ways that support their sense of autonomy and competence.

Further, the finding that acculturating Chinese international students in this study perceived the *spoken* component of English as the greatest problem in negotiating academic situations and social relationships during their academic acculturation amplifies the urgent need for higher Canadian education stakeholders to proactively mitigate the potential negative impact of inadequate oral English capacity on international students' academic acculturation. For international students' admission, many Canadian higher education institutions require a lower spoken English test score than for reading, writing and listening. This may send a misleading message to future international students regarding what is truly needed to succeed in Canadian academic contexts. Higher education institutions in Canada should consider a more stringent requirement for the spoken score of English proficiency language to proactively tackle the primary acculturative stressor that impedes international students' learning and academic acculturation. Similarly, designing and making accessible specific and effective oral English language support programs that incorporate international students' needs and perspectives may prove beneficial for facilitating successful academic acculturation on Canadian campuses.

LIMITATIONS

Due to the in-depth narrative nature of this study, only a small number of international students were included. This study was also limited by solely looking at undergraduate students' academic acculturation experiences. Additionally, this research was limited by its focus on participants with low English communication capacity and a Chinese educational and cultural background. Therefore, the findings from this study cannot be generalized to a wider international student population in Canadian higher education. understanding, and telling of our participants' narratives. The findings from this study can only be interpreted with the specific research contexts in mind.

CONCLUSION

Researchers have repeatedly identified the increasing recruitment of international students in the higher education systems must be accompanied by corresponding infrastructure and support services (e.g., Arthur, 1997; Arthur, 2004; Du, 2019; Xing et al., 2019). Striving to accommodate the needs of international students that experience psychological stress due to a lack of autonomy, competence, and relatedness is a way to move towards education equity in the increasingly diverse post-secondary context in Canada. As one of the participants in our study explained, "my academic capacity is suppressed here in Canada by at least fifty percent. I am not able to demonstrate and utilize my academic intelligence like domestic students, which takes a toll on both my grades and my self-esteem."

Aside from the common psychological problems associated with academic acculturation, researchers have uncovered concerns for more serious psychiatric disorders among international students on higher education campuses. Leong and Chou (1996) speculated decades ago that academic acculturation stress could put international students at risk for the onset of mental illness. Mental health issues such as serious depression, anxiety syndromes, and suicide attempts have all been found within the international student population (e.g., Arthur, 2004; Chen et al., 2015; Choy & Alon, 2019; Oropeza, Fitzgibbon, & Baron, 1991). There have been a great number of studies into challenges facing international students during their academic acculturation within new educational systems, identifying issues such as language difficulty, academic and social differences, and financial constraints (Kim, 2018). All these challenges interact with one another in a new environment in complex ways, making academic acculturation a precarious process for international students.

The adjustments required to accommodate and facilitate the transition experiences of international students recruited into Canadian higher education are multifaceted. Policy change, staff training, curriculum accommodation, and social and language support are all important areas for improvement. International students experience adaptation challenges that involve a complex and idiosyncratic interplay between academic and non-academic experiences (Cheng & Fox, 2008). Only when adequate infrastructure and support are in place to meet acculturating international students' need for autonomy, competence, and relatedness can Canadian universities truly become the equitable and inclusive communities they claim to be.

REFERENCES

Arthur, N. (1997). Counseling issues with international students. *Canadian Journal of Counselling, 31*(4), 259–273.

Arthur, N. (2004). *Counselling international students: Clients from around the world*. Plenum Publishers. doi:10.1007/978-1-4419-8919-2

Aubrey, R. (1991). International students on campus: A challenge for counselors, medical providers, and clinicians. *Smith College Studies in Social Work, 62*(1), 20–33. doi:10.1080/00377319109516697

Barone, T. E., & Eisner, E. W. (2012). *Arts-based research*. Sage.

Beech, S. E. (2019). *The geographies of international student mobility: Spaces, places and decision-making*. Springer Nature Singapore. doi:10.1007/978-981-13-7442-5

Bertram, D. M., Poulakis, M., Elsasser, B. S., & Kumar, E. (2014). Social support and acculturation in Chinese international students. *Journal of Multicultural Counseling and Development, 42*(2), 107–124. doi:10.1002/j.2161-1912.2014.00048.x

Bolden, B. (2008). Suds and Stan: Musically enhanced research. *Journal of Creative Arts in Education, 8*(1). http://www.jcae.ca/08-01/bolden.html

Bolden, B. (2017). Music as method: Musically enhanced narrative inquiry. *International Journal of Education & the Arts, 18*(9), 1–19.

Bresler, L. (2006). Embodied narrative inquiry: A methodology of connection. *Research Studies in Education, 27*(1), 21–43.

Canadian Bureau for International Education. (2019). *Another record year for Canadian international education.* https://cbie.ca/another-record-year-for-canadian-international-education/

Carter, A. (2016). Students learning English in Canada: Grounding decisions in evidence and lived experience. *Journal of Professional, Continuing, and Online Education, 1*(1), 1–14. doi:10.18741/P93W2B

Charmaz, K. (2003). Qualitative interviewing and grounded theory analysis. In J. A. Holstein & J. F. Gubrium (Eds.), *Inside interviewing: New lenses, new concerns* (pp. 311–330). Sage.

Chen, J. A., Liu, L., Zhao, X., & Yeung, A. S. (2015). Chinese international students: An emerging mental health crisis. *Journal of the American Academy of Child and Adolescent Psychiatry, 54*(11), 879–880. doi:10.1016/j.jaac.2015.06.022 PMID:26506576

Cheng, L., & Fox, J. (2008). Towards a better understanding of academic acculturation: Second language students in Canadian universities. *Canadian Modern Language Review. Canadian Modern Language Review, 65*(2), 307–333. doi:10.3138/cmlr.65.2.307

Choy, Y., & Alon, Z. (2019). The comprehensive mental health treatment of Chinese international students: A case report. *Journal of College Student Psychotherapy, 33*(1), 47–66. doi:10.1080/87568225.2018.1427513

Creswell, J. W. (2007). *Qualitative inquiry and research design: Choosing among five approaches.* Sage.

Deci, E. L., & Ryan, R. M. (2002). *Handbook of self-determination research.* University Rochester Press.

Du, X. (2019). International students' daily negotiations in language, culture, and identity in Canadian higher education. In M. T. Kariwo, N. Asadi, & C. E. Bouhali (Eds.), *Interrogating models of diversity within a multicultural environment* (pp. 275–297). Springer International Publishing AG. doi:10.1007/978-3-030-03913-4_14

Elliot, D., Reid, K., & Baumfield, V. (2016). Beyond the amusement, puzzlement and challenges: An enquiry into international students' academic acculturation. *Studies in Higher Education, 41*(12), 2198–2217. doi:10.1080/03075079.2015.1029903

Gallagher, M. (2016). Sound as affect: Difference, power and spatiality. *Emotion, Space and Society, 20*, 42–48. doi:10.1016/j.emospa.2016.02.004

Gao, Y. (2019). Experiences of Chinese international doctoral students in Canada who withdrew: A narrative inquiry. *International Journal of Doctoral Studies, 14*(1), 259–276.

Gareis, E., & Jalayer, A. (2018). Contact effects on intercultural friendship between east Asian students and American domestic students. In Y. Ma & M. A. Garcia-Murillo (Eds.), *Understanding international students from Asia in American universities* (pp. 83–106). Springer International Publishing AG. doi:10.1007/978-3-319-60394-0_5

Gershon, W. S. (2013). Vibrational affect: Sound theory and practice in qualitative research. *Cultural Studies ↔ Critical Methodologies, 13*(4), 257-262.

Gershon, W. S., & Van Deventer, G. (2013). The story of a poet who beat cancer and became a squeak: A sounded narrative about art, education, and the power of the human spirit. *Journal of Curriculum and Pedagogy, 10*(2), 96–105. doi:10.1080/15505170.2013.782593

Gopal, A. (2017). Canada, US and UK: Canada's immigration policies to attract international students. In *Understanding higher education internationalization* (pp. 231–233). Sense Publishers. doi:10.1007/978-94-6351-161-2_50

Han, X., Han, X., Luo, Q., Jacobs, S., & Jean-Baptiste, M. (2013). Report of a mental health survey among Chinese international students at Yale University. *Journal of American College Health, 61*(1), 1–8. doi:10.1080/07448481.2012.738267 PMID:23305539

Ho, H. J. (2017). *Promoting international college students' academic adjustment from self-determination theory* (Doctoral dissertation). Purdue University. https://docs.lib.purdue.edu/dissertations/AAI10608059/

Houshmand, S., Spanierman, L., & Tafarodi, R. (2014). Excluded and avoided: Racial microaggressions targeting Asian international students in Canada. *Cultural Diversity & Ethnic Minority Psychology, 20*(3), 377–388. doi:10.1037/a0035404 PMID:25045949

Ippolito, K. (2007). Promoting intercultural learning in a multicultural university: Ideas and realities. *Teaching in Higher Education, 12*(5-6), 749–763. doi:10.1080/13562510701596356

Joshee, R. (2004). Citizenship and multicultural education in Canada: From assimilation to social cohesion. In J. Banks (Ed.), *Diversity and citizenship education: Global perspectives* (pp. 127–156). Jossey-Bass.

Kim, E. (2018). Korean students' acculturation experiences in the U.S. In *Understanding International Students from Asia in American Universities* (pp. 127–147). Springer International Publishing AG. doi:10.1007/978-3-319-60394-0_7

Knight, J. (2012). Student mobility and internationalization: Trends and tribulations. *Research in Comparative and International Education, 7*(1), 20–33. doi:10.2304/rcie.2012.7.1.20

Lee, J. (2015). International student experiences: Neo-racism and discrimination. *International Higher Education, 2015*(44), 3-5.

Li, G., Chen, W., & Duanmu, J. (2010). Determinants of international students' academic performance: A comparison between Chinese and other international students. *Journal of Studies in International Education, 14*(4), 389–405. doi:10.1177/1028315309331490

Li, M. (2015). A case of difficult acculturation: A Chinese student in a New Zealand university. In E. Christopher (Ed.), *International management and intercultural communication* (pp. 41–61). Palgrave Macmillan. doi:10.1007/978-1-137-55325-6_4

Ma, Y. (2018). Paradigm shift: Learning is a two-way street between American universities and Asian international students. In Y. Ma & M. A. Garcia-Murillo (Eds.), *Understanding international students from Asia in American universities* (pp. 1–11). Springer International Publishing AG. doi:10.1007/978-3-319-60394-0_1

Meng, Q., Zhu, C., & Cao, C. (2018). Chinese international students' social connectedness, social and academic adaptation: The mediating role of global competence. *Higher Education, 75*(1), 131–147. doi:10.100710734-017-0129-x

Nilsson, P. A., & Stålnacke, B. M. (2009). Life satisfaction among inbound university students in northern Sweden. *Fennia, 197*(1), 94–107. doi:10.11143/fennia.70337

Oropeza, B. A. C., Fitzgibbon, M., & Baron, A. J. Jr. (1991). Managing mental health crises of foreign college students. *Journal of Counseling and Development, 69*(3), 280–284. doi:10.1002/j.1556-6676.1991.tb01506.x

Polkinghorne, D. (2007). Validity issues in narrative research. *Qualitative Inquiry, 13*(4), 471–486. doi:10.1177/1077800406297670

Poyrazli, S., & Kavanaugh, P. R. (2006). Marital status, ethnicity, academic achievement, and adjustment strains: The case of graduate international students. *College Student Journal, 40*, 767–780.

Razfar, A., & Gutiérrez, K. (2003). Reconceptualizing early childhood literacy: The sociocultural influence. In N. Hall, J. Larson, & J. Marsh (Eds.), *Handbook of early childhood literacy* (pp. 34–47). Sage. doi:10.4135/9781848608207.n4

Rosenthal, D. A., Russell, V. J., & Thomson, G. D. (2006). *A growing experience: The health and the well-being of international students at the University of Melbourne*. The University of Melbourne.

Sam, D. L. (2001). Satisfaction with life among international students: An exploratory study. *Social Indicators Research, 53*(3), 315–337. doi:10.1023/A:1007108614571

Sawir, E., Marginson, S., Forbes-Mewett, H., Nyland, C., & Ramia, G. (2012). International student security and English language proficiency. *Journal of Studies in International Education, 16*(5), 434–454. doi:10.1177/1028315311435418

Smith, R. A., & Khawaja, N. G. (2011). A review of the acculturation experiences of international students. *International Journal of Intercultural Relations, 35*(6), 699–713. doi:10.1016/j.ijintrel.2011.08.004

Tannock, S. (2018). *Educational equality and international students: Justice across borders?* Springer International Publishing AG. doi:10.1007/978-3-319-76381-1

Teixeira, J. P., Carraca, V. E., Markland, S., Silva, N. M., & Ryan, M. R. (2012). Exercise, physical activity, and Self- Determination Theory: A systematic review. *The International Journal of Behavioral Nutrition and Physical Activity*, (9), 1–30. PMID:22726453

Telbis, N. M., Helgeson, L., & Kingsbury, C. (2014). International students' confidence and academic success. *Journal of International Students, 4*(4), 330–341.

Thomas, D. (2006). A general inductive approach for analyzing qualitative evaluation data. *The American Journal of Evaluation, 27*(2), 237–246. doi:10.1177/1098214005283748

Torrance, H. (2013). Qualitative research, science, and government: Evidence, criteria, policy, and politics. In N. K. Denzin & Y. S. Lincoln (Eds.), *Collecting and interpreting qualitative materials* (4th ed., pp. 355–380). Sage.

Trainor, L. (2010). The emotional origin of music. *Physics of Life Reviews, 7*(1), 44–45. doi:10.1016/j.plrev.2010.01.010 PMID:20374924

Wargo, J. M. (2018). Earwitnessing (in)equity: Tracing the intra-active encounters of 'being-in-resonance-with' sound and the social contexts of education. *Educational Studies, 54*(2), 1–14.

Xing, D. (2017). *Exploring academic acculturation experiences of Chinese international students with low oral English proficiency: A musically enhanced narrative inquiry* (Master's thesis). Queen's University, Kingston, Canada. https://qspace.library.queensu.ca/handle/1974/15922

Xing, D., & Bolden, B. (2019). Treading on a foreign land: A multiple case study of Chinese international students' academic acculturation experiences. *Student Success, 10*(3), 25–35. doi:10.5204sj.v10i3.1406

Xing, D., Bolden, B., & Hogenkamp, S. (2019). The sound of silence: A musically enhanced narrative inquiry into the academic acculturation experiences of Chinese international students with low oral English proficiency. *Journal of Curriculum and Pedagogy*. Advance online publication. doi:10.1080/15505170.2019.1627616

Yan, K., & Berliner, D. C. (2011). Chinese international students in the United States: Demographic trends, motivations, acculturation features and adjustment challenges. *Asia Pacific Education Review*, *12*(2), 173–184. doi:10.100712564-010-9117-x

Yang, R., Noels, K., & Saumure, K. (2006). Multiple routes to cross-cultural adaptation for international students: Mapping the paths between self-construals, English language confidence, and adjustment. *International Journal of Intercultural Relations*, *30*(4), 487–506. doi:10.1016/j.ijintrel.2005.11.010

Yeh, C. J., & Inose, M. (2003). International students' reported English fluency, social support satisfaction, and social connectedness as predictors of acculturative stress. *Counselling Psychology Quarterly*, *16*(1), 15–28. doi:10.1080/0951507031000114058

Zhang, Z., & Beck, K. (2014). I came, but I'm lost: Learning stories of three Chinese international students in Canada. *Comparative and International Education / Éducation Comparée et Internationale*, *43*(2), 1-14.

Zimmerman, S. (1995). Perceptions of intercultural communication competence and international student adaptation to an American campus. *Communication Education*, *44*(4), 321–335. doi:10.1080/03634529509379022

ADDITIONAL READING

Hayes, A. (2019). *Inclusion, epistemic democracy and international students: The teaching excellence framework and education policy*. Springer International Publishing AG. doi:10.1007/978-3-030-11401-5

Kariwo, M. T., Asadi, N., & Bouhali, C. E. (Eds.). (2019). *Interrogating models of diversity within a multicultural environment*. Springer International Publishing AG. doi:10.1007/978-3-030-03913-4

Madgetta, P. J., & Bélanger, C. (2008). International students: The Canadian experience. *Tertiary Education and Management*, *14*(3), 191–207. doi:10.1080/13583880802228182

Popadiuk, N., & Arthur, N. (2004). Counseling international students in Canadian schools. *International Journal for the Advancement of Counseling*, *26*(2), 125–145. doi:10.1023/B:ADCO.0000027426.05819.44

Spencer-Oatey, H., Dauber, D., Jing, J., & Lifei, W. (2017). Chinese students' social integration into the university community: Hearing the students' voices. *Higher Education*, *74*(5), 739–756. doi:10.100710734-016-0074-0

Sullivan, C., & Kashubeck-West, S. (2015). The interplay of international students' acculturative stress, social support, and acculturation modes. *Journal of International Students*, *5*(1), 1–11.

Trilokekar, R. D. (2010). International education as soft power? The contributions and challenges of Canadian foreign policy to the internationalization of higher education. *Higher Education*, *59*(2), 131–147. doi:10.100710734-009-9240-y

Yan, K. (2017). *Chinese international students' stressors and coping strategies in the United States*. Springer Nature Singapore. doi:10.1007/978-981-10-3347-6

KEY TERMS AND DEFINITIONS

Academic Acculturation: A dynamic psychological adaptation process that international students experience when migrating to study in an academic setting in a foreign country.

Academic Contexts: Settings where scholastic activities are the main focus or purpose.

Acculturation: A dynamic psychological adaptation process that one experiences when migrating into new cultures.

Cultural Distance: The degree of similarity that two cultures share in terms of values and communication norms.

English Proficiency: The ability one has to engage in listening, speaking, reading, and writing in English.

International Student Mobility: The opportunity that a student has to undertake academic studies broad in a foreign country that range from short-term experience programs to long-term degree programs.

Linguistic Distance: The degree of similarity that two languages share in terms of linguistic features.

Section 2
Classroom–Based Experiences

Chapter 4

Connecting Best Practices for Teaching International Students With Student Satisfaction:
A Review of STEM and Non–STEM Student Perspectives

Clayton Smith

https://orcid.org/0000-0002-7611-9193

University of Windsor, Canada

George Zhou

https://orcid.org/0000-0002-4594-633X

University of Windsor, Canada

Michael Potter

University of Windsor, Canada

Deena Wang

University of Windsor, Canada

Fabiana Menezes

https://orcid.org/0000-0002-9596-6275

University of Windsor, Canada

Gagneet Kaur

University of Windsor, Canada

ABSTRACT

This chapter explores promising teaching practices for teaching linguistically and culturally diverse international students by identifying the teaching practices that have high levels of international student satisfaction and student perceptions of learning for science, technology, engineering, mathematics (STEM)

DOI: 10.4018/978-1-7998-5030-4.ch004

and non-STEM international students. Research was conducted by an international, student-learning community, with guidance from a faculty-led research team. Data was collected through a qualitative research design that included focus groups and individual interviews conducted at a mid-sized Canadian comprehensive university. A total of 28 students participated (14 STEM students and 14 non-STEM students). Researchers examined differences between STEM and non-STEM students on 22 promising teaching practices regarding student satisfaction and students' perceptions of learning. Recommendations for professional practice are discussed, along with potential areas for further research.

BACKGROUND

As international student enrollment in Canadian and U.S. colleges and universities grows, institutions are becoming increasingly more culturally and ethnoculturally diverse (Canadian Bureau of International Education, 2016; Institute of International Education, 2016). Despite this trend, few instructors have received training for teaching international students (Paige & Goode, 2009), which may produce an inadequate environment for intercultural learning. In order to achieve higher student satisfaction and perceptions of learning, instructors need to implement new teaching strategies that may better engage international students. Educational leaders also need to analyze their role in facilitating students' learning experiences abroad.

Culture shock may be the first big discomfort faced by international students when they arrive in the new host country; even so, this will not be the only challenge they face. As soon as they move abroad to study, international students must adapt to new social and academic environments. Beyond living arrangements, socialization, language barriers, changes in eating practices, and in communication, international students also must face issues regarding their academic life. They will not only deal with new methods of teaching used by their instructors, in a foreign language, but they will also have to alter their learning strategies and preferences to a new learning environment (Lin & Yi, 1997; Rao, 2017; Smith, Zhou, Potter, & Wang, 2019).

Smith, Zhou, Potter, and Wang (2019) identified some of the teaching practices that have high levels of student satisfaction and perceptions of learning. They found that instructors who use these teaching practices will create a more accessible learning environment for international students. In a subsequent research report (Smith, Zhou, Potter, Wang, Pecoraro, & Paulino, 2019), they found that by examining individual student characteristics (e.g., country of origin, the field of study, level of study), the preferred teaching practices, rated by the respondents, varied significantly. In addition, they revealed 22 promising teaching practices where there was a significant difference between the responses of STEM and non-STEM students regarding student satisfaction and perceptions of learning.

Although there are studies that confirm variability in student satisfaction and perceptions of learning by the students' field of study, the literature is deficient regarding investigating the experiences of international students. The purpose of this chapter is to discuss the different teaching and learning preferences of international students, with specific attention to the differences between STEM and non-STEM students' preferences, to identify the most promising teaching practices for teaching linguistically and culturally diverse international students.

The following two research questions guided this study:

1. What are the promising teaching practices for teaching linguistically and culturally diverse international students that have high international STEM student satisfaction and students' perceptions of student learning?
2. What are the promising teaching practices for teaching linguistically and culturally diverse international students that have high international non-STEM student satisfaction and students' perceptions of student learning?

LITERATURE REVIEW

The academic and non-academic challenges faced by international students during their education-abroad experience often impacts students' educational success and retention. Some of the academic challenges international students encounter include language challenges (Zhang, & Zhou, 2010), exclusion from group discussions (Yates & Thi QuynhTrang, 2012), cultural-related learning differences (Koul & Fisher, 2005), academic support issues (Zhang & Zhou, 2010), and adjustment to new educational systems (Hofstede, 1997). They also face several non-academic challenges, including cultural adjustment (Zhang & Zhou, 2010), social issues (Fritz, Chin, & DeMarini, 2008; Zhang & Goodson, 2011), and finances (Choudaha & Schulmann, 2014). While international students engage more in educationally purposeful activities than their domestic student colleagues (Zhao, Kuh, & Carini, 2005), they report greater academic challenges, more interactions with instructors, more engagement in diversity-related activities, and greater gains in personal and social development, practical competence, and general education.

North American post-secondary educational institutions have demonstrated that they can attract international students by developing strong strategic enrollment management initiatives. However, to achieve diversity, inclusivity, and internationalization goals, educational leaders must also enhance the international-student academic experience. This will require paying more attention to the international-student success factors. Satisfaction of international students within the classroom and across the student experience will also need to be an important consideration. Institutions are increasingly looking at ways to enhance the international student academic experience by making use of promising international student-teaching practices, connected to student learning preferences, as a pathway for achieving higher levels of student satisfaction and retention (Smith, 2020).

Learning Preferences

Cultural differences are an important factor that can influence the learning process for international students. The way learners absorb content is different according to their cultural background (Foster & Stapleton, 2012). It is also important to consider that international students prefer the teaching practices and approaches that they are accustomed to in their home countries (McKinnon, 2013). This suggests that any other approach used by instructors can cause an estrangement to international students, seeming foreign and incompatible.

The Asian educational system, especially the Chinese system, follows Confucianism values. These values, when reflected in the classroom, provide students with a learning environment quite different from what is found in North American postsecondary educational institutions. Confucianism gives professors the authority to be the holders of knowledge; their wisdom must never be questioned. As part of this learning environment, Chinese students tend not to question their instructors, and maintain silence for most of the class (Le Ha & Li, 2012). The learning styles and preferences of Chinese students may also be affected by the exam culture, that is, their learning strategies are more related to memorization, in order to get excellent marks on their exams (Lee, 1996). Research conducted with Chinese business students enrolled at a Canadian university concluded that Western practices, such as case analysis, presentations, and in-class discussions, are very different from the experience they have in their native-country classrooms. Therefore, Asian students require more direction from their instructors when studying abroad (Liang & McQueen, 1999).

Learning styles and preferences may vary according to the student's field of study (Kulturel-Konak, D'Allegro & Dickinson, 2011). One study, developed at the University of Bahrain, sought to identify differences in learning styles among students. The researchers found that there were statistical differences in the learning styles of students enrolled in different areas of study. While education and information technology students were more active learners, law and science students were more reflective learners (Alumran, 2008). The author implied that a possible reason for these results is that information technology students must focus on computer skills and activities involving hands-on application, and education students must also use new methodologies and activities to teach children in the classroom. Therefore, active learning techniques were commonly used by these groups of students. Surprisingly, the same logic could not be applied to science students, who were found to be very active with running experiments and practical analysis. In this case, science students proved to be more reflective learners.

Another study, conducted at the University of Oklahoma, sought to find the similarities and differences in learning styles among students in STEM fields. The sample in this study included engineering, mathematics, physics, and chemistry students. Although the study concluded that there are differences between students in these four areas of study, the most significant difference was found between engineering and mathematics' students. Engineering students preferred more active and concrete learning styles, while mathematics students were more intuitive (Harvey, Ling, & Shehab, 2010). The researchers explained that the way mathematics students absorb information presented in class is different from engineering students. As mathematics students must deal with more abstract ideas, they become more abstract learners. On the other hand, engineering students are more visual, because in their coursework they are required to interpret graphs and diagrams. The author suggests that mathematics-instructors use visual approaches when teaching engineering groups, so that students can understand the different concepts and content properly.

A more recent study focused on students enrolled in a summer term at a university in Iran. The student sample included representation from various fields, including the arts and humanities, science, engineering, social sciences, and English as a foreign language. Findings showed that, among this sample of students, no statistical significance was found regarding the differences in the areas of study and learning styles used by Iranian students (Sahragarda, Khajavia, & Abbasian, 2016). A possible explanation for this, according to the researchers, is that as learning styles and strategies are highly individualized (Wintergerst & DeCapua, 2001), they cannot be changed easily. That is, it is not solely a result of a student's chosen field of study that the teaching and learning preferences of students vary.

Teaching Approaches

Recent research suggests that STEM and non-STEM students have different preferences for teaching practices. Smith, Zhou, Potter, Wang, Pecoraro, and Paulino (2019) identified 22 promising teaching practices for which there are student satisfaction differences between STEM and non-STEM students.

Further, Debdi, Paredes-Velasco, and Velázquez-Iturbide (2016) concluded that the teaching practices used by instructors in engineering and computer science courses were unaligned with the learning preferences of the students.

Felder and Spurlin (2005) stated that the traditional teaching approaches that have been used in engineering courses are reflective, verbal, intuitive, and sequential. Instructors used lecture-based lessons, along with theoretical and abstract approaches in their classes, yet students preferred hands-on, and active engagement activities. This disparity among the teaching practices used by instructors, and the learning strategies and styles used by students, can negatively affect the learning environment and students' perceptions of learning. In fact, their study found that traditional practices of teaching engineering, including lectures and practical exercises, were perceived as somewhat outdated to students. The authors also suggested that instructors use non-traditional approaches, such as providing less lecture-heavy classes, practical activities, and concrete examples in order to teach those students in a more effective way. Pollard, Hains-Wesson, and Young (2018) further concluded that engineering instructors should use creative teaching practices in order to help their students better understand the content. The authors also recommend that changing teaching approaches can be hard and challenging, but students require new methodologies and pedagogies in STEM disciplines.

While STEM students appear to prefer teaching practices that implement hands-on, active learning, non-STEM students are more reflective and abstract learners who prefer teaching approaches that emphasize lectures, papers, and discussions. According to one study (Fox & Rokowsky, 1997), political science students have learning preferences for approaches related to abstract thinking, but in a contextualized environment, using real examples to illustrate their explanations. Another study (Nelson Laird, Shoup, Kuh, & Schwarz, 2008) found that students who major in non-STEM fields of study tend to use "deep approaches to learning" (p. 489) to a greater degree than those majoring in STEM fields. Deep learning, according to Biggs and Tang (2011), is an approach whereby students engage meaningfully with the subject matter by using various learning strategies (e.g., reading widely, combining a variety of resources, discussing ideas with others, reflecting on how individual pieces of information relate to larger constructs or patterns, applying knowledge in real world situations).

Although the literature corroborates the idea that there is a need for different teaching approaches for STEM and non-STEM fields, attempting to match the learning preferences of students with instructors teaching approaches can be challenging, since learning practices evolve and change (Vincent-Lancrin, Urgel, Kar, & Jacobin, 2019). Instructors must take into consideration the individuality of their students and be aware of how to facilitate learning so that every student can absorb the content efficiently.

The field of study is an important factor that may relate to the learning styles and strategies of students. Further, the teaching approaches used by instructors may influence students' learning processes. However, little is known about how preferred teaching and learning practices vary according to the area of study among international students, and which teaching methods optimize student satisfaction and perceptions of learning among this group.

THEORY

This study is based on the belief that the most effective teaching practices for teaching linguistically and culturally diverse international students are where promising teaching practices, international student satisfaction, and student perceptions of learning meet. It is based on Tinto's (1993) student integration model, which was built on Durkheim's suicide model (1951). It suggests that individual departure from postsecondary-educational institutions results from a lengthy process of interactions between the individual and her/his connection with an institution's academic and social systems. He explained that students who achieve academic and social integration, both formal and informal, increase their commitment to their careers and educational goals, and their postsecondary educational institutions. Figure 1 shows how promising teaching practices, student satisfaction, and student perceptions of learning come together to create the necessary academic and social integration to achieve student retention.

Figure 1. Identifying effective teaching practices

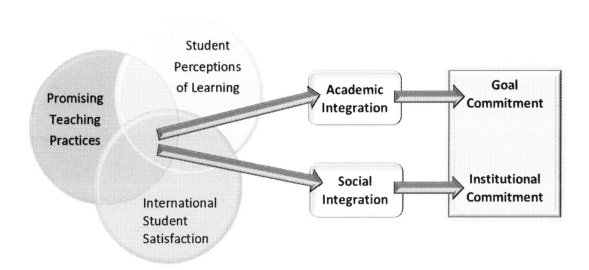

METHOD

The purpose of this chapter is to discuss the different teaching and learning preferences of international students, with specific attention to the differences between STEM and non-STEM students' preferences, to identify the most promising teaching practices for teaching linguistically and culturally diverse international students. As this is an exploratory study related to the impact of area of study regarding STEM v. non-STEM on student satisfaction with selected teaching practices, researchers focused primarily on student preferences for specific teaching and learning methods (e.g., "quiet" vs. 'active' participation, individualistic vs. collective orientations to learning).

Participants

Research participants are international students who study at a mid-sized, comprehensive university in Ontario, Canada. They included students from a wide array of countries of origin, study levels, programs, study times, study stages, and ages. Most (23) research participants were graduate students enrolled in thesis-based or course-based master's degree programs. Undergraduates who participated were in third or fourth-year undergraduate studies. A total of 28 students participated (14 STEM students, and 14 non-STEM students) in the study.

Procedures

Step 1: The participants of this study were recruited by e-mail to participate in focus groups and individual interviews. Participants were recruited by the following methods:

- an individual email invitation was sent to all international students, with a link to a survey questionnaire, including two reminder emails, for students to indicate their interest in participating in the study;
- a broadcast message was sent to the institution's learning management system's international student group, inviting international students to participate in the study;
- an email was sent to all international student-serving offices encouraging staff to share the invitation with potential research participants; and
- an email was sent to the institution's graduate assistants and teaching assistants encouraging them to share the invitation with potential research participants.

Step 2: Focus groups and individual interviews were held between November 2019 and March 2020. Each focus group and individual interview lasted approximately one hour in length. They were digitally recorded, and then transcribed, after which the recordings were destroyed.

Step 3: Data was coded and analyzed, which resulted in a thematic analysis.

Step 4: A prize draw was awarded upon the conclusion of the study.

RESULTS

Data from a prior research study (Smith, Zhou, Potter, Wang, Pecoraro, & Paulino, 2019) revealed 22 promising teaching practices where there was a statistically significant difference between the responses of STEM and non-STEM international students regarding student satisfaction and perceptions of learning. In this study, researchers explored these teaching practices to learn more about why STEM and non-STEM students have different levels of satisfaction and students' perceptions of learning levels. Study findings for some overall topics, including overall impression of teaching received, most enjoyable memory, teaching practices most preferred, teaching practices least preferred, and recommended teaching practice changes, are presented. In addition, student satisfaction with each of the selected teaching practices is described. Student comments in general terms are presented below, which represent the themes students identified during the focus groups and individual interviews.

Overall Impression of Teaching Received

In general, the student respondents said that their experience with the teaching practices they experienced was positive. They reported satisfaction with their professors' use of the student-centered teaching paradigm, which differed from the teacher-centered paradigm used by professors in their home countries.

Some of the comments made by STEM students included:

- "Back in India, there is a theoretical part, and it was very less practical. In our courses, we actually apply those things, and it was very useful."
- "Teachers are very good and always open to questions."
- "We were given group partners who did not always participate."
- "Teaching methods were good. Both courses had projects and so, we practiced what we learned."
- "I think the teaching is very good, but the classes are huge."
- "I expected more practical and less theoretical."
- "There was a lot of differences in the terminology from what was used back home. I need to learn those things."
- "Teaching methods vary from one course to another."
- "Industrial experience is key. I am satisfied due to practical applications."
- "They don't spoon-feed us. Just give us an overview of the topic and let us study on our own."

Some of the comments made by non-STEM students included:

- "In general, it is very good. One of the teachers was the best teacher I have ever had."
- "Sometimes instructors speak very fast."
- "When I started, with permission from the instructor, I recorded the lectures. Then I go back and study again. If there is more hands-on, or maybe more visuals. I think when you are a second-language learners, it makes you a visual learner."
- "The depth of the program is well thought of."
- "Really satisfied."
- "Back home, what the professor says is everything. You go against what the professor says, you are probably going to fail that class. Over here, particularly in my economics classes, you have more freedom to explore. So, I actually prefer what I am getting here to back home."

Most Enjoyable Memory

While the length of time studying outside of their home countries varies, all respondents were able to describe an enjoyable memory associated with the teaching they had experienced. One engineering student spoke about a professor who knew the names of all the students in a class where there were more than 100 students enrolled. A business student told of how a professor used story-telling as a way of conveying course content. Another engineering student described a tower-building activity that took place in the first-class meeting, which resulted in a team-building experience. Nearly all respondents had similar stories to share with the researchers.

Some of the comments made by STEM students included:

- "They do this peer review thing. Helps me to see mistakes he does, but allows me to see what mistakes I am making. Helps a lot."
- "Like two-way communication where there is not just a slide-read."
- "Professor shared industry experience."
- "Use of interactive technology, such as Kahoot."
- "Liked continuous feedback."

Some of the comments made by non-STEM students included:

- "Well-structured class."
- "Discussion-based and presentations that include diversity. I feel like I learned a lot, especially through the discussions."
- "I used to go to his office all the time. We would dialogue and debate on different issues."
- "I took one class with Professor…and boom that was it. The passion with which he spoke about the subject. It was not just about facts. It was just so beautiful. Literally, he changed my life."
- "Professors paid attention to students."

Student Satisfaction with Selected Teaching Practices

In this study, researchers explored the teaching practices, identified by Smith, Zhou, Potter, Wang, Pecoraro, and Paulino (2019), where STEM and non-STEM students have statistically significant different levels of student satisfaction and perceptions of learning, to better understand the reasons for their varying responses. Findings suggest both similarities and differences between STEM and non-STEM students regarding their experiences with the selected teaching practices. Table 1 provides a summary of student satisfaction comments with the selected teaching-practices for STEM and non-STEM respondents.

Teaching Practices Most Preferred

A wide array of teaching practices was described as most preferred by the student respondents. Some of the common responses included the use of two-way communications between students and professors, incorporation of discussion and student-faculty engagement, and development of a positive and inclusive classroom environment.

Some of the comments made by STEM students included:

- "Two-way communication where students and teachers interact with each other."
- "Using visualizing tools, because some concepts are difficult to understand."
- "Labs. So, if we have any questions, we can learn how to apply theories. So, the labs are very beneficial."
- "The storytelling method, since it will always remain in your mind."
- "The seating arrangement where everyone can see each other."
- "The professor engages with us and tries to help us present ourselves in a better way."

Some of the comments made by non-STEM students included:

- "Reviewed one chapter per class. Managed the timing and covered the full amount of time. Managed the tempo of the class."
- "Able to crack a joke."
- "Uses a two-way communication style."
- "Uses a lot of team-work. Projects make the difference."
- "Use of rubrics."
- "Classes that have different structures."

Table 1. Student satisfaction with selected teaching practices by STEM and non-STEM respondents

Teaching Practice	STEM Respondents	Non-STEM Respondents
Makes time for students to share their backgrounds during class	"I would prefer it even though I haven't experienced it." "Would like to share information, but not easy with large classes." "Never share background beyond our names."	"Every single professor did it. Maybe too much." "It is important to know students from a cultural diversity perspective." "Sometimes people get offended by being put on the spot." "As an ice-breaker."
Uses fair assessment practices	"They are pretty much fair." "Assessments are graded properly." "Sometimes, the finals are way too hard.".	"Depends on the professor. Do better by going to the professor and asking for help." "Prefer to have fewer assignments in classes I do well in, and more assignments in more difficult classes."
Designs assessments that recognizes and validates cultural differences in writing and communication styles	"There is not much cultural difference in computers because the coding is pretty much the same." "Mainly affected project management and technical communications. There are so many ways our culture affects our writing."	"Rubrics need to be mindful of international students where English is not their first language." "Some of the classes mention different economic climates."
Collects written questions about the lecture at the end of class	"At the end of each section, sometimes." "I haven't seen that yet." "Professor asks at the end if anyone has questions."	"Sometimes." "People who ask you for feedback use that feedback."
Actively invites students to come to faculty office hours	"Mentions office hours in the first class and does not mention it again." "Every time we have any kind of struggle, they promote them." "They really ask us to come to office hours."	"Most do." "About 75% would encourage us to come to office hours." "Sometimes, especially when they are rushing to another class, they would say come to office hours."
Takes every opportunity to enhance student-teacher dialogue outside of the classroom	"Almost nothing outside of the classroom." "Sometimes, career counseling." "Professors are very busy, so not much opportunity." "Informal discussion." "Just a formal 'Hi' or 'How are you doing."	"Some of them." "Varies by program." "Some professors do not want to see you after class." "I have seen about 5 professors outside of class or office hours" (over 3 years). "For those who have been available, it is really nice."
Engages in cross-cultural communications and learning	"I don't think this has anything to do with engineering; no such thing really." "I think that cross-cultural communications are essential for engineers." "It is not possible in such a big-class."	"Yes, they do." "Some engage students culturally outside of class." "They initiate discussions." "When there are few international students in class, professors may not want to put too much attention on them."
Appreciates that students come to higher education with a range of educational experiences and expectations	"Appreciate is a strong word. They understand and try to work with it." "Communication between a professor and students is almost always one-way. It needs to be two-way." "Try to relate our working experience with the teaching material." "In class we never share our backgrounds."	"On an individual basis." "Not all of them."
Focuses on how we can become global professionals	"Give insights." "One professor really focuses on that." "It is very important."	"Prepare people to work everywhere." "We have some courses based on cultural differences." "In our French classes, we compare Quebec French and international French, which is a lot different." "Talking about the whole world."
Models tolerance for responses that have more than one meaning	"I don't think it has application in engineering." "Most have very good tolerance." "Open to different ideas and responses is a good thing."	"They are thinking about what students are saying, then puts it into context." "We do talk about our cultural differences." "None of my professors shun conflict. Most allow us to express our views in such areas as abortion and police brutality."
Provides opportunities for students to reflect on, and gain a better understanding of their own multiple (e.g., cultural, personal, disciplinary) identities	"Don't think this is relevant to engineering." "Lifestyle matters. I started volunteering in lots of things. An improvement for me."	"I feel that it is not important for them to put them in a unique perspective." "Would help me learn better." "They don't expect you to already be a master of the material."
Uses inclusive language to help create a positive classroom climate	"STEM is cut and dried." "I feel like I belong in the classroom."	"They ask what pronouns you want for yourself. Everyone feels safe." "When it comes to gender, almost everyone is inclusive." "But maybe not in terms of research methods. It is usually Western."
Invites guest speakers with various perspectives to enrich course content	"I did not have, but I think it is a good idea." "In first-year classes." "I like having guest speakers."	"Some of them. Some were helpful; some not so much." "Guest speakers can talk about real world experiences." "Many invite us to on-campus sessions outside of class."
Provides feedback often using multiple techniques	"Very lacking in formative feedback." "Most feedback is summative." "I would like timely feedback, so I can improve." "Feedback – only give marks, right or wrong."	"Depends on your willingness to receive feedback." "Feedback is sometimes spotty." "Only way you get feedback is by going to office hours." "One gave me feedback through Blackboard." "Professors write notes on your paper."
Encourages public feedback	"They clarify with public feedback, anonymous." "We got public feedback, using a comparison method." "They always discuss the mid-term in class."	"Feedback to class can be useful. But sometimes people don't want to be embarrassed with public feedback." "General feedback is better." "Most give public feedback after mid-terms."
Provides students with a list of relevant dictionaries or other reference materials	"No textbooks or glossaries." "Usually through lecture slides."	"Do in their slides and presentations." "One provided a list of terms on Blackboard." "For language classes, you can find what you need with a translator."

continued on following page

Table 1. Continued

Teaching Practice	STEM Respondents	Non-STEM Respondents
Uses verbal signposts, such as "this is an essential point" to underscore important information	"No. It is all important." "They stress things that are more important." "Tells us to focus on certain things and tells us to research certain topics and become more familiar."	"Yes. Would say this is very important." "Some of them do that. The professor talking about this thing, so you get the idea." "Practically all of my classes."
Makes lecture slides available to students	"A very good idea to post slides before. You can then bring your laptop and take notes. But not experienced it." "We have a skeleton type so we can concentrate on the lecture during class."	"Slides usually provided before the lecture." "Some profs give slides before, others during or after class."
Makes lectures available by audio or video outside of class	"Would be good for those unable to make class. Or a combination of in class and video lectures."	"No. Slides only." "Only when they are hybrid classes – audio only." "Recordings are helpful. You can go back in and study from them."
Offers a question and asks students to write a response silently for a few minutes, which is followed by class discussion focusing on the responses	"No experience." "Happens sometimes." "Uses surprise quizzes." "About half of my classes use this."	"Very common." "One professor uses Top Hat."
Creates a peer support/mentor program for lecture note-taking	"No. But could be useful." "Don't need to take notes because the slides have everything." "In case you miss a class, you can ask for other students to share their notes." "Yes. We have a group of students on WhatsApp. So, in case we miss a class, we ask other students if they can post the solutions."	"No. But if you have a doctor's note, that is a different thing. But only available to students with documentation. I wish it were otherwise." "Only have 2 classes where someone takes notes."
Ensures that notes written on the board or flipcharts are legible from the furthest seat in the room	"There are some classes where we cannot see the board. In large classes, more an issue." "Sometimes it is hard to see from the back due to the angle." "It can be seen, but it is not clear. The professor jokes about is and says, 'use your imagination.'" "The angle and the reflection on the board sometimes. So, the professor tells us to come forward."	"Yes." "You can see everything." "When it is written on the white board, sometimes lighting affects whether you can see it."

- "Group projects when I can pick my group members."
- "Professor's approach."

Teaching Practices Least Preferred

There were several teaching practices that students said they did not prefer. Some of these are related to the differences between their home-country learning experience and the one they found at their new postsecondary institution. Others resulted from their expectations not being met by the new learning environment.

Some of the comments made by STEM students included:

- "Courses are heavily memorization-based."
- "Written assignments because everyone is going to cheat from each other."
- "Lectures that do not fully cover the content."
- "Professor's accent, which I could not fully understand."
- "Presentation of lecture slides without full explanations."
- "The method of not sharing notes and being told to write everything the professor is reciting."

Some of the comments made by non-STEM students included:

- "Didn't cover the book at all."
- "No feedback."
- "Where students did most of the teaching. Seems like there was no teaching."
- "Lectures that are only theory-based."

- "Where there is little opportunity for engagement."
- "The main thing is having to know it is because that is how it is."

Recommended Changes to Teaching Practices

At the conclusion of the focus groups and interviews, the researchers asked student participants to suggest some teaching practices they thought their professors should change. Some of these suggestions touched on institutional decisions, such as class size and availability of university-wide international connections, while many recommendations focused on specific teaching approaches individual professors could implement.

Some of the comments made by STEM students included:

- "Provide lecture notes in addition to slides."
- "More concentration on the technical stuff."
- "Professors should be available during the last 15 minutes for questions."
- "Professor should be more clear and articulate properly."
- "Focus more on theory in class."
- "Reduce class size."
- "Share some teaching material so we can refer to it for better understanding."
- "Providing more opportunities to learn more outside of the class. It is a good idea to provide learning outside of class."
- "More applied learning opportunities."
- "Have the GA's and professor resolve the question in the same way."
- "Posting lecture slides online."
- "Improve class organization."

Some of the comments made by non-STEM students included:

- "Standardize how the grading goes, less different between different classes."
- "Would want my professors to use more discussions, and to be more engaged. If professors would take more time to focus on their students, it would help."
- "Communicating outside of the classroom and having a place to talk to professors."
- "Having more international connections, socializing, in the university in general."
- "Those who are not engaging to become engaging. If it is more of a dialogue, that would work better."

DISCUSSION

This research sought to examine the different teaching preferences of international students, with specific attention to the differences between STEM and non-STEM students' preferences, to identify the promising teaching practices for teaching linguistically and culturally diverse international students. Building on an earlier study (Smith, Zhou, Potter, Wang, Pecoraro, & Paulino, 2019), the researchers examined differences between STEM and non-STEM students on 22 promising teaching practices where there is a statistically significant difference between STEM and non-STEM international students regarding student satisfaction and students' perceptions of learning.

Findings from this study echoed several literature findings. First, the field of study appears to be an important factor in understanding both the learning styles and teaching preferences of international students. Second, there is a need to use different teaching practices when teaching STEM and non-STEM students. Third, there are teaching practices used by non-STEM instructors that, if used by STEM instructors, could result in more deep and efficient content learning.

In general, the student respondents said that their experiences with the teaching practices they encountered were positive. They reported satisfaction with their professors' use of student-centered teaching methods to enhance classroom learning. There was little difference in responses made by STEM and non-STEM students regarding their most preferred and least preferred teaching practices, or recommended teaching practices' changes. Some of the practices identified by both groups included: use of two-way communications, formative feedback, sharing lecture slides in advance, matching lecture topics with textbook topics, course organization, student engagement, managing speed of lecturing, and opportunities for applied or hands-on learning. In addition, STEM students identified reducing class sizes, terminology explanations, industrial experiences, use of interactive technology, visualization tools, lecture-notes sharing, and out-of-class learning opportunities. Non-STEM students stressed program depth, discussion-based and team-work activities, focus on diversity topics, use of humor, opportunities to engage with professors outside the classroom, and having more opportunities for socializing beyond home-country students.

Looking at the 22 teaching practices in which there is a statistically significant difference between STEM and non-STEM students regarding student satisfaction and students' perceptions of learning, the study identified many similar responses. In cases where students did not experience the teaching practice, there was some agreement on the value of using the teaching practice. Often, different responses focused on the extent the specific teaching practice should be used. For instance, non-STEM respondents wanted to see more use of discussion and group presentations, but while STEM students also liked this approach, they preferred knowledge transmission from the professor. The teaching practices where there was a clear difference in responses are in the areas of culturally responsive teaching, as well as diversity and inclusion, with non-STEM students preferring these, and STEM students seeing them as less important.

RECOMMENDATIONS

Faculty members looking to improve their teaching could benefit from a review of this study's research findings. Those teaching STEM students are encouraged to review the STEM student responses, while those teaching non-STEM students may want to look closely at the non-STEM student responses. A close examination of responses regarding the 22 teaching practices in which there is a statistically significant difference between STEM and non-STEM students on student satisfaction and students' perceptions of learning could be especially useful.

Faculty who teach STEM students should consider implementing the following: reducing class sizes, adding terminology explanations, playing up industrial experiences, using interactive technology and visualization tools, sharing lecture-notes, and enhancing out-of-class learning opportunities.

Faculty who teach non-STEM students should consider ensuring program depth, engaging in discussion-based and team-work activities, focusing on diversity topics, using humor, enhancing opportunities to engage with students outside of the classroom, and increasing opportunities for students to socialize with students from beyond their home-country.

Looking across both respondent types, faculty who teach international students should embrace the use of student-centered teaching methods, use two-way communications, engage in formative feedback, share lecture slides in advance, match lecture topics with textbook topics, ensure solid course organization, promote student engagement, manage lecture-delivery speed, and increase opportunities for applied or hands-on learning.

CONCLUSION AND FURTHER RESEARCH

This research sought to examine the different teaching preferences of international students, with specific attention to the differences between STEM and non-STEM students' preferences, to identify the promising teaching practices for teaching linguistically and culturally diverse international students. Researchers found that the student respondents described their experiences with the teaching practices they experienced as positive. There was little difference in responses made by STEM and non-STEM students regarding their most preferred and least preferred teaching practices, or recommended teaching practices' changes. Looking at the 22 teaching practices in which there is a statistically significant difference between STEM and non-STEM students regarding student satisfaction and perceptions of learning, the study identified many similar responses, with differences, noted primarily, in knowledge transmission, culturally-responsive teaching, as well as diversity and inclusion.

As North American postsecondary educational institutions continue to expand enrollment of international students and work to increase student retention, there is a growing need to ensure that instructors incorporate promising practices for teaching international students into their teaching. In order to achieve higher student satisfaction and perceptions of learning, instructors need to implement new teaching strategies that better engage international students and analyze their role in facilitating their learning experiences. This will require use of teaching strategies appropriate to the area of study. This is true for instructors who teach both STEM and non-STEM subjects.

As further research is contemplated, there is a need to learn about international student preferences for both STEM and non-STEM students at other levels, including additional language instruction, lower-level undergraduate studies, and upper-level undergraduate studies. It may also be helpful to examine student teaching preferences for STEM and non-STEM students at other institutional types (e.g., community colleges), as well as within secondary schools. Future research could also examine differences between STEM and non-STEM student satisfaction levels regarding country of origin, study levels, programs, study times, study stages, and ages.

This study had limitations that need to be acknowledged, which may limit generalization of the results. It was conducted at one mid-sized, Canadian university and incorporated responses from only 28 student participants, most of which were students in course-based or thesis-based graduate programs. Also, responses did not take into account faculty teaching contexts (e.g., class size, lecture v. seminar format, undergraduate v. graduate instructional levels). While research findings help to understand differences between the students' preferences regarding the selected teaching practices, care should be taken in generalizing results beyond the research site.

Notwithstanding these limitations, this study demonstrates that there is little difference between STEM and non-STEM responses on most of the promising teaching practices. Differences noted are more in terms of priority given by each group, with STEM students more focused on knowledge transmission and non-STEM students preferring to construct knowledge through student engagement, group work, and class discussions. The research also found a clear preference by non-STEM students for culturally responsive teaching, and teaching practices that consider diversity and inclusion.

REFERENCES

Alumran, J. (2008). Learning styles in relation to gender, field of study, and academic achievement for Bahraini University students. *Individual Differences Research*, 6(4), 303–316.

Biggs, J. B., & Tang, C. (2011). *Teaching for quality learning at university: What the student does* (4th ed.). Open University Press.

Canadian Bureau of International Education. (2016). *A world of learning: Canada's performance and potential in international education*. Canadian Bureau of International Education.

Choudaha, R., & Schulmann, P. (2014). Bridging the gap: Recruitment and retention to improve student experiences. Washington, DC: NAFSA: Association of International Educators.

Debdi, O., Paredes-Velasco, M., & Velázquez-Iturbide, J. Á. (2016). Influence of pedagogic approaches and learning styles on motivation and educational efficiency of computer science students. *IEEE Revista Iberoamericana de Tecnologias del Aprendizaje*, 11(3), 213–218. doi:10.1109/RITA.2016.2590638

Durkheim, E. (1951). *Suicide: A study in sociology*. Routledge.

Felder, R. M., & Spurlin, J. (2005). Applications reliability and validity of the index of learning styles. *International Journal of Engineering Education*, 21(1), 103–112.

Fox, R., & Ronkowski, S. (1997). Learning styles of political science students. *PS, Political Science & Politics*, 30(4), 732–737. doi:10.1017/S1049096500047363

Fritz, M. V., Chin, D., & DeMarini, D. (2008). Stressors, anxiety, acculturation and adjustment among international and North American students. *International Journal on Teaching and Learning in Higher Education*, 24(3), 301–313. doi:10.1016/j.ijintrel.2008.01.001

Harvey, D., Ling, C., & Shehab, R. (2010). Comparison of student's learning style in STEM disciplines. *IIE Annual Conference Proceedings*, 1-6.

Hofstede, G. (1997). *Cultures and organizations: Software of the mind*. McGraw-Hill.

Institute of International Education. (2016). *Open doors 2016*. Institute of International Education.

Koul, R., & Fisher, D. (2005). Cultural background and students' perceptions of science classroom learning environment and teacher interpersonal behavior in Jammu, India. *Learning Environments Research*, 8(2), 195–211. doi:10.100710984-005-7252-9

Kulturel-Konak, S., D'Allegro, M. L., & Dickinson, S. (2011). Review of gender differences in learning styles: Suggestions for STEM education. *Contemporary Issues in Education Research*, 4(3), 9–18. doi:10.19030/cier.v4i3.4116

Le Ha, P., & Li, B. (2012). Silence as right, choice, resistance and strategy among Chinese 'Me Generation' students: Implications for pedagogy. *Discourse (Abingdon)*, *35*(2), 233–248. doi:10.1080/01596 306.2012.745733

Lee, W. O. (1996). The cultural context for Chinese learners: conceptions of learning in the Confucian tradition. In D. Watkins & J. Biggs (Eds.), *The Chinese learner: Cultural, psychological and contextual influences* (pp. 25–41). The Comparative Education Research Centre, Faculty of Education, University of Hong Kong.

Liang, A., & McQueen, R. J. (1999). Computer assisted adult interactive learning in a multi-cultural environment. *Adult Learning*, *11*(1), 26–29. doi:10.1177/104515959901100108

Lin, J.-C. G., & Yi, J. K. (1997). Asian international students' adjustment: Issues and program suggestions. *College Student Journal*, *31*(4), 473–479.

McKinnon, S. (2013). A mismatch of expectations? An exploration of international students' perceptions of employability skills and work-related learning. In J. Ryan (Ed.), *Cross-cultural teaching and learning for home and international students: Internationalisation of pedagogy and curriculum in higher education* (pp. 211–224). Routledge.

Nelson Laird, T. F., Shoup, R., Kuh, G. D., & Schwarz, M. J. (2008). The effects on deep approaches to student learning and college outcomes. *Research in Higher Education*, *49*(6), 469–494. doi:10.100711162-008-9088-5

Paige, R. M., & Goode, M. L. (2009). Intercultural competence in international education administration-cultural mentoring: International education professionals and the development of intercultural competence. In D. Deardorff (Ed.), *The SAGE handbook of intercultural competence* (pp. 333–349). SAGE Publications.

Pollard, V., Hains-Wesson, R., & Young, K. (2018). Creative teaching in STEM. *Teaching in Higher Education*, *23*(2), 178–193. doi:10.1080/13562517.2017.1379487

Rao, P. (2017). Learning challenges and preferred pedagogies of international students: A perspective from the United States. *International Journal of Educational Management*, *31*(7), 1000–1016. doi:10.1108/IJEM-01-2016-0001

Sahragard, R., Khajavi, Y., & Abbasian, R. (2016). Field of study, learning styles, and language learning strategies of university students: Are there any relations? *Innovation in Language Learning and Teaching*, *10*(3), 255–271. doi:10.1080/17501229.2014.976225

Smith, C. (2020). International students and their academic experiences: Student satisfaction, student success challenges, and promising teaching practices. In U. Galuee, S. Sharma, & K. Bista (Eds.), *Rethinking education across borders: Emerging issues and critical insights on globally mobile students* (pp. 271–287). Springer., doi:10.1007/978-981-15-2399-1_16

Smith, C., Zhou, G., Potter, M., & Wang, D. (2019). Connecting best practices for teaching linguistically and culturally diverse international students with international student satisfaction and student perceptions of student learning. *Advances in Global Education and Research*, *3*, 252–265.

Smith, C., Zhou, G., Potter, M., Wang, D., Pecoraro, M., & Paulino, R. (2019). Variability by individual student characteristics of student satisfaction with promising international student teaching practices. *Literacy Information and Computer Education Journal, 10*(2), 3160–3169. doi:10.20533/licej.2040.2589.2019.0415

Tinto, B. (1993). *Leaving college: Rethinking the causes and cures of student attrition.* University of Chicago Press.

Vincent-Lancrin, S., Urgel, J., Kar, S., & Jacobin, G. (2019). *Measuring innovation in education 2019: What has changed in the classroom?* Paris: Educational Research and Innovation, OECD Publishing. . doi:10.1787/9789264311671-en

Wintergerst, A., & DeCapua, A. (2001). Exploring the learning styles of Russian-speaking ESL students. *The CATESOL Journal, 13*, 23–46.

Yates, L., & Thi Quynnh Trang, N. (2012). Beyond a discourse of deficit: The meaning of silence in the international classroom. *The International Education Journal: Comparative Perspectives, 11*(1), 22-34.

Zhang, J., & Goodson, P. (2011). Predictors of international students' psychosocial adjustment to life in the United States: A systematic review. *International Journal of Intercultural Relations, 35*(2), 139–162. doi:10.1016/j.ijintrel.2010.11.011

Zhang, Z., & Zhou, G. (2010). Understanding Chinese international students at a Canadian university: Perspectives, expectations, and experiences. *Comparative and International Education, 39*(3), 1–16.

Zhao, C.-M., Kuh, G. D., & Carini, R. M. (2005). A comparison of international student and American student engagement in effective educational practices. *The Journal of Higher Education, 76*(2), 209–232. doi:10.1353/jhe.2005.0018

KEY TERMS AND DEFINITIONS

Active Learning: Activities that students do to construct knowledge and understanding.

Deep Learning: Learning that promotes deep understanding of content and facilitates active learning through applied educational experiences.

International Students: Students enrolled in postsecondary educational institutions, located in a country other than their home country.

Non-STEM Students: Students enrolled in a postsecondary educational institution in an academic program other than science, technology, engineering, or mathematics.

Promising Teaching Practices: Teaching practices that have been, or are being, evaluated, and for which strong quantitative and/or qualitative data shows positive learning outcomes.

STEM Students: Students enrolled in a postsecondary educational institution in a science, technology, engineering, or mathematics academic program.

Student Engagement: Meaningful student involvement throughout the learning environment that results in students making a psychological investment in their learning.

Student Perceptions of Learning: Students' perceptions of the quantity and quality of learning they have acquired while enrolled in a postsecondary educational institution.

Student Satisfaction: Students' subjective evaluation of the outcomes and experiences associated with postsecondary education.

Chapter 5
Why Don't They Participate in Class?
A Study of Chinese Students' Classroom Participation in an International Master of Education Program

George Zhou
iD https://orcid.org/0000-0002-4594-633X
University of Windsor, Canada

Zongyong Yu
University of Windsor, Canada

Glenn Rideout
University of Windsor, Canada

Clayton Smith
University of Windsor, Canada

ABSTRACT

This study explores how Chinese international graduate students participate in Canadian classrooms, what factors promote and inhibit their participation, and what approaches can help to improve their participation. Eight student participants and two of their instructors were interviewed individually. Data analysis revealed that all participants appreciated the significance of classroom participation for their learning, but they were quieter than domestic students. Many factors were mentioned that possibly influenced their participation including their English language ability, differing education context and pedagogy between Canada and China, class environment, their personal work experience, part-time job commitments, personal interest, and emotional state. It is critical for instructors to distinguish and observe why their students participate less, then adjust their teaching practice in different situations to improve the participation level.

DOI: 10.4018/978-1-7998-5030-4.ch005

INTRODUCTION

With high-quality educational programs and a safe and multicultural environment, Canada has attracted a significant number of international students from around the world (Global Affairs Canada, 2014). In 2018, 572,415 international students were present in Canada at a variety of educational organizations, representing a growth of 16% compared to 2017 and a 154% increase since 2010. Approximately 25% of international students in Canada are from China (Canadian Bureau for International Education, 2019). This may be one reason why many scholars have recently focused their research on the study of Chinese international students (e.g., Baker, 2017; Zhou & Zhang, 2014).

While many studies have reported the experiences and challenges Chinese international students encounter on North American campuses (Zhang & Zhou, 2010; Zhou & Zhang, 2014), there has been minimal research particularly focusing on classroom participation among Chinese students. In addition, most past studies focused on international education at the undergraduate level; there is much less research on international students at the graduate level. In our previous study (Zhou, Liu, & Rideout, 2017) of Chinese international graduate students, we explored their experiences and challenges in a middle-sized comprehensive university. Among many other findings, participants reported the differences between Canadian and Chinese classrooms and raised a concern regarding lack of participation in classroom interactions. As follow-up research, this study was particularly designed to explore classroom participation of Chinese international graduate students. The study was guided by three key questions: How do Chinese international graduate students participate in class at a Canadian university? What factors promote or hinder their participation? What strategies may improve their participation?

LITERATURE REVIEW

At the beginning of this century, Liu (2002) pointed out that Chinese international students tend to keep silent in North American classes. There are many possible explanations for Chinese students' silence, but "it is unclear whether their lack of classroom participation is due to their unwillingness, or inability to speak up in class, or a combination of both" (p. 38). He warned that "the speculation that Chinese students are likely to be silent in classrooms could be plainly erroneous and dangerously misleading if the types of social contexts in which silence regularly occurs and the silence is derived from are not taken into consideration" (p. 37). Following Liu's observation, some research has been conducted to explore Chinese students' class participation, which will be reviewed below.

Cultural Differences

Past studies indicate that cultural differences influence Chinese international students' classroom participation. Huang and Brown (2009) pointed out that teachers in China were models for their students, not only in terms of knowledge, but also in terms of virtuosity. 'One day's teacher, a lifetime master.' This Chinese proverb illustrates that students should always respect the teacher no matter how long he/she teaches them. Challenging teachers in classroom is considered impolite in traditional Chinese culture. On the other hand, Huang and Brown (2009) noted that Chinese students often feel shameful when they cannot understand what the teacher is talking about in class. Therefore, it is quite natural for them to keep silent or simply agree in order to pretend they understand everything (Xiang, 2017).

Chinese students attempt to have good relationships with others. They seldom criticize each other, even from a purely academic perspective (Holmes, 2006; Huang & Klinger, 2006). They preferred to simply praise others and their opinions. Grez, Valcke, and Roozen (2012) studied the assessment of oral academic presentations and found that peer assessment by Chinese students was typically much higher than teacher assessment. Coming from such a cultural and educational context, Chinese international students were often noticed to lack the critical thinking experience and spirit found in western classes (Huang & Brown, 2009).

Language Barrier

English language ability affects academic and social confidence and achievements, and sometimes even those with high TOEFL or IELTS scores struggle to become accustomed to the new academic and social environment (Huang & Klinger, 2006). Liu (2002) stated that the linguistic factor, which includes issues such as English proficiency, English accent and dialogue competence, was troublesome for Chinese students. Andrade (2006) concluded that Chinese students' "adjustment challenges are primarily attributable to English language proficiency" and that their "achievement is affected by English proficiency" (p. 131). He found that Chinese students had more language barriers than expected and attributed their lack of classroom participation to language weaknesses and their sensitivity about their abilities. Moreover, Baker (2017) found that if Chinese international students could communicate in English with locals and other international students confidently, they were more likely to feel comfortable during their university study experiences. Liu (2006) found that the more proficient in English the students were, the less anxious they seemed to be when they responded to the teacher or were singled out to speak English in class.

Oral academic presentations (OAPs) are among the most popular activities in post-secondary classrooms. It requires students to share their understanding of an article that was pre-assigned by the instructor and as well lead class discussion on the article. Morita (2000) found that English as a second language affected international students during OAPs, despite their attempts to compensate by rehearsing their presentation, bringing reference documents for themselves, and even writing out other extra notes to overcome nervousness. Some of their study participants "were conscious of specific areas of linguistic problems… whereas others were more concerned with their overall lack of fluency and limited ability to elaborate." Another concern was that their English was "too simple" or "childish" and that their OAP might be "not very academic sounding" as a result (p. 298).

Group work is another popular form of class participation activity for developing and sharing ideas (Kim, 2006; Kingston & Forland, 2008). Elliott and Reynold (2014) found that although instructors and students preferred to mix domestic and international students within groups, students would choose group members who shared a similar ethnic background as themselves. As one study participant said: "When you kept quiet in a group you felt intense stress. I became nervous and totally lost confidence in myself. Especially when someone in the group tends to dominate, I am afraid to speak out" (p. 313).

Life Management and Psychological Issues

Chinese international students face more stress than domestic students because of the social and cultural adjustment they need to go through. Mori (2000) identified five difficulties that created special mental pressures for international students: language, different academic requirements, socialization in new communities, financial concerns, and new relationships with western students and instructors. Zhang and Goodson (2011) found that connections with local students and instructors were correlated with the level of cultural and psychological adjustments students made. But, low language proficiency led to students' lack of self-confidence, which then affected their communication with instructors and classmates in class. It was hard for them to make friends with local students and often suffer from loneliness and homesickness (Zhang & Zhou, 2010; Zhou & Zhang 2014). According to Yuan (2011), Chinese students thought their chances to socialize with local students were very limited. Holmes (2006) stated that it was challenging to make friends with domestic students. The difficulty with forging lasting friendships with Canadians exacerbated emotional difficulties, loneliness, and anxiety (Huang & Klinger, 2006). These emotional difficulties are among the main reasons Chinese students keep silent in class (Liu, 2002).

Li, Chen, and Duanmu (2010) noted that many Chinese students were financially supported by their families who demanded them to complete the program successfully. Family expectation placed immense pressure on Chinese students. Zhang and Brunton (2007) stated "living management issues" (p. 133) led to trouble for Chinese students because they lacked related experiences. In China, parents look after all issues so that children can paid full attention to their study; thus, being forced to deal with living problems such as cooking, laundry, and shopping in Canada often affected their mood. Liu (2002) stated that mental problems could lead to classroom silence for Chinese students. Unfortunately, international students often ignore mental health, not daring to ask for help for fear of losing face, and this usually leads to silence in class and isolation in social contexts (Zheng & Berry, 1991).

Past Learning Experience

Tatar (2005) pointed out that the educational context in different countries should be considered a significant factor influencing learning results. Liu (2002) stated that past learning experiences is a key factor influencing Chinese students' classroom participation. Huang and Klinger (2006) also noted that classroom participation problems occurred for Chinese international students because organization of the class in North America differs greatly from that in China. Zhang and Xu (2007) drew major comparisons between Chinese and North American classes in three aspects: learner responsibilities, learner engagement, and learner assessment. They concluded that Chinese requirements for students' preparation for class, participation in class, and assignments after class were starkly different from those in North America. Due to the exam-oriented education, Chinese students tend to be passive in class and listening to the instructor was their most significant task.

Yang (2017) found that pedagogical difference was a major obstacle to Chinese students' classroom engagement. Before they arrived at the host universities, few were prepared effectively, especially with regard to the western teaching and learning classroom environment. The interactive teaching method, which was popular and recommended by most English teachers, was incompatible with Chinese students' learning habits and rarely fulfilled learning objectives (Li, 2003). Wong (2004) found that the learning habits of Chinese international students were a principal challenge influencing their classroom performance. Fortunately, Gu (2009) pointed out that learning habits of Chinese students could change gradually over two or more semesters. As familiarity with Canadian education and society increased, Chinese students started to behave differently in the classroom, participating in the class more frequently and positively as time passed (Lu & Han, 2010).

Micro-Aggression

Although all North American universities have relevant policies to ensure equity of all students, international students often feel excluded or avoided. In comparisons between Chinese and American students, Poyrazli and Lopez (2007) found that Chinese students were at a much higher risk of discrimination than American students. Younger students with lower language proficiency reported more discrimination, while increased years of residence decreased feelings of discrimination. In a recent study exploring micro-aggressions that Chinese students face at a Canadian university (Houshmand, Spanierman, & Tafarodi, 2014), Chinese international students reported they felt excluded in many aspects. On one hand, the activities they participated in were often organized by an international student society and most of the participants were thus international students. On the other hand, when classroom activities involved white peers, domestic students played the dominant role and most international students were ignored. To cope with such challenge, Houshmand et al. found that Chinese international students dealt with being "excluded and avoided" by staying together with students from the same community, for example, sitting together in class. Since they shared the same origin and values, they could easily understand each other and felt comfortable and relaxed. Myles and Cheng (2003) found that this coping method was quite popular but noted that it caused other problems by making it even more difficult for Chinese students to be academically involved in class or socially engaged after school, even after they had stayed in Canada for an extended period of time.

Instructor Influence

Xiang (2017) stated that teaching pedagogies largely influenced classroom participation. Tatar (2005) found the climate of the classroom played a dominant role for classroom participation. Therefore, instructors should be much thoughtful in classes that enroll international students. However, in practice Love and Arkoudis (2006) noticed that although the academic teachers knew international students had more difficulties at the linguistic level, they were uninterested in teaching language in their academic areas. Subject teachers seldom worked with language teachers to help students bridge the gap between language and academic subjects. Kingston and Forland (2008) suggested that the notion that Chinese students from a teacher-centered education system performed worse than domestic students was misleading. Instructors' expectations need "a move away from viewing international students as problematic and toward a more positive viewpoint in which they can add a fresh perspective" (pp. 216-217).

To improve Chinese international students' classroom participation, direct engagement by instructors is essential. Myles and Cheng (2003) studied the relationship between Chinese students and their Canadian instructors and supervisors, concluding that "it has become essential for faculty to make a conscious effort to learn about students' cultures and cultural differences to become more aware of their own ethnocentric behavior" (p. 252). Kingston and Forland (2007) suggested that instructors should know their students, value their personal opinions, and adopt flexible teaching methods to involve a wider range of culturally diverse students in class. Moreover, Vita (2000) demonstrated that strong relationships between students and instructors were important for students to interact effectively in the classroom. To facilitate this, Vita (2000) told his students to call him by his first name and encouraged students to ask questions, share their experiences, and help each other. To reduce their tension and nervous feelings, Vita (2000) divided students into small groups during class discussions and gave positive remarks to all students' answers.

METHODOLOGY

The university where this study took place is located in southern Ontario. It has a Master of Education (MEd) program for international students. This program has attracted many Chinese students since it started several years ago. In most cohorts, students were all from China. The international cohort students take some courses with domestic students, but more courses with their cohort peers only. This program creates a unique context for this study. The study adopted a case study design with one international cohort that started the program in September of 20XX. Case study research is a qualitative approach in which the researchers explore a rea-life case or cases through detailed in-depth data collection often involving multiple source of information (Creswell, 2013). In order to increase the trustworthiness of data, the study explored Chinese international graduate students' classroom participation from the views of both students and instructors.

Participants

The 20XX cohort enrolled 26 Chinese graduate students in the fall semester and eight course instructors taught the cohort. Among them, eight students and two instructors were recruited through class visits and personal emails to voluntarily participate in the study. To protect participant identification, the eight student participants were assigned letters A-H (Table 1) and the two instructor participants were marked as A and B. Both instructors were male and had over 10 years of teaching at the university. Instructor A was a tenured professor and B was a sessional instructor. Both of them immigrated to Canada over 15 years ago. They taught the MEd program including such courses as Comparative and International Education, Research in Education, etc.

All student participants were female. Most of them were in their 20s except for students A and C in 30s. They were in their first semester of the MEd program at the time of data collection. As indicated in Table 1, two student participants did not have formal work experience before coming to Canada, four had less than three years' work experience, and two had more than ten years. Their work experiences were all related to language teaching, either as English teachers or Chinese teachers. In regards to their education background, five participants majored in English or English education, two majored in Teaching Chinese as a Second Language, which involve high requirement of English. One student majored in elementary education. Seven student participants provided their parents' education background. Six pairs of their parents had high school or lower diplomas, and only one pair had university degrees. With regard to parents' careers, participants provided various responses including housewife, business manager, business owner, accountant, or construction worker. Three student participants had been in Canada for approximately five months and the rest been in Canada for about a year. The five participants who came to Canada earlier took part in the English Language Improvement Program (ELIP). To worthy of noting, the participant H had a MEd from UK before coming to Canada.

Data Collection

Data were collected through semi-structured one-on-one interviews. Student interviews took place in the independent group discussion room in the university library while instructor interviews were conducted in their offices. Each interview lasted from 30 to 90 minutes. All interviews were audio recorded. Field notes were taken to capture the data that audio recording might miss, such as gestures and expressions.

Table 1. Demographic information of student participants

Participant	Prior work experience	Undergraduate major	Parent highest education degree	Length in Canada (months)	English improvement program
A	15 years as English teacher	English education	High school	11	Yes
B	No work experience	English	(Information missing)	12	Yes
C	13 years as a Chinese teacher	Elementary education	Middle school	12	Yes
D	One year as a Chinese teacher	Chinese as second language	Middle school	16	Yes
E	3.5 years as English teacher	English	Elementary school	5	No
F	No work experience	English	High school	5	No
G	2 years as a English tutor	English education	High school	15	Yes
H	0.5 year as English tutor	Chinese as second language	University bachelor's degree	5	No

Interview Protocols

The interview protocols for students and instructors were developed and validated by the research team. The student protocol consisted of 24 open-ended questions. Among them, five questions sought demographic information including family background, past education and work experience, length of stay in Canada, and motivation to take the program. One question asked participants about how they were doing in the program. One question asked participants what differences they noticed between Chinese classes and Canadian classes. Three questions asked participants to reflect upon their perspective regarding classroom participation and the factors that help or hinder their classroom participation. Eight questions collected information on their actual classroom performance related to raising questions, answering questions, providing feedback to others' work in class, and group work performance. Five questions aimed to identify instructors' efforts to encourage Chinese graduate students' participation and participants' suggestion for instructors about how to promote their participation. The last question provided participants a chance for further comments.

The instructor protocol had 14 questions. It collected information about such items as instructors' observation of the differences between Canadian and Chinese graduate students, their participation in various classroom activities including raising questions, response to questions, providing feedback to classmates in class, and factors that might influence Chinese graduate students' classroom participation, and what they did to promote such participation.

Data Analysis

Data were analyzed using a content analysis approach which involved a process of coding and re-coding. First, the researchers got themselves merged in the interview transcripts through reading and re-reading.

Once they got a sense of data, they started to code the data. They broke the text into different segments, highlighted the key sentences, and noted with key words or phrases. Later, they organized the initial codes to different categories which lead to the themes of the findings. The interview texts from students and instructors were analyzed separately first and then were cross-linked for the purpose of triangulation.

STUDY RESULTS

General Impression about the Program

Participants were asked to describe their overall experience in the program. Six participants used the following words to describe their experiences in this program: "a lot of challenges," "sometimes very hard," "much difficult," "very stressful," "didn't find the right way," and "not used to it." One student described her experience as "not too bad and not so good" and the last student simply said "good." An overload of reading materials and critical writing style were mentioned most frequently by all student participants as elements that made the program particularly challenging for them. Participant B said:

I find it's very hard sometimes, especially when I face the due dates. Yeah, it is almost like the national exam for getting to university in China for me. I can't sleep well, and I have to read a lot of materials. However, I don't like reading and that's the biggest problem. So most of them it is hard for me.

Student C also reported that a lot of reading materials caused her a great deal of trouble because her English was poor, even though she spent much more time on reading than other students. Some students found that they were always struggling. For example, Student A said: "At the very beginning I did not understand teachers' instructions, and after three months I still worried about my final paper." Student G said: "the professor didn't tell us the right way to do."

Student D had a better situation. She stated that she initially felt very stressed about the program but she gradually accepted the different teaching and learning environment, attaining acceptable grades on her assignments. Student H reported a positive comment about the program: "I think it's good. I adjusted myself very quickly to this program because I had such relevant experience before." She indicated that her past experience in international study played a significant role in her ability to catch up in the program easily.

Differences Between Canadian and Chinese Classes

Student participants were asked about their observations and perceptions about the differences between Chinese and Canadian classes. All participants agreed that teacher-centered pedagogies dominated Chinese classes while in Canada student-centred instructional methods were widespread. Participants approached these questions from various angles including classroom arrangement, learning atmosphere, the roles of teachers and students, instructional emphases, assessment, and so on. Student F said Chinese classes "focus more on teacher-centred teaching," where "students sit down and take notes," being silent most of the time. Thus, there is a lack of engagement compared to Canadian classes, where student-centred learning facilitates group work, presentations, workshops, and brainstorming sessions with peers. Moreover, Student F stated that while teachers prepared class content in China, Canadian students were expected to prepare class presentations themselves. Student H added, Canadian students sit in all kinds of patterns in the classroom including circles, squares, and groups whereas Chinese students always sit in rows and lines.

Student A noticed the emphasis on critical thinking in Canadian classes. She said: "In Canada, from class presentation to after-class homework, teachers emphasized critical thinking. Every time, I was encouraged to critique the designated articles, their authors, even other students' presentations in class." She compared this with her learning experience in China, where she and her classmates tried to be docile, followed instructors, listened to lectures, and took notes with no critical thinking. Student B expressed her similar observation by stating that in Canada you could question teachers while in China you could only say 'yes' to instructors.

Students A and B also talked about the difference in teamwork. They noticed that there was a great deal of teamwork inside and outside Canadian classes, but Chinese students usually finished their assignments independently or separately. Student C commented on the difference in assessment, stating that "in Canada, there were many assessments: presentations, essays, quizzes, papers, classroom participation marks, projects and so on to compose a final course grade. In China, mostly the final examination would decide a student's final grade." Student C elaborated that this was why she was always busy studying in Canada while in China she usually studied during the last two weeks of each semester.

There might be some differences between Canadian and Chinese students who grew up in different teaching and learning educational environments. When being asked about the differences they had noticed between Chinese and Canadian students, participating instructor A said:

Canadian students often have an opinion about anything. Even if they're not necessarily well-informed, they can give you an opinion and probably fairly easily. Where Chinese students, some are more comfortable with communicating their thoughts on an idea than others, and others hope not to be asked.

He also stated that Canadian students were usually more assertive. Their presence was more willingly than their Chinese peers. He found that Chinese students who were a little bit older, with work experience and possibly some international experience, came closer to domestic students in terms of mentality and performance.

Instructor B expressed the same impression as instructor A. He observed that Chinese students were quieter than Canadian students. Few spoke in class. He pointed out that Chinese students' English writing was inferior compared with domestic students because English was not their first language. Instructor B noticed that Chinese students generally had a great deal of respect for authority. He illustrated this point by saying that:

Chinese students are much less likely to contest their grades and to fight with me about their work. If they get a bad grade, it's more likely a Canadian student will come and argue about the grade. Chinese students... can get very bad grade... they'll come to me and say "Oh, what can I do better?"

Perceptions of Classroom Participation

Participating students were asked about their perception of classroom participation. All eight participants agreed that classroom participation was essential to learning. They mentioned various opportunities classroom participation could offer them. Student D talked about working with partners in addition to listening to instructors; student F mentioned sharing ideas after reading class materials; student G connected answering questions with new knowledge generation; and student H believed classroom participation promoted independent thinking. Student A said:

There are two reasons for participation. First, teachers here highlight classroom participation: attendance and discussion in classroom usually occupy 20% of the final score. Second, I should participate in the classroom because this is how we learn here. Every time you participate in the activity, you can learn new things.

Students B and C thought classroom participation was a good opportunity to practice and improve their English since they could discuss topics with "Canadian students in a natural English-speaking environment."

Status of Classroom Participation

Although all student participants recognized the importance of classroom participation, they provided different responses when they were asked about whether they actively participated in class. Four students responded affirmatively. Student A said she was well-prepared before she entered the classroom. When teachers raised questions or organized group-work, she took part in every activity and did her best to speak as much as possible. Student F said: "When my classmates are giving presentations, they will give some questions to discuss. Every time, I share my ideas because sharing helps me learn from others through dialogue."

Three students responded to this question with "it depends." Student D declared that if she was interested in the topics covered in that class, she might participate in the discussion. Student G stated that if she had related work experience with the discussion topics and was familiar with them, she was keener to participate. Student E said that she enjoyed participating in one of her instructors' classes because he created a very welcoming classroom climate to relax students. There was only one participant (student C) who responded to this question with *no*. She explained that her inactivity was due to the fact that it was difficult for her "to organize and to express" ideas in English and was therefore afraid of wasting class time. She was not majored in English and believed she could not catch up to other students.

The results from student participants' interviews were correlated to those from instructor participants. With regard to whether Chinese students actively participated in the classroom, Instructor A said:

I think some did, some didn't. I would say a smaller portion did sort of naturally. And it comes out of that experience, age, work, intercommunication, and maybe international experience. So those ones were, I would say, pretty, pretty good, if not very good. Then you have the other ones that are kind of afraid and silent and that they hope they don't get asked publicly to express themselves.

Raising Questions

Raising questions may be one of the most obvious indicators of classroom participation. In response to the question "did you often raise questions in class?" only participant F responded affirmatively. She said she raised questions from time to time in class. All other student participants responded negatively. Student C made it clear that she only raised questions when she was asked to. Student B said she did not want to interrupt the class or be the focus of attention. Like B, student E thought it was impolite to interrupt the class with her own questions. Student G explained that she did not want to embarrass her teacher or classmates by asking questions that they might not be able to answer. When being asked about what to do if they had questions, most said they would ask for help from classmates or pose questions to the instructors after class. Sometime, they "just let it go" to avoid embarrassment or save face.

The interview with Instructor A confirmed student participants' answers. This instructor noticed that the students who did not raise questions during class sometimes came up to him after class to discuss the question they had. While he did not mind this practice, he encouraged them to ask questions in classes by saying "your classmates will benefit from your thoughts, your context, and your experience if you asked your question in class."

When asked if Chinese students often raised questions in class, both instructors gave negative responses. Instructor A reported that Chinese students seldom raised questions in class. He echoed the sentiment expressed by student participants about avoiding embarrassment: "My understanding is that … nobody wants to look like they don't know something, or they're not informed, or they're less smart than the person beside them." Instructor B also found that Chinese students raised fewer critical questions, and their questions were often simply clarification questions, such as what the professor wanted or expected in assignment. He added that this limited Chinese students' creativity and originality, which was critical for their university studies and their life after graduation.

Response to Questions

Student participants were asked who often responded when instructors posted questions in class, and their responses suggested that Chinese students were more hesitant to respond than others. Student H noticed a general order of student responses in a multicultural class. Domestic students would always respond first, other international students after, and Chinese students would always be the last to respond to instructors' questions. Student G added that, among Chinese students, a few responded quite often, and most responded occasionally or not at all.

Student participants A, B, E, and F stated that if the class was composed of Canadian students and Chinese students, the Canadian students would usually respond first and more frequently. Alternately, if the class was composed of only Chinese students, most would respond to instructors' questions. Students A and B agreed that students' frequency of response depended on the students' work experiences: if they had work experiences, they would answer more. If they did not understand systems or situations, they would speak less, regardless of nationality. Student B took one of her classes as an example: the assigned reading was discussing Chinese education, and during classroom discussion, Canadian students seldom spoke.

Instructor A replied to questions about Chinese students' responses to questions by agreeing with the student participants: "If you had 50-50, Canadian and Chinese students, more than likely the hands would go up faster with the Canadian students… the exception to the rule are those what you could call statistically outliers, those individuals who are an exception to the norm in terms of Chinese." Instructor B responded with the same idea.

For the intention to respond, seven student participants and two instructor participants agreed that Chinese students intended to respond to the questions posed by instructors. Student E said she was trying to respond every time, but she might not get the chance to respond sometimes because of time limitations. Only Student C said she had no intention to respond because she thought she could not express her ideas in English very fluently. Instructor B hypothesized that the lack of responses from Chinese students might have been due to "nervousness about speaking in a public setting," given that "English is not… their first language."

Feedback to Classmates

When asked if they often provided feedback to their classmates' work, all eight student participants and two instructor participants said Chinese students would provide feedback regularly, but they had different opinions about how to provide that feedback, how often to give feedback, and how to assess work for feedback. Student D stated that, whether she agreed with her classmates or not, she would always give some feedback, while Student A said she offered her classmate different ideas. Student F said she would just give some praises so as not to make them lose face. This was a trend observed by Instructor A, who reported that Canadian students were generally more willing to address a negative aspect of student performance than Chinese students were. For the frequency to provide feedback to peers, four students used "often" and four students and one instructor used "sometimes."

Student E said providing feedback to classmates depended on the class climate: "If the atmosphere is friendly and relaxed, I always do this. For some serious teachers, actually we don't say anything." In addition, Chinese students were more inclined to provide feedback after class or through emails, which is a factor corroborated by Students A and G. Instructor B noticed that if students were forced to provide written feedback, they were more likely to provide more because they would not be exposed in a public setting.

Group Work

Participants were asked how they felt about group work in class. All eight student participants loved group work even though some of them mentioned struggling in some cases. They unanimously thought it was an efficient method to help Chinese students participate more in the classroom. Students E and F said group work allowed students to benefit from their peers with different backgrounds and experiences, which usually resulted in new ideas and mutual learning experiences. Students D and H thought group work was an excellent chance to practice their English because there were just a few students in one group and all of them had many chances to converse and raise their concerns. Student H also mentioned that many Chinese students were afraid of speaking in public, so group work could provide them the opportunity to express their feelings or ideas with less fear.

Most participants preferred a mixed group with domestic students. Student A mentioned that one of her instructors encouraged Chinese students to work with Canadian students. This offered her and other Chinese students the opportunity to learn from Canadian students. She also stated that this was the only way she had a reliable chance to work with Canadian students. However, student D thought forming the group by student themselves would make them feel at ease, as opposed to the instructor assigning groups. With respect to group work, five students reported that they were free to form their own group, while two reported that the instructors would assign groups. Student F used "it depends" to describe this difference:

In some classes, most students were Chinese students, so the instructor just let us go whatever we wanted and organize our own group. In other classes, Chinese students were blended with Canadian students so the instructor usually appointed groups... in order to ensure Canadian and Chinese students had chances to share different opinions.

Student E added that in some course, Chinese students and Canadian students sit separately in different sections of the classroom, and they seldom rearranged their seats throughout the course. Student A thought the instructor should try to mix them into assigned groups to avoid the situation where otherwise "Chinese students sit together and Canadian students sit together."

The two instructor participants had different perspective on teacher's intervention with student grouping. Instructor B would let students form their own group and did not consider influencing the process as an important factor affecting the effectiveness of group discussion. Instructor A thought instructors should pay attention to how to assign students into different groups. First, he never said: "you're Chinese, you go with the Canadian student because I know it will be good for you," because he thought that would be patronizing. Second, he tried to mix personalities. He elaborated: "If I think somebody is very shy, I don't put all shy people in the same group." Third, he made attempts to bring students out of their comfort zones. For example, "I know those three young women are friends, I don't necessarily just keep them in the same group, because part of the experience is interacting with people that you don't know." Fourth, he would always use different methods to assign groups to improve the efficiency of group discussion. Instructor A shared a phenomenon in one of his classes with four Canadian and 20 Chinese students. He assigned groups in a way that there would be a Canadian student in each group. In this context, every group chose the Canadian student as their representative for their group reports. Instructor A considered this to be problematic.

Factors That Influence Classroom Participation

Student participants listed six factors that influence their class participation: language proficiency, working experience, self-confidence, mood, interest, and classroom atmosphere:

- Language proficiency: Language proficiency was mentioned by all participants as a key factor that influences Chinese students' classroom participation. For example, student A said that low proficiency in verbal English prevented her from class participation. Student E said: "Fluent spoken English would help me to participate."
- Working experience: Participants' working experience could influence classroom participation. Student B noted that sometimes she would not participate because she "lacked hands-on experiences related to the issue that was discussed in class."
- Self-confidence: Language proficiency and work experience could also shape students' self-confidence, which in turn impacted participation. Student H stated that self-confidence affected students' classroom participation. If they were self-confident, they would participate more in the classroom, and if they were not self-confident, they would keep silent and seldom involve themselves in the class.
- Mood: Mood could influence classroom participation. Student E said: "Sometimes I felt happy and I spoke up more, while sometimes I was in a bad mood and less inclined to participate." She added that language proficiency affected self-confidence and self-confidence usually shaped her mood.

- Interest: Participants also identified interest as an influential factor in classroom participation. Student B said: "if I'm interested in it [the discussion topic] I will participate more. But if it is not my interest, like a very specific theory, I don't want to participate." Likewise, Student H argued that if the topic was too boring, she might lose the interest and not participate.
- Classroom atmosphere: Student G stated, "If I felt there is a relaxing classroom climate and other students are positive in terms of involving themselves, I am far more likely to participate." Similarly, student E reported that friendly classmates often encouraged her to ask more questions, share more ideas, and provide more feedback to peers' works. Student G commented that if the instructor was open-minded and could give reasonable feedback and explain any confusion, she was more likely to involve herself. Otherwise, she often refused to participate. It seems that both classmates and the instructor shape the classroom atmosphere, which had an impact on classroom participation.

What Instructors Have Done to Improve Classroom Participation

All eight student participants stated that their instructors encouraged Chinese students to participate in class, and both instructor participants confirmed that they consistently engaged in this practice. Student participants reported that their instructors applied several approaches: some specifically designed different group work, some instructors included presentations as assignments with a specific requirement of interactive activity, some asked questions and follow-up questions to involve students, some organized discussions in class or on the Blackboard website, some gave comments and feedback to students to encourage deeper thinking, and some explained questions in detail and provided examples to help students understand the work.

Both instructors agreed that specific pedagogical methods should be adapted when teaching Chinese students. Instructor A explained what he did to encourage Chinese students' classroom participation: "I don't just take students who put up their hand. I expect everybody to contribute to the class, but it's also my responsibility to build a relationship with those students so they don't mind talking." He commended that if the teacher monitored their group discussion from time to time, more Chinese students would contribute whether there were domestic students present or not. Knowing this, he often walked around to observe their discussion and sometimes would join them to encourage participation from all group members. Instructor B described what he did to involve Chinese students' participation in class. He said: "I structure the class in a way that… requires a lot of discussion… I also intervene in their discussions and presentations with stories and jokes and try to keep it in a conversational format so it's not someone talking, someone listening."

What Instructors Should Do to Improve Classroom Participation

When asked how they felt teachers could improve the participation of Chinese students, student A said instructors should try to assign students to different groups every time, which would help Chinese students learn to communicate with Canadian students and other international students. Student D suggested classroom participation should be a significant portion of the final evaluation in the class, such as 20% or even 30%. This would ensure students could not ignore the requirement to participate. Students E, F, and H said the instructors should choose some materials related to China, some practical cases to clarify theories, and some activities to make the classroom climate fun and encouraging. Student G suggested that instructors should call upon students individually to ensure each student participates. She also added that discussing in pairs, rather than in large groups, would more effectively encourage students to speak out.

Instructor A said it was important for non-Chinese professors to understand the different types of behaviours of Chinese students in the class because a wide range of reasons may shape their behaviours. He noted that these reasons might include discomfort in speaking out due to the difference between the teacher-centered pedagogy used in China and the student-centered pedagogy employed in Canada. Likewise, they may have simply not done the work and therefore do not know the answer. In addition, there might be personal reasons related to feeling self-conscious or avoiding being embarrassed. Thus, Instructor A pointed out that it is critical "that professors don't simplify and say, 'Oh, well, they're Chinese. They don't have that experience,' because some students do."

What Students Should Do to Improve Classroom Participation

"Personality" and "character" were two words mentioned frequently by almost all student participants. They thought Chinese students were shy and docile, so they seldom spoke out in class because they had been trained for most of their lives to act this way. Student B suggested that whether one was extroverted or introverted in real life, Chinese students must adjust themselves to be "academically extroverted" within Canadian education. Student A said: "I think we should encourage ourselves, no matter we want to immigrate, find a good job, or experience the host culture." She suggested: "We'd better focus on our study, not part time jobs. We should participate actively in the classroom. We have spent energy, time, and money to study abroad, so we should pay our attention to the academic requirements. For example, we must read all the required materials before class and bring questions and comments to the classroom discussion." Student D stated:

It is very important to improve our English. After I finished the ELIP program, I thought I could catch up the academic courses, but I couldn't in fact. There are so many new words and it really make me in the trouble to read through some textbooks and articles. I think we still need to learn English all the time.

Student D mentioned that one must respect others and others' work. When classmates were presenting, one should always listen to them and interact with them despite lack of interest. She thought this was the very basic mutual respect principle expected within Canadian classrooms. Student H shared her opinions:

I think we should share our ideas and experiences so that other students can learn from our thinking. Teacher questions often do not require a right-and-wrong answer. Therefore, you can just raise your hand to answer the question and don't be afraid of losing face. That is also the way we learn from other students when they answer questions.

CONCLUSION AND DISCUSSION

Classroom Participation

A majority of the student participants had some difficult experiences with the MEd program. While the primary mentioned reason for such difficulty was the large amount of reading materials, participants provided a complex picture about their classroom participation. Kuo and Roysircar (2004) found that English language reading ability was one of the main challenges for the acculturation of Chinese adolescent immigrants. Zhang and Zhou (2010) and Zhou and Zhang (2014) reported that international student language proficiency significantly influenced their social and academic integration on Canadian campuses. Similarly, in this study, Chinese graduate students, like Chinese undergraduate students, experienced challenges due to the language issue. Failing to complete the required course readings on time and developing an accurate understanding of them affected their class participation.

Similar to the finding of Zhang and Xu (2007), participants in this study noticed the differences between the teacher-centred pedagogy in China and the student-centred pedagogy in Canada. Particularly, the requirement for critical thinking in Canadian graduate courses put study participants in a difficult position. Their past educational experiences and cultural values lead to the lack of critical mindsets and ability (Yang, 2017). Both student and instructor participants commented that Chinese students were much quieter than Canadian students in class. Chinese students seldom raised questions or responded to questions in class. When they did have problems, they often asked their peers for help or just searched for answers on the internet. This pattern was also identified in previous studies (Andrade, 2006; Huang & Klinger, 2006; Zhou & Zhang, 2014). All participants liked group work and reported that they felt more comfortable to share ideas in small group settings.

It is not difficult to understand that in this study more experienced participants reported that they were more active in classes. Participants' interests in the discussion topics and their mood on the class day influenced their participation in class. Even though all of them appreciated the significance of classroom participation for their learning, they reported the lack of relevant experience or knowledge about the topic, low confidence with their language ability, not being interested in the topic, and low mood as the factors preventing their participation. Personality is another significant factor. If participants were outgoing in daily life, they would usually be active participants in class. However, if they were shy and did not socialize with others easily, they would often keep silent in class and seldom state their ideas. Gu (2009) also found personality was correlated to students' classroom participation, but also found that students could adapt their personalities within one or two semesters of studying abroad.

Even though student participants did not have to support themselves financially, many of them had part-time jobs. They wanted to gain Canadian experiences and learn more about local community through work. This limited their time for study. In addition, as Myles and Cheng (2003) found, almost all Chinese students worked in Chinese companies who did not employ local Canadians. This did nothing to help them communicate with local communities or Canadians.

Improvement of Classroom Participation

This study found that participants were more willing to participate in classes in an encouraging, considerate, and relaxing classroom environment. Therefore instructors can promote classroom participation by shaping the classroom climate and learning atmosphere. An empathic and positive class climate can relax students, assuaging fear and anxious feelings to make it easier to share opinions without pressure. Instructors should make effort to build a relationship of trust with international students, as Vita (2000) did in his teaching. Chinese students are used to respecting authorities and they seldom engage in critiques. This makes the relationship of trust a key factor to influence the frequency of Chinese students' participation. Turner (2006) studied Chinese international students by socializing with them so that he heard students' voices through "discussion with the students about any aspect of their lives" (p. 29).

He found that during and after these designed listening sessions, he became friends with the Chinese students to some extent and gained trust from them. This trust led Chinese students to relax and gain the self-confidence to communicate in class or during academic workshops.

Since most student participants felt overloaded in terms of reading tasks and could not finish them before class, one solution might be for instructors to consider reducing the quantity and difficulty of reading, especially in the first semester. The authors of this paper are aware that such a solution might impinge on the academic rigour of the course and program structure, since this would likely diminish the likelihood that learning outcomes would be accomplished to the same level. In the particular case for this study, there would then be a difference between the international cohort and domestic cohort courses, a problem which would be exacerbated by including students from both programs in the same classes in order to achieve some of the other acculturation goals.

The emotional state of students affects classroom participation as well. Most Chinese students are still quite young, so emotion might be a key influencing factor both in and out of class. For example, if a student just had a dispute with a landlord before class, that student may be less likely to either connect with the material or participate during class. Mori (2000) found that Chinese students experienced many mental health issues. It is therefore essential for instructors to do warm-up activities at the beginning of the class to facilitate positivity in class. For example, random chatting can help students feel relaxed and focus their attention on what the instructor is talking about.

Instructors may educate themselves about China. Kinston and Forland (2008) and Myles and Cheng (2003) state that instructors should be familiar with their students' social and cultural backgrounds to be effective in teaching. The Chinese educational system is quite different from the Canadian educational system, and so Chinese culture is from Canadian culture (Li, 2012). Some basic knowledge about Chinese cultural and education in advance will help instructors involve Chinese students in class. When they are presenting something about Canadian or Western education, it would be effective to make comparisons with parallel conditions in China. Grayson (2008) claimed that such comparative teaching methods were an efficient way to solve multicultural problems. It should be a good way to engage international students in education classes as well. Chinese students are familiar with Chinese education, so engaging with Chinese topics is one way to keep them interested and encourage their participation.

Another tactic is to call on students directly to participate. Some students regularly raised their hands and spoke often in class while others kept silent; however, this can result from differences in personalities. If instructors sometimes call students' names to answer questions, Chinese students may be more likely to focus on class content and keep alert. This solution uses their fear of losing face productively.

Participants reported that Chinese and domestic students often sit separately in class. Instructors might assign students into groups rather than allowing them to choose their own to achieve mixed groups. Elliott and Reynolds (2014) recommended blending international students with domestic students into mixed groups for better learning experience for students. Most participants in this study expressed their preference for working with domestic students. Kim (2006) also suggests that teachers should purposefully design or intervene in the classroom activities. Instructors should participate in group discussions to encourage and monitor each group member's contribution.

As far as students are concerned, they should be improving their English at all times. English is an additional language for most Chinese students, so language barriers are ever-present, as Andrade (2006) observes. Students should focus on academic courses and their requirements. They need to guarantee enough time to preview the required materials before class, to participate in class, and to complete the assignments after class. This means not prioritizing part-time work, which can significantly interfere with one's classroom performance. Students should work to be "academically extroverted," which means simply that they should perform actively in class. Even if one is timid and seldom communicates with others in daily life, one must engage in classroom participation in order to improve their learning efficiency.

REFERENCES

Andrade, M. S. (2006). International students in English-speaking universities. *Journal of Research in International Education, 5*(2), 131–154. doi:10.1177/1475240906065589

Baker, C. A. (2017). *Understanding the study abroad experience for international students from China at the University of Vermont* (Undergraduate thesis). University of Vermont. Retrieved from http://scholarworks.uvm.edu/hcoltheses/132

Canadian Bureau for International Education. (2019). *International students in Canada.* Retrieved from https://cbie.ca/infographic/

Creswell, J. W. (2013). *Qualitative inquiry and research design: Choosing from five approaches.* SAGE Publications.

Elliott, C. J., & Reynolds, M. (2014). Participative pedagogies, group work and the international classroom: An account of students' and tutors' experiences. *Studies in Higher Education, 39*(2), 307–320. doi:10.1080/03075079.2012.709492

Global Affairs Canada. (2014). *Canada's international education strategy.* Retrieved fromhttp://international.gc.ca/global-markets-marches-mondiaux/assets/pdfs/overview-apercu-eng.pdf

Grayson, J. P. (2008). The experiences and outcomes of domestic and international students at four Canadian universities. *Higher Education Research & Development, 27*(3), 215–230. doi:10.1080/07294360802183788

Grez, L. D., Valcke, M., & Roozen, I. (2012). How effective are self- and peer assessment of oral presentation skills compared with teachers' assessments? *Active Learning in Higher Education, 13*(2), 129–142. doi:10.1177/1469787412441284

Gu, Q. (2009). Maturity and interculturality: Chinese students' experiences in UK higher education. *European Journal of Education, 44*(1), 37–52. doi:10.1111/j.1465-3435.2008.01369.x

Holmes, P. (2006). Problematizing intercultural communication competence in the pluricultural classroom: Chinese students in a New Zealand university. *Language and Intercultural Communication, 6*(1), 18–34. doi:10.1080/14708470608668906

Houshmand, S., Spanierman, L. B., & Tafarodi, R. W. (2014). Excluded and avoided: Racial microaggressions targeting Asian international students in Canada. *Cultural Diversity & Ethnic Minority Psychology, 20*(3), 377–388. doi:10.1037/a0035404 PMID:25045949

Huang, J., & Brown, K. (2009). Cultural factors affecting Chinese ESL students' academic learning. *Education, 129*(4), 643–653.

Huang, J., & Klinger, D. A. (2006). Chinese graduate students at North American universities: Learning challenges and coping strategies. *Canadian and International Education. Education Canadienne et Internationale, 35*(2), 47–61.

Kim, S. (2006). Academic oral communication needs of East Asian international graduate students in non-science and non-engineering fields. *English for Specific Purposes, 25*(4), 479–489. doi:10.1016/j.esp.2005.10.001

Kingston, E., & Forland, H. (2008). Bridging the gap in expectations between international students and academic staff. *Journal of Studies in International Education, 12*(2), 204–221. doi:10.1177/1028315307307654

Kuo, B. C. H., & Roysircar, G. (2004). Predictors of acculturation for Chinese adolescent in Canada: Age of arrival, length of stay, social class, and English reading ability. *Journal of Multicultural Counseling and Development, 32*(3), 143–154. doi:10.1002/j.2161-1912.2004.tb00367.x

Li, G., Chen, W., & Duanmu, J. L. (2010). Determinants of international students' academic performance: A comparison between Chinese and other international students. *Journal of Studies in International Education, 14*(4), 389–405. doi:10.1177/1028315309331490

Li, J. (2012). *Cultural foundations of learning: East and West.* Cambridge University Press. doi:10.1017/CBO9781139028400

Li, M. (2003). Culture and classroom communication: A case study of Asian students in New Zealand language schools. In *NZARE AARE Conference 2003: Educational research, risks, & dilemmas* (pp. 1-19). Auckland, New Zealand: Australian Association for Research in Education.

Liu, J. (2002). Negotiating silence in American classrooms: Three Chinese cases. *Language and Intercultural Communication, 2*(1), 37–54. doi:10.1080/14708470208668074

Liu, M. (2006). Anxiety in Chinese EFL students at different proficiency levels. *System, 34*(3), 301–316. doi:10.1016/j.system.2006.04.004

Love, K., & Arkoudis, S. (2006). Teachers' stances towards Chinese international students: An Australian case study. *Linguistics and Education, 17*(3), 258–282. doi:10.1016/j.linged.2006.11.002

Lu, C., & Han, W. (2010). Why don't they participate? A self-study of Chinese graduate Students' classroom involvement in North America. *Brock Education, 20*(1), 80–96. doi:10.26522/brocked.v20i1.147

Mori, S. (2010). Addressing the mental health concerns of international students. *Journal of Counseling and Development, 78*(2), 137–144. doi:10.1002/j.1556-6676.2000.tb02571.x

Morita, N. (2000). Discourse socialization through oral classroom activities in a TESL graduate program. *TESOL Quarterly, 34*(2), 279–310. doi:10.2307/3587953

Myles, J., & Cheng, L. (2003). The social and cultural life of non-native English speaking international graduate students at a Canadian university. *Journal of English for Academic Purposes, 2*(3), 247–263. doi:10.1016/S1475-1585(03)00028-6

Poyrazli, S., & Lopez, M. D. (2007). An exploratory study of perceived discrimination and homesickness: A comparison of international students and American Students. *The Journal of Psychology, 141*(3), 263–280. doi:10.3200/JRLP.141.3.263-280 PMID:17564257

Tatar, S. (2005). Classroom participation by international students: The case of Turkish graduate students. *Journal of Studies in International Education, 9*(4), 337–355. doi:10.1177/1028315305280967

Turner, Y. (2006). Chinese students in a UK business school: Hearing the student voice in reflective teaching and learning practice. *Higher Education Quarterly, 60*(1), 27–51. doi:10.1111/j.1468-2273.2006.00306.x

Vita, G. D. (2000). Inclusive approaches to effective communication and active participation in the multicultural classroom: An international business management context. *Learning in Higher Education, 1*(2), 168–180. doi:10.1177/1469787400001002006

Wong, J. K. (2004). Are the learning styles of Asian international students culturally or contextually based? *International Education Journal, 4*(4), 154–166.

Xiang, B. (2017). *Classroom engagement and participation among Chinese international graduate students: A case study*. Retrieve from Scholarship at UWindsor. (6028)

Yang, X. (2017). *Problems Chinese international students face during academic adaptation in English-speaking higher institutions* (Master thesis). University of Victoria, Canada. Retrieved from https://dspace.library.uvic.ca/handle/1828/8086

Yuan, W. (2011). Academic and cultural experiences of Chinese students at an American university: A qualitative study. *Intercultural Communication Studies, 20*(1), 141–157. https://web.uri.edu/iaics/files/11WenliYuan.pdf

Zhang, J., & Goodson, P. (2011). Acculturation and psychosocial adjustment of Chinese international students: Examining mediation and moderation effects. *International Journal of Intercultural Relations, 35*(5), 614–627. doi:10.1016/j.ijintrel.2010.11.004

Zhang, Z., & Brunton, M. (2007). Differences in living and learning: Chinese international students in New Zealand. *Journal of Studies in International Education, 11*(2), 124–140. doi:10.1177/1028315306289834

Zhang, Z., & Xu, J. (2007). Understanding Chinese international graduate students' adaptation to learning in North America: A cultural perspective. *Higher Education Perspective, 3*(1), 45–59.

Zhang, Z., & Zhou, G. (2010). Understanding Chinese international students at a Canadian university: Perspectives, expectations, and experiences. *Canadian and International Education. Education Canadienne et Internationale, 39*(3), 43–58.

Zheng, X., & Berry, J. W. (1991). Psychological adaptation of Chinese sojourners in Canada. *International Journal of Psychology, 26*(4), 451–470. doi:10.1080/00207599108247134

Zhou, G., & Zhang, Z. (2014). A study of the first year international students at a Canadian university: Challenges and experiences with social integration. *Canadian and International Education. Education Canadienne et Internationale, 43*(2), 7.

KEY TERMS AND DEFINITIONS

Classroom Participation: Classroom participation refers to the behaviours that students engage themselves in class. This behaviour can take many formats, such as raising questions, responding to others' questions, participation in discussions, providing feedback, and so on.

Cultural Differences: For international students who grew up in their home countries, many cultural aspects they get used to are often different from what they will experience in the host country.

International Cohort: Refers to international students who join a program as a group. They follow the same curriculum path for their study program.

International Students: These are students who left their home country and come to the host country for their education.

Language Barriers: International students have a mother tongue that is different from the main language in the host country. Often, their inadequate proficiency in the main language can cause many challenges for their academic and socialization efforts.

Life Management Skills: These skills refer to students' ability to look after themselves when they live away from home. Life management can be about academic, individual, or social matters.

Micro-Aggression: Although most universities in North America have policies in place in regards to equity, diversity, and inclusion, international students can suffer from some discrimination or hostility at the micro level, which often take place in their daily life context. For example, international students can be stereotyped and ignored by mainstream faculty and students.

Oral Academic Presentations (OAPs): They are among the most popular activities in post-secondary classrooms. It requires students to share their understanding of an article that was pre-assigned by the instructor as well lead a class discussion on the article.

Chapter 6
Multilingual International Students From the Perspective of Faculty:
Contributions, Challenges, and Support

Vander Tavares
York University, Canada

ABSTRACT

This chapter explores the experiences and perceptions of 14 faculty members toward multilingual international students at River University—a large, research-focused university in Ontario. Data was collected through an online survey and analysed thematically. Responses were categorised under three broad categories with respect to faculty's (1) perceptions of multilingual international students' contributions to River's academic community, (2) challenges surrounding faculty's interactions with multilingual international students, and (3) strategies developed and implemented to support students' academic success. Overall, findings were consistent with those in the current research literature, in which language proficiency was identified by faculty as a major concern, and multilingual international students were considered important for the enhancement of cultural and intellectual diversity, and for the internationalisation of higher education.

BACKGROUND

Canadian colleges and universities have experienced a rapid growth in their international student enrolment. According to data from Statistics Canada (2018), international student enrolment numbers in higher education rose to 245,895 in the academic year of 2016/17, resulting in a growth rate higher than that of domestic students. The Canadian Bureau of International Education (CBIE, 2020) reported that the number of international students pursuing post-secondary education in Canada exceeded 498,000 in 2019. This steady increase has helped broaden the focus of research concerned with international students and higher education in Canada with the aim of enhancing our understanding of the multidi-

DOI: 10.4018/978-1-7998-5030-4.ch006

mensionality of international students' experiences, particularly those experiences of a socio-academic and linguistic nature.

Recent research about international students' socio-academic dimension of lived experience in Canada has explored a variety of important topics. For instance, some scholars have examined the affordances of informal learning contexts for international students' development of social and professional skills (Fu, 2018), discrimination by members of international students' host academic communities, whether in or outside the classroom (Houshmand, Spanierman, & Tafarodi, 2014), the lack of an internationalised curriculum (Guo & Guo, 2017), and international students' adjustment to new social and academic expectations specifically within the graduate classroom (Alqudayri & Gounko, 2018). Investigations such as these have productively offered key insight into some of international students' experiences in Canada from the perspective *of the student*. However, as this very research demonstrates, international students' socio-academic experiences are co-constructed in interaction with other members of the academic community, such as local students, support staff, and faculty. Among these, the perspectives of faculty remain underexplored in the Canadian literature, despite the significance of the multiple institutional roles played by faculty to the socio-academic experiences of international students (Glass, Kociolek, Wongtrirat, Lynch, & Cong, 2015).

This chapter seeks to contribute to this line of research by exploring the experiences and perspectives of 14 faculty members at a large research-oriented university in Ontario. During the winter term of 2019, a study was conducted through an electronic survey forwarded by email to faculty in all departments in the institution under consideration in this study. Prior to describing the methodological design of the study, this chapter provides an overview of the literature related to faculty and international students' interaction in English-medium universities. In closing, the chapter offers a discussion in light of the findings, which highlights the perspectives of faculty on the ways in which multilingual international students contribute to their institution, the challenges faculty reported encountering in working with the students, and the support mechanisms developed and implemented to enhance faculty and student inter-group experiences. The study presented in this chapter was guided by the researcher's concern and interest to explore faculty's experiences and perspectives on multilingual international students.

FACULTY'S PERSPECTIVES ON INTERNATIONAL STUDENTS

Exploring faculty's perspectives on and experiences with multilingual international students can offer unique insight into the (co-constructed) international student experience. The following paragraphs aim to contextualise such insight by foregrounding three important inter-related dimensions of socio-academic experience commonly found in the scholarly literature. First, this review will discuss the influence which multilingual international students' interactions with faculty can have on the students' perceptions of their academic performance, both inside and outside the classroom. Second, it will identify some of the challenges faculty have reported to encounter while working from their multiple roles with multilingual international students. And third, this review will present some of the benefits faculty associate with the multilingual international student presence in academic communities. Altogether, the findings in this section help illustrate some of the complexity inherent in faculty-international student interactional experiences.

For international students, positive relationships with faculty may significantly enhance their sense of a positive academic experience. By exploring international students' perspectives on their social and academic experiences with faculty at an American university, Glass, Kociolek, Wongtrirat, Lynch, and Cong (2015) found that international students tend to view faculty not only as sources of academic knowledge, but also of practical advice and even emotional support as the students transition and progress through their academic journeys. While international students interact frequently with other groups within their institutions, such as support staff and local students, Glass and colleagues found that the students interviewed had approached professors "more frequently than [their] U.S. peers" (p. 363), and that when the outcomes of their interactions with faculty were positive, international students generally felt more socially and academically included as a result.

Additionally, international students' experiences with faculty, specifically in the classroom, can influence students' satisfaction with their overall academic experience. The international students interviewed by Glass et al. (2015) who felt more generally connected to their academic community did so when they also considered the teaching practices employed by their instructors to be more equitable and inclusive. In turn, the increased sense of belonging experienced by the international students, but facilitated pedagogically by faculty, related positively to students' perceptions of better academic and interpersonal performance. The students' experiences illustrate the importance placed by international students on their relationships with faculty, whom international students may see as "role models and gatekeepers" (p. 363) to successful academic acculturation.

For some faculty, however, obstacles to fostering a positive teaching and learning experience for international students in the classroom persist. Among these, insufficient proficiency in the English language on the part of the students, and by extension, in the academic register of English, has been commonly identified as a major challenge for supporting international students' academic success (Starr, 2009; Jeong et al., 2011). In her study exploring faculty's experiences working with multilingual international graduate students, Trice (2003) found that faculty identified insufficient linguistic proficiency as the most common challenge, regardless of the department with which the faculty interviewed were associated. Language was considered a significant barrier for international students' interaction with faculty as well as their classroom peers, even for disciplines wherein conversational peer interaction may be considered to occur less frequently (e.g., Tavares, 2019, 2016).

Yet, linguistic challenges have been reported to impact faculty's experiences beyond teaching. Faculty are known to sometimes necessarily spend more time marking, advising, and communicating with multilingual international students outside the classroom, such as during office hours, because of language-related issues (Del Fabbro, Mitchell, & Shaw, 2015; Jin & Schneider, 2019; Nguyen, 2013; Trice, 2003). In the classroom, however, faculty may modify their language in an effort to better support multilingual international students' learning experiences. Modifying language can include the simplification of oral or written language, such as during a lecture or on examinations, respectively (Bosher & Bowles, 2008; Tavares, 2017). Still, little is known whether the strategies employed by faculty actually meet multilingual international students' needs in terms of linguistic support (Tavares, 2020).

In her study, Trice (2003) found that faculty were concerned about international students' segregation from their domestic peers. While some faculty related the lack of intergroup mingling to a lack of language proficiency on the part of multilingual international students, others suggested that cultural differences might be the greatest barrier to intergroup socialisation. When identifying possible cultural challenges for international students, some faculty cited the informality characteristic of student-faculty interactions in the American academic context which, for students coming from teacher-centred cultures, may seem initially conflicting. However, despite all concern raised around segregation between students,

Trice noted that some faculty incorrectly believed that international students simply wished to remain with their co-nationals, despite research strongly suggesting otherwise.

Faculty perceptions of international and domestic students may differ when faculty act also as advisors to international students. Nguyen (2013) found that faculty in her study broadly characterised international graduate students as more motivated and hard-working than their domestic peers, essentially because "they [international students] have to be hard-working in order to get to where they are currently" (p. 106). Some faculty in the study also reported that international students in general are more respectful and polite students, regardless of whether the faculty member is the student's advisor or instructor. As for challenges, faculty cited language as a major barrier for the international students they advise formally. Furthermore, faculty identified international students' previous educational acculturation in their home countries as having a strong influence on the students' views of higher education, especially when it comes to plagiarism.

The impact of international students' financial difficulties on their academic studies has also been cited as a concern. In a study with international graduate students and faculty at a university in Ontario, Faiza (2015) noted that the high cost of tuition and fewer scholarships designated exclusively for international students were some of the concerns faculty reported based on their experience in teaching and advising international students. Cuts to higher education funding in general were another issue that affected faculty in their recruitment of now significantly fewer international graduate students than they desired or needed for the continuity of their research projects. From the perspective of the international students in Faiza's study, high tuition costs, fewer scholarships, and less funding, when coupled with fewer job opportunities on and off campus and limited work hours, rendered the international student experience challenging and stressful.

Despite the challenges, research points to a strong consensus among faculty in terms of their beliefs about the positive contributions international students make to their academic communities. Contributions such as offering international perspectives to classroom discussions; diversifying the ethnic, cultural, and linguistic profile of the student body; helping establish international research ties with faculty; and enhancing cross-cultural interaction and communication on campus have been commonly identified by faculty not only as important, but sometimes also as unique to multilingual international students (Faiza, 2015; Nguyen, 2013; Trice, 2003). In closing, exploring faculty's experiences—based on their interactions, expectations, perceptions, and challenges—with multilingual international students affords us a unique kind of insight into how the international student experience may be enhanced both in and outside the academic classroom.

METHODOLOGY

River University, founded in the 1950s, is a large, research-oriented university with two campuses in Ontario. The smaller campus of the two is known for its bilingual profile, offering courses in French and English. According to River University's web site, the university also has two international campuses: one in Costa Rica and one in India.[1] From the university's web site, the following figures were available regarding its campus population and international affiliations as of 2019: over 45,000 undergraduate students, approximately 6,000 graduate students, 6,200 international students from almost 200 countries, 280 international university partners, and about 7,000 faculty and staff. Within its immediate communities, River University has been known distinguishably for its multicultural and multilingual profile, a kind of visibility sustained across all institutional groups.

The recruitment of participants consisted of an invitation distributed by email to all faculty at River University. Insights from faculty were sought for the purpose of understanding, learning about, and expanding the range of voices, experiences, and perspectives that help contextualise the multilingual international student experience at River University. The recruitment process entailed the compilation of email addresses for full- and part-time faculty from all 11 faculties at River University. Both full- and part-time faculty were included in order to increase the pool of participants and potentially diversify the range of perspectives shared. The email message which faculty received contained a link to an electronic survey along with an explanation and purpose of the study.

Prior to starting the survey, consent was given by participants electronically. All faculty participants have been assigned pseudonyms. Participants include 14 faculty members. Eight of them were in the faculty of Liberal Arts—River University's largest faculty—three were in the faculty of Health, one in the faculty of Law, one in the faculty of Environmental Studies, and one in the faculty of Visual Art. The majority ($N=9$) taught undergraduate-level courses only, and the remaining five taught both undergraduate and graduate courses. All participants reported teaching both international and domestic students in their classes.

For this study, online surveys were chosen on the basis of convenience as a large number of individuals needed to be reached. Wyatt (2000) identified a few advantages to using online surveys in qualitative research, all of which were directly applicable to this study: online surveys are more inclusive, as they can include suitable participants who may not be physically present in the research setting at the time of a study; they are cost-effective, often free; the data are "captured directly in electronic format, making analysis faster and cheaper" (p. 427); they are interactive, allowing the researcher to check the responses easily and quickly; they allow material related to the study to be included onto the survey interface, such as external links; and lastly, surveys allow the researcher to modify any of its content with ease, should the need arise.

The surveys contained both closed- and open-response questions. Close-response questions were intended to capture participants' academic and demographic information, such as the length of their time at River University up to the time of the study, their faculty or departmental association, and teaching load status, consisting of check boxes and limited-choice items on a drop-down menu. On the other hand, open-response questions were intended to explore an area of concern more closely. As Brown (2009) has pointed out, open-response questions can enrich the data "by not restricting the respondents to a set of answers but asking them to express their own ideas more fully or inviting them to elaborate or explain their answers to closed-response items in their own words" (p. 202).

In developing the questions, the concerns guiding this research were prioritised. Generally speaking, these concerns related to the topics of academics, culture, social interaction, psychological experiences, and language. Findings and gaps from the studies reviewed in preparation for this study were carefully considered to help narrow down the questions to a point in which they could be usefully applied to the context of River University. The underlying intention was not to generalise or compare the open responses from faculty members, but rather to learn and develop a sense of the personal experience each individual participant had toward the topics included in the survey. Once the list of questions was formulated, they were shared with a fellow researcher for feedback. The questions were then adjusted as necessary and transferred to Google Forms.

All open responses were compiled and analysed thematically (Creswell, 2013) in connection with the concerns guiding the study. The analysis process helped reduce the amount of data to more manageable and understandable information. The broader concerns mentioned previously were used as general categories under which the emergent themes from the responses were organised. When a response suggested a theme which did not easily fit in any of the pre-established categories, a new category was created. At the last stage of data analysis, the categories were collapsed into three groups which flowed logically from the data organisation process: first, faculty's perspectives on the contributions made to River University by multilingual international students; second, on the challenges faced by the students; and third, the support mechanisms implemented by faculty. All findings are based on self-reported data by faculty and are interwoven analytically with findings from previous research to help situate and compare the context of River University.

FINDINGS

Contributions to River's Academic Community

Overall, faculty members characterised multilingual international students as a valuable group within River's community. In particular, they spoke of multilingual international students as contributing to an increased visibility of multiculturalism and multilingualism on campus. These contributions were considered organic in that they related to the very essence of being international: a student who was international at River was likely someone who was studying in a language other than their first one and whose cultural experiences were likely more internationally diverse, encompassing those experienced at home and in Canada. Furthermore, the students' contributions were not considered to be restricted to a particular dimension of the academic experience. Instead, they were argued to be important to the community as a whole:

One of River's strengths is its multicultural diversity. Students benefit from being with students who may be different from them in a variety of ways and may learn to view things from different perspectives. Especially in small classes, they have to move outside the bubble of their earlier life experiences. (Professor Gallant)

They are a vivid representation of true multiculturalism, and bring much awareness of other ways of thinking and being in the world. (Professor Li)

As with all aspects of life, diversity teaches tolerance, flexibility, empathy. I think these are essential skills for all students (and professors!), and ultimately a successful society. (Professor MacArthur)

Multilingual international students' contributions were also considered important in the context of the academic classroom. For Professor Campbell, multilingual international students contributed by providing unique international insight into the classroom experience, normally by means of giving specifically cultural examples. In fact, she considered her teaching to be its "best" when these contributions were present. She drew multilingual international students' languages into teaching and learning by asking students to translate foreign advertising content. In a similar vein, for Professor Frescatti, teaching multilingual international students was also advantageous as they possessed linguistic and cultural knowledge that could benefit pedagogical practices:

My best teaching is when I use them to bring in global examples. They offer unique perspectives. Sometimes I use images with other languages in them and ask students what they say – I teach advertising so this is easy. (Professor Campbell)

Multilingual international students contribute to the university's multiculturalism and multilingualism. In my case, it's a huge benefit to be able to count on them to speak their languages and to share their culture to those who want to learn it. (Professor Frescatti)

However, despite the notion that multilingual international students were a valuable addition to the academic community, for some, contribution was a matter of choice. For instance, from viewing multilingual international students as one large cultural group, Professor Nboni commented that their contribution to diversifying academic discourse depended on their understanding of the active role expected of students in a learner-centred academic culture. As research suggests, however, international students transitioning from teacher-centred academic cultures tend to encounter conflicting expectations around teaching and learning in English-medium, learner-centred environments, especially around the extent to which students are expected to actively and orally participate in their academic communities (e.g., Tatar, 2005; Wu, 2009). Professor Nboni argued as follows:

Diversity and multiplicity of viewpoints reflecting a broad range of value orientations, world views and life experiences brought by multilingual international students contribute to the academic discourse – if and when these students overcome often strongly ingrained attitudes of reserve and deference to authority. (Professor Nboni)

The characterisation of multilingual international students as a more reserved group prevails in the research literature. The absence of an active, often vociferous, behaviour whether in the classroom or in other academic spaces has often been uncritically ascribed primarily to a lack of linguistic proficiency or intelligence on the part of multilingual international students. However, "passivity" or "disengagement" by means of silence is a complex social, cultural, and linguistic behaviour (Harumi, 2010). Bista (2012) argued that international students cannot simply isolate the sociocultural aspects informing their identities in a new cultural environment, especially students from an Asian background, who typically view instructors and elders as being more knowledgeable and respectable based on their cultural values. He further argued that instructors might be better equipped to work with multilingual international students' silence if they are more critically aware of students' cultural and linguistic backgrounds, and of how these may inform their beliefs concerning classroom behaviour and student-instructor interactions.

For Professor Gylys, the students' contribution to enriching the academic community was also a matter of choice. In her experience, not all multilingual international students "choose" to participate in their host communities by sharing their cross-cultural perspectives. However, analogous to the previous point, a more critical understanding of engagement should be considered. Engagement may not be a construct defined equally by all members of an academic community. Definitions may depend on the institutional position from which one is (un)able to engage and speak, as well as on the sociocultural resources made available to the individual on the basis of their group identity (e.g., nationality, language, race).

In fact, community engagement by multilingual international students should be understood from a place of reciprocity. For example, in a study exploring the experiences of multilingual and minority university students at an American university, Oropeza, Varghese, and Kanno (2010) found that the multilingual students would not invest in their academic communities when their investments would result in the extended institutional construction of themselves as ESL students. Because ESL students did not collectively enjoy the same range of academic support services at the university as native-speaker students did, the ESL students refused to use the exclusive services in place for them. The authors stressed that "a lack" of engagement was a form of resistance to services that implicitly sustained marginalisation. Professor Gylys proposed that:

Students who choose to engage in the community bring a richness of perspectives to everything. (Professor Gylys)

Challenges

This section presents faculty's perspectives on the challenges faced by multilingual international students at River University. In general, faculty expressed a concern primarily in relation to language proficiency. This did not refer only to insufficient proficiency to express oneself in casual interactions in English, but also proficiency in the academic register of higher education. For Professor MacArthur, for example, insufficient language proficiency was not an issue for all multilingual international students. Yet, those students for whom it was, she considered the impact to be significant, affecting students' clarity of communication. Professor MacArthur reported that language proficiency was particularly problematic for her when she could not understand students' ideas. As for challenges of a social nature, she believed that the majority of students did not seem to experience them considering the visibility of their membership in small groups:

It really depends, as many multilingual students speak English well (they just also speak a second or third language). For those for which English is a difficulty, I think this has an impact on them academically – I can see this reflected in the quality of their writing, and confidence in their public speaking. Although I try to be more forgiving, but it can be an issue when I simple do not understand the ideas and concepts they are attempting to convey. This may translate to difficulties professionally. It appears that most have cliques of friends however, so I don't think the social aspect is as challenge. (Professor MacArthur)

Furthermore, while language was viewed as a common challenge, it was rarely considered a challenge to occur by itself. In particular, language-related challenges were accompanied by unfamiliar cultural expectations of classroom participation between the context of River and of where the students lived prior to moving to Canada. Professor Nboni mentioned that in her teaching experience, many multilingual international students did not have sufficient language proficiency and did not engage in typical western-based classroom behaviour, such as in asking questions or challenging the points of view expressed by instructors during lectures.

Linguistic challenges: many international students have marginal command of writing skills in the English language required to express themselves in written assignments. And cultural challenges: from some cultures, students are not used to questioning and challenging their teachers even if/when they have doubts about the assertions made by instructors. (Professor Nboni)

Professor Gallant's experience closely mirrored that of Professor Nboni. She reported that many of the multilingual international students specifically from China lacked sufficient language skills and preferred more "passive" engagement with learning. She associated the students' choice of studying economics to their limited language skills. Indeed, some multilingual international students whose academic language skills require further improvement might opt for less linguistically-demanding academic programs—programs wherein oral communication is less frequently expected, such as mathematics and computer science—in order to minimise the potential for linguistic challenges (Zhang & Mi, 2010). Additionally, Professor Gallant mentioned that multilingual international students were often minimally involved in the other dimensions connected to the experience of being a university student:

Many of the students coming from China, especially through River's language institute, enrolling in economics do so because their English language skills are limited. They strongly prefer equations delivered by lecture method and multiple choice tests to a more engaged classroom encouraging critical thinking through discussion. Socially, educationally, professionally, these students stay quite apart from the university learning experience. (Professor Gallant)

For other faculty, some of the identified challenges could not be ascribed exclusively to multilingual international students. Professor Li commented specifically on challenges around social and cultural integration into the academic community, which may be a new experience for both domestic and international undergraduate students alike. However, she argued that this challenge might be greater for newly arrived international students, and cited age as one of the possible reasons. A consensus among researchers suggests that younger immigrants tend to acculturate to the host society with fewer challenges in comparison to older immigrants (Kuo & Roysircar, 2004; Scot & Scot, 1989; Yeh, 2003). In the case of international students, this may be true as well. The older the international student, the higher the probability of experiencing greater social and cultural adjustment issues in the new academic environment (Yeh & Inose, 2003).

Those born in Canada have fewer challenges than new newly arrived immigrants. It seems that social and cultural integration would be the most challenging for recent immigrants at the age level of our undergraduate students. (Professor Li)

Professor Gylys highlighted linguistic challenges as one of her central concerns. She explained that multilingual international students with whom she had worked often possessed insufficient proficiency in academic English despite passing internationally recognised language exams. In the research literature, personal accounts shared by multilingual international students with respect to their academic English language-related experiences strongly suggest that international language exams for college and university admittance fall short of realistically testing students for the complex and specialised register of English utilised in the academy (Lee, 2009; Li, 2004; Liu, 2011). However, Professor Gylys also reported encountering this kind of challenge in monolingual, native speakers of English:

Linguistic difficulties—receiving acceptable grades in the IELTS and TOEFL tests does not in my experience necessarily translate into adequate levels in English language comprehension or oral and written expression for post-secondary study. To be fair, these skills are sometimes lacking in native unilingual speakers of English as well. (Professor Gylys)

Finally, challenges were also identified specifically at the graduate level. To exemplify, Professor Campbell expressed some concern toward multilingual international students' communication skills in the form of written language. She characterised their writing as a distinguishably marked, "awkward" variation of standard written English, in the same way that some non-native speakers may speak the target language with an accent. However, she reported approaching written discourse in a second language in a manner that positioned difference as an expression of identity—the material production bore the identity of the producer—rather than as a language deficit. Moreover, she suggested that the expectation that all academic writing in English should be native-like could potentially silence the multicultural "voice" embedded in the writing produced by international students.

For grad students, the biggest challenge I think is the question of their writing, which is good, but written as a second language speaker. I am of the camp that I don't want to erase that voice – of being an international student – to make it sound like a native Canadian. But others think that the writing should be flawless. I am not talking about improper grammar, but awkward writing, because the student is an international student: the writing equivalent of an accent. (Professor Campbell)

Another concern focused on challenges resulting from an incongruence between students' former and current education. In particular, Professor Nboni referred to the lack of uniformity in the labelling of course names by different institutions as a potential disadvantage for multilingual international graduate students. In this sense, she argued that a multilingual international graduate student who began graduate studies in the same discipline, but at a foreign institution (i.e., outside Canada), might not be able to progress in a given course as linearly as their other peers who advanced to graduate studies within the same educational and linguistic context.

Especially at the graduate level, international students may have taken courses with the same labels as our courses but which have very different content. For example, in my discipline a course titled "Syntax" may have been a general history of thought with regard to the subject matter rather than learning how to analyze data and apply theory to new data. They are thus at a disadvantage in that they may not have the same background preparation as other students. (Professor Nboni)

Supporting Achievement of Academic Success

While the previous section focused on identifying challenges, this section highlights the strategies adopted by faculty in support of multilingual international students in the academic community. Faculty's responses suggest that supporting the students' achievement of academic success is a complex task. Additionally, responses illustrated that support mechanisms were context-dependent, rather than employed uniformly all around, despite most challenges previously identified being of a linguistic nature.

The ability to support multilingual international students was considered to depend on several factors. These factors were more or less influential in accordance with the specific teaching context of each individual faculty member. For some, class size was a significant factor. Professor Gylys, who taught a first-year lecture, reported supporting multilingual international students in her 400-student class was "impossible." Comparably, Professor Campbell reported it was difficult to support these students in her large classes. She mentioned resorting to the teaching assistants to provide individual support and to evaluate the students' writing differently. Furthermore, she expressed that it would be helpful, in her context, if students themselves could explain their needs and preferred strategies for individual support *in writing*.

Not in a classroom of 400. (Professor Gylys)

In a big class, this is really hard. I try to work with the TAs to support them and have different expectations of their writing. I think what would be great, is if there is a way for us as professors to hear these students' voices. Maybe a page that has quotes from these students of their challenges. Or a list of 5 things that they would like us to do to support them. It is easy to just teach and forget about all the ways that students need support – which are constantly changing. (Professor Campbell)

For Professor Li, supporting students equated to providing personal guidance and encouraging the use of support services for those with language-related challenges. However, in relation to support services, some research suggests that multilingual international students may not always take part in the services because such services are normally developed and promoted only to students who are considered deficient. For instance, among many important findings, Roberts and Dunworth (2012) found that a lack of student-friendly language and an emphasis on failure contributed to both students' and staff members' negative perceptions of the effectiveness of support services at an English-medium university. In parallel, Oropeza, Varghese, and Kanno (2010) argued that services which position multilingual students inferiorly may only contribute to the exclusion of the very same students they seek to support. As emphasised previously, some of the students in the study by Oropeza and colleagues refused services as an act of resistance to institutionalised marginalisation.

In addition to personal guidance, I always encourage students with poor English skills to take advantage of the many services available at the university: learning commons, writing centre, etc. (Professor Li)

Professor MacArthur reported drawing on "teach-back" as a strategy to ensure that students understand course content. However, despite the support provided, she expressed that the "poor" communication skills on the part of multilingual international students posed challenges to the overall quality of teaching and learning in her classes. Peters and Anderson (2017) identified language as one component by which "rigorous standards of academic excellence" of higher education are maintained (p. 46), and argued that embedding language-focused resources in the curriculum from the very beginning of a course may help maintain the high standards of academic education when concerns about the possible impact of language proficiency on teaching and learning exist.

I try to explain things many times over, and use a "teach-back" method to try and ensure that ideas were understood. Often they use their own representative analogies to a concept and I can confirm if they have grasped the content. Honestly, it is very challenging for me as a professor to teach students when their communication skills (or English skills) are so poor that information cannot be conveyed. I think while there are clear benefits to diversity, on campus, socially, academically, but it can also introduce challenges that affect the quality of education. (Professor MacArthur)

Challenges by multilingual international students in regards to understanding and developing proficiency in academic language have been reported by both faculty and students themselves. In response, some faculty opt to modify the language of instruction by simplifying it. For instance, in a university-wide survey, Peters and Anderson (2017) found that some faculty adopted simpler language in quizzes and tests, and when this was not feasible, other faculty allotted extra time during exams in an attempt to foster better comprehension. Unruh (2015) found the faculty in her study adopted language-related strategies in the form of posting announcements on the board and avoiding the use of slang. Professor Nboni reported supporting multilingual international students by drawing on a similar strategy, while also acknowledging and encouraging students to express their opinions.

As much as is practicable to use simpler English in teaching; encourage and reinforce efforts made by students to express themselves even if their difficulty with the English language might be manifested in inefficiency and ineffectiveness in expression. (Professor Nboni)

In Professor Gallant's experience, many of the multilingual international students who lacked language proficiency also happened to not attend class. Consequently, she contemplated assigning points for participation as a strategy to help mitigate attendance issues. Additionally, she differentiated the level of cross-cultural contribution to the class between multilingual, multicultural international students and multilingual, multicultural first-generation students. She argued the contributions made by the latter group were more meaningful, and reported modifying her teaching to include practices aimed at inviting contributions by this group.

I am clearly differentiating between those students who do not yet have the English language facility (many of the international students in economics) from the many first generation students from many other countries who are quite broadly capable at the university level. The latter group enriches the discussion and so changes to teaching include ways to bring the varying perspectives into the classroom. The former do not attend class at all, but only show up for the tests... I suppose I could try giving points for participation... (Professor Gallant)

Professor Gallant's experience, however, contrasts with findings of earlier research conducted with over 1,000 students in four universities in Canada, including River University. In the study, Grayson (2011) found that domestic first-generation students were the least academically engaged by means of attending lectures and tutorials, studying outside class times, and visiting the library. Conversely, international students who were not first-generation—the term meaning "the sons and daughters of parents with less than post-secondary education" (p. 605)—had the highest level of academic involvement according to the measures developed by the researcher.

DISCUSSION AND CONCLUSION

This chapter presented findings from a study which focused on exploring faculty's experiences with and perceptions of multilingual international students at River University. This study was operationalised through a survey completed by fourteen faculty members at River University, a large, research-oriented university in Ontario, recognised within its immediate community for its cultural, ethnic, and linguistic diversity across and within all institutional groups: faculty, students, and support staff. Overall, the findings reveal that among faculty, those who participated in the study considered multilingual international students' contributions to River University positively and important for the continuous development and enhancement of intercultural experience, teaching and learning, and intellectual diversity at the institution.

Additionally, findings reveal that faculty encountered ongoing challenges in working with multilingual international students. Consistent with the literature, most of these challenges revolve around the English language, particularly with respect to students' development and use of an academic register of English. Faculty reported feeling concerned about the great extent to which insufficient proficiency in English seems to affect international students' academic success. Other challenges involve different social and cultural behaviours which faculty also identified as having an impact on students' academics. These social and cultural differences translated into what some faculty characterised as a less active style of participation in the classroom, but also outside in terms of the students' involvement in campus life, when compared to that of a typical local student.

Nevertheless, faculty also reported supporting multilingual international students in their achievement of academic success. Support strategies varied across experiences, but were primarily of a linguistic nature. Faculty reported using simpler language whenever possible, both in oral and written communication with students. Other strategies in the immediate context of the classroom were pedagogical in nature, which included the integration of methods aimed at facilitating teaching and learning. Furthermore, faculty reported drawing on their teaching assistants and directing students to university-wide support programs when the needs of international students were considered difficult to meet through instructor-led initiatives alone. In alignment with findings from previous research, understanding and responding to the needs of multilingual international students continues to be a complex task for faculty.

This study highlights some important areas that continue to require attention as we strive to better understand the multilingual international student experience in Canada. To begin with, at least in the context of River University—but likely in those of many other institutions of English-medium higher education in Canada as well—more and better institutional support around the development of multilingual international students' academic language proficiency is still needed. Faculty identified language as a major factor to successful faculty-international student interaction, as well as to multilingual international student success in general. If such support were already available at River University, it is also central to consider the ways in which international students experience and perceive the effectiveness of language support programs. Further research can examine the experiences of support staff in this regard, and the existing links, if any, between support staff and faculty in their effort to collaboratively support multilingual international students.

English language proficiency exams are required for multilingual international students who speak English as an additional language and seek admission to River University. Yet, it is worth considering how accurately those exams can prepare international students for academic studies in English at the university. It seems to be the case that while many international students pass those exams, they still struggle with language once they begin their studies (Tavares, 2016), which then directly affects faculty's experiences as well. Moreover, one faculty member also expressed concern about international students who joined River University through the university's language bridging program and whether the students had chosen their program of study on the basis of a less linguistically demanding curriculum. It is unclear whether River's language program staff worked collaboratively with faculty in order to (sufficiently) prepare students to be able to choose their academic programs regardless of linguistic demands. Both faculty and staff in preparatory language programs can work together to enhance this aspect of the multilingual international student experience.

Still in relation to support, but specifically that which is offered by faculty, it remains unclear whether such support efforts realistically meet the needs of multilingual international students. Consequently, better mechanisms which can more frequently and more systematically access and bring the needs of international students to the attention of faculty may contribute to the development of more appropriate, context-sensitive academic support strategies for international students' classroom experience. As the findings suggest, faculty seem generally not only concerned about international students' success, but also willing to help. However, a gap still exists with respect to how this support may be bridged successfully. Further research can investigate this area of concern.

In closing, this study also reinforces the essential role multilingual international students play in contributing to the internationalisation of higher education in Canada. The presence and participation of international students in their host academic communities contribute to campus diversity in numerous dimensions, including the cultural, ethnic, linguistic, and professional. Also, multilingual international students help enhance teaching and learning for both faculty and domestic students by offering first-hand international perspectives that can challenge traditional thinking in academe. Moving forward, researchers can explore multilingual internationals students' contributions to Canadian higher education from the perspectives of Canadian students and staff members. The number of participants in this study was limited, and findings were framed within the context of River University only, although they cannot represent the experiences of all faculty members at the institution. Consistent with the objective of the study, the accounts shared by the participants were sought in order to understand interpersonal interaction as specifically situated (i.e., at River University) and individually experienced exchanges only.

REFERENCES

Alqudayri, B., & Gounko, T. (2018). Studying in Canada: Experiences of Female Graduate Students from Saudi Arabia. *Journal of International Students*, *8*(4), 1736–1747.

Bista, K. (2012). Silence in teaching and learning: Perspectives of a Nepalese graduate student. *College Teaching*, *60*(2), 76–82.

Bosher, S., & Bowles, M. (2008). The effects of linguistic modification on ESL students' comprehension of nursing course test items. *Nursing Education Perspectives*, *29*, 165–172. PMID:18575241

Brown, J. D. (2009). Open-response items in questionnaires. In J. Heigham & R. Croker (Eds.), *Qualitative research in applied linguistics: A practical introduction* (pp. 200–219). Palgrave MacMillan.

Canadian Bureau of International Education. (2020). *International students in Canada continue to grow in 2019*. Retrieved from https://cbie.ca/international-students-in-canada-continue-to-grow-in-2019/

Creswell, J. W. (2013). *Qualitative inquiry & research design: choosing among five approaches*. Sage.

Del Fabbro, L., Mitchell, C., & Shaw, J. (2015). Learning among nursing faculty: Insights from a participatory action research project about teaching international students. *The Journal of Nursing Education*, *54*(3), 153–158. PMID:25693177

Faiza, O. (2015). *Building rapport between international graduate students and their faculty advisors: Cross cultural mentoring relationships at the University of Guelph* (Unpublished master's thesis). University of Guelph, Guelph, Canada.

Fu, J. (2018). *The role of two extracurricular programs in international students' informal learning experiences in Atlantic Canada* (Unpublished master's thesis). Mount Saint Vincent University, Halifax, Canada.

Glass, C. R., Kociolek, E., Wongtrirat, R., Lynch, R. J., & Cong, S. (2015). Uneven experiences: The impact of student-faculty interactions on international students' sense of belonging. *Journal of International Students*, *5*(4), 353–367.

Grayson, J. (2011). Cultural capital and academic achievement of first generation domestic and international students in Canadian universities. *British Educational Research Journal*, *37*(4), 605–630.

Guo, Y., & Guo, S. (2017). Internationalization of Canadian higher education: Discrepancies between policies and international student experiences. *Studies in Higher Education*, *42*(5), 851–868.

Harumi, S. (2010). Classroom silence: Voices from Japanese EFL learners. *English Language Teaching Journal*, *65*(1), 1–10.

Houshmand, S., Spanierman, L. B., & Tafarodi, R. W. (2014). Excluded and avoided: Racial microaggressions targeting Asian international students in Canada. *Cultural Diversity & Ethnic Minority Psychology*, *20*(3), 377–388. PMID:25045949

Jeong, S. Y. S., Hickey, N., Levett-Jones, T., Pitt, V., Hoffman, K., Norton, C. A., & Ohr, S. O. (2011). Understanding and enhancing the learning experiences of culturally and linguistically diverse nursing students in an Australian bachelor of nursing program. *Nurse Education Today*, *31*(3), 238–244. PMID:21078536

Jin, L., & Schneider, J. (2019). Faculty views on international students: A survey study. *Journal of International Students*, *9*(1), 84–99.

Kuo, B. C., & Roysircar, G. (2004). Predictors of acculturation for Chinese adolescents in Canada: Age of arrival, length of stay, social class, and English reading ability. *Journal of Multicultural Counseling and Development*, *32*(3), 143–154.

Lee, G. (2009). Speaking up: Six Korean students' oral participation in class discussions in US graduate seminars. *English for Specific Purposes*, *28*, 142–156.

Li, Y. (2004). Learning to live and study in Canada: Stories of four EFL learners from China. *TESL Canada*, *22*(2), 25–43.

Liu, L. (2011). An international graduate student's ESL learning experience beyond the classroom. *TESL Canada Journal*, 77–92.

Nguyen, H. M. (2013). Faculty advisors' experiences with international graduate students. *Journal of International Students*, *3*(2), 102–116.

Oropeza, M. V., Varghese, M. M., & Kanno, Y. (2010). Linguistic minority students in higher education: Using, resisting, and negotiating multiple labels. *Equity & Excellence in Education*, *43*(2), 216–231.

Peters, B., & Anderson, M. (2017). *Supporting non-native English speakers at the University of Minnesota: A survey of faculty & staff.* University of Minnesota.

Roberts, P., & Dunworth, K. (2012). Staff and student perceptions of support services for international students in higher education: A case study. *Journal of Higher Education Policy and Management*, *34*(5), 517–528.

Scott, W. A., & Scott, R. (1989). *Adaptation of immigrants: Individual differences and determinants.* Pergamon.

Starr, K. (2009). Nursing education challenges: Students with English as an additional language. *The Journal of Nursing Education*, *48*, 478–487. PMID:19645373

Statistics Canada. (2018). *Canadian postsecondary enrolments and graduates, 2016/2017.* Retrieved from https://www150.statcan.gc.ca/n1/daily-quotidien/181128/dq181128c-eng.htm

Tatar, S. (2005). Classroom participation by international students: The case of Turkish graduate students. *Journal of Studies in International Education*, *9*(4), 337–355.

Tavares, V. (2016). *The role of peer interaction and second language learning for ESL students in academic contexts: An extended literature review* (Unpublished Master's thesis). York University, Toronto, Canada.

Tavares, V. (2017). Reflecting on international students' experiences: Strategies that support academic success. *International Journal of Multidisciplinary Perspectives in Higher Education, 2.*

Tavares, V. (2019). A review of peer interaction and second language learning for ELL students in academic contexts. *Canadian Journal for New Scholars in Education*, *10*(2), 111–119.

Tavares, V. (2020). *International students in higher education: Language, identity, and experience from a holistic perspective* (Unpublished doctoral dissertation). York University, Toronto, Canada.

Trice, A. (2003). Faculty perceptions of graduate international students: The benefits and challenges. *Journal of Studies in International Education*, *7*(4), 379–403.

Unruh, S. (2015). Struggling international students in the US: Do university faculty know how to help. *Athens Journal of Education*, *2*(2), 99–110.

Wu, X. (2009). The dynamics of Chinese face mechanisms and classroom behavior: A case study. *Evaluation and Research in Education*, *22*(2), 87–105.

Wyatt, J. C. (2000). When to use Web-based surveys. *Journal of the American Medical Informatics Association*, *7*, 426–430. PMID:10887170

Yeh, C. J. (2003). Age, acculturation, cultural adjustment, and mental health symptoms of Chinese, Korean, and Japanese immigrant youths. *Cultural Diversity & Ethnic Minority Psychology, 9*(1), 34. PMID:12647324

Yeh, C. J., & Inose, M. (2003). International students' reported English fluency, social support satisfaction, and social connectedness as predictors of acculturative stress. *Counselling Psychology Quarterly, 16*(1), 15–28.

Zhang, Z., & Mi, Y. (2010). Another look at the language difficulties of international students. *Journal of Studies in International Education, 14*(4), 371–387.

ADDITIONAL READING

Hegarty, N. (2014). Where we are now: The presence and importance of international student to universities in the United States. *Journal of International Students, 4*(3), 223–235.

Houshmand, S., Spanierman, L. B., & Tafarodi, R. W. (2014). Excluded and avoided: Racial microaggressions targeting Asian international students in Canada. *Cultural Diversity & Ethnic Minority Psychology, 20*(3), 377–388. doi:10.1037/a0035404 PMID:25045949

Le Ha, P. (2009). English as an international language: International student and identity formation. *Language and Intercultural Communication, 9*(3), 201–214.

KEY TERMS AND DEFINITIONS

Academic English: The register of the English language used in academic contexts. When in writing, this register is governed by specific writing conventions around vocabulary, syntax, and argumentation strategies.

Domestic Student: Normally a student who is a citizen or a permanent resident of the country in which they study.

Faculty: The teaching staff of a particular institution. In addition to teaching, faculty members may also advise and supervise international students.

IELTS: International English Language Testing System. An international, standardised language test developed to measure proficiency in the English language whose scores are used for admission of speakers of English as an additional language to an English-medium institution.

International Student: A student who holds a student visa and/or a study permit at a university outside their home country.

Multilingual: An individual who possesses contextualised knowledge of multiple languages and linguistic varieties as a single, hybrid competence.

TOEFL: Test of English as a Foreign Language. An international, standardised language test for those who speak English as an additional language and wish to study at an English-medium college or university.

ENDNOTE

[1]   River University's web site has been excluded from the reference list for anonymity reasons.

Chapter 7
Chinese Graduate Students at a Canadian University:
Their Academic Challenges and Coping Strategies

Wei Yang

McGill University, Canada

Xiaoli Jing

McGill University, Canada

ABSTRACT

With the growing trend of globalization and internationalization of education, an increasing number of Chinese students choose to pursue higher education in Canada. In order to explore Chinese international students' academic challenges and coping strategies in Canadian universities, the authors conducted semi-structured interviews with 16 students studying graduate programs in one Canadian university. The findings reveal that Chinese graduate students encounter a number of academic challenges due to their limited English language proficiency, and the different educational norms and practices between China and Canada. By employing the theory of student agency as the theoretical framework, the study finds that Chinese graduate students possess the agency to cope with their academic challenges. The coping strategies can be grouped into two categories: the first category is to rely on students' personal improvement and the second category is to resort to external resources. The chapter concludes with implications for future research.

INTRODUCTION

With the growing trend of globalization, internationalization and neoliberalism, an increasing number of Chinese students choose to pursue higher education abroad with the aim of enhancing their competitive advantages in the labour market. According to the latest statistics, the number of Chinese students studying abroad rose from approximately 39,000 in 2000 to 662,100 in 2018 (Liu & Liu, 2016; Ministry

DOI: 10.4018/978-1-7998-5030-4.ch007

of Education of China, 2019). Among the major destinations of Chinese international students, Canada ranks fourth following the United States, Australia, and the United Kingdom, hosting nearly 170,000 Chinese studying in 2018 (Immigration, Refugees, and Citizenship Canada, 2019; Institute of International Education, 2018). As shown in Figure 1, the number of Chinese students studying in Canadian educational institutions has increased rapidly in the recent decade, among which university students have been the largest student group.

Figure 1. The number of Chinese students in Canadian educational institutions (2000-2018)
Data source: Immigration, Refugees, and Citizenship Canada. (2019). Canada: Study permit holders with China as country of citizenship by province/territory of destination, study level and calendar year 1998-2019. Ottawa, Canada: Immigration, Refugees, and Citizenship Canada.

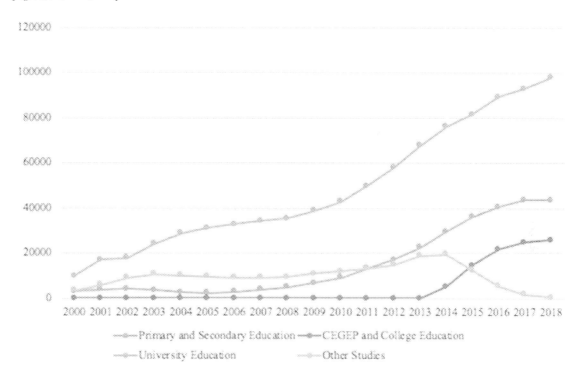

Despite this large enrolment, only several studies have been conducted to investigate Chinese students' academic challenges and coping strategies as part of their learning experiences in Canadian universities. These several relevant papers describe Chinese students' learning experiences in Canadian universities from both positive and negative perspectives. On the one hand, they highlight the positive elements of the Canadian educational system that Chinese students feel comfortable with, such as the opportunity to participate in classroom discussion (Foster & Stapleton, 2012), more chances to make class presentations (Foster & Stapleton, 2012), the rigorous academic requirements (Zheng, 2010), constant support from professors (Li, DiPetta, & Woloshyn, 2012). On the other hand, the difficulties and problems Chinese students encounter while studying at Canadian universities are also mentioned. Among them, the students' limited English language proficiency (Huang & Cowden, 2009; Li, 2004; Li, DiPetta, & Woloshyn, 2012; Yang, 2010; Zhang & Zhou, 2010), lack of critical thinking skills (Huang & Klinger,

2006; O'Sullivan & Guo, 2010), unfamiliarity with the Canadian education system (Liu, 2016; Huang & Cowden, 2009; Huang & Klinger, 2006; Yang, 2010), disinclination to engage in classroom discussion (Foster and Stapleton, 2012; Liu, 2016), and unwillingness to communicate with local students (Zhang & Zhou, 2010; Zheng, 2010) are frequently discussed.

With regard to the strategies to cope with these academic challenges, Liu (2016) depicts that in addition to spending more time on reading and assignments, Chinese students tend to talk with instructors and classmates to clear up their confusion. They would also like to use university services, particularly those offered by the library, the writing support desk, and the international student center. Huang and Klinger (2006) report that Chinese students found strategies such as forcing themselves to adapt to the new classroom environment, spending more preparation time, and interacting with local students, which are very useful in improving their academic performance. When there is no peer support, they would employ strategies such as reading extensively about a topic, asking questions whenever it is possible in class, and spending more time before and after class. It is worth noting that Chinese students also use some learning strategies that were acquired in China such as note taking, memorization of basic concepts, pre-class reading, self-study, and review. These strategies are identified as effective in North American universities.

These research findings are of great value to inspire further exploration towards Chinese students' academic challenges and coping strategies in Canadian universities. However, one underlying problem is that these findings are scattered in many different papers. No studies have been conducted to systematically investigate Chinese students' academic challenges and coping strategies in Canadian universities. Considering the various struggles Chinese students have been experiencing and the large number of Chinese graduate students in Canadian universities (Yang, 2018), we decided to conduct a qualitative research project to examine the academic challenges Chinese graduate students encounter in Canadian universities, and further identify the strategies they develop to cope with these challenges and to achieve academic success. The research findings are expected to provide prospective Chinese graduate students with effective strategies to cope with similar academic challenges.

This paper is organized in five sections. The first section describes the theory of student agency as the theoretical framework of this study. In the second section, this paper sets out the research method by which the participants were recruited as well as the way the data was collected and analyzed. In the following two sections, we present and discuss the findings resulting from the thematic analysis of the data. The paper concludes with contributions of this study and suggestions for future research.

THEORETICAL FOUNDATION

The theory of student agency provided the theoretical foundation for us to analyze the coping strategies developed by Chinese graduate students in addressing their academic challenges in Canadian universities. The theory of student agency was extended from social cognition theory and sociological theories of human agency that emphasizes human beings' capacity to exercise control over events (Klemenčič, 2015). Bandura (1986), an expert working on social cognition theory, points out that the most central mechanism of human agency is people's self-efficacy beliefs about their capabilities to exercise the behaviours necessary to bring about a desired outcome. Each individual is assumed to have a certain capacity to take control of his life and influence the course of events by his actions.

Drawing from the theory of human agency, student agency is conceptualized as a process of students' intentional action and interaction during studentship (Klemenčič, 2015). Students' intentionality may not be supported by a clear idea of goals and action plans, but some anticipation of likely outcomes and some beliefs in one's efficacy are crucial. According to Klemenčič's explanation, student agency encompasses two variables: one is students' agentic orientation ("will"), which is the way that students relate to past, present and future when making choices of action and interaction, and the other is agentic possibility ("power"), which is students' perceived power to achieve the intended outcomes in a particular context of action and interaction. Similar to the theory of human agency, the theory of student agency emphasizes that students seek to exert some influence on their immediate and larger social surroundings, educational trajectories, and future lives, and strive to realize their desired educational outcomes although the influence can be stronger or weaker (Klemenčič, 2015).

When students have more knowledge, better skills and easier access to information, they can make better judgments with regard to the context of their actions and make more informed decisions on how to act to achieve their desired outcomes. The theory of student agency has been used to study many educational practices, such as student-centered learning (Klemenčič, 2017) and online learning (Lindgren, & McDaniel, 2012). Tran and Vu (2018) also use it to analyze international students' lived experiences. They argue that although the notion of agency is not often explicitly explained or adequately theorized in the context of international education, international students have the potential to exercise different forms of agency to cope with the challenges they face during their sojourn and to respond to the emerging needs in the new academic context. Considering the fact that the new academic context involves cross-cultural educational spaces and transnational relationships, international student agency appears to be distinctive compared to other forms of student agency. More importantly, when international students transition to a completely new academic environment, their agency is reshaped and reactivated in correspondence to new emerging needs.

The application of theory of student agency in this study would provide the theoretical basis for analyzing the coping strategies Chinese graduate students develop to address their academic challenges in Canadian universities. On the one hand, the theory can be used to analyze how Chinese graduate students would make efforts to overcome their academic challenges by connecting their previous learning experiences, current situations, and desired learning outcomes. On the other hand, the theory can also be used to examine Chinese graduate students' capabilities to exercise control over their own endeavors and the environments that affect their learning to achieve their desired learning outcomes. In brief, the two important variables of agentic orientation and agentic possibility in the theory of student agency would provide unique perspectives to analyze Chinese graduate students' coping strategies to address their academic challenges in Canadian universities and thus deepen the understanding of the research topic.

RESEARCH METHOD

Research Methodology

We adopt case study as the research methodology to capture the complexities of Chinese graduate students' academic challenges and coping strategies in Canadian universities. According to Yin (2014), case study is an empirical inquiry that is used to 'investigate a contemporary phenomenon in depth and within its real-life context, especially when the boundaries between phenomenon and context are not clearly evident' (p. 16). The analysis unit in case study research is 'a bounded system' (Stake, 1995, p. 2), which can be an individual, group, program, project, organization, institution, partnership, community, or policy (Merriam, 2009; Simons, 2009; Stake, 1995; Yin, 2014). According to the number of cases, case study research is divided into single case study and multiple case study. Single case study is appropriate when 'the case represents (a) a critical test of existing theory, (b) an extreme or unusual circumstance, (c) a common case, or the case serves a (d) revelatory or (e) longitudinal purpose' (p. 56). The fundamental goal of conducting case study is to gain an in-depth and holistic understanding of participants' perspectives about research questions (Brown, 2008; Harrison, Birks, Franklin, & Mills, 2017; Hentz, 2016). To achieve this goal, diverse research methods such as interviews, focus groups, observations, document analysis, archival records, and physical artifacts are recommended to be used in the data collection process (Merriam, 1997; Simons, 2009; Stake, 1995; Yin, 2014), among which interview is recognized as one of the most important sources (Yin, 2014). This is because participants in interviews are expected to have unique experiences and to tell special stories (Stake, 1995), through which researchers can gain diverse insights about research questions.

In this study, we chose the Faculty of Education at McGill University as the case. Chinese graduate students studying at this selected institution were invited to participate in the study. We have three rationales to make this selection. The first one is previous research indicates that students from humanities and social sciences such as educational field encounter more challenges compared to the students from other departments such as engineering, or chemistry (Huang, 2005). Considering this fact, we have narrowed our research focus on the Faculty of Education. The second one is the representativeness of the case. The Faculty of Education at McGill University is a very common institution among the Faculty/Department of Education in Canada. It ranks No.3 among Canadian Faculty/Department of Education in the QS World University Ranking by Subject in Education 2020, following Ontario Institute for Studies in Education of the University of Toronto and Faculty of Education of the University of British Columbia (Quacquarelli Symonds, 2020). The academic challenges Chinese graduate students encounter in this institution are very likely to happen to Chinese graduate students studying in other Faculty/Department of Education. The third rationale is data accessibility. The Faculty of Education at McGill University hosts around 40 Chinese graduate students every year. This provides us with sufficient candidates from whom to collect data. In addition, since both authors are studying at the selected institution, it is easier for us to recruit participants in the same institution.

Participants

After obtaining the ethics approval from the university research ethics board, we started to recruit participants via two methods: (1) through distributing a "Call for Participants" advertisement in WeChat[1] groups consisting of Chinese graduate students studying at the Faculty of Education in McGill University; (2) through emailing the target participants by purposive sampling approach. In total, 16 Chinese students studying for master's degree in the university were recruited to participate in the study. The students were chosen based on the following three criteria: (a) they came from Mainland China; (b) they finished their undergraduate studies in China; (c) they did not have parents whose native language was English. The detailed background information of the student participants is presented in Table 1.

Overall, the student participants' ages ranged between 23 and 30, and they started their second academic year at the time of the interview. They had obtained a bachelor's degree in Mainland China and most of them did not have overseas studying experiences before coming to Canada except that student participant 8 and student participant 14 studied in the United States for several months as exchange students. Their undergraduate majors were mostly related to English literature and many of them had one-year working experiences relevant to English language teaching. These students were motivated by different factors to pursue graduate degrees in Canada. The motivational factors are summarized into six major categories: improving English proficiency, experiencing western-style education, getting a foreign graduate degree, enriching life experience, pursuing a better career prospect, and seeking opportunity to immigrate to Canada.

Data Collection and Analysis

Specifically, we adopted semi-structured interviews to seek an in-depth and holistic understanding of Chinese graduate students' academic challenges and coping strategies in the selected university. Compared to structured interviews, semi-structured interviews can, on the one hand, give the participants great flexibility to share their experiences of studying in the Canadian university, and on the other, guide the participants to share their experiences without going off-track from the research questions. The semi-structured interview questions were mainly concerned about three aspects: (a) students' demographic information, educational trajectory, and motivations to pursue graduate degree in Canada; (b) their academic challenges in the Canadian university; (c) their corresponding coping strategies. The interviewer also asked some follow-up questions whenever appropriate in order to obtain more meaningful data. The face-to-face interviews were conducted individually in either Chinese or English depending on the interviewees' choice with the aim to make them feel comfortable and easy to communicate with. The language choice also helped interviewer build a harmonious relationship with each participant, which was crucial to the data collection process. Each interview lasted about one hour and was audio-recorded.

Upon completion, the interviews were transcribed verbatim and thematically analyzed in the qualitative analysis tool NVivo 11.0. The two authors read and re-read all the transcripts together to identify the major themes, based on which the coding matrix was developed, and then worked independently to code the interviewee narratives into an appropriate code. Once all the transcripts were coded, a coding comparison query was conducted in N-Vivo 11.0 to assess inter-rater reliability. The Kappa coefficient across all nodes was reported to be 0.71, indicating a substantial agreement between both coders (Landis & Koch, 1977). With regard to the disagreements, the two authors discussed the discrepancy codes and revised them until consensus was reached. In order to further examine the validity and reliability of the analysis, we shared our interpretations with the participants after the paper was completed, inviting them to clarify or modify their initial responses.

FINDINGS

Academic Challenges

The results indicate that Chinese graduate students encounter a number of academic challenges in the selected Canadian university. These challenges can be grouped into two categories depending on the root cause from which they are generated. The first category of challenges derives from the students' limited English language proficiency and the second category stems from the different educational norms and practices between China and Canada.

Table 1. The profile of student participants

No.	Age	Undergraduate Program	Graduate program	Working experiences	Motivations
SP1	24	English literature	Second language education	One-year experience as a Mandarin and English teacher	To obtain overseas experience; To get a better job; To immigrate
SP2	23	English literature	Education and society	Three-months' part-time work experience as an English teaching assistant	To get a foreign graduate degree
SP3	26	Spanish	Second language education	None	To learn about western educational theories
SP4	23	Teaching Chinese as a second language	Second language education	One-month experience as a Chinese tutor at a Canadian university	To seek a better career prospect
SP5	23	English education	Second language education	Eight-months' experience as a study advisor for English teaching	To improve English language proficiency; To experience western-style education
SP6	25	English literature and language	Second language education	One-year experience as a primary school teacher	To enrich life experience
SP7	23	English literature	Second language education	Two-months' internship as a middle school English teacher	To seek better job opportunity
SP8	24	English literature	Second language education	One-month summer internship as an English teacher	To get a foreign graduate degree; To experience a new lifestyle
SP9	28	English literature	Second language education	Two-years' experience as an English teacher for IELTS listening	To enrich life experience; To improve English language proficiency
SP10	23	English literature	Education and society	Two-years' internship and part-time work experience related to English	To experience western-style education
SP11	30	Teaching English as a foreign language	Second language education	Seven-years' experience as an English and Mandarin teacher	To get a foreign graduate degree; To experience western-style education
SP12	23	English literature	Second language education	None	To accomplish her father's will
SP13	24	English literature	Education and society	None	To immigrate
SP14	23	Major: Chinese literature Minor: English	Educational leadership	None	To enrich educational experience
SP15	25	Applied psychology	Educational psychology	One-year experience as an English teacher	To experience western-style education
SP16	23	English literature	Second language education	None	To enrich life experience

Challenges Generated From Limited English Language Proficiency

As previously introduced, most of the student participants obtained a bachelor's degree related to English literature in China, signifying their higher level of English language proficiency. Moreover, they met their program's English proficiency requirements such as IELTS with a minimum overall band of 7.0 or

TOFEL with a total score of 92. Even so, after starting graduate studies in Canada, the students gradually realized that their English language proficiency was still limited, and this limitation caused many academic challenges such as struggles in understanding teaching content, hesitation in participating in classroom discussion, incompetence to answer questions during presentation, spending more time on reading materials, and frustration in writing term papers.

Struggles in Understanding Teaching Content

Understanding professors' lectures and classmates' discussion is the basis for students to achieve academic success. However, many Chinese students found it difficult to follow up with their professors and classmates during classroom teaching in the Canadian university. For example, SP2 reported that, "I cannot understand some professors and classmates' main points due to my lower English level. Of course, not everyone has this problem, but some Chinese students indeed have this difficulty and are likely to miss some important course information." Some students further explained that their difficulty in understanding the teaching content was caused by the slangs and jargons used as well as their professors and local students' speaking speed and accent. SP6 stated that "In the beginning, I could not understand them [professors and classmates] very well because they have very strong accent. And local students speak very fast when most students are native speakers."

Hesitation in Participating in Classroom Discussion

In addition to listening to professors' lectures and classmates' discussion, Chinese students are also expected to share their insights in class. This will not only enhance their understanding of the teaching content, but also foster cross-cultural communication. Yet, some students reflected how the insufficient English ability increased their hesitation in participating in classroom discussion. For instance, SP9 stated that "I always feel that during group discussions, I cannot reach the exact point that I want to cut into. Even though I think over the question very deeply, when I speak it out, it becomes very superficial. Hence, I gradually lose the confidence to speak." SP8 shared the same feeling and further added that she chose not to speak in the end. "Because my English is not very good, I lack the confidence to participate in group discussions. Sometimes I also think about the questions, but I am not willing to express my own ideas. I always feel that I cannot get the point, so it's better to listen to others."

Incompetence to Answer Questions During Presentation

When talking about making presentations in class, some students expressed their concerns about their inability to understand and answer the random questions posed by their professors and classmates. SP2 mentioned that "Because my English is not good, I need to write a note for the presentation in advance and recite it. During my presentation, if the audience ask me questions that I did not prepare, I would become very panic." Echoing this view, SP9 also indicated that "There is usually a Q&A session after each presentation. When it comes to this session, I would get very nervous because for most of the times, I am not prepared for the questions. Moreover, you know, my English is not as fluent as native speakers, so I cannot organize my ideas very quickly in a short time. I always recall my answers after the presentation and assume that I should have answered the question in another way. That would be much better."

Spending More Time on Reading Materials

The challenges caused by the limited English language proficiency not only occur in class, but also take place after class, such as finishing the weekly reading materials. Take SP11 as an example. She expressed that "In the beginning, I could not finish all the readings. Even though I knew every word, I could not understand the meaning of a full sentence or a whole paragraph." SP1 confirmed this by stating that "There are a lot of new concepts in the readings, which I did not hear of before. So, I need to spend much more time than local students on the same article. Sometimes, I would read the articles for several times. In spite of this, however, I could not totally understand the articles' key points." SP8 analyzed that the difficulty in finishing reading materials was caused by her English reading skills. She explained that "I do not know how to efficiently read English articles. Some local students told me that they just needed to skim the beginning and ending of the article, and then they could get to know what the article was talking about. But when I use this strategy, I cannot get the point."

Frustration in Writing Term Papers

With regard to the academic challenges incurred by the limited English language proficiency, some students also mentioned their frustration in writing term papers. The students understood that as graduate students, they should be dedicated to improving their academic writing skills. But writing term papers in English was a huge challenge for them. This was especially true when professors set very high requirements for them. For example, SP7 presented that "While many professors would not pay too much attention to language, grammar or writing format, one professor had very high expectations and requirements for us. She was strict with almost every aspect of the paper. That was very challenging." SP10 expressed her frustration after receiving feedback from his supervisor. He described that, "My supervisor made so many changes for the paper to which I devoted a lot of time and effort. Some of them were caused by language issues while others were not. I felt pretty frustrated at that moment."

Challenges Caused by Different Educational Norms and Practices Between China and Canada

Apart from the challenges caused by their limited English language proficiency, Chinese students are faced with another set of academic difficulties resulting from the new educational norms and practices prevailing in Canadian universities. When Chinese students come to Canada, they bring with their previous learning habits, and traditional ways of thinking. When the old habits encounter a new context that is culturally distant from China, the students feel challenged. Specifically, these challenges include inadequate participation in classroom activities, difficulty in writing research papers in APA style, lack of confidence in learning about educational theories, and struggles in relating working experiences with academic studies.

Inadequate Participation in Classroom Activities

All of the student participants reported that participating in classroom activities was a great challenge for them. While this challenge was partially caused by their limited English language proficiency, it was also owing to the different educational norms and practices between China and Canada. For example,

SP9 pointed out that when she was studying in China, instructors usually taught a lot whereas students did not have many opportunities to speak in class. However, there were many classroom discussions in the Canadian university. So, she spent several months getting used to this new teaching style. SP10 explained why Chinese students tended not to speak in class. He stated that "This is because in China, students are expected to provide right answers to the instructors' questions or raise some very good questions that other students do not consider. They believe that they should not spend time asking some naïve questions that other students may have already known the answers. Otherwise, they will feel that they are losing face. However, in Canada, students can talk about whatever they want to share with the class." SP5 confirmed this viewpoint and asserted that "I often think the students are wasting time in class. Some students were just chatting about something else rather than discussing the teaching content. Every time this occasion happens, I feel annoyed and do not want to listen to them anymore."

Difficulty in Writing Research Papers in APA Style

Writing research papers in APA style was reported to be a major challenge for many Chinese international students. As SP5 stated, "I am not familiar with the writing style. So, I have to spend much more time than local students in managing the new writing format. That's why I am feeling very stressful." SP10 also confirmed that due to his unfamiliarity with APA style, English academic writing was very challenging for him. He further compared the academic writing in China and Canada. He indicated that "I feel the Chinese professors were not strict with my undergraduate thesis. But the Canadian professors are very strict with almost every aspect in academic writing, including the writing structure and writing format. For now, after studying in Canada for more than a year, I still cannot do it skilfully. Whenever I think of my thesis, I feel headache. I am not worried about the content, but about the APA format and punctuations." SP2 mentioned that citation was somewhat difficult for her. "To avoid plagiarism, I have to paraphrase or summarize many articles. But it is very difficult to summarize a number of ideas into several sentences." Some students also expressed their concerns about the writing style difference between Canada and China. SP2 described that "local students tend to write details and repeatedly illustrate an idea. But in Chinese academic writing, we don't need to use many words to repeat one idea. The writing styles are very different."

Lack of Confidence in Learning About Educational Theories

The student participants recognized that their programs put much emphasis on theories which they did not know about before. SP9 complained about this. "Because I worked as an English teacher before coming to Canada, I know some practical knowledge about how to teach. However, after arriving here, I have to make great effort to learn about theories and I am not sure whether these theories will be applied into my future teaching." SP7 mentioned that, "Because my concentration is second language education, I expected to learn how to teach English as a second language. But the program is more relevant to research. It is very academic. You know, I don't have a strong theoretical background before coming here, so I have to spend much time in understanding the theories that I have not heard of before." SP2 also found that, "The courses here are very theoretical. Hence, I have been striving to figure out their connection with my future teaching. This is not easy."

Struggles in Relating Working Experiences With Academic Studies

Chinese students regarded themselves at a disadvantaged position in comparison to local students due to their lack of working experiences. These Chinese students felt that in addition to the language barrier, their struggles in understanding teaching content and expressing their opinions were partly due to their lack of teaching experiences. SP3 indicated that "If you have teaching experiences, when you come to the class, you can share your experiences with your classmates and use them to illustrate the theories taught in class. You will also be able to have a good understanding of the teaching content. But the question is I don't have any teaching experiences. So, it is rather difficult for me to understand some of the teaching content." SP6 also mentioned that "Many of my classmates are school teachers. They can talk a lot about their school teaching. But because I do not have any teaching experiences in Canada, I cannot speak anything during class and can only listen to them." SP10 expressed a similar viewpoint, indicating that "most of the local students who are studying for graduate degrees in education are working in schools and they come to study to further improve their teaching. But Chinese students tend to finish studies first and then look for a job. So when the instructors ask us to present some teaching examples, I don't have much information to share."

Coping Strategies

Following the theory of student agency, we find that Chinese graduate students possess the agency to respond to their academic challenges. The process of developing coping strategies reflects the students' "agentic orientation," through which students relate their past experiences to the current situations with the aim of addressing their academic challenges in the selected Canadian university. When one strategy does not work, the students choose to modify their strategies to better adapt to the new environment. This manifests the students' "agentic possibility," by which students make their choices of action and interaction to achieve academic success. Specifically, Chinese students' coping strategies in response to the above-mentioned academic challenges can be grouped into two categories: to rely on the students' personal improvement and to resort to external resources, respectively.

Relying on Students' Personal Improvement

Chinese graduate students emphasized the importance of their personal improvement in coping with their academic challenges. Almost all the student participants indicated that it should be their responsibility to address their learning difficulties and to achieve academic success. Specifically, their personal improvement strategies include pushing oneself out of the comfort zone, devoting more efforts to academic tasks, developing innovative learning strategies, and utilizing self-psychological therapies.

Pushing Oneself out of the Comfort Zone

Since Chinese graduate students believed that some of their academic challenges were caused by the different educational norms and practices between China and Canada, they tried to push themselves out of their comfort zone and to integrate into the new academic context. SP1 confirmed this by stating that "In class, I have to push myself to walk out of the comfort zone. In the beginning, I did not feel very good. But I practiced a lot and gradually got improved." Depending on the types of their academic challenges, the students chose to use different strategies. For example, in order to improve her English language proficiency, SP9 pushed herself to sit beside local students and to seize the opportunity to speak English; with the aim to better adapt to the new classroom environment, S1 encouraged herself to interrupt professors whenever she had questions and to express her opinions without too much hesitation.

But not everyone would like to force themselves to use this strategy. As SP1 pointed out, "Because people differ in personality, I don't think everyone needs to compel himself/herself to speak in class if he/she is not that type of person." Therefore, Chinese students also need to use other strategies to overcome their academic challenges.

Devoting More Efforts to Academic Tasks

Devoting more efforts to study is another coping strategy that Chinese students frequently used when they were challenged with the academic difficulties. Just as SP1 said, "What you need to do is to read more and write more. There is no shortcut." She further depicted that in order to better understand one article, she read it again and again until she grasped its meaning. SP12 also mentioned that when she did not know how to write a literature review, she spent a few more days in the library to read papers and to complete the assignment. SP13 reported that she chose to recite any new words in the reading materials in order to expand her academic vocabulary.

Developing Innovative Learning Strategies

In addition to devoting more efforts to academic tasks, Chinese students developed many innovative learning strategies when they realized their weakness in the new academic environment. For example, SP16 turned to watching English dramas to improve her English listening and speaking ability; SP13 chose to take note of useful expressions that she might use later to enhance her academic writing quality. SP12 shared her technique to deepen understanding of some new terminologies. She introduced that "When coming across new concepts in educational sociology, I will search on YouTube to watch relevant videos. Some videos only last for 2 or 3 minutes. I feel watching such videos more useful than reading a 30-pages article. While watching the videos, I prefer to write down some interesting points that I can share in class. This is really helpful, and it is my unique strategy."

Utilizing Self-psychological Therapies

While some Chinese students overcame their academic difficulties after employing the above-mentioned learning strategies, others still felt uneasy about integrating into the new environment and participating in classroom activities. In this situation, the students tended to employ some self-psychological therapies to comfort themselves. SP8 emphasized the importance of accepting who you really are. "In the beginning, I felt rather embarrassed for speaking nothing in class. Later I tried to analyze the reasons behind this problem. I found it was not because I did not know what to say but was caused by my personality. Even if I were in China, I would still sit there quietly. Therefore, I learned to understand myself instead of pushing myself to become someone else." SP7 expressed a similar viewpoint, stating that "I found it was always the several local students that were active in participating in classroom activities. So, I think it is more about culture. It also depends on the education that students receive. If I were in China, I would not speak either. But I would probably not notice this problem."

Resorting to External Resources

Chinese graduate students were pretty sensitive to what was possible to achieve in a given situation. They constantly adjusted their coping strategies in accordance with the situation change. When not being able to address their academic difficulties by themselves, they turned to resort to external resources, such as friends, classmates, faculty, staff, and other institutional services.

Seeking Help From Friends and Classmates

Friends and classmates were reported to be the most significant social support sources of Chinese graduate students in the Canadian university. The students repeatedly expressed their appreciation to their friends and classmates' assistance. SP6 claimed that "I have some seniors from China. They are incredibly generous to share their study experiences with me. Their suggestions are super helpful for addressing my academic concerns." The student participants further revealed that friends could not only share valuable information, but also help students with in-class participation. SP2 shared how co-national friends supported her to better participate in classroom discussions. She reported that, "If there is another Chinese I am familiar with in a group, I will feel more comfortable and safer to speak out my opinions". By contrast, SP9 depicted how local friends and classmates supported her to participate in classroom discussions. She stated that "I usually join a group with one or more local students who I am familiar with. When I am in a group with some familiar classmates, I will have more courage to express myself. In this occasion, I can at least speak with them whenever necessary. This also offers me great opportunity to improve my English." SP2 shared how local classmates helped her after class. She described that "I have a Canadian classmate who is originally from Vancouver. When I cannot understand some teaching content, I prefer to ask her after class. She always helps me with patience. Moreover, she would like to proofread my assignments and give me detailed feedback. She helps me a lot."

Seeking Support From Faculty Staff and the University

Apart from seeking help from friends and classmates, Chinese students also noted the strong support they received from faculty, staff and the university. SP15 mentioned that when she did not know how to proceed with an assignment, she emailed the professor to ask for advice. She appreciated that the professor had offered her a prompt response together with some valuable suggestions. SP13 reported on her interactive experiences with her supervisor. "Whenever I talk with my supervisor about my thesis, he helps me clarify my thoughts and provides me with many articles related to my research topic." Other than the support from professors, the institutional resources provided by the library, writing centre, teaching and learning services, as well as the counselling clinic were frequently used by the student participants. SP11 introduced that when he had difficulty in searching for journal articles, there would be a librarian ready to help him. SP1 described that she often used the writing tutorial service provided by the writing center. The tutors could proofread her work and improve the quality of her writing. SP13 illustrated that she often went to attend the workshops offered by the teaching and learning services. These workshops enriched her knowledge to a large extent. SP 14 found that the university counselling service helped alleviate her stress and anxiety.

DISCUSSION

From the above descriptions, we find that while an increasing number of Chinese students choose to pursue graduate studies in Canada, they encounter many academic challenges in Canadian universities. These challenges are grouped into two categories. The first category of challenges, such as struggles in understanding teaching content, hesitation in participating in classroom discussion, incompetence to answer questions during presentation, spending more time on reading materials, and frustration in writing term papers, is generated from the students' limited English language proficiency. The second category of challenges is caused by the different educational norms and practices between China and Canada. This can be evidenced by inadequate participation in classroom activities, difficulty in writing research papers in APA style, lack of confidence in learning about educational theories, and struggles in relating working experiences with academic studies. It is notable that many of these challenges were found in previous studies related to Chinese international students in North America (Huang & Klinger, 2006; Heng, 2017, 2018).

Chinese graduate students' diverse coping strategies are grouped into two categories depending on the power source of changes. The first category is to rely on the students' personal improvement, such as pushing oneself out of the comfort zone, devoting more efforts to academic tasks, developing innovative learning strategies, and utilizing self-psychological therapies. The second category is seeking support from external resources including friends, classmates, faculty staff, and the university. These research findings reflect the importance of student agency in coping with academic challenges regardless of the power source of changes. The strategies reveal that Chinese graduate students not only have the "agentic orientation" to address their academic challenges, but also have the "agentic possibility" to impact their learning trajectories.

By incorporating their past studentship, which is characterized by being diligent and enduring, into their present situation, Chinese graduate students made consistent endeavours to achieve their desired outcome of academic success. After utilizing diverse strategies, the students perceived a high degree of accomplishment. In addition, it is interesting to notice how the students differentiated their choice of coping strategies when facing similar challenges. When students had difficulties in academic writing, some sought help from the writing center whereas others asked guidance from their professors. This finding refutes earlier research results which indicate that Chinese international students' academic challenges were partially caused by their passive and dependent personality (Heng, 2017; Tweed & Lehman, 2002). Our findings highlight that Chinese students are not passive learners. Instead, they are active and creative problem solvers. The students have the capacities to choose different coping strategies according to their personal preferences and evaluations of current situations. This finding is also consistent with the theory of student agency which indicates that students would make proper choices of their actions on the basis of their analysis and judgement of their current situations.

CONCLUSION

In the context of an increasing number of Chinese students pursuing higher education in Canada, this study explored the academic challenges Chinese graduate students faced when studying in a Canadian university and further identified the strategies they developed to cope with these challenges by using the theory of student agency as the theoretical foundation. This study is of great significance for prospective

Chinese graduate students as the research results will provide them with the effective strategies to cope with similar academic challenges that they might encounter in Canadian universities. Future research is suggested to include Chinese graduate students' local peers and professors to investigate their perceptions of Chinese graduate students' academic challenges in Canadian universities. Also, studies should be conducted to examine what Canadian universities and faculty members can do to help Chinese graduate students better integrate into the new academic environment.

REFERENCES

Bandura, A. (1986). *Social foundations of thought and action: A social cognitive theory*. Prentice-Hall.

Brown, P. A. (2008). A review of the literature on case study research. *The Canadian Journal for New Scholars in Education*, *1*(1), 1–13.

Foster, K. D., & Stapleton, D. M. (2012). Understanding Chinese students' learning needs in western business classrooms. *International Journal on Teaching and Learning in Higher Education*, *24*(3), 301–313.

Harrison, H., Birks, M., Franklin, R., & Mills, J. (2017). Case Study Research: Foundations and Methodological Orientations. *Forum Qualitative Social Research*, *18*(1), 19.

Heng, T. T. (2017). Voices of Chinese international students in USA colleges: 'I want to tell them that … '. *Studies in Higher Education*, *42*(5), 833–850. doi:10.1080/03075079.2017.1293873

Heng, T. T. (2018). Different is not deficient: Contradicting stereotypes of Chinese international students in US higher education. *Studies in Higher Education*, *43*(1), 22–36. doi:10.1080/03075079.2016.1152466

Hentz, P. (2016). Overview of case study research. In M. De Chesnay (Ed.), *Nursing research using case studies: Qualitative designs and methods in nursing* (pp. 1–10). Springer Publishing Company. doi:10.1891/9780826131935.0001

Huang, J. (2005). Challenges of academic listening in English: Reports by Chinese students. *College Student Journal*, *39*(3), 553–569.

Huang, J., & Cowden, P. (2009). Are Chinese students really quiet, passive and surface learners? A cultural studies perspective. *Canadian and International Education. Education Canadienne et Internationale*, *38*(2), 75–88.

Huang, J., & Klinger, D. (2006). Chinese graduate students at North American universities: Learning challenges and coping strategies. *Canadian and International Education. Education Canadienne et Internationale*, *35*(2), 48–61.

Immigration, Refugees, and Citizenship Canada. (2019). *Canada: Study permit holders with China as country of citizenship by province/territory of destination, study level and calendar year 1998-2019*. Ottawa, Canada: Immigration, Refugees, and Citizenship Canada.

Institute of International Education. (2018). *Project atlas: Infographics and data*. Retrieved from https://www.iie.org/Research-and-Insights/Project-Atlas/Explore-Data

Klemenčič. M. (2015). What is student agency? An ontological exploration in the context of research on student engagement. In M. Klemenčič., S. Bergan., & R. Primožič (Ed.), Student engagement in Europe: Society, higher education and student governance (pp. 11-29). Strasbourg, France: Council of Europe Publishing.

Klemenčič, M. (2017). From student engagement to student agency: Conceptual considerations of European policies on student-centered learning in higher education. *Higher Education Policy*, *30*(1), 69–85. doi:10.105741307-016-0034-4

Landis, J., & Koch, G. G. (1977). The measurement of observer agreement for categorical data. *Biometrics*, *33*(1), 159–174. doi:10.2307/2529310 PMID:843571

Li, X., DiPetta, T., & Woloshyn, V. (2012). Why do Chinese study for a master of education degree in Canada? *Canadian Journal of Education*, *35*(3), 149–163.

Li, Y. (2004). Learning to live and study in Canada: Stories of four EFL learners from China. *TESL Canada Journal*, *22*(2), 25–43. doi:10.18806/tesl.v22i1.164

Lindgren, R., & McDaniel, R. (2012). Transforming online learning through narrative and student agency. *Journal of Educational Technology & Society*, *15*(4), 344–355.

Liu, B., & Liu, Q. (2016). Internationalisation of Chinese higher education in the era of globalisation. In S. Guo & Y. Guo (Ed.), Spotlight on China: Chinese education in the globalised world (pp. 85-106). Rotterdam, Netherlands: Sense Publishers.

Liu, T. (2016). *Learning experience of Chinese international students in Master of Education program at a mid-sized Ontario university* (Unpublished master's thesis). University of Windsor, Windsor, Canada.

Merriam, S. B. (2009). *Qualitative research: A guide to design and implementation* (2nd ed.). Jossey-Bass.

Ministry of Education of China. (2019). *Annual report on the development of Chinese students studying abroad (2018)*. Retrieved January 13, 2020, from http://www.moe.gov.cn/jyb_xwfb/gzdt_gzdt/s5987/201903/t20190327_375704.html

O'Sullivan, M., & Guo, L. (2010). Critical thinking and Chinese international students: An East-West dialogue. *Journal of Contemporary Issues in Education*, *5*(2), 53–73.

Simons, H. (2009). *Case study research in practice*. Sage. doi:10.4135/9781446268322

Stake, R. E. (1995). *The art of case study research*. Sage.

Symonds, Q. (2020). *QS World University Ranking by Subject in Education 2020*. Retrieved from https://www.topuniversities.com/university-rankings/university-subject-rankings/2020/education-training

Tran, L. T., & Vu, T. T. P. (2018). "Agency in mobility": Towards a conceptualisation of international student agency in transnational mobility. *Educational Review*, *70*(2), 167–187. doi:10.1080/00131911.2017.1293615

Tweed, R. G., & Lehman, D. R. (2002). Learning considered within a cultural context: Confucian and Socratic approaches. *The American Psychologist*, *57*(2), 89–99. doi:10.1037/0003-066X.57.2.89 PMID:11899565

Yang, L. (2010). Doing a group presentation: Negotiations and challenges experienced by five Chinese ESL students of commerce at a Canadian university. *Language Teaching Research*, *14*(2), 141–160. doi:10.1177/1362168809353872

Yang, W. (2018). *Investigating academic challenges and coping strategies of Chinese international graduate students in Canadian universities* (Unpublished master's thesis). McGill University, Montreal, Canada.

Yin, R. K. (2014). *Case study research: Design and methods*. Sage Publications.

Zhang, Z., & Zhou, G. (2010). Understanding Chinese international students at a Canadian university: Perspectives, expectations, and experiences. *Canadian and International Education. Education Canadienne et Internationale*, *39*(3), 43–58.

Zheng, J. (2010). Neoliberal globalization, higher education policies and international student flows: An exploratory case study of Chinese graduate student flows to Canada. *Journal of Alternative Perspectives in the Social Sciences*, *2*, 216–244.

KEY TERMS AND DEFINITIONS

Academic Challenges: The problems students encounter in meeting their institutions' expectations.

Academic Success: The evaluation of students' academic performance in terms of their institutions' expectations. It is usually measured by testing scores, GPA, course grade, teacher evaluations, etc.

Coping Strategies: People's cognitive and behavioural efforts to master, tolerate, reduce, or minimize the adverse impact of particular stressful events.

International Students: Students who move out of their country of origin for the purpose of education and are enrolled in an accredited educational institution in another country.

Internationalization of Higher Education: A process of integrating an international, intercultural, or global dimension into the purpose, functions, or delivery of postsecondary education. Specific activities involve international branch campuses, cross-border education delivery, programs for international students, English-medium programs and degrees, etc.

Student Agency: Students' capacity to set a goal, reflect and act to make changes.

Student Mobility: In the context of increasingly globalization and internationalization, students move across their national boundaries to another educational institution to study for a limited time. This is regardless of their study purpose to obtain a full degree or to participate in a short-term exchange program.

ENDNOTE

[1]   WeChat is the largest social media platform in China with over one billion monthly active users. It has similar functions to Facebook and Twitter.

Chapter 8
Chinese International Graduate Students' Perceptions of Classroom Assessment at a Canadian University

Yue Gu

(iD) https://orcid.org/0000-0001-8327-483X

University of Windsor, Canada

ABSTRACT

The purpose of this chapter is to investigate Chinese international students' perceptions of classroom assessment in Canadian higher education. Data collection for the study took place in a Canadian university and was comprised of two parts: an online survey for the collection of quantitative data, and semi-structured interviews for the collection of qualitative data. Sixty-two participants (n=62) voluntarily finished the online questionnaire and ten interview participants took part in semi-structured interviews. The exploration into the participants illustrated that Chinese graduate students held positive perceptions of classroom assessment at the Canadian university where the study was conducted, in terms of congruence with planned learning, authenticity, student consultation, transparency, and diversity.

BACKGROUND

Classroom assessment serves as an integral constituent of the teaching and learning process in higher education (Cheng & Fox, 2017). During their time in the college or university classroom, students are exposed to several kinds of assessment tasks. Students build their own opinions about the significance, usefulness, value, and shortcomings of these tasks when processing them (Alkharusi et al., 2014; Mertler, 2003). Such assessments are not only considered a means of evaluating and awarding marks in order to decide whether students have accomplished objectives; they have also developed into a tool for learning (Watering, Gijbels, Dochy, & Rijt, 2008).

DOI: 10.4018/978-1-7998-5030-4.ch008

Teachers, administrators, and policies overwhelmingly determine what forms and tasks of classroom assessment are applied in higher education; however, students' experiences with the process are central to determine the effectiveness of a pedagogical approach and how to improve it. Thus, educators in higher education must recognize students' perceptions of assessment if they seek to construct an involving and high-quality learning environment (Biggs & Tang, 2011; Hayward, 2012). Students should also understand the assessment processes and the meanings for themselves as learners in order to maximize learning (Fisher, Waldrip, & Dorman, 2005; Schaffner, Burry-Stock, Cho, Boney, & Hamilton, 2000). It is therefore important to recognize and examine students' perceptions of classroom assessment in higher education; however, few studies have thoroughly investigated this topic (Torkildsen & Erickson, 2016).

With an increasing number of international students studying abroad, internationalization has seen a significant expansion, particularly in Western universities since 2000. This provides a substantial source of revenue to receiving countries and universities (Biggs & Tang, 2011). In Canada, the internationalization of higher education is developing at a high pace (Y. Guo & S. Guo, 2017). One indication of the recent expansion of internationalization is the increasing enrolment of international students in Canadian institutions of higher education. According to a report given by the Canadian Bureau for International Education in 2019, there were 572,451 international students in Canada at all levels of study in 2018, and Chinese international students comprised 143,104 (25%) of those students. Given the substantial number of Chinese international students entering Canadian educational institutions, investigating how Western pedagogical approaches, particularly assessment, impact these students is becoming increasingly important.

This chapter focuses on an examination of Chinese international graduate students' perceptions of classroom assessment in Canadian higher education. This vein of research is critical to the success of Chinese international students as Western and Chinese pedagogies are drastically different in many respects: Western education is known as student-centered and quality-oriented, while Chinese education has long been considered teacher-centered, content-based and exam-oriented (Wang & Kreysa, 2006). Consequently, assessment is primarily executed in the form of examinations in Chinese schools (Kennedy, 2007). Whether this gap between the two pedagogies could lead Chinese international students to hold different perceptions of classroom assessment at in Canadian higher education is the major concern for this chapter to explore.

INTRODUCTION

In order to examine how Chinese international students perceive classroom assessment, it is important to establish some of the fundamental elements that characterize this issue. Firstly, it is critical to define assessment itself, as well as the different formats of assessment. It is then necessary to outline the importance of students' perceptions of classroom assessment. Finally, an in-depth investigation requires an understanding of the factors of classroom assessment that can motivate students' learning, and assessment and learning in China.

Definitions of Assessment

Teachers can use assessment tools to gather accurate information about students' learning, understanding, and skills (Cheng & Fox, 2017). By locating students' positions in their learning process, teachers can arrange and adjust their instruction to support and enhance students' learning. Students can use assessments to find their strengths and weaknesses and to support their learning progression.

Black and William (1998) broadly define assessment as processes that either teachers or students employ to assess the learning process and that in turn provides insights that can inform the pedagogical approaches employed in class (as cited in Cheng & Fox, 2017, p. 1). This is consistent with Hill and McNamara's (2012) definition of "classroom-based assessment," also known as "classroom assessment," which is framed as instances where teachers and/or learners reflect on learners' work for "teaching, learning (feedback), reporting, management, or socialization purposes" (p. 396). Cheng and Fox (2017) think that assessment may be conducted by both teachers and students and can come in three forms: teacher-student, or teacher-assessment; student-student, or peer-assessment; and student-self, or self-assessment. However, it is important to note that peer-assessment may lead to competition rather than personal improvement (Black & William, 1998).

This definition is narrowed by Allen (2004), Linn and Miller (2005), Dhindsa at al. (2007), and Lambert and Lines (2013), who regard assessment as a systematic process of data collecting about students' progress. Allen (2004) and Lambert and Lines (2013) underscore the systematic elements of this process by noting that empirical data should be recorded and then interpreted to measure knowledge, skills, and attitudes in order to improve student learning by refining pedagogical approaches. When considering these classifications of assessment, it is reasonable to define assessment as a systematic process of gathering information relating to student achievement and interpreting assessment results and students' responses, and then using the findings to adjust teacher instruction with the aim of enhancing students' learning.

Students' Perceptions of Classroom Assessment

Dorman and Knightley (2006) note that in schools, students normally acknowledge how they are assessed. However, they also observe that students often want to understand why a given assessment task is important, fair, reflective of what they have been learned and the connection to real world/industry application. Therefore, Dorman and Knightley (2006) built and validated an instrument to assess students' perceptions of assessment tasks, which is named Perceptions of Assessment Tasks Inventory (PATI). It involved 35 items with regard to five dimensions, which are: congruence with planned learning, authenticity, student consultation, transparency, and diversity, and had been tested with a sample of 658 science students from 11 English secondary schools in Essex, England.

Although Dorman and Knightley (2006) examined students' perceptions of assessment tasks in science classrooms in the secondary school context, PATI is suitable for any curriculum area, and these researchers expect that validation work could be done in other curriculum areas, year levels, education contexts, and even other countries in the future. Consequently, this chapter will conduct PATI within a group of Chinese graduate students at a university in southern Ontario.

There are some past studies on student perception of classroom assessment based on the five dimensions. Alkharusi and Al-Hosni (2015) surveyed 2753 Omani students from grade 10 and 11, and of the students they examined, 80% believed their classroom assessments were authentic. However, Gao (2012) found that most students did not believe their classroom assessments in math were related to real-life situations. These contrasting results could be due to a significant gap in sample sizes, different subject areas, and distinct social contexts. These results also may be due to a gap between teachers' perceptions of authenticity and that of students', which means that teachers believe assessment tasks are authentic, but students may not because authenticity relies on personal experience to some degree (Gulikers et al.,

2008). As a result, when teachers design assessment tasks and decide assessment processes, they should acknowledge the real-life situations on which their students focus.

The second contentious dimension is student consultation. Almost 50% of students believe that they were consulted with respect to assessment tasks (Alkharusi & Al-Hosni, 2015). However, Dhindsa et al. (2007) used mixed methods to study 1,028 upper secondary students' perceptions of science classroom assessments. Using quantitative data, they found that students could not frequently consult their teachers about their assessments, which was also confirmed by interviews and observations. Dhindsa et al. (2007) noted that teachers referred to giving information about the schedules and types of assessments as student consultation; however, students did not think that was enough and that they needed more details about assessments. The gap caused students to believe that they were not consulted with respect to assessment tasks.

Alkharusi and Al-Hosni (2015), Dhindsa et al. (2007), and Gao (2012) found similar results regarding diversity, though in Dhindsa et al.'s (2007) study, the quantitative data were not supported by interviews and observations. Students thought that classroom assessments provided by teachers only considered their diversity some of the time; however, based on teachers' interviews and observation data, teachers believed that they took students' diversity into account. Thus, it is important to give teachers some strategies about how to design assessments in order to cater to students' diversity, which means the degree to which each student has an equivalent opportunity to finish assessment tasks.

In juxtaposition, consistency exists with respect to congruence with planned learning and transparency. Alkharusi and Al-Hosni (2015), Dhindsa et al. (2007), and Gao (2012) found that students firmly thought that classroom assessments accorded with their planned learning, and "they almost always or often understood what was expected and needed to successfully accomplish assessment tasks" (Gao, 2012, p. 64). Student academic achievement can be improved by a congruence between instruction and assessment by raising students' attitudes and effectiveness in learning because students tend to take more time and energy to engage with their learning activities when they believe class content will appear in their assessment tasks.

In general, by using PATI, previous research studies had not established consistent conclusions on students' perceptions of classroom assessment based on five dimensions: congruence with planned learning, authenticity, student consultation, transparency and diversity. It is therefore necessary for this chapter to test them further.

Assessment and Learning

The initial and primary goal of assessment in education is to motivate students' learning (Black & William, 2012). Thus, assessments should not only be considered a way to evaluate and award marks in order to decide whether students accomplish objectives, but more importantly, they should be a tool for learning (Watering, Gijbels, Dochy, & Rijt, 2008). As such, it is critical to understand how classroom assessment motivates student learning.

Stiggins (2001) asserts that assessments are the most effective means through which teachers can promote or discourage students' desires to learn more rapidly and more constantly. According to Ames (1992), four specific classroom assessment practices were best able to increase student motivation to learn: developing a sense of efficacy, referring to the task as being significant and meaningful, decreasing test anxiety, and underlining deep meaning and understanding rather than surface meaning and rote memorization (as cited in Alkharusi, 2013, p. 22). She suggests that teachers design assessment tasks that include challenge, diversity, innovation, and active involvement, provide students with opportunities to make options and decisions regarding their learning, and allow for time to change assessment tasks to conform with the nature of the task and student needs.

Furthermore, using a path analysis technique to research a model to clarify the effect of students' perceptions of the assessment environment on their motivational orientations, Greene, Miller, Crowson, Duke, and Akey (2004) discovered that students who thought the assessment tasks were meaningful and motivating had mastery motivational orientations.

To conclude, assessment can influence student learning strategies and motivation to learn. Black and William (1998) explain how particular assessment practices increase or decrease student motivational orientations and learning strategies. To improve student learning approaches and motivation, they suggest that teachers engage in five key assessment practices, which are (1) to clarify how learning will be evaluated, (2) to give specific feedback following an assessment activity, (3) to employ moderately difficult assessments, (4) to utilize many assessments rather than a few major tests, and (5) to use authentic assessment tasks.

Western education is known as student-centered and quality-oriented, while Chinese education has long been considered teacher-centered, content-based and exam-oriented (Wang & Kreysa, 2006). This has led to significant differences between the West and China in terms of assessment and learning. Traditionally, education in China has primarily relied on examinations; consequently, learning depended largely on preparing for exams and memorization. This has led students to become surface learners, meaning students focus on developing the ability to repeat information without understanding the meaning or making connections between the previous and new knowledge (Kennedy, 2002).

However, these views produce stereotypes of Chinese approaches to learning. Though memorization is required and is viewed as a deep approach, learning through memorization and through understanding can be intertwined with and related to each other (Sit, 2013). Chinese students may employ strategies that appear to be surface oriented but actually have a deep orientation (Biggs & Tang, 2011), which helps them succeed academically, particularly in mathematics and science (Mehdizadeh & Scott, 2005). Furthermore, Chinese educational philosophy and learning traditions had been deeply influenced by Confucianism, which emphasized modesty, diligence, hierarchical order, and respect to authorities. Hence, Chinese classroom activities have normally been controlled by teachers, featured limited questions or discussions, and saw students treat teachers as professionals while unquestioningly accepting the knowledge conveyed by teachers (Zhou & Zhang, 2014). In order to keep order and harmony, students were typically allowed to speak up when being called upon; however, most of them asked questions privately after class rather than during class (Sit, 2013).

As a result, when Chinese students study in Canada and engage with the different pedagogical elements of Western education, their learning can be impacted by their perceptions of classroom assessment. Thus, in order to improve their learning outcomes, it is crucial to examine classroom assessment and their perceptions of it.

METHODOLOGY

Research Methods

In order to investigate Chinese international students' perceptions of classroom assessment at a Canadian university, a mixed-method research was designed in this chapter. It is because a mixed-method design effectively merges the advantages of both quantitative and qualitative approaches, and it is ideal for interpreting the issue, which allows researchers to summarize the findings and develop comprehensive visions as to the meaning of a phenomenon or the conception for individuals (Creswell, 2007). Therefore, for the study, an online survey based on PATI was the method of data collection for the quantitative data set while semi-structured interviews were used for the qualitative data set.

A purposive sample is a group of people specially selected as participants who have a particular characteristic that makes them appropriate for the study (Creswell, 2012; Nardi, 2014). Due to the unique features of analysis, the proposed study recruited Chinese graduate students at a university in southern Ontario in Canada. According to the information provided by the International Student Center (ISC), most of the Chinese international students at the university were graduate students. Therefore, this group of students was chosen as research subjects to represent the Chinese international students at the university in very general terms. After the researcher received the approval from the university's Research Ethics Board (REB), participants were recruited with the help of the ISC via email. After the ISC sent the initial recruitment email, there were 62 online survey participants and 10 interview participants.

An online survey was conducted to collect quantitative data about Chinese graduate students' perceptions of their classroom assessment. The survey was formed and hosted by using Qualtrics, an online survey platform provided by the university. The online survey was in English and consisted of four sections. Section 1 was the welcome and information section of this research. Section 2 was based on Dorman and Knightley's (2006) PATI, which had 35 items. PATI had five scales: congruence with planned learning, which spoke to the extent to which assessment tasks aligned with the goals, objectives, and activities of the learning program (items 1–7); authenticity, which referred to the extent to which assessment tasks featured real-life situations (items 8–14); student consultation, or the extent to which students were consulted and informed about the forms of assessment tasks being employed (items 15–21); transparency, or the extent to which the purposes and forms of assessment tasks were defined and made clear to the learner (items 22–28); and diversity, which spoke to the extent to which all students had an equal chance at completing assessment tasks (items 29–35). These items employed a five-point Likert scale response: 'strongly disagree', 'disagree', 'neutral', 'agree' and 'strongly agree'. Pilot tests had been conducted with a small group of Chinese graduate students ($n=4$) whose characteristics were similar to the survey participants. As a consequence, the 35 items were revised to improve clarity and idiomatic expressions to Chinese participants. Section 3 consisted of five demographical questions that collected information on the participants' gender, age, year in the program, and program. Providing demographic questions at the end of the survey experience made the task easier for the survey respondents; therefore, demographic data were collected at the end of the survey (Nardi, 2014). Section 4 provided expressed appreciation to the participants for their completion of research participation.

A semi-structured interview was conducted to collect qualitative data in order to provide a more in-depth understanding of the findings of the survey. As Schensual, Schensual, and LeCompte (1999) note, "Semi- structured interviews combine the flexibility of the unstructured, open-ended interview with the directionality and agenda of the survey instrument to produce focused, qualitative, textual data at the factor level" (p. 149). Due to the limited research on how Chinese graduate students perceive their classroom assessment at Canadian universities, the current study was considered and designed to be an open-ended and explanatory investigation. Because of its essence, a qualitative study was necessary to explore Chinese graduate students' in-depth opinions, struggles, and helpful suggestions about their classroom assessment. It was also beneficial for the researcher to collect in-depth data by asking questions and listening to participants' opinions in their own language and about their own positions, which allowed for more authentic responses (Patton, 2002).

After receiving the recruitment email, ten participants who contacted the researcher and wanted to voluntarily participate in the interview were selected. When selecting the participants, the researcher ensured that interview participants were from different faculties and the study had a balanced representation of gender. The interviews were held individually at a time suited to participants' schedules and needs. Each interview was approximately one hour. Interview locations were chosen based on convenience, comfort, and privacy. Each of the participants was a graduate student and met the admission requirement established by the university. The international graduate students were considered to possess high levels of English proficiency, so interview participants had enough English proficiency to be interviewed in English. With participants' consent, all interviews were audio-taped for transcription.

All questions were open-ended and concerned the research topic. According to Berg (2007), open-ended interviews enable researchers to direct the flow of the conversation to some degree but also encourage participants to freely understand the questions and express their general views or perspectives in details. Relying on the responses from each participant, the researcher followed up with probing questions. Participants were allowed to decline to answer any question that they were unwilling to answer or that made them feel uncomfortable or unpleasant.

In order to examine how do Chinese graduate students perceive their classroom assessment, descriptive statistics relating to means, standard deviations, and percentages were computed to examine students' perceptions of classroom assessment. In addition, a conventional content analysis approach was employed in the study for qualitative data analysis. The analysis process involved selecting key ideas, summarizing the field notes, recognizing and sorting codes into themes, counting the frequency of the codes, relating categories to analytic frameworks in current literature, generating a point of view, and presenting the data.

FINDINGS

The online survey was conducted to collect data from Chinese graduate students who were registered in the winter semester of 2018 at a Canadian university ($N=500$). The sample was made up of 62 participants ($n=62$) who voluntarily finished the online questionnaire from the link shown in the initial recruitment email and the reminder email. Five programs were represented in the sample: the Masters of Education program (MED), the Masters of Engineering program (MEG), the Masters of Management program (MOM), the Masters of Science program (MSC), and the Masters of Sociology program (SOCIO). There was one participant who did not report gender and 23 participants who did not show their program of study. Thus, data collection generated a survey response rate of 12.40%, with a survey completion rate of 61.29% ($n=62$).

The average scale-item mean values were greatest for congruence with planned learning (3.82±0.51), authenticity (3.63±0.59), and transparency (3.77±0.57); the mean values were lowest for student consultation (3.26±0.66) and diversity (3.15±0.75). This suggests that, generally, Chinese graduate students perceived that class assessment at this Canadian university was congruent with their learning goals and objectives, could reflect real-life situations, and was transparent. In contrast, the lower values for student consultation and diversity imply that students were not consulted and informed adequately about the forms of assessment tasks being employed, and teachers were not adequately concerned about students' diversity with regard to issues such as students' different abilities and the time required to finish their assessments. Thus, the overall analysis of students' perception data advises a scope for improvement in student consultation and diversity.

The current study recruited ten Chinese graduate students as interview participants, who respectively came from five different programs: the Masters of Education program, the Masters of Engineering program, the Masters of Management program, the Masters of Science program, and the Masters of Sociology program. In addition, there was a sufficient gender balance: six females and four males. The duration of each interview was approximately one hour. For the sake of confidentiality, the study allotted each participant a random alphanumeric code, ranging from "Participant A" to "Participant J." The findings of the one-on-one interviews conducted with Chinese graduate students were categorized into four factors: fairness of grading, assessment guidance, purposes for studying in Canada, and preference of assessment.

Fairness of Grading

Participants expressed particular concern with regard to the fairness of grading. First, many participants noted that some teachers did not always mark carefully because in a class of 80 students, they would sometimes receive the grading result within three hours of submitting a paper, suggesting that there simply was not enough time to thoroughly and thoughtfully mark each paper. Second, some teachers had several teaching assistants or graduate assistants, but they did not unify the scoring standard for their assistants, nor did they supervise their assistants' scoring. This led to two students in the same group receiving different scores despite finishing and submitting the same assignment. Another example given by Participant F was that he had two friends who copied each other's assignment, but the same answer led to two different scores, and the one who had better hand writing had 15% higher scores. Third, some participants noticed that some students cheated during the midterm or final exams, but teaching assistants or graduate assistants did not find this problem and did not take their responsibility to invigilate the exam. Their observation of such unchecked cheating led some participants to view the marking and evaluation process as unfair and inconsistent. Last, some participants thought that their teachers over scored them, as demonstrated by Participant C. He observed that he often outperformed his Canadian classmates. This caused him to wonder if he truly performed at a higher level, or if his professor was trying to encourage him or lowering the standards due to Participant's C status as an international student. He hoped that he would receive authentic score responses as this is the only way he believes he will be able to recognize how much he has learnt.

Assessment Guidance

As for assessment guidance, all students appreciated direction and instruction that was provided by teachers before and during assessment preparation. Participant D offered an anecdote that underscores the importance of the feedforward guide process for international students. In his first class, he was required to participate in class discussion via an online forum. At least one post had to be an original thread, and another had to be a response to another student's post. However, because Participant D had never used that particular forum before, he did not know how to navigate the website, an issue that many international students had, and so he raised the question to the instructor. In response, the instructor explained the process and guided the international students through the process in the class. Participant D suggested that "Teachers should present every assignment in details in the syllabus, including objectives, guidelines and explanations, rather than only description, due date and score value" and that "every international student needs the guidance, because [they] are from different country and experience different education" that may be drastically different from Western modes of education.

Meanwhile, some participants were concerned with the limited guidance that they received from their instructors. This was disappointing as they assumed that instructors would provide them with enough support to facilitate and encourage their independent learning. Furthermore, students hoped that guidance could be given early or in advance because it would help them accept and effectively apply the advice so as to improve their current and future work.

Other than assessment guidance, students hoped that they could consult instructors about their assessments. All participants acknowledged that teachers had absolute authority and final decision about how, why, what, when, and where an assessment could be done, but they also would like to be involved in the assessment process. For example, they hoped to be asked what their preferred form of assessment was, how each assignment should be weighted into the final grade, and what content would be included in exams. That did not mean that students would control assessments, merely that instructors would consider student input or consult them about assessment. This seemed reasonable to the participants given that students and teachers have the same goal: facilitating students' learning. However, Participant F observed that even when one instructor did solicited student' opinions, that instructor did not incorporate them. Participant F assumed it was simply a 'symbolic' strategy meant to appease students and discourage them from complaining that the instructor did not consider their perspectives.

Purposes for Studying in Canada

The participants' responses mainly concentrated on three advantages that studying in Canada had the potential to offer them, particularly with respect to the advance programs and knowledge offered in Western education, the opportunity to become proficient in English, and a potential path to citizenship.

Chief among these reasons are new knowledge and Western education. When studying the advanced academic subjects that the participants wished to pursue in Canada, they were afforded the ability to attend courses of much better quality than the ones provided by colleges in China. This collective view was exemplified by Participant A, who stated that an internet search suggested that Canada was advanced in education, particularly education administration and theory, which was her field of interest. She stated that theory is abstract and challenging to apply, and she was happy to see that instructors encouraged students to "analyze some cases which were related to... theories first, then taught... theories in details." This allows the students to be able to identify and, more importantly, understand Western education models and theories that they were not familiar with. This experience left Participant A optimistic: "In the future, I will be an educator in China. I will bring pedagogy, cases and knowledge about western education to China, and I hope I can combine Chinese and Western education very well in my class."

In order to improve their English proficiency, all the participants were willing to study in Canada. After studying in a foreign country for a relatively long period, the participants were likely to be fluent in English. This would give them a distinct advantage over their peers who took graduate programs at Chinese universities or could help them integrate into Western societies should they chose to work outside of China. This was reinforced by the co-op opportunities given by some programs, which allowed them to develop their English language skills in a professional setting. In addition, the Ontario Immigrant Nominee Program (ONIP) provided by Ontario Immigration enticed some participants to study in Canada. ONIP is an immigration program that allows graduate students to apply for provincial nomination after their graduation if they have a post-secondary degree in Ontario. This could be a strong motivator for students who wish to settle outside of China permanently.

Preference of Assessment

According to participants' responses, there were three significant factors that caused them to prefer some specific assessment models: timeliness, score, and authenticity.

All participants preferred assessments that offered them reasonable and sufficient time to prepare and finish, rather than urgent assessments. Other than the timeliness, the frequency of assessment was an important factor for the participants. For example, Participant G complained that a teacher in his program always required students to take a quiz in every class, which made him nervous and anxious, and consequently made him reluctant to attend class. In addition, Participant E preferred the classroom assessments used in her Chinese university, in which the overall grade was constituted of a midterm exam, a final exam, and attendance. Compared with classroom assessment that consisted of various assignments, she thought she could more effectively utilize her preparation time by concentrating on two exams or assignments. This kind of approach put her at ease.

Participants were more willing and likely to take part in the assessment with grades or scores. This point could be best illustrated by an example of Participant A. One of her classes featured a bonus-mark assignment. It was a relatively simple assignment that asked students to submit a short introduction about themselves with a photo of them doing something they enjoyed. If the students submitted this assignment to the course's online forum, they would earn two bonus points, which would be added to their grade at the end of the course. Participant A expressed her favor to this assessment and explained the reasons in details. First, she thought that it was an effective way for her to get to know her classmates and a successful way for her to begin to familiarize with the course's online forum, which she had never used before, but was able to understand from her teacher's comprehensive and detailed guidance. Second, the bonus marks assignment was a way to promote engagement and motivate student learning. Last, through the bonus marks assignment, she could acknowledge that the teacher had studied some pedagogy and students' psychology, which underscored the teacher's professional qualifications. This, in turn, encouraged the students to trust this teacher's instruction and assured them that the instructor cared about their learning outcomes.

The high authenticity of assessment was another main reason why all interview participants favored particular assessments. For example, Participant D reported that a teacher in one of his selective courses required students to do case studies that "took place in the 1990s or 1980s." He was shocked as the cases were older than he was, which caused him to view the case studies as out-of-date cases and irrelevant to contemporary issues. Participant D felt that if these case studies were reflective of the current situation, then the instructor should explain this to the students beforehand so that they can apply them in practice. Thus, because Participant D did not feel these case studies were current enough to be applicable in a contemporary setting, he did not view the assessment as authentic and hence did not value it.

This was echoed by Participant F. In one of his engineering courses, the instructor taught a number of formulas and the reasoning processes behind them, and then assessed the students based on how well they remembered and applied the formulas. However, having worked in the field for five years, Participant F noted that he had never "seen a company required their employees to remember these formulas, because [they] all had a particular software in the computer [that] had already installed these formulas." Therefore, one was simply required to "input some figures and wait for the result." He noted that his instructor did not tell the students about this, which led him to believe these assessments did not have real-world applications. Thus, because he did not see these assessments as authentic, he failed to see the value in them.

The Whole Picture

Triangulating the quantitative and qualitative data reported in the current research via a thorough discussion can provide important insights with respect to the Chinese international students' perceptions of classroom assessment in Canadian higher education. The quantitative data suggests that Chinese graduate students' perception of classroom assessment at a Canadian university was congruent with their learning goals and objectives, which was supported by participants' interview responses. During the interviews, all students reported a strong association between their assessment and study.

Also, this finding was consistent with previous studies, such as Alkharusi and Al-Hosni (2015), Cheng, Wu and Liu (2015), Dhindsa et al. (2007), and Gao (2012). These past studies found that students firmly believed that classroom assessments accorded with their planned learning, and that "they almost always or often understood what was expected and needed to successfully accomplish assessment tasks" (Gao, 2012, p. 64). Student academic achievement could be improved by affirming a more cognizant congruence between instruction and assessment by raising students' attitudes and effectiveness in learning (Koul & Fisher, 2006). This would be effective because students tended to take more time and energy to engage with their learning activities when they believed class content would appear in their assessment tasks (Brookhart & Bronowicz, 2003; McMillan, 2000).

Furthermore, when this research identified that classroom assessment at a Canadian university was congruent with Chinese graduate students' learning goals and objectives, it became necessary to examine what their learning goals and their purposes for studying in Canada were. According to the results of qualitative data, Chinese graduate students principally focused on three advantages: the advantages gained from studying in advance programs and offered in Western education, the opportunity to become proficient in English, and a potential path to citizenship. Although students generally believed that classroom assessment was congruent with their purposes for studying in Canada, they also hoped that some teachers and faculties could value and focus on their voice more when designing classroom assessment and study program. Specially, in order to improve students' comprehensive English proficiency, teachers could balance oral and written forms of assessment rather than only offering one form, and for the sake of helping students to integrate into Canada and the Canadian work environment, faculties and university could supply more co-op opportunities.

As for authenticity, the quantitative data suggests that students perceived classroom assessment was linked to real-life situations. This quantitative result was confirmed by the qualitative data as interview participants thought that classroom assessment at their Canadian university generally reflected the real-world situations.

With respect to authentic classroom assessment, the current study offered generally positive responses, which correlated with some previous studies, but was in stark contrast to others. Alkharusi and Al-Hosni (2015) surveyed 2,753 Omani students from grade 10 and 11 whose subjects were Arabic language, English language, Islamic education, mathematics, science, and social studies, and they found that 80% of the students they examined believed their classroom assessments were authentic. However, in a survey of 248 high school students around northeast Arkansas, Gao (2012) found that most students did not believe their classroom assessments in math were related with real-life situations. Although these studies took place in the secondary school context and it seems inappropriate to compare them with the current study which is in the post-secondary context, there is only a small number of research studies done to examine students' perceptions of classroom assessment, so it is feasible, reasonable, and necessary to contrast them to draw a whole picture for this study. As for these contrasting results, they could be due to a significant gap in sample sizes, different subject areas, and distinct social contexts. These results also may be due to a gap between teachers' perceptions of authenticity and that of students', which means that teachers believe assessment tasks are authentic, but students may not because authenticity relies on personal experience to some degree (Gulikers et al., 2008). As a result, when teachers design assessment tasks and decide assessment processes, they should acknowledge the real-life situations on which their students focus.

The qualitative data in this research also showed that in some cases, there was a gap between teachers' perceptions of authenticity and that of students'. Two of the participants reported that their teachers required students explore case studies that "took place in the 1990s or 1980s." which were older than the participants were. Teachers then assessed the students based on how well they remembered and applied the engineering formulas, which though applicable in contemporary engineering context, were usually performed by computer programs. It was possible that these teachers wanted their students be able to perform critical analysis about past cases in order to apply them into the contemporary society, or wanted their students to understand the formulas rather than just punch numbers into a computer, but teachers did not clarify and indicate their final or potential teaching goals and objectives to students effectively. Consequently, students may have misunderstood their designed instruction and assessment. To address this, teachers need to clearly explain and illustrate the value of lessons to students at the beginning of every class and assessment. This is an example of how strengthened communication with students can improve learning outcomes and students' perceptions of assessment.

The participants' responses to student consultations had an average scale-item mean of 3.26±0.66. These data propose that students were not adequately consulted and informed about the forms of assessment tasks being employed, which are also supported by the qualitative data reported in the previous paragraphs.

During the interviews, all participants acknowledged that although teachers had absolute authority and final decision about how, why, what, when, and where an assessment could be done, they also would have preferred being involved in the assessment process. For example, they hoped to be asked how each assignment should be weighted into the final grade, what their preferred form of assessment was, and what content would be included in exams. They specified that teachers should design and arrange the distribution of scores reasonably and scientifically, rather than randomly and groundlessly. For instance, some teachers awarded 70% of the overall grade to final paper and 20% to class attendance. Therefore, students hoped teachers could pay attention to these problems when they consulted with students about classroom assessment.

In terms of transparency, the quantitative data on students' perception (3.77±0.57) imply that Chinese graduate students perceived that there was transparency in assessment. When data from interviews were triangulated, these results were confirmed and were consistent with past studies, which found that students almost always or often understood what was expected and needed to successfully complete assessment tasks (Alkharusi & Al-Hosni, 2015; Cheng et al., 2015; Dhindsa et al., 2007; Gao, 2012). During the interviews, participants reported that they were not only informed in advance about how, why, and when they would be assessed and what they would be assessed on, but also received teachers' support and explanation in details about assessment.

With regard to diversity, the average scale-item mean of 3.15±0.75 implies that teachers did not adequately express concern about or consider students' diversity, which include students' different abilities and the time they required to finish assessments. However, this result was not supported by qualitative data, in which participants reported that teachers paid attention to their international student status and therefore created different assessments that considered the fact that students' abilities were at different levels. One participant even reported that teachers graded international students too easily as a means to encourage them.

This inconsistent result between quantitative and qualitative data supported a finding offered by Dhindsa et al. (2007), who state that "students perceived that assessment only sometimes catered for student diversity, while the teachers' interviews and observation data (analysis of tests, homework, and classwork) did not support this value" (p. 1276). Other studies also found that it was difficult for teachers to paint a clear picture as to whether the needs associated with student diversity had been met, and teachers usually believed that they took students' diversity into account even in instances where students did not. Therefore, it is important for faculties and universities to provide teachers with some strategies regarding the design of assessments so as to address the needs associated with students' diversity.

SOLUTIONS AND RECOMMENDATIONS

The current study found that Chinese graduate students generally hold positive perceptions of classroom assessment at the Canadian university in terms of congruence with planned learning, authenticity, student consultation, transparency, and diversity. Furthermore, four factors of classroom assessment should be considered by educators: fairness of grading, assessment guidance, Chinese international students' purposes for studying in Canada, and their preference of assessment for the sake of enhancing students' learning and motivation to learn.

Classroom assessment is not only considered a means of evaluating and awarding marks in order to decide whether students have accomplished objectives, but that they are used as a tool to promote learning in higher education. Thus, Chinese international students should not only pay attention and express high engagement to summative assessment, but also to formative assessment, which can help and support their learning. Moreover, although they must meet the university's admission requirement for English proficiency before enrolment, they should continue to practice and learn English diligently because English proficiency can influence their perceptions of classroom assessment, which in turn impacts their learning and motivation to learn.

As an assessment with high authenticity means a smooth transition for Chinese international students integrating into Canadian society and work environments, teachers and educators in Canadian higher education could design the assessment including the present and updated contents and information from the real Canadian society in order to meet students' needs and trigger their self-determined extrinsic motivation to learn. This kind of motivation can encourage students to participate in order to achieve another goal: learning to adapt and integrate into Canadian life (Ryan & Deci, 2000).

Universities and faculties could train and help teachers to be supportive and sensitive to intercultural students in Canada's multicultural context. Some specific departments, like ISC and the Center of Teaching and Learning, could offer more services, training, and opportunities to help teachers who do not have experiences teaching international students and help international students who are newcomers to adapt to their new studying and living environment. Universities could also help teachers design and implement assessments that support and enhance students' learning, which not only benefits international students, but also domestic students. In addition, the Chinese higher education system should also reflect profoundly students' perceptions of classroom assessment, support and develop diverse forms of assessment, and lessen the importance of exam scores. This might not only help Chinese students integrate into international environments more effectively, but also has the potential to improve China's higher education system.

FUTURE RESEARCH DIRECTIONS

Although Dorman and Knightley (2006) examined students' perceptions of assessment tasks in science classrooms, PATI is suitable for any curriculum area, and they expect that validation work could be done in other curriculum areas, year levels, education contexts, and even other countries in the future. Consequently, future studies should continue to conduct PATI in different curriculum and year levels within different Canadian universities, colleges, and institutions in order to better examine Chinese international students' perceptions of classroom assessment in Canadian higher education. Furthermore, other Western universities could replicate this study easily, especially those who have not examined Chinese international students' perceptions of classroom assessment and are missing important information from a key group of students at their universities.

CONCLUSION

Chinese graduate students held positive perceptions regarding classroom assessment at the Canadian university where the study was conducted in terms of congruence with planned learning, authenticity, student consultation, transparency, and diversity. However, the lower values for student consultation and diversity imply that students were not consulted and informed adequately about the forms of assessment tasks being employed, and teachers were not adequately concerned about students' diversity with regard to issues such as students' different abilities and the time required to finish their assessments. In addition, in order to enhance Chinese international students' learning and motivation to learn in Canadian higher education, this chapter suggests that four factors of classroom assessment should be considered: fairness of grading, assessment guidance, Chinese international students' purposes for studying in Canada, and their preference of assessment. These factors can also help universities, colleges, and institutions in Canada construct an involving and high-quality learning environment for international students, and strengthen the Canadian education brand of quality education.

REFERENCES

Alkharusi, H. (2011). Development and datametric properties of a scale measuring students' perceptions of the classroom assessment environment. *International Journal of Instruction, 4,* 105–120.

Alkharusi, H. (2013). Canonical correlational models of students' perceptions of assessment tasks, motivational orientations and learning strategies. *International Journal of Instruction, 6,* 21–38.

Alkharusi, H., Aldhafri, S., Alnabhani, H., & Alkalbani, M. (2014). Modeling the relationship between perceptions of assessment tasks and classroom assessment environment as a function of gender. *The Asia-Pacific Education Researcher, 23*(1), 93–104. doi:10.100740299-013-0090-0

Alkharusi, H. A., & Al-Hosni, S. (2015). Perceptions of classroom assessment tasks: An interplay of gender, subject area, and grade level. *Cypriot Journal of Educational Sciences, 10*(3), 205–217. doi:10.18844/cjes.v1i1.66

Allen, M. J. (2004). *Assessing Academic Programs in Higher Education.* Jossey-Bass.

Ames, C. (1992). Achievement goals and the classroom motivational climate. In D. H. Schunk & J. Meece (Eds.), *Student perceptions in the classroom* (pp. 327–348). Erlbaum.

Berg, B. L. (2007). *Qualitative research methods for the social sciences.* Pearson.

Biggs, J., & Tang, C. (2011). *Teaching for Quality Learning at University* (4th ed.). SRHE & Open University Press.

Black, P., & William, D. (1998). Inside the black box: Raising standards through classroom assessment. *Phi Delta Kappan, 80*(2), 139–148.

Black, P., & William, D. (2012). Assessment for learning in the classroom. In J. Gardner (Ed.), *Assessment and Learning* (pp. 11–32). SAGE Publications Ltd. doi:10.4135/9781446250808.n2

Brookhart, S. M., & Bronowicz, D. L. (2003). I don't like writing: It makes my fingers hurt: Students talk about their classroom assessments. *Assessment in Education: Principles, Policy & Practice, 10*(2), 221–242. doi:10.1080/0969594032000121298

Canadian Bureau for International Education. (2019). *A world of learning: Canada's performance and potential in international education 2019.* Retrieved from http://cbie.ca/what-we-do/research-publications/research-and-publications/#awol

Cheng, L., Wu, Y., & Liu, X. (2015). Chinese university students' perceptions of assessment tasks and classroom assessment environment. *Language Testing in Asia, 5*(13), 1–17. doi:10.118640468-015-0020-6

Creswell, J. W. (2007). *Qualitative inquiry and research design: Choosing among five traditions* (2nd ed.). Sage.

Creswell, J. W. (2012). *Educational research: Planning, conduction, and evaluating quantitative and qualitative research* (4th ed.). Pearson Education.

Dhindsa, H., Omar, K., & Waldrip, B. (2007). Upper Secondary Bruneian Science Students' Perceptions of Assessment. *International Journal of Science Education, 29*(10), 1261–1280. doi:10.1080/09500690600991149

Dorman, J. P., & Knightley, W. M. (2006). Development and validation of an instrument to assess secondary school students' perceptions of assessment tasks. *Educational Studies, 32*(1), 47–58. doi:10.1080/03055690500415951

Fisher, D. L., Waldrip, B. G., & Dorman, J. P. (2005). *Student perceptions of assessment: Development and validation of a questionnaire.* Paper presented at the annual meeting of the American Educational Research Association, Montreal, Canada.

Gao, M. (2012). Classroom assessments in mathematics: High school students' perceptions. *International Journal of Business and Social Science, 3,* 63–68.

Greene, B. A., Miller, R. B., Crowson, H. M., Duke, B. L., & Akey, K. L. (2004). Predicting high school students' cognitive engagement and achievement: Contributions of classroom perceptions and motivation. *Contemporary Educational Psychology, 29*(4), 462–482. doi:10.1016/j.cedpsych.2004.01.006

Gulikers, J. T., Bastiaens, T. J., Kirschner, P. A., & Kester, L. (2008). Authenticity is in the eye of the beholder: Student and teacher perceptions of assessment authenticity. *Journal of Vocational Education and Training, 60*(4), 401–412. doi:10.1080/13636820802591830

Guo, Y., & Guo, S. (2017). Internationalization of Canadian higher education: Discrepancies between policies and international student experiences. *Studies in Higher Education, 42*(5), 851–868. doi:10.1 080/03075079.2017.1293874

Hayward, L. (2012). Assessment and learning: The learner's perspective. In J. Gardner (Ed.), *Assessment and Learning* (pp. 125–139). SAGE Publications Ltd. doi:10.4135/9781446250808.n8

Hill, K., & McNamara, T. (2012). Developing a comprehensive, empirically based research framework for classroom-based assessment. *Language Testing, 29*(3), 395–420. doi:10.1177/0265532211428317

Kennedy, K. J. (2007). *Barriers to innovative school practice: A socio-cultural framework for understanding assessment practices in Asia.* Paper presented at the Redesigning Pedagogy: Culture, Understanding and Practice Conference, Nanyang Technological University, Singapore.

Kennedy, P. (2002). Learning cultures and learning styles: Myth-understandings about adult (Hong Kong) Chinese learners. *International Journal of Lifelong Education, 21*(5), 430–445. doi:10.1080/02601370210156745

Koul, R. B., & Fisher, D. L. (2006). Using student perceptions in development, validation, and application of an assessment questionnaire. In S. Wooltorton & D. Marinova (Eds.), *Sharing wisdom for our future. Environmental education in action: Proceedings of the 2006 Conference of the Australian Association of Environmental Education* (pp. 294–305). Retrieved from http://www.aaee.org.au/docs/2006%20 conference/32_Koul_Fisher.pdf

Lambert, D., & Lines, D. (2013). *Understanding assessment: Purposes, perceptions, practice.* Routledge. doi:10.4324/9780203133231

Linn, R. L., & Miller, M. D. (2005). *Measurement and assessment in teaching* (9th ed.). Pearson Prentice Hall.

McMillan, J. A. (2000). Fundamental assessment principles for teachers and school administrators. *Practical Assessment, Research & Evaluation, 7*(8), 89–103. https://PAREonline.net/getvn.asp?v=7&n=8

Mehdizadeh, N., & Scott, G. (2005). Adjustment problems of Iranian international students in Scotland. *International Education Journal, 6*(4), 484–493.

Mertler, C. A. (2003). *Preservice versus inservice teachers' assessment literacy: Does classroom experience make a difference?* Paper presented at the meeting of the Mid-Western Educational Research Association, Columbus, OH.

Nardi, P. (2014). *Doing survey research: A guide to quantitative methods* (3rd ed.). Paradigm Publishers.

Patton, M. Q. (2002). *Qualitative research and evaluation methods* (3rd ed.). Sage.

Schaffner, M., Burry-Stock, J. A., Cho, G., Boney, T., & Hamilton, G. (2000). *What do kids think when their teachers grade?* Paper presented at the annual meeting of the American Educational Research Association, New Orleans, LA.

Schensual, S. L., Schensual, J. J., & LeCompte, M. D. (1999). *Essentials ethnographic methods observations, interviews, and questionnaires*. Sage.

Sit, H. H. W. (2013). Characteristics of Chinese students' learning styles. *International Proceedings of Economics Development and Research, 62*(8), 36–39. doi:10.7763/IPEDR

Stiggins, R. J. (2001). *Student-involved classroom assessment* (3rd ed.). Merrill Prentice Hall.

Torkildsen, L. G., & Erickson, G. (2016). 'If they'd written more…'– On students' perceptions of assessment and assessment practices. *Education Inquiry, 7*(2), 27416. doi:10.3402/edui.v7.27416

Wang, V. C. X., & Kreysa, P. (2006). Instructional strategies of distance education instructors in China. *Journal of Educators Online, 3*(1), 1–25. doi:10.9743/JEO.2006.1.4

Watering, G., Gijbels, D., Dochy, F., & Rijt, J. (2008). Students' assessment preferences, perceptions of assessment and their relationships to study results. *Higher Education, 56*(6), 645–658. doi:10.100710734-008-9116-6

Zhou, G., & Zhang, Z. (2014). A study of the first year international students at a Canadian university: Challenges and experiences with social integration. *Canadian and International Education / Education Canadienne et International, 43*(2), Article 7.

KEY TERMS AND DEFINITIONS

Authenticity: The degree to which assessment tasks include real-life states that are related to the learner.

Classroom Assessment: A systematic process of gathering information relating to student achievement and interpreting assessment results and students' responses, and then using the findings to adjust teacher instruction with the aim of enhancing students' learning.

Congruence With Planned Learning: The degree to which assessment tasks are consistent with the study programs' purposes and intentions.

Diversity: The degree to which each student has an equivalent opportunity to finish assessment tasks.

Motivation to Learn: Forceful stimuli from intrinsic and/or extrinsic powers which confer on students force to study successfully.

Student Consultation: The degree to which students are asked and notified about the practices of assessment tasks being used.

Transparency: The degree to which every student has an identical probability to finish assessment tasks.

Section 3
Beyond the Classroom

Chapter 9

The Role of Two Extracurricular Programs in International Students' Informal Learning Experiences in Atlantic Canada

Junfang Fu

https://orcid.org/0000-0002-4957-7113

Mount Saint Vincent University, Canada

ABSTRACT

This chapter is composed with a strong empirical base on international students' experiences at Canadian higher education institutions. It focuses on international students' sociocultural adjustment, development in intercultural awareness and professional skills, and integration within the community. A qualitative methodology has been applied in the study of 10 international student participants from two extracurricular programs in Halifax, the city with the most higher education institutions in Atlantic Canada. The author holds a unique perspective on this subject for her triple identity as a former international student, program organizer, and practitioner in international education for over 10 years.

BACKGROUND

Over the past two decades, Canada has become one of the world's top five destinations for international students (Gopal, 2016; Johnstone & Lee, 2014), experiencing a dramatic rise in the number of international students in higher educational institutions. For most international students in Canada, formal learning is their primary goal. For example, through learning, international students can improve and develop language and professional skills in such a way that if their mother tongue is neither English or French, their further education delivered in one of these two languages in Canada can help enable them to achieve some of the necessary linguistic competencies, such as well as adequate job skills, for the Canadian workplace.

DOI: 10.4018/978-1-7998-5030-4.ch009

For international students in Canadian universities and colleges, learning can happen both through formal and informal experiences. For instance, attending structured classes in university may be considered a kind of formal learning as it occurs through a pedagogically structured approach. On the other hand, volunteering in the community, interacting with people in the neighborhood, or watching YouTube channels on the internet may be considered an informal way of learning for these experiences are generally not pedagogically designed. Beyond the learning in formal educational contexts, the possible ways international students learn through informal experiences, particularly through extracurricular activities, have become a primary concern for some educators. The purpose of this chapter is to present a study which examined informal learning of international students through extracurricular activities in Halifax, Nova Scotia.

In this chapter, the author conducts a critical assessment of two innovative experiential learning programs as part of international students' informal learning experiences in Canada. These two extracurricular programs include the Interfaith Engagement Program (IEP) in Halifax, Nova Scotia, and the International Student Volunteer Program (ISVP) at Mount Saint Vincent University (MSVU, or the Mount), also in Halifax. The research interest stems from the author's experience as an international graduate student in a Canadian university, and from the need to better understand international students' learning experiences in Canadian higher education from a new perspective.

INTRODUCTION

Canada has seen a significant growth in the foreign student population, which has risen at both the national and regional levels, as table 1 shows.

Table 1. International students in Canada by province, 2004–2005 and 2013–2014

Province of Study	International Students (Percentage)	
	2004–2005	**2013–2014**
Can.	7.4	11.0
N.L.	4.4	10.7
P.E.I.	5.7	11.8
N.S.	9.3	15.3
N.B.	10.8	16.0
Que.	8.2	11.0
Ont.	6.4	8.9
Man.	7.0	10.0
Sask.	6.6	11.2
Alta.	6.0	9.7
B.C.	10.9	17.6

Source: Statistics Canada (2016)

At the national level, the total amount of international students is rising sharply in Canada. International students made up 11% of all students in Canadian universities in 2013–2014, which is 4% higher than its portion in 2004–2005 (Statistics Canada, 2016). Geographically speaking, almost half of all international students are studying in Ontario, 24% in British Columbia, 12% in Quebec, and the rest 16% are distributed across Canada (Canadian Bureau for International Education [CBIE], 2018; cited in Fu, 2018).

Among all international students in Canada, three quarters of them are at post-secondary levels of studies (CBIE, 2018). In 2014, Canada's International Education Strategy (IES) indicated that the number of international students in Canada at all levels would double from around 239,000 in 2011 to over 450,000 by 2022 (Government of Canada, 2014). Amazingly, IES's target was accomplished five years early, as the international student population reached 494,525 by the end of 2017, leading to a total of 572,415 international students in 2018 (CIBE, 2020).

At the regional level, international students are an integral component of 16 universities in the Atlantic Canada provinces, which include Nova Scotia (NS), New Brunswick (NB), Prince Edward Island (PEI), and Newfoundland and Labrador (NFL). According to the Preliminary Enrollment Survey of the Association of Atlantic Universities [AAU] (2019), in all these 16 Atlantic Canadian universities, there were 19,000 full-time visa students enrolled in the 2018–2019 academic year, which accounts for 24.5% of all full-time university students enrolled in the same academic year and for an increase of 14% from ten years ago.

Take Mount Saint Vincent University as an example. It is a small public university located in Halifax, Nova Scotia, with around 4,000 students from over 50 countries (MSVU, 2020). In the 2008–2009 academic year, the Mount had enrolled 256 full-time international students, which made up 13% of the University's full-time student population (2009). In the year of 2018–2019, the number of full-time international students reached 672, accounting for 26% of all the full-time students at the university (AAU, 2019).

Therefore, from Canada's west to east coast, all provinces have experienced strong growth in the numbers of international students during the last ten years. This growth has played a decisive role in the development of Canadian higher education, regardless of the institution's location or size.

Challenges in and Contributions to the Host Country

In contrast, despite the benefits listed above, living and studying in another country often comes up with unpredictable situations and challenges. Migrating from one's motherland to another country brings the individual some frequent issues, such as feelings of being away from the family, detachment from accustomed social structures, beliefs and traditions, and lack of accesses to social supports from the host country (Schwartz, Montgomery, & Briones, 2006). When working with international students in New Zealand, Lewthwaite (1996) stated that "the differences in values, attitudes and beliefs between home and host cultures were seen as great and coupled with the sense of loss of the familiar (including food) put considerable pressure on the student" (p. 182).

Wu, Garza, and Guzman's (2015) research unveils that most international students in the U.S. have been faced with a feeling of frustration and challenge in the process of adjustment and adaptation to the local culture. In their study with international students in the UK, Gu, Schweisfurth, and Day (2010) report that half of their participants experienced a dissatisfaction with "social life," and one third of the participants reported feeling "powerless" or "lack of a sense of belonging" in Britain (p. 17). These findings help understand some of the complexity associated with studying in another country.

Specifically in Canada, international students have played a significant impact on the economy in boosting employment and consumption. International students have spent 12.8 billion dollars and 15.5 billion dollars, respectively, in 2015 and 2016 on study and life in Canada, and accordingly the annual spending of these students has generated over 141,000 career opportunities in 2015 and 168,860 in 2016 for the Canadian market (Citizenship and Immigration Canada [CIC], 2017). In 2016, the initial economic impact of the Atlantic region's less than 25,000 international students is 690 million dollars, and it has been translated into about 7,500 jobs in Atlantic Canada (CIC, 2017). Since all four Atlantic provinces are faced with demographic challenges such as aging and out-migration (Chira, 2016), an increasing retention rate of international graduates in this region could help to revitalize the local labour market and sustain the economic growth (Siddiq et al., 2012). According to CBIE (2018), 60% of the international students in Canada are prepared to apply for Canadian permanent residence. Compared with the local Canadian labour force and immigrants from other streams, international students stand out as they own Canadian credentials and Canadian experiences and are in a younger demographic (Arthur & Flynn, 2011).

INFORMAL AND EXPERIENTIAL LEARNING

International students' learning starts much earlier than when they attend the first class in the host country. Whenever they step onto the new country and become aware of all the changes, geographically or mentally, they probably begin to import new information and adjust their behaviours consciously or unconsciously, which could be called a kind of informal learning in the absence of a teacher.

A rough distinction between formal and informal learning is that formal learning occurs in the classroom, while informal learning happens beyond the classroom (Eshach, 2007). Learning in the formal settings, including primary, secondary, and post-secondary schools, is closely related to learning through a structured curriculum, class activities, and academic assessment, which makes it formal learning (Gerber, Marek, & Cavallo, 2001). On the contrary, informal learning is less structured and often takes place in a variety of locations other than in a classroom, and learners take the initiative to acquire knowledge themselves (Gerber et al., 2001). Eraut (2004) puts informal learning and formal learning to each end of a learning continuum, and informal learning is closer to the informal end than the formal end, when informal learning shows its characteristics as "implicit, unintended, opportunistic and unstructured learning and the absence of a teacher" (p. 250).

Informal learning activities are those "involving the pursuit of understanding, knowledge or skill which occurs outside the curricula of educational institutions, or the courses or workshops offered by educational or social agencies" (Livingstone, 1999, p. 50). For many students, significant amounts of their time are spent beyond formal learning, since informal learning plays an important role in developing students' potentials. However, more studies have to be done on informal learning to help us understand its role for university students, especially for international students (Gerber et al., 2001), because international students also learn outside the academic classroom as they navigate life in the new community.

Experiential learning is "an idealized learning cycle or spiral" process, and the learner experiences, reflects, thinks, and acts "in a recursive process that is responsive to the learning situation and what is being learned" (Kolb & Kolb, 2005, p. 194). Chavan (2014) presents experiential learning as a process consisting of multiple stages: "experiential learning happens when (1) a person is involved in an activity,

(2) he/she looks back and evaluates it, (3) determines what was useful or important to remember, (4) and uses this information to perform another activity" (p. 202; see also Kolb, 1984). In brief, experiential learning means to learn by doing and by reflecting on the experience. Learning by doing can enable international students to change and grow. From firsthand experience, the learners can accumulate related knowledge, and through reflective thinking on what has happened, they may gain insight that can be useful for making sense of new experiences.

METHODOLOGY

Research Methods, Research Questions, and Participants

To explore the ways whether and how international students develop intercultural awareness and transferrable professional skills through community engagement and volunteering in Halifax, the author uses qualitative methodology to investigate two educational programs. The first is the Interfaith Engagement Program (IEP) and the second is the International Student Volunteer Program (ISVP), both of which are organized or co-hosted by a local university, MSVU.

The research method of case study has been applied to investigate the two extracurricular programs. Focus group interviews and semi-structured in-depth interviews act as the main tools for data collection. First, the participants were organized into two groups according to the program they had been in, and the two groups got together with the researcher respectively for a focus group interview. After the focus group interview, each participant met with the researcher on a one-on-one basis for a semi-structured in-depth interview.

Under the overarching research question on how international students gain knowledge from informal learning, four interrelated research topics are developed to better explore this main theme: (a) the motivation to move to Canada, (b) the reasons to join in the IEP or the ISVP, (c) the experience in the program, and (d) the impact of the IEP or the ISVP experience on them. Of the above four, the first two topics were discussed within the two focus groups, and the last two topics more related to personal feelings and experiences were brought to the semi-structured in-depth interview with each research participant in a more private way.

After all the interviews were done, the recordings were transcribed verbatim by the researcher. The gathered qualitative data were scanned thoroughly, leading to several main themes and clusters being generalized during the coding process, which followed the three procedures of qualitative data analysis — data reduction, data display, and conclusion drawing and verification (Miles & Huberman, 1994). Then the themes and clusters were analyzed to portray international students' experiences in Canada, including their reasons to study in Atlantic Canada, challenges in life and study, informal learning experiences, perspective changes, and gains after participating in extracurricular activities.

The IEP is an experiential education opportunity for participants to enroll in a week-long free program, in which they visit designated sacred spaces citywide, and engage in spiritual and worship practices in Halifax (IHH, 2020). The ISVP is a project-based program initiated by the International Education Centre (IEC) of MSVU in 2017, and provides volunteer opportunities, training, and consulting supports to cultivate international students' professional skills in a Canadian working environment, so that they reap the skills that could be transferred to future employment (Fu, 2018).

Neither program is mandatory for international students. They both happen in informal learning environments beyond the classroom, without any syllabus, textbook or teacher, and they are not credit-related. All participants voluntarily sign up for the program, and use their spare time on the events or volunteer work, which means that their involvement totally depends on the autonomy and interest of each individual. In both programs, participants will visit a place or practice something that might be novel to them, and they learn from what they have experienced in the program. All of them have to attend an intro session in the beginning and a post-session in the end, and the facilitated sessions help the participants to exam their original beliefs, to pose questions, to exchange ideas, and to reflect on their experiences and changes. Therefore, the IEP and the ISVP can play active roles in promoting international students' informal and experiential learning, which will serve to further develop students' cultural competence and transferrable skills.

Five international student participants from each program, for a total of ten, have been invited to attend a focus group interview and a semi-structured in-depth interview. Challenges of the research may include the limitations of qualitative methods, small samples of participants, English as a Second Language (ESL) for both the researcher and most international student participants, as well as the author's insider role and personal bias as an international student and program organizer for both programs (Fu, 2018). Since the research participants are all from outside Canada, and each one has a unique social and cultural identity, it is very important for the researcher to create a respectful and trustful atmosphere in the meetings. To reduce probable misunderstandings caused by language, the researcher would paraphrase some unclear points and ask for clarification, or follow up with more questions during the interviews. In the one-on-one interviews, certain participants used Mandarin if they could not find the right words to express some ideas in English, since Mandarin is the shared mother tongue for both the participant and the researcher; in the transcription and analysis process, the author would contact some participants for elaboration on some answers to avoid misinterpretation. The focus group interview lasted about 1.5 to 2 hours, while each individual interview lasted about 0.5 to 1 hour.

Admissions criteria on research participants include: (a) international students over 19 years old, who (b) held student visa when participating in the IEP or the ISVP, (c) had been in Canada for at least six months, and (d) had participated either in the IEP or the ISVP (Fu, 2018). Below is a table (Table 2) listing some basic demographic data of the participants, including pseudonym, gender, region of origin, level of study (i.e., undergraduate [UG] or postgraduate [GD]). Participants were all between the ages of early 20s to mid-30s, while the gender ratio between male and female is 3:7. Six of them were at undergraduate level, and four at graduate level. The IEP participants came from four different colleges and universities in Halifax, while all ISVP participants were from MSVU.

RESEARCH FINDINGS

The study generates several clusters of themes, which include (a) international students' motivations to study in Atlantic Canada, (b) dilemma in new environment, and (c) their informal learning experiences in the IEP or ISVP.

Table 2. Research participants from IEP and ISVP

IEP			
Name	**Gender**	**Region of Origin**	**Level of Study**
Ahmad	Male	Middle East	GD
Fox	Female	East Asia	UG
Julia	Female	East Asia	GD
Meredith	Female	East Asia	UG
Yolanda	Female	East Asia	UG
ISVP			
Name	**Gender**	**Region of Origin**	**Level of Study**
Andy	Male	East Asia	UG
April	Female	East Asia	UG
Dr. T.	Male	Middle East	GD
Lola	Female	Africa	GD
May	Female	North America	UG

Motivations to Choose Atlantic Canada

What might be distinct from the traditional impression on international students' motivations to choose Canada is that six out of the ten research participants mentioned that the most important reason to study in Atlantic Canada was not for immigration but its high quality of education or their individual preference for certain academic programs. Two participants cited personal or family reasons, and only one confirmed immigration as the main purpose to study in this region.

In the discussion about his reasons to come to Canada, Ahmad mentioned that his choice of university and academic program have more value than the location.

I chose to come to Canada because it offers the best learning opportunities, and Canada is a welcoming country, and diverse country, multicultural. So I decided if I want to further my education, I should be choosing a country with that criteria, and the country, Canada was the best choice that I made and I don't regret further time. … I spoke with the supervisors, and they offered me the research topic I was interested. So it's more Dalhousie [University] than Halifax.

Unlike those who chose Canada as a primary destination of study, Lola had originally planned to study in the UK but changed her mind so that she could be away from other family members in the UK and become more independent in a new country. She said:

I told my dad, I don't want to live with all of you. I just want to be separate from all of you. I want to be independent, at least be able to stand on my own, not be depending on you guys all the time. Then I applied for master's program here in Halifax … and I got admissions here, and then I came to do women and gender studies, being a great experience for me.

The only participant that mentioned immigration outweighed all other reasons to Atlantic Canada was Fox, an IEP participant:

Actually, I chose the city more than university, because I applied a lot of colleges in Ottawa. But the agency told me Halifax is the city for you to go. It's easier to get immigration. I said, "Fine, OK." And there is a university, the NSCAD is one of the famous design universities in Canada. So I said, "OK, I can, I can go to NSCAD." And then, I came.

Although only one participant placed immigration as the main reason to study in Atlantic Canada, nine out of ten claimed that they want to stay after graduation. By the end of 2019, eight participants have already graduated from their programs. Seven of the eight graduates have found employment in Canada: six in Nova Scotia, and one who moved out of Atlantic Canada after a few years of work here. Only one of the eight has left Canada and gone back to his native country, but this participant reiterates that he plans to return to work or visit if possible.

Dilemma in New Environment

The challenges faced by international students in the host country may include academic barriers, social barriers, and cultural barriers (Wu et al., 2015). This research reveals that the participants are in similar dilemma in Atlantic Canada, when they have experienced academic barriers, feelings of isolation, and institutional or systematic obstacles.

Academic Barriers

Language issues and lack of cultural context have been widely discussed by the participants, and stood out as two major academic barriers for these international students.

As a non-native English speaker, Julia regarded the English language as the greatest challenge for her study in Canada. Besides her unfamiliarity with academic English, insufficient academic preparation before beginning classes and professors' disregard for the differences in each international student's English ability were also considered as factors. At the very beginning, she could only understand 30% of the professor's lecture. Even two years later, she had to make extra efforts and be more "focused" in class or be "prepared earlier" before class so she could "understand better."

It depends on the professor, because some of them may be considering that you are an international student and they would talk not that quickly. But some of them, they just think, as you have the ability to engage in our program, maybe you have no problem to join the class. So they would just talk as normal. … And terminology is the most important one. Actually, if translated into Chinese, I would know that, but it's just new in English for me. Even when I studied another course called Nutrition Medical Therapy, it's related to medical therapy which I am familiar with in Chinese, but when it's talked in English, I couldn't understand all the terminologies in medicine. Because we learned them in Chinese, not in English. (Julia)

Even with a relatively high level of English, May was upset when being treated differently by the local people because English was not her first language.

The first time that I encounter a problem was when I did my first co-op. The people I worked with didn't understood that even though I had good level of English, they expected me to not have errors. I didn't like them treating me as I was a different person just by the fact that English wasn't my first language. (May)

Although English was her "lingua franca," Lola had some tough moments in Canada, when people exhibited a stereotyped attitude on international students' English proficiency and their accents. She said:

I struggle with people always. I was usually ... Right, because I'm African, I can't speak English. Like someone asked me,

[Started in this way] Do you speak English?

[I said] Well, this is my lingua franca.

[They continued] What? What do you mean by lingua franca?

[I said] I mean, you didn't know? English is my adopted language. I studied in English. I grew up speaking English, and I can speak and see.

[They said] Your English is so different.

[I said] You know, English is English.

It was hard for me to get used to that. Because when my country is dominantly black, so coming to a different country where you have people from different cultures or races, it's difficult to assimilate other people, and then people will judge you based on the color of the skin and all of that. (Lola)

Concerns about the lack of Canadian cultural context were also mentioned by the participants. At their Canadian Higher Education institutions, more or less, they have noticed the differences in the ways of teaching and learning from the education received in their home country. Some participants felt regretful when relating to their lack of presentation skills and learning skills. Some talked about how they tried to do things in a more "Canadian way" and the challenges in "catching up" or building up knowledge on the local culture. According to Yolanda, it was "a risk" for her when the time came to do presentations. Compared to her Canadian classmates, who had accumulated abundant experiences in presenting since a much earlier age, she was deficient in presentation skills and public speaking, and had never been exposed or trained in this aspect in her home country.

[When] I took the business courses, unlike some students here in Halifax, they all had presentations since primary school, or middle school, or high school, but we didn't have those presentations skills, when we were back in China. So the local students, they know how to prepare for presentation, they will not be nervous to do the presentation. But for us, it's totally a risk. (Yolanda)

Some external factors are likely to have situated the international students in unfriendly, exclusive, and oppressive learning environments. One participant used the metaphor "riding the bicycle" to depict her experience in Canada, in which her Canadian counterparts—the students with Canadian "cultural context"—were those bicyclists riding following the wind and with an added impulse pushing them forward. This participant, as an international student, labelled herself as the one "without the cultural context," and her study in Canada was similar to cycling against the wind, which had placed her in a disadvantaged situation.

And you feel that you have to catch up with the others, and they have over twenty years to accumulate all those cultural contexts. But looking at you, if you want to get to the same finish line, you need to set a lot more hard work than anymore else trying to catch up. It's like you are riding the bicycle, everyone has the wind on their back pushing them forward, but you have the wind to the opposite direction, and it's constantly drawing you back, and you have to work harder just trying to catch up on the same way, so you don't end up being too behind. (Meredith)

To "catch up" with her peers and make up for her insufficient knowledge on local culture, Meredith had to give up listening to music and sacrifice much of her spare time to learn the "Canadian context."

I used to talk to my colleague that I don't know why I stopped listening to music, but the thing is, I guess, is the intense fear that you are a dummy in a room that people are talking about things that they all seem to know, and you have no clue what's going on, because you don't grow up with the same culture. And when you are expected to be the expert to teach people, you really have a lot of catch up to do. So there is no time for music. Because music, those kind of leisure things, you cannot afford. You have to use the time to catch up on the Canadian context. (Meredith)

Feelings of Isolation

Even though the research participants had been immersed among both Canadian students and students from other countries in classes or extracurricular activities, many of them still identified difficulties in making friends with local students or other Canadians. Some participants considered their classmates as nodding acquaintances instead of friends, and some referred to "Hi and bye" people who would never gather again after school. Most of them expressed the feeling of alienation, and a few admitted that they did not have any Canadian friends, even after two or more years living in Canada.

According to Ahmad, he was from a community where people were closely related to each other, but to study in Canada means to start a new life, and he had been challenged by the Canadian "individualized" social life.

The other challenges in life outside school is to find as I said a community, a company, or friendship, because we are international students, and we are alone. Back home we were with everybody, the big family, the long friendship from school time. So this is the challenge that you are here alone, start again. … Social life here is more individual, sometimes, especially when we are talking about students, it's more individualized. And I am a person who loves to be with a community. (Ahmad)

"Lonely" was a frequently used word that appeared in several participants' statements in relation to their first few days in Canada. Loneliness had been attributed to the weather, snow, a sense of alienation, biases from the locals, and unpleasant experiences with the locals. A participant noticed that people from different origins tended to have their own "cliques," and it's harder to "penetrate" them in university than in high school.

I felt so lonely for two weeks. I didn't talk to no one for two weeks. That's was ... bad. And it was really difficult to communicate to people, because the weather didn't help, and it was my first time seeing snow. ... I tried so hard to make friends but the whole thing was new to me. (Dr. T)

It's very common. Even though everyone says hi to you. You think that's being nice, but it's not, like the locals just wanna say hi, but they don't wanna me to be your clique. You [the locals] don't want to talk to that person. You [the locals] don't want to get to know the person... even in school here, it's the same thing. Hi. Pass by. If you don't say Hi, and you two just pass by. The next time you see each other, you don't. (Lola)

It's difficult. ... I think I have a similar problem as yours. I think the biggest difficulty is to make friends or communicate with local people here. It is easy for me to talk to Chinese or Asian, when I have difficulty, or I have question. But it is a problem until now. ... It is hard for me to communicate with the locals, or to be really a friend ... or having a deeper relationship with them, because ... they are all friendly, and they're willing to talk with me, or having a group with me, or we do assignment together. This is not a problem. But I think the difficult part is that you have a deeper relationship, like making friends, or really talking something out of the class, or out of the assignment. So I'm still learning how to start a conversation with them comfortably, and to learn about their culture. I think this is still a difficult thing, or still a thing for me to learn until now. (Dr. T.)

The distant responses from their Canadian peers is only one cause the international students' feelings of isolation. Situations might become worse when they feel abandoned due misunderstanding, hostile or opposing attitudes from their original ethnic groups or even their families.

And another lonely is, I guess, breaking away from the pack, and having a very different experience compare[d] to a lot of other international students in a way, you have less people understanding how you feel, and you see less people are like you. And then it kind of making you feel that you are very lonely. ... A lot of the experience that I have, I don't think that my parents are able to understand that, [because] they never need to learn how to live with racism, they never need to learn to live with a system that set against them. (Meredith)

I am trying to adopt the believes, and the ideas that I really want to choose for myself, not the same set I have been told for the beginning, since the beginning of life. But the new challenge is, when you change, how others are going to see this change, and what their reaction will be, whether the people you knew before, or even the people that you have been with them for quite some time. So this is a little bit challenging, the new you change in you, outgoing to impact others, what the other reaction will be on that. (Ahmad)

Institutional and Systematic Obstacles

Systematic obstacles in the higher education institution have been pointed out by the international students as hindrance to their study in Canada. These obstacles include the high expectation of academic performance despite their prior knowledge, a one-size-fits-all teaching style and a single standard set up for all learners, and lack of support from the school and instructors.

Because here, they expect you already know. Especially in postgraduate studies, this is the first point. The second point, the content is too much. Finishing four chapters in one session. I was never exposed to this during my undergraduate. … It was so intense, and the level of expectation is so high, as you already know. And if you don't, it's your problem, you have to follow up. So I found it's very challenging to just move on. (Ahmad)

A participant had been told by the professor that if expecting to succeed, just "leave the pack of people" from her home country, "because they don't know the Canadian way of thinking."

You set up these policies. … This policy can work its own magic, even the people who have the good meaning or never intend to hurt you. But the thing is we live in the system, and then the system function in the way and this proportionately affect you. … Looking back, just like the program that I was in. In order to get into the internship program, you have to demonstrate those academic, employment, and volunteer experiences. … They have to look at every single application and then compare one and another. So the standard is set. However, if you are local student or you are Canadian born, you have a lot more years to accumulate all these employment, volunteer. (Meredith)

It's more than just reading books. If it's just book, I can handle that. But … [Canadian] people have a lot more time to accumulate that. That's how the set system is set against us. At the first place, you have to use all those very limited hours or years that you have, in order to catch up, because you only have that, say, two or fewer years, but the other people have lots longer. They could draw to things all the way from their high school or middle school, that's the thing, then they demonstrated they have the leadership skills. (Meredith)

Many participants in this research requested more support from the higher education institution, which implied that Canadian higher education providers need to understand more about international students' demands, in order to offer sufficient and appropriate assistance and create more channels to connect international students with the local community.

We're not given the kind of attention they give all the Canadian students here. But we pay more money, double or triple of what normal Canadian students pay. But we are not really taken good care of, not really given that attention. We're paying more and just dumping in the system and not given the right information, that is why the Afrocentric group [support group at her university] is very important to African students. And also I feel like there should be other groups, other students from some other countries, that will help them, because most students are going through a lot because they don't know their rights. (Lola)

As an international student, I think it's very difficult to find volunteer works, because I tried to actually volunteer many times, but the problem is the university doesn't provide like a volunteer centre. (Dr. T.)

I feel some people just don't know anything about this program, so maybe to use social media or something to let more people know about it … like some university students, can know by some big posters in the university. … I don't really see a lot of international students to come here. (Yolanda)

In their educational institutions, international students commented that some teachers did not provide enough attention to international students. The faculty's lack of responses, misunderstandings, or stereotypes of international students might have negatively affected international students' learning enthusiasm and experiences in Canada in other possible ways.

And the system set up in a way that doesn't help with at all. They would think that, as the teacher would say, "Well, the Chinese students are very quiet, so they must not have a lot of opinions, they must not be willing to contribute to the experiences of the class." But the fact is, we grow up in a classroom where the students are expected not to speak. They are expected to be obedient, they are expected to listen to the teacher. (Meredith).

Informal Learning in the IEP/ISVP

In these two extracurricular programs, the ten participants had a few reasons to attend the program, and all of them confirmed experiencing some positive results from the informal learning experience.

Reasons to Attend the IEP/ISVP

The IEP enables the participant to have firsthand experience of diverse cultures and religions. All participants can voluntarily visit some faith groups and attend their religious practices, and they have to attend an intro session and a closing session to receive a certificate of completion from the Interfaith Harmony Halifax (IHH) committee at the end (IHH, 2020). One of the main reasons for the five IEP participants to join the IEP was curiosity about religions and culture, and a second was the opportunity to meet different people and share experiences.

At the first time, I was just curious about some [faiths]. … I could find the introduction about each religion online, but I really wanted to connect with their people, to know what their believes are. … Do they really love their religions or just follow their traditions? (Yolanda)

I really enjoyed everything in the week, and I just have gone to some places I'm interested in, and I wanted to share [my experiences] with the other people through the ending session. (Julia)

I feel I should go to some places to travel and eat their traditional food, because their food, like the dessert in the Indian community, is super good. (Fox)

The ISVP is more project-oriented, and it tries to connect international participants with local volunteer opportunities, which helps them to build on professional skills and better prepare for future employment in Canada. Each participant takes the initiative to organize an activity or assist in a project, in which they have to cooperate with other people, and an intro and a debriefing session are compulsory for the participants. In the end, qualified participants receive a volunteer certificate and a reference letter from the MSVU International Education Centre. The most popular reasons listed by the five ISVP participants to be engaged in the program are: to make more connections with people, to gain Canadian experiences, and to receive the reference letter and volunteer certificate.

First of all, to make friends, and to help other international students to get into the community here in Halifax at the Mount. Because I know the feeling, when I was here as an international student … they, most of them I hear, are alone, so they came to Halifax, to Canada by themselves usually. So I know they want to make friends. They want to know the local culture, and, where should they go have food and go to movies, things like that. (Andy)

I just felt at home studying, playing a game, that's it. I know it's weird the reason why I joined this is because I want to meet new people actually. This is one of the main goals. Yeah, I met a lot of people from my country too. They were like very, nice, I had a great time with them. And the experience I received from this activity, Photoshop, Snapchat. Now I know how to add a filter in a snapshot … and I opened an Instagram page. (Lola)

The most I think is the work experience and the reference letter. Because I think it is so difficult for international students here to find a job after we graduate. I think it is easier in Toronto or Vancouver. … The population of international is bigger, and there are different companies from different countries … but here it is still developing. So I think I need more experience to prove that I'm capable of working here, and talking in English. … I have some part time jobs, during these three years, but I still think this program can help me to develop more professional skills, so that that leads me to join this program. Because I think it is really useful for my future career, if I want to find a job, or if I want to stay here. So I decided to participate in this program. (Dr. T.)

The reference letter. That's why I applied, as Participant 3 said, it's hard for international students to get jobs here, because Halifax is a very small city, and they don't have so many job prospects. So I think that's why most international students move out of the province once they are done. So I thought it would be a very good experience for me to do something out of my comfort zone, because I've never coordinated a campaign before, doing anything like that. So it was a good experience for me. (April)

Informal Learning Experiences

Through the IEP and the ISVP, participants reported that they gained experience in intercultural aware-ness, developed transferrable professional skills through different activities, and expanded connections with people in Canada. Some participants believed that they have deepened their understanding of other cultures and become more tolerant to people from other backgrounds. A participant changed her previous view on a religious group that was described by media as "very dangerous people," but after a visit and having a conversation with the members, she found "they were really friendly," not "like the news said."

It was my first time attending a harmony program with different interfaiths engaged together. So the program that I have attended before, it was more oriented into one religion, one interfaith. And also here I love the diversity that exists within this group. And I love how everybody was open to one another, with curiosity to know humbleness, which is the most important thing. To humble ourselves in front of others, and not seeing ourselves superior than others, so this is the special thing that I like with this program. (Ahmad)

It's very very powerful, and I still constantly quoting the theme of this year, and also the banner from the mosque. When I was at work, and I have to bring up things as how we can achieve racial equity in the organization, and how we need to truly embrace the community that we want to welcome to our organization. I feel like I go back to constantly quoting that, like "exploring similarity and celebrating diversity," quoting "Don't just hear about us, hear from us." And I feel like that's the message, that I would love other people from my organization to get to learn a little bit better. Because it speaks very much to my heart. By now that I guess, when you work in an organization and people have different levels of understanding on things, because they have very different experiences, sometimes they don't really get it in a way you get it. (Meredith)

We don't really need to have the same believes, but we all respect each others, and share our loves. (Yolanda)

Through community engagement and interacting with people, the participants may become more confident in dealing with people and facing unknown situations, because they have practiced skills in real life situations, which can benefit their future career. For international students without a Social Insurance Number (SIN) such as Dr. T., it was almost impossible to accumulate Canadian work experience from jobs, but the ISVP was "a good thing," because work permit or visa issues were no longer a concern.

First of all, organization skills and time management skills. Because we have to do many stuff day by day. We have to make a group plan for what's we are going to do each day to achieve our goals. And also marketing skills and interpersonal skills.... We have to have communication with the other people, or with other staff or students. And we have to express what we think and what we want, then to have them to support us ... also communication skills, as well as intercultural communicating skills. (Andy)

So ... time management, because I was taking actually three courses that semester, one of them was research method, which took a lot of my time. And I also had a lot of work to do with the international volunteer program. So time management was definitely one of the skills that I gained. Because I created time to work on the ISVP task, and my assignments from other courses. Also, how to communicate with my team. So some of my team you know they have been not working probably, but I discussed with them because they were also busy fighting ... on their assignments. ... So we found time to meet, and discussed all the things. ... The third thing I learned was how to work in a team, how to be a team player. (Dr. T.)

I would like to keep going with this program, to learn more about how it's running, to build something similar in the future by my own. (Ahmad)

I learn to sit with the discomfort better and better over the times. And I just get a lot prepared. I am able to speak about certain issues, like a lots of the very very hard issues that I will never feel to bring it up seriously. (Meredith)

That's why work experience is different from class experience. You're trying to get a job, and they ask you, "Do you have work experience?" OK. I studied women and gender studies for example, I did not have any volunteer experience or have any experience. I don't have any work experience. I will not get a job. Someone with my (work) experience will get a job, because the person has worked and done all those things in the office, has done awareness campaign, has been able to coordinate an event, has done so many things. While (if) I have never done it before, then how do I start it. (Lola)

DISCUSSION

The analysis of the international students' informal learning experiences through two extracurricular programs results in some important points to consider. Although for most of participants the primary objective of studying in Nova Scotia was to attain education rather than immigration, all of them have been faced with academic challenges, feelings of isolation, or the barriers derived from the institutional or educational system. After realizing their unfavourable and culturally disadvantaged situation in the host country and the imperative need to change, these individuals took the initiative to join such extra-curricular programs to expand social networks by socializing with people in collaborative activities or volunteering work. Through such kinds of informal learning experiences, they are reporting becoming more adaptable and more culturally tolerant to unknown situations, and their confidence in communicating and professional abilities have also reportedly improved.

Based on the students' experiences, success in education and personal growth were valued more than eventual immigration to Canada. It is important for Canadian universities and colleges to recognize the changes in international students' essential needs, so that they could adjust the academic courses or curriculum accordingly, and offer more adequate or enhanced supporting services, such as EAL or a bridging program, settlement and community engagement activities, career training, and counselling.

The findings validate previous research on challenges experienced by international students. The cultural shock associated with emotional frustration in the host country is a typical and predictable process before international students may find unhindered integration into Canadian education and social life. These needs of the international students in Canadian universities and colleges should be recognized and accommodated by education providers. The cultural dissonance and the lack of Canadian experiences could be exacerbated in their educational path, and impede their success in education, eventual employment, and immigration in Canada.

Extracurricular programs such as the IEP and the ISVP may help international students in their attempt to adjust to a new culture or social environment, and to build up necessary skills for future employment and immigration in Canada. The research findings add to the literature concerning international students' informal learning in Canadian higher education. It is important to design appropriate curricula and programs to help support international students' intercultural awareness development and employment transitions, which might also help retain international students as prospective young immigrants and relieve the labour shortages in Atlantic Canada. In general, the findings are also helpful for higher education providers and practitioners, educational program developers, Canadian education policymakers and other stakeholders in a wider context as the students' accounts relate to the international student experience in general, as in their needs, challenges, and expectations in and beyond the academic classroom.

LIMITATIONS AND FUTURE RESEARCH DIRECTIONS

This study is not without shortcomings. First, the study sample is small and does not reflect the full multicultural span of international students in Atlantic Canada. Second, all participants were from early 20s to mid-30s in terms of age, and may be older than their international student peers who move to Canada shortly after high school. Third, the research is based on a medium-sized metropolitan city in Canada, which does not represent international students in small-sized cities and suburbs. Lastly, the qualitative research methodology has its disadvantages in lack of representativeness, accuracy, and objectivity. Therefore, future research could be carried out within larger participant groups, by taking in more diversity in terms of ethnicity, age, and gender. Further studies may be undertaken at a wider selection of universities or colleges in smaller cities or rural areas of Canada to understand what informal and experiential learning opportunities may be available for students in those locales, and other formats of informal and experiential learning within higher education can be investigated to help diversify findings.

CONCLUSION

This study explored the active role of informal learning in international students' sociocultural growth and integration in the host country. The findings support the initial assumption that self-directed cultural immersion, volunteering, and community engagement would facilitate participants' learning experiences and sociocultural adjustment in Canada. The extracurricular programs helped international students to build up intercultural awareness, cultivate some transferrable skills, and stimulate their adaptation and integration to the life and study in Canada. It is expected that more extracurricular programs and positive changes will be created to improve international students' satisfaction within Canadian colleges and universities, which will in turn increase Canada's competitiveness in the world international education industry and enhance its inclusiveness to be an ideal destination for higher education, immigration, employment, and settlement in the long-term.

REFERENCES

Arthur, N., & Flynn, S. (2011). Career development influences of international students who pursue permanent immigration to Canada. *International Journal for Educational and Vocational Guidance*, *11*(3), 221–237. doi:10.100710775-011-9212-5

Association of Atlantic Universities. (2019). *AAU survey of preliminary enrolments*. https://www.atlanticuniversities.ca/statistics/aau-survey-preliminary-enrolments

Canadian Bureau for International Education. (2018, March 16). *International students surpass 2022 goal*. https://cbie.ca/international-students-surpass-2022-goal/

Carlson, J. S., & Widaman, K. F. (1988). The effects of study abroad during college on attitudes toward other cultures. *International Journal of Intercultural Relations, 12*(1), 1–17. doi:10.1016/0147-1767(88)90003-X

Charles-Toussaint, G. C., & Crowson, H. M. (2010). Prejudice against international students: The role of threat perceptions and authoritarian dispositions in U.S. students. *The Journal of Psychology, 144*(5), 413–428. doi:10.1080/00223980.2010.496643 PMID:20806848

Chavan, M. (2014). Alternative modes of teaching international business: Online experiential learning. In V. Taras & M. Gonzalez-Perez (Eds.), *The handbook of experiential learning in international business* (pp. 202–222). Palgrave Macmillan.

Chira, S. (2016). *In a class of their own: International students, class identity and education migration in Atlantic Canada* [Doctoral dissertation, Dalhousie University]. DalSpace. http://hdl.handle.net/10222/72176

Citizenship and Immigration Canada. (2017). *Economic impact of international education in Canada: 2017 update.* https://www.international.gc.ca/education/report-rapport/impact-2017/index.aspx

Dwyer, M., & Peters, C. (2004). The benefits of study abroad. *Transitions Abroad, 27*(5), 56–57.

Eraut, M. (2004). Informal learning in the workplace. *Studies in Continuing Education, 26*(2), 247–273. doi:10.1080/158037042000225245

Eshach, H. (2007). Bridging in-school and out-of-school learning: Formal, non-formal, and informal education. *Journal of Science Education and Technology, 16*(2), 171–190. doi:10.100710956-006-9027-1

Foster, M. (2014). Student destination choices in higher education: Exploring attitudes of Brazilian students to study in the United Kingdom. *Journal of Research in International Education, 13*(2), 149–162. doi:10.1177/1475240914541024

Fu, J. (2018). *The role of two extracurricular programs in international students' informal learning experiences in Atlantic Canada* [Master's thesis, Mount Saint Vincent University]. E-commons. http://hdl.handle.net/10587/1932

Gerber, B., Marek, E., & Cavallo, A. (2001). Development of an informal learning opportunities assay. *International Journal of Science Education, 23*(6), 569–583. doi:10.1080/09500690116959

Gopal, A. (2016). Visa and immigration trends: A comparative examination of international student mobility in Canada, Australia, the United Kingdom, and the United States. *Strategic Enrollment Management Quarterly, 4*(3), 130–141. doi:10.1002em3.20091

Government of Canada. (2014). *Canada's international education strategy: Harnessing our knowledge advantage to drive innovation and prosperity* (Cat. No.: FR5-86/2014). http://international.gc.ca/global-markets-marchesmondiaux/assets/pdfs/overview-apercu-eng.pdf

Gu, Q., Schweisfurth, M., & Day, C. (2010). Learning and growing in a "foreign" context: Intercultural experiences of international students. *Compare: A Journal of Comparative Education, 40*(1), 7–23. doi:10.1080/03057920903115983

Ingraham, E., & Peterson, D. L. (2004). Assessing the impact of study abroad on student learning at Michigan State University. *Frontiers: The Interdisciplinary Journal of Study Abroad, 10*(1), 83–100. doi:10.36366/frontiers.v10i1.134

Interfaith Harmony Halifax. (2020). *Interfaith engagement educational opportunity.* http://ihhalifax.ca/home/interfaith-engagement-program

Johnstone, M., & Lee, E. (2014). Branded: International education and 21st-century Canadian immigration, education policy, and the welfare state. *International Social Work, 57*(3), 209–221. doi:10.1177/0020872813508572

Kolb, A. Y., & Kolb, D. A. (2005). Learning styles and learning spaces: Enhancing experiential learning in higher education. *Academy of Management Learning & Education, 4*(2), 193–212. doi:10.5465/amle.2005.17268566

Kolb, D. A. (1984). *Experiential learning: Experience as the source of learning and development.* Prentice Hall.

Lewthwaite, M. (1996). A study of international students' perspectives on cross-cultural adaptation. *International Journal for the Advancement of Counseling, 19*(2), 167–185. doi:10.1007/BF00114787

Livingstone, D. (1999). Exploring the icebergs of adult learning: Findings of the first Canadian survey of informal learning practices. *Canadian Journal for the Study of Adult Education, 13*(2), 49–72.

Miles, M. B., & Huberman, M. (1994). *Qualitative Data Analysis: A Sourcebook of New Methods* (2nd ed.). Sage Publications.

Mount Saint Vincent University. (2020). *Quick facts.* https://www.msvu.ca/en/home/aboutus/universityprofile/quickfacts.aspx

Nunan, P. (2006). *An exploration of the long term effects of student exchange experiences* [Paper presentation]. *Australian International Education Conference*, Perth, Australia.

Schwartz, S. J., Montgomery, M. J., & Briones, E. (2006). The role of identity in acculturation among immigrant people: Theoretical propositions, empirical questions, and applied recommendations. *Human Development, 49*(1), 1–30. doi:10.1159/000090300

Siddiq, F., Nethercote, W., Lye, J., & Baroni, J. (2012). The economic impact of international students in Atlantic Canada. *International Advances in Economic Research, 18*(2), 239–240. doi:10.100711294-012-9344-5

Statistics Canada. (2016). *International students in Canadian universities, 2004/2005 to 2013/2014.* http://www.statcan.gc.ca/pub/81-599-x/81-599-x2016011-eng.pdf

Vincenti, V. B. (2001). Exploration of the relationship between international experiences and the interdisciplinary work of university faculty. *Journal of Studies in International Studies, 5*(1), 42–63. doi:10.1177/102831530151004

Wu, H., Garza, E., & Guzman, N. (2015). International student's challenge and adjustment to college. *Education Research International, 2015*, 1–9. doi:10.1155/2015/202753

ADDITIONAL READING

Canadian Bureau for International Education. (2019, February 15). *Another record year for Canadian international education*. https://cbie.ca/another-record-year-for-canadian-international-education/

Canadian Bureau for International Education. (2020a). *Facts and figures*. https://cbie.ca/infographic/

Canadian Bureau for International Education. (2020b). *International students in Canada*. https://cbie.ca/wp-content/uploads/2018/09/International-Students-in-Canada-ENG.pdf

Institute of International Education. (2016). *Open doors 2016 report on international education exchange*.

Kambouropoulos, A. (2014). An examination of the adjustment journey of international students studying in Australia. *Australian Educational Researcher*, *41*(3), 349–363. doi:10.100713384-013-0130-z

Levatino, A. (2017). Transnational higher education and international student mobility: Determinants and linkage. *Higher Education: The International Journal of Higher Education Research*, *73*(5), 637–653. doi:10.100710734-016-9985-z

McDonald, I. (2014). Supporting international students in UK higher education institutions. *Perspectives: Policy and Practice in Higher Education*, *18*(2), 62–65. doi:10.1080/13603108.2014.909900

Suárez-Orozco, C., Todorova, I., & Louie, J. (2002). Making up for lost time: The experience of separation and reunification among immigrant families. *Family Process*, *41*(4), 625–643. doi:10.1111/j.1545-5300.2002.00625.x PMID:12613121

The Organisation for Economic Co-operation and Development. (2017). *Education at a Glance 2017: OECD Indicators*. OECD Publishing., doi:10.1787/eag-2017-

Trilokekar, R., & Rasmi, S. (2011). Student perceptions of international education and study abroad: A pilot study at York University, Canada. *Intercultural Education*, *22*(6), 495–511. doi:10.1080/14675986.2011.644951

KEY TERMS AND DEFINITIONS

Case Study: An in-depth study to describe and analyse a series of phenomena, such as a person, a program, an organization, a process, etc.

Experiential Learning: The ability to learn from practice, to gain new insights from observation, to refine perspectives from reflection, to transfer existed skills in new situation.

Extracurricular Activity: Activities for international students to expand social connections, develop valuable skills, and gain Canadian experience, which falls outside the realm of the standard curriculum of school, college, or university education.

Focus Group: A small group of people who have been invited to participate in a facilitated discussion whose purpose is to collect participants' opinions and experiences on a certain topic.

Formal Learning: Structured and compulsory learning with objectives and goals, usually teacher-centered, happening within a school, university, or college.

Informal Learning: Non-institutionalized and voluntary learning, learning through participation, student-centered, self-directed, and meaningful experiences integrated in community life.

Retention of International Students: To keep international students in the local labour market after they complete study in Canadian universities or colleges, and the conversion of international graduates into productive labour force in Canada, which helps to alleviate the demographic issues, such as the aging society and out-migration.

Chapter 10
Within Discipline and Within Culture Advanced Academic Writing for Asian International Students

Dawn Julie Andrews

ⓘD https://orcid.org/0000-0003-2314-2303

Thompson Rivers University, Canada

ABSTRACT

The purpose of this chapter is to challenge the Western education system to better understand the needs of international students, particularly from Asian countries. Higher education has become a big business, and many schools have popped up to meet the demand. North America's traditional universities are now well and truly dependent upon international students to fund full programs, and universities have come to rely on international dollars. International students are looking to the West for high-quality education, but may arrive in the West unprepared to face the challenge of writing advanced academic essays.

INTRODUCTION

This chapter focuses on the problem reported in the graduate higher education literature that Asian graduate students studying in Canada and the United States are not adequately prepared for western expectations of advanced essay writing when in their western graduate program (Gao, 2012; Lax, 2002; Santos, 1988; Rahimi & Goli, 2016; Rawlings & Sue, 2013; Zhang, 2008). Contradictory evidence exists regarding what issues underlay this problem. Yang and Chung (2015) suggested that the problem was the lack of cross-cultural programs between international academic partners. The cultural tension model suggested that the problem was that the West favours one cultural viewpoint over another (Montgomery, 2013). A collectivist perspective suggested that the problem was an individual versus a collective self-identification by students (Kim & Markus, 1999). Others have suggested that the student's lack of ethics and their

DOI: 10.4018/978-1-7998-5030-4.ch010

resorting to plagiarism and cheating were the main concern (Ngo, 2016; Ramzan, Munir, Siddique, & Asif, 2012). Finally, Knowlton (2017) stated that it was students failing courses.

Taking the form of a critical literature review, this chapter seeks to propose answers and recommendations in response to the concern of how and why international students struggle in advanced academic writing. Additionally, this chapter investigates what leaders in North American higher education can do to improve student outcomes with the understanding that recruitment and retention are both at-risk. This review was narrowed to literature from the United States, Canada, and content from Asia to offer Canadian scholars both a balanced view of the works and to help rule out extraneous educational systems. The advanced academic writing core competency section is limited to primary research studies to avoid comparison to unstudied professional opinions.

This literature review places the context within the teaching of international graduate students in the West. It implores leadership accountability to meet the academic needs of international students. The literature review begins by exploring how Canada's higher education system and the big business of higher education impact the internationalization of pedagogy and curriculum. The focus then shifts to advanced writing core competencies to explore bachelor versus master-level curriculum and writing proficiency within the discipline/within the culture. Recommendations are specifically for advanced writing. Improvements include attention to core competencies through pre-writing, drafting, resourcing, and scaffolding ideas.

CANADA'S HIGHER EDUCATION SYSTEM

Canada's elementary, secondary, and post-secondary educational systems are a provincial and territorial responsibility, which results in regional autonomy with differences between regions. In Canada, no federal department of education exists, except for responsibility for military and Indigenous studies. International enrollment in public higher learning and stand-alone international schools encompasses public/private institutions such as language schools, transnational institutions with satellite campuses, career/technical institutes, community colleges, and traditional public universities; hence, the provinces are responsible for administering international higher education. For example, in British Columbia (BC), institutions are required to meet and hold the Education Quality Assurance (EQA), a designation necessary to host international students. However, Mohamedbhai (2017) states that the boundaries between public institutions and private providers of higher education have become blurred regarding quality, governance, and funding, with some non-traditional institutions making their own rules and ignoring compulsory standards. The BC Degree Quality Assurance Board (DQAB) is responsible for ensuring that all degree programs at higher learning institutions meet high-quality criteria; however, the sheer amount of stand-alone international start-ups seriously challenges oversight.

Across Canada, there are higher education campuses comprised almost entirely of international students that have popped up to meet the demand over the past ten years (Andrews, 2019). Whether an academic branch of the public, a not-for-profit university, a stand-alone for-profit university, or an insular certificate/diploma program, many of these institutions are enrolling almost exclusively international students. Green (2014) warns that the West is squandering the quality advantage by not investing more in the academic internationalization of higher education and is lagging in reported measures of international infrastructure, dedicated office space, a specific budget, use of an evaluation system, and specific targets or the benchmarks to assist educational leaders with decision-making regarding education policies for international students, which encourages stand-alone international programming.

Students' self-funding of tuition, living expenses, and travel can create a burden that is, in part, offset if students can work during and after their studies. In Canada, students can work twenty hours per week and up to three years full-time after competition of a degree (Government of Canada, 2020a), unlike more stringent policies in other countries. Canada's immigration system also has speed-up the *Permanent Residency* application process, which interests many students seeking long-term employment. However, because of class schedules, students often work part-time, low-paid, low-status work, despite often holding a previous bachelor's degree in their own country.

LITERATURE REVIEW

The literature review uncovers glaring gaps in the topic of advanced academic writing. Instead of focusing on these gaps, the body of literature reviewed focused primarily on undergraduate language attainment. There is a large body of international research that focuses on instruction in English language literacy (Kuo, 2011; Lee, 2014; Lopez & Bui, 2014; Lu, 2013; Martirosyan, Hwang, & Wanjohi, 2015; Rahimi & Goli, 2016; Webb, 2015; Yang, 2014;). However, a significant difference exists between English language fluency and advanced academic writing, particularly at the graduate level (Gao, 2012; Kim, 2006; Webb, 2015).

The individual deficit model of teaching English to international graduate students dominates the literature on writing pedagogy (Badenhorst, Moloney, Rosales, Dyer, & Ru, 2014). The Western differences in the knowledge framework inevitably assign international students to a disadvantaged position (Zhu & Flaitz, 2005). However, Lu (2013) expounded that ESL studies that are focused on grammar and grammatical structure alone are ineffective at producing advanced academic writing skills. However, a significant shortfall exists at the graduate level of agreed-upon advanced writing core competencies (Ondrusek, 2012). Wang (2014) looked at postgraduate advanced academic writing in China and confirmed that most studies there also tended to focus on undergraduate language attainment versus the synthesis of knowledge that is necessary at the graduate level.

In addition to other research, this review also amasses advanced core writing competencies by including and comparing Ondrusek's (2012) and Andrews' (2019) previous literature reviews. Ondrusek from the United States reviewed literature between 1981-2007. Andrews from Canada reviewed the literature between 2010-2016. The commodities are shown in Table 2 and Table 3. The inclusion of Sardiko's (2004) comparison between bachelor and master level writing offers an additional rationale for missing skills in Table 1.

BIG BUSINESS OF HIGHER EDUCATION

International higher education in Canada and the United States is big business. In 2018, international students contributed 44.7 billion to the US economy (Institute of International Education (IIE), 2019). The *Canadian Bureau of International Education* (CBIE) (2019) reported that in December of 2018, there were 571,215 international students in Canada, a 16% increase over the year before. The Institute of International Education's (IIE) (2019), The *Open Door* (2019) report informs that the total number

Table 1. Comparison of core competencies between bachelor and master academic writing

Bachelor Level/Declarative	Master Level/Procedural
Writes from personal experience – private thoughts and feelings - first person tense	Writes from a content perspective – third person tense
Writes about what is already known/familiar	Summarize and paraphrase the main points of an argument
Thesis comes from own head	The thesis is draft from research articles
Looks up and uses definitions	Research theories use multiple resources
May have many or loosely connected ideas	According to – notes authors and year
Repetitive description, ideas may not be cited	Multiple views - more logical based
May have multiple grammar mistakes	Grammar mistakes are minimal
May have extensive quotes, mistakes, or missing APA	Paraphrases with the correct use of in-text APA citations
Straightforward descriptive discussion	Critical reflection of authors, ideas, research
May fail to cite figures, statistics, and images	Facts used to support points and are cited and referenced
Shows solid attempt at APA	Shows few APA errors in citations and references
May employs online non-academic resources	Uses scholarly peer-reviewed and academic research

New table adapted from written prose in Sardiko (2004).

of international students in the US in 2018/19 was 1,095.299, a 0.05 increase from the previous year. In Canada, international students contribute $21.6 billion to Canada's GDP (Government of Canada, 2020b).

The tightening of US immigration, the lack of popular support for immigrants, strict work permit policies, and an unstable political climate have created an advantage for Canada as a destination of choice for international students (Wermund, 2018). Ghazarian (2014) named the most significant asset of North American academia as being the quality of education. However, a lack of quality perceived by the international student has the potential to effect future recruiting because of the interconnectivity of Asian families who extensively share critiques (Andrews, 2019). Moreover, the world pandemic of Covid-19 has created an environment where faculty must develop the additional expertise of online instruction, while in-person instruction restrictions remain in place.

The importance of international graduate students in Canada is undeniable. Canada, and the United States, are now well and truly dependent upon international students to fund full programs (Redden, 2013), and universities have come to rely on international dollars (Ghazarian, 2014; Wu, Garza, & Guzman, 2015). To remain competitive, Canada needs to meet the academic needs of international students (Ortiz, Chang, & Fang, 2015). "Year over year government funding declines as a percentage of our operating budgets, and so these kinds of lines of revenue are critical to maintaining the standards of teaching excellence we pride ourselves on" (The Pie News, 2019, para. 6). Cantwell (2015) warns that a short-sighted cash-cow mentality omits recognition that program quality directly impacts future recruiting, and Li (2013) encouraged Canada and the United States to increase the number of international students numbers within their existing knowledge-based economies.

Transnational universities, for-profit and not-for-profit, in-person and online education are a popular education model where the central administrative office of an academic institution is in one country, and the academic branch institution is in another country. This centralized business model means that international student tuition money, in part, can be funnelled back to the home country of the university to help fund domestic programs or to investors (Cantwell, 2015). For-profit universities, either stand-alone institutions or conglomerates, seek dividends for their shareholders, which has driven the big business model for international higher education, which produces a *bottom-line* focus. However, Wilmshurst, Vice-president of Camosun College, a BC public institution, stated that "Every penny earned has gone back into the college as investments either to support domestic and international student success or to improve our infrastructure" (The Pie News, 2019, para. 7).

Unfortunately, low-paid part-time contract staff are often the norm in the international higher education field in Canada who typically are not paid for curriculum development (Basen, 2014). Many instructors are contract-based, non-union positions, lacking raises, or benefits, with no pension, no seniority, no research time, and no job security despite the fact many are doctorate holders with many years of teaching experience (McKeen, 2018). These part-time instructors may carry full teaching course loads allowing tenured faculty the time to perform research (Webb, Wong, & Hubball, 2013), but are not empowered by the education system to enhance their potential. Institutions that follow these cost-cutting practices will result in transitory or disgruntled staff, inadequately empowered to meet the needs of international students (Doran, 2017).

WESTERN ACADEMIC CULTURE

Western teaching of writing exists in academic silos separated by business, academic, professional, and creative disciplines. According to Badenhorst, Moloney, Rosales, Dyer, and Ru (2014), writing has become a problem that needs fixing, suggesting viewing writing through a problem-solving approach that locates both the deficit and the solution inside the individual, which disallows the perspective that problems are a product of the broader education system; hence, minimizing accountability. The onus must be that once a student is on a western campus that western leaders assist adaption to the western education model not by blaming students, assimilating students, or describing students' skills using a deficit model, but by providing tutorage that acknowledges the multilingual intellectual ability of international students and assists transition to new educational practices (Cigdem, 2017). Once in Canada, graduate students must compete on par with domestic students. Professional and popular literature reinforce and sensationalize international students as failing, being expelled, or disheartened by the western system of education (Goodboy, Martin, & Johnson, 2015).

On the surface, institutions carefully craft accreditation applications, academic policies, cultural activities, and training for both international students and faculty. However, behind closed doors, the availability, quality, and consistency of these resources are often limited or low quality (Andrews, 2019). Montgomery (2013) addressed the dilemma of institutional, systematic irresponsibility suggesting the need to remove blame from the student and blame from the staff (Scoggin & Styron, 2006). Blame can block movement forward toward a partnership model that is capable of balancing competing demands (Montgomery, 2013; Qi, 2015). However, institutions removing money from students and society must be held accountable to promote excellence in the classroom (Green, 2014).

THE INTERNATIONALIZATION OF PEDAGOGY AND CURRICULUM

Pedagogy is an all-encompassing concept. It primarily refers to a purposeful undertaking to develop understanding within a specific culture or society (Institute for Education Planning, 2020). International students have unique historical, linguistic, social, and cultural practices as well as educational systems that affect the writing of their graduate academic essays (Ariza, 2010). Education policies, constitutional principles, health care, societal norms, business practices, curriculum development, and the instructor's interaction style in Canada tend toward an egocentric perspective. The individual perspective differs significantly from collectivists' principles common in Asia cultures and a more formal student-instructor interaction (Na et al., 2015). As the International Institute for Education Planning (2020) notes:

Learning is dependent on the pedagogical approaches teachers use in the classroom. A variety of peda-gogical approaches are common in schools, but some strategies are more effective and appropriate than others. The effectiveness of pedagogy often depends on the particular subject matter to be taught, on understanding the diverse needs of different learners, and on adapting to the on-the-ground conditions in the classroom and the surrounding context. (para. 1)

An age-old issue with extreme complexity exists around creating uniformity for writing curriculum. Different disciplines teach different styles of citations, references, and discussion discourse; it has always been so. A student who learns to cite and use bibliography in English class later enters a social science class only to find that the American Psychological Association (APA) standards of citation and refer-ences are mandatory. Moreover, faculty tend to interpret the APA rules differently, even using different editions of the APA manual. Consensus, although highly prized, is missing, and conformity could ease much confusion for international students.

Differences also exist between bachelor and master level writing. Sardiko (2004) found significant disparities between the bachelor level and master level of academic writing, which can also explain stu-dents' difficulties, in which case, both bachelor and master level programs may benefit from a broader application of writing within a culture and within the curriculum. Academic leaders can plan to develop a curriculum that can also address the gulf between bachelor and master level writing to bridge students' needs.

Declarative knowledge of substance suggests that the writer already possesses knowledge of the content and the meaning (Smith, Wilhelm, & Fredricksen, 2013). The student focuses on their opinion of the content versus a critique of the literature (Caffarella & Barnett, 1997). The content may be personalized using the first-person tense. If the student also understands the literary context, then the student can reason and write based on existing knowledge and abilities. This style of writing is notable in undergradu-ate studies (Sardiko, 2004). Scardamalia (as cited in Ondrusek, 2012) discussed knowledge-telling as a writing style for less experienced students because it rests on shared knowledge and personal feelings.

Procedural knowledge, on the other hand, shows how to put declarative thinking into practice (Smith, Wilhelm, & Fredricksen, 2013). Procedural reasoning at the sentence-level refers to the ability to con-struct complete and varied sentences (Smith, Wilhelm, & Fredricksen, 2013). Students can conceptual-ize complex writing based on the inclusion of theory from resources. Instructors who are sensitive to students' diverse ethnicities are more likely to assess their students' grasp of knowledge and facilitate pedagogy of how to complete tasks by focusing on writing content versus opinion (Waring & Evans, 2015). Oxford (2011) referred to the need for faculty to promote cultural understanding, self-knowledge, task comprehension, and multidimensional process that represents the individuals' interaction among cognitive-affective and social-cultural constructs within the context of the curriculum.

PEDAGOGY FOR ADVANCED WRITING

The pedagogy for advanced academic writing practices is rarely in evidence in the research literature about graduate programs (Belcher, 1994; Chittum & Bryant, 2014; Lou & Ma, 2012). Advanced academic writing is considered central to many graduate disciplines (Monrow, 2003), and the evaluation of advanced writing is an essential skill for faculty to possess (Ondrusek, 2012). The importance of writing at the tertiary level, decimating arguments, accrediting ideas, and the use of complex synthesis are traditional skills necessary for obtaining a master's degree (Hyland, 2007). Curriculum development for international students needs to be comparable with curriculum for citizens. Rather than the wider focus of teaching advanced writing within culture and within discipline, curriculum development may be relegated to a form of orientation for second language learners rather than leaders addressed the core system issues. Gal (2020) notes;

The internationalization of the curriculum should not be viewed only as something that supports internationalization in higher education. Instead, it is a contemporary approach to curriculum design that takes into consideration the multiple complexities of different contexts and encourages academic teams to reflect critically on curriculum development. (pp. 13-14)

WRITING PROFICIENCY INSIDE THE CURRICULUM

Baynham, Beck, Gordon, and Miguel (1995) discussed the need for faculty to comprehend and help the essay writer from within the written context of a particular discipline. Stoller, Horn, Grabe, and Robinson (2005) discussed the trend for a marriage between disciplines transforming into interdisciplinary contexts between two or more academic disciplines, which the authors say increases the challenge for the academic writer. Ball, Dice, and Bartholomae (1990) informed that a student not only has to learn to write but must also immerse themselves within the discourse for that specific discipline. According to Buzzi, Grimes, and Rolls (2012), writing across the curriculum and writing within the discipline have fallen into two categories. The faculty are either content to leave the writing to the writing experts or faculty want writing embedded within their courses. If English language tutorage is given precedence over advanced writing core competencies or seen as a similar concept; then, separate writing classes will be viewed as the gold standard to follow for advanced academic writing, which will delegate curriculum-based writing to the shadows (Gao, 2012; Webb, 2015).

International students writing within a different culture are often challenged to transfer language learning into discipline-specific learning; therefore, the two may remain cognitively separate. Troia, Lin, Cohen, and Monroe (2009) rationalize the scarcity of peer-reviewed evidence-based research literature specific to advanced essay practices on the difficulty of studying the conceptual abilities necessary for advanced essay writing practices. However, smaller studies are available where faculty anecdotally report personal use teaching techniques (Lee, 2014). Western education leaders recruiting and accepting international students into their graduate programs need the insight that students from Asia have an internal steady state based on being taught and learning in specific ways within their education system (Cigdem, 2017), which requires adjustment to the western education system.

WRITING PROFICIENCY WITHIN THE CULTURE

Cheng and Erben (2012) inform that graduate students often arrive with incomplete or wrong information regarding the Canadian education system and culture, which can quickly deter confidence and reduce the students' ability to communicate efficaciously. Kuo (2011) found that listening comprehension in-class lectures caused poor results for learners. The accent and rate of speech by faculty and other students can be problematic, suggesting faculty need to speak slower, explain unusual words, and announce clearly (Andrews, 2019). Alberts and Hazen's (2006) research found that some students express a feeling of alienation due to language skills in the classroom. Some graduate students reported difficulty understanding other cultures when in group activities (Andrews, 2019). Asian master students that enter Canada to attend graduate education must also be seen to be entering into a markedly different cross-cultural teaching system (Cheng & Erben, 2012).

The western higher education institution expects international students to be able to write intra-culturally immediately upon arrival and negates the student's previous learning. Students taught by their home educational system should not receive blame for the educational standards (Andrews, 2019). Students who have not been raised in or exposed to another education system and culture are not prepared to write interculturally and immediately acclimatize to new standards. Long-term habits, societal ethics, incorrect assumptions, little or no knowledge of western writing practices, and a collectivist practice that tends to ask each other rather than instructors, can all get in the way of international writers' success (Andrews, 2019). Schein (2010) reported a particularly important point that relates well to international students, that the "Human mind needs cognitive stability and any challenge of a basic assumption will release anxiety and defensiveness [for the student]. Many change programs fail for that very reason" (p. 24).

Montgomery (2013) informed that academic discourse is moving away from internationalization toward a global citizenry that highlights the need for the cultural competence of both domestic and international students in a rapidly globalizing society (Carr, 2011). Paradigms for the acquisition of cultural proficiency are throughout the globalization literature (Azevedo, 2015; Dietrich & Olson, 2010; Dimitrov, Dawson, Olsen, & Meadows, 2014; Hail, 2015; Lum, 2015; Sullivan & Kashubeck-West, 2015). Dietrich and Olson (2010) reported that to be considered culturally competent, a person needs to demonstrate comprehension of the economic and political interplay among global governments and organizations. An individual requires an understanding of world values, intercultural beliefs, local practices, and human rights (Dietrich & Olson, 2010). The individuals need to formulate critical cultural frames of reference to problem solve using four modes of learning; speaking (productive), listening (receptive), reading (receptive), and writing (productive) (Dietrich & Olson, 2010; Lum, 2015). Dietrich and Olson (2010) also informed that regardless of advancements in higher education, no consensus has been reached to articulate an exact cultural measurement of international education goals, attitudes, and knowledge.

WRITING CHALLENGES

The expertise required to teach advanced academic writing beyond learning English grammar, essay structure, and documenting sources necessitates a discussion of the criteria required to empower advanced international learners. Students stated that their perceived skill in undergraduate writing at the bachelor level was later discovered in graduate school to be much less than they had self-perceived (Andrews, 2019). Students expressed a severe lack of written feedback in Asia from faculty on bachelor writing, not detailing mistakes, possible corrections, skill level, or how the student may acquire writing growth; most students suggested a grade was the direct feedback (Andrews, 2019). Students suggested that verbally asking the professor for feedback may have been possible. However, many students were scared to ask their professors because of the perceived power of the professor in the Asia education system (Andrews, 2019).

Feedback through a letter grade minus possible corrections for logical flow, synthesis, and a discussion of structure fails to recognize students' needs to evolve advanced writing (Andrews, 2019). Detailed rubrics, highlighting errors, and written feedback all require significant time for faculty to grade assignments. An opportunity for a closer inspection of student's work uncovers attainment already present within the international student's writing style that may not be obvious at first glance due to cultural differences (Andrews, 2019). He or she may be an accomplished writer. However, the faculty's lack of experience with international writers and linguistic differences may result in blaming or shaming the student whose base knowledge does not fit the western ideology (Andrews, 2019). Higher education leadership must involve its' understanding of the gulf and build bridges between writing within another culture to promote intercultural writing competence (Institute for Education Planning, 2020), realizing that internationalization of the curriculum is not a narrow concept, such as teaching in English or supporting student mobility needs, but rather an opportunity to challenge existing knowledge paradigms and push the boundaries of the curriculum (Gal, 2020).

Asian writers report that their domestic schools generally did not address the need for intellectual property rights (Andrews, 2019). Western educators need awareness that Asian students' educational systems allowed students to copy and paste, use any source without citing, and did not strictly manage cheating, which may intuitively seem wrong by Western standards; however, these practices are grounded within another culture (Andrews, 2019). Moral arguments aside, students struggle to acculturate to western practices, but not because they are morally void. Students report preferring the Western system after indoctrination; however, change does take time (Andrews, 2019). Others may experience a challenge to transform from the cultural-education system they knew since birth, especially if they experience homesickness (Andrews, 2019).

CORE WRITING COMPETENCIES

Advanced academic writing needs to address the organization of information, argument style/logic, writing to the audience, content versus personal experience, the mechanics of grammar, the conceptualization of ideas, the pre-writing process, accuracy of formatting, scholarly identity, use of resources, expression, critique/peer review, previous experience, feeling uncertain, how to incorporate feedback, writing comprehension, and intercultural importance (Ondrusek, 2012). However, insight and identification are the first steps in the process of advancing academic knowledge. Students need to learn what they are doing wrong and how to correct it within the context of the discipline. According to Bucher (2012), special attention should be directed toward information literacy to enhance critical thinking because students who lack multifaceted skills in early life can be unable to discriminate between scholarly research and superfluous materials.

Collectivist Asian culture tends to envision the self as interdependent with others, potentially requiring more extensive hands-on writing instruction rather than the more individualistic style of knowledge attainment common in the West (Kim & Markus, 1999). Students from restrictive cultural backgrounds may experience the most duress trying to adjust philosophically to an independent model of thinking, learning, and academic content that goes beyond rote and punitive learning that actively discourages independent thinking (Ellis, 2009).

Ondrusek's (2012) literature review from 1981-2007 was reviewed (see Table 2) and compared to Andrews' (2019) core competencies literature review from 2010-2016 (see Table 3) to amass a best-practice list only primary research studies were included. A comparison between the two tables helps to substantiate graduate core writing competencies across time to determine the stability of recommended best-practices for advanced core writing competencies.

Table 2. Core competencies of advanced writing (1981-2007)

Core competencies	Peer-Reviewed Articles on Advanced Writing Skills								
	Bynum and Ferguson, 1981	Casanave and Hubbard, 1992	Koncel and Carney, 1992	Jones et al., 1995	Shaw, 1999	Caffarella and Barnett, 1997	Rose and McClafferty, 2001	Linder, Murphy, Wingenbach, and Kelsey, 2004	Lavell and Bushrow, 2007
1. Organization	X	X	X	X	X		X		
2. Argument / Evidence / Logic		X	X		X		X	X	
3. Audience / Voice					X		X	X	X
4. Content	X	X	X			X			
5. Mechanics / Grammar	X				X		X	X	
6. Conceptualization / Developing ideas / Pre-writing		X	X				X		
7. Process		X				X			X
8. Accuracy				X	X				X
9. Identity as Scholar							X	X	
10. Sources				X				X	
11. Expression	X	X							
12. Critique						X	X		

What the research reveals about graduate students, writing skills: A literature review (Ondrusek, 2012. Used with Permission).

Areas of commonality include the organization of information, argument style/logic, writing to the audience, content versus personal experience, the mechanics of grammar, the conceptualization of ideas, the pre-writing process, accuracy of formatting, identity as a scholar, use of resources, expression, critique/peer review, previous experience, feeling uncertain, how to incorporate feedback, writing comprehension, and intercultural importance.

Some institutions have been investing in and view writing centres as the holy grail. In part, because it is much easier to operationalize a centralized writing centre versus address the core issues that exist below the curriculum within departments. However, teaching language separate and apart from the class content is not enough to fill the gap for core competencies. Badenhorst et al. (2014) informed that successful writers need to (1) become discourse analysts; (2) develop authorial voice and identity, and (3)

Table 3. Core competencies of advanced writing (2010-2016)

Comparison to Ondrusek (2012)	Palmer (2016)	Lee (2014)	Huang (2010)	Lin & Scherz (2014)	Zhang (2011)
1. Organization					X
2. Argument / Logic	X				X
3. Audience / Voice				X	X
4. Content/Personal Experience	X	X	X	X	X
5. Mechanics / Grammar					X
6. Conceptualization / Developing ideas /	X		X	X	X
7. Pre or rewriting/Process	X	X	X	X	
8. Accuracy			X		
9. Identity as Scholar	X	X			
10. Sources/Resources		X	X	X	X
11. Expressions	X			X	X
12. Critique/ Peer Review /Group Discussion	X		X	X	X
13. Previous Experience	X	X	X		X
14. Feeling Uncertain/ Self-perception	X			X	X
15. Incorporating Feedback				X	
16. Writing Comprehension			X		
17. Intercultural Importance	X			X	
Origin of Study	Chinese in Canada	Korean In the US	Taiwanese in the US	Chinese in the US	Chinese in Canada

Advanced Writing for Asian Graduates in Canada and the United States: A Qualitative Case Study (Andrews, 2019. Used with permission).

acquire critical competence before becoming advanced writers. A challenge exists for academic higher education leaders to address the more difficult problem of writing embedded in the curriculum. According to Kellogg (2018), competency-based education must concentrate on what students understand and what students can achieve instead of the length of time it took to learn like the Carnegie credit model where students spend a required time in each course.

RECOMMENDED STRATEGIES FOR ADVANCED WRITING

Pre-Writing

Understanding of activities that surround pre-writing includes thinking, conceptualizing, and organizing concepts was not widely displayed by students who reported the use of fill-in-the-blanks type templates in the Asia education system (Andrews, 2019). Williams (2014) noted that significant time and effort are necessary for pre-writing activities. Huang (2014) named self-confidence, self-rated language, and perceived language proficiency as aspects that concern students about writing performance. The authors suggested that pedagogical changes may necessitate leadership to create environments that are more culturally and linguistically open to all students and empower faculty through increased time to prepare curriculum for classes (Lin & Scherz, 2014; OECD, 2013). Logan (2016) informed that an underlying challenge in the West was to educate international students by flipping the script to approach student interactions by learning from and about international students based on a non-centric Western standpoint instead of demanding written cultural conformity.

Drafting

Students described a lack of knowledge of how to approach drafting, editing, and writing to an audience in their written work (Andrews, 2019). International students were familiar with a list of bullets but lacked knowledge of how to advance the bullets into a draft (Andrews, 2019). Suggested writing activities are thesis statement, outline, and annotated bibliography to begin to develop goals and an argument structure based on pre-writing activities (Singleton Jackson, Lumsden, & Newson, 2009). The organization of ideas requires international students to develop a conceptual framework using a fair amount of new knowledge and ability (Palmer, 2016; Zhang & Zhang, 2013; Zhou & Zhang, 2014). Chen (2010) incorporated peer-peer feedback in her study at the draft stage. Chen (2010) found that peer to peer feedback tends to be cautious, and students were uncertain whether to believe the other student's comments. Kaur and Singh (2015) recommend that the student prepare multiple drafts with frequent feedback from faculty and recommend multiple revisions to achieve the final draft.

The ability to edit one's writing requires a redrafting loop; however, international students tend to focus on familiarity, rhetoric, and differences in linguistics rather than use unfamiliar methods (Gao, 2012), which can result in little to no editing. Horwitz (as cited in Huang, 2012) noted that an accuracy focus created a belief that students need to have absolute precision of language, which produced fear of failure in students. McMartin-Miller (2014) studied feedback provided to international students and reported pedagogical implications; students needed to know what and how instructors are marking their errors when using feedback; orally, written on assignments, and provide explanations of both styles within the course syllabus (McMartin-Miller, 2014). The consensus in intercultural research was that students needed direct and explicit instructions (e.g., grading rubrics, marking mistakes and comments on their essays) on how to edit their work (McMartin-Miller, 2014).

Resourcing Ideas

Students reported distress around the concept of plagiarism, and many feared expulsions. However, they did not have enough training to avoid issues, and the amount of time to adjust was reported longer than the graduate program (Andrews, 2019). Procedural knowledge of substantive writing relates to knowing what and how to retrieve information for evidence to support or craft an argument using the knowledge of context and purpose (Smith, Wilhelm, & Fredricksen, 2013). Many students were reporting using websites to search for information (Andrews, 2019). Graduate students not familiar with the western APA style of writing and documenting may struggle to connect research from peer-reviewed journal articles focused on best-practice with writing about their ideas (Abase & Graves, 2008).

Students are required to learn that academic writing requires a review of scholarly articles and not merely popular literature available on the Internet. The effort to connect ideas across many resources may create a burden for the international students who try to determine what is relevant and valid information

(Howard, Serviss, & Rodrique, 2010; Krol & Krol, 2012). Direct support must be given that teaches students how to validate research contents based on the originality of the article, academic credentials, the merit of the publisher, research funding, and adherence to methodological practices (Andrews, 2019).

Scaffolding Ideas

Students unfamiliarity with scaffolding techniques expressed interest in instruction that shows what and how to write synthesizing multiple texts into one essay (Nguyen, 2013). Smith, Wilhelm, and Fredricksen (2013) described the difference between procedural knowledge and declarative knowledge vis-à-vis form and substance in essay writing. A sentence-level of declarative style refers to the cognizance of the rules of grammar and how each of these rules may relate to each other in the academic writing of essays (Smith, Wilhelm, & Fredricksen, 2013). Lin and Scherz (2014) stated that faculty might be consciously unaware of linguistic and cultural differences, and therefore, not attempt to scaffold knowledge to advocate student success, thereby missing a learning opportunity to turn the classroom into a community of learning (Weiss, Visher, Weissman, & Wathington, 2015). Ibrahim and Nambiar's (2011) model includes how to plan, act, observe and reflect on writing using scaffolding through genre analysis directly with students.

Scaffolding techniques, direct and indirect, may include visual supports, online resources, group interaction, practical activities, explicit instruction, rubrics, and guided feedback (Ibrahim & Nambiar, 2011). Vygotsky (1978) described scaffolding as an interactive process of individuals sharing social and cultural communication to promote and enhance cognitive growth. Ohta (2000) confirmed that genre is the proficiency in a language and content knowledge that develops through interactions with faculty and peers, and rhetorical patterns include arguments, discourse, narrative, and exposition. Ibrahim and Nambiar's (2011) findings informed that many international students do not benefit from the professor's use of an indirect method of pedagogy. Students reported craving practical application of knowledge, which teaches individuals how to operationalize theory (Andrews, 2019). Ibrahim and Nambiar (2011) recommend that intercultural rhetoric (Connor, 2004) is needed to unite with genre analysis.

SIGNIFICANCE

This literature review collects information currently spread throughout multiple academic disciplines that focused on advanced core competencies for academic writing skills. The literature included journal articles that focus on advanced writing practices existing in communication, higher education, journalism, international studies, student mobility, global studies, policy, as well as educational leadership. The literature is brought together in this study to produce a cohesive whole that helps to build a knowledge base for future advanced academic writing researchers; academic literature is included from Asia, Canada, and the United States.

RECOMMENDATIONS

Students all have access to a cell phone and desire using it in the classroom to access academic websites, peer-reviewed journal articles, Microsoft Word documents, libraries, and all manner of scholarly pursuits (Chua, 2014). Njoku (2015) noted that cell phone technology can have a positive influence when facilitated by faculty and can be used for access to handouts, classroom discussions, note-taking, group work, and retrieval of resources that will help fulfil the student's desire to use technology.

Whether through a university's learning management system or a stand-alone program (e.g., *Drop-Box*), faculty can create a repository of pre-selected learning tools. It is recommended that the resources be uploaded weekly not to overwhelm the students. Each week faculty add resources to folders such as *PowerPoints*, links to articles on the world-wide-web, group work activities, or direct links to videos that augment the class lecture (Andrews, 2019). These resources are available both in-class and online and offer support to students who sometimes reported not being able to follow the class content (Andrews, 2019). In partnership with university librarians, tools also can be made available to students—two cautionary notes, first that each university's policy around copying and disseminating information tutorage needs to be available to faculty and students, and the second recommendation is that less is more. Do not overwhelm the international student with too much information (Andrews, 2019).

Many Asian students have not previously experienced academic groups and are lacking in the knowledge of group norms (Andrews, 2019). Students expressed initial fear of working with other cultural groups, displayed as avoidance or conflict, and worried grades would be affected by other students' performance (Andrews, 2019). It is recommended, based on student feedback, that groups should have a small writing activity every week and be given group time in class to bond and perform the activity (Andrews, 2019). Faculty can clarify directions, offer support by mentoring groups, and answer questions. In contrast, group members have the opportunity to develop writing and group skills that enhance international and academic experience (Njoku, 2015).

Faculty should resist the urge and students' initial complaints to group like students with like because it does not mimic real-world experience (Andrews, 2019). Students reported overcoming fears and reported successful outcomes when the weekly group method was used as part of class time (Andrews, 2019). Asian students described a tendency toward a cultural expression of blame and excuses, so faculty will need to mentor individual responsibility, especially when things go wrong (Andrews, 2019). Faculty are encouraged to select groups that consist of different ages, gender, nationalities, languages, religious backgrounds, races, and undergraduate degrees (Andrews, 2019). A class introduction can take place in the first class to facilitate faculty preparing groups for the second class or use a randomization computer tool. Faculty mentorship of acceptance, tolerance, and sharing is necessary for successful verbal intercultural communication (Njoku, 2015).

CONCLUSION

This chapter aims to provide information to educate higher education practitioners, and leaders about the needs and challenges for international students' advanced academic writing and to postulate examples of remediation. The higher education field must hear the call of Millennials from all countries demanding quality education (Andrews, 2019). Higher education leaders need to accept the responsibility for the past cost savings of contract employees and move this part of the system to a practitioner-educator model in the classroom to provide an opportunity to develop culturally advanced curriculum practices (Andrews, 2019). Education leaders must take up the challenge to improve conformity of practice, to better fund curriculum development, to better train new faculty, and to evolve evaluation programs that enhance educational practices using a positive framework for growth (McFadden, Maahs-Fladung, & Mallet, 2012). To do otherwise, risks limiting future recruitment and graduating international students not ready for the marketplace. Sixty-six percent of students state that they would remain in Canada if good work were available (CBIE, 2019). The Canadian education system must take ownership that it is preparing students for the western marketplace; unlike the past, many students do not plan to return home after their studies. As future permanent residents and citizens, our education system must assist students in becoming productive members of society.

REFERENCES

Abase, A. R., & Graves, B. (2008). Academic literacy and plagiarism: Conversations with international graduate students and disciplinary professors. *Journal of English for Academic Purposes, 7*(4), 221–233. doi:10.1016/j.jeap.2008.10.010

Alberts, H., & Hazen, H. (2006). Visitors or immigrants: International students in the United States. *Population Space and Place, 12*(3), 201–216. doi:10.1002/psp.409

Andrews, D. J. (2019). *Advanced writing for Asian graduates in Canada and the United States: A qualitative case study.* Available from Dissertations & Theses @ University of Phoenix. ProQuest Central. ProQuest Dissertations & Theses Global. (2243910750). Retrieved from https://search.proquest.com/docview/2243910750?accountid=35812

Ariza, E. N. (2010). *Not for ESOL teachers: What every classroom needs to know about the linguistically, culturally, and ethnically diverse students* (2nd ed.). Allyn & Bacon.

Azevedo, A., Hurst, D., & Dwyer, R. (2015). Competency-based training program for international students. *International Business Research, 8*(3), 11-28. doi:10.5539/irb.v8n3p11

Badenhorst, C., Moloney, C., Rosales, J., Dyer, J., & Ru, L. (2014). Beyond deficit: Graduate student research writing pedagogies. *Teaching in Higher Education, 20*(1), 1–11. doi:10.1080/13562517.2014.945160

Ball, C., Dice, L., & Bartholomae, D. (1990). Developing discourse in adolescence and adulthood. In R. Beach & S. Hynds (Eds.), *Advances in Discourse Processes, 39.* Ablex.

Basen, I. (2014). *Most university undergraduates now taught by poorly paid part-timers.* Retrieved from https://www.cbc.ca/news/canada/most-university-undergrads-now-taught-by-poorly-paid-part-timers-1.2756024

Baynham, M. D., Beck, K., Gordon, A. L., & Miguel, C. S. (1995). Constructing a discourse position: Quoting, referring and attribution in academic writing. In K. Chanock (Ed.), *Integrating the teaching of academic discourse into courses in the disciplines. Proceedings of the conference.* La Trobe University.

Belcher, D. (1994). The apprenticeship approach to advanced academic literacy: Graduate students and their mentors. *English for Specific Purposes, 13*(1), 23–34. doi:10.1016/0889-4906(94)90022-1

British Columbia Education Quality Assurance. (2018). *Policy and procedures manual.* Retrieved from https://www2.gov.bc.ca/assets/gov/education/post-secondary-education/institution-resources-administration/eqa/eqa-policy-and-procedures-manual.pdf

Bucher, K. (2012). The importance of information literacy skills in the middle school curriculum. *The Clearing House: A Journal of Educational Strategies, Issues and Ideas*, *73*(4), 217–221. http://www.jstor.org/stable/30189549. doi:10.1080/00098650009600955

Buzzi, O., Grimes, S., & Rolls, A. (2012). Posts of departure: Writing for the discipline in the discipline. *Teaching in Higher Education*, *17*(4), 479–484. doi:10.1080/13562517.2012.711932

Caffarella, R. S., & Barnett, B. G. (1997). Teaching doctoral students to become scholarly writers: The importance of giving and receiving critiques. *Studies in Higher Education*, *25*(1), 38–52. doi:10.1080/030750700116000

Canadian Bureau for International Education. (2020). *International students in Canada*. Retrieved from https://cbie.ca/infographic/

Canadian Bureau for International Education (CBIE). (2019). *Annual report*. Retrieved from https://cbie.ca/who-we-are/annual-report/

Cantwell, B. (2015). Are international students cash cows: Examining the relationship between new international undergraduate enrollments and institutional reviews at public colleges and universities in the US. *Journal of International Students*, *5*(4), 512–525.

Carr, S. C. (2011). A global community psychology of mobility. *Intervención Psicosocial*, *20*(3), 319–325. doi:10.5093/in2011v20n3a8

Chen, C. Y. (2010). Graduate students' self-reported perspectives regarding peer feedback and feedback from writing consultants. *Asia Pacific Education Review*, *11*(2), 151–158. doi:10.100712564-010-9081-5

Cheng, R., & Erben, A. (2012). Language anxiety: Experiences of Chinese graduate students at US higher institutions. *Journal of Studies in International Education*, *16*(5), 477–497. doi:10.1177/1028315311421841

Chittum, J. R., & Bryant, L. H. (2014). Reviewing to learn: Graduate student participation in the professional peer-review process to improve academic writing skills. *International Journal of Teaching and Learning in Higher Education*, *26*(3), 473-484. Retrieved from http://www.isetl.org/ijtlhe/

Chua, A. Y. K. (2014). Expectations, dispositions, and experiences of international graduate students. Handbook of Research on Education and Technology in a Changing Society. doi:10.4018/978-1-4666-6046-5

Cigdem, H. N. (2017). *Former English language learners: A case study of the perceived influence of developmental English programs on academic achievement and retention*. Retrieved from https://search.proquest.com/docview/1896654315

Connor, U. (2004). Intercultural rhetoric research: Beyond texts. *Journal of English for Academic Purposes*, *3*(4), 291–304. doi:10.1016/j.jeap.2004.07.003

Dietrich, J. W., & Olson, C. (2010). In quest of meaningful assessment of international learning: The development and implementation of a student survey and e-portfolio. *The Journal of General Education*, *59*(3), 143–158. https://muse.jhu.edu/. doi:10.1353/jge.2010.0015

Dimitrov, N., Dawson, D. L., Olsen, K. C., & Meadows, K. N. (2014). Developing the intercultural competence of graduate students. *Canadian Journal of Higher Education, 44*(3), 86–103. https://www.tru.ca/__.../Nanda_Dimitrov_Developing_Intercultural_Co

Doran, L. M. (2017). *A case study of adjunct faculty: Community and collegial support.* Available from Dissertations & Theses @ University of Phoenix; ProQuest Central; ProQuest Dissertations & Theses Global. (2019629158). Retrieved from https://search.proquest.com/docview/2019629158?accountid=35812

Easley, J., & Tulowitzki, P. (2013). Policy formation of intercultural and globally minded educational leadership preparation. *International Journal of Education, 27*(7), 744–761. doi:10.1108/IJEM-04-2012-0050

Ellis, R. (2009). Measuring implicit and explicit knowledge of a second language. In R. Ellis, S. Loewen, C. Elder, R. Erlam, J. Philp, & H. Reinders (Eds.), *Implicit and explicit Knowledge in second language learning, testing and teaching* (pp. 31–64). Multilingual Matters. doi:10.21832/9781847691767-004

Gal, A. M. (2020, January 18). The road less travelled to the internationalisation of HE. *University World News, 581.* Retrieved from https://www.universityworldnews.com/post.php?story=2020011308103575

Gao, L. (2012). Investigating ESL graduate students' intercultural experiences of academic English writing: A first-person narration of a streamlined qualitative study process. *Qualitative Report, 17*(24), 1–25. http://www.nova.edu/ssss/QR/QR17/gao.pdf

Gavan, P., Watson, L., & Kenny, N. (2014). Teaching critical reflection to graduate students. *Collected Essays on Learning and Teaching, 7*(1), 56-61. Retrieved from www.gavan.ca/wp-content/uploads/2014/01/Academic-Vitae.pdf

Ghazarian, P. G. (2014). Actual vs. ideal attraction: Trends in the mobility of Korean international students. *Journal of International Studies, 4*(1). https://jistudents.org/fall2014vol41/

Goodboy, A., Martin, M., & Johnson, Z. (2015). The relationships between workplace bullying by graduate faculty with graduate Students: Burnout and organizational citizenship behaviours. *Communication Research Reports, 32*(3), 272–280. doi:10.1080/08824096.2015.1052904

Government of Canada. (2020a). *Immigration and citizenship.* Retrieved from https://www.canada.ca/en/immigration-refugees-citizenship/services/study-canada/work/work- off-campus.html#hours

Government of Canada. (2020b). *Immigration and citizenship.* Retrieved from https://www.canada.ca/en/immigration-refugees-citizenship/news/notices/pgwpp-rules- covid19.html

Green, M. F. (2014). The best in the world: Not in internationalization. *Trends & Insights: For International Education Leaders.* Retrieved from http://www.nafsa.org/Explore_International_Education /Trends/TI/The_Best_in_the_World_Not_in_Internationalization/

Hail, H. C. (2015). Patriotism abroad: Overseas Chinese students' encounters with criticisms of China. *Journal of Studies in International Education, 19*(4), 311–326. doi:10.1177/1028315314567175

Hegarty, N. (2014). Where we are now – the presence and importance of international students to universities in the United States. *Journal of International Students, 4*(3). https://jistudents.org/2014-volume-43/

Hosny, M., & Fatima, S. (2014). Attitude of students towards cheating and plagiarism: University case study. *Journal of Applied Sciences (Faisalabad)*, *14*(8), 748–757. doi:10.3923/jas.2014.748.757

Howard, R. M., Serviss, T., & Rodrique, K. (2010). Writing from sources, writing from sentences. *Writing & Pedagogy*, *2*(2), 177–192. doi:10.1558/wap.v2i2.177

Huang, T. (2012). Motivation-orientated teaching model for certification education. *International Education Studies*, *6*(2). Advance online publication. doi:10.5539/ies.v6n2p84

Huang, Y. (2014). Taiwanese graduate students' personal experiences on culturally related language anxiety and adjustment. *Journal of Educational and Developmental Psychology*, *4*(1), 258–271. doi:10.5539/jedp.v4n1p258

Hyland, K. (2007). Genre pedagogy: Language, literacy, and L2 writing instruction. *Journal of Second Language Writing*, *16*(3), 148–164. doi:10.1016/j.jslw.2007.07.005

Ibrahim, N., & Nambiar, R. (2011). Writing in foreign lands: The case of postgraduate international students and the introductory sections of a project paper. *Procedia: Social and Behavioral Sciences*, *18*, 626–632. doi:10.1016/j.sbspro.2011.05.092

Institute of International Education (IIE). (2019). *Open door report: Enrollment.* Retrieved from https://www.iie.org/Research-and- Insights/Open-Doors/Data/International-Students/Enrollment

International Institute for Educational Planning. (2020). *Effective and appropriate pedagogy*. Retrieved from https://learningportal.iiep.unesco.org/en/issue-briefs/improve- learning/teachers-and-pedagogy/effective-and-appropriate-pedagogy

Kaur, M., & Singh, M. (2015). International graduate students' academic writing practices in Malaysia: Challenges and solutions. *Journal of International Studies*, *5*(1), 12–22. https://jistudents.org/

Kellogg, S. E. (2018). *Competency-based education: Best practices and implication strategies for institutions of higher education.* Retrieved from https://digitalcommons.csp.edu/edd/3

Kim, H. S., & Markus, H. R. (1999). Deviance or uniqueness, harmony or conformity? A cultural analysis. *Journal of Personality and Social Psychology*, *77*(4), 785–800. doi:10.1037/0022-3514.77.4.785

Knowlton, M., & Collins, S. B. (2017). Foreign-educated graduate nursing students and plagiarism. *The Journal of Nursing Education*, *56*(4), 211–214. doi:10.3928/01484834-20170323-04 PMID:28383744

Krol, E. S., & Krol, L. M. (2012). Referencing and citation for graduate students: Gain without pain. *Collected Essays on Learning and Teaching (CELT)*, *5*, 64-68. Retrieved from http://webcache.google-usercontent.com/search?q=cache:6xVvkn9FwsgJ:celt.uwindsor.ca /ojs/leddy/index.php/CELT/article/view/3403+&cd=1&hl=en&ct=clnk&gl=ca

Kuo, Y. (2011). Language challenges faced by international graduate students in the United States. *Journal of International Studies*, *1*(2), 38–42. http://jistudents.org

Lax, J. (2002). Academic writing for international graduate students. *Frontiers in Education*, *32*(2), 8–12. doi:10.1109/FIE.2002.1158212

Lee, J. (2014). Experiences of intensive English learners: Motivations, imagined communities, and identities. *English Language Teaching*, *7*(11). Advance online publication. doi:10.5539/elt.v7n11p28

Lin, S., & Scherz, S. D. (2014). Challenges facing Asian international graduate students in the US: Pedagogical considerations in higher education. *Journal of International Students*, *4*(1), 16–33. https://jistudents.org/

Logan, S. W. (2016). Where in the world is the writing program: Administering writing in global contexts. *College English*, *78*(3), 290–297. http://www.ncte.org/library/NCTEFiles/Resources/Journals/CE/0783 jan2016/CE0783Review.pdf

Lopez, I. Y., & Bui, N. H. (2014). Acculturation and linguistic factors on international students. self-esteem and language confidence. *Journal of International Students*, *4*(4), 314–329.

Lou, X., & Ma, G. (2012). Comparison of productive vocabulary in Chinese and American advanced English academic writings. *Theory and Practice in Language Studies*, *2*(6), 1153–1159. doi:10.4304/tpls.2.6.1153-1159

Lu, A. (2013). A functional grammar approach to analyzing Asian student's writing. *American Journal of Educational Research*, *1*(2), 49–57. doi:10.12691/education-1-2-3

Martirosyan, N. M., Hwang, E., & Wanjohi, R. (2015). Impact of English proficiency on performance of international students. *Journal of International Students*, *5*(1), 60–71.

McFadden, C., Maahs-Fladung, C., & Mallett, W. (2012). Recruiting international students to your campus. [Retrieved from]. *Journal of International Students*, *2*(2), 157–167.

McKeen, A. (2018, November 1). Majority of Canadian university appointments now precarious gigs. *The Star Vancouver*. Retrieved from https://www.thestar.com/vancouver/2018/11/01/majority-of-canadian-universityappointments-now-precarious-gigs.html

McMartin-Miller, C. (2014). How much feedback is enough: Instructor practices and students' attitudes toward error treatment in second language. *Assessing Writing*, *19*, 24–35. doi:10.1016/j.asw.2013.11.003

Mohamedbhai, G. (2017, Nov. 3). The changing landscape of private higher education. *Inside Higher Ed*. Retrieved from https://www.universityworldnews.com/post.php?story=2017103110332862

Monroe, J. (2003). Writing and the disciplines - In peer review, Fall 2003, 4-7. *An Association of American Colleges and Universities Publication*. Retrieved from https://www.aacu.org/publications

Montgomery, C. (2013). International students and higher education: New perspectives on cultures and communities. *Journal of International Students*, *3*(2). https://jistudents.org/

Na, J., Kosinski, M., & Stillwell, D. J. (2015). When a new tool is introduced in different cultural contexts: Individualism-collectivism and social network on Facebook. *Journal of Cross-Cultural Psychology*, *46*(3), 355–370. doi:10.1177/0022022114563932

National Center for Education Statistics (NCES). (2015). *Digest of education statistics: Outcomes of education*. Retrieved from http://nces.ed.gov

Ngo, M. N. (2016). Eliminating plagiarism in programming courses through assessment design. *International Journal of Information and Education Technology (IJIET), 6*(11), 873–880. doi:10.7763/IJIET.2016.V6.808

Njoku, C. P. U. (2015). Information and communication technologies to raise quality of teaching and learning in higher education institutions. *International Journal of Education and Development Using Information and Communication Technology, 11*(1), 122–147. https://www.learntechlib.org/p/151050

OECD. (2013). Executive summary. In *Leadership for 21st-century learning*. OECD Publishing. doi:10.1787/9789264205406-

Ohta, A. S. (2000). Rethinking interaction in SLA: Developmentally appropriate assistance in the zone of proximal development and the acquisition of L2 grammar. In J. P. Lantolf (Ed.), *Sociocultural theory and second language learning* (pp. 51–78). Oxford University Press.

Ondrusek, A. L. (2012). What the research reveals about graduate students; writing skills: A literature review. *Journal of Education for Library and Information Science, 53*(3), 176–188. http://www.jstor.org/stable/23249110

Ortiz, A., Chang, L., & Fang, Y. (2015). International student mobility trends 2015: An economic perspective. *WES Research & Advisory Services.* Retrieved from http://wenr.wes.org/2015/02/international-student-mobility-trends-2015-an-economic-perspective/

Oxford, R. L. (2011). *Teaching and researching language learning strategies*. Pearson Longman.

Palmer, Y. M. (2016). Student to scholar: Learning experiences of international students. *Journal of International Students, 6*(1), 216–240. https://jistudents.org/

Qi, L. (2015, May 29). US schools expelled 8,000 Chinese students. *The Wall Street Journal*. Retrieved from http://blogs.wsj.com/chinarealtime/2015/05/29/u-s-schools-expelled 8000-Chinese-students-for-poor-grades-cheating/tab/comments/

Rahimi, M., & Goli, A. (2016). English learning achievement and EFL learner's cheating attitudes and cheating behaviours. *International Education Studies, 9*(2), 81–88. doi:10.5539/ies.v9n2p81

Ramzan, M., Munir, M. A., Siddique, N., & Asif, M. (2012). Awareness about plagiarism amongst university students in Pakistan. *Higher Education, 64*(1), 73–84. doi:10.100710734-011-9481-4

Rawlings, M., & Sue, E. (2013). Preparedness of Chinese students for American culture and communicating in English. *Journal of International Students, 3*(1), 29–40. https://search.proquest.com/docview/1355441919?accountid=458

Redden, E. (2014). Teaching international students. *Inside Higher Education*. Retrieved from https://www.insidehighered.com/news/2014/12/01/increasing-international-enrollments-faculty-grapple-implications-classroom

Santos, T. (1988). Professors' reactions to the academic writing of nonnative-speaking students. *TESOL Quarterly, 22*(1), 69–90. doi:10.2307/3587062

Sardiko, L. (2004). *Guidelines on writing a term paper, a bachelor paper, a master paper*. Daugavpils, Latvija: Daugavpils University. Retrieved from https://du.lv/en/

Schein, E. H. (2010). *Organizational culture and leadership* (4th ed.). Jossey-Bass.

Schilmann, P., & Choudaha, R. (2014). *International student retention and success: A comparative perspective*. Retrieved from http://wenr.wes.org/2014/09/international student-retention-and-success-a-comparative-perspective/

Scoggin, D., & Styron, R. (2006). Factors associated with student withdrawals from community college. *The Community College Enterprise, 12*, 111-25. Retrieved from www.schoolcraft.edu/pdfs/cce/12.1.111-124.pdf

Singleton-Jackson, J., Lumsden, D. B., & Newson, R. (2009). Johnny still can't write, even if he goes to college: A study of writing proficiency in higher education graduate students. *Current Issues in Education (Tempe, Ariz.), 12*(10). https://cie.asu.edu/ojs/index.php/cieatasu/article/view/45/9

Smith, M. W., Wilelm, J. D., & Fredricksen, J. (2013). The common core: New standards, new teaching. *Phi Delta Kappan, 94*(8), 45–48. doi:10.1177/003172171309400811

Stoller, F., Horn, B., Grabe, W., & Robinson, M. S. (2005). Creating and validating assessment instruments for a discipline-specific writing course: An interdisciplinary approach. *Journal of Applied Linguistics, 2*(1), 75–104. doi:10.1558/japl.v2i1.75

Sullivan, C., & Kashubeck-West, S. (2015). The interplay of international students' acculturative stress, social support, and acculturation modes. *Journal of International Studies, 5*(1), 1–11. https://jistudents.org/

The Pie News. (2019). *Canada: BC Institutions post $340m surpluses*. Retrieved from https://thepienews.com/news/british-columbia-post-340m-surpluses

Troia, G. A., & Olinghouse, N. (2013). The common core standards and evidence-based educational practices: The case of writing. *School Psychology Review, 42*(3), 343–357. https://www.researchgate.net/.../258148583_The_Common_Core_State

Vygotsky, L. S. (1978). *Mind in society: The development of higher psychological processes. Cambridge.* Harvard University Press.

Wadhwa, R. (2016). Understanding decision-making and process and destination choice of Indian students. *Higher Education Council, 3*(1), 54–75. doi:10.1177/2347631115610221

Wang, Y. (2014). A survey of postgraduates' state of language learning at graduate school, Chinese academy of social science. *Theory and Practice in Language Studies, 4*(1), 160–166. doi:10.4304/tpls.4.1.160-166

Waring, M., & Evans, C. (2015). *Understanding pedagogy: Developing a critical approach to teaching and learning*. Routledge.

Webb, A. S., Wong, T. J., & Hubball, H. T. (2013). Professional development for adjunct teaching faculty in a research-intensive university: Engagement in scholarly approaches to teaching and learning. *International Journal of Teaching and Learning in Higher Education, 25*(2), 231-238. Retrieved from http://www.isetl.org/ijtlhe

Webb, R. K. (2015). Teaching English writing for a global context: An examination of NS, ESL, EFL learning strategies that work, *PASAA Journal – Chulalongkorn University Language Institute, 49*, 171-198. Retrieved from http://www.culi.chula.ac.th/publicationsonline/home_p1.php

Weiss, M. J., Visher, M. G., Weissman, V., & Wathington, H. (2015). The impact of learning community for students in developmental education: A synthesis of findings from randomized trails at six community colleges. *Educational Evaluation and Policy Analysis, 37*(4), 520–541. doi:10.3102/0162373714563307

Wermund, B. (2018, April 23). *Trump blamed as US colleges lure fewer foreign students.* Retrieved from https://www.politico.com/story/2018/04/23/foreign-students-colleges-trump-544717

Williams, J. D. (2014). *Preparing to teach writing: Research, theory and practice.* Routledge. doi:10.4324/9780203082683

Wu, H., Garza, E., & Guzman, N. (2015). International student's challenge and adjustment to college. *Education Research International*, 3-9. doi. doi:10.1155/2015/202753

Yang, B. (2014). Using non-finites in English academic writing by Chinese EFL students. *English Language Teaching, 7*(2), 42–52. doi:10.5539/elt.v7n2p42

Yang, K., & Chung, S. H. (2015). Key factors for developing a cross-cultural education program. *International Journal of Educational Management, 29*(2), 222–233. doi:10.1108/IJEM-12-2013-0177

Zhang, Z. (2008). *Finding the critical edge: Helping Chinese students achieve optimal development in academic writing* [Unpublished Master Thesis]. Retrieved from The University of Western Ontario, London, ON, Canada.

Zhang, Z., & Zhang, W. (2013). I am not what you thought I should be: Learning accounts of Chinese international students. *The International Journal of Social Sciences (Islamabad), 3*(6), 576–581. doi:10.7763/IJSSH.2013.V3.306

Zhao, C., Kuh, G. D., & Carini, R. M. (2005). A comparison of international student and American student engagement in effective educational practices. *The Journal of Higher Education, 76*(2), 209–231. doi:10.1353/jhe.2005.0018

Zhou, G., & Zhang, Z. (2014). A study of the first year international students at a Canadian university: Challenges and experiences with social integration. *Canadian and International Education. Education Canadienne et Internationale, 43*(2), 1–17. http://search.proquest.com.contentproxy.phoenix.edu/docview/1566312980/fulltext/4FCF 3CF7E58443E7PQ/8?accountid=458

Zhu, W., & Flaitz, J. (2005). Using focus group methodology to understand international students' academic language needs: A comparison of perspectives. *Teaching English as a Second or Foreign Language, 8*(4), 1–11. Retrieved from http://tesl-ej.org/ej32/a3.html

KEY TERMS AND DEFINITIONS

Advanced Academic Essay Writing: Refers to the ability to structure and write an essay at the master level in any academic discipline, usually following APA standards.

Asian: The whole Asian continent; North Asia, East Asia, Central Asia, Middle Asia, and Southwest Asia.

Core Competencies: The specific skills required to write academic essays that have been documented in primary research studies listed in the document.

English Speakers of Other Languages (ESOL): International graduate-level students. Their functional English meets entrance criteria. Many students also speak additional languages beyond their mother tongue. Hence, their abilities can be multilingual.

International Students: In this context, refer to graduate students who have travelled from the Asian continent to the North American continent and have already received their bachelor's degree in Asia.

Steady-State: An internal feeling of consistency between one's sense of identity, culture, values, and lived experience.

Writing Across the Discipline: Writing experts (e.g., writing centres) teaching writing skills generally and not specific to a subject matter, which can create a divorce between subject matter and write for advanced writers.

Writing Within the Discipline: Instructors teaching advanced academic writing within their subject knowledge, and writing is embedded within their course and discipline.

Chapter 11
International Turkish Student Experience in Canadian Higher Education

Aylin Çakıroğlu Çevik
https://orcid.org/0000-0003-0967-0169
TED University, Turkey

ABSTRACT

This study explores and discusses the experience of students from Turkey in Canadian higher education. It is known that international student experience is a complex and multidimensional issue and is influenced by various fixed or unfixed factors that vary at individual and national levels. Drawing on Jones's classification of international student experience (i.e., academic, pastoral/living, social experience) and the factors affecting these types of experience (i.e., personal, familial, institutional, and national milieus), the qualitative research method, namely in-depth interview, was used to acquire detailed knowledge about the issue by using the purposive sampling technique. The findings of this study basically indicate that personal, institutional, and national dimensions have a strong effect on the experience of international Turkish students in Canadian higher education.

INTRODUCTION

According to statistics reported by the Organization for Economic Co-operation and Development (OECD, 2019), the number of international students in higher education worldwide has greatly expanded in the past few decades, increasing from 2 million in 1998 to 5.3 million in 2017. Drawing on multidimensional factors related to the globalization of higher education, this massive international mobility has been addressed by different disciplines such as education, international relations, politics, economics, psychology, and sociology. The findings of previous studies in different disciplines point at numerous reasons for this international student flow/mobility which can be categorized from different perspectives as "push-pull factors" or "domestic-external factors." It is possible to state these factors in general terms as follows: increasing demand for highly skilled labour by knowledge-based and innovation-driven

DOI: 10.4018/978-1-7998-5030-4.ch011

economies across the world, insufficient capacity to meet this growing demand, getting a high-paid job, working permanently in the receiving/host country, employability in the globalized labour market, political and economic stability of countries, cultural differences and/or similarities between host and sending countries so forth (Abbott & Silles, 2016; Dreher & Poutvaara, 2005; Findlay et al., 2012; Perkins & Neumayer, 2014; UNESCO, 2013). It seems that every part of the international student mobility process (from the individual to the global world) offers different challenges and benefits in terms of human capital, integration, and socioeconomic development.

The general trend for international students is to study in English-speaking countries. According to official figures, more than 40% of all mobile students in the OECD and partner countries have been studying in the United States, the United Kingdom, Australia, and Canada in decreasing order of number of students (OECD, 2019). Besides linguistic and socioeconomic factors, Canada as an important receiving country is attractive to students for the opportunity to work during and after study (CBIE, 2018a; Lu et al., 2015) as well as to obtain permanent residency. For instance, approximately one-quarter of international students who arrived in the 1990s and 2000s became permanent residents within 10 years after their first study permit (Hou & Lu, 2017). Additionally, the number of registered international students in Canada has been gradually rising since 2014 (34%) (CBIE, 2018b). All these indicate that Canada plays an important role in international student mobility/flow processes across the world.

Canada's international student population in 2017 consisted of 494,524 registered students at all levels of study. These students are 28% from China, 25% from India, 5% from South Korea, 4% from France, 3% from the USA, 2% from Nigeria, 1% from Pakistan, 1% from Turkey, 1% from Hong Kong, 1% from Taiwan, and so forth (CBIE, 2018b). It is evident that Canada has a diverse international student population. Therefore, each study on these students coming from different countries would be valuable for candidates and Canada alike because of the heterogeneity of the international student population, which is expected to increase across the world in the next decades (Brown, 2004; Chapman, 1999; Lu & Hou, 2015). Overall, more research would be helpful in enhancing our understanding of some of difficulties students may face, such as language and adaptation problems, academic and financial difficulties, cultural challenges, and social exclusion (Sherry, Thomas, & Chui, 2010). Additionally, international student is too broad a conceptualization to understand students coming from diverse national, cultural, and social backgrounds (Hanassab, 2006). Due to the under-exploration of studies on any international minority group in Canada, studies about this group would be valuable to make both students and their experiences visible and give them a voice as well as foster inclusive policies. As a first step towards filling this gap in the literature, this exploratory study will focus on students coming from Turkey as one of the minority international groups.

This chapter, which consists of four parts, explores and discusses the experience of students from Turkey in Canadian higher education, specifically universities. In the first part, the theoretical framework of the experience of international students will be introduced. In the next part, the method and research process of the study will be defined. In this part, the design of the study, including sampling, data collection procedure, and limitations of the study, will be presented in detail. The third part will present the main findings and discussions based on the theoretical framework. In the last part, the findings and suggestions for further studies will be assessed.

THEORETICAL FRAMEWORK

Increasing globalization of higher education has led to new study interests as well as concerns on both individual and structural levels. As Mills (1959) argued, however, this phenomenon highlights the complexities of life and the interdependency of the individual (i.e. "private troubles") and structural (i.e. "public issues") levels. Furthermore, international student mobility has promoted various intersections between the sending and receiving countries, socioeconomic and sociodemographic factors. One of the fields in which intersections occur is the experience of international students in higher education. In this respect, Jones's (2017) categorization of international student experience can be used to study international Turkish students' experience in Canadian higher education.

According to Jones (2017), the international student experience consists of the academic, pastoral/living, and social dimensions, all which are related to each other. These three dimensions of experience are influenced by a wide range of interrelated factors. Jones classifies these factors into four milieus which address "the environmental factors arising from personal history, family context, institutional nature and country location of the study destination" (Jones, 2017, p. 936). She identifies these four milieus as follows:

Each of these has a role to play. The national context will frame language, education system, sociocultural and other environmental aspects, while institutional values, facilities, support and other services can provide a study environment which is more or less welcoming for students. Family context, history and experience will vary, with some having siblings or parents who have studied abroad setting the tone well before the student's arrival in the host country. Individual personality and other factors will also play a part in the student's overall experience. (p. 936)

Note that each milieu is very broad in scope. For this reason, Jones (2017) lists aspects of each milieu affecting the student experience in detail as in Table 1 below. It should be kept in mind that all aspects are interdependent. In addition, a wide range of variants in each section indicates the plurality of influences on international student experience and heterogeneity.

According to Jones (2017), personal and familial milieus given in the first and second columns are relatively stable and unchangeable in relation to factors such as age, gender, mother tongue, number of siblings, and socioeconomic background of the family. In other words, the personal and family dimensions are constant, compared to institutional and national dimensions. In this sense, the personal and family milieus including sociodemographic and socioeconomic background, level of study, disability, degree of freedom, networks and social capital, language, parents' prior experience abroad, expectation/pressure of family to succeed, contact with family, and so forth can be considered as the fundamental dimension of student experience.

Conversely, the institutional dimension given in the third column is subject to change. That is to say, this milieu including curriculum, learning culture, pedagogic approach, inclusivity, student clubs/unions, academic staff experience, support of staff, accommodation, food, scholarship and health policies, and so forth would be subject to change by institutions (i.e. as the concern of higher education management). Moreover, some aspects of this milieu may affect the choice of the student to study. For example, a student may choose one university which supports part-time work or has a low accommodation cost.

Finally, the national milieu given in the fourth column, including language, climate, visa requirements, opportunities to work and become permanent resident, security and health systems, educational

Table 1. Effect of personal, familial, institutional and national milieus on student academic, pastoral and social experience (not an exhaustive list)

	Personal	Familial	Institutional	National (Country of study)
Academic	Level of study – undergrad, postgrad research etc. Length of study: short-term vs part-time vs full degree or full-time Study discipline Prior study experience Awareness of/attitude towards any learning disability Awareness of regulatory environment	Expectations and pressure to succeed Prior parent/sibling study experience at home or abroad Desire for contact with the institution (may conflict with legal responsibility of institution	Language of instruction Academic and learning culture Curriculum relevance Inclusivity 'Enrolment intensity' – number of international students in total or those from the same country Academic staff experience Orientation and ongoing support provided	Equivalence of education system with home country Familiarity of education system Whether institutions are 'in loco parentis' (having the legal responsibility to take on some of the functions and responsibilities of a parent)
Pastoral/ living	Gender Language Ethnicity Religion Sexual orientation Personality factors and (inter)cultural capital Financial security/need to obtain paid work	Frequency and quality of contact Familiarity with study destination Extent of desire for parental involvement	Location – city or regional General support and responsiveness Accommodation policy Financial support Offer of work opportunities for students Access to Students' Union	Language Climate Visa requirements Post-study work visas and job opportunities Health system Food and restaurants
Social	Willingness to socialize Perception of personal safety Mental or physical health Friendship groups Degree of contact with friends at home Degree of freedom (real or perceived) Networks and social capital	Language Number of siblings in family Ethnicity Socio-economic background	Opportunities to socialise Availability of relevant clubs and societies Diversity on campus Degree of welcome and/or role models for students	Embracing of multiculturalism Degree of cultural inclusivity Degree of structural discrimination towards salient aspects of identity Familiarity with/attitude towards social support and authority (e.g. police, medical, etc.)

Source: Jones (2017, pp. 937-939)

system, cultural inclusivity, and so forth, is relatively fixed (Jones, 2017). Furthermore, all these aspects influence the choice of students. For example, a student may choose to study in a country that is ethnically diverse and welcoming as well as has a policy for granting permanent residence to international students after their graduation.

Regarding all these three main experience dimensions, namely academic, pastoral/living and social experiences, it can be clearly seen that the international student experience is a complex and multidimensional issue and is influenced by various fixed or unfixed factors that vary at individual and national levels. In other words, different combinations of the factors lead to different experiences that vary with individual personality as well as nationality of the international student.

METHOD

Research Design

In view of the aim of the study, the most appropriate way to collect data is the qualitative method. Semi-structured interview method which helps the researcher to acquire in-depth knowledge about the issue was used. Considering the target population and their accessibility, a purposive sampling technique, which is helpful to "get all possible cases that fit particular criteria" for "a difficult-to-reach specialized population" (Neuman, 2014, p. 169), was utilized to find and reach the participants of the study.

Procedure

Drawing on Jones's (2017) classification of experience, the semi-structured interview questions consisted of two parts. The first part was made up of questions on the sociodemographic and socioeconomic background of the respondents such as age, gender, parents' educational and occupational level, number of siblings, accommodation type, length of stay in Canada, field of study, university, and so forth. The second part of the interview, which included four open-ended questions, tried to capture students' academic, pastoral/living and social experiences. The questions were general at first. For instance, "How is your academic life in Canada? For example, lectures, peers, instructors, etc." Therefore, the respondents were allowed to freely express their own realities and experiences.

After determining the interview questions, ethical permission was taken from TED University Human Subjects Ethics Committee (HREC) to collect data as of December 12th, 2019. The students from Turkey were invited through an email sent to the Turkish student unions/associations of universities in Toronto, Vancouver, Montreal and Ottawa which are highly preferred by international students (CBIE, 2018b) and have high ratings among all universities (THE, 2019). This mailing was followed by two more email messages, one and three weeks later, to ensure that the invitation was received and seen and also to achieve a higher return rate. At first, a consent form was sent to those who volunteered. Upon respondents' approvals, interviews were conducted via either email or Skype as new generation online interview tools (Janghorban, Roudsari, & Taghipour, 2014). The respondents were assured of the confidentiality of their responses and identity, so the participants' profiles will not be given in detail.

To analyze the data, the illustrative method in qualitative analysis (Neuman, 2014, p. 489) was used because of having predetermined theoretical concepts and themes from Jones's classification for international students' experience. In this sense, 52 pages of interview transcripts were read in detail and classified based on the categorization of dimensions (i.e. academic, pastoral/living and social experiences) which is given in the Table 1 above. In this sense, as the first step of the analysis, a table of personal experiences was constructed for each participant in terms of each dimension which was specifically asked during the interviewing process in the form of open-ended questions. The cases were compared for similarities and differences.

Limitations of the Study

The main limitation of the study is that participants are mostly at the graduate level. Therefore, this study remains limited in representing the experience of students at the undergraduate level. Furthermore, this study had to be carried out from Turkey, and the time gaps in the academic calendar due to Christmas or the final exam period affected the number of students reached and the return rate negatively. Additionally, although there was an attempt to reach participants through the student unions of the universities where there is a large number of Turkish students, the low response rate may also call into question the relationship of students with the unions. Despite all these limitations, this study is still important by virtue of its aim to explore the experience of Turkish students in Canadian higher education.

Respondents

For this research study, ten students receiving education in Canada have been interviewed. These students are living in different cities of Canada and studying in different universities. General characteristics of the respondents in question can be summarized as follows:

For the study, seven female and three male students between ages 18-37 have been interviewed. These students are studying in five different universities in Toronto, Montreal, Vancouver, and Ottawa. The distribution of the students by universities is as follows: The University of British Columbia (three students), Concordia University (three students), McGill University (two students), Carleton University (one student), and University of Toronto (one student). Of these students who are majoring in social sciences, natural sciences or engineering, four are registered in undergraduate, two in master's and four in doctorate programs. One of these students is in her first year in Canada and has been living in Canada for only five months. All of the others have been studying in Canada for more than two years. Those who have been living the longest in Canada are in their fourth year. Thus, the time span of the examined student experience covers a range of 5 months-4 years.

The general information about the students' lives in Turkey and families is as follows: from a socio-economic standpoint, the students mainly belong to middle and lower class families. As a matter of fact, all of the graduate students were in Canada by virtue of the scholarships they receive while undergraduate students had not received a scholarship and all their expenses were covered by their families. The families in general supported the students' decision to study in Canada. The families of three graduate students did not like this idea much on grounds of distance and being apart, but they respected their children's decision and gave their support. In addition, communication with family is regular (once in two days on the average) by virtue of technological means (such as WhatsApp and Skype).

EXPERIENCES OF TURKISH STUDENTS

The findings of the current study, which depend on Jones's (2017) categorization of experience, are presented under three main headings. The statements of students themselves form a significant part of these in order to give in-depth information about their experience. Hence, the goal of "giving a voice," which is one of the principal aims of the study, is attempted through their own words.

Academic Experience of Students

Generally speaking, whether international or non-international, the academic experience of each student and their feelings and thoughts about the education system in relation to this experience is different (Jones, 2017). However, it is possible to infer a general trend from the imparted experiences. In this context, the following can be said about the academic experience of students in Canada.

First of all, as in almost every respect, the perspectives of undergraduate and graduate students on academic experience diverge considerably. That is to say, since undergraduate students do not have prior university experience in Turkey, they cannot make a comparison and accept almost any aspect of academic life as natural. Graduate students, however, compare academic life in Canada with that in Turkish universities and consequently they arrive at positive or negative judgements. For example, while undergraduate students give positive opinions about orientation programs, which are an important part of starting university and basically have the purpose of "introducing and informing" new students, the majority of graduate students expressed that they find these programs ineffectual. The general opinion of the students who find orientation programs ineffectual is that orientation is a process aimed at providing the order and continuity of the university system rather than giving something to students. That is to say, orientation is perceived as a "preliminary warning" process which underlines what students ought or ought not to do rather than making their life easier. Actually, these warnings are intended to make the students' life easier; however, students, especially graduate students, generally state that they felt confused and worried after the orientation process rather than informed and relieved. Nevertheless, there are also graduate students who give positive opinions about orientation programs. For example, a female student from Concordia University says the following about the orientation period together with campus life:

Orientation programs were very enjoyable and productive. I was surprised to find that the University has lots of different offices, facilities, and richness for students. I have plenty of opportunities to improve myself for free by attending workshops in dozens of different subjects each semester besides my academic life. The University offers free seminars in dozens of subjects from budget keeping to CV preparation, from Photoshop programming to healthy living.

The education system implemented in Canadian universities which relies on practice and team work rather than theory generally leaves a positive impression on students, and this impression even reaches the level of admiration in undergraduate students. Generally speaking, this educational approach which provides international students with the opportunity to acquire more information about the labour market and develop a social network is also one of the reasons Canada is preferred by international students (Hou & Lu, 2017). For instance, a female undergraduate student from The University of British Columbia conveys the following views about her academic experience concerning this matter:

In Turkey, there is a rote learning based educational system. You have to memorize many things to be able to answer the questions in exams. Here, however, memorizing is not necessary. What matters is how you approach the subject and what kind of a solution methodology you develop to solve the problem. Moreover, here we extensively do projects related to our lessons. These projects are geared towards production and our future professional life. We have courses that focus on projects only. Education in Turkey is not this developed in terms of projects; training is mostly at the theoretical level. The projects here improve me a lot; I can also turn my theoretical knowledge into practice. This way I feel more competent in my field. The laboratory facilities here are also more advanced, effective and in better condition than those in Turkey.

A female student from McGill University makes a general comparison between university lives in Canada and Turkey as follows:

The instructors are very helpful and friendly. There is no distance or stern attitude between instructors and students. [...] Additionally, in Turkey they place great emphasis on exams. In Canada, assignments, projects and presentations are more important than exams. They encourage you not to memorize something but to investigate and present it, to convince the group.

Graduate students who had studied in Turkish universities with curricular systems similar to those in Canada adapt to the academic system in Canada more easily. A female student from Concordia University makes the following assessment:

Language of instruction in the universities I had studied in Turkey was English. Not only their language but also their educational systems were similar to those in Canada. Because of this, I didn't feel much like an outsider in my university life. I didn't have difficulty in delivery of lectures or submission of assignments and projects. However, it is possible for most university students from Turkey to have such difficulties.

The greatest difficulty concerning academic life encountered by all respondents is with respect to language. This difficulty experienced probably by all international students is basically about English not being their mother tongue. Much as Turkish students who study here speak English due to their prior education experience, they do not have full command of this language because English is not their mother tongue. Although this causes a problem with the students' self-confidence, especially early on, this problem is surmounted substantially in time. For example, in the universities, a large number of students and instructors are not native speakers of English and this makes it easier for students to contact and understand each other. In this context, a female student from The University of British Columbia makes the following assessment:

There are instructors and students whose mother tongue is English. Active involvement in these instructors' lectures is very difficult for students in my situation. These instructors conduct the lesson mainly with students whose mother tongue is English because they have a different and much smoother communication channel among them. However, there are also instructors like us, whose mother tongue is not English. These instructors more readily empathize with international students like us and help us more. And we express ourselves more easily in these instructors' lectures.

The interviewed students generally give a positive opinion about thesis supervision, which is applicable especially to graduate students and is an important dimension of instructor-student relationship apart from courses. However, they convey that some of their friends have severe problems with their supervisors, if not themselves. In this context, they express that a general assessment such as "all are good or all are bad" that lumps all instructors and supervisors together cannot be made because there are very considerate and guiding instructors as well as totally indifferent ones. Yet, they express that instructors and supervisors are mostly considerate, supportive, and guiding individuals.

It can be noticed that the main personal factors that affect academic experience for respondents are level of study (undergraduate vs. graduate students) and prior university study experience in relation to that. For academic experience it can also be said that the institutional dimension is very influential and dominant: Factors of institutional dimension such as language of instruction in English, curricular structure, a project-and-practice-based learning culture (unlike Turkey), approaches of academic staff to native and non-native speakers of English, and orientation programs are noteworthy with regard to academic experience. While undergraduate students compare the educational system with the rote learning approach at the high school level and say that there is an enormous difference in between, graduate students express based on their prior experience that they had received a similar university education in a foreign language and that they therefore do not have difficulty in the academic sphere.

Pastoral/Living Experience of Students

Living in a foreign country definitely brings some difficulties in daily life. These difficulties are felt acutely especially early on, but they usually decrease in time as the person adapts to the environment and the circumstances (Gale & Parker, 2014). Turkish students in Canada also face various difficulties in their daily life as they come from a different sociocultural environment. These difficulties are mainly related to the students' entering into an environment in Canada that is different from the cultural environment and living conditions they are accustomed to in Turkey. Bourdieu and Passeron's (1977) concept *habitus* is critical in terms of differences in experience and the encountered difficulties. As a matter of fact, it can be observed that cultural differences and economic constraints underlie the encountered difficulties.

Depending on the statement of the respondents, these difficulties can be considered under four headings: high cost of living, rigidness of rules, problems with the health system, and harsh climate conditions. To these headings, difficulties related to the French language can be added, faced by students in the province of Québec, in which French is the official language and is used extensively in daily life.

All of the students interviewed express that living in Canada is very expensive in comparison to the living standards in Turkey. However, it should also be mentioned that many students say that in terms of cost of living, Canada is better than many other countries they could go to for education. In other words, Canada is an expensive country but is cheaper than many countries they could study in as international students. However, since high cost of living bears on every aspect of students' life from meeting their basic needs to their academic and social experiences, it is named as the foremost difficulty.

The Turkish students in this study are mostly scholarship holders. Graduate students in particular are on full scholarship. They pursue their education here with the help of various scholarships they receive from Canada or Turkey. However, they find these scholarships insufficient in general. They say that because of this, they have to work in extra jobs on and/or outside the campus. In this context, a male graduate student from Concordia University says the following about the high cost of living:

Life is very expensive in Canada. I live in Montreal though. Here it is much cheaper than cities like Toronto and Vancouver but still it's expensive. The scholarship I get is about 400 dollars below the minimum wage here. So, it is almost impossible to subsist on a scholarship only, you need to work extra jobs. As extra jobs, we graduate students can become teaching assistants or serve as proctors. But most of the time even these are not enough and we have to work outside the campus.

However, this student who lives in Montreal tells of the problems he has about French in relation to working outside the campus as follows:

Here the language of daily life is French. This is a tough situation for people like me who don't speak French well enough. At the university English is spoken, so no problem, but we have severe problems in the city, in daily life. Actually, the biggest difficulty is finding a job. If you don't speak French, working somewhere is very hard, nay not possible. While French-speaking students can easily find part-time jobs, we can't. Even if we find a job somehow, we can't work there for a long time or regularly since we don't speak French.

Students' thoughts about finding and working at a part-time job vary according to their personal experience as well as the city they live in. So, a female graduate student living in Vancouver says the following on this subject:

Students are permitted to work full-time on campus and part-time outside the campus. I served as a teaching assistant constantly except for the first semester. As for off-campus jobs, pizza and döner kebab shops owned by the Turks are widespread, Turkish students can easily work in those places.

Except for the high cost of living and necessity to work, economic problems of Turkish students in Canada seem to arise mostly from the accommodation problem–high accommodation cost. Students naturally stay at dormitories or off-campus houses. From the interviews conducted, it is understood that the number of dormitories is insufficient, and the existing dormitories are not very comfortable. As to residing in a house, it is difficult for students because of high rents. Moreover, while undergraduate students prefer to stay at dormitories especially in their first year, graduate students reside at houses as a necessity rather than preference. In this context, a female student, again from Concordia University, gives the following information about staying at a dormitory or a house:

Dormitory facilities for students are very limited. Generally students who are younger, who come from farther away and who have limited financial means stay at dormitories. However, the dormitories here are arrayed as apartments. I mean, students who stay here are responsible for all kinds of chores of the place, including cleaning. In Turkey, the management is always involved with everything, there are rules, there are regular inspections. Here, dormitories are much more flexible, nobody even thinks of obeying rules.

A female graduate student from The University of British Columbia who lives in Vancouver answers the question about accommodation as follows:

Accommodation is the BIGGEST problem. After Vancouver was publicized as the most livable city, there has been a great migration to here from the Far East. For this reason, in the city you can see people from all nationalities, Far East countries and India first and foremost. Far Eastern population is so dense that when you first arrive you ask, "Am I in Canada or China?" Since the city is squeezed between the ocean and mountains, it is not easy to expand it. So, living space is scarce.

Staying at a dormitory also has advantages and disadvantages for a student. In this context, an undergraduate student who is studying at Carleton University and staying at the dormitory tells about his dormitory experience as follows:

I'm staying at the dormitory. The dormitories of Carleton University are inside the campus; as far as I know, it's like that in other universities, too. I think the best thing about our dorm is this: The dorm is connected with other buildings of the school through underground tunnels. So, I can go to classes from the dorm without being exposed to the cold outside. Staying at the dormitory is also good for my budget because of low transportation costs. But there are also many problems at the dorms. The walls are too thin and you can't get rid of the noises from the rooms next door.

For Turkish students in Canada, the second daily life problem after the high cost of living is the rules they encounter in their daily life both in the university and the city and the strict enforcement of these rules. This situation being named by the students as a difficulty arises from the fact that in their country of origin rules can be bended to a certain extent. Not being able to continue this mentality and their habits they had in Turkey naturally in Canada creates some tension in these students. A male graduate student from Concordia University says the following about the rules, their application, and the pressure they cause:

Here the rules are very strict, no flexibility at all. If you violate a rule, you may face prosecution that may even lead to deportation. This is very troubling for students coming from countries like ours. You always feel the pressure "I should not make a mistake, or I may face serious problems."

A female graduate student, again from Concordia University, makes a comparison with Turkey and gives the following example about rules pertaining to daily life:

For example, you question your habit of crossing the street as a pedestrian and even change it. Because in Canada you can't cross the street at places where there is no crosswalk, and you can't cross if there is a traffic light and it's not green. People here have absolutely internalized these simple rules.

Another major problem faced by Turkish students in Canada concerns the health system. Perceptions of this as a problem also stem from the fact that Turkish students compare the circumstances in Canada with their experience in Turkey. The main issue students express about the health system is that it is very difficult to reach doctors in hospitals and appointments are made for months later. A female graduate student from Concordia University conveys her experience and thoughts about the health system in Canada as follows:

The health issue is one of Canada's biggest problems. You have to wait 7-8 hours to see a doctor even at the emergency service. They say you have to wait for months for an operation or an appointment with a specialist. I went to the emergency service twice; I waited for five hours in one of them, and eight in the other. Since I am a student, I can see a doctor in the University's health center after waiting for one or two hours. Of course this is a boon given this country's conditions. But to be honest, because of these problems in Canada's health sector, I have my medical examinations and get my prescriptions in Turkey where the health sector is much more advanced and in Canada I use the drugs I bring from Turkey.

Another difficulty Turkish students in Canada face in their daily life is the harsh climate conditions. Climate conditions in Canada, which is a country where winters are very cold and long, are very unusual for Turkish students. Of course this situation may vary according to the region or city the students live in. For example, a female undergraduate student who lives in Montreal and studies at McGill University says the following about the climate conditions:

This is a very cold city. Air temperature falls to as low as -30, -35 ^0C during winter. It is extremely cold. What is more, winter lasts too long. It snows for at least six months and everywhere is covered with snow. This is something I am not accustomed to in the least. The snow and cold become very depressing after a while. Because I don't want to go outside if I don't have to and I don't. I sometimes feel helpless because of this.

Contrary to the views of this student from Montreal, a female graduate student who lives in Vancouver compares the climate and geography of the city she lives in with those of Turkey as follows:

Here it resembles the Eastern Black Sea Region in Turkey; at one side is the ocean and at the other side are high mountains and forests. The city is very different from other cities in Canada in terms of climate. It's not cold in winter like other places in Canada and it almost never snows. So, I don't feel much different than in Turkey. The climate being like this made it easier for me to get used to life here.

Daily life of students in Canada is not always full of difficulties and problems of course. They certainly experience many positive things in their daily life as well. The most important positive information the students give about their daily life is that in general everybody treats each other with respect and tolerance in a multicultural social structure. For example, a female graduate student from Concordia University conveys her observations and experience about daily life in Montreal as follows:

Montreal is a multicultural, colourful and lively city. There are districts with different concepts. One district provides an environment where gay individuals live peacefully while another creates an environment where art buffs can make art even on the street. There are various parts of the city such as the city center, financial district, Chinatown, Italian quarter, hipster district, English language quarter, Jewish quarter or French quarter. But none of these differences cause any quarrels or disturbance. And that's the beauty of it. Dozens of different cultural elements existing peacefully side by side together and becoming a richness.

Another positive thing the students convey about their daily life is that people are generally kind and helpful. They attribute this to the fact that there is a dense immigrant population and that people who had faced or are facing similar problems naturally show solidarity. As can be seen, institutional and national dimensions effectively shape the pastoral/living experience of students. While geographical and cultural structure of the city lived in, accommodation policy, economic conditions such as scholarship and job opportunities are the most emphasized institutional dimension factors. Factors such as a language other than English being spoken in the city lived in, the climate of the country and flaws of the health system can be enumerated as the national dimension.

Social Experience of Students

Social experience of Turkish students in Canada has supporting and limiting aspects just like other kinds of experience. It should first be mentioned that social experience in particular may vary depending on many factors such as the city the students are living in, the university and department they are studying at, current level of education (undergraduate or graduate), age, and gender. Nevertheless, some generalizations can be made because there are common points.

A general picture can be drawn about the social experience of these students as follows: Undergraduate students can participate in social life actively because they have a denser course schedule and they attend lessons on a continuous basis. Graduate students are in a similar situation with undergraduate students during the course periods and can also participate in social life actively. However, if graduate students are in their thesis stage, they are cut off from social life to a great extent because of having to concentrate on their theses along with some other reasons. According to the information given by the graduate students interviewed, their social life is inhibited because of a number of principal reasons. These reasons can be enumerated as follows:

- The students are not financially well-off regarding the socioeconomic status of their families. The scholarship they receive is insufficient even to meet their basic needs. Accordingly, they have to work extra jobs and earn money. They stay away from social environments that require them to spend money because of both the scarcity of their scholarship and the necessity to work.
- Thesis preparation at the graduate level is an exhausting process that requires too much time and concentration. For this reason, graduate students must focus entirely on their theses after the course period. This requires staying at home to study and away from social environments.
- The circle of friends of the students here is mostly made up of international students from various countries like themselves. Everybody has a busy schedule including their own courses, assignments, projects, extra jobs on or off campus, thesis studies, etc. So, most of the time it is not possible to find a common free time in which more than one person can come together. When a student has free time, their friend does not or vice versa. This makes it difficult to come together in a social environment.
- Climate conditions are generally harsh. Winters are very long and cold. Students who are not accustomed to such heavy winter conditions in Turkey are reluctant to go out and join in social environments because of winter, alongside other reasons. Moreover, because of the difficulties of reaching the relevant doctor concerning the health system, they are not very eager to go out in order to be cautious against the risk of getting sick by staying outside in the cold weather for a long time.

Because of all these challenges/limitations, students have to accept their situation after a while and settle on a more introversive lifestyle. For instance, a male graduate student from Concordia University evaluates all these processes of his social experience and summarizes as follows:

As a doctoral student at his thesis stage in Montreal, I can say this: I don't feel as if I am living in Canada or Montreal but in a house in Montreal. I mean, I don't have anything to do with the outside and social life even if I want to.

Apart from their limitations in social life, the students express that the cities they live in have very active social life. For example, they say that Montreal is a lively city of culture and art, there are activities for all kinds of styles and personalities and anyone can participate in those activities.

In friendship relationships, which constitute a part of social life, although there are personal differences, they usually tend to prefer Turkish students or citizens of countries such as Iran which are culturally and geographically close to Turkey. In this context, a female graduate student studying at The

University of British Columbia gives the following information about the limitations on social life and choosing friends:

My friends at school and I all work hard and we can't spend too much time together except on special occasions. At school I eat lunch with my friends who work at the same laboratory or we go swimming in the school's pool after school. Apart from this, I spend time usually with my Turkish friends.

Of course not every Turkish student has their circle of friends made up of students from Turkey or cultures similar to Turks. This depends on the circumstances as well as that person's preferences. For example, a female graduate student from Concordia University states the following about her own social life as well as that of Canadians:

Here I have a multinational circle of friends. Most of my friends are Latin Americans or Western Europeans. It is not quite possible to get close to Canadians, Montrealers. Although they look warm and friendly, I think they have invisible walls. They don't get into close relationship with anyone, even among themselves. I mean this is a cultural thing. But the multiculturalism of the city makes you feel problems about this at the minimum level.

Canada is a country where there are many people from diverse cultures. This can be easily felt in the texture of the cities as well as university campuses. However, it is also possible that some faculties or departments, where there are a great number of students from certain countries, are dominated by the culture of those countries. In this context, a female graduate student, again from Concordia University, makes the following assessment about her own campus and the general profile of graduate students in Canada:

At the campus you feel the predominance of the nations from which there is the largest number of students. For example, in my faculty the ratio of students coming from India and Iran is 75%, maybe even more. Therefore, it is really difficult to meet Canadian or American students at the campus.

The most pleasing social experience for Turkish students in Canada is that a social environment has been created in which people from diverse countries and cultures respect others and live in harmony without marginalizing each other and feeling alienated or segregated. For example, a female undergraduate student from The University of British Columbia voices the following views:

In Canada I never felt alienated. People are very warm and tolerant. There is no segregation. An egalitarian perspective is dominant. I think the school has a share in this because there are always egalitarian activities at school.

A female graduate student from Concordia University expresses the following about safety, alienation, and segregation, which are major parts of social life:

In Canada I feel at least ten times safer than I did in Turkey. It is not a problem to be outside at late hours for any reason. For example, in Canada I can lock the cafe I work in at 23:30 by myself under the eyes of passers-by, put the key in my pocket and go to the metro by a ten minute walk through a park and go to my home safely. [...] In Canada sexual harassment is punished heavily, so nobody risks even disturbing a woman. And this makes me feel free and secure. [...]. I think the discrimination I face as a woman is the same as everywhere, of course less than that in Turkey. I can say that Canada is the place I felt least segregated because I see how all sorts of people can exist together in peace and happiness. [...] The most basic difference I experience in Canada is that people respect each other's differences. When they ask something about any of my differences only because they are curious about it, they first apologize timidly and ask later. This makes me feel comfortable while I answer politely.

All the information Turkish students convey about their social experience in Canada can be interpreted in general together with a description of Canada as follows: Canada, which hosts people from diverse cultures, is a country where people feel safe, and where there is a large number of immigrants or international students. Hence, the students believe that nobody feels alienated because everyone is like the majority in this respect, and nobody is segregated.

To sum up, while social experience is related to personal dimension factors such as gender, level of study, degree of freedom, and perceptions of safety, it can be said that institutional and national factors are at least as influential as personal factors. While opportunities to socialize at the university are important, Canadian politics supporting a multicultural environment, cultural inclusivity and the legislation they enforce to create this environment are major factors in the national dimension.

DISCUSSION AND CONCLUSION

This study aimed to explore and discuss the experience of international Turkish students in Canadian higher education informed by Jones's (2017) classification of experience. Drawing on the qualitative approach, semi-structured interviews were conducted with ten students, of which seven are females and three are males; and six are graduate students and four are undergraduate students. Therefore, the findings obtained represent predominately the experiences of graduate and female students.

It was observed that being a graduate or undergraduate student is a strong determining factor on all dimensions/parameters of the research. In other words, having prior university study experience or not is found to be a factor that makes a notable difference in academic experience and determines the interpretation of other types of experience and variables. This is due to the fact that graduate students have previously been undergraduate and/or graduate students in Turkey and have knowledge and experience about higher education. Additionally, graduate students have more experience than undergraduate students also in terms of social relationships and daily life, which are shaped by academic experience. Some of the comparisons that concern particularly the institutional milieu make student experience in Canada harder (i.e. "cultural shock" and adaptation problem because of values, interests, and customs) (Poyrazli et al., 2001; Zhou et al., 2008), and some make it easier. This finding is consistent with those from a study by Pelling (2000) on the cultural shock of international students in Canada. As stated, language, fear of contact, misunderstanding, and social-cultural differences are the factors of cultural shock. In this study, for example, similarities between the language of instruction in the universities they had previously studied in Turkey and are currently studying in Canada make it easier while differences in curriculum and pedagogical approaches make it harder.

Another important factor for academic experience is the institutional milieu ("institutional habitus" in Reay's (1998) words). It is well-known that receiving education in a language other than one's mother tongue and living in a multicultural social environment are difficult in many respects (Pelling, 2000; Windle et al., 2008, Wu, Garza, & Guzman, 2015). As Cheng, Myles, and Curtis (2004) found, for international students in Canada, although writing and speaking are difficult tasks in academic life, it can be compensated by class presentions and improved over time. For students from Turkey, even if they have a general grasp of English, they sometimes have difficulty because they are not well-acquainted with the cultural background as language is not just knowledge "learnt" from dictionaries and grammar books but also a cultural skill acquired through a process (i.e. cultural capital (Bourdieu & Passeron, 1977)). Furthermore, the academic culture as the part of the institutional habitus in Canada, whose approach based on practices, projects and assignments, is another important factor for experience of students from Turkey. This factor is also consistent with the study of Windle et al. (2008), which highlighted the differences of Chinese and Canadian education system. Moreover, in the universities, the academic staff attitudes and some sociodemographic characteristics such as not being native speaker of English, ethnicity and class ("teacher's habitus" in Kayaalp's (2014) words) play an important role in students' adaptation to academic environment and social life, as Schutz and Richards (2003) and Xu (2015) stated for international students in Canada.

Considering the pastoral/living experience of Turkish students in Canada, the main factor is the personal milieu such as having prior university study experience, accommodation type, working experience and economic resources. For instance, undergraduate students live in dormitories and graduate students live in houses both due to accommodation policies (for example, scarcity of dormitories) and personal preferences. Additionally, undergraduate students who have busier course schedules spend more time at the university and thus increase their academic and social experience. Moreover, graduate students usually study by means of scholarships they receive from various institutions in Canada or Turkey. As for undergraduate students, all the expenses of these students are covered by their families. As economic means is a factor that affects social life directly, undergraduate students have more opportunities for socializing. Furthermore, in the students' pastoral/living experience, factors relating to both institutional and national milieus as well as comparisons with Turkey are prominent. For example, there are difficulties concerning climate and the great number of rules in Canada. In addition, problems concerning the health system in Canada are among the difficulties most frequently pronounced by Turkish students. Another conclusion they reached via comparison with Turkey is that in Canada diverse cultures manage to live together in harmony.

It can be observed that many factors may affect students' social experience. Both preferences and the population in the region inhabited (faculty, campus, dormitory, home, etc.) are influential in forming a circle of friends or a social network. In this context, it is seen that Turkish students usually make friends with the Turks or students they feel culturally close to themselves such as the Iranian. However, some students personally prefer to form a multinational and multicultural circle of friends and social network. In addition, gender is also a major variable affecting social experience, such that female students express that they feel safer and freer in Canada, which is important for them. In addition, the most underlined institutional and national factor affecting social experience is the multicultural structure of Canada in general and its universities in particular and the non-segregating, egalitarian environment established within this multicultural structure. This social texture that supports a culture of solidarity constitutes a significant experience for Turkish students. While communal living enables students to live together with people they perceive as different, this approach also provides a perspective which makes them comprehend that there is not a "single dominant habitus" which excludes them and a "perception of themselves within the field" (Thomas, 2002, p. 436). This fact is outlined in the words of a respondent as: "because everyone is a foreigner."

To conclude, it is not easy to define students' academic, pastoral/living and social experiences as disconnected and clear-cut experience types. In other words, we have to talk about an integral "life space" or "dynamic experience" (Zhou et al., 2008, p. 65) affected by many interconnected fixed and unfixed factors. In brief, for these students going from Turkey to Canada for education, experience processes and the encountered difficulties and/or conveniences are basically shaped by personal, institutional, and national milieu factors.

FUTURE RESEARCH DIRECTIONS

This study aimed to at investigate the experience of Turkish students in Canadian higher education. The study was conducted from Turkey and mediated by Turkish student associations in universities where there are a large number of Turkish international students. Since the majority of the students who participated voluntarily in this study are graduate students, other in-depth studies on the subject can be conducted to better understand the experience of undergraduate students. Additionally, experience can be studied through the gender perspective in order to understand the demographic or personal milieu effect in more detail. For example, the relationship between field of study and gender can be studied for the cases of international students from different countries or only Turkish students in Canadian higher education. Their experience can be evaluated in relation to Science, Technology, Engineering, Arts, Mathematics (STEAM) education and compared with Turkey.

In brief, the case of Turkish students going abroad is a little-studied subject on the whole. As for the particular case of Canada, despite the increasing interest of Turkish people in Canada, studies on this subject are insufficient. In-depth studies to be made in this field will be illuminating for Turkish students who will go to Canada in the future as well as Canadian institutions making policies about education, social life, and short-term immigrants. I believe that in order to obtain more data through a broader sample and therefore deepen the analyses, it will be very helpful to conduct field studies on-site, namely in Canada, and to plan these studies as an interdisciplinary collective work together with partners from different universities.

REFERENCES

Abbott, A., & Silles, M. (2016). Determinants of international student migration. *World Economy, 39*(5), 621–635. doi:10.1111/twec.12319

Bourdieu, P., & Passeron, J. C. (1977). *Reproduction in education, society and culture*. Sage.

Brown, L. I. (2004). Diversity: The challenge for higher education. *Race, Ethnicity and Education, 7*(1), 21–34. doi:10.1080/1361332042000187289

Canadian Bureau for International Education (CBIE). (2018a). *The student's voice: National results of the 2018 CBIE international student survey*. Canadian Bureau for International Education.

Canadian Bureau for International Education (CBIE). (2018b). *International students in Canada*. Canadian Bureau for International Education.

Chapman, M. P. (1999). The campus at the millennium: A plea for community and place. *Planning for Higher Education, 2,* 25–31.

Cheng, L., Myles, J., & Curtis, A. (2004). Targeting language support for non-native English-speaking graduate students at a Canadian university. *TESL Canada Journal, 21*(2), 50–71. doi:10.18806/tesl. v21i2.174

Dreher, A., & Poutvaara, P. (2005). *Student flows and migration: An empirical analysis.* Discussion Paper series. IZA.

Findlay, A. M., King, R., Smith, F. M., Geddes, A., & Skeldon, R. (2012). World class? An investigation of globalisation, difference and international student mobility. *Transactions of the Institute of British Geographers, 37*(1), 118–131. doi:10.1111/j.1475-5661.2011.00454.x

Gale, T., & Parker, S. (2014). Navigating change: A typology of student transition in higher education. *Studies in Higher Education, 39*(5), 734–753. doi:10.1080/03075079.2012.721351

Hanassab, S. (2006). Diversity, international students, and perceived discrimination: Implications for educators and counselors. *Journal of Studies in International Education, 10*(2), 157–172. doi:10.1177/1028315305283051

Hou, F., & Lu, Y. (2017). International students, immigration and earnings growth: The effect of a pre-immigration host-country university education. *IZA Journal of Development and Migration, 7*(5), 1–24.

Janghorban, R., Roudsari, R. L., & Taghipour, A. (2014). Skype interviewing: The new generation of online synchronous interview in qualitative research. *International Journal of Qualitative Studies on Health and Well-being, 9*(1), 24152. doi:10.3402/qhw.v9.24152

Jones, E. (2017). Problematising and reimagining the notion of 'international student experience'. *Studies in Higher Education, 42*(5), 933–943. doi:10.1080/03075079.2017.1293880

Kayaalp, D. (2014). Educational inclusion/exclusion of Turkish immigrant youth in Vancouver, Canada: A critical analysis. *International Journal of Inclusive Education, 18*(7), 655–668. doi:10.1080/136031 16.2013.802031

Lu, Y., & Hou, F. (2015). *International students who become permanent residents in Canada.* Insights on Canadian Society (December). Statistics Canada Catalog no. 75-006-X.

Mills, C. W. (1959). *The sociological imagination.* Oxford University Press.

Neuman, L. W. (2014). *Basics of social research: Qualitative and quantitative approaches.* Pearson: Allyn and Bacon.

Organization for Economic Co-operation and Development (OECD). (2019). *Education at a glance 2019: OECD indicators.* OECD Publishing.

Pelling, A. C. (2000). *Cultural shock of international students in Canada* (Unpublished Master's Thesis). University of Lethbridge, Lethbridge, Canada.

Perkins, R., & Neumayer, E. (2014). Geographies of educational mobilities: Exploring the uneven flows of international students. *The Geographical Journal, 180*(3), 246–259. doi:10.1111/geoj.12045

Poyrazli, S., Arbona, C., Bullington, R., & Pisecco, S. (2001). Adjustment issues of Turkish college students studying in the United States. *College Student Journal, 35*(1), 52–62.

Reay, D. (1998). "Always knowing" and "never being sure": Familial and institutional habituses and higher education. *Journal of Education Policy, 13*(4), 519–529. doi:10.1080/0268093980130405

Schutz, A., & Richards, M. (2003). International students' experience of graduate study in Canada. *Journal of the International Society for Teacher Education, 7*(1), 56–63.

Sherry, M., Thomas, P., & Chui, W. H. (2010). International students: A vulnerable student population. *Higher Education, 60*(1), 33–46. doi:10.100710734-009-9284-z

Thomas, L. (2002). Student retention in higher education: The role of institutional habitus. *Journal of Education Policy, 17*(4), 423–442. doi:10.1080/02680930210140257

Times Higher Education (THE). (2019). *World university rankings 2019*. Retrieved December 1, 2019, from https://www.timeshighereducation.com/world-university-rankings/2019/worldranking#!/page/0/length/25/sort_by/rank/sort_order/asc/cols/stats

United Nations Educational, Scientific and Cultural Organization (UNESCO). (2013). *The international mobility of students in Asia and the Pacific*. UNESCO.

Windle, S., Hamilton, B., Zeng, M., & Yang, X. (2008). Negotiating the culture of the academy: Chinese graduate students in Canada. *Comparative and International Education/Éducation Comparée et Internationale, 37*(1), 71-90.

Wu, H. P., Garza, E., & Guzman, N. (2015). International student's challenge and adjustment to college. *Education Research International, 2015*, 1–9. doi:10.1155/2015/202753

Xu, L. (2015). Transitional challenges faced by post-secondary international students and approaches for their successful inclusion in classrooms. *International Journal for Leadership in Learning, 1*(3), 1–28.

Zhou, Y., Jindal-Snape, D., Topping, K., & Todman, J. (2008). Theoretical models of culture shock and adaptation in international students in higher education. *Studies in Higher Education, 33*(1), 63–75. doi:10.1080/03075070701794833

KEY TERMS AND DEFINITIONS

Academic Experience: All sorts of student experience relating to education life.

Familial Milieu: All factors relating to family. For example, occupation of parents, educational level of parents, socioeconomic status, family's support or pressure, prior parent/sibling study experience, etc.

Institutional Milieu: All factors relating to university. For example, language of instruction, curriculum, attitude of academic staff, pedagogic approach, inclusivity, orientation, location, student unions, scholarships, etc.

National Milieu: All factors relating to country. For example, climate, language, inclusivity, discrimination sense, multicultural structure, health system, accommodation policy, etc.

Pastoral/Living Experience: All kinds of student experience relating to daily life.

Personal Milieu: All personal factors. For example, age, gender, level of study, religion, ethnicity, department, socioeconomic status, mental or physical health, etc.

Receiving/Host Country: Country where people go to especially because of pull factors. In the case of international students, country where students go to for education.

Sending Country: Country whose citizens go abroad because of push factors. In the case of international students, their country of origin.

Social Experience: All kinds of student experience relating to social life.

Section 4
Student Support and Development

Chapter 12
Teaching and Learning Professional Development for International Graduate Students:
The Role of Teaching and Learning Centres

Lianne Fisher
Brock University, Canada

ABSTRACT

In this chapter, Bakhtin's metatheoretical framework of dialogism is offered as a frame in which to consider the work of Centres for Teaching and Learning (CTLs) on university campuses. Dialogism keeps front and centre the co-construction of student learning and teaching and the ways in which international graduate students' knowledges and experiences enhance and inform university teaching and learning. The chapter outlines CTL professional development activities that support the scholarship of international teaching assistants (ITAs). A discussion of the differences and tensions between learning a language and using language to learn is offered. CTLs are often seen as sites for instrumental and pragmatic instructional purposes, rather than the sites where ITAs are invited into the teaching and learning scholarly community; this later idea will be highlighted throughout.

INTRODUCTION

Centres for Teaching and Learning (CTLs) are positioned to support campus members in their teaching and learning outcomes. Most broadly, the mandate of teaching and learning centres is the support and advancement of teaching and learning. For graduate students (GS), more generally, inviting them into this scholarly teaching community, supports their own professional development and advances teaching and learning. The discussions that take place in one-on-one consultations between instructors/GSs and CTL staff might focus on instructional strategies, online course design, or assessment rubrics.

DOI: 10.4018/978-1-7998-5030-4.ch012

Often the roles of CTLs are seen as pragmatic and instrumental in that they transmit current standards for instructional strategies and better practices or support the use of Learning Management Systems (Schroeder, 2011). CTLs' involvement in numerous university committees, for example, teaching and learning policy, academic integrity, or the Faculty of Graduate Studies, is not always visible. CTL staff engage with various partners at the university to inform teaching practice, which can include a focus on classroom and campus climate to support student learning and, by extension, student retention. Also, CTLs foster the investigation of ways to support student learning through the Scholarship of Teaching and Learning (SoTL), typically engaging in and supporting faculty members' investigations of student learning and teaching practice.

Welcoming graduate students, both local and international, into the scholarly community and the practice of teaching and learning is an important goal of CTLs. The role of CTLs in supporting International Graduate Students as they embark on and progress through their academic and professional journey is multi-faceted and of particular interest. This chapter will outline the kinds of professional development and programming offered by CTLs that support the teaching and learning of international students who are engaged in teaching and will discuss methods of general and target teaching and learning supports in this context. Bakhtin's metatheoretical framework of *dialogism* operates as a socio-cultural backdrop to this exploration of teaching and learning. Framing teaching and learning through dialogism keeps front and centre the importance of the co-construction of knowledge, thereby problematizing colonial practices and interrupting perceptions of CTLs as instrumental sites of pedagogical strategy transmission. The particular use of language in academic settings is central to this discussion. After outlining the more generic types of professional development offered to graduate students working as teaching assistants, this chapter will focus on how this work supports international teaching assistants (ITAs).

REFLECTION AS METHOD

This chapter takes the form of a critical practitioner reflection. It addresses the themes that emerge from my work as an educational developer for the past decade, which includes working with international graduate students. Up until recently, the CTL at Brock University has been a small centre, with less than 8 individuals, whose work, for example, focuses on instruction, curriculum, and educational technologies. The context of the work of educational development is the support and advancement of teaching and learning at the: university; national (e.g., Society for Teaching and Learning in Higher Education); and international (e.g., International Society for the Scholarship of Teaching and Learning) level. When teaching is:

defined as scholarship... teaching both educates and entices future scholars . . . Teaching is also a dynamic endeavor involving all the analogies, metaphors,and images that build bridges between the teacher's understanding and the student's learning. Pedagogical procedures must be carefully planned, continuously examined and relate directly to the subject taught . . .knowing and learning are communal acts...teachers encourage students to be critical, creative thinkers, with the capacity to go on learning after their college days are over. Further, good teaching means that faculty, as scholars, are also learners. (Boyer, 1990, pp. 23-24)

Educational developers support faculty, teaching assistants, and ITAs in this kind of scholarship. This work is complex and wondrous. Themes related to the work of educational development arise across time and within particular contexts, in this chapter themes related to supporting and learning from ITAs are shared and reflected on.

PURPOSE OF CENTRES FOR TEACHING AND LEARNING (CTLS)

CTLs are typically independent administrative departments as their mandate is not to police or determine teaching (Schroeder, 2011) but rather, through a cross disciplinary approach, to provide a critical perspective on the functioning of teaching and learning in the university setting (Schroeder, 2011). Often learning management systems (LMS) are also within the purview of CTLs. CTL staff might be seconded faculty, staff members who are educational developers, instructional designers, or consultants, or educational technologists. Drawing on these diverse and professional backgrounds, CTL staff primarily work with faculty members, instructors, sessional instructors, teaching assistants, and other staff members who engage in instruction on campus. This support can occur through reflection on individual teaching needs; examination of how teaching or strategies fit within or extend a particular disciplinary practice; or working with instructors on specific teaching goals. Supporting individual instructor's goals is an important component of this educational development work, and the use of a reflective practice that engages with the questions: *'how do you know you are an effective teacher?'* or *'why is effective teaching important?* are central.

Recent research suggests that CTLs are moving toward a *leadership* mandate and away from *service* orientations (Forgie et al., 2018). CTLs function within the broader university context and can inform key institutional decisions; however, CTLs are often marginalized (e.g., Schroeder, 2011) and seen as only providing instrumental help for teaching strategies, curriculum review, and/or LMS support. Identifying how a CTL is positioned in an institution and the roles and influence of CTL staff can provide insight into the ways that teaching is valued and privileged within an institution. As building peer teaching and learning communities of practice (CoP) is often an important goal of CTLs, CTL staff can share practices and resources, and work through pedagogical challenges and successes. CTL programming can also assist in developing and maintaining CoPs and provide pedagogical context, knowledge and evidence to support teaching.

The professional development detailed throughout this paper is offered to all teaching assistants unless indicated otherwise. The focus of this chapter is on ITAs and therefore they are the focus of the discussion. It is important to remember that this teaching and learning professional development is for all graduate students.

TEACHING AND LEARNING PROFESSIONAL DEVELOPMENT FOR TEACHING ASSISTANTS

The teaching and learning needs of International Graduate Students are predominantly similar to those of most graduate students. Graduate students arrive into their programmes with varying degrees of experience and exposure to post-secondary teaching, and in some cases, experience as a learner in a classroom might be the only knowledge a graduate student has of university teaching. This lifetime of experience of teaching from the *student* perspective may result in graduate students teaching the way they were taught. Like other students, many ITAs have not had the experience of being a student in a seminar but have had experience listening in a lecture hall. In fact, a teaching assistant (TA) workshop, TA Day, or TA Orientation may be the first time a TA engages in professional development for post-secondary teaching, which means that they may be drawing on a different model of instruction that is of limited use in the seminar environment. Part of the CTL mandate is to engage TAs with a variety of instructional and teaching methods to facilitate student learning, simultaeneously providing the TA with their own successful/informing teaching experience.

Not all Canadian Universities have seminar systems like Brock University in Ontario, or Simon Fraser University in British Columbia, where graduate students (GS) can get teaching experience, particularly at the Master's level. Similarly, doctoral programmes are increasingly including teaching comprehensive options in their programs, providing PhD students the opportunity to design and co-instruct a course, in some cases linking these experiences with professional development programming from CTLs. The opportunity to teach is often a welcomed addition to a GSs academic career at the University, and some GSs report that this opportunity influenced their selection of a particular university and programme. Although a TAship can be seen as a monetary activity and not necessarily part of a scholarly journey, CTLs offer a variety of opportunities to bring graduate students into the scholarly community of teaching and learning. As such, CTL staff are often in contact with GSs who have a teaching assistant contract (or contract as a marker-grader or tutorial leader) as part of their graduate funding package. At Brock University, for example, GSs facilitate the learning of small groups of students through seminars of approximately 20 students, or tutorials or labs of approximately 40 students. TAs might facilitate discussion of readings, demonstrate laboratory procedures, work through statistical or math problems in tutorials, and grade and provide feedback on papers, assignments and in-class presentations.

ITAS AND TEACHING AND LEARNING PROFESSIONAL DEVELOPMENT

Often the support ITAs receive from CTLs focuses on instructional needs and the development of skills and competencies (e.g., Ross & Dunphy, 2007). Classrooms are increasingly diverse and inter-cultural approaches are important for new ITAs; as such, traditional CTL programming does not necessarily meet the specific needs of ITAs. In fact, CTLs tend to provide inter-cultural teaching professional development through programming that focuses on cultural differences (e.g., Dimitrov & Haque, 2016), but this is generally designed to support instructors' cultural sensitivity and is not necessarily designed for international instructors/teaching assistants new to the university. In addition, professional development for ITAs (and TAs) takes on the characterization of instrumental and pragmatic; when content, for example, active learning strategies, academic integrity, or marking and grading focuses primarily on the the learning of undergraduate students (both national and international), rather than to prioritize the professional development and pedagogical knowledge growth of these newer members of our scholarly community an important pedagogical element is missing. The importance of using reflection to foster culturally sensitive classrooms and for effective teaching is identified as an important practice (Dimitrov & Haque, 2016; Lee, 2017). Reflection forms an important basis for supporting the scholarly development and teaching and learning work of ITAs. Seeing TAs/ITAs as new(er) teaching and learning scholars frames this CTL work differently.

Supporting the professional development of GSs and ITAs can take place in several ways. For example, Brock University offers a TA Day at the beginning of the Fall semester; a Certificate in Teaching and Learning in Higher Education, which requires attendance at 8 workshops (1 credit each); and an Advanced Certificate in Teaching and Learning, which requires attendance at an additional 8 workshops and the submission of a statement of teaching philosophy (16 credits total). Also, teaching and learning professional development is offered through the Instructional Skills Workshop (ISW). The ISW is an intensive 24-hour program, often conducted over a 3 or 4 day period, where small groups of instructional faculty, students, or staff come together in small, peer-based groups to try out different teaching approaches and receive feedback in multiple formats (e.g., written, verbal, and a digital copy of their teaching). Also, practica and graduate courses in the *Theory and Practice of University Teaching* may culminate in the compilation of a teaching dossier and often involve investing in reflective practice and teaching observations. CTL staff also offer individual consultations. Consultations with CTL staff are often flexible and agile enough to work from where ITAs are in their teaching approaches and address their changing needs as they move through their teaching careers.

The multiple benefits of teaching and learning professional development benefits individuals who are exploring their teaching effectiveness, and are valuable for ITAs. As noted the development of new(er) scholars can be obscured through the lens of pedagogical professional development in service of (undergraduate) student learning; however, although student learning (typically undergraduate) is an important goal, so is the teaching and learning scholarship for ITAs. Part of the role of CTLs is to invite in and engage with ITAs in the scholarly community of teaching and learning—a vital academic endeavour.

DISCOURSES OF TEACHING AND LEARNING

As noted above, CTLs support and advance teaching and learning, typically in consultation with people instructing and educating on campus, with the goal of sharing better practices in teaching and learning. These practices come from different scholarly approaches, including learning and cognitive science and socio-cultural perspectives. CTL staff support the use of strategies to engage memory and other cognitive processes, for example, the use of story and narrative, and metacognition (see Bjork, Dunlosky, & Kornell, 2013), or the use of metaphor in providing feedback on student work.

The goal of consultation between individuals steeped in their discipline (e.g., an ITA and CTL staff member) is not to provide a list of strategies or *how to* resources. Rather, this consultation is to facilitate an instructor's search for ways to engage with instructional strategies or to design an assessment that works for their specific pedagogical needs. This context of teaching and learning consultation is achieved in active collaboration and reflection, and has the ability to address the unique and individualized goals of ITAs. Instructors and ITAs have enormous disciplinary knowledge and experience that allows them to engage in pedagogical design in ways that CTL staff cannot achieve alone. Such educational development is the context for co-construction and offers the opportunity for furthering innovative teaching. When working with ITAs, cultural and educational differences foster increased complexity in pedagogy thinking and open new possibilities for instruction. ITAs help drive initiatives to enhance intercultural pedagogy on campus and inform understanding.

ITAs teach and learn in complex situations, they are students in the university and employees at the same time. Teaching expectations may differ markedly from ITAs prior experiences or they may have no teaching experience in post-secondary education. It is not unusual for all TAs to feel less than competent in the teaching and learning vocabulary of the university, or with the content of their teaching assignment. Not all ITAs who engage with teaching have the same experiences; many come with rich teaching experiences and receive a teaching assignment that fits well with the content knowledge of their discipline. Remembering that ITAs bring diverse teaching experience to the university is important for CTLs.

The scholarship of teaching and learning points to many ways of aiding learning, whether it be at the undergraduate level or for graduates/professionals seeking instructional development. Research suggests that understanding who the learners are in the classroom or in consultation (e.g., ITAs) is an important factor for developing effective strategies to facilitate enduring learning (e.g., Ambrose et al., 2010; Soderstrom & Bjork, 2015) and practice. Activating and engaging with individuals' existing knowledges and experiences rather than propagating transmission models of teaching and learning aligns with Bakhtin's dialogism (2004). Bakhtin's proposes that *meaning* is not found in dictionary definitions of words but is rather actively constructed in interaction between speaking (dialogic) individuals.

Approaching ITA teaching and learning support through the metatheoretical framework of *dialogism* (Bakhtin, 2004) helps disrupt the conception of ITAs as blank slates. The co-construction of pedagogical meaning allows for the development of innovative practice in teaching and learning rather than the transmission of static pedagogical strategies. As such, a dialogic approach helps CTLs engage with the professional development of ITAs more fully.

BAKHTIN'S DIALOGISM

Education scholars sometimes promote some pedagogical method or "best practice," citing quite good research that shows "it" works better. But there is no "it," standing alone; other things are never equal. No method—active learning, small classes, whatever—is actually practiced independently of the teacher using it." (Chambliss & Takacs, 2014, p. 75)

In alignment with Bakhtin's idea that meaning as unfixed, it is difficult to find a definitive definition of dialogue (dialogue and dialogism are used interchangeably; Shields, 2007) in Bakhtin's work. For the context of CTLs, Shields' (2007) definition of dialogic relation as "a way of relating to one another in the fullness of each person's existence and in the fullness of differences among people" (p. 66) is helpful. Bakhtin offers meaning as constructed in dialogic interaction, not 'held' in the word or sentence; rather meaning is a process of understanding between the speaker and the addressee. In dialogic interaction, meaning is an inherently responsive process (Bakhtin, 2004). An utterance is an event, an act, that takes place in the social sphere; in the context of teaching and learning, an utterance can be conceived as a site, an event, of teaching *and* learning.

Bakhtin (2004) acknowledges the unwieldiness of meaning co-construction in dialogic interaction and offers speech genres as a way to contain the active co-construction of an utterance. Speech genres are typical spheres of language (e.g., teaching and learning, business correspondence, or casual greetings) in which particular utterance(s) are used and thus provide accepted or conventional forms in which utterances and meaning can be generated. For example in consultation, meaning is co-constructed between CTL staff and an ITA, and offers an opportunity for new ways of thinking about, and approaching, teaching to take place. Bakhtin suggests such discourses might be internally persuasive, authoritative, or monologic. The discourse of teaching and learning, for example, is internally persuasive when:

... entirely different possibilities open up in the everyday rounds of our consciousness, the internally persuasive word is half-ours and half-someone else's. Its creativity and productiveness consist precisely in the fact that such a word awakens new and independent words, that it organizes masses of our words from within, and does not remain in an isolated and static condition. It is not so much interpreted by us as it is further, that is, freely, developed, applied to new material, new conditions; it enters into interanimating relationships with new contexts ... this discourse is able to reveal ever newer ways to mean. (Bakhtin, 2002, pp. 345-346)

In comparison, *authoritative discourse*

[d]emands that we acknowledge it, that we make it our own; it binds us, quite independent of any power it might have to persuade us internally; we encounter it with its authority already fused to it. The authoritative word is located in a distanced zone, organically connected with a past that is felt to be hierarchically higher. It is, so to speak, the word of the fathers. Its authority was already acknowledged in the past. It is a prior discourse. (Bakhtin, 2002, pp. 342)

When pedagogical professional development and discourse are only authoritative, the opportunity for innovation is lost and teaching as a set of strategies through which knowledge is transmitted and reproduced takes hold. Here the voice of *a best pedagogy* dominates rather than the opening of possibilities and innovation. Heteroglossia, multivoicedness, gives way to a flattened monologic pedagogy.

Monologic discourse suggests "a single authoritative voice or perspective that is remote, fixed, and distant" (Shields, 2007, p. 40). In contrast, the heteroglossia that Bakhtin speaks of: "is not a particular voice within, but a particular way of combining many voices within" (Morson & Emerson, 2002, p. 221). Thinking of teaching strategies in a generic form (e.g., group work as active learning), strips them of their active, responsive, and pedagogical qualities when used by a particular instructor, who has a particular disciplinary, historical, and cultural context, who interacts with a particular group of students who have particular histories and cultures, who are learning within a particular discipline, within a particular institution, etc. Dialogism keeps the complexity of meaning, difference, and teaching and learning visible and is wary of reductionist, context-free teaching and learning. Indeed, while active learning, for example, is an accepted pedagogical strategy to enhance student learning, investigation of active learning demonstrated that background pedagogical knowledge was necessary for persistent student learning gains (Andrews et al., 2011).

Active learning becomes authoritative when it is implemented without attention to multivoiced pedagogical concerns. Active learning is stripped of active responsivity when its context and dialogue are removed from its use—with a particular instructor with a particular group of students. To put his another way, the implementation of an active learning strategy is authoritative, without the instructor supporting students to engage their exisiting knowledge with a particular active learning strategy chosen for a particular use. Allowing students time to learn more about a topic and to try out and explore with such knowledge in the context of their own lived experience opens up an opportunity for internally persuasive dialogue. Without these additional opportunities to engage in the process of active learning, knowledge cannot be internally persuasive.

Bakhtin's (2004) metatheoretical framework of dialogism keeps the idea of the co-construction of knowledge foregrounded. Course content cannot be transmitted, taught, and learnt effectively in an unadulterated format passing from from teacher to student; learning is enhanced and more enduring when students apply the knowledge to different situations and engage with knowledge in various modes and formats (Bjork et al., 2013). In terms of Bakhtin's approach of active responsivity, a student, for example, is not a passive recipient, but actively engages and is in dialogic interaction with the teaching and the contexts of teaching and learning. ITAs are asked to bring their knowledge and experience to their teaching and in this way interanimate their own professional development through and with the support of CTL staff. The work of the CTL is also interanimated through this exchange and the scholarly practice of all is enhanced.

Informing the work of CTLs from a dialogic metatheoretical framework assumes and prioritizes diversity (Shields, 2007). Diversity in the classroom is not exceptional. The ways in which institutions function, and how policies and procedures are developed and implemented, impact the ways in which diversity and sameness are privileged (see byrd, 2019; Henry et al., 2017). When working with ITAs and pedagogy, there are opportunities to disrupt privileged pedagogical approaches to teaching and learning.

Supporting and advancing teaching and learning with ITAs takes on different forms when approached from a dialogic framework. Thinking of teaching and learning, as ways of being, that inform an individual's practice of teaching, moves away from seeing individuals only as teachers or only as students, that possess some internal essentialist characteristics. Co-construction and dialogic exchanges remove the ideas of pedagogy as being a continuous series of replacements of a newer best practice, and keep the focus in the needs of lived pedagogy. Such a framework informs the work of CTLs and interrupts practices that are, or are potentially, colonial and monolithic. When ITAs and CTL staff collaborate, ITAs may bring multilingual (heteroglot) approaches to teaching and learning as well as individualized experiences of effective instruction and/or experiences of discrimination, which can inform their own practice and also be shared with the scholarly community. ITAs offer multiple approaches and experiences that facilitate innovative pedagogy, especially from an intercultural standpoint, which highlights the importance of using dialogism to challenge the restrictions of accepted teaching and learning discourses.

Teaching from the position of authoritative discourse aligns with transmission models based on the idea that knowledge/information is unchanged when transmitted between individuals. Additionally, this position assumes that ITAs must take on Western pedagogies or identities uncritically (Fei et al., 2012) and authoritatively or without engaging with their own experiences. The varied cultures and background of ITAs can inform and support students in the classroom, some of whom are also international. When the idea of instructional practice is systematized through dominant views of CTLs as functioning through expert models, rather than the fostering of opportunities for co-creation, collaboration, and the scholarship for ITAs our work dulls and stagnates.

The idea that knowledge is actively co-constructed does not mean that memory and cognitive do not exist or are not needed; indeed, memory and cognition are imperative for many forms of learning but these processes should not be equated with learning. When consulting in CTLs, the goal is to support ITAs and others to find internally persuasive discourses that are meaningful to them and that reach for more complex forms of learning and investigation and to encourage ITAs to engage with their own teaching. Pedagogical knowledge and practice is necessary for the learning gains. As already discussed, research examining the use of active learning to promote enduring learning suggests that the implementation of active learning without pedagogical knowledge is troublesome (Andrews et al., 2011). Engagement with pedagogical dialogue is imperative. Using this form of reflective and layered practice, that is to work dialogically, can scaffold and deepen knowledge when new learning is recast in exsiting practices and using existing knowledge for both CTL staff and ITAs.

The importance of active learning has been highlighted in SoTL and the findings provide evidence that the pedagogical knowledge and experience of instructors is an essential component for its successful use for enduring learning (Andrews et al., 2011; Auerbach et al., 2018; Prince, 2004). As Prince (2004) notes, "[T]eaching cannot be reduced to formulaic methods and active learning is not the cure for all educational problems" (p. 229). In fact, an effective teaching and learning strategy cannot work in every situation and should not be applied without intention, purpose and understanding of the learning outcomes. When CTLs move beyond these authoritative discourses, the co-construction and development of pedagogical knowledge with ITAs becomes possible and offers exciting opportunities for engaging in the pedagogical process.

Framing teaching and learning through dialogism helps to prioritize the need for active consultation rooted in disciplinary knowledges (or speech genres), of which teaching and learning in post-secondary education is one. By extension, when working with ITAs, the risk of reproducing racist, sexist, and colonial pedagogy, for example, can be interrupted when CTLs think of pedagogy as informing, co-constructing, and generating pedagogical meaning.

ADVANCING TEACHING AND LEARNING

Bakhtin (2006) focuses on meaning in co-construction and how meaning is mediated through language. This position has implications for international students and the different kinds of knowledges and information they may need as they work and learn in multiple languages and/or educational structures. Knowledge and experience, for ITAs, is often mediated within two layers of language. It is not the goal or even necessary for the educational developer (or other CTL staff) to understand all elements of an ITA's teaching; instead, it is to guide and engage with ITAs in ways that allow them to understand and develop their own teaching. Language, therefore, becomes one facet rather than the focus of CTL and ITA interactions, and reflective practice to understand pedagogy in the form of a teaching dossier, becomes imperative.

Importance of Reflective Practice

The development of a teaching dossier as a reflective practice creates space for dialogue and reflection and the opportunity to answer the question: '*How do you know you are an effective teacher?*' As the Canadian Association of University Teachers (CAUT; 2016, 2018) notes, "[T]he recording of competence and effectiveness in teaching is more difficult than research" (p. 5). Indeed, CAUT considers the teaching dossiers as "the gold standard" (p. 2) for communicating and understanding teaching effectiveness. A teaching dossier contains a *statement of teaching philosophy* that provides context for the whole of the dossier. In a statement of teaching philosophy, the instructor (ITA) shares their beliefs about teaching and learning, and examines the ways in which these beliefs inform teaching practice. The writing of a statement of teaching philosophy is an important step in the creation of a teaching dossier and provides ITAs and other developing instructors an opportunity to examine the assumptions and experiences they bring to their teaching practice. The rest of the dossier is pedagogical evidence for what is said in the philosophy, usually in the form of a list of teaching experience, formative feedback, strategies used in teaching, lesson plans, a course syllabus, professional development in teaching and learning, and/or unsolicited feedback from learners. As a reflective practice, the process of compiling the materials allows an instructor to consider and reflect on effectiveness and directions for change.

As CAUT (2018) suggests, "[t]he teaching dossier provides a comprehensive approach to evaluation much more likely to result in genuine 'quality control' than any other so-called productivity measure" (p. 9). While CAUT focuses on evaluation, as they see the value afforded teaching in the ability to assess, reflective practice is a valuable practice in and of itself. Inviting ITAs into the scholarly practice of teaching and learning can be done by supporting ITAs to create and engage in the development of a teaching dossier. This process support the scholarly development of, and engages ITAs in the post-secondary scholarly community through a dialogic and reflective exercise especially when asking the question: *why is your teaching important?* In higher education, however, developing a teaching dossier as documentation of *learning* of teaching, is often neglected. Teaching dossiers can be used as reflective practice for post-secondary instructors as a way to reflect on and change their own teaching. Some practitioners suggest the development of teaching dossiers also can improve "the quality of [the] educational institution" (de Rijdt et al., 2006, p. 1091). Reflecting on the importance of teaching in the university engages ITAs in a fuller scholarship.

Teaching dossiers are the outcome of teaching assistant learning; for the TA Practicum and the graduate course in the *Theory and Practice of University Teaching*, at Brock University and ITAs frequently take part in these forms of professional development. Along with the TA Workshop series, the practicum and course are designed to support academic and non-academic career journeys, and provide a place where GS can both discuss the ways in which they are effective in their teaching and document their experiences. The TA Practicum combines the TA/ITA Workshop series with the Instructional Skills Workshop (described earlier) and teaching observations of faculty members (often award winners and who give their consent to be observed). Teaching observation is an important scholarly practice for teaching and learning. Although many elements may be the same and different between the practicum and the course, the goal is to allow for flexibility in the compilation of a teaching dossier so ITAs can participate in ways that are meaningful to them and they can document their professional development.

Reflective practice takes place, well—in the practice (Brookfield, 1995; Schon, 1986), and everyday engagement with teaching and learning, or what Bakhtin (2004) would describe as the mundane, that is, in the everyday use and response to utterances. It is not the generic activity of teaching and learning, it is the teaching and learning of the particular ITA with all the individualized and co-created meaning brought to this endeavour that is a continuous dialogic process.

Often TA workshops orient students to focus on their roles and responsibilities as an employee and student of the university. Topics of TA workshops generally include grading for assessment, academic integrity, and instructional strategies. In addition, other members of the university community, including the university library, learning services, and human rights and equity services, may come to facilitate workshops. These other campus services provide information on how they support ITAs in their teaching and also how ITAs can use the services to support their own teaching.

Separate ITA workshops have been developed to support teaching but this is not without tension and controversy. Inclusive workshops for all TAs (including ITAs) is preferable as the co-construction and sharing of knowledge and experiences is beneficial to all. In my professional context, there have been instances, however, where discrimination takes place (both intentionally and unintentionally) that impacts the learning of ITAs. Providing an opportunity for ITAs to come together and discuss issues and needs specific to their situation can be valuable. These ITA workshops allow ITAs to have discussions about the racism they encounter on campus and/or in their teaching, without the additional demands of explaining and/or having to justify why particular behaviours are discriminatory and display disrespect for cultural difference. It is not that ITAs do not want to share and discuss with their peers, and they do, do so, in other workshops, rather it is important for ITAs to have other opportunities and spaces that focus on their particular needs with others who have similar experiences. Also, these workshops offer a community in which to share and try out pedagogical strategies.

Discussion between CTLs and ITAs regarding languages of teaching and the development of meaning, student engagement, and active learning often centre around ITAs' concerns about accents or word pronunciation. One workshop developed with ITAs to dislodge and disrupt Eurocentric ways of teaching and learning, particularly when verbal transmission models are heralded as the gold standard of teaching, is called the *Languages of Teaching*. This workshop highlights for ITAs the myriad ways that learning can take place and provides particular strategies for individualized needs when requested. A focus of this workshop is to outline how meaning is constructed through active learning, the importance of the learning environment/climate, and ways to allow students to take ownership of their own learning. There is much more involved in teaching and learning beyond the verbal transmission of knowledge, and this is important to understand for ITAs who are concerned about their language fluency. Limiting teaching to verbal transmission ignores the important evidence that multiple forms of content representation are important for learning (Ambrose et al., 2010, CAST, 2020).

That language is seen as the primary vehicle of teaching and learning, especially when talking of culture and accents on campus, makes it an important site for examining the ways in which these ideas foster deficit and discriminatory thinking. Discussions around language and learning using a socio-cultural as frame of reference are important and, in addition to findings from learning science, can effectively support the mandate of a diverse and inclusive campus.

Historically, classrooms in Western universities have been homogenous but it is important to note the student population is increasingly diverse and using multiple modalities to teach is both practical and effective. For example, instrumental teaching strategies such as writing new vocabulary or words that pose difficulty in pronunciation on a whiteboard to enhance student learning are a sound pedagogical practice, not activities to hide a perceived teaching deficit of the instructor. With this in mind, Universal Design for Learning (UDL; CAST, 2020) and the promotion and facilitation of UDL for teaching and learning is key to CTL and ITA partnerships. Using multiple forms of representation, engagement, and action and expression, supports more students more of the time, whether students have learning, social class, or cultural differences. The use of UDL supports the work of ITAs in the classroom, and contributes to promoting diverse and inclusive teaching and learning approaches (see Fovet, 2019).

Experienced instructors can find it difficult not to see themselves as imposters or novice teachers. The idea that teachers are born and do not spend a long time honing their teaching craft and practice is pervasive. CTLs can help ITAs who experience feelings of impostership to gain experience and knowledge that fosters their own understanding of teaching and learning through the development of pedagogical knowledge, namely the kinds of practices that facilitate student learning. CTL workshops developed with ITAs, dialogically, address their current teaching needs, allow for increased nuance and focus, and facilitate this professional growth. Here CTLs advance teaching and learning in "ever newer *ways to*" teach (Bakhtin, 2002, p. 346). As part of the TA workshop series at Brock University, workshops such as *TAs Teaching about Teaching* provide ITAs with the opportunity to design and teach in the context of professional development in higher education. Here pedagogy is fostered so that ITAs can try out pedagogical practices with peers, with a goal to move toward an internally persuasive practice.

Unfortunately, when CTL are seen as places that instructors attend when they are *not* good teachers, engagement can be difficult. Informal activities, *meet and greets* with other services, pedagogical walks and talks or book clubs, for example, can be ways to engage with ITAs. As noted, reflective practice is an important component of CTLs, and workshops on *Developing a Statement of Teaching Philosophy* and *Documenting your Teaching* (Teaching Dossiers) are included in the Brock TA workshop series. These are designed to be delivered in time for ITAs to prepare teaching dossiers to apply for teaching awards.

For ITAs who have not had any teaching experience or would like to have more experience to reduce stress before leading a class for the first time, the Instructional Skills Workshop (ISW) provides that opportunity and experience. Not only do ITAs *receive* feedback on their teaching in multiple formats, they also repeatedly *provide* feedback in multiple formats, an important component of ITAs' work on campus. Participants often report involvement in an ongoing community beyond the duration of the ISW group as members continue to meet socially. Individuals garner social support through their common interests in teaching and learning. In some ways, ISW participation can begin the formation of a community of practice (Macpherson, 2011).

Some departments encourage and arrange for new GSs and ITAs to participate in an ISW before the first term begins. ITAs and TAs often participate in the ISW together. Participants report this experience as being pivotal to feeling part of a community and gaining confidence before teaching a small group seminar or a tutorial for the first time in the university setting. Feedback from ISW participants suggests that the ISW was fundamental in reducing their social isolation. The ISW is also an important component of professional development in that it is an internationally recognized certificate. ISWs can be found around globe (e.g., China, Africas, West Indies), and the design elements of the ISW are often looked for in job talks in post-secondary education.

In addition, it is common for ITAs to take internship courses with CTLs, and when possible, CTLs provide occasional employment for interested students. Whichever ways ITAs engage with CTL offerings, that engagement demonstrates a commitment to teaching and learning. Much of the programming offered by CTLs provides ITAs the opportunity to develop different academic communities, social interactions, and support, which they report as contributing positively to their experiences (e.g., Moglen, 2017).

REFLECTIONS ON LANGUAGE, TEACHING, AND ITAS

ITAs may have the goal to increase English fluency or the goal to 'learn' English when attending particular universities. Sometimes when ITAs use their first language(s) to enhance their own learning, this behaviour can be seen as being in opposition to that goal of learning the official language of instruction at their institution. Practising and trying out a new language in cultural and social contexts is important, but sometimes learning about teaching, for example, is mediated more fully through the ITAs' first language(s) and in dialogic interchange with peers. In teaching and learning, and professional development, it is useful when ITAs (and visiting faculty members) use translators on their phones and translate for each other, when clarification is required for comprehension. Activating peoples' own knowledges and backgrounds has positive impacts for enduring learning (see Ambrose et al., 2010; Bjork, Dunlosky, & Kornell, 2013).

The continued focus on language is an important reminder that language remains a marker of privilege; and therefore, a site in which racism and prejudice can be experienced. Obviously, not all language use is a site of discrimination. However, within educational institutions, it is important to consider the ways in which international graduate students may encounter colonialism and racism in unexamined ways, especially when they teach. It is still frequent for the use of "standard" language (both spoken and written) and particular dialects (e.g., English spoken with particular accents) to be seen as the dominant mode for teaching. In Bakhtin's terms, these languages are authoritative in that they already have their authority and privilege fused within. By extension, the use of particular languages carries much social capital (see Fei, Siong, Kim, & Yaacob, 2012) and also this use is still seen as the dominant mode of teaching, despite it also being a potential site for discrimination.

Teaching and learning has moved beyond the unidirectional verbal transmission models of teaching (Andrews et al., 2011). Communicating in English may support an individual's goals, provide social capital, for example, with racial, gendered, and colonial underpinnings, and at the same time, discriminate. Language does not only represent an object in the world, for example, for Bakhtin (2004) language, an utterance, is an event. An utterance is active and productive--it does things in the world. Dialogism highlights how meaning is constructed through its use and use may differ depending on the context, or the ability and mastery of those in dialogic interaction. Respect for multiple language use is imperative for co-constructing meaning in teaching and learning.

It is important to distinguish between learning a new language and learning through language. Sociocultural perspectives, like that of Bakhtin, remind us that meaning is constituted through language; thus, language for learning, say the speech genres of teaching and learning in higher education, would be scaffolded and deepen when first and subsequent languages are used. Positing first language use as detrimental on campus is troublesome and suggests authoritative discourses.

ITAs are not a monolithic group, even when students identify as coming from the same culture or being born in the same country. Some ITAs do come to English-speaking universities to learn English with more fluency, depth, or nuance, but this is not the goal of every International Graduate Student. In fact, even when learning English more fully is a goal, it is not the only goal. Bakhtin's (2004) concept of speech genres helps to keep in mind that the language needs of ITAs are multiple. Learning the speech genre for campus students services, especially when in need of help for health, mental health, and university or student visa services, should not be limited to English. As an example, when essential student services and supports are offered only in English, we are not fully supporting the ITAs we invite to our campuses. CTLs can help outline the multiple roles of language by talking about how language mediates learning and inclusivity.

Vygotsky's zone of proximal development (ZPD) (Lantolf, 2000) is accepted doctrine in pedagogical circles. The idea that a peer who is also an international student who has been on campus and has developed multiple language skills is able support new ITAs in accessing and using campus services is sound pedagogy because increased experience is helpful. Peers are important cultural brokers. Even when a student is proficient in multiple languages, stress and change can interfere with language abilities. When an individual is under duress (e.g., an illness, adjusting to a new environment, teaching for the first time) new language abilities and development may be strained (Buttaro, 2004). Indeed, illness can impact the language abilities of any instructor. When an institution has an official language, naturally this language is used in teaching contexts (e.g., lecture, seminar, etc), but for students to also use a language that they are fluent in (but not the official language of the institution) is supported by socio-cultural approaches to learning (Bakhtin, 2004; Lantolf, 2000).

Seeking out friends, peers, or teaching assistants who can help explain concepts in a fluent language scaffolds learning. Most students who speak English as their dominant/first language do this all the time: they ask their peers for help or have discussions about content they are learning in their first language.

Many international students will have two textbooks, one in a language they feel competent in and one in the language of the institution; they scaffold their own learning in this way. Another way to scaffold learning is the use of multiple languages. For example, during office hours, if an ITA can describe a concept in a dominant language that is not English, but the language is a first language the ITA and the student share, learning is enhanced. The use of multiple languages on campus is important for learning and by championing this approach, CTLs can inform institutional policy and, by extension, enhance learning for all. Learning and performance are intertwined and have important differences (Soderstrom & Bjork, 2015), and language for learning, specifically learning mediated through socio-cultural processes, can help better support more students more of the time.

By extension, materials used by ITAs to gather, record, and reflect on their teaching experiences, namely teaching dossiers, can and possibly should be compiled in a multilingual fashion. A CTL staff member does not necessarily have to be able to read the teaching dossier as it is the reflective practice of that particular individual, but the staff can inform the process through dialogic interaction and consultation. Bakhtin (2004) suggests words carry the voices of others; in this way, the compilation of a teaching dossier carries the voices of CTL staff and by extension knowledge of numerous and better pedagogical practices in its design. As Bakhtin (2002) notes:

Language is not an abstract system of normative forms but rather a concrete heteroglot conception of the world. All words have the "taste" of a profession, a genre, a tendency, a party, a particular work, a particular person, a generation, an age group, the day and hour. Each word tastes of the context and contexts in which it has lived its socially charged life; all words and forms are populated by intentions . . . serving other people's intentions: it is from there that one must take the word, and make one's own. (pp. 293-294)

Some researchers (e.g., Tomasello, 2019) posit joint attention, collaboration, and intentionality as the hallmark of human learning. Unfortunately, we often ask that individuals perform (e.g., use a new language) before they have learnt. Learning and performance can happen at the same time, but often we privilege this simultaneity rather than allowing time and space for learning. Learning a language, learning new disciplinary content, or learning a more sophisticated disciplinary vocabulary all take time, no matter how engaged or motivated a student is. By opening opportunities for learning in multiple modalities and recognizing the importance of time for learning. CTLs can inform and transform the ways in which ITAs and the broader GS community learn on campus.

"Dialogical and inquiry-based professional development approaches… provide a social context in which teachers are able to construct… first hand experiential knowledge" (Greenleaf & Katz, 2004, p. 198). Through their interactions with CTLs, ITAs can "author their own pedagogical change" (Greenleaf & Katz, 2004, p. 199) and come to their own internally persuasive pedagogical engagement.

ITAS INFORM THE WORK OF TEACHING & LEARNING CENTRES

Working with international graduate students in the realm of teaching and learning challenges CTLs to be explicit and make visible the assumptions of teaching and learning in the Canadian context. The services and leadership provided by CTLs are enhanced because of the willingness and generosity of international graduate teaching assistants who ask questions and share teaching experiences. It is these dialogic encounters that inform the development of programming for graduate student teaching at the university and provide a richer and more developed teaching experience for undergraduate students.

CLOSING THOUGHTS

This chapter offered an approach that conceives of the professional development of ITAs through Bakhtin's (2004) dialogic lens. Teaching and learning centres support ITAs primarily through teaching and learning professional development; however, the broad context of welcoming ITAs into the scholarly community of teaching and learning is just as important. Also, discussed were the ways in which CTLs can inform policy and procedures; for example, by highlighting that not all ITAs come to Western Universities to learn English and that language is important for learning as it mediates understanding.

Bakhtin's (2004) concept of dialogism is offered to keep visible the co-construction of meaning and knowledge, and the importance of co-construction to (international) student learning. Along with Bakhtin's metatheoretical framework of dialogism, Universal Design for Learning (UDL) is suggested as a framework from which to support more students' learning more of the time. Dialogism helps frame the work of CTL and the scholarly development of ITAs from a position of co-construction, a scholarly endeavor—and not only, the sharing of tips, tricks, and strategies. Dialogism, like pedagogy and UDL, is an approach, it is a way of being, knowing, and doing, that informs rather than dictates.

That ITAs take on instructional roles in the university offers the opportunity for new and innovative approaches to teaching and learning. The dialogic perspective highlights how *meaning* is made through teaching and learning centre staff and the participation of, and engagement with, international graduate students. A dialogic perspective can dislodge the perspective of teaching professional development as a one-way transmission of pedagogical and cultural knowledge to "unknowing" or "uninformed" international graduate students. This perspective also highlights the ways in which international graduate students contribute to informing and enhancing teaching and learning in the academy. The mandate of CTLs in partnership with other campus partners and services can foster climates informed by models of pedagogy that foster inclusion and diversity and address the very real issues faced in the classroom and curriculum, and by extension, in the social contexts of international students outside their immediate academic communities.

The knowledges from CTL staff support ITAs in their professional development through dialogue and individualized needs and desires. ITAs' academic outcomes and desires are not all the same, just as their cultural and linguistic backgrounds, genders, sexualities, social classes, and abilities are all diverse. Among many possibilities, CTLs provide a place where individuals, who may face discrimination in the classroom and who may also be asked to address and transverse these occurrences when teaching, can share their experiences, develop resources, and participate in changing campus culture from a supported position. When CTLs are positioned as places to receive teaching and learning information, rather than as part of the scholarly community, ITAs may not know to seek support. It is important to note here that ITAs, even without the support of CTLs and the wider institution, often help interrupt and displace discriminatory actions in the classroom and curriculum. ITAs bring their own sophisticated knowledges and experiences—their lived experiences—to inform and foster different ways to be, teach, and learn on a university campus. Many international students cannot and do not don the mantle of English-speaking privilege, as they live in cultures and worlds that do not require this (Fei, Siong, Kim, & Yaacob, 2012).

As such, they inhabit a unique position with a potential, if they so choose and are simulatenously adequately supported by their communicaties, to radically shift dominatant campus culture.

Discourses of diversity and inclusion have their own *speech genres*, and this include speech genres within teaching and learning. Having CTL members with experiences and knowledges in diversity, inclusion, and indigeneity, helps develop and engage with pedagogic consultation to foster diverse and inclusive ways of knowing, being, and teaching. ITAs also have this potential, though they may be constrained by the demands and pressures of their graduate programs; therefore, engaging ITAs in developing teaching assistants workshops informs the work of CTLs and has a wide-reaching impact on the university campus. Furthermore, engaging in reflective practice, through internal and external dialogues as well as the development of teaching dossiers, fosters the professional development of ITAs, strengthens the offerings of CTLs, and builds a strong community of teaching and learning.

It is not uncommon for reflective practice to be appropriated and, in some ways, it has become an authoritative discourse through its use in other contexts. However, this is not to say that reflective practice or a more dialogic discourse in many other domains are not useful. In fact, human beings reflect constantly to great effect. The issue is when reflective practice is co-opted instrumentally as a checklist for measures of accountability. When used this way, the process of reflection to answer the question *how do you know you are an effective teacher* is diminished and the product, a teaching dossier that operates as an individual's reflection and compilation of how an individual's pedagogy is mediated through their own knowledges (which includes different cultural and linguistic knowledges) and experiences, is reduced to a product in service of dominant ways of being. Here, innovative teaching and learning may be appropriated within academic climates that privilege dominant, and inaccurate, understandings of teaching and learning pedagogy, that is, they interfere with the purpose of teaching dossiers for reflection.

Dimitrov and Haque's (2016) observation that the "contemporary classroom is an interdisciplinary community of diverse learners and instructors" (p. 1) is important. A focus on competencies can cause concern, whether they are intercultural or teaching and learning competencies, when competencies are framed, positioned, and used as enduring characteristics and qualities of individuals. Competency, like language ability, is too often positioned and re-inscribed on an individual as deficit rather than abilities learnt through the dialogic exchange. Often competencies are infused with authoritative discourse as having fixed meaning rather than being co-constructed through internally persuasive discourses that bring individual experiences and knowledges to the fore. All too often competencies are assigned rather co-constructed and taught.

At times the diversity of students in the university classroom is forgotten. Often 'student' is envisioned as a standard, default, entity. The presence of international graduate students who lead seminars, tutorials, and labs, can enhance undergraduate learning experiences. In fact, undergraduate students have shared that it was indeed an international teaching assistant's ability to speak in their own language (English was an subsequent language for both) that allowed them to come to a fuller understanding of the course materials. Insights such as these allow post-secondary educators to understand *Global Education* more fully and more accurately. Often, concerns over ability to express course content in English (the predominant language of instruction at Brock University, for example) with a "foreign accent" are raised. Such linguistic dominance is commonly framed as necessary for student learning without acknowledgement of the multiple accents of students in our classrooms. Also, the assumption that learning takes place via the verbal transmition of information remains unchallenged. CTLs can highlight the multiple languages of learning, and the ways in which learning can take place.

ITAs often graduate and leave the university and, after several years of working closely with these individuals who are committed to teaching and learning, it is often difficult for us to say goodbye. However, that ITAs move forward and share their pedagogical experience and experiences with other communities of learning is a rewarding and positive outcome. Teaching and learning as a dialogical exchange, not a strict reproduction of what was taught but a collection of what was learnt, tried out, and re-cast and re-envisioned from the ITAs' (and all TAs) own knowledges and experiences, runs the "risk" of fostering ever new approaches to teaching and learning. ITAs take their pedagogical scholarship forward, and CTLs are lucky and privileged in the roles they play in this process.

REFERENCES

Ambrose, S. A., Bridges, M. W., DiPietro, M., Lovett, M. C., & Norman, M. K. (2010). *The Jossey-Bass higher and adult education series. How learning works: Seven research-based principles for smart teaching*. Jossey-Bass.

Andrews, T. M., Leonard, M. J., Colgrove, C. A., & Kalinowski, S. T. (2011). Active learning not associated with student learning in a random sample of college biology courses. *CBE Life Sciences Education, 10*(4), 394–405. doi:10.1187/cbe.11-07-0061 PMID:22135373

Auerbach, A. J., Higgins, M., Brickman, P., & Andrews, P. C. (2018). Teacher knowledge for active-learning instruction: Expert-novice comparison reveals differences. *CBE Life Sciences Education, 17*(12), 1–14. doi:10.1187/cbe.17-07-0149 PMID:29420184

Bakhtin, M. M. (2002). *The dialogic imagination: Four essays* (M. Holquist, Ed., EmersonC.HolquistM., Trans.). University of Texas.

Bakhtin, M. M. (2004). *Speech Genres and other Late Essays (V. W. McGee, Trans.,)* (C. Emerson & M. Holquist, Eds.). University of Texas.

Bjork, R. A., Dunlosky, J., & Kornell, N. (2013). Self-regulated learning: Beliefs, techniques, and illusions. *Annual Review of Psychology, 64*(1), 417–444. doi:10.1146/annurev-psych-113011-143823 PMID:23020639

Boyer, E. L. (1990). *Scholarship reconsidered: Priorities of the professoriate*. Princeton University Press.

Brookfield, S. D. (1995). *Becoming a critically reflective teacher*. Jossey-Bass.

Buttaro, L. (2004). Second language acquisition, culture shock, and language stress of adult female Latina students in New York. *Journal of Hispanic Higher Education, 3*(1), 21–49. doi:10.1177/1538192703255525

byrd, d. (2019). Uncovering hegemony in higher education: A critical appraisal of the use of "institutional habitus" in empirical scholarship. *Review of Educational Research, 89*(2), 171-210.

Canadian Association of University Teachers. (1986). *The CAUT guide to the teaching dossier: Its preparation and use*. Author.

Centre for Applied Special Technology (CAST). (2020). http://www.cast.org/our-work/about-udl.html

Chambliss, D. F., & Takacs, C. G. (2014). *How college works*. Harvard University Press. doi:10.4159/harvard.9780674726093

Dimitrov, N., & Haque, A. (2016). Intercultural teaching competence: A multidisciplinary model for instructor reflection. *Intercultural Education, 27*(5), 437–456. doi:10.1080/14675986.2016.1240502

Fei, W. F., Siong, L. K., Kim, L. S., & Yaacob, A. (2012). English use as an identity marker among Malaysian undergraduates. *3L. The Southeast Asian Journal of English Language Studies, 18*(1), 145–155.

Forgie, S. E., Yonge, O., & Luth, R. (2018). Centres for teaching and learning across Canada: What's going on? *The Canadian Journal for the Scholarship of Teaching and Learning, 9*(1), 1–18. doi:10.5206/cjsotl-rcacea.2018.1.9

Fovet, F. (2019). Not just about disability: Getting traction for UDL implement with International Students. In K. Novak & S. Bracken (Eds.), *Transforming higher education through universal design for learning: An international perspective* (pp. 179–200). Routedge. doi:10.4324/9781351132077-11

Greenleaf, C. L., & Katz, M.-L. (2004). Ever new ways to mean: Authoring pedagogical change in secondary subject-area classrooms. In A. F. Ball & S. W. Freedman (Eds.), *Bakhtinian perspectives on language, literacy, and learning* (pp. 172–202). Cambridge University Press. doi:10.1017/CBO9780511755002.009

Henry, F., Dua, E., James, C. E., Kobayashi, A., Li, P., Ramos, H., & Smith, M. S. (2017). *The equity myth: Racialization and indigeneity at Canadian Universities*. UBC Press.

Korpan, C. (2011). *TA professional development in Canada*. https://www.stlhe.ca/wp-content/uploads/2011/05/TA-ProD-in-Canada-Report_July-2011.pdf

Lantolf, J. P. (2000). Introducing sociocultural theory. In J. P. Lantolf (Ed.), *Sociocultural theory and second language learning* (pp. 1–26). Oxford University Press.

Lee, A., Poch, R., O'Brien, M. K., & Solheim, C. (2017). Teaching interculturally: A framework for integrating disciplinary knowledge and intercultural development. *Stylus (Rio de Janeiro)*.

Macpherson, A. (2011). *The instructional skills workshop as a transformative learning process* [Unpublished doctoral dissertation]. Simon Fraser University.

Moglen, D. (2017). International graduate students: Social networks and language use. *Journal of International Students, 7*(1), 22–37. doi:10.32674/jis.v7i1.243

Morson, G. S., & Emerson, C. (1990). *Mikhail Bakhtin: Creation of a prosaics*. Stanford University Press.

Prince, M. (2004). Does active learning work? A review of the research. *Journal of Engineering Education, 93*(3), 223–231. doi:10.1002/j.2168-9830.2004.tb00809.x

Ross, C., & Dunphy, J. (2007). *Strategies for teaching assistant and international teaching assistant development: Beyond micro teaching*. Jossey-Bass.

Schon, D. A. (1986). *Education the reflective practitioner: Toward a new design for teaching and learning in the professions*. Jossey-Bass.

Schroeder. (2011). *Coming in from the margins: Faculty development's emerging organizational development role in institutional change*. Stylus.

Shields, C. M. (2007). *Bakhtin primer*. Peter Lang.

Soderstrom, N. C., & Bjork, R. A. (2015). Learning versus performance: An integrative review. *Perspectives on Psychological Science*, *10*(2), 176–199. doi:10.1177/1745691615569000 PMID:25910388

Tomasello, M. (2019). *Becoming human: A theory of ontogeny*. Harvard. doi:10.4159/9780674988651

KEY TERMS AND DEFINITIONS

Dialogism: Meaning is constructed in dialogic interaction, in the every day interaction of people. Meaning is not 'held' in the word or sentence; rather meaning is a process of understanding between the speaker and the addressee.

Reflective Practice: Ways in which a person considers, thinks about, and comes to an understanding of their effectiveness in a profession. Reflection is also a process via which to consider needs for change or development. Reflection uses multiple forms of evidence.

Teaching Dossier: A dossier comprised of multiple forms of evidence; for example, a statement of teaching philosophy, formative feedback, and instructional strategies, to reflect on teaching effectiveness. It may also be used for functions other than reflection, for example, in consideration for tenure and promotion.

Chapter 13
Plagiarism and Information Literacy Workshops for International Students

Guoying Liu
University of Windsor, Canada

Zuochen Zhang
University of Windsor, Canada

Clayton Smith
University of Windsor, Canada

Shijing Xu
University of Windsor, Canada

Karen Pillon
University of Windsor, Canada

Haojun Guo
https://orcid.org/0000-0002-7182-2023
University of Windsor, Canada

ABSTRACT

The population of international students has increased significantly at the University of Windsor in recent years, and the university takes a variety of actions to address several key issues of interest to international students, including academic integrity, English language development, and writing support. This chapter reports findings from a multi-year collaborative project that was designed to enhance international students' library and academic literacy, with a focus on the understanding of plagiarism and measures to prevent it. A number of workshops that involved students at different levels were delivered to students from the English language improvement, undergraduate, and graduate programs. Research data col-

DOI: 10.4018/978-1-7998-5030-4.ch013

lected from these workshops indicate that students benefited from the workshops, although at different degrees because of various factors, such as academic discipline, English language proficiency, previous educational experience. Further research can be conducted to explore ways to optimize such programs to meet the needs of students, particularly international students.

INTRODUCTION

International Students in Canada

Colleges and universities in North America are increasingly becoming culturally diverse, which is partially due to increasing enrolment of international students. Currently, 494,525 international students choose to study at all levels at Canadian educational institutions, which increased by 17 percent between 2016 and 2017, and by 34 percent between 2014 and 2017 (Canadian Bureau of International Education, 2018). Most international students study in university programs. Globally, the United States is currently the top destination for study abroad while Canada ranks sixth (Institute of International Education, 2017). Top countries of origin for Canada include China, India, South Korea, France, and Vietnam. Several factors contribute to international students' choice of Canada as their destination, including "programs, policies put in place to increase their numbers, the quality of postsecondary education, and the appeal of Canada as a study destination" (Statistics Canada, 2018, para. 3).

This has led many institutions to make internationalization a strategic priority. Knight (2003) identifies internationalization as a process "of integrating an international or intercultural dimension into teaching, research, and services functions of an institution" (p. 3). Dr. Paul Davidson, President of Universities Canada, suggests:

Globalization has become a pervasive force shaping higher education. Today almost all institutions in Canada and around the world engage to some degree in activities aimed at forging global connections and building global competencies among their students, faculty, and administrative units. Developing such activities at many levels within universities is now a central part of institutional planning, structures, and programming – a phenomenon known as the internationalization of higher education. (Association of Universities and Colleges of Canada, 2014, p. 3)

The enrollment of international students contributes to the increasing multiculturalism and diversity on campus, while providing a global perspective in the classroom. Additionally, international student enrolment can help in the development of global cultural skills throughout the student body, both in and outside of the classroom. The presence of international students represents a cost benefit for the institutions and Canada. Roslyn Kunin and Associates (2017) reports that $15.5 billion was spent by international students who studied in Canada in 2016. Today, most postsecondary institutional leaders see the enrollment of international students to be an institutional priority.

International Students at the University of Windsor

The University of Windsor has benefitted from a sizable growth in international students in recent years. Students attending with a student visa grew by 26 percent, from 950 students in 2009 to 3,595 in 2018 (University of Windsor, 2020c). This has led the university to address several key issues of interest to international students, including academic integrity, English language development, immigration support, mental health services, social support, and writing support. This study focuses on academic integrity, especially on the following three sub-areas: plagiarism, academic writing, and information literacy.

At the University of Windsor, we expect our students, faculty, and staff to contribute to a positive environment where academic integrity is upheld in all our work. The university created an Academic Integrity Office which advocates for academic integrity through honest, education, and enforcement. Similar to what is happening at other higher education institutions, plagiarism is an important issue to address at University of Windsor, and Zhang and Almani (2018) suggest that "this issue is becoming more serious because of the increasing number of international students and easy access to online resources" (p. 1). According to the *Ninth Annual Comprehensive Student Discipline: 2012-2013* at University of Windsor submitted by Arbex (2014), 74 disciplinary cases investigated are involved with plagiarism which "continues to be the most prevalent integrity violation among all complaints" (p. 4), and 39% (i.e., 29) of these cases were engaged by international students, whose population constitutes 14% of the total students enrolled in that year.

Hayes and Intrano (2005) assert that cultural differences play a role in international students' plagiarism. A study of Chinese students at University of Windsor indicates that they do not take full advantage of library resources and are "often unaware of legal and ethical issues surrounding the access and use of information" due to language limitations and cultural differences (Liu & Winn, 2009, p. 571). Amysberry (2009) points out that "cultural, educational, and linguistic" barriers create difficulties for international students to comprehend the academic integrity and plagiarism guidelines properly (p. 32). The rapid developments of digital technologies for teaching, learning, and research may also promote plagiarism (Power, 2009; Sulikowski, 2008). Sutherland-Smith (2010) suggests that universities take a "holistic" approach to "implementing sustainable reform" (p. 13) in their plagiarism management, moving out of merely replying on legal discourse, an approach still adopted by many universities.

Even if they are aware of the concept of plagiarism, many international students are unaware of the importance of citing information correctly and have difficulties with referencing in academic writing (Liu & Winn, 2009). The university has created a Writing Support Desk in its main library years ago, which helps international students to analyze and integrate sources, enhance citing, and strengthen their research papers and theses through workshops, class visitations, and individual consultations.

In addition to what has been mentioned above, the University of Windsor provided Strategical Priority Fund (SPF) grants to support projects that aimed to help international students succeed in their program of study. International students tend to experience significant difficulty developing their information literacy skills in Western institutions (Han, 2012). Libraries and librarians can play a key role in these areas by helping international students prevent plagiarism and improve their information literacy skills (Chen & Van Ullen, 2011; Zimmerman, 2012). This chapter reports on the "Library and Academic Literacy Enhancement Program for International Students", a multi-year collaborative SPF project that was carried out by librarians and other researchers from different units across the campus to support international students' development of literacy skills.

LITERATURE REVIEW

Challenges Faced by International Students

Research has found that international students cannot be made information-literate in the same way as English native students, due to the challenges such as "difficulty with the English language, unfamiliarity with [foreign] library systems, lack of comfort with technology, and tendency toward plagiarism" (Badke, 2002, p. 60). Some findings suggest that not all international students, upon arrival at their host universities, have proper information retrieval skills to take advantage of online public access catalogue systems (Allen, 1993; Battle, 2004). Many international students arrive with erroneous beliefs about the functions of Western academic libraries (Jiao, Onwuegbuize, & Lichtenstein, 1996). Findings from more recent studies reveal that international students have strong technology skills, but remain unfamiliar with library resources, services, and online library information search and retrieval interface (Hughes, 2010). Ishimura and Barlett (2014) argue that because of their lower English proficiency, international students may have difficulty working out their own research needs in relation to assignment requirements. Liu and Winn's (2009) study found that cultural differences are still a barrier when it comes for Chinese students to fully take advantage of existing library resources. Furthermore, international students tend to lack understanding about librarians' role and their "research expertise," "subject specialties," and "contributions to academic knowledge" (Datig, 2014, pp. 355-356). Compared to domestic students, these students face unique challenges in information retrieval and evaluation as well as information use in terms of comprehending and citing information (Zhao & Mawhinney, 2015). In short, international students generally experience significant difficulty developing their information literacy skills in Western institutions (Han, 2012).

However, library instructions and information literacy training programs for international students are usually very brief and general, and they tend to treat international students the same as their domestic counterparts, instead of differentiating and responding to the different needs. As students themselves tend to expect course-related or subject-specific training, Han (2012) suggests that rather than only focusing on basic information skills, the training should consider different needs within a research context. Badke (2002) argues that, to help international students with their academic success, librarians and higher education institutions should provide them with compulsory and comprehensive training to gain understanding of Western approach to education, and skills for library use.

Information Literacy and International Students

The Association of College and Research Libraries (ACRL) (2016) defines information literacy as:

[T]he set of integrated abilities encompassing the reflective discovery of information, the understanding of how information is produced and valued, and the use of information in creating new knowledge and participating ethically in communities of learning. (p. 3)

Information literacy is urgently demanded in response to the rapid increase of information resources and ways of access (Bundy, 2004). It is important for international students to learn how to complete a comprehensive literature review, to evaluate information in the context of their subjects and projects of learning and research, and to appropriately utilize and cite sources of information in their own academic work (Battle, 2004; Rempel & Davidson, 2008). Generally speaking, students are learning how to seek information in academic contexts (Julien & Barker, 2009), so it is necessary for information literacy skills to be regarded and accepted as core competency to be offered systematically at universities (Breivik, 2005). Usually we have rationale for such program, and we design it, bring it into effect, and evaluate students' learning outcomes. In that sense, information literacy can be discussed in each step, from framework design to assessment system, or from people who should be involved to what materials should be used in the program.

The roles of librarians and instructors in higher education institutions have been frequently mentioned in previous research, but there is not much discussion about how they could cooperate with each other, or how they view the training programs related to information literacy. For example, Badke (2002) points out that librarians are in a unique position to initiate the development of training programs that move beyond the basics of information literacy to academic literacy, and Johnston (2014) recommends that librarians, English language instructors and other academic support professionals consider the aspects of international students' learning approaches, various levels of experiences and knowledge, language limitation, and other challenges in information literacy curriculum development.

Plagiarism and International Students

Plagiarism has various definitions, but it seems they all share the main focus on:

[T]he practice of directly copying and then presenting an existing production without accurate citing or referencing, and/or passing off the product as one's own, without permission from the original producer. (Copyleaks, n.d., para. 2)

Evering and Moorman (2012) argue that plagiarism is a concept that is socially constructed and not universally recognized, and "the way today's students learn, think, and work" (p. 39) should be taken into consideration. Therefore academic institutions need to explicitly explain what their definition of plagiarism is to help students have a clear understanding of it, so as to avoid unintentional or unconscious plagiarism due to the lack of sufficient information regarding plagiarism (Weidler, Multhaup, & Faust, 2012). The major contributing factors to the plagiarism and academic integrity issues associated with international students could be unintentional plagiarism, cultural differences, and insufficient supporting programs specific to them (Fatemi & Saito, 2019).

Cultural shocks are normal to the students in a new academic environment which has different practices in instructional methods, assignment requirements, and writing styles that are different from what they experienced in their home countries, making it difficulty for them to identify and adapt to the rules and expectations on plagiarism-free papers (Chen & Van Ullen, 2011). Because of their cultural background, it is possible that international students may attribute sources inappropriately (Abasi & Graves, 2008), and may face more challenges regarding the plagiarism issues.

Youmans (2011) argues that plagiarism is usually determined by the employment of programs such as Turnitin.com, and it is possible that the overlapped content identified among papers could be coincidental. Hu and Lei (2011) assert that the conceptualization of plagiarism may be difficult for international students as their interpretation of the concept and meaning associated with plagiarism varies, as the link between plagiarism and stealing other people's ideas and expressions could be perceived differently.

Referencing sources of information is essential in academic writing, as citation does not only acknowledge the original authors' work, but also offers evidence of the source as well as avoids plagiarism (Vardi, 2012). However, international students may experience challenge to cite sources of information properly, due to their limited understanding on the indirect use of other people's ideas and the particular parts being referenced (Vardi, 2012). Lack of English proficiency could place another obstacle for international students to synthesize and use source information properly, which may lead to plagiarism (Lund, 2004).

A number of measures have been taken to help develop students' information literacy so as to deal with plagiarism issues. Risquez, O'Dwyer, and Ledwith (2013) developed a course for students across all disciplines to promote academic integrity using a critical and creative approach to reference and citation rather than punitive approach. The University of Albany designed new workshops on the research process and plagiarism focused on international students, and the results indicated that participating students showed significant improvement in their knowledge of information literacy and how it related to their course work and research (Chen & Van Ullen, 2011). Online information literacy and plagiarism tutorials become favorable for instructors because they enable students to recognize plagiarism cases (Risquez, O'Dwyer, & Ledwith, 2011). Garber, Berg, and Chester-Fangman (2017) created an online academic honesty video tutorial titled "Plagiarism: Making the Right Choices" to help students learn about academic honesty and dishonesty, which mainly emphasizes responsible decision making rather than negative consequences. The video tutorial was embedded in the university's learning management system as well as availed on the library's website, and it was configured to be accessible from a variety of electronic devices. Lambert's (2014) "Combating Student Plagiarism: An Academic Librarian's Guide" provides very useful information on how to help instructors and students combat plagiarism.

Instead of merely relying on guidelines and punishment mechanisms, information literacy education can be employed to help students to get a good understanding of what plagiarism is, and also how to avoid it (Davis, 2011). To make it more effective, institutions can take actions such as encouraging collaboration among faculties, libraries and other academic supporting units on campus, organizing workshops designed and delivered by libraries, making plagiarism a mandatory component in related courses, such as technical communications, research methods, or literature review (Zhang & Almani, 2018). Developing online library tutorials, workbook and web pages specifically for international students is another pathway to support them (Bordonaro, 2019), and it may be more beneficial if institutions require anti-plagiarism instruction as an integral component of their curriculum (Lampert, 2004; Zhang & Almani, 2018). Academic integrity can also be promoted through "more meaningful assignments and experiences" (Evering & Moorman, 2012, p. 39).

BACKGROUND

The Library and Academic Literacy Enhancement Program for International Students

In April 2013, a group of researchers from Leddy Library, Faculty of Education, and International Student Centre at University of Windsor collaboratively made an initiative titled "the Library and Academic Literacy Enhancement Program for International Students". The initiative was supported by the Deans of the Library, Faculty of Education, and other faculties who have a large percentage of international students. The project aimed to enhance the library and academic literacy skills of international students at the University, who would obtain an understanding of information and its proper use in an academic context. In this project, the library and academic literacy refers to the ability to: (1) understand the library's function and structure; (2) retrieve, evaluate, and use information; (3) deal with issues of copyright; and (4) carry out academic writing by properly using citations and references. The project was supported by the University of Windsor SPF grant.

With the support of the grant, three Research Assistants were recruited to join the team assisting with various tasks, including environmental scan, workshop development and delivery, and data collection. The team started the project with a comprehensive review of related literature and other resources about academic integrity and information literacy of international students, such as library and information science literature, comprehensive student discipline reports at the University, and web resources provided by universities in Ontario and Canada. Subject librarians were consulted about existing library instructions and other services to international students at the Library. The team also reached out to instructors and academic supporting staff who worked closely with international students on campus regarding the issues of and services to international students at the University. Based on the information collected through these activities and the researchers' own experiences working with international students, the team agreed that it is critical to help international students understand the concept of plagiarism and obtain skills to avoid it.

The first action the team took was to develop a series of workshops on plagiarism covering the topics of definition, types, possible causes, potential consequences, and examples of plagiarism, as well as how to prevent plagiarism from happening. Two members in the team led the workshop development with the contribution from other members via their feedback and comments on the workshop. There were two portions in the workshop, including the workshop presentation and the survey tests. The survey tests were designed to measure the effectiveness of the workshop and were in form of a pretest and a post-test. Each test consisted of nine multiple choice questions about plagiarism and related topics taught in the workshop presentation. The same test was given to the students in the class before and after the workshop presentation. The tests were anonymous, and their results were calculated upon the total correct answers of all the students in the classroom who handed in their tests. In the workshops, students were asked to practice the techniques of quoting, paraphrasing, patch-writing, and summarizing sentences to avoid plagiarism. A tip sheet with related resources available at the Library and the University designed for students' future reference was distributed at the workshops. These workshops were customized to address specific needs of classes in different programs in terms of subject areas and duration that class instructors assigned to them.

In 2014-2016, the workshops were presented to over 1,000 international students enrolled in a variety of programs, including the English Language Improvement Program (ELIP), business, education, and engineering programs at the University. For example, through discussion with the Centre for English Language Development, the advanced level of the ELIP program (i.e., ELIP 3) was determined as best suitable to this workshop. The team taught the plagiarism workshops to ELIP3 students registered in different sections of the class. In collaboration with the Business Librarian and a professor at Odette School of Business, a series of 75 minutes of plagiarism workshops following 45 minutes of library instructions on business resources were delivered to students registered in the course "Managing Employees" in the Master of Management (MoM) program. Besides regular classes, the team also reached out to the Graduate Student Society and the International Student Centre to host a one-hour open session on plagiarism to international students from various graduate and undergraduate programs on campus.

Over 200 students participated in the open session. Data were collected through pre- and post-test to measure the effectiveness of the workshops at some of the classes.

In addition to plagiarism workshops, a series of information literacy workshops were also developed to help students establish a fuller understanding on ethical and legal issues associated with information use, and to further enhance their library and academic literacy skills required in Canadian universities. The workshop is rooted on the information literacy competency standards for higher education by the ACRL, American Library Association (2000). Online tutorials offered by other academic libraries were also consulted, particularly the Information Literacy Portal created by University of Idaho (n.d.). The information literacy workshop developed in this project contains six modules covering the following topics: (1) what is information? (2) matching information to your topic; (3) how to search successfully; (4) locating the right information for your information need; (5) evaluating your resources; and (6) sharing your ideas using citation.

Because facilitation required a large amount of time to go through all modules of the information literacy workshop in classroom, the team encountered difficulty finding classes to fit the workshop in. With the assistance of a professor at the Faculty of Education, a workshop including two half-day sessions were established and delivered to a small group of graduate education students outside of their coursework. Pre- and post-tests were applied to each module to measure the effectiveness of the information literacy workshop. Due to the small size of the participants, researchers were able to collect additional information about these sessions and other issues students may have encountered via class observations.

Table 1 summarizes the objectives, modules, number of questions, data collection method, grading system, and participants of the plagiarism workshop and the information literacy workshop in this study.

DATA ANALYSIS AND RESULTS

Plagiarism Workshop

At the beginning of each workshop, students were asked to complete a test sheet. At the end, they were given the same questions on another test sheet labelled post-test. Each test included the following nine questions:

1. What is plagiarism?
2. Is submitting one of your assignments into two different courses considered plagiarism?
3. Is buying a paper or assignment considered plagiarism?
4. Is translating material in a paper from one language to another and submitting it as your own work considered plagiarism?
5. How can a sentence be paraphrased?
6. What is patch-writing?
7. What are the reasons that can justify plagiarism?
8. Which one of these are citation styles: American Psychological Association (APA), Modern Language Association (MLA), IEEE, American Society of Civil Engineers (ASCE), American Sociological Association (ASA), Chicago?
9. How can you help yourself to avoid plagiarism?

Table 1. Plagiarism workshop and information literacy workshop

Workshop	Plagiarism Workshop	Information Literacy Workshop
Objectives	Help students understand the concept of plagiarism and obtain skills to avoid it	Help students establish a fuller understanding on ethical and legal issues associated with information use and to further enhance their library and academic literacy skills
Module(s)	One module covers the definition, types, possible causes, potential consequences, and examples of plagiarism as well as how to prevent plagiarism from happening	Six modules cover the following topics: (1) the concept, types and formats of information; (2) selecting topics and key concepts pertinent to a research; (3) the concept and coverage of databases and techniques of database search; (4) locating information and understanding citations; (5) evaluating information; and (6) citing information and avoiding plagiarism
Number of Questions in the Tests	Eight questions in total	Modules 1-4 and 6: eight questions in each module Module 5: nine questions 49 questions in total
Data Collection Method	Pre- and post-tests on the same set of questions	Pre- and post-tests on the same set of questions, Class observations
Grading System	Each question was worth one point. The average percentage score by all participants for each question was used in the data results and analysis.	Each question was worth one point. The average percentage score by all participants for each question was used in the data results and analysis.
Duration	One hour to one-and-a-half hours for each workshop	Five hours in total for six modules of the workshop
Participants	About 128 students in ELIP3 program About 140 students in MoM program	Six graduate education students (five international and one domestic students) participated in Modules 1-3 Five graduate education students (four international and one domestic students) participated in Modules 4-6

The Appendix provides the complete pretest and post-test questions along with their predefined answers for plagiarism workshops. The tests were conducted in both ELIP 3 and MoM classes at ELIP and MoM programs respectively in Fall 2014.

ELIP 3 is the most advanced level of English language improvement program offered at the University of Windsor. It prepares undergraduate and graduate international students to meet the English proficiency requirements for their admissions to university study (University of Windsor, 2020a). The plagiarism workshop was delivered to the ELIP 3 class which included two sections. A total of 125 valid pretest sheets and 128 valid post-test sheets were received. The numbers of pre- and post-test sheets received were slightly different because a couple of students arrived late to the class and missed the pretest. Figure 1 illustrates the average scores for pre- and post- tests in this class.

MoM program is a professional master's degree program offered by Odette School of Business at University of Windsor (University of Windsor, 2020b). The workshops were conducted in all three sections of the course "Managing Employees" for MoM students. All students enrolled in this course were international students. One hundred and thirty-eight valid pretest and 140 valid post-test sheets were collected in the workshop. In these sections, a couple of students left early so they missed the post-test while a few other students arrived late and missed the pretest. Figure 2 illustrates the average percentage scores of the tests at MoM class.

Figures 1 and 2 indicate that although the average scores for individual questions in the two student groups may be different, the patterns of the test results before and after the workshops are similar for

Figure 1. Test Results for ELIP 3 Class

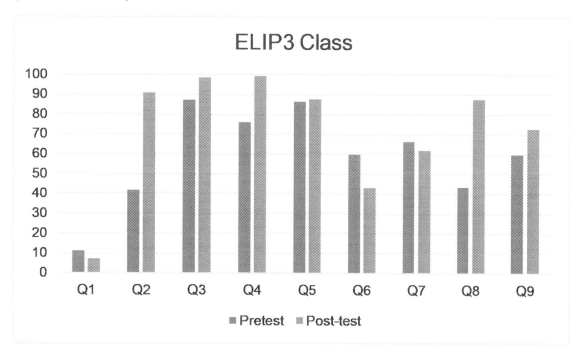

Figure 2. Test Results for MoM Class

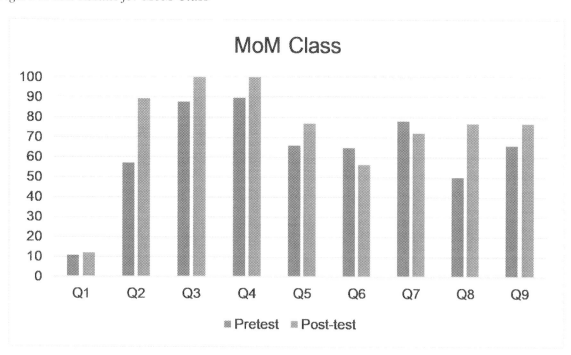

each question.

Question 1 is about the definition of plagiarism. Most students in ELIP 3 and MoM chose the wrong answer even after the workshops. A closer examination reveals that students might be confused with the terms of plagiarism, copyright, and patent. Many of them chose "unauthorized use of patented or copyrighted materials" as well as "use of another person's written work without acknowledging the source" for the question "what is plagiarism?" Further explanation on these terms with examples may help address the issue in future workshops. If the patent and copyright part is not considered, then almost all students chose the correct answer after the workshops in those classes.

Questions 2-4 target on what kind of behaviours are considered plagiarism, which is important to enable students to avoid plagiarism in their study or research. Figures 1 and 2 indicate noticeable improvement after the workshops compared to what had been before the workshops for both groups, especially for Question 2, "submitting one of your assignments into two different courses is considered plagiarism." The test scores for this question went up from 41.6 to 90.6 in the ELIP 3 class and up from 57.2 to 89.3 for MoM class. The post-test results for Questions 3 and 4 reached over 98 for both classes.

Questions 5 and 6 are about paraphrase and patch-writing. The results show no meaningful improvement for either group. The test scores for Question 6 even got worse after the workshop. This result suggests that it is hard for students to learn techniques of paraphrasing and avoid patch-writing in a very short timeframe. More examples and exercises would be helpful for students to comprehend the concept. In addition, students may have trouble understanding the meaning of the term patch-writing precisely. The results do not necessarily imply that students do not understand the concept, but may indicate they need further instructions and practices on how to quote, paraphrase, and summarize text from other people's work. One class, which combined many other concepts, was far from enough to teach students this concept and related skills. The language barrier faced by international students may play a role here as well. It needs further investigation.

Question 7 is about what may cause plagiarism. The average scores for MoM students were much higher than those for ELIP 3 students. However, both groups got lower scores after the workshop. The question and its predefined answers for students to make selections from might not have been clear to students. Some students wrote the meaning of "justify" in other languages on the test sheets which indicates they did not understand this English word. It might be beneficial if the questions themselves could be made clearer to students in the future.

The test scores for Question 8, citation styles, went up remarkably for both groups. The results show that students get to know more types of citation styles, to name a few, APA, MLA, and Chicago, after the workshops. Prior to the workshops, most of the students only recognized one or two citation styles.

Question 9 is about ways to get help to avoid plagiarism. The scores for both groups increased over 10% after the workshops. The answers students picked also indicate that asking friends is still an important way for many students to seek help for their academic work. Figure 3 illustrates the pretest results for MoM and ELIP students.

In pretest, the scores of MoM students for most questions, including Questions 2-4 and Questions 6-9 are higher than those of ELIP students, especially Question 2, Question 4, and Questions 7-9. This could be interpreted that MoM students might have had a better understanding on plagiarism-related concept prior to the workshop compared to students enrolled in ELIP programs. Figure 4 shows the post-test results for both groups. The results show that the scores of Question 2, Question 4, and Question 9 got closer for both groups after the workshop. ELIP students' scores of Question 2 and Question 8 are even higher than MoM students' in the post-test, although their scores were lower than MoM students in the

Figure 3. Pretest results for MoM and ELIP Students

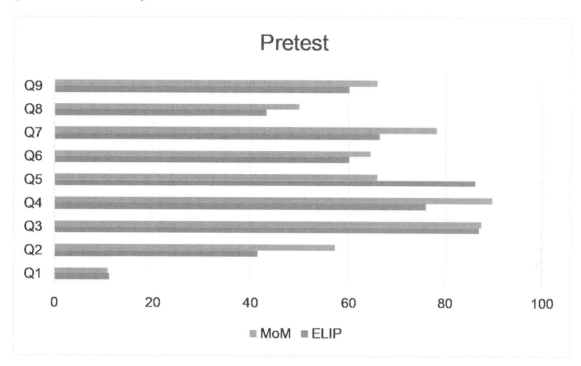

Figure 4. Post-test results for ELIP and MoM students

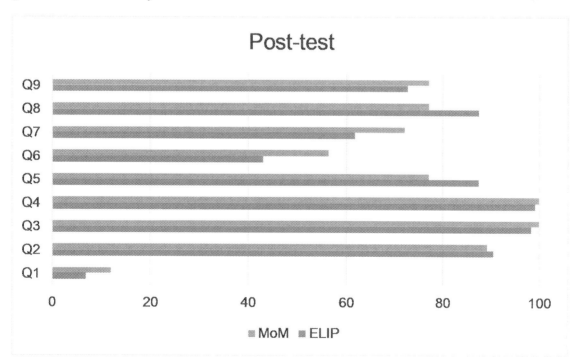

pretest. The workshops were most effective in terms of improving students' understanding of what kinds of behaviours are considered plagiarism, various citation styles, and where to get help to avoid plagiarism to both groups. Although there is no improvement in the post-test for either group, MoM students got much higher scores for Question 7 in both pre- and post-test. They exhibit a better understanding about excuses of plagiarism than students registered in ELIP programs.

Generally speaking, a one-time plagiarism workshop embedded in regular classes can be effective for students to become more knowledgeable on different types of plagiarism and ways to avoid plagiarism. This can apply to students already enrolled in graduate programs or students in language improvement programs which prepare for them to meet the English proficiency requirements for undergraduate or graduate academic programs at the University. However, results suggest that such workshops may not be sufficient for students to improve their quoting, paraphrasing, and summarizing skills. Further instructions or writing help are necessary for international students in language improvement programs or regular academic programs.

Information Literacy Workshop

The information literacy workshop consists of the following six modules:

1.   What is information?

This module covers popular and scholarly information, primary and secondary information, and different formats of information.

2.   Matching the information to your topic

This module focuses on the concept of research, using topics, broadening and/or narrowing research topics, and choosing keywords.

3.   How to search successfully?

This module talks about the database's concept and coverage, creating search queries and search strategies.

4.   Locating the right information for your information need

This module includes reading citations, locating sources, and library classification.

5.   Evaluating your resources

This module covers the elements required to evaluate a resource, such as authorship, publishing body, point of view, knowledge of the literature, accuracy, and currency.

6.   Sharing your ideas using criteria

This module includes the concept of citation, quoting, paraphrasing, and summarizing. Definition, types and reasons of plagiarism as well as the concept of copyright are also included in this module.

In the Fall of 2015, the information literacy workshop was delivered to a group of graduate students from the Faculty of Education at the University of Windsor. There were two sessions and each session lasted two-and-a-half hours. There were six participants in the first session on Modules 1-3, including five international students enrolled in the graduate program in Education. The second session designated for Modules 4-6 was hosted in the following week. Four international students attended the second session which included three who had attended the first session. Although the workshop was intended for international students, one domestic student participated in both sessions for all six modules. The test results of the domestic student are presented in comparison with international students' results in this chapter, which may help reveal the necessity of developing information literacy instruction specific to international students.

Similar to the plagiarism workshop described in the previous section, pre- and post-tests were conducted to measure the success of the information literacy workshop. Except for Module 3, which contained nine questions, the other five modules had eight questions in each. All questions were multiple-choice. These questions were distributed to students prior to the start of each module and then students were asked to complete the same questions on the post-test sheets right after the instruction of each module. The completed test sheets were collected after each session.

Students in both sessions were very engaged. Several students asked questions related to defining and searching topics for their thesis projects during break. In the sessions, the researchers observed that a few students kept looking up the meaning of terms on the test sheets in online dictionaries using their cellphones during the pretest. There were translations in languages other than English written beside a

Figure 5. Test Results of Information Literacy Workshop (International Students)

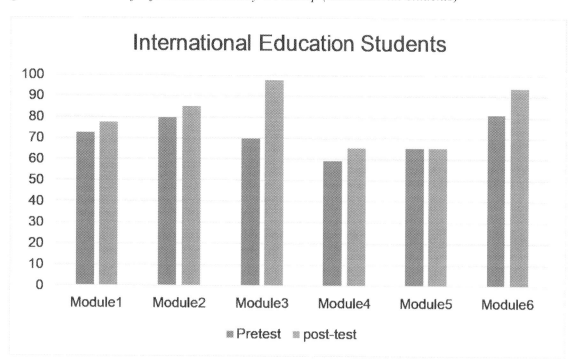

couple of terms on the test sheets submitted after the sessions, such as translations for primary, reputable, cons, etc. It was observed that some students also looked up words from the PowerPoint slides during the workshop.

Figure 5 illustrates the test results of international students for all six modules. The results show that the test scores went up after the sessions for international students, except for Module 5 in which the score remained the same in the post-test. Module 3 recorded a most noticeable improvement after these sessions.

Figure 6 shows the results of the domestic student who participated in the sessions. The student received full mark in four out of the total six modules, including Modules 1, 2, 4, and 6 in the post-test after the workshop. However, the scores for the remaining two modules dropped after the sessions. The reason for this needs further investigation.

Figure 6. Test Results of Information Literacy Workshop (Domestic Student)

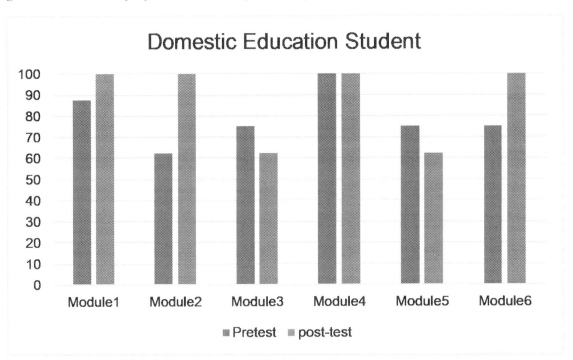

Module 1 is about what information is and the types and formats of information. Further analysis on students' answers to the questions shows that students understood well on website-related issues, but did not perform well on what kind of information resources are considered primary sources and/or scholarly sources. Figures 5 and 6 show that international students improved slightly on their understanding on this topic after the workshop while the domestic student received full mark after the session.

Module 2 focuses on selecting research topics, including choosing keywords, and broadening and narrowing topics. Narrowing topics and choosing keywords seem to be the most difficult parts for students. The test results indicate that international students gained a better understanding in this area and the domestic student got full mark after the workshop (see Figures 5 and 6).

Module 3 teaches the concepts and techniques of databases, fields, and advanced search. Figure 5 demonstrates a meaningful improvement of test scores received by international students after attending the workshop. However, the score received by the domestic student dropped in the post-test for this module. Due to the small sample size of data collected, future investigation is necessary to reveal the issues and causes.

Module 4 is about how to locate information, including understanding citations, locating a source at the Library, and understanding the concept of library classification system. The results suggest that international students participating in this study did not comprehend the library classification system adopted in academic libraries in Canada. In addition, they seemed to not know library websites and collections are an important place to start their research according to the answers they selected for the questions in the tests. On the other hand, the test questions included in this module seemed quite straightforward to the domestic student who answered all of them correctly in both pre- and post-tests. This indicates that libraries need to reach out to international students to provide library instructions specifically designed for these students in order to improve their knowledge about academic libraries in Canada.

Module 5 targets on information evaluation. Both international and domestic students did not show any improvement after the session. The domestic student received a lower score in the post-test (see Figures 5 and 6). The results imply that a one-time workshop may not be sufficient to teach students such a topic. More examples and practices included in the workshop might be helpful for students to better understand this topic. Further investigation is needed on how to improve the information evaluation skills for students effectively.

Module 6 is about citing information and avoiding plagiarism. Figures 5 and 6 demonstrate a good understanding of both international students and the domestic student on the topics covered in this module after the workshop. The workshop helped students improve their knowledge and skills in citing information correctly to avoid plagiarism.

Figure 7 illustrates the pretest results for both domestic and international students who attended the workshop, while Figure 8 compares the post-test results of both groups. Figures 7-8 indicate that the domestic student has a better understanding than international students on topics covered in most modules, including Modules 1, 3, 4, and 5 prior to the workshop. Full mark was received by the domestic student in the post-test of the following four modules: Modules 1, 2, 4, and 6. International students received higher grades on Modules 3 and 5 in the post-test although the grades were lower than the domestic student's in pretest. Compared to domestic students, international students may need more library instructions on locating information and where to search scholarly information for their own research.

The sample size for this workshop is quite small so the results can hardly be generalized to all students. Data collected from more students and student groups would help further identify issues related to both international and domestic students. Nonetheless, the data collected in this project indicate that one-time information literacy workshop helps improve international students' information literacy skills in most areas, especially knowledge and skills related to how to locate information and where to start their research using library resources. More in-depth instructions and research help on information evaluation in addition to one-time workshops are necessary for domestic students as well as international students.

Figure 7. Pretest Results of Information Literacy Workshop

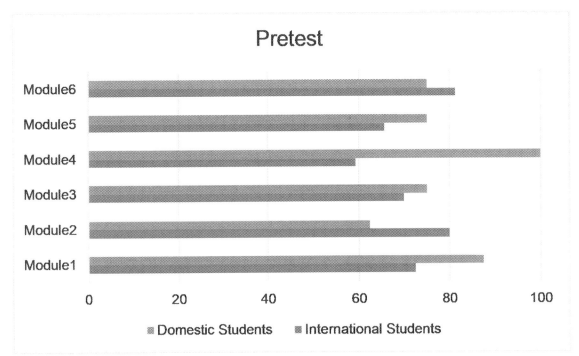

Figure 8. Post-test Results of Information Literacy Workshop

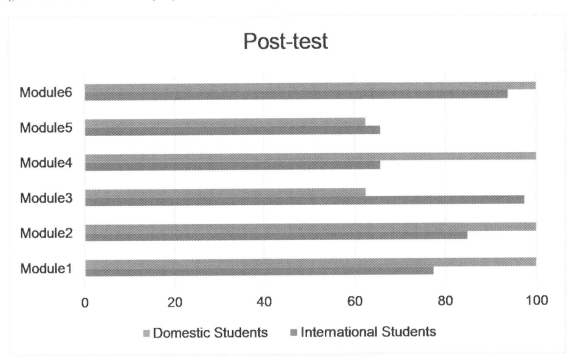

DISCUSSION AND CONCLUSION

In this study, we investigated the knowledge of academic integrity and information literacy in international students. This research suggests that one-time plagiarism workshops can improve international students' understanding of what behaviours are considered plagiarism and how to avoid them. Results also indicate that additional instructions and writing support are needed for these students to improve their citation skills. The data collected from the information literacy workshop demonstrate that providing specialized library instructions on Canadian academic libraries' resources and services to international students would be beneficial to them. Further instructions on information evaluation may be valuable to both international and domestic students. The findings from both plagiarism and information literacy workshops suggest that language limitation is still a barrier for international students to be more aware of plagiarism and become more information literate in higher education in Canada. Furthermore, this project implies that faculty and librarian collaboration play a critical role in the development and delivery of workshops to enhance international students' library and academic literacy skills.

We understand that the method of assessment for the workshops used in this study needs to be improved to yield more meaningful and useful results (Storm, Friedman, Murayama, & Bjork, 2014). The small sample size also places limitations on the findings of the information literacy workshop. Moreover, international students by no means should be considered a homogeneous group. Awareness regarding international students can be raised in the higher education context with the promotion of intercultural pedagogy (Lee, 2017). By learning not only content, but also study strategies, students could become more effective learners (Dunlosky, 2013; Dunlosky, Rawson, Marsh, Nathan, & Willingham, 2013).

Future study may utilize additional assessment methods to gain better understanding on the international students' knowledge and their ability to implement the skills learnt from the workshops in their academic work, for example, online surveys, face to face interviews, and adding evaluation on search strategies and information literacy to the writing assignments in communications, literature review, or other suitable classes through the collaboration between librarians and instructors. Another direction is to create and experiment with online tutorials based on the workshops developed in this project and integrate them into the learning management system, which instructors can incorporate into their curricula, and students can study based on their own individual needs and time flexibilities. The test questionnaire can be implemented in the online environment to gather data for analysing and improving the online tutorials. It would also be worthwhile to explore the possibility of embedding plagiarism and information literacy workshops to the curriculum of programs in faculties that have large percentage of international student population at the University of Windsor or other Canadian institutions.

Acknowledgment

The project described in this paper was supported by the University of Windsor Strategic Priority Fund.

REFERENCES

Abasi, A., & Graves, B. (2008). Academic literacy and plagiarism: Conversations with international graduate students and disciplinary professors. *Journal of English for Academic Purposes, 7*(4), 221–233. doi:10.1016/j.jeap.2008.10.010

Allen, M. B. (1993). International students in academic libraries: A user survey. *College & Research Libraries, 54*(4), 323–333. doi:10.5860/crl_54_04_323

American Library Association. (2000). *ACRL standards: Information literacy competency standards for higher education.* Retrieved from https://crln.acrl.org/index.php/crlnews/article/view/19242/22395

Amsberry, D. (2009). Deconstructing plagiarism: International students and textual borrowing practices. *The Reference Librarian, 51*(1), 31–44. doi:10.1080/02763870903362183

Arbex, D. (2014). *Ninth annual comprehensive student discipline report: 2012-2013.* Retrieved from https://www.uwindsor.ca/secretariat/sites/uwindsor.ca.secretariat/files/apc140410-5.3a_-_comprehensive_student_discipline_report_9th_annual.pdf

Association of College and Research Libraries. (2016). *Framework for information literacy for higher education.* Retrieved from http://www.ala.org/acrl/sites/ala.org.acrl/files/content/issues/infolit/Framework_ILHE.pdf

Association of Universities and Colleges of Canada. (2014). *Canada's universities in the world, AUCC international survey 2014.* Ottawa: Association of Universities and Colleges of Canada. Retrieved from https://www.univcan.ca/wp-content/uploads/2015/07/internationalization-survey-2014.pdf

Badke, W. (2002). International students: Information literacy or academic literacy. *Academic Exchange Quarterly, 6*(4), 60–65.

Battle, C. J. (2004). *The effect of information literacy instruction on library anxiety among international students* (Doctoral dissertation, University of North Texas, Denton, the United States). Retrieved from https://search.proquest.com/docview/305138026?pq-origsite=gscholar

Bordonaro, K. (2019). Forging multiple pathways: Integrating international students into a Canadian university library. In Y. Luckert & L. T. Inge (Eds.), *The globalized library: American academic libraries and international students, collections, and practices* (pp. 85–97). Association of College & Research Libraries.

Breivik, P. S. (2005). 21st century learning and information literacy. *Change, 37*(2), 21–27. doi:10.3200/CHNG.37.2.21-27

Bundy, A. (Ed.). (2004). *Australian and New Zealand information literacy framework: Principles, standards and practice* (2nd ed.). University of South Australia.

Canadian Bureau of International Education. (2018). *International students in Canada.* Ottawa: CBIE. Retrieved from https://cbie.ca/wp-content/uploads/2018/09/International-Students-in-Canada-ENG.pdf

Chen, Y., & Van Ullen, M. K. (2011). Helping international students succeed academically through research process and plagiarism workshops. *College & Research Libraries, 72*(3), 209–235. doi:10.5860/crl-117rl

Copyleaks. (n.d.). *What is plagiarism?* Retrieved from https://copyleaks.com/education/what-is-plagiarism

Datig, I. (2014). What is a library?: International college students' perceptions of libraries. *Journal of Academic Librarianship, 40*(3–4), 350–356. doi:10.1016/j.acalib.2014.05.001

Davis, L. (2011). Arresting student plagiarism: Are we investigators or educators? *Business Communication Quarterly, 74*(2), 160–163. doi:10.1177/1080569911404053

Dunlosky, J. (2013). Strengthening the student toolbox: Study strategies to boost learning. *American Educator, 37*(3), 12–21.

Dunlosky, J., Rawson, K., Marsh, E., Nathan, M., & Willingham, D. (2013). Improving students' learning with effective learning techniques: Promising directions from cognitive and educational psychology. *Psychological Science in the Public Interest, 14*(1), 4–58. doi:10.1177/1529100612453266 PMID:26173288

Evering, L. C., & Moorman, G. (2012). Rethinking plagiarism in the Digital Age. *Journal of Adolescent & Adult Literacy, 56*(1), 35–44. doi:10.1002/JAAL.00100

Fatemi, G., & Saito, E. (2019). Unintentional plagiarism and academic integrity: The challenges and needs of postgraduate international students in Australia. *Journal of Further and Higher Education*, 1–15. Advance online publication. doi:10.1080/0309877X.2019.1683521

Garber, G., Berg, E., & Chester-Fangman, C. (2017). Rethinking plagiarism in information literacy instruction: A case study on cross-campus collaboration in the creation of an online academic honesty video tutorial. In T. Maddison & M. Kumaran (Eds.), *Distributed learning: Pedagogy and technology in online information literacy instruction* (pp. 341–360). Chandos Publishing. doi:10.1016/B978-0-08-100598-9.00019-2

Han, J. (2012). Information literacy challenges for Chinese PhD students in Australia: A biographical study. *Journal of Information Literacy, 6*(1), 3–17. doi:10.11645/6.1.1603

Hayes, N., & Introna, L. D. (2005). Cultural values, plagiarism, and fairness: When plagiarism gets in the way of learning. *Ethics & Behavior, 15*(3), 213–231. doi:10.120715327019eb1503_2

Hu, G., & Lei, J. (2011). Investigating Chinese university students' knowledge of and attitudes toward plagiarism from an integrated perspective. *Language Learning, 62*(3), 813–850. doi:10.1111/j.1467-9922.2011.00650.x

Hughes, H. (2010). International students' experiences of university libraries and librarians. *Australian Academic and Research Libraries, 41*(2), 77–89. doi:10.1080/00048623.2010.10721446

Institute of International Education. (2017). *2017 Project Atlas infographics.* New York: Institute of International Education. Retrieved from https://www.iie.org/Research-and-Insights/Project-Atlas/Explore-Data/Infographics/2017-Project-Atlas-Infographics

Ishimura, Y., & Bartlett, J. C. (2014). Are librarians equipped to teach international students? A survey of current practices and recommendations for training. *Journal of Academic Librarianship, 40*(3-4), 313–321. doi:10.1016/j.acalib.2014.04.009

Jackson, P. A. (2005). Incoming international students and the library: A survey. *RSR. Reference Services Review, 33*(2), 197–209. doi:10.1108/00907320510597408

Jiao, Q. G., Onwuegbuzie, A. J., & Lichtenstein, A. A. (1996). Library anxiety: Characteristics of 'at-risk' college students. *Library & Information Science Research, 18*(2), 151–163. doi:10.1016/S0740-8188(96)90017-1

Johnston, N. (2014). *Understanding the information literacy experiences of EFL students* (Unpublished doctoral dissertation). Queensland University of Technology, Brisbane, Australia.

Julien, H., & Barker, S. (2009). How high-school students find and evaluate scientific information: A basis for information literacy skills development. *Library & Information Science Research, 31*(1), 12–17. doi:10.1016/j.lisr.2008.10.008

Knight, J. (2003). Updated internationalization definition. *Industry and Higher Education, 33*, 2–3.

Lampert, L. (2004). Integrating discipline based anti-plagiarism instruction into the information literacy curriculum. *RSR. Reference Services Review, 32*(4), 347–355. doi:10.1108/00907320410569699

Lee, A. (2017). *Teaching interculturally: A framework for integrating disciplinary knowledge and intercultural development.* Stylus Publishers.

Liu, G., & Winn, D. (2009). Chinese graduate students and the Canadian academic library: A user study at the University of Windsor. *Journal of Academic Librarianship, 35*(6), 565–573. doi:10.1016/j.acalib.2009.08.001

Lund, J. R. (2004). Plagiarism: A cultural perspective. *Journal of Religious & Theological Information, 6*(3-4), 93–101. doi:10.1300/J112v06n03_08

Power, L. G. (2009). University students' perceptions of plagiarism. *The Journal of Higher Education, 80*(6), 643–662. doi:10.1080/00221546.2009.11779038

Rempel, H., & Davidson, J. (2008). Providing information literacy instruction to graduate students through literature review workshops. *Issues in Science and Technology Librarianship, 53.* Retrieved from https://pdxscholar.library.pdx.edu/ulib_fac/137/

Risquez, A., O'Dwyer, M., & Ledwith, A. (2011). Technology enhanced learning and plagiarism in entrepreneurship education. *Education + Training, 53*(8/9), 750–761. doi:10.1108/00400911111185062

Risquez, A., O'Dwyer, M., & Ledwith, A. (2013). 'Thou shalt not plagiarise': From self-reported views to recognition and avoidance of plagiarism. *Assessment & Evaluation in Higher Education, 38*(1), 34–43. doi:10.1080/02602938.2011.596926

Roslyn Kunin & Associates, Inc. (2017). *Economic impact of international education in Canada: 2017 update.* Vancouver: RKA, Inc. Retrieved from https://www.international.gc.ca/education/report-rapport/impact-2017/index.aspx?lang=eng

Statistics Canada. (2018). *Canadian postsecondary enrolments and graduates, 2016/2017.* Ottawa: Statistics Canada. Retrieved from https://www150.statcan.gc.ca/n1/daily-quotidien/181128/dq181128c-eng.htm

Storm, B. C., Friedman, M. C., Murayama, K., & Bjork, R. A. (2014). On the transfer of prior tests or study events to subsequent study. *Journal of Experimental Psychology. Learning, Memory, and Cognition, 40*(1), 115–124. doi:10.1037/a0034252 PMID:23978234

Sulikowski, M. M. (2008, Spring). Copy, paste, plagiarize. *Vanderbilt Magazine.* Retrieved from https://news.vanderbilt.edu/vanderbiltmagazine/copy_paste_plagiarize/

Sutherland-Smith, W. (2010). Retribution, deterrence, and reform: The dilemmas of plagiarism management in universities. *Journal of Higher Education Policy and Management, 32*(1), 5–16. doi:10.1080/13600800903440519

Universities Canada. (2014). *Canada's universities in the world: AUCC internationalization survey.* Ottawa: Universities Canada. Retrieved from https://www.univcan.ca/wp-content/uploads/2015/07/internationalization-survey-2014.pdf

University of Idaho. (n.d.). *Information literacy.* Retrieved from https://www.webpages.uidaho.edu/info_literacy/modules/module1/1_0.htm

University of Windsor. (2020a). *English language improvement program (ELIP).* Retrieved from https://www.uwindsor.ca/englishlanguagedevelopment/301/elip

University of Windsor. (2020b). *Master of management.* Retrieved from http://odette.uwindsor.ca/366/master-management

University of Windsor. (2020c). *Overall – 10 year historical.* University of Windsor Office of Institutional Analysis.

Vardi, I. (2012). Developing students' referencing skills: A matter of plagiarism, punishment and morality or of learning to write critically? *Higher Education Research & Development, 31*(6), 921–930. doi:10.1080/07294360.2012.673120

Weidler, B., Multhaup, K., & Faust, M. (2012). Accountability reduces unconscious plagiarism. *Applied Cognitive Psychology, 26*(4), 626–634. doi:10.1002/acp.2842

Youmans, R. (2011). Does the adoption of plagiarism-detection software in higher education reduce plagiarism? *Studies in Higher Education, 36*(7), 749–761. doi:10.1080/03075079.2010.523457

Zhang, Z., & Almani, A. (2018). Information literacy education and plagiarism issues: Inputs from international graduate students. *International Journal of Research in Engineering and Technology, 7*(7), 1–7. doi:10.15623/ijret.2018.0707001

Zhao, J. C., & Mawhinney, T. (2015). Comparison of native Chinese-speaking and native English-speaking engineering students' information literacy challenges. *Journal of Academic Librarianship, 41*(6), 712–724. doi:10.1016/j.acalib.2015.09.010

Zimmerman, M. (2012). Plagiarism and international students in academic libraries. *New Library World, 113*(5), 290–299. doi:10.1108/03074801211226373

KEY TERMS AND DEFINITIONS

Academic Integrity: Understanding of ethical and legal issues associated with information use.

Academic Library: A library belonging to a higher education institute to support teaching, learning and research.

Academic Literacy: The ability to understand, interpret, and construct meaningful text.

Academic Writing: A clear, concise, focussed, and structured kind of written discourse, normally backed up by evidence. Academic writing usually follows discipline-specific conventions.

Information Literacy: The expertise to perceive, retrieve, evaluate, and apply information effectively.

International Students: Students studying in a country under non-immigrant status.

Library Literacy: Familiarity with library resources, services, and material organization.

APPENDIX

Pretest and Post-test Questions for Plagiarism Workshop

1) What is plagiarism?
   A) Use of another person's written work without acknowledging the source
   B) Unauthorized use of patented or copyrighted materials
   C) All of the above
   D) None of the above
2) Submitting one of your assignments into two different courses is considered plagiarism
   A) TRUE
   B) FALSE
   C) It depends on other factors
3) Is buying a paper or assignment considered plagiarism?
   A) Yes
   B) No, because you paid for it
   C) No, because you are planning to only use parts of it
4) Is translating material in a paper from one language to another and submitting it as your own work considered plagiarism?
   A) Yes
   B) No, because you will paraphrase it
   C) No, because you are planning to only use the parts that translated correctly
5) How can a sentence be paraphrased?
   A) Use synonyms of the words found in the text
   B) Change the structure and grammar of the text
   C) All of the above
   D) None of the above
6) What is patch-writing?
   A) Copying a sentence from somewhere else and quoting it
   B) Summarizing few sentences from somewhere without citation
   C) Paraphrasing with too much reliance on the original text
   D) Taking parts of an original text and putting them together to form a new text
7) Which one of these reasons can justify plagiarism?
   A) I was too close to due date of the project or assignment
   B) I had a lot of stress and my workload was large
   C) I lack enough English language skills
   D) All of the above
   E) None of the above
8) Which one of these are citation styles?
   A) APA

B)   MLA
C)   IEEE
D)   ASCE
E)   ASA
F)   Chicago
G)   All of the above
H)   None of the above

9)   How can you help yourself to avoid plagiarism?
A)   Learn about referencing and quotation rules
B)   Use online software to check your papers
C)   Ask your friends if they have plagiarized
D)   All of the above
E)   Only A and B

Chapter 14

Effect of Provision and Utilization of Support Areas on International Students' Perceived Academic Success:
A Case Study of a Canadian Community College

Taiwo O. Soetan

https://orcid.org/0000-0002-4270-8213

Red River College, Canada

ABSTRACT

This study examined the effect the provision and utilization of different support areas had on the perceived academic success of international students at a large community college in Canada. The study considered the effect of the provision of support areas on one hand, and the utilization of these support areas on the other hand on the perceived academic success of international students. A quantitative study was conducted to measure the effect of the provision and utilization of support areas on international students' perceived academic success. A target sample size of 399 international students who were pursuing different academic programs at a large community college in Canada was recruited to participate in a hard copy, one-on-one survey in the winter semester of 2019. The Canadian government's strategy at both the federal and provincial/territorial levels of increasing international students' presence in Canada as a way of addressing the aging workforce and population challenge in Canada would be more successful with increased investments in these support areas.

DOI: 10.4018/978-1-7998-5030-4.ch014

INTRODUCTION

Community colleges in Canada belong to Colleges and Institutes Canada (CICan), formerly the Association of Canadian Community Colleges (ACCC). CICan, the national, voluntary membership organization representing publicly supported colleges, institutes, CEGEPS (i.e. *Collège d'enseignement général et professionnel,* in Quebec), and polytechnics in Canada, and internationally, is also the umbrella body for Canada's community colleges and institutes serving domestic, indigenous, and international students in various campuses across the country. Community colleges are sometimes called institutes, institutes of technology, technical colleges, regional colleges, university colleges or colleges.

In Canada, community colleges play important roles in supporting economic development and innovation based on their ties and links to their communities (CICan, n.d.; Universities Canada, 2015). Community colleges provide over 10,000 different higher education and training programs to a wide variety of students ranging from high school graduates, and adult learners to international and indigenous students and university graduates including professional and on-going training for professionals in the workforce in both the private and public sectors of the economy (CICan, n.d.). Academic programs in community colleges are usually developed through industry connections and collaborations, and internship opportunities. Programs range from health, business, technology, trades, academic upgrading, university preparation, applied and creative arts, hospitality and social sciences (Atlantic Colleges Atlantique, ACA, 2018; CICan, n.d).

Furthermore, community colleges are government-regulated and the higher education programs they offer are one to two year academic and pre-professional certificates, diplomas, two to three year associate degrees, four year bachelor's degrees, post graduate certificate (PGC), post graduate diploma (PGD) programs, and master's degree programs (CICan, n.d.). This study considered the effect of provision and utilization of support services on the perceived academic success of international students in community colleges in Canada using the Bronfenbrenner theory of human development.

Research Questions

The Bronfenbrenner's theory of human development provided theoretical orientations for forming research questions for this study. These questions address support areas and programs as well as policies that were available at the micro-level (individual), meso-level (institutional), and macro-level (government/societal) to international students attending a community college.

These questions were:

1. Do international students utilize identified support areas available to them at the micro (individual), meso (institutional), and macro (government/societal) levels?
2. Which support area(s) is/are most strongly related to international students' academic success?

Purpose of the Study

The purpose of this study was to examine the effect of the provision and utilization of support areas as well as policies/programs that influence international students' perceived academic success in community colleges in Canada. Although Bronfenbrenner (1979) identified four levels that influence an individual's development in his theory of human development, this study focused on only three of these levels (i.e., the micro-, meso-, and macro-levels). This is because the exo-level was subsumed in the other levels.

Rationale for the Study

The current literature shows that there is not much research conducted regarding the effect of the provision and utilization of support areas available to international students in Canadian community colleges and the effect of these support areas on their perceived academic success. This is unlike information available in literature regarding the support areas that are available to international students at the university and graduate school levels. The need to understand and determine the effect of support areas on international students at the community college level of higher education informed the reason for this research study.

The determination of the impact of the support areas available to international students at the various levels in which they operate, both on and off campus, on their perceived academic success is germane to this study. This would require a theoretical framework that is both relevant and applicable to international students at the community college level. That requirement informed the decision to consider the Bronfenbrenner's theory of human development as the theoretical framework for this research study.

Limitations of the Study

This study collected responses to a hard copy Qualtrics survey that 399 international students who were pursuing different academic programs at a large community college in Canada completed. However, different academic programs admit international students at different times of the year because some academic programs admit international students year-round (i.e., August, January, and May), while some academic programs admit students only in August. Due to the differences in admission dates across different departments and academic programs, some international students in the community college under consideration in this study may have taken advantage of the support areas more than some others, which may have had an impact on their perceived academic success.

INTERNATIONALIZATION IN CANADA

The Canadian Bureau of International Education report (CBIE, 2016) revealed that internationalization has become a central pillar of Canadian education. According to the report, several provinces in Canada have developed international education strategies to complement the federal government's initiatives, such as the Canada's first federal international education strategy. Regarding the internationalization strategy of the Canadian government, an expert advisory panel on international education was set up by the government in 2011 (Shaw, 2014). The final report of the Advisory Panel on Canada's International Education (2013) defined internationalization as "the process of bringing an international dimension into the teaching, research and service activities of Canadian institutions" (p. 8). The Advisory Panel's report further stated that the survey of higher education institutions in Canada revealed that the top three priorities of these institutions were:

1. International students' recruitment;
2. Increasing the number of Canadian students who are engaged in education abroad; and,

3.   The internationalization at home in Canada including the internationalization of the curriculum.

The impact of the internationalization of higher education by the Canadian government, with the active support of provincial/territorial governments, has led to the increasing enrolment of international students in Canada's higher education institutions. CBIE (2016) stated that over 66,000 international students studied at the community college level out of the over 353,000 international students that studied at all levels of educational study in Canada in 2015. The report further stated that figure was a 92% increase in the international student population between 2008 and 2015.

In addition to the above, CBIE (2019) revealed there were 494,525 international students at all levels of study in Canada in 2017. The report further stated that the figure, which already exceeded the 450,000 target of international students in Canada by 2022 by the federal government, was a 20% increase over the previous year and a 119% increase between 2010 and 2017.

Recruitment of International Students by Community Colleges

In Canada, international student enrolment grew in the 1960s and 1970s from just 10% of Canadian institutions reporting to have international students to 82% by 1986 (Hurabielle, 1998). Today, virtually every higher education institution in Canada has international students with the internationalization agenda of the federal and provincial/territorial governments playing a significant role in that regard. Hurabielle (1998) averred that the recruitment of international students to Canadian post-secondary institutions was historically based on liberal humanism and humanitarian concerns.

From the mid-1980s to date, there was a shift in the focus of recruiting international students to Canada from "aid to trade" as international student recruitment became commoditized (Fisher & Rubenson, 1997; Galway, 2000; Knight, 1997) and community colleges moved away from the less lucrative and government funded projects to the marketing of programs at full cost recovery rates to international students (Cudmore, 2005).

Impact of International Students in Canada

International students continue to make an impact on the economy (Adams, Banks, & Olsen, 2011; Paltridge, Maysons, & Schapper, 2012; Trilokekar & Kizilbash, 2013). Tables 1 and 2 below revealed that after accounting for Canadian scholarships and bursaries from the Canadian government, international students spent about $15.5 billion on tuition, accommodation and discretionary spending in 2016 which translated to $12.8 billion contribution to Canada's GDP in 2016. Global Affairs Canada (GAC, 2018) stated that GDP contributions of these international students include both direct and indirect impacts, where firms supplying goods and services to the education services and other sectors are also taken into consideration. Furthermore, international students from India, especially those studying at the community college level, made the most contribution with Ontario accounting for the biggest increase in the number of international students.

Table 2 shows that Ontario, with the highest number of international students, made the largest contribution to Canada's GDP at $6.3 billion, representing 49.7% of the total $12.8 billion, followed by British Columbia at $2.7 billion, representing 21.6%, and Quebec at $1.6 billion, representing 13.0%. Also, the number of international students' overall spending translated to 168,861 jobs that were supported by the Canadian economy in 2016. International students' annual spending directly and indirectly

Table 1. Number of international students and total annual spending in Canada by province and territory in 2016 in ($million)

Province/Territory	All Students	Total Annual Spending ($M)
Ontario	223,226	$7,806.8
British Columbia	145,691	$3,726.6
Quebec	67,534	$1,887.2
Alberta	30,342	$823.6
Nova Scotia	14,063	$413.4
Manitoba	14,298	$374.8
Saskatchewan	8,063	$222.6
New Brunswick	5,178	$136.4
Newfoundland & Labrador	3,227	$72.6
Prince Edward Island	2,270	$68.3
Yukon Territory	60	$1.4
Northwest Territory	19	$0.4
Nunavut Territory	0	$0.0

Source: Global Affairs Canada, 2018.

contributed $2.8 billion in tax revenue in Canada in 2016 (GAC, 2018). The GAC report indicated that international students' expenses represent revenue for goods and services from abroad because they are Canadian exports of education services. Also, according to the report, in 2016, long-term international students accounted for 93.4% of the total spending by international students and they contributed $12.0 billion to Canada's economy, supporting 158,300 jobs.

Challenges Confronting International Students in Canada

The challenges that international students face range from micro-level (individual) to the meso-level (institutional) and the macro-level (government/societal). The support areas of international students at their various community colleges are developed in response to the challenges that they face. For example, at the micro-level, international students face challenges that are often taken for granted by domestic students (i.e., the significant challenges that international students face are not as significant to domestic students since domestic students are not usually confronted with the challenges which international students are confronted with) (Grayson, 2008; Habib, Johannessen, & Ogrim, 2014; Hendrickson, Rosen, & Aune, 2011). These challenges include emotional (i.e. home sickness), psychological (i.e. acculturative stress), personal, family, and academic (Andrade, 2006; Bai, 2016; Lin & Yin, 1997; Popadiuk & Arthur, 2004).

At the meso-level, some of the challenges that international students face are related to social interactions, integration, social network and relationship, and social connectedness (Liu, 2009; McFaul, 2016; Perry, 2016). Some of the challenges that international students face at the macro-level include study and work permits, ability to work legally to support their academic study, acceptance in the local community where their community college campuses are located, and the political rhetoric of the host

Table 2. Combined direct and indirect economic impact of all International Students in Canada, by province and territory in 2016 in ($Million)

Province/Territory	2016 GDP	2016 Employment (Jobs)
Ontario	$6,349.4	79,034
British Columbia	$2,764.1	40,499
Quebec	$1,664.9	25,102
Alberta	$945.0	10,094
Nova Scotia	$318.2	4,378
Manitoba	$306.3	4,250
Saskatchewan	$197.1	2,350
New Brunswick	$122.1	1,650
Newfoundland & Labrador	$62.9	762
Prince Edward Island	$44.9	663
Yukon Territory	$2.0	27
Northwest Territory	$4.2	21
Nunavut	$1.1	8
Canada	$12,783.0	168,865

Source: Global Affairs Canada, 2018.

country government toward international education and international students (Coffey & Perry, 2013; Guo & Chase, 2011; Trilokekar & Kizilbash, 2013).

Support Areas for International Students in Community Colleges in Canada

The support areas of international students in community colleges in Canada range from the micro-level (individual) to the meso-level (institutional) and the macro-level (government/societal). These support areas in Table 3, which cut across the micro-, meso-, and macro-levels, include family, faculty, peer, mentoring supports at the micro-level, academic advising, networking, mental health and counselling supports at the meso-level, and study permit, work permit, public health insurance, and immigration supports at the macro-level (Andrade, 2006; Guo & Chase, 2011; Hegarty, 2014; Kusek, 2015; Liu, 2009; Mori, 2000; Tolman, 2017; Trilokekar & Kizilbash, 2013).

THEORETICAL FRAMEWORK

Urie Bronfenbrenner (1917-2005) was a Russian born American developmental psychologist. He developed the Bronfenbrenner's theory of human development. He argued that an individual's environment had an impact on the individual's process of development. He identified four levels of environmental influences as contributors to an individual's development. These are micro-, meso-, exo-, and macro-levels.

Table 3. International students' support areas at the micro-, meso-, and macro-levels

Levels	Support Areas
Micro	Family Support Faculty Support Peer Support Mentoring Support
Meso	Academic Advising Support Networking Support Mental health/Counselling Support
Macro	Study Permit Support Work Permit Support Health Insurance Support Immigration Services Support

Micro-level

Bronfenbrenner identified the micro-level as the first and most immediate level of the four levels. It encompasses an individual's human relationship, interpersonal interactions, and immediate surroundings. An example of the micro-level would be an international student's relationship with his/her immediate and extended family members; room, course and classmates; faculty, staff, and administrators in their college environment.

Meso-level

This level is the second level after the micro-level and it involves the various activities and interactions that take place between an individual and the immediate environment that the individual operates in. For example, this level examines the impact of the relationship that may exist between an international student and college activities such as co-curricular or extra-curricular activities, and the impact of this relationship on the international student's perceived academic success. The activities that international students are engaged in at the meso-level are institutional and are often organized or promoted by college administrators, faculty or student associations.

Exo-level

The exo-level is the third level that was identified by Bronfenbrenner after the meso-level. This level contains elements of the micro-level that do not affect an individual directly but may have an indirect effect. For example, an international student may suddenly find themselves in an embarrassing financial situation because their parents lost their jobs or have financial challenges that make it difficult or impossible to provide support to the student to enable them to continue with their academic study. While the student is not directly affected by the job loss or financial difficulty of their parents, the negative impact or effect still robs off on the student's study and ability to achieve perceived academic success.

Macro-level

This is the fourth and outermost level and it is believed to have an all-encompassing effect on an individual. This level includes cultural and societal attitude, beliefs, norms, and practices that impact an individual's development. For example, the policies, programs, and support areas that are provided to international students by the federal, provincial/territorial, and local governments. The government policies in that regard, for example, the introduction of work permits for international students is also making a number of business organizations to be more receptive to the idea of hiring international students to work for them both when they are still studying in their various community colleges as part-time workers, and upon graduation as full time workers.

The Bronfenbrenner's theory of human development was applied to this study by examining the impact of support areas at the micro-, meso-, and macro-levels on the perceived academic success of international students at the community college level. Each of these levels were examined distinctly and independently. The exo-level was not examined distinctly and independently in this study because that level was subsumed in the other micro-, meso-, and macro-levels.

APPLICATION OF BRONFENBRENNER'S THEORY

There are different support areas that affect international students' academic success at the micro-, meso-, and macro-levels as identified and explained by Bronfenbrenner (1979) in his theory of human development. With the increasing number of international students in community colleges in Canada, it is imperative to study the kind of support areas that are available to these students at each of the levels identified by Bronfenbrenner. For example, at the micro-level (individual), literature shows that a significant number of international students face challenges interacting and communicating effectively with their classmates and instructors, which possibly affects their intrapersonal well-being and interpersonal skills.

These students also miss the social supports provided back in their home country by friends and family members. As a result, language training/communication, intercultural/multicultural, and tutorial programs and activities are organized and provided to these international students to help them address the challenges that they face (Andrade, 2006; Fox, 1994; Hechanova-Alampey, Beehr, Christiansen, & Van Horn, 2002; Robertson, Line, Jones, & Thomas, 2000; Zhao, Kuh, & Carini, 2005. At the meso-level (institutional), literature reveals that international students have inclusion and integration challenges as far as orientation programs, college services (e.g., health and recreation programs) are concerned in terms of having a sense of belonging and being able to participate actively in various activities and programs (Bai, 2016; Bhochibhoya, Dong, & Branscum, 2017; McFarlane, 2015; Sullivan & Kashubeck-West, 2005; Thomson & Esses, 2016; Zhang, 2015).

Also, at the macro-level (government/societal), literature reveals that international students face challenges that have to do with immigration, employment, integration, and settlement (Cudmore, 2005; Hegarty, 2014; Kusek, 2015; Legusov, 2017; Paltridge et al, 2012; Schindler, 1999; Trilokekar & Kizil-bash, 2013). These three levels have various challenges that international students are confronted with in their efforts to obtain international academic credentials in their host country, Canada.

METHODS

Data Collection and Analysis

A questionnaire was developed and provided to the participants to complete. A hard copy of the question-naire was distributed by the researcher to participants in class prior to the start of their classes following a prior arrangement with the instructor teaching the class. Data were collected from international students across different academic departments and levels of study in the community college where the study was conducted. A questionnaire was developed and hard copies of the questionnaire were distributed by the researcher to participants in class to complete (copies are available from the researcher upon request). The questionnaire was divided into three parts A, B, and C. Part A consists of 9 questions on student variables and 7 questions on perceived academic success. Part B consists of 33 questions on partici-pants' awareness of, use of, and future use of supports at the micro, meso, and macro levels. In Part C, participants were asked to complete their responses to statement items based on a five-point Likert scale (1=Strongly Disagree, 2=Disagree, 3=Somewhat Agree, 4=Agree, 5=Strongly Agree).

For example, at the micro-level, there were four items each at the faculty, mentoring, and family support areas while the peer support area had five items. At the meso-level, there were four items each at the mental health/counselling, academic advisor, and networking support areas. At the macro-level, there were also four items each at the work permit, study permit, immigration services, and public health insurance support areas. The survey instrument was adapted from a research study on perceived suc-cess in the MBA/MPA program by Butz, Stupnisky, Peterson, and Majoris (2014). The adapted survey instrument was then used to determine the perceived academic success of participants in this study at the end of their first semester.

Survey data were analyzed in three parts using SPSS version 25. The first part involved descriptive statistics to provide a general description of participants' characteristics in terms of their age, gender, country of origin, sources of support, length of stay in Canada, and evaluation of variable distribution. The second part utilized reliability statistics to determine the internal consistency of the summated rating scale. The third part used correlation and linear regression to determine the correlation between sup-port areas at the micro, meso, and macro levels and international students' perceived academic success.

Participants

The participants in this study were drawn from the international student population in the main campus of a large community college in Canada who were studying across different academic programs at the certificate, diploma, and post-graduate diploma levels. There were over 1,500 international students in the community college under consideration at the time they were surveyed in the winter academic semester of 2019. A total of 399 international students were recruited to participate in this study.

Peers (1996) stated that sample size is an important feature of a study design with the capacity to influence the detection of significant differences, relationships or interactions. In determining sample size calculations, it is important to determine the influence of categorical variables in data analysis (Bartlett, Kotrlik, & Higgins, 2001). Furthermore, if a categorical variable plays a role in data analysis, categorical sample size formulas should be used to determine sample size (Bartlett et al, 2001).

Based on the categorical sample size formula that was used for a population size of about 1,500 with a margin of error of .05 for categorical data with $p = .50$ and $t = 1.96$, it was suggested that the sample size for a population of about 1,500 should be 306 (Bartlett et al, 2001). The response rate of the Qualtrics survey that were distributed was very high and hugely successful because 399 international students were recruited from the community college where the participants were drawn.

Demographic Characteristics of the Sample

Table 4 displays the demographic review of the participating students in the survey. The sample involved predominantly male students who were older than traditionally-aged students. The majority of the students were from Asia, which was not surprising as the national trends in Canada show that the majority of international students comes from the Asian countries with India being the largest supply followed by China being the second largest supply (CBIE, 2019; Katem, 2018). Also, most of the students in the sample did not have any financial aid which may be the reason why most of them worked part-time.

Table 4. Demographic characteristics of the sample (n=399)

Characteristics	n	%
Gender		
Male	235	58.9
Female	157	39.3
Choose not to identify	2	.5
Missing	5	1.3
Age in Years		
18 to 19	58	14.6
20 to 21	85	21.3
22 to 24	103	25.8
25 to 29	74	18.6
30 to 39	49	12.6
40 to 49	13	3.5
50 to 59	2	.6
Missing	15	3.8
Ethnicity		
African/Caribbean/Black	11	2.3
Asian	331	83
Mexican	2	.5
Middle East	9	2.3
South American	23	5.8
White/Caucasian	12	3
Other	5	1.3
Missing	6	1.5
Employment Status		
Unemployed	153	38.3
Working Part-time	240	60.2
Missing	6	1.5
Financial Aid		
Yes	113	28.3
No	278	69.7
Missing	8	2.0

Academic Characteristics of the Sample

Tables 5 to 7 provide a summary of the academic characteristics of the participants in this study.

Academic Qualifications

Table 5 provides a summary of the academic qualifications that the international students were pursuing and expecting to achieve upon successful completion of their studies. The majority of the students were studying for a diploma academic credential. That is understandable because virtually every community college offers a diploma qualification with the exception of a few, such as the community college in this study that offers post-graduate diploma, degree, diploma, and certificate qualifications. However, international students are not typically admitted to degree programs in the community college where this study was conducted, which explained why there were no data regarding students pursuing degree programs.

Table 5. Academic qualification pursued

Academic Qualification	n	%
Post-graduate diploma	98	24.6
Diploma	231	57.9
Certificate	70	17.5
Total	399	100.0

Academic Programs

As indicated in Table 6, the majority of the students were pursuing their academic programs in Business and Applied Arts, which was the largest department in this community college. A major reason for the high number of students in that particular academic program was because students were typically admitted year round (i.e., in August, January, and May) in this program. This was unlike other programs where students were admitted only once a year, usually in August.

Table 6. Academic programs

Academic Program	n	%
Business & Applied Arts	175	43.9
Skilled Trades & Tech.	118	29.6
Educations, Arts & Science	40	10.0
Hospitality & Culinary Arts	27	6.8
Continuing Education	24	6.0
Health Sciences	15	3.8
Total	399	100.0

Academic Semester

Table 7 provides a summary of the academic semester of the participating students in this study. It shows that all the participants had spent at least more than a semester in the community college where the study was conducted, which guaranteed more thoughtful responses to the survey questions pertaining to their community college experience and perceptions of academic success.

Table 7. Academic semester

Academic Semester	n	%
2nd Semester	288	72.2
3rd Semester	49	12.3
4th Semester	52	13.0
5th Semester	9	2.3
Missing	1	0.3
Total	399	100.0

Variables of Interest

Statistical analysis of this study included items from the Qualtrics survey that probed students' agreement with the importance of various support areas. Table 8 provides information regarding the classification of various support areas into the three levels as per the theoretical framework, such as the micro-level, meso-level, and macro-level. These levels were the Independent Variables (IVs) in this study. For example, within the micro-level, there were four items in the faculty support, four items in the mentoring support, four items in the family support, and five items in the peer support. In all, there were 17 items in the support areas at the micro-level that consisted of faculty support, mentoring support, family support, and peer support. Within the meso-level, there were four items in the mental health/counselling support, four items in the academic advisor support, and four items in the networking support as well. In all, there were 12 items in the support areas at the meso-level that consisted of mental health/counselling support, academic advisor support, and networking support.

Also, within the macro-level, there were four items in the work permit support, four items in the study permit support, four items in the immigration support, and four items in the public health insurance support. In all, there were 16 items in the support areas at the macro-level that consisted of work permit support, study permit support, immigration support, and public health insurance support. A dependent variable (DV), perceived academic success was the outcome.

Reliability Measures and Data Analysis Procedures

The survey data were analyzed in three parts. The first part was the descriptive part of the sample that provided a general description of the characteristics of the participants' data that were collected in terms of their age, gender, country of origin, sources of support, and length of stay in Canada. The second part

Table 8. Three-level classification of support areas

Level	Support Area Items (IVs)	Outcome (DV)
Micro	Faculty Support Mentoring Support Family Support Peer Support	Perceived Academic Success
Meso	Mental health/Counselling Academic Advisor Support Networking Support	Perceived Academic Success
Macro	Work Permit Support Study Permit Support Immig. Services Support Health Insurance Support	Perceived Academic Success

was the reliability statistics that was used to determine the internal consistency of the summated rating scale, while the third part was the correlation and linear regression analysis to determine whether the support areas had relationship with international students' perceived academic success. The correlational study measured international students' perceived academic success in terms of their support areas at the micro-, meso-, and macro-levels. Descriptive statistics was run to evaluate variable distributions. The descriptive part of the survey was at the end of the survey because of the assumption that respondents would feel more comfortable to provide personal background information after they know what the purpose of the research study was after answering the research questions first (Xu, 2016).

Data collection was cross-sectional, that is: data were collected from international students across different academic departments and levels of study in the community college where the study was conducted. As expected, the results from the analysis showed international students' perceived academic success was impacted by support areas. The results from the analysis also revealed the awareness level of international students regarding these support areas. Finally, the results from the analysis revealed the most strongly related support areas to international students' perceived academic success in order to be able to graduate, and join the Canadian workforce upon the successful completion of their academic study.

The Cronbach's alpha, often symbolized by the lower case Greek letter α, is commonly used to determine the internal consistency (reliability measures) of summated rating scales (Cronbach, 1951). The

Table 9. Reliability statistics at the micro-Level

Cronbach's Alpha	Number of Items	Mean	Variance	Std. Deviation
.836	17	64.78	91.492	9.565

Table 10. Reliability statistics at the meso-Level

Cronbach's Alpha	Number of Items	Mean	Variance	Std. Deviation
.920	12	39.64	103.583	10.178

Cronbach alpha is excellent if $0.9 \leq \alpha$, good if $0.8 \leq \alpha < 0.9$, and acceptable if $0.7 \leq \alpha < 0.8$. As Table 9 indicates, the Cronbach alpha for the 17 items at the micro-level was 0.8.

The Cronbach's alpha for the 12 items at the meso-level area of support was 0.9 which shows that the internal consistency or reliability measure of these items was excellent (See Table 10).

The Cronbach's alpha for the 16 items at the macro-level was 0.9 which shows that the internal consistency or reliability measure of these items was also excellent (See Table 11).

Table 11. Reliability Statistics at the Macro-Level

Cronbach's Alpha	Number of Items	Mean	Variance	Std. Deviation
.895	16	62.23	121.461	11.021

Findings

As shown in Table 12, the majority of the international students in the sample provided positive responses regarding their perceived academic success. The highest responses of *strongly agree* were in the survey items "as an international student, you are pursuing an academic program in the college?" and "as an international student, when it comes to knowing that you made an honest effort to make progress during the year?" and "as an international student, in doing all the works, meeting deadlines, keeping up with the reading, studying etc.?"

Furthermore, the highest responses of *agree* in the survey items were "as an international student, about the grades you got on tests and assignments in your academic program?" and "as an international student, in achieving the learning goals that you set for yourself?" and "as an international student, when it comes to knowing that you made an honest effort to make progress during the year?" in addition to "as an international student, in doing all the work, meeting deadlines, keeping up with the reading, studying etc.?"

The highest responses of *strongly disagree* in the survey items were "as an international student, about the grades you got on tests and assignments in your academic program?" and "as an international student, in achieving the learning goals that you set for yourself?" respectively. Finally, the highest responses of *disagree* was in relation to the survey item that had to do with "as an international student, in achieving the learning goals that you set for yourself?"

Research Question One

This research question was as follows: Do internationals students utilize identified support areas at the micro (individual), meso (institutional), and macro (government/societal) levels. To answer research question one, the researcher analyzed the data via SPSS version 25 using descriptive statistics to determine percentage distribution of international students' awareness of, current utilization, and potential utilization of the support areas at the micro-, meso-, and macro-levels. See Tables 13 - 15 for a summary of the response distributions.

Content

Table 12. Perceived academic success survey item responses in percentage (n=399)

Survey	Strongly disagree (%)	Disagree (%)	Somewhat agree (%)	Agree (%)	Strongly agree (%)	No response (%)	Total (%)
…you are pursuing an academic program in the college?	1.3	.5	10.8	38.8	**48.1**	.5	100
…about the grades you got on tests and assignments in your academic program?	1.5	2.5	16.0	**48.6**	31.1	.3	100
…in achieving the learning goals that you set for yourself?	1.5	5.3	16.8	**47.4**	28.8	.3	100
…when it comes to knowing that you made an honest effort to make progress during the year?	.8	1.0	9.8	41.9	**46.1**	.5	100
…in doing all the work, meeting deadlines, keeping up with the reading, studying, etc.?	1.3	2.5	12.8	40.6	**42.6**	.3	100

Table 13 and Figure 1 show that international students did not utilize all the support areas at the micro-level. This was revealed by an examination of each of the support areas at the micro-level (i.e., faculty, mentoring, family, and peer supports). For example, the majority of the students indicated that they were aware of supports provided by faculty, some students indicated that they were not aware of supports provided by faculty, while very few students did not complete that portion of the survey. Also, more than half of the students indicated that they utilized faculty support, about a third of the students indicated that they did not, while a tiny number of the students did not provide any response. However, the majority of the students indicated that they would take advantage of faculty support in the future, a small number of students indicated that they would not, while a smaller number of students did not complete that portion of the survey.

Regarding mentoring support, not all the students in the sample used this support as well. From Table 13, a higher number of students indicated that they were aware of the support, about a fifth of the students surveyed indicated that they were not, a tiny number of students did not complete that portion of the survey. Furthermore, less than half of the students surveyed indicated that they used the support, more than half of the students surveyed indicated that they did not, while very few students did not provide any response. A greater number of the students who were surveyed indicated that they would use the mentoring support in the future, about a fifth of the students surveyed indicated that they will not, while a few number of the students surveyed did not provide any information in that regard.

Another support area at the micro-level that was examined in the survey was the family support where the majority of the students indicated that they were aware of their family support, less than a fifth of the students surveyed indicated that they were not aware, and a tiny few number of students did not respond. Moreover, the majority of the students indicated that they use their family support, less than a third of the students indicated that they did not, while a few number of the students who were surveyed did not respond. A greater number of the students surveyed indicated that they will use their family support in the future, less than a fifth of the students surveyed indicated that they will not, while a very few number of the students surveyed did not complete that portion of the survey.

Finally, the last support area at the micro-level was the peer support where the majority of the students surveyed indicated that they were aware of peer support, less than a fifth of the students indicated that they were not aware, and a tiny few number of the students did not complete that portion of the survey. Also, the majority of the students indicated that they use peer support, about a third of the students did not, while a few number of the students did not provide any response. As obtained in the other support areas under the micro-level, a greater number of the students who were surveyed indicated that they will use peer support in the future, less than a fifth of the students surveyed indicated that they will not use the support in the future, while a few number of the students who were surveyed did not respond.

Table 13. Distribution of Students' awareness of, use of, and future use of supports at the micro-level in numbers and percentages

Micro-Level Support Area	Awareness of Support (n)	Use of Support (n)	Future Use of Support (n)	Awareness of Support (%)	Use of Support (%)	Future Use of Support (%)
Faculty						
Yes	338	265	326	84.7	66.4	81.7
No	54	124	55	13.5	31.1	13.8
Missing	7	10	18	1.8	2.5	4.5
Total	399	399	399	100.0	100.0	100.0
Mentoring						
Yes	307	168	298	76.9	42.1	74.7
No	80	217	83	20.1	54.4	20.8
Missing	12	14	18	3.0	3.5	4.5
Total	399	399	399	100.0	100.0	100.0
Family						
Yes	328	275	308	82.2	68.9	77.2
No	63	115	75	15.8	28.8	18.8
Missing	8	9	16	2.0	2.3	4.0
Total	399	399	399	100.0	100.0	100.0
Peer						
Yes	310	247	309	77.7	61.9	77.4
No	76	136	72	19.0	34.1	18.0
Missing	13	16	18	3.3	4.0	4.5
Total	399	399	399	100.0	100.0	100.0

Note: Percentage distribution of international students showing their awareness, use of, and future use of support areas at the micro-level.

The trend observed in Table 13 was also repeated in Table 14, which revealed that international students did not utilize all the support areas at the meso-level. For example, the majority of the students surveyed indicated that they were aware of mental health/counselling support, about a third of the students surveyed indicated that they were not aware, while a tiny few number of students did not respond. Also, about a fifth of the students who were surveyed indicated that they utilize the mental health/counselling support, the majority of the students indicated that they did not utilize the support while a few number of students did not complete that portion of the survey. However, a larger number of the participants i.e. students indicated that they would utilize the mental health/counselling support in the future, about a third of the students indicated that they would not, while a few number of students did not complete that portion of the survey.

Regarding the use of academic advisor support, the majority of the students indicated that they were aware of the support, less than a fifth of the students were not aware, and a tiny few number of students did not respond. Also, close to half of the students who were surveyed indicated that they use the support, about half of these students indicated that they did not use the support, while a tiny few number of the students did not complete that portion of the survey. Moreover, the majority of the students indicated that they would use the academic advisor support in the future, less than a fifth of the students indicated that they would not, while a tiny few number of the students did not complete that portion of the survey.

The last support area under the meso-level that was examined in the survey (i.e., networking), refers to events organized by the community college such as welcome party for new international students, orientation, excursions, alumni events, and other events organized through the student association. Table 14 reveals that the majority of the students were aware of the networking support, while less than a fifth of the students were not aware of the support. Additionally, more than half of the students surveyed

Table 14. Distribution of students' awareness of, use of, and future use of supports at the meso-level in numbers and percentages

Meso-Level Support Area	Awareness of Support (n)	Use of Support (n)	Future Use of Support (n)	Awareness of Support (%)	Use of Support (%)	Future Use of Support (%)
Mental Health/Counseling						
Yes	280	87	257	70.2	21.8	64.4
No	111	296	125	27.8	74.2	31.3
Missing	8	16	17	2.0	4.0	4.3
Total	399	399	399	100.0	100.0	100.0
Acad. Advisor						
Yes	321	191	318	80.5	47.9	79.7
No	71	199	68	17.8	49.9	17.0
Missing	7	9	13	1.8	2.3	3.3
Total	399	399	399	100.0	100.0	100.0
Networking						
Yes	329	229	342	82.5	57.4	85.7
No	70	168	54	17.5	42.1	13.5
Missing	0	2	3	0	.5	.8
Total	399	399	399	100.0	100.0	100.0

Note: Percentage distribution of international students showing their awareness, use of, and future use of support areas at the meso-level.

indicated that they use the networking support, less than half of these students did not, while a very tiny few students did not indicate any response. Finally, a greater number of the students indicated that they would use the networking support in the future, few students indicated that they would not, while a very tiny few students did not respond to that portion of the survey.

Table 15 reveals that international students did not utilize all the support areas at the macro-level as well. An examination of the support areas at the macro-level (i.e., work permit, study permit, immigration, and public health insurance supports) revealed that international students did not utilize all these support areas. Regarding work permit, more than a third of the students surveyed indicated that they had a work permit, more than half of these students indicated that they did not, while a small number of students did not complete that portion of the survey. Also, about a tenth of the students who were surveyed indicated that they had renewed their work permit, the majority of the students had not renewed their work permit, while less than a tenth of the students surveyed did not complete that portion of the survey. However, a greater number of the international students who participated in the survey indicated that they would renew or obtain a work permit in the future, about a fifth of the students indicated that they would not, while a small number of students did not complete that portion of the survey.

On study permit, virtually all the students indicated that they had a study permit, while a noticeable few number of students did not. Moreover, about a third of the students indicated that they had renewed their study permit, the majority of the students indicated that they had not, while a few number of students did not provide any response. Finally, less than half of the students surveyed indicated that they would renew their study permit in the future, less than half of the students would not, while a few students did not complete that portion of the survey. The students who indicated that they will not renew their study permit in the future were most probably students who were about completing their academic study at the time they were surveyed.

The other support areas at the macro-level are immigration services and public health insurance supports. Regarding immigration services support, which referred to the government sponsored and organized events, such as seminars on how international students can stay in Canada in the course of their study as legal temporary residents and later transition to permanent residents, the majority of the students indicated that they were aware of the support, while about a quarter of the students surveyed indicated that they were not aware. Furthermore, about half of the students surveyed indicated that they used the support, less than half of the students surveyed indicated that they did not, while a tiny few students did not provide any response. A greater number of the students, however, indicated that they would use the immigration support in the future, a few number of students indicated that they would not, while a very tiny few students did not provide any response to that aspect of the survey.

Public health insurance refers to the provision of health insurance by the provincial government so that international students do not have to incur any additional expense of having to pay for their health insurance from their pockets. In this study, majority of the students indicated that they were aware of the support, about a quarter of the students were not aware, while a very tiny few students did not provide any response. Also, less than half of the students indicated that they use the support, more than half of the students indicated that they did not, while a very tiny few number of the students surveyed did not provide any response to that portion of the survey. Finally, a greater number of the students who participated in the survey indicated that they would use the support in the future, few students indicated that they would not, while a tiny few students did not respond to that portion of the survey.

Thus, the results of this analysis provided the answer to research question one, which was that the international students in the sample did not utilize all the support areas at the micro-, meso-, and macro-

Table 15. Distribution of students' awareness of, use of, and future use of supports at the macro-level in numbers and percentages

Macro-Level Support Area	Awareness of Support (n)	Use of Support (n)	Future Use of Support (n)	Awareness of Support (%)	Use of Support (%)	Future Use of Support (%)
Work Permit						
Yes	152	44	297	38.1	11.0	74.4
No	222	321	76	55.6	80.5	19.0
Missing	25	34	26	6.3	8.5	6.5
Total	399	399	399	100.0	100.0	100.0
Study Permit						
Yes	397	123	189	99.5	30.8	47.4
No	2	274	192	.5	68.7	48.1
Missing	0	2	18	0	.5	4.5
Total	399	399	399	100.0	100.0	100.0
Immigration						
Yes	305	205	380	76.4	51.4	95.2
No	94	189	17	23.6	47.4	4.3
Missing	0	5	2	0	1.3	.5
Total	399	399	399	100.0	100.0	100.0
Public Health Insurance						
Yes	289	190	380	72.4	47.6	95.2
No	108	204	15	27.1	15.1	3.8
Missing	2	5	4	.5	1.3	1.0
Total	399	399	399	100.0	100.0	100.0

Note: Percentage distribution of international students showing their awareness, use of, and future use of support areas at the macro-level.

levels. This could be due to acculturation issues (Bai, 2016) or the length of stay of the students in Canada (Bhochhibhoya et al., 2017) since the majority of these students had spent less than two years in the country at the time they were surveyed. However, many students indicated that they were aware of the support areas and planned to use in the future.

Research Question Two

Which of these support area(s) is/are most strongly related to international students' perceived academic success? To answer research question two, the researcher analyzed the data via SPSS version 25 by running linear regression statistics to determine the most strongly related support areas to international students' academic success.

The support areas at both the micro-, and macro-levels were significant at (p=.000) were the most strongly related levels of supports to international students in terms of their perceived academic success (See Table 16). The other support areas at the meso-level did not show any statistical significance regarding these students' perceived academic success.

Table 16. Linear regression using perceived academic success as dependent variable and micro, meso, & macro levels as independent variables

Level	Unstandardized Coefficients		Standardized Coefficients		
	B	Std. Error	Beta	T	Sig.
Micro	.094	.020	.302	4.732	.000
Meso	-.008	.019	-.025	-.392	.695
Macro	.059	.016	.213	3.623	.000

Dependent Variable: Perceived Academic Success

In Table 17, R shows a moderate positive relationship between the support areas at the micro-level and perceived academic success although the micro-level was the most important support area to determine international students' perceived academic success. The adjusted R square confirmed that the variation in perceived academic success was explained by the variation at the micro-level.

Table 17. Model summary showing determination of R and adjusted R square

Level	R	R Square	Adjusted R Square	Std. Error of the Estimate
Micro	.421[a]	.177	.172	2.84503

a. Predictors: (Constant), Tot_Macro, Tot_Micro

Based on the data presented in Tables 18 and 19, the results of the linear regression analysis showed that the support areas at the micro-level (individual) and the macro-level (government/societal) were statistically significant and most strongly related to international students' perceived academic success.

Figure 1 shows the relationship between support areas at the micro-, meso-, and macro- levels and perceived academic success. There is an insignificant relationship between the support areas at the meso-level and perceived academic success although there is a significant relationship between the support areas at the micro-level and perceived academic success, and the support areas at the macro-level and perceived academic success respectively.

CONCLUSION

This study explored the impact of support areas at the micro-level, meso-level, and macro-level on international students' academic success in community colleges. The research was conducted on the site of a large community college in Canada. The support areas at the micro-level (individual) and the

Figure 1. Model of environmental factors predicting perceived academic success

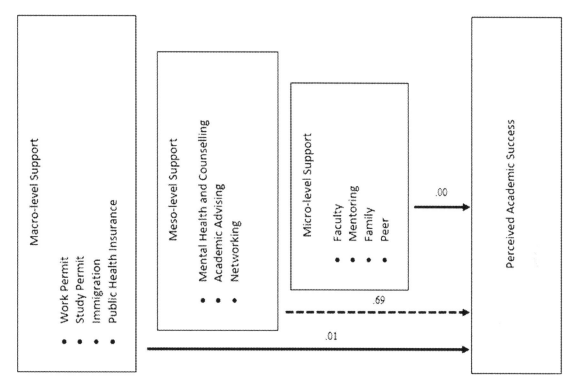

Note: Solid lines represent significance at the .00 and .01 level and dashed lines represent non-significant relationships.

macro-level (government/societal) were more statistically significant to international students' perceived academic success.

The findings from this study showed that the support areas at the micro-level and macro-level were most strongly related to international students' perceived academic success. The reason for the inverse relationship between the support areas at the meso-level and international students' perceived academic success could be due to the fact that international students from Asia (who constituted a majority of the students surveyed in this study) socialized more amongst themselves, thereby providing social support to each other, and were less engaged with the campus-environment than other international students (Andrade, 2006; Bai, 2016). Another reason could be that in spite of the enormous supports that several higher education institutions have put in place at the meso-level (institutional) to provide social supports to international students, language and cultural barriers still prevent these students from adequately utilizing these supports (Lee & Ciftci, 2014; Lin & Scherz, 2014; Lin & Yi, 1997; Mori, 2000; Soetan, 2020).

In future research, a replication of this study should be conducted with a survey designed to gather more detailed information about international students in order to gain a better understanding of other variables that were not accounted for within the results of this study. For example, various demographic variables such as the effect of types of dependents (spousal and children), and the types of work (internships or work placement) and location of work (on-campus or off-campus) were not taken into account in the statistical analysis, but future research may take them into consideration and run multiple regression with interaction effects. Furthermore, academic success could be measured in terms of actual (official GPA) and satisfaction (in terms of both academic and non-academic experiences) of these students. The addition of these demographic elements should better connect the findings of these studies to prior research (Soetan, 2020).

Replication of this study using the Bronfenbrenner's theory of human development should be conducted from data from a single large community college or a collection of community colleges from the provinces with the highest number of international students across the country with the inclusion of a qualitative analysis from the community college or colleges. This is because it is only through a mixed-approach/method could a researcher gain a clearer picture of the perceived academic success of international students.

Community college leaders and administrators can use the results of this study to both affirm and re-affirm their strategies and institutional programming efforts and initiatives for international students on their campuses. For example, they can increase their macro-level support areas by increasing their participation in federal and provincial/territorial governments' initiatives in immigration services by ensuring that these programs and initiatives of the Canadian government become a regular feature and occurrence on their campuses in order to enhance international students' confidence in their perceived academic success. Government rhetoric and an increased investment in these important support areas are therefore essential in both making Canada a competitive destination of choice for international students and also ensuring the success of these students when they study in community colleges in Canada.

REFERENCES

Adams, T., Banks, M., & Olsen, A. (2011). Benefits of international education: enriching students, enriching communities. In D. Davis & B. Mackintosh (Eds.), *Making a difference: Australian international education* (pp. 9–46). University of New South Wales Press Ltd.

Advisory Panel on Canada's International Education Strategy Final Report. (2013). *International Education: A key driver of Canada's future prosperity*. Retrieved on 4/9/18 from http://www.international.gc.ca/education/report-rapport/strategystrategie/index.aspx?lang=eng

Andrade, M. S. (2006). International students in English-Speaking universities: Adjustment factors. *Journal of Research in International Education*, 5(2), 131–154. doi:10.1177/1475240906065589

Atlantic Colleges Atlantique. (2018). *Fact sheet. The economic value of Atlantic colleges Atlantique*. Author.

Bai, J. (2016). Perceived support as a predictor of acculturative stress among international students in the United States. *Journal of International Students*, 6(1), 93–106.

Bartlett, J. E., Kotrlik, J. W., & Higgins, C. C. (2001). Organizational research: Determining appropriate sample size in survey research. *Information Technology, Learning and Performance Journal*, 19(1), 43–50.

Bhochhibhoya, A., Dong, Y., & Branscum, P. (2017). Sources of social support among international college students in the United States. *Journal of International Students*, 7(3), 671–686.

Bronfenbrenner, U. (1979). *The ecology of human development: Experiments by nature and design.* Harvard University Press.

Butz, N. T., Stupnisky, R. H., Peterson, E. S., & Majerus, M. M. (2014). Self-determined motivation in synchronous hybrid graduate business programs: Contrasting online and on campus students. *Journal of Online Learning and Teaching / MERLOT, 10*(2), 211–227.

Canadian Bureau of International Education. (2016). *A world of learning: Canada's performance and potential in international education.* Retrieved on 19/2/18 from http://net.cbie.ca/download/World-of-Learning-2016-EN.pdf

Canadian Bureau of International Education. (2019). *International students in Canada: Where do inbound students come from?* Retrieved from https://cbie.ca/infographic/

Coffey, R., & Perry, M. (2013). *The role of education agents in Canada's education systems.* Council of ministers of education, Canada. Retrieved from https://www.cmec.ca/Publications/Lists/Publications/Attachments/326/The-Role-of Education-Agents-EN.pdf

Colleges and Institutes Canada. (n.d.). *What we do.* Retrieved from https://www.collegesinstitutes.ca/

Cronbach, L. J. (1951). Coefficient alpha and the internal structure of test. *Psychometrika, 16*(3), 297–324. doi:10.1007/BF02310555

Cudmore, G. (2005). Globalization, internationalization, and the recruitment of international students in higher education, and in the Ontario colleges of applied arts & technology. *Canadian Journal of Higher Education, 35*(1), 37–60.

Fisher, D., & Rubenson, K. (1998). *The changing political economy: The private and public lives of Canadian universities. In Universities and Globalization: Critical Perspectives.* Sage Publications Inc.

Fox, H. (1994). *Listening to the world: Cultural issues in academic writing.* National Council of Teachers in English.

Galway, A. D. (2000). *Going global: Ontario colleges of applied arts and technology, international student recruitment and the export of education.* Ontario Institute for Studies in Education, University of Toronto.

Gleazer, E. J. (1980). *The community college: Values, vision and vitality.* American Association of Community and Junior Colleges.

Global Affairs Canada. (2018). *Economic impact of international education in Canada –2017 update.* Retrieved on 24/3/18 from http://www.international.gc.ca/education/report- rapport/impact-2017/toc-tdm.aspx?lang=eng

Grayson, J. P. (2008). The experiences and outcomes of domestic and international students at four Canadian universities. *Higher Education Research & Development, 27*(3), 215–230. doi:10.1080/07294360802183788

Guo, S., & Chase, M. (2011). Internationalization of higher education: Integrating international students into Canadian academic environment. *Teaching in Higher Education, 16*(3), 305–318. doi:10.1080/13 562517.2010.546524

Habib, L., Johannsen, M., & Ogrim, L. (2014). Experiences and challenges of international students in technology-rich learning environments. *Journal of Educational Technology & Society, 17*(2), 196–206.

Hechanova-Alampay, R., Beehr, T. A., Christiansen, N. D., & Van Horn, R. K. (2002). Adjustment and strain among domestic and international student sojourners: A longitudinal study. *School Psychology International, 23*(4), 458–474. doi:10.1177/0143034302234007

Hegarty, N. (2014). Where we are now-The presence and importance of international students to universities in the United States. *Journal of International Students, 4*(3), 223–235.

Hendrickson, B., Rosen, D., & Aune, R. (2011). An analysis of friendship networks, social connectedness, homesickness, and satisfaction levels of international students. *International Journal of Intercultural Relations, 35*(3), 281–295. doi:10.1016/j.ijintrel.2010.08.001

Hurabielle, J. (1998). *Canada's public colleges and postsecondary technical institutions' involvement in international education* (Unpublished doctoral dissertation). University of Alberta, Alberta, Canada.

Katem, E. (2018). *Canada is home to nearly half a million international students: An update from the Canadian Bureau of International Education reveals the total number of international students in the country exceeds Canada's 2022 target*. Retrieved on 7/9/19 from https://www.canadastudynews. com/2018/03/19/canada-is-home-to-nearly-half-a- million- international-students/

Kusek, W. A. (2015). Evaluating the struggles with international students and local community participation. *Journal of International Students, 5*(2), 121–131.

Lee, J., & Ciftci, A. (2014). Asian international students' socio-cultural adaptation: Influence of multicultural personality, assertiveness, academics self-efficacy, and social support. *International Journal of Intercultural Relations, 38*, 97–105. doi:10.1016/j.ijintrel.2013.08.009

Legusov, O. (2017). The growing reliance of Ontario colleges of applied arts and technology on educational agents for the recruitment of international students. *The College Quarterly, 20*(1), 1–21.

Lin, J. G., & Yi, K. Y. (1997). Asian international students' adjustment: Issues and program suggestions. *College Student Journal, 31*(4), 473–479.

Lin, S., & Susan, D. S. (2014). Challenges facing Asian international graduate students in the U.S. *Journal of International Students, 4*(1), 16–33.

Liu, M. (2009). Addressing the mental health problems of Chinese international college students in the United States. *Advances in Social Work, 10*(1), 69–86. doi:10.18060/164

McFarlane, A. M. (2015). Internationalization and the role of student affairs professionals: Lessons learned from the international student engagement meeting initiative. *Journal of Student Affairs in Africa, 3*(1), 83–91. doi:10.14426/jsaa.v3i1.94

McFaul, S. (2016). International students' social network: Network mapping to gage friendship formation and student engagement. *Journal of International Students*, *6*(1), 1–13.

Mori, S. C. (2000). Addressing the mental health concerns of international students. *Journal of Counseling and Development*, *78*(2), 137–144. doi:10.1002/j.1556-6676.2000.tb02571.x

Paltridge, T., Maysons, S., & Schapper, J. (2012). Covering the gap: Social inclusion, international students and the role of local government. *Australian Universities Review*, *54*(2), 29–39.

Peers, I. (1996). *Statistical analysis for education and psychology researchers*. Falmer Press.

Popadiuk, N. E., & Arthur, N. M. (2004). Counselling international students in Canadian schools. *International Journal for the Advancement of Counseling*, *26*(2), 125–145. doi:10.1023/B:ADCO.0000027426.05819.44

Raby, R. (2000). Globalization of the community college model: Paradox of the local and the global. In N. P. Stramquist & K. Monkman (Eds.), Globalization and education: Integration and contestation across cultures (pp. 149-173). New York, NY: Rowman & Little field Publishers Inc.

Shaw, K. (2014). Internationalization in Australia and Canada: Lessons for the future. *The College Quarterly*, *17*(1), 1–17.

Soetan, T. O. (2020). Impact of support areas on the perceived academic success of international students in community colleges in Canada. *NAFSA Research Symposium Series*, Vol 4, 161-176.

Sullivan, C., & Kashubeck-West, S. (2015). The Interplay of international students' acculturative stress, social support, and acculturation modes. *Journal of International Students*, *5*(1), 1–11.

Thomson, C., & Esses, V. M. (2016). Helping the transition: Mentorship to support international students in Canada. *Journal of International Students*, *6*(4), 873–886.

Tolman, S. (2017). The effects of a roommate-pairing program on international student satisfaction and academic success. *Journal of International Students*, *7*(3), 522–541.

Tompson, H. B., & Tompson, G. H. (1996). Confronting diversity issues in the classroom with strategies to improve satisfaction and retention of international students. *Journal of Education for Business*, *72*(1), 53–57. doi:10.1080/08832323.1996.10116826

Trilokekar, R. P., & Kizilbash, Z. (2013). IMAGINE: Canada as a leader in international education. How can Canada benefit from the Australian experience? *Canadian Journal of Higher Education*, *43*(2), 1–26.

Universities Canada. (2015). *Universities and colleges: Partners in education*. Retrieved on 14/7/18 from https://www.univcan.ca/universities/universities-and-colleges-partners-in education/

Xu, Y. J. (2016). Attention to retention: Exploring and addressing the needs of college students in STEM majors. *Journal of Education and Training Studies*, *4*(2), 67–76.

Zhang, Y. (2015). Intercultural communication competence: Advising international students in a Texas community. *NACADA Journal*, *35*(2), 48–59. doi:10.12930/NACADA-15-007

Zhao, C., Kuh, G. D., & Carini, R. M. (2005). A comparison of international and American student engagement in effective educational practices. *The Journal of Higher Education*, *76*(2), 209–231. doi:10.1353/jhe.2005.0018

KEY TERMS AND DEFINITIONS

Bronfenbrenner's Theory of Human Development: The application of a developmental theory to international students' experience in Canada. Urie Bronfenbrenner posited that every individual's development is influenced by the environment in which the individual operates.

International Students: Students who are studying away from their home country and require a study and work permit visas to be able to legal temporary residents to enable them study and work in the course of their academic study.

Internationalization: The strategy of the Canadian government to bring a global and multicultural dimension to the operations and activities of Canadian higher education.

Macro-Level Support Area: The last and outermost level of support of international students.

Meso-Level Support Area: The second level of support of international students.

Micro-Level Support Area: The first and immediate level of support of international students.

Perceived Academic Success: Perceptions of academic success by international students are different from their actual success. Literature reveals that international students are usually academically successful when they perceive themselves to be academically successful and that informed the survey design for this study.

Section 5
Student Satisfaction and Recruitment

Chapter 15
International Undergraduate Student Choice of Alberta for Post–Secondary Education

Darren Howes
Medicine Hat College, Canada

ABSTRACT

In this chapter, the author provides an overview of the decision-making process that international students will go through when choosing a country, province, and ultimately, an institution for their international higher learning education. After conducting exploratory qualitative research from an Alberta perspective, it was determined that international students are influenced by (1) safety, (2) quality, (3) knowing someone locally, (4) jobs and strength of the economy, and (5) cost. Subsequently, the author will also consider the factors that would influence international students to enjoy or remain in a province after their studies. Having an understanding of the factors that influence international student choice can help the reader understand some of the marketing implications of recruiting international students to institutions and how international students end up studying in the Canadian post-secondary system.

INTRODUCTION

Walking through the halls of one of the twenty-seven publicly funded post-secondary institutions in the province of Alberta, and seeing a plethora of diverse international students, it crossed the researcher's mind "how in the world did this many students from around the globe end up here?" As a faculty member for over fifteen years at this institution, where the institution is great and the community is beautiful, but it is not necessarily a destination for tourism or travel. And yet the international student population within the business program has grown from four percent to over forty percent in that fifteen-year time frame. There are other Albertans in the province who are not necessarily sure where the community is or that a post-secondary institution exists here, so then, how is it that these international students managed to locate and choose to study here? Those students cannot possibly be sitting in their bedroom in Delhi, India, or their kitchen in Beijing, China, or at their school in Osaka, Japan, dreaming of coming to this

DOI: 10.4018/978-1-7998-5030-4.ch015

specific institution. Maybe this happens to institutions like Harvard, but certainly not here. This pondering led the researcher to ask that exact research question to try to understand the factors that influence international students to choose Alberta, Canada, as their choice for higher learning.

The objective of this chapter is to provide an overview of how international students come to study higher learning in Alberta, Canada. Understanding the motivations and factors that influence international students' choice of destination for schooling can provide some insight into how administrators can market to those students. Or perhaps, just help everyone to better understand the cohort of students filling classrooms and some of their rationale for studying in Canada. The chapter will also discuss the aspects that international students like about studying in the country as well as what existing factors would allow them to want to continue to stay in Canada post-graduation.

BACKGROUND

International students have been choosing Canada as a destination for higher education for many years and this number continues to increase. According to the Canadian Bureau for International Education (CBIE, 2019) in 2018 there were 571, 215 international students enrolled in Canadian post-secondary schools representing a 16% increase over 2017. Research has previously been conducted in several different ways to try to understand the choice of institution by international students (Cubillo, Sanchez, & Cervino, 2006; Eder, Smith, & Pitts, 2010) and further research has been conducted to understand location choice, which means the selection of country or province where students will attend schooling (Abubakar, Shanka, & Muuka, 2010; Bohman, 2010). The challenge, however, is that the flows of students from the sending countries will change over time. In 2018, India surpassed China as the largest contributor to international students attending Canadian post-secondary institutions (CBIE, 2019). It seems that as soon as research is conducted, the flows of students tend to change. What impact will the next United States election have on international student flows? The political relationships between countries can ebb the flow of students or help to increase it. What about the impact of COVID-19 or whatever the next global health pandemic? We know that Severe Acute Respiratory Syndrome (SARS), a contagious respiratory coronavirus that impacted both Asia and Canada in 2002 and 2003, had a negative impact on international student enrollment in Canada the following year. There will always be the next thing.

Internationalization of the higher learning education system in Canada is important to administrators within the Canadian federal government and in October 2011 a panel was formed to develop a domestic "international education" strategy. So, although there is a national level strategy, the authority for post-secondary education (PSE) lands under provincial governments in Canada to coordinate and regulate PSE with their provincial jurisdictions (Kirby, 2007, Shanahan & Jones, 2007). In Alberta, specifically, even though there is a recognized gap that exists between the goals of the federal and provincial governments, the Ministry of Advanced Education and Technology (MAET) felt there has not been a concentrated effort by government to assure marketing of PSE with the province's institutions of higher learning towards international learners (Alberta Advanced Education and Technology, 2012).

By understanding the reasons why international students choose to study in Canada, a province, and then down to a specific institution is becoming increasingly more important for institutions of higher learning administrators due to increases in competition. Understanding the factors which international learners consider when they make their choice for higher education in Alberta can be beneficial to administrators in the creation of future recruitment strategies of institutions (Greene & Kirby, 2012;

Madgett & Belanger, 2008). There is increasing competition between countries (United States, United Kingdom, and Canada for example), but also for institutions within countries for international students and there are new ways to market to these students (Hemsley-Brown & Oplatka, 2006; McCarthy, Sen, & Garrity, 2012). Access to information using the internet has significantly changed the competitive nature of institutions competing to attract international learners (Steele, 2010). Access to online information and increasing online programming increases the competition not only between countries but also between institutions (Flynn & Vredevoogd, 2010). It has just become that much easier for international students to gather information about institutions and cities for them to be able to find the right fit of institution. In addition, institutions of higher learning in Canada are having a difficult time adapting to changing educational expectations and education needs of students (Tagg, 2008). Some institutions may be better than others at communicating to future learners, but many institutions are often slow to make significant changes.

Further to this, a decline in birth rates and immigration from 2006 and 2011 will negatively impact enrollments of domestic students due to negative growth rates (Chagnon & Milan, 2011). The diminishing number of traditional aged students (students between the ages of 18-24) enrolling in PSE moving forward will create further challenges for academic institutions. With lower domestic student enrolment in institutions of higher learning, unprecedented challenges will be created for Canadian schools (Steele, 2010). Whether immigration, increased domestic participation, or international student recruitment will mitigate the negative population growth has yet to be concluded (Steele, 2010). The sustainability of Albertan post-secondaries into the future with less traditional domestic students available comes into question unless attempts are made to increase other potential student populations.

The participation rate for post-secondary education in Alberta is the lowest of the 10 Canadian provinces in relation to 18-34-year olds. Alberta's participation rate is also lower than the Canadian average of 22.7%, leaving Alberta in a vulnerable position in relation to population declines (MAET, 2010). Previously, that low participation rate has been blamed on a robust oil and gas sector resulting in fewer males entering post-secondary education due to the availability of good paying jobs in that sector (Steele, 2010). With the decline in the oil and gas sector currently within the province what impact will that have on participation rates? The current Alberta government has also removed tuition caps on Albertan post-secondary institutions resulting in likely 7% increases on tuition in the province for the next three years (Government of Alberta, 2019). These are some factors on both sides that will either aid or hinder further participation rates in the province.

LITERATURE REVIEW

To try to understand the decision-making process utilized by students to select higher learning opportunities, many different models have been created. These include econometric models (Chapman, 1979), marketing models (Cubillo et al., 2006; Hossler, Braxton, & Coopersmith, 1989), and sociological models (Flint, 2002). To understand international student choice to study abroad, push-pull factors have been used (Li & Bray, 2007; Maringe & Carter, 2007; Mazzarol & Soutar, 2002). In the decision-making process of international students, the push factors often occur first. A push factor is a reason why international student will look outside of their home country to choose to study and could include the belief that an international credential will provide better job opportunities thus leading to pull factors from a host country and subsequently a host institution to attract a foreign student which may include the academic quality of an institution or an immigration process (Lam, Arrifin, & Ahmad, 2011). Push-pull factors have also been used in the Canadian context to help explain flows of international students (Chen, 2007; Wang, 2009).

To understand the factors that influence international students to leave their home countries to study abroad, Lam et al. (2011) found that (1) enhancement of future job prospects, (2) better environment to study in, (3) higher status for the student in the future, and (4) ability to improve language skills were the reasons students looked to study abroad. These are the most likely reasons students were 'pushed' to start looking to study abroad. Once students are pushed to look for education outside of their home country, pull factors from countries or institutions start playing a role in the decision-making process. The most common pull factors include (1) research and academic quality at institutions of higher learning, (2) the facilities and academic infrastructure at the institutions, (3) the reputation and image of the institutions, and (4) the fit of the academic programs to the learner (Lam et al., 2011).

Location is an important factor influencing international student choice (Abubakar et al., 2010). Once students decide to start looking abroad for their higher education needs, they start comparing countries to one another. From a Canadian perspective, Canada is in competition with several other countries. The United States has traditionally been the leader in international student enrollment holding around 22% of the market: but competition is increasing from other nations with the U.K. recruiting 13%, France at 9%, Australia at 8%, and Germany at 7% (McCarthy et al., 2012). In 2017, Canada attracted around 370,000 international students compared to close to 1.1 million in the U.S. and 500,000 to the U.K. (CBIE, 2018). Previous research determined some of the influencers that international students used to decide to study in Canada, as can be seen in Table 1.

Table 1. Factors influencing choice of Canada by Asian international students

Key influencers for choosing Canada	Sample factors related to key influencers
1. Perceived Characteristics of Canada	Safe place to study, studious environment, diverse and multicultural, quality of life, strong economic and political ties to home country.
2. Internal factors	Economics, marketing, and information that includes tuition costs, visa processing, living expenses, reputation and quality of higher education institutions.
3. Other significant factors	Recommended by friends, family, or professor; friends, family, or relatives living in Canada.

Adapted from Chen (2007)

Once international learners decide on a country to study in, it is only at that time that the students start to consider the institution in which they will study. In a research conducted by Bohman (2010), the decision making process for students follows the previously described push-pull model: first considering whether or not to leave the home country deciding on pull factors of countries before ultimately deciding on the type and then specific institution. Table 2 provides the four-step process that influences the choice of an international learner to community colleges in the United States.

Table 2. Four step process influencing choice of community colleges in the USA

Step – Key question	Elements
1. Should I study abroad?	The global identity of the student and push-pull factors.
2. Where should I go?	Students' perception of countries and pull factors.
3. What type of school is best?	Students obtain information about types of schools, relying on outside sources.
4. What school should I attend?	Students' personal preferences and institutional pull factors including costs, location, and institutional responsiveness.

Adapted from Bohman (2010)

METHODOLOGY

Understanding the previous research that had been conducted on international student choice is extremely useful in providing a general understanding of the individual's decision-making process. It confirmed that students were not dreaming of studying at any specific institution, but instead the learners followed a pattern of decision making that ultimately led them to choose Canada and subsequently a specific institution of higher learning. The previous research and literature did not consider Alberta specifically in the students' decision-making process. What were the factors specific to Alberta that drive students to choose to study in the province? If administrators of institutions understand the factors driving students to Alberta, what can be done to increase the number of international students studying in the province? What can be done to keep the students in the province after they complete their studies? Is there a systematic difference between students studying at one institution versus students who choose to study at other institutions within the province? Or are the factors consistent among all the schools? These were the questions at the heart of the research conducted that will be discussed in this section.

Having worked in higher education for over 12 years, initially in recruitment and then as a faculty member in a business program, my understanding was that the decision-making process of students on where to study abroad was an individual one, but it appeared that there were some similarities. National data, although relatively plentiful, did not necessarily explain factors influencing international students to study at a specific institution but was aggregate in nature. Further to this, in discussions with managers of international education, their perceptions seemed to be anecdotal in nature. In trying to answer the questions above, exploratory qualitative research was conducted at three different types of post-secondary institutions in Alberta using focus groups. According to Myers (2009), the qualitative method is best when the research is exploratory, and the study is being conducted on one or a few organizations. The institutions were found using convenience sampling and included: one community college, one university, and one polytechnic. These institutions each had between three to eight percent of the overall undergraduate student population in the province of Alberta. A qualitative multiple case study was used in this research.

The study sample consisted of international undergraduate students studying at the participating institutions. Once the institutions were selected, the researcher worked with the managers of the participating international education offices to send a recruitment email to the international students offering for them to participate in structured interviews for the study. Purposeful sampling was used to select the participants based on their knowledge and experience in choosing Alberta for the post-secondary education which was determined after a brief screening process. Semi-structured focused interview questions were created using the literature review as a guide and were based off previous research questions by Chen (2007) and Wang (2009). The questions were field-tested by three experts including two English as a second language (ESL) instructors and one linguistics instructor. Since the research was exploratory, semi-structure interview questions were the best option to allow flexibility in the response pattern (Frey & Fontana, 1993).

Twelve students were selected to be interviewed for the study. The questions followed a questioning route created by Krueger and Casey (2009). The study sample had an equal number of male and female participants with an average age of 23 and 24 respectively. Countries of origin included: Nigeria, Brazil, China, Vietnam, Mexico, South Africa and, Thailand. All interviews were conducted in English.

According to Baker and Edwards (2012), interviewing 12 students is enough to develop themes, but the results will be further respected if additional qualitative tools are used. Therefore, the data collected were triangulated by collecting secondary data using focused interviews with three managers of international education offices, and an evaluation of marketing materials was analysed to view how institutions communicated with international students. Managers were interviewed to ascertain their perspective as to why international students choose to study in Alberta. A rubric was created to evaluate the marketing materials of the three participating institutions.

From the research conducted, five common themes were found to exist: (a) safety, (b) quality of education, (c) knowing someone locally, (d) jobs and the strength of the economy, and (e) the cost of the education (Howes, 2015). In addition to these five themes, there were several other factors that permeated throughout the research conducted but to a lesser extent. These factors included partnership agreements between the home and host institutions, weather, and having good infrastructure and transportation networks.

Factors Influencing International Student Choice

In retrospect, looking back at the results of the research that was conducted, some of the responses of students were very predictable while other responses were not expected. Some of the factors that were discussed by the international students would not be factors that Canadian students if studying abroad would consider. Safety is an important factor for students choosing to study in Canada. Some of the push factors from students' home countries could be the violence, corruption, and inequality (this can be both economic but can also include gender inequality) that exists. In a study conducted by Howes (2015) one student reported about studying in Alberta:

I was looking for a country that had less problems with violence and corruption and inequality and things like that. Especially safety. Safety was a big one. I wasn't very comfortable living where I was living so I had to go somewhere else. (p. 79)

The perception that Canada is a safe country which is generally free from discrimination against foreigners was prevalent. Unfortunately, many of the respondents stated that they had been exposed to discrimination during their studies in Canada, but mostly the international students felt safe in their communities and at their institutions. A particularly challenging story to hear was from a female South African student who mentioned that had she chosen to study in her home country, she likely would have been sexually assaulted on the public transportation during her studies in her home country. This is not something Canadian learners necessarily try to avoid when choosing a post-secondary institution to study in, but was a reality for this international learner. One perspective that perhaps had not been considered was the perception of the parents of international students were extremely important. Parents are influencers in a prospective learner's life and their perceptions around safety certainly influenced student choice. Managers of international education felt that safety was important, and the marketing materials of the institutions also stated safety as a factor that would aid in recruiting international students (Howes, 2015).

Education quality is a factor that influences an international student's decision-making. Students spoke of quality of education being a reason to leave their home country but also used quality of education as a comparison between countries and ultimately institutions. One student mentioned that her perception of the quality of Canadian post-secondary education was higher than that of the United States which prompted her to choose Canada over the United States (Howes, 2015). Quality of the education was also found to be a key factor in an earlier study by Mazzarol and Souter (2002). Although quality of education seems like an obvious factor, only one of three managers stated that quality of education was important to international student choice (Howes, 2015). It is possible that the more obvious a factor such as quality of education appears to be, the more it could allow for oversight from marketers of post-secondary institutions. So how do institutions communicate quality? Perhaps this is why there seems to be a push towards ensuring institutions do well in University rankings.

Knowing someone locally in the host country is another important factor influencing student choice of higher learning. This includes either family or friends of the international learner. If a student knows someone who has previously been to a community or institution and had a positive experience, that positive experience may be communicated to prospective students creating a potential future flow of students. All but one of the students in the study had family in Canada which made their decision to study in the country easier (Howes, 2015). On numerous occasions, it has been seen that one student from an international city attends an institution, then the brother comes, then the cousin comes. This flows based on word of mouth and positive experiences is an extremely useful tool for recruiters of international students at post-secondary institutions. The key is that the students must have a positive experience. The reasons international students provided for wanting to know someone locally was to reduce the culture shock of their experience, and to have support of people they know (Howes, 2015).

International students will also pay attention to the economy and the types of jobs that are available for them upon graduation. In some instances, students are interested in obtaining their Canadian credential and then heading back to their home country whereas in other circumstances the students are hoping to remain in the host country post graduation. One student from Brazil chose to study in Canada due to the strong oil and gas sector that existed in the province at the time and since the education and training that would be received in Canada would be transferable back to similar industries from the student's home country:

I guess, when I did look into Alberta there were a lot of job opportunities as well like, especially when I go into the oil fields. If I go in Alberta, I'll probably be able to get a better knowledge I'd say and like the oil fields because the majority of it is in Alberta. So that is one thing like the job possibilities. (Howes, 2015, p. 81)

Other industry sectors that were discussed by students as being a draw are the health sectors and sciences. I can only assume that these industries would vary based on the geographic location of the institutions of higher learning across Canada. In talking with the managers of international education offices, the types of jobs available in the country did not appear to be a factor for recruitment initiatives for institutions. So, although students were interested in attending schools with similar economies, and even though this could be a selling feature in them choosing a country or province, this is not something currently practiced.

I believe that anyone that reads this chapter would not be surprised by the fact that the cost of education was a factor that showed up in the research results. What was however, a little surprising is there appeared to be a difference between institutions as to whether international learners felt that cost was a significant factor in their decision to study at that institution (Howes, 2015). It seemed that at smaller schools, cost was an important factor whereas at bigger institutions the cost of study was less likely to show up in the responses of the international students. Perhaps quality of education was more important to some learners, or that the family financial situation was different enough that cost was not significant, this was not determined in the results, but there definitely was a difference as to whether cost was a factor between institutions. So, cost of education will be something that some institutions need to consider. Currently in Alberta, the cost of education is going to be increasing relatively significantly over the next several years as the current government has stated that there will be an 11% increase in 2020 in the cost of post-secondary education with subsequent increases of nearly 5% for the following two years (Government of Alberta, 2020). What will this mean for institutions? Based on what can be derived from above, enrollments of international learners at some institutions may be impacted differently with reductions in student enrollments whereas enrollments at other institutions of higher learning may not be significantly influenced.

The remaining factors that were discovered in the research were (a) partnership agreements between home country and host country institutions, (b) weather, and, (c) having good infrastructure and transportation (Howes, 2105). The flow of international students is impacted by the partnership agreements that exist between institutions. My firsthand knowledge at the campus under consideration here is there was a significant flow of students from a city in China where there was a partnership arrangement. Since the end of that partnership arrangement, the flow of students has completely depleted that -the institution no longer has any students from that city. Partnerships provide a safety net for students and a comfortability with their decision. In several instances, they knew someone previously who had attended the institution, personnel at the institution are typically more knowledgeable about the partner institution which created an easier decision for the international learner.

In several instances the weather in Canada came up as a factor that influences students' decision to study in the country. Not surprisingly, in discussing weather with the managers of international education offices, weather was a factor that was assumed to be overcome by the international recruitment offices whereas the results showed that in some cases weather was a favorable or compelling factor in international students' decision to come to Canada (Howes, 2015). The opportunity for students coming from a country where they only experience one season year-round and have never seen snow, the weather and seasons are a positive. One other factor that came up in the conversation on weather was the air quality in Canada. Air quality is likely not a factor that weighs into Canadian students when choosing an institution of higher learning in Canada, but air quality was a factor that influenced international students to study in the country. The final factor that was uncovered in the research was having good infrastructure and transportation for example, where a respondent answered that they expected "good roads, like transportation methods, like safe transportation methods" (Howes, 2015, p. 83).

What do International Students Like About Studying in Alberta?

Understanding what international students like about studying in Canada can help marketers of institutions focus marketing messages or can help administrators of institutions create an environment within their institutions that can help foster a better environment for international learners. Four main themes emerged from previous research: (a) physical environment, (b) quality of education, (c) quality of life, and (d) the economy (Howes, 2015).

Based on students' responses, the physical environment consists of the air quality, physical landscape including mountains and lakes, and the weather. The physical environment was an important factor about what students enjoyed while studying in Alberta with statements around enjoying the scenery through going on hikes, comparisons to air quality in the student's home country, and the fact of enjoying the different seasons in Canada. Some students stated that the weather and climate of Alberta (specifically the winter months) were something that they did not like about studying in the province, but there were enough positive factors in relation to the physical environment that in general it seemed as a positive (Howes, 2015). Through the analysis of marketing materials, Albertan institutions promote the physical environment by showing pictures of mountains, lakes, and rivers (Howes, 2015).

Students' perceptions of the quality of education as a factor in their decision to study in the province were corroborated with students stating that their experiences confirmed their perception. A student stated that they liked the quiet college environment and "learned a lot here, knowledge of English and business administration, and I got the education that my parents expect" (Howes, 2015, p. 87). If students are expecting a certain level of education, and those expectations are being met by the Canadian institutions, then that will help with future recruitment efforts through word-of-mouth advertising.

The quality of life in Canada was mentioned by all the students as a factor that the students enjoyed about studying in the country. Quality of life included safety and social development as areas the students enjoyed.

I personally like the western lifestyle more than eastern in some point, like I appreciate where I'm from and the country I'm from. But I personally like to be independent and the eastern culture don't give me that much. So I actually like it here so much. (Howes, 2015, p. 84)

Quality of life was a comparison strictly between the home country and the host country. Perhaps there could be some difference between different regions in Canada, but that was not established in the results of this particular case study.

The last factor that students identified as being a factor that they enjoyed about studying in Canada was the economy. At the time of the research, Alberta economy was relatively strong with a decent industry around oil and gas. The opportunities in that sector as well as the tax bracket that existed in the province at the time were of interest to some of the students interviewed in the research. As the price of oil and gas has decreased since that time and the unemployment rate in Alberta has increased significantly, it remains to be seen if the Alberta economy will continue to draw international students to the province.

LIMITATIONS

Issues with the research that has been discussed above can be the scrutiny of the credibility of the researcher, rigorousness of the research methods, and the perceived value of qualitative research (Patton, 2002). In order to ensure reliability and validity, qualitative triangulation can be used (Merriam, 1998). In the case study discussed, triangulation was achieved by using multiple institutions, using focused in-depth interviews with managers of international education office, and from the evaluation of marketing materials from the participating institutions.

With the research only being conducted at three institutions within the province, this could be another limitation. No research was conducted at the privately funded post-secondary institutions in the province and with the limited sample size of three schools it may be difficult to determine if the results would be generalizable across the 26 publicly funded institutions in the province or if the results could be generalized across Canada. With the students being interviewed while already in Canada, their memories of the factors influencing their choice of Canada and institution could have changed over time (Howes, 2015). If students were interviewed after their decision to study in Canada was made, but before they began their studies here, this could be a more accurate depiction of the factors that ultimately influenced their decision to study in the province. There could be additional benefits in trying to interview students that considered Canada but decided not to study in the country.

The sample size of the study being relatively small (the number of students interviewed compared to the number of international students at each institution) could also be a limitation of the study. The study was limited by the methodology chosen as exploratory research therefore a larger sample size was not required. Saturation was followed to determine if the sample size was big enough, whereby if no new information was being obtained from the interviews the sample size was considered large enough (Glaser & Strauss, 1967; Mason, 2010).

Other problems with the research results could be the ever-changing flow of international students to countries or destinations. Like the painting of the San Francisco Bridge, as soon as the research has been completed, it could begin again to determine if there have been any changes to the factors influencing choice. A change in government, a global conflict, a global health pandemic can all change the perceptions around safety and reputation which can change the flow of students for a short time or forever.

SOLUTIONS AND RECOMMENDATIONS

Although international learners have been attracted to Albertan post-secondary institutions, there is reason to believe that administrators at those institutions will need to continue to attract a greater number of international learners. The reason for this it to make up for enrollment shortages, declining birthrates in the province and to deal with the impact of higher tuition costs across the province. Understanding international students' choice and the factors influencing international learners to study in the province, will help marketers within the post-secondary landscape to better communicate with potential learners. The author proposes several recommendations that could aid the increase in number of international students studying in the province which include: (a) focus marketing efforts on countries with similar jobs and economies as Alberta (an example of this would be Brazil for the oil and gas industry), (b) pay attention to the relationship and relationship building aspect of international students, (c) collaboration between post-secondary institutions within the province to create a Brand Alberta, (d) creating a marketing campaign aimed at undergraduate students currently studying in Alberta to promote the high quality of graduate studies in the province, and (e) aid in the development of relationship building within institutions toward current international students (Howes, 2015).

Although international students mention that they are interested in attending post-secondary institutions in locations that have similar economies than their home countries (Howes, 2015), it does not appear that the marketing departments of the Albertan higher learning organizations factor home country economies and industries and look for comparisons to the host province or country. This slight change in recruitment focus could aid in the recruitment and therefore increase in number of international learners into the province. So from an Alberta perspective, this could mean recruiting from countries with oil and gas, agriculture, and health services which could lead to a higher conversion rate than countries with dissimilar industries as only one institution mentioned post-graduation employment in its marketing materials (Howes, 2015).

Relationships or knowing someone locally is an important factor in the decision of international students in choosing the destination of their higher education institution. This provides a couple of opportunities for post-secondary institutions to market to the international learner. One way to create a flow of students between institutions is to create more partnership agreements between institutions in a home and host country. These partnerships help with the flow of students between countries as it increases the flow of students. If the students have positive experiences, the word of mouth advertising and ease in which students can typically move to partner institutions (as there is typically easier transfer credit or degree and diploma completion opportunities that exist). Another opportunity is to work with foreign nationals to promote the benefits of living and studying in Alberta to those individuals' network of friends and family.

Greater collaboration between Albertan institutions to market the province and Albertan higher education would be another recommendation to administrators of higher learning institutions in the province. Previous research concluded that the majority of international students will first choose the country and province before finally choosing the institutions in which they will study (Abubakar et al, 2010; Bohman, 2010). By increasing the number of students studying in the province, there should be a trickle-down effect to individual schools. The collaboration of a Brand Alberta should lower marketing costs for administrators of institutions and have a positive impact on the number of international learners who would look to study in Alberta. Based on previous research, factors that could be highlighted within the Brand Alberta could be the physical environment of the province, job opportunities and industries within the province, and the quality of education (Howes, 2015).

One practical recommendation is to create a marketing campaign aimed towards undergraduate international students to promote graduate studies and immigration policies to increase awareness around the quality graduate level education opportunities that exist within the province (Howes, 2015). Marketing literature of post-secondaries rarely focus on the next steps for international learners' post graduation from their undergraduate studies. This strategy again could increase the number of international students studying in the province.

Students having a positive experience in the host country and at the host institution is critical for the international students to remain in the province for future learning or to remain in the province post-graduation. Administrators must find ways to ensure that students are able to develop relationships with domestic students as well as their international student cohort. It is recommended that institutions focus on mentorship programs for their international learners. One heartbreaking story that was discussed with an international learner was that after two years, that student had not made one Canadian friend over two years of studying at the school. Obviously, that student's experience could not have been a positive one and it was hard not to feel that institution had let that student down even though some responsibility would lie with the student in question.

FUTURE RESEARCH DIRECTIONS

Future research in the area of international decision making and choice of province and institution is quite substantial. The exploratory research discussed above was the first that focused on the choice of Alberta for post-secondary education and ultimately added to the body of research around the marketing of higher education institutions toward international learners. Since the study was exploratory and qualitative, more in-depth research could be conducted using quantitative analysis at all Alberta institutions (or for that fact all institutions across Canada) to determine if the factors discussed hold true across the 26 publicly funded institutions in Alberta. Although there appeared to be some differences between factors between the different institutions, further research could be conducted to determine if there are systematic differences between different types of post-secondary institutions (in Alberta these are the comprehensive academic and research institutions, baccalaureate and applied studies institutions, polytechnic institutions, comprehensive community institutions, independent academic institutions, and specialized arts and culture institutions). Future researchers could further study whether these differences could change the marketing messages of individual institutions. This increase of institutions (and therefore students) would add to the credibility of the study by adding to the results; and although the factors determining international student choice of this study replicated results in previous research, better determining factors such as cost of education across institutions could be better understood. Administrators of higher learning institutions may be able to understand what impact changes to tuition rates on international learners will have, which could aid in their recruitment and retention efforts.

The inclusion of graduate students would give a better understanding regarding the differences that may exist dependant on the type of qualification the international learner is trying to attain. Perhaps some of the factors are identical, however, there could be a difference in the importance of quality of education or reputation of the institution for a higher degree among other differences. Of course, that is just speculation until future research is conducted. Lastly, by interviewing students before they come to Canada may give a more accurate depiction of the factors influencing the international learners without any possible bias that may have creeped in since coming to study in the province.

CONCLUSION

The purpose of this chapter was to provide some understanding how international students choose to study at specific institutions within the province of Alberta. Analysis of previous research concluded that international students will typically follow a push-pull model whereas the students will first determine that they would like to leave their home country (push factors) before ultimately deciding on the appropriate country to study in (pull factors). Although there are several factors that were discussed above that will ultimately aid in the decision of where to study for international students, there are many factors that constantly change and evolve that will make the choice of destination change over time. As soon as administrators of higher education institutions feel like they have it figured out, internal or external factors can change leading to a change in the flow of international student. Safety, reputation for quality, politics, cost of education, and the overall health of the economy can all be factors that will affect the international student choice. In the current context of Alberta, many of these factors are constantly changing, in 2020 unemployment in the province is rising, government funding to post-secondary is decreasing, and tuition is increasing (Government of Alberta, 2020). It remains to be seen what impact this will have on future international student recruitment, but alas the underlying factors should continue to hold even as the flows of students will continue to evolve.

ACKNOWLEDGMENT

This research received no specific grant from any funding agency in the public, commercial, or not-for-profit sectors.

REFERENCES

Abubakar, B., Shanka, T., & Muuka, G. (2010). Tertiary education: An investigation of location selection criteria and preferences by international students - The case of two Australian universities. *Journal of Marketing for Higher Education, 20*(1), 49–68. doi:10.1080/08841241003788052

Alberta Advanced Education and Technology. (2012). *Campus Alberta Planning Resource.* Retrieved from http://eae.alberta.ca/media/299589/capr2012.pdf

Baker, S. E., & Edwards, R. (2012). *How many qualitative interviews is enough?* National Centre for Research Methods.

Bohman, E. (2010). Headed for the heartland: Decision making process of community college bound international students. *Community College Journal of Research and Practice, 34*(1-2), 64–77. doi:10.1080/10668920903385848

Canadian Bureau for International Education. (2018). *International students in Canada.* Retrieved from https://cbie.ca/wp-content/uploads/2018/09/International-Students-in-Canada-ENG.pdf

Canadian Bureau for International Education. (2019). *Annual Report.* Retrieved from https://cbie.ca/wp-content/uploads/2019/11/CBIE-0299---AR-Eng.pdf

Chagnon, J., & Milan, A. (2011). *Population growth: Canada, provinces, and territories, 2010.* Retrieved from https://www.statcan.gc.ca/pub/91-209-x/2011001/article/11508-eng.html

Chapman, R. G. (1979). Pricing policy and the college choice process. *Research in Higher Education, 10*(1), 37–57. doi:10.1007/BF00977498

Chen, L. (2007). East-Asian students' choice of Canadian graduate schools. *International Journal of Educational Advancement, 7*(3), 271–306. doi:10.1057/palgrave.ijea.2150071

Cubillo, J., Sánchez, J., & Cerviño, J. (2006). International students' decision-making process. *International Journal of Educational Management, 20*(2), 101–115. doi:10.1108/09513540610646091

Eder, J., Smith, W., & Pitts, R. (2010). Exploring factors influencing student study abroad destination choice. *Journal of Teaching in Travel & Tourism, 10*(3), 232–250. doi:10.1080/15313220.2010.503534

Flint, T. A. (1992). Parental and planning influences on the formation of student college choice sets. *Research in Higher Education, 33*(6), 689–708. doi:10.1007/BF00992054

Flynn, W. J., & Vredevoogd, J. (2010). The future of learning: 12 views on emerging trends in higher education. *Planning for Higher Education, 38*(2), 4–10.

Frey, J., & Fontana, A. (1993). The group interview in social research. In D. L. Morgan (Ed.), *Successful focus groups* (pp. 20–34). Sage. doi:10.4135/9781483349008.n2

Glaser, B., & Strauss, A. (1967). *The discovery of grounded theory: Strategies for qualitative research.* Aldine.

Government of Alberta. (2019). Budget 2019. Fiscal plan: A plan for jobs and the economy. Edmonton, Canada.

Government of Alberta. (2020). Budget 2020. Fiscal plan: A plan for jobs and the economy. Edmonton, Canada.

Greene, M., & Kirby, D. (2012). The impact of tuition fees on access and student migration: Lessons from Canada's Atlantic coast. *Widening Participation and Lifelong Learning: the Journal of the Institute for Access Studies and the European Access Network, 14*(2), 72–90. doi:10.5456/WPLL.14.1.72

Guest, G., Bunce, A., & Johnson, L. (2006). How many interviews are enough? An experiment with data saturation and variability. *Field Methods, 18*(1), 59–82. doi:10.1177/1525822X05279903

Hemsley-Brown, J., & Oplatka, I. (2006). Universities in a competitive global marketplace: A systematic review of the literature on higher education marketing. *International Journal of Public Sector Management, 19*(4), 316–338. doi:10.1108/09513550610669176

Hossler, D. R., Braxton, J., & Coopersmith, G. (1989). Understanding student college choice. In J. C. Smart (Ed.), *Higher education, handbook of theory and research* (pp. 231–288). Agathon Press.

Howes, D. (2015). *A multiple case study of international undergraduate student choice of Alberta, Canada for post-secondary education* [Doctoral Dissertation. Northcentral University]. Proquest Dissertations Publishing, 3713980.

Kirby, D. (2007). Reviewing Canadian post-secondary education: Post-secondary education policy in post-industrial Canada. *Canadian Journal of Educational Administration and Policy, 65,* 1–24.

Krueger, R., & Casey, M. (2009). *Focus groups: A practical guide for applied research* (4th ed.). Sage Publications.

Lam, J. S., Ariffin, A. M., & Ahmad, A. j. (2011). Edutourism: Exploring the push-pull factors in selecting a university. *International Journal of Business & Society, 12*(1), 63–78.

Li, M., & Bray, M. (2007). Cross-border flows of students for higher education: Push–pull factors and motivations of mainland Chinese students in Hong Kong and Macau. *Higher Education, 53*(6), 791–818. doi:10.100710734-005-5423-3

Madgett, P. J., & Belanger, C. (2008). International students: The Canadian experience. *Tertiary Education and Management, 14*(3), 191–207. doi:10.1080/13583880802228182

Maringe, F., & Carter, S. (2007). International students; motivations for studying in UK HE: Insights into the choice and decision making of African students. *International Journal of Educational Management, 21*(6), 459–475. doi:10.1108/09513540710780000

Mason, M. (2010). Sample size and saturation in PhD studies using qualitative interviews. In *Forum Qualitative Sozialforschung/Forum: Qualitative. Social Research, 11*(3).

Mazzarol, T., & Soutar, G. N. (2002). "Push-pull" factors influencing international student destination choice. *International Journal of Educational Management, 16*(2), 82–90. doi:10.1108/09513540210418403

McCarthy, E. E., Sen, A. K., & Garrity, B. (2012). Factors that influence Canadian students' choice of higher education institutions in the United States. *Business Education & Accreditation, 4*(2), 85–95.

Myers, M. (2009). *Qualitative research in business and management.* Sage Publications.

Shanahan, T., & Jones, G. A. (2007). Shifting roles and approaches: Government coordination of post-secondary education in Canada, 1995-2006. *Higher Education Research & Development, 26*(1), 31–43. Advance online publication. doi:10.1080/07294360601166794

Steele, K. (2010). The changing Canadian PSE landscape. In J. Black (Ed.), *Strategic Enrolment Intelligence.* Retrieved from https://www.academica.ca/strategic-enrolment-intelligence

Tagg, J. (2008). Changing minds in higher education: Students change, so why can't college? *Planning for Higher Education, 37*(1), 15–22.

The Ministry of Advanced Education and Technology. (2010). *Advanced education and Technology Business Plan, 2010-2013.* Retrieved from http://www.advancededucation.gov.ab.ca/apps/publications/PublicationItem.asp?ID=912

Wang, X. (2009). *Institutional recruitment strategies and international undergraduate student university choice at two Canadian universities* (Doctoral dissertation). University of Toronto. ProQuest Dissertations and Theses database. Retrieved from https://search.proquest.com/docview/375478075?accountid=28180

KEY TERMS AND DEFINITIONS

Higher Learning Institutions: Post-secondary institutions within Alberta include institutions from the six-sector model: comprehensive academic and research institutions, baccalaureate and applied studies institutions, polytechnical institutions, comprehensive community institutions, independent academic institutions, and specialized arts and culture institutions.

International Students: International students include visa students who are studying outside of their home country.

Physical Environment: The physical environment includes the physical landscape such as mountains, air quality and weather.

Post-Secondary Institutes: Post-secondary institutions within Alberta include institutions from the six-sector model: comprehensive academic and research institutions, baccalaureate and applied studies institutions, polytechnical institutions, comprehensive community institutions, independent academic institutions, and specialized arts and culture institutions.

Push-Pull Model: The push-pull model explains the motivations, decisions, and flow of international students where push factors drive students' decision to study abroad and pull factors are characteristics of a host country that attract international students.

Saturation: The concept of determining whether data collected from focus groups or surveys is presenting any new information. If no new information is being collected, saturation has been achieved and no more data collection is required.

Six Sector Model: The government of Alberta's institutional arrangement explaining the geographic region of service, main credential offerings, as well as the program, delivery, and research responsibilities the publicly funded institutes of higher learning.

Chapter 16
Beyond Recruitment:
Career Navigation and Support of International Students in Canada

Philipp N. Reichert
UBC Okanagan, Canada

Rohene Bouajram
UBC Vancouver, Canada

ABSTRACT

In this chapter, the authors provide an overview of internationalization efforts and the impact of substantial immigration policy shifts to support, recruit, and retain international students in Canada. Consideration is given to how higher educational institutions, and other key stakeholders play a role in supporting career exploration as well as the factors that influence international students' ability to stay in Canada post-graduation. Future directions and research are explored to further highlight the importance of understanding the international student lifecycle in the Canadian context.

INTRODUCTION

As long-standing professionals in the field of international education in Canada and having first-hand experience of being an international student, the authors are humbled to contribute with a chapter that honours a field that has evolved and grown, as students, shifts in global forces, and multiple key stakeholders have impacted the exchange of ideas, learning, and culture. This chapter will elucidate the Canadian context in light of intensified, fierce global competition to recruit and retain international students amongst many Organization for Economic Co-operation and Development (OECD) countries. Simply put–international education has become critical to Canada's future of a skilled workforce (DFAIT, 2012; Kunin, 2012; OECD, 2014).

This chapter is designed as a practitioner reflection based on research that both authors have completed. Our reflection offers a contextualized overview of the key literature in the field and addresses: first, concerns related to the international student experience in the Canadian context; and second, is-

DOI: 10.4018/978-1-7998-5030-4.ch016

sues related to employability more broadly. The bulk of the chapter will explore graduate employability outcomes, career navigation, and factors that contribute to international students' transition to work by focusing on responsive programming delivered in Canadian post-secondary institutions. Dedicated space will also be given to the decision-making process of international students in choosing to stay in Canada or return home, an area of research and understanding that continues to grow. Lastly, reflections on future research directions and concluding remarks will be provided with a sense of hope that understanding the international student lifecycle in Canada remains a vital area of exploration as international education will likely become more complex in an ambiguous and ever-changing global terrain.

BACKGROUND

Over the past 40 years, forces of globalization have intensified in all aspects of the human experience. International trade, the movement of people, technology, environmental catastrophes, and conflicts have become increasingly intertwined. This interconnectedness has increased in many spheres, not least in higher education. During the past 20 years and particularly in the past decade, the number of international students has risen dramatically around the world as many students are making the choice to study outside the country of their citizenship. Henceforth, international students in the context of this paper refers to individuals not holding Canadian or permanent resident status and select Canada as their destination of multiple levels of study. In 2016, over five million students attended Higher Education Institutions (HEIs) internationally. That number is expected to continue increasing for many of the top receiving countries of international students (OECD, 2018).

Internationalization activities, faculty and student exchanges, research agreements, international student enrolments, and international rankings have become increasingly important for many HEIs across Canada and in many western countries. A number of factors have influenced the amplified importance of internationalization, including an increased focus on international rankings (international student enrollments, research, and collaboration influence rankings systems), the financial benefits of growing international enrollments, declining domestic enrolments, and the goal of preparing students for the globalized economy (often referred to as creating "Global Citizens") (Altbach & Knight, 2007; AUCC, 2014; CBIE, 2016a; Hudzik, 2014). All of these factors have and continue to influence internationalization efforts at HEIs across Canada.

The relationship between HEIs, governments, and students are often symbiotic in nature, with students looking to develop their careers, HEIs looking for diversified income and increasing prestige/rankings, and governments looking to retain skilled labour to support their national economies (Arthur & Flynn, 2011; Hawthorne, 2012; Suter & Jandl, 2008). Closely related to the implementation of internationalization initiatives is the degree of interconnectivity of government policies, bureaucratic processes, and institutional programs. Internationalization plans have been launched across the country, including Canada's International Education Strategy, Provincial International Education Strategies, and individual institutional plans, yet the impact of the interconnected nature of these different aspects of internationalization has not been extensively examined. Promoting academic migration (retention of international students) is an important goal of federal and provincial immigration policies and strategies that will in turn impact the types of services, such as career services, immigration advising, as well as general support that is needed by students to navigate their transition to Canada as long-term immigrants (Chaoimh & Sykes, 2012; Morris-Lange & Brands, 2015).

It is critical to highlight that international students are by no means a monolithic entity that can be simply lumped into one category. The level of concerns differs greatly and is dependent on a combination of age, nationality, and personal experiences. Many international students may not have work experience in the Canadian labour market or have knowledge of professional settings in Canada, while other international students may. As a result, the career-focused programming of international student services is important for preparing students wherever their needs may be to be successful in their transition into their professional setting if academic migration is to occur.

The importance of employability and the role of employment outcomes for graduates have increased rapidly over the past few years. Numerous articles, reports, and presentations at conferences indicate the increasing importance of the various aspects of international student employability (Berquist et al., 2019; Linney, 2019; Mattis, 2019; Nilsson & Ripmeester, 2016; Pollock, 2014; Ripmeester & Leese, 2018; TRA, 2019). With various ranking systems emerging that allow graduates to highlight their satisfaction with their experience, the importance of ensuring that international students are being supported in the area of employability and careers should be increasingly important for HEI administrators who are concerned with ongoing success of recruiting top students (Crace, 2017). Furthermore, the impact of career-focused programming could help support the recruitment goals of many HEIs who are interested in attracting more students. Many of these students are focused on gaining work experience in Canada, as the potential for immigration is an increasingly important recruitment tool benefiting Canadian institutions (Attfield, 2016; CBIE, 2018c; Chiose, 2016b). Thus, it is critical to understand the landscape of international education in the Canadian context as the ubiquitous relationship between education, immigration and the labour market has become salient over the years.

International Education in Canada

Canada's immigration policies offer international students a somewhat clear path to permanent residency. Since 2008, the Canadian government has implemented several changes to make studying in Canada more attractive for international students, including the creation of lucrative "study and stay" programs which have given Canada a distinct competitive advantage in recruiting international students. Canada's choice to have a more open policy towards international students has made it an international education power house, particularly given the change in atmosphere and polices in the United States and the United Kingdom in the past four years (Civinini, 2018). The goals outlined in the 2014 Internationalization Strategy of reaching 450,000 students by 2022 was surpassed in 2017 with over 494,000 students opting to study in Canada, and in 2018, enrollment jumped again to 572,415[1] international students studying in Canada, the most recent data from Immigration, Refugees and Citizenship Canada (IRCC) indicated that this number has increased to 642,480[2] study permit holders in Canada (CBIE, 2018a, 2018c). Student surveys provide clear indications that attractive and open immigration policies play a central role to increased enrolments (CBIE, 2018a).

Rapidly increasing changes have led to more open and less restrictive Canadian immigration policies across the different status categories of the current pathway international students navigate. Each immigration program sets out different eligibility criteria, requirements for compliance, caps/quotas, conditions and the type of activity the international student can engage in. Such changes are related to making Canada an attractive study destination, enriching the Canadian study experience and providing a straightforward and less stressful adaptation into the Canadian labour market. One example of the programming implemented to attract international students is the creation of the Post-Graduation Work

Permit (PGWP), which allows international students who have graduated with a qualification from a Canadian designated learning institution (DLI) to work in Canada for up to three years after graduation. The PGWP allows students to gain work experience to make them eligible for immigration through various pathways, such as the Canadian Experience Class (CEC). The emphasis from governmental policy makers on recruiting international students is not just about the initial economic impact that students have, but also the retention of international students as skilled workers as part of an overall immigration strategy (Hawthorne, 2010; IRCC, 2018c; Kunin, 2017; She & Wotherspoon, 2013).

International students and internationalization are strategically important to the future of Canada's economic development and prosperity. Canada's interest in the retention of international students as skilled immigrants after they have completed their studies has been matched with the release of significant strategies, both for recruiting international students and for retaining them long-term (Birchard, 2005; CBIE, 2015; CBIE, 2016a; Lokhande, 2016). Numerous immigration pathways geared towards recruiting and retaining international students are promoted at the federal and provincial levels (Desai-Trilokekar & El Masri, 2016; Seidle, 2013; She & Wotherspoon, 2013). Since 2015, all the Ministers (McCallum, Hussen and currently Mendicino) who have led Immigration, Refugees and Citizenship Canada (IRCC) have made and continue to make it clear that international students form an important part of the government's immigration strategy (Donovan, 2016; IRCC, 2017; IRCC, 2018c). Canada is not alone in this regard. The study-and-stay immigration approach is being utilized in other countries as well, including countries that are viewed as competitors in recruiting international students such as Australia and New Zealand (Civinini, 2018c, 2018d).

The prominence of the economic impact of international education in Canada is a significant contributor to the economic landscape of many regions across Canada. Yet the potential for increased benefits through the effective integration of international graduates into the Canadian workforce as skilled immigrants is an area that is still to be fully realized. It is important to highlight the inherent assumption embedded within the immigration policies–the view that international students will integrate with less difficulty than their immigrant counterparts in the Canadian labour market due to their acquired Canadian education, proficiency in one of the official languages and relevant Canadian work experience (DFAIT, 2014). While there are many layers to consider how international students adapt to a new status of worker and the impact of policies on their transitional experiences; one area of support that has the potential to make an impact is the creation of career-focused programing that supports international students in their transition from studies to work/immigration benefits all stakeholders involved, including HEIs, students, and governments.

Motivations and Challenges of Increasing International Enrolments

A major focus of internationalization activities in the Canadian context has been a focus on increasing international enrolments (Government of Canada, 2014). The recruitment of international students for immigration impacts government policy makers and HEI leadership as they often work in tandem to promote the retention of international students (Desai-Trilokekar & El Masri, 2016; Desai-Trilokekar & Kizilbash, 2013). Many countries, including Canada, have created international education strategies that are focused on promoting themselves as a place to study, but also promoting programs to retain students as skilled immigrants after they have completed their studies (Birchard, 2005; CBIE, 2016; Government of Canada, 2014; Lokhande, 2016). Significant financial benefits and a rise in international rankings/reputation are motivating factors. In strategic plans, articulated reasons for focusing on internationalization include: preparing students for global citizenship, increasing intercultural understanding, international research, exchanges between HEIs, and international rankings (Altbach & Knight, 2007; Deardorff, Goodman, Charles, & Gee, 2018). With the clear focus of many institutions increasing international enrollments, there has to be a recognition of the duty of care associated with their recruitment practices. The provision of in-depth support for academic, personal and career needs of international students should be addressed in light of the significant role they in play in the Canadian economy.

Increased international enrolments result in a diverse student-body at HEIs whose needs for career-focused programming are different from domestic students who typically have accessed the services, including career services. In many cases, international student programming/support or increased funding for frontline staff has not increased at the pace of increased international enrolments (Lowe, 2011). Many institutions are intent on continuing to increase enrolment, so adequate supports/programming for international students during their studies are necessary to enhance the institutional experience for students, faculty, and staff. These supports ran the gamut of the student experience including orientation activities, academic supports, health/wellness (including mental health).

The promotion of academic migration could influence the types of services that HEIs provide to their international student population such as career services, immigration advising, and general support to navigate the transition to long-term immigrants (Chaoimh & Sykes, 2012; Desai-Trilokekar & El Masri, 2016). Although there has been an increase in the student supports provided to international students by HEIs, the level of programming and support varies between different levels and sizes of institutions, and may be focused on their initial start as students, rather than later in their student career when post-graduation employability becomes an increasing concern (El Masri, Choubak, & Litchmore, 2015). Programs and support for international students have often struggled to keep pace with the rapid increase in the number of international students attending HEIs in Canada, as well as staying up to date with changes to immigration policy and the limitations placed on HEIs as to which staff members are able to provide immigration advice.

While challenges exist within and across institutions, much of this is also impacted by what occurs at the provincial and federal level. Frequent changes to immigration policies and procedures, as well as the 2013 shift towards the regulation of immigration advising have influenced the international student experience, and specifically the area of career transitions in many ways. First, immigration policies directly influence every aspect of the student experience during their studies, from start to finish; international students are faced with additional stress of navigating the muddle of immigration policy and making sense of policies and procedures that are often lacking in clarity and are riddled with ambiguity. Second, international students' ability to work during and after their studies are impacted by immigration policies, as Immigration, Refugee and Citizenship Canada (IRCC) documentation with the proper comments on the study permit allows students to work part-time during studies, in co-op programs, and qualify for the Post-Graduation Work Permit (PGWP) after completing their studies. Conversely, documentation with missing or incorrect comments can often take months to correct, impacting student's ability to study, work, and apply for health insurance. Third, changes to policies and/or delays in the processing of IRCC documents can affect the ability of international students to take advantage of career options and qualify for immigration programs in Canada.

For all immigration programs, there are tight deadlines and often a lack of communication from IRCC throughout the process. These delays and challenges often result in employers being hesitant to hire international students, as they are concerned about these extra challenges and delays. As a result, having knowledgeable and experienced international student support, including regulated immigration advisors who are able to explain the process to students and employers, is an important service for institutions to provide. At the heart of international student advisory services at HEIs is the provision of professional, current, and accurate advice to students with respect to their immigration documentation, especially in their transition to the workforce Embedded support and competence in understanding what international students need to successfully transition from a student to a worker allows for a duty of care that extends nationally to institutionally. In many ways, the recognition of what is needed for an international student to succeed during their studies (and beyond) through formal supports facilitates the strategic interest in enhancing graduate employability that will lead to attaining skilled jobs and eventually qualifying for Canadian permanent residency–thereby allowing the two-step migration process in Canada to be achieved in high numbers that match the increased enrollments felt by many stakeholders.

Increasing Importance of Graduate Employability Outcomes

The importance of both employability and of the role of employment outcomes for graduates has increased rapidly over the past few years. Numerous articles, reports, and presentations at conferences indicates the increasing importance of the various aspects of international student employability (Berquist et al., 2019; Linney, 2019; Mattis, 2019; Nilsson & Ripmeester, 2016; Pollock, 2014; Ripmeester & Leese, 2018; TRA, 2019). With many countries adopting policies to increase international student enrollments and retain them as skilled labour after graduation, the importance of "getting it right" has sparked a recent increase in the focus on career outcomes for international students (Berquist et al., 2019; Nilsson & Ripmeester, 2016; Norvaisaite & Ripmeester, 2016; Ripmeester, 2019b; Ripmeester & Leese, 2018). The use of the term employability has become increasingly common with educators, researchers, and employers and it refers to the knowledge, skills, and abilities required to look for work and continue successfully in a career (Ripmeester, 2019a, 2019b). As noted by Ripmeester (2019b), employability was an emerging trend in 2018, has been gaining momentum in 2019 and is predicted to stay important for a number of years to come due to the expectations of the current generation of students who anticipate career outcomes as part of their international degree.

The importance of student recommendations and reviews of their experience at an HEI have been highlighted in the most recent 2018-2019 International Student Barometer (ISB) survey with 195,182 students in 21 countries. Results indicated that employability-related responses rank number one when it comes to recommendation of a higher education institution to prospective students (Ripmeester, 2019b). With various ranking systems emerging that allow graduates to highlight their satisfaction with their experience, the importance of ensuring that international students are being supported in the area of employability and careers should be increasingly important for HEI administrators who are concerned with ongoing success of recruiting top students (Crace, 2017).

With the increasing importance of employability outcomes for international students, institutional, provincial, and national internationalization plans (often focused on immigration), it makes strategic sense for HEIs to turn their attention on career-focused programming for international students for several reasons. First, the link between potential permanent residency, the ability to work in Canada, and the decision to study in Canada is important for many students. In the most recent CBIE survey of international students studying in Canada, 60 percent of students indicated they intend to apply for Permanent Residency (PR) after graduation (CBIE, 2018c). Of the students surveyed, 75 percent indicated that the ability to work in Canada was "essential" (42 percent) or "very important" to their decision to study in Canada (CBIE, 2018c).

Second, from a reputational and ethical perspective, HEIs would be prudent to focus on the holistic international student experience. This whole experience includes the extra level (in comparison to domestic students) of support that is unique and required by international students during their time in Canada. Extra layers include the empowered attention to maintaining immigration documentation, building a support network, and navigating a new health care system.

Third, students who are able to successfully transition to work or further studies reflect positively on the institution as a whole. Graduate employment has become an increasing focus for institutions as certain aspects of their reputation are tied to employment outcomes for their alumni, yet it continues to be an area that in many cases could be improved (Berquist et al., 2019; Crace, 2017; Linney, 2019; Mattis, 2019; Nilsson & Ripmeester, 2016; Ripmeester & Leese, 2018).

Finally, career transition for international students in Canada has been identified as being fraught with challenges. Policy makers continue to make the point that international students are ideal or "designer" immigrants with their education, language abilities and cultural experiences, but this does not paint a complete picture (Chaoimh & Sykes, 2012; Levatino, 2015; Nunes & Arthur, 2013). A 2019 study from StatsCan examining early career outcomes for three groups of students, Canadian citizens, permanent residents, and international students, appears to further highlight concerns related to career outcomes for international students in Canada (Frenette, Lu, & Chan, 2019). The StatsCan research examined enrolment, graduation, and postgraduate earnings related to five postsecondary programs international students. The study found that international students generally possessed more characteristics associated with higher earnings than Canadian students, yet, international students earned less than domestic students six years after graduation after controlling for demographics and qualifications (Frenette et al., 2019).

More broadly, the challenges international students face when looking at study-career transitions have been effectively identified in a study conducted by the Expert Council of German Foundations on Integration and Migration (SVR), which looked at the experiences of students in 238 HEIs in four countries (Germany, Canada, Netherlands, and Sweden) (Morris-Lange & Brands, 2015). These challenges include: insufficient language skills; lack of host country work experience; hesitant employers; lack of personal and professional networks; lack of job entry support; legal barriers; and dropping out of academic studies. The prominence of employability as a motivator for international students, career advising, as well as immigration related advising provided by institutions is an essential support for students during their studies.

Career-focused Programming for International Students

The combination of quality institutions, safe and secure environment, an open and tolerant society, and attractive work options after graduating have all added to Canada's appeal as a study destination (CBIE, 2018c; 2018d). CBIE reports have highlighted some of the key factors influencing student intentions of working and applying for permanent residency in Canada, highlighting some of the key variables that play a role in international students deciding to stay in Canada including academic, socio-cultural, economic, and demographic variables (Esses et al., 2018). Arthur and Flynn (2011) identified four key themes in their study of international student's career development and intentions to remain in Canada including: enhanced quality of life, career related opportunities, enhanced work environment, and safety and political stability. While the decision process of the student to stay in Canada is important, as Nunes and Arthur (2013) asserted, key stakeholders such as employers and career service personnel play a central role in supporting international students and their ability to succeed long-term and transition to permanent residency (Nunes & Arthur, 2013). As governments are creating immigration programs and strategies targeting the retention of international students, career-focused programming for international students is becoming an increasingly important area of programing HEIs across Canada (Desai-Trilokekar, Thomson, & El Masri, 2016a).

Although there has been an increasing focus on the topic of general career transitions and immigration prospects in receiving countries such as the US, UK, Canada, New Zealand and Australia, the examination of the actual components of the career programming at HEIs provided to international students is limited. Challenges, immigration policies, and labour market outcomes have been identified, but we know little about the way in which services and programming have changed at institutions to address the needs of international students (El Masri et al., 2015; Hawthorne, 2010, 2012; Hawthorne & To, 2014). The number of articles published on the topic of career and employability outcomes for international students increased rapidly over the past five years. Since 2015, there have been a number of reports, articles, surveys, rankings, and other work that have been focused on the importance of employability outcomes for international students and various programming approaches (Dietsche & Lees, 2017; Kisch, 2015; Morris-Lange & Brands, 2015; Nilsson & Ripmeester, 2016; Ripmeester, 2019a)

One of the most prominent authors and presenters on the subject of international student employability is Nanette Ripmeester who published a number of reports and articles on the topic of international student employability over the past few years (Nilsson & Ripmeester, 2016; Norvaisaite & Ripmeester, 2016; Ripmeester, 2019a, 2019b; Ripmeester & Leese, 2018). Ripmeester presented at the 2019 CBIE Atlantic regional conference, providing an overview of some of the latest updates regarding the motivations around international students with regard to career outcomes and the selection of an institution. As noted in the presentation at "Future career impact is the biggest motivator for prospective international students in selecting a higher education institution. Between 2016/17 and 2018/19 International Student Barometer (ISB) results show a paradigm shift in students' expectations around the ROI of their study" (Ripmeester, 2019c). The prominence of career outcomes for international students and the interconnected nature of universities, governments, employers, and students was noted throughout the keynote at the conference in June 2019.

One of the most recent examples of the prominence of the topic of employability is the report "Global Perspectives on International Student Employability" which provided a broad overview of the current global context of employability (Berquist et al., 2019). This report indicated that Canada currently leads market perception for favorable visa settings, including post study work, and transition to residency that have been part of Canadian government policies related to international students as potential immigrants (Berquist et al., 2019). Specifically, it was noted in the report that the current Canadian policies are in stark contrast to the current policies and rhetoric coming out of the US, which have played a role in the increasing popularity of Canada as a study destination (Berquist et al., 2019). All of these factors portray the opportunity for students to come to Canada in a positive light, but with the continued increase of international students, there are also challenges post-graduation. One of the key challenges surrounding the issue relates to post-graduation opportunities with international graduates being able to find permanent residence qualifying work after their studies. The post-graduation work challenges are not unique to Canada, and are highlighted in a report that was recently published in New Zealand. The 2019 report entitled "Employer Perception of Hiring International Graduates" was commissioned by Education New Zealand. This report is an excellent example of new research that is being completed on the topic of international student career transitions/employability, specifically addressing one of the most prominent issues, namely the employer perceptions of hiring international students (TRA, 2019).

The rapidly changing nature of this field of research, especially the connection with immigration policy, and influenced by national political environments, means that there continues to be a need for ongoing and updated research to support practitioners in the field, as well as institutional decision makers. The importance of establishing a professional network, adequate advising/support services, the development of soft skills and establishing connections between HEIs and employers and immigration documentation processing times are well-documented (Desai-Trilokekar & El Masri, 2016; Desai-Trilokekar et al., 2016a). Furthermore, the different roles and responsibilities among stakeholders in the provision of services to international students (including career services) is confusing, highlighting a need for better communication (Desai-Trilokekar et al., 2016a). Additionally, traditional approaches to career services need to be adjusted to the unique needs of international students, by revisiting the type, composition, and timing of programs and services that are provided (Desai-Trilokekar et al., 2016a). Understanding the services and programming provided to international students would strengthen our understanding of international students' experiences in transitioning to the labour market and their experiences at Canadian HEIs with faculty, staff, and domestic students.

Challenging Transitions to the Workforce for International Graduates in Canada

Although many countries and HEIs are benefiting from the increase in international students, there are indications that international students are not as well prepared for the workforce as domestic students (Chiose, 2016; El Masri et al., 2015; Nunes & Arthur, 2013). Simultaneously, while immigration policies provide the legal means to make this transition possible, how it materializes becomes the responsibility of each individual student.

In 2016, the Globe and Mail published a story on a Citizenship and Immigration Canada (CIC), now IRCC, report highlighting problems with the PGWP program. The report showed that statistically many international students who study in Canada and receive the Post-Graduation Work Permit (PGWP) end up in lower paying jobs than their domestic counterparts, with many of them not gaining the required work experience to become permanent residents (Chiose, 2016). More recently these concerns were echoed in a study from *StatsCan*, published in September 2019 which highlighted differences in the earnings, and challenges for international students in early career outcomes in Canada (compared to Canadian citizens and permanent residents) (Frenette et al., 2019). A lack of success in the labour market also negatively impacts international students' ability to immigrate to Canada long term via various immigration programs. Even with some adjustments made to the Express Entry System that should benefit students, in the most recent data from IRCC, the number of former international students who have transitioned to PR has decreased from the previous year (IRCC, 2018a; 2018b).

The challenges international students face when looking at study-career transitions have been effectively identified in a study conducted by the Expert Council of German Foundations on Integration and Migration (SVR), which looked at the experiences of students in 238 HEIs in four countries (Germany, Canada, Netherlands, and Sweden) (Morris-Lange & Brands, 2015). These challenges include:

- insufficient language skills;
- lack of host country work experience;
- hesitant employers;
- lack of personal and professional networks;
- lack of job entry support;

- legal barriers; and
- dropping out of academic studies.

Many students are unaware of the existence (or importance) of the career development supports and activities in which they can participate until their final year, at which point it is too late to set themselves up for a successful study to work transition (Arthur & Flynn, 2011; Nunes & Arthur, 2013). Because international students pay much higher fees for their education than domestic students, it is not surprising that they expect increased support/programming to support them during their time studying in their host country. Many of the challenges identified could be substantially mitigated with intentional programming from HEIs to assist international students in their career transitions.

The challenges faced by international students suggest an opportunity for HEIs to create innovative programs that will benefit their students and in turn be a "selling point" for their institution and what it can offer potential students. Some HEIs address these specific needs with the creation of career related programming for international students through the implementation of a needs-based career support for international students with a combination of general support services for all students, support services that are specifically designed for international students and lastly, individual counselling that is culturally responsive (Morris-Lange & Brands, 2015).

One area that traditional career advising for students typically overlooks is the immigration-related issues that many international students face in transitioning to the Canadian work force (Desai-Trilokekar, Thomson, & El Masri, 2016b; El Masri et al., 2015). These barriers add a level of complexity and expense to the already stressful endeavor of trying to start a career out of university. In comparison to their domestic counterparts, an added layer of holding temporary status if they qualify for a Post-Graduation Work Permit (PGWP) can result in more pressure for international students in Canada to make the transition quicker and easier. Although immigration policies have been set-up to facilitate a student-worker-permanent resident pathway, the experience of each individual student remains subjective and influenced by multiple factors with a paucity of research that contributes to the lived experience of Canadian international graduates.

To Stay or To Go: Influential Factors

As an attractive study destination, Canada is also chosen for the opportunities to seek employment or permanently stay upon completion of studies. These intentions are often on the minds of prospective international students prior to arriving in Canada; 60% of international students surveyed by the Canadian Bureau for International Education (CBIE) indicated a long-term goal of becoming a permanent resident (CBIE, 2018c). Often, the intention to settle permanently in any host country is part of an ongoing decision-making process throughout the period of stay that is influenced by professional, societal and personal motivating factors (Alberts & Hazen, 2005; Hazen & Alberts, 2006; Soon, 2012). Conventional push and pull factors such as better employment opportunities, higher salaries, better benefits for dependents and economic or political stability in one's home country play a role in this decision (Lu, Zong, & Schissel, 2009). Simultaneously, parental expectations and family conditions play a role too (Lu et. al, 2009).

In a qualitative study of 20 international students conducted by one of the authors (Bouajram, 2015), the research question "How do former international students experience the transitional years of post-graduation work authorization in Canada?" was explored with additional sub-research questions. Using a semi-structured interview approach, all participants held a Canadian PGWP at the time of the study and shared that both internal and external factors contributed to their ability to ease into the student-to-worker transition as well as influenced their decision to stay in Canada. Bouajram (2015) highlights that internal factors included shifting one's mindset to the adaptation process to becoming a worker as well as increasing their coping strategies particularly when faced with not receiving call backs for job applications. External factors such as Canadian networks and support systems of family and friends as well as familiarity with the Canadian labour market were seen as critical in both the job search post-graduation as well as influential in considering the possibility of remaining in Canada (Bouajram, 2015). In addition, having Canadian work experience during post-secondary studies positively impacted the participants' transition to becoming a worker.

A salient theme that emerged from this study, albeit a small qualitative study, was that participants would likely base their intentions to stay or leave on being successfully employed and financially stable, with the stakes being even higher if they had family and dependents to consider as well. Thus, choosing to stay or go for Canadian international students is not as simple as the two-step migration process embedded in current Canadian immigration policies, multiple moving parts and stakeholders such as the government, employers and higher education, become invaluable influencers as international students rely on internal resources and adaptive activities to make the transition and personal decision to stay or leave smooth and attainable.

Consequences of Internationalization

Career programming prepares international students to capitalize on opportunities provided by Canadian immigration programs. However, there are key concerns that arise out of the discussion of internationalization more broadly, including brain drain, neocolonialism, an increasing focus on for-profit programs and the commodification of higher education, and an increased level of nativist political movements in many receiving countries (Altbach & de Wit, 2017; Altbach & Knight, 2007; De Wit, 2019; Knight, 2013). Study and stay programs in receiving countries which encourage international students to stay following their studies contribute to the movement of talent from south to north and often continue to solidify the strength of already dominant institutions (Altbach, 2016; Hudzik, 2014). All of these concerns may present themselves differently depending on the specific context, but all play into the experiences of international students, and play a role in the employability outcomes for international students.

The experiences of international students during their studies, including anti-immigrant political movements may in turn play a role in the retention of international students in the specific country and may cause them to look for opportunities elsewhere. The role of political rhetoric and the hiring of international students has been highlighted, as the overall political attitudes towards immigrants and newcomers will influence their ability to find work and be hired (Crace, 2019). Anti-immigrant attitudes that have become part of mainstream politics in many countries have also had a negative impact on the political environment for international students and will likely impact their ability to find post-graduation employment (Altbach & de Wit, 2017; Crace, 2019) With some traditional receiving countries implementing protectionist trade and economic policies, including the reduction of work options for international students post-study, they may also likely see a decrease in the number of students looking to them as a destination of study.

As part of the discussion, there has to be an acknowledgement that negative consequences of internationalization will also play a role in career-focused programming. When educated and skilled individuals from (often) developing regions choose to leave their countries for better opportunities in Canada, a brain drain and movement of skills usually from the Global south to the Global north occurs. This transfer supports the status quo, namely a situation where developed countries reap many of the benefits of internationalization while developing countries often lose out (Altbach, 2016; Altbach & Knight, 2007; Brandenburg & De Wit, 2015; Knight, 2013). The complexities, challenges, and concerns around international education and internationalization and their impact on global inequity continue to be of concern, with more students studying internationally than ever before (Altbach & Knight, 2007; Knight, 2007; OECD, 2018). One traditional approach to internationalization, focused on supporting students from developing countries to complete a degree in another country and return home to contribute to their national development, is becoming increasingly less of a priority, as many receiving countries are actively trying to retain the top talent to support their continued economic development and innovation activities (Altbach, 2016; Knight, 2013). Career-focused programming can be an ethical response to recruitment practices that benefit from opportunities for immigration, treating students with dignity and equipping them with the skills that they can use if they chose to stay in Canada, return home, or end up settling elsewhere. Such support can also address how international students can navigate the very real gaps that still exist in hiring practices, diversification of industries and disparaging recognition of non-Canadian work experience.

Another critique of internationalization in its current form is the homogenizing or westernizing impact that it can have on other cultures through the perpetuation of a western style of education. Education has traditionally been seen as a method of acculturation. Rather than creating hybrid cultures, it is a form of neo-colonialism when western HEIs dominate the landscape (Altbach, 2016; Knight, 2013). Scholars and educators have raised concerns around the commodification and commercialization of higher education. The commodification and commercialization of education are closely linked, with an increase in the number of private, for profit institutions, students being treated as consumers, the utilization of rankings in promoting an institution, and marketing plans playing an increasingly important role for many institutions. The conflation of an international-focused marketing or branding plan with an internationalization plan is a key issue that was addressed by Knight (2015), examining five myths of internationalization and the pitfalls associated with a lack of critical examination of activities falling under the umbrella term of internationalization.

A key piece of the concern around the commodification of education is the increasing emphasis on the income generating side of internationalization activities. This concern has been raised by many scholars and is something that HEIs will have to address in the coming years, as an overwhelming dependency on certain countries has been highlighted as an area of risk (Altbach, 2016; Brandenburg & De Wit, 2015; Hudzik, 2014; Knight, 2013). These concerns were noted in the most recent Canadian International Education Strategy, with specific points and references to diversifying source countries of international students and have identified the vulnerabilities associated with a lack of diversity. Specifically in the area of international recruitment, the past decade has seen an increased recruitment effort on students who are able to pay the high fees allocated to international students, moving away from supporting the education of students from developing countries (Altbach, 2016; Altbach & Knight, 2007; Deardorff et al., 2018; Hudzik, 2014). The presence of political conflicts between countries, regional instability, and other concerns have led to concerns over the long-term sustainability of international education without diversification (Government of Canada, 2019; Redden, 2018). Additionally, the high cost of studying in many of the most popular countries, including the US, UK, Canada, and Australia, provides a level of self-selection and creates a barrier for many economically disadvantaged students who wish to study internationally. If students are discouraged by high costs, then genuine social, cultural, and economic diversity cannot be realized on campuses through current approaches to international recruitment and become the echo chambers of the global elite from countries around the world.

Finally, nationalist and anti-immigration attitudes have negatively impacted the climate for international education (Altbach & de Wit, 2017; Deardorff et al., 2018). Several major political changes that have affected international education and immigration policies include Brexit, the ongoing fallout of the refugee crises in the EU, the Trump Presidency, and the rise of right-wing nationalist parties in many European countries. These political shifts have had a negative impact on the number of students choosing to study in those countries (Altbach & de Wit, 2017; Crace, 2019; Kennedy, 2019a, 2019b, 2019c, 2019d). At the same time, Canada has become the net benefactor of these political shifts, seeing increasing international enrolments. Canada has a more attractive set of programs to promote students to study and stay in Canada and the reputation of having a welcoming and multicultural society (CBIE, 2018b; CBIE, 2018d; Desai-Trilokekar & El Masri, 2016; Morris-Lange & Brands, 2015). However, Canada is not immune to negative populist attitudes: news stories about issues related to anti-immigrant attitudes in Canada are becoming more prevalent and the challenges faced by international students and immigrants in their search for work, as well as everyday life are becoming increasingly prevalent (Nakonechny, 2019; Shingler, 2019). The election results in Ontario and Quebec are examples of shifts in the political landscape that have already influenced international education policies and approaches away from the open and welcoming society vision of Canada that has been an important part of the national marketing strategy for Canada as a location of study.

The results of the 2019 federal election emphasized the challenges faced in a geographically dispersed country like Canada. The regional divisions across the country were highlighted, including differing stances on issues like immigration, multiculturalism, climate change and numerous related issues. Given that the Liberal party emerged in a minority position following the election, it is unlikely that any major changes in immigration programs will take place in the near future, but the topics addressed during the election campaign could highlight areas of concern in the coming years. These regional divisions may influence the development of international education in Canada. Specifically, given that education is a provincial jurisdiction, provincial politics and funding decisions have the potential to impact international education. A shift in the political environment and the mainstreaming of negative attitudes towards immigrants or newcomers could also consequently influence the experiences of international students studying and working in Canada, and subsequently their transition from study to work. Career-focused programming for international students is an opportunity for institutions to try to mitigate some of the challenges that will face graduates, while also playing an important role in the local community, creating a positive economic impact of international students/alumni on their local economies.

When looking at the role of HEIs and internationalization, and specifically the recruitment of international students, policymakers at HEIs would be prudent to take note of these concerns and look at ways to mitigate them and engage with critical perspectives on current educational approaches. Practitioners at HEIs need to be aware of and responsive to the experiences of students at their institutions, including classroom and staff interactions, and help students navigate the labyrinth of government bureaucracy related to their immigration status. HEIs are often a hub of their communities, subsequently HEIs have a unique opportunity to support their students in their transition from study to work, capitalizing on their position to connect students with employers. HEIs can also play an important role in debunking myths that exist around immigration patterns, combating populist and isolationist tendencies by highlighting the benefits of immigration at the local and national level. Overall, concerns related to internationalization will continue to influence the international education landscape and will present both challenges and opportunities to HEIs as they continue to increase their international student enrollments.

The combination of generous study and stay immigration options in the form of various work permit and immigration programs, and the desire of HEIs to continue to increase the number of international students studying at their institutions have worked in synergy with one another, with Canada emerging as an international education powerhouse. Increasingly, students are choosing Canadian institutions for the opportunity to work during and after their studies, as well as to potentially settle in Canada (CBIE, 2018c). The transition from study to work is challenging for many international students, and key challenges identified in previous research could be addressed with targeted, career-focused programming for international students. Little is known about the approaches HEIs are taking to provide comprehensive career-focused programming for international students to address the issues that have been identified as challenges for international students. As HEIs are continuing to benefit financially from increasing international student enrollments, the importance of employability and career supports will become an increasingly important feature of the international student experience. With international students indicating the importance of post-graduation work opportunities and immigration options for their decision to study in Canada, universities can adjust their programming to support their future alumni.

FUTURE RESEARCH DIRECTIONS

With the majority of Canadian institutions focused on various internationalization activities, including increasing their international student enrollments, the importance of addressing challenges associated with one of the key motivators (immigration/employment) for international students is critical. Future research in this field would benefit from an examination of the student perspective and experiences with career programming provided by universities. Such research could engage with currents students and international graduates at various points of time post-graduation to gain a better understanding of what factors have allowed them to be successful or have hindered their progress. Focusing future research on students and outcomes will allow university administration to make better-informed decisions about funding opportunities and strategic engagement with community partners.

Another area for future research and one that will become increasingly relevant is the long-term outcomes of former international students. Specifically, the students who have become PRs or citizens via one of the immigration pathways that is geared towards international students and their earnings compared to other immigrant streams and their domestic counterparts. It will be particularly interesting to see if the issues highlighted in previous research in regard to a low rate of conversion from student to PR and issues related to the lower earnings of Canadian educated international students continue into the future.

Australia is an example of a country where poor labour market outcomes of former international students negatively impacted recruitment of international students for an number of years (Desai-Trilokekar & Kizilbash, 2013; Hawthorne, 2010). Part of the challenge in Australia was that some colleges and universities opened up new programs with insufficient resources and support services in order to attract more international students for revenue generation (Desai-Trilokekar & Kizilbash, 2013). The similarities between Australia and Canada (politically and historically) allow for a good comparison. As noted in the Australian experience, the challenges associated with lackluster outcomes in the labour market for graduates provided challenges for institutions and governmental policy makers. New Zealand and their new international education strategy (2018), with a focus on the economic impact, also emphasizes the maintenance of the quality of the education and satisfaction of international students, which may be a good example for the Canadian context. Policy makers in government and HEIs in Canada would benefit to learn from the experiences of other countries, examine the successes and explore ways to emulate them, while examining the pitfalls, challenges, and take steps to mitigate repeating them.

Finally, given the rapid growth that Canadian institutions have seen in the past decade, it may be a good opportunity for institutions to pause and take stock of their current situations, and having a realistic look at the supports they are able to provide students to ensure positive student outcomes. With the current issue of low conversion rates with approximately 25% of former international students to PR via the Express Entry system, there may be other concerns that arise in the coming years (Toughill, 2019). The connection between recruitment practices including the allure of PR and the outcomes for students may highlight a problematic disconnect.

Overall, the rapidly changing arena of international education, including career and employability outcomes for international students, will likely provide areas for future research that are not yet recognized. Given the influence of national politics and geopolitics on international education, there are potential disruptions that will in turn create new areas of concerns and potential solutions and new areas of research.

CONCLUSION

The expectations of students, recruitment activities of universities, employers looking for a skilled work force, and the desire of governments to retain international graduates in their regions post-graduation forms a symbiotic relationship. The connection between universities and regionally focused programs was highlighted as one of the key areas of further development. For many universities, the coordination of efforts, redesigning or development of programming to address the needs of students, and improving international graduate outcomes are all areas of improvement that need to be taken under consideration. With the importance of graduate employability outcomes for international students and the role it plays in student selection of institutions, it is prudent for universities to address these challenges now, as part of their internationalization activities. These programs will need strategy, funding, and a coordinated approach, but need to be viewed as part of the requirement of recruiting and retaining international students. There are many opportunities for universities to create meaningful and coordinated programming, bringing together international and domestic students to create graduates with competences that will be increasingly applicable in the diverse and globally connected world particularly at a time when it is needed the most for international students–the post-graduation transitional years where no clear roadmap exists and a deadline in the form of an expiry date is imposed.

REFERENCES

Alberts, H. C., & Hazen, H. D. (2005). "There are always two voices…": International Students' Intentions to Stay in the United States or Return to their Home Countries. *International Migration (Geneva, Switzerland)*, *43*(3), 131–154. doi:10.1111/j.1468-2435.2005.00328.x

Altbach, P. G. (2016). *Global perspectives on higher education*. JHU Press.

Altbach, P. G., & de Wit, H. (2017). Trump and the coming revolution in higher education internationalization. *International Higher Education,* (89), 3-5.

Altbach, P. G., & Knight, J. (2007). The internationalization of higher education: Motivations and realities. *Journal of Studies in International Education, 11*(3-4), 290–305. doi:10.1177/1028315307303542

Arthur, N., & Flynn, S. (2011). Career development influences of international students who pursue permanent immigration to Canada. *International Journal for Educational and Vocational Guidance, 11*(3), 221–237. doi:10.100710775-011-9212-5

Berquist, B., Hall, R., Morris-Lange, S., Shields, H., Stern, V., & Tran, L. T. (2019). *Global perspectives on international student employability.* Retrieved from https://www.ieaa.org.au/research/global-employability

Birchard, K. (2005). Canada seeks more foreign students. *The Chronicle of Higher Education, 51*(34).

Brandenburg, U., & De Wit, H. (2015). The end of internationalization. *International Higher Education,* (62). doi:10.6017/ihe.2011.62.8533

Canadian Bureau of International Education. (2016). *From permits to permanency: Supporting the international student in status transition.* Retrieved from https://cbie.ca/wp-content/uploads/2016/07/Immigration-RiB.pdf

Canadian Bureau of International Education. (2018a). *Facts and figures.* Retrieved from https://cbie.ca/media/facts-and-figures/

Canadian Bureau of International Education. (2018b). *International students in Canada.* Retrieved from https://cbie.ca/wp-content/uploads/2018/09/International-Students-in-Canada-ENG.pdf

Canadian Bureau of International Education. (2018c). *The student's voice: National results of the 2018 CBIE international student survey.* Retrieved from https://cbie.ca/wp-content/uploads/2018/08/Student_Voice_Report-ENG.pdf

Canadian Bureau of International Education. (2018d). *A World of Learning: Canada's performance and potential in international education.* Retrieved from https://cbie.ca/wp-content/uploads/2018/04/Infographic-inbound-EN.pdf

Chaoimh, E. N., & Sykes, B. (2012). *Mobile talent? The staying intentions of international students in five EU countries.* Retrieved from https://www.svr-migration.de/wp-content/uploads/2014/11/Study_Mobile_Talent_Engl.pdf

Chiose, S. (2016, Mar. 31). International student work program creating low-wage work force: report. *The Globe and Mail.* Retrieved from https://www.theglobeandmail.com/news/national/international-student-work-program-needs-overhaul-report-says/article29463566/

Civinini, C. (2018). Canada threatens to overtake UK as top study destination – QS. *PIE News.* https://thepienews.com/news/canada-threatens-to-overtake-uk-as-top-study-destination-qs/

Crace, A. (2017). Canada best and worst in IAJN international alumni satisfaction report. *PIE News.* https://thepienews.com/news/canada-best-and-worst-in-iajn-graduate-satisfaction-report/

Crace, A. (2019). Political rhetoric is "substantial barrier" to int'l grad employment – report. *PIE News.* https://thepienews.com/news/politics-employer-barrier-employment/

De Wit, H. (2019). Dutch cuts to internationalization send the wrong message. *Inside Higher Ed.* https://www.insidehighered.com/blogs/world-view/dutch-cuts-internationalization-send-wrong-message

Deardorff, D. K., Goodman, A. E., Charles, H., & Gee, E. G. (2018). *Leading internationalization: A handbook for international education leaders.* Stylus Publishing.

Desai-Trilokekar, R., & El Masri, A. (2016). Canada's international education strategy: Implications of a new policy landscape for synergy between government policy and institutional strategy. *Higher Education Policy, 29*(4), 539–563. doi:10.105741307-016-0017-5

Desai-Trilokekar, R., & Kizilbash, Z. (2013). Imagine: Canada as a leader in international education. How can Canada benefit from the Australian experience? *Canadian Journal of Higher Education, 43*(2), 1–26.

Desai-Trilokekar, R., Thomson, K., & El Masri, A. (2016). *International students as "ideal" immigrants: Ontario employers' perspective.* Academic Press.

Dietsche, P., & Lees, J. (2017). *Insight into Canadian post-secondary career service models: Final report.* Retrieved from https://ceric.ca/project/insight-into-canadian-post-secondary-career-service-models/

El Masri, A., Choubak, M., & Litchmore, R. (2015). *The global competition for international students as future immigrants: The role of Ontario universities in translating government policy into institutional practice.* Retrieved from http://www.heqco.ca/SiteCollectionDocuments/Global%20Competition%20for%20IS%20ENG.pdf

Esses, V., Sutter, A., Ortiz, A., Luo, N., Cui, J., & Deacon, L. (2018). *Retaining international students in Canada post-graduation: Understanding the motivations and drivers of the decision to stay.* Retrieved from https://cbie.ca/wp-content/uploads/2018/06/Intl-students-post-graduation-RiB-8-EN-1.pdf

Frenette, M., Lu, Y., & Chan, W. (2019). *The postsecondary experience and early labour market outcomes of international study permit holders.* Retrieved from https://www150.statcan.gc.ca/n1/en/pub/11f0019m/11f0019m2019019-eng.pdf?st=U-s22c6O

Government of Canada. (2014). *Canada's international education strategy: Harnesssing our knowledge advantage to drive innovation and prosperity.* Ottawa, ON: Government of Canada Retrieved from https://international.gc.ca/global-markets-marches-mondiaux/assets/pdfs/overview-apercu-eng.pdf

Government of Canada. (2019). *Building on Success: Canada's International Education Strategy (2019-2024).* Ottawa, ON: Government of Canada Retrieved from https://www.international.gc.ca/education/strategy-2019-2024-strategie.aspx?lang=eng

Hawthorne, L. (2010). Two-step migration: Australia's experience. *POLICY, 39.*

Hawthorne, L. (2012). Designer immigrants? International students and two-step migration. In D. K. Deardorff, H. de Wit, J. D. Heyl, & T. Adams (Eds.), *The SAGE handbook of international higher education* (pp. 417–435). SAGE. doi:10.4135/9781452218397.n23

Hawthorne, L., & To, A. (2014). Australian employer response to the study-migration pathway: The quantitative evidence 2007-2011. *International Migration (Geneva, Switzerland), 52*(3), 99–115. doi:10.1111/imig.12154

Hudzik, J. K. (2014). *Comprehensive internationalization.* Routledge. doi:10.4324/9781315771885

Immigration Refugees and Citizenship Canada. (2018a). *Backgrounder: Study and stay program* [Press release]. Retrieved from https://www.canada.ca/en/atlantic-canada-opportunities/news/2018/07/study-and-stay-program.html

Immigration Refugees and Citizenship Canada. (2018b). *Speaking notes for Ahmed Hussen, Minister of Immigration, Refugees and Citizenship* [Press release]. Retrieved from https://www.canada.ca/en/immigration-refugees-citizenship/news/2018/06/speaking-notes-for-ahmed-hussen-minister-of-immigration-refugees-and-citizenship.html

Kennedy, K. (2019a). Post-study work restrictions cost the UK £150 million a year. *PIE News.* https://thepienews.com/news/restrictions-post-study-work-cost-uk-150-million-year-report/

Kennedy, K. (2019b). UK home secretary backs call for post-study work restrictions to be lifted. *PIE News.* https://thepienews.com/news/uk-home-secretary-calls-for-a-lifting-of-psw-restrictions-on-international-students/

Kennedy, K. (2019c). Universities UK warns against 'no-deal' consequences. *PIE News.* https://thepienews.com/news/brexit-briefing-uuk/

Kennedy, K. (2019d). US could have lost US$5.5bn in value from declining market share – NAFSA. *PIE News.* https://thepienews.com/news/international-students-in-us-decline-considered-threat/

Kisch, M. (2015). Helping international student navigate career options. *International Educator,* 66-69.

Knight, J. (2007). Internationalization: Concepts, complexities and challenges. In *International handbook of higher education* (pp. 207–227). Springer.

Knight, J. (2013). The changing landscape of higher education internationalisation – for better or worse? *Perspectives: Policy and Practice in Higher Education, 17*(3), 84–90. doi:10.1080/13603108.2012.753957

Levatino, A. (2015). Transnational higher education and skilled migration: Evidence from Australia. *International Journal of Educational Development, 40,* 106–116. doi:10.1016/j.ijedudev.2014.11.009

Linney, S. (2019). Why your graduate employability matters more than ever. *QS.com.* https://www.qs.com/employability-important-higher-education/

Lokhande, M. (2016). *Policy Brief des SVR-Forschungsbereichs - Engagiert gewinnt Bessere Berufschancen für internationale Studierende durch Praxiserfahrungen.* Retrieved from http://www.stifterverband.de/study_work/policy_brief_study_and_work_engagiert_gewinnt.pdf

Lowe, S. J. (2011). Welcome to Canada? Immigration incentives may not be enough for international students to stay. *Canadian Diversity / Canadian Diversité, 8*(5), 20-24.

Mattis, G. (2019). Why is employablity important in higher education? *QS.com.* https://www.qs.com/employability-important-higher-education/

Morris-Lange, S., & Brands, F. (2015). *Train and retain: career support for international students in Canada, Germany, the Netherlands and Sweden.* Retrieved from Berlin: https://www.svr-migration.de/wp-content/uploads/2015/06/study_Train-and-Retain-svr-research-unit-web.pdf

Nakonechny, S. (2019). Suspension of Quebec graduate program leaves international students in limbo. *CBC News.* https://www.cbc.ca/news/canada/montreal/suspension-of-quebec-graduate-program-leaves-international-students-in-limbo-1.5210839

Nilsson, P. A., & Ripmeester, N. (2016). International student expectations: Career opportunities and employability. *Journal of International Students, 6*(2), 614–631.

Norvaisaite, V., & Ripmeester, N. (2016, Summer). Satisfaction is in success, not in canteen food. *Forum: Member Magazine (EAIE),* 14-16.

Nunes, S., & Arthur, N. (2013). International students' experiences of integrating into the workforce. *Journal of Employment Counseling, 50*(1), 34–45. doi:10.1002/j.2161-1920.2013.00023.x

OECD. (2018). *Education at a glance 2018.* OECD Publishing.

Pollock, A. (2014). *Student employability is a necessity, not a choice.* Retrieved from http://www.labourmobility.com/student-employabilitynecessity-choice

Redden, E. (2018). For international students, shifting choices of where to study. *Inside Higher Ed.* https://www.insidehighered.com/news/2018/08/24/international-enrollments-slowing-or-declining-some-top-destination-countries-look

Ripmeester, N. (2019a). Employability and Alumni Relations. *Career Professor.* https://careerprofessor.works/employability

Ripmeester, N. (2019b). Essential ingredients for global talent. *LinkedIn.* https://www.linkedin.com/pulse/essential-ingredients-global-talent-nannette-ripmeester/?trackingId=VevkhGQCQcWaJz%2F9av5FGQ%3D%3D

Ripmeester, N. (2019c). *Setting s ail for success: key employability trends & ways to help international students thrive in the workplace.* Paper presented at the 2019 CBIE Atlantic Regional Meeting, Halifax.

Ripmeester, N., & Leese, B. (2018). *What's cooking? A recipe book for employability by Study Queensland.* Retrieved from Queensland: https://www.tiq.qld.gov.au/iet-strategy/wp-content/uploads/2019/06/Study-Qld_Cookbook-for-Employability-AW-WEB.pdf

Shingler, B. (2019). CAQ's plan to slash immigration levels threatens Quebec economy, business groups say. *CBC News.* https://www.cbc.ca/news/canada/montreal/quebec-immigration-levels-hearings-1.5243632

Toughill, K. (2019). Express Entry stalls for student immigrants to Canada. *Polestar Student Immigration News.* https://studentimmigration.ca/express-entry-international-student-canada/

TRA. (2019). *Employer perceptions of hiring international graduates.* Retrieved from New Zealand Education: https://intellilab.enz.govt.nz/document/583-tra-enz-employer-value-book-pdf?_ga=2.90425946.1569402105.1562193360-1689215942.1528279883

KEY TERMS AND DEFINITIONS

Canadian Bureau for International Education (CBIE): The national non-profit organization in Canada dedicated to leadership and education service in international education.

Canadian Experience Class (CEC): A federal immigration stream program that individuals with Canadian work experience can qualify for permanent residence.

Citizenship and Immigration Canada (CIC): The federal government department that oversees Canadian immigration, citizenship and refugee policies in Canada; now referred to as Immigration, Refugee and Citizenship Canada (IRCC).

Express Entry (EE): Refers to the application management system used to assess applicants applying to select federal programs for permanent residence.

Higher Educational Institutions (HEIs): Educational institutions at the post-secondary level; that is, college and university.

Permanent Resident (PR): An individual who has been given permanent resident status by immigrating to Canada, but is not a Canadian citizen. Permanent residents are citizens of other countries.

Post-Graduation Work Permit (PGWP): An open work permit that is available post-graduation to international students who complete eligible Canadian higher education programs.

ENDNOTES

[1] CBIE Figures based on IRCC data as of December 2018.

[2] IRCC data as of December 2019: https://open.canada.ca/data/en/dataset/90115b00-f9b8-49e8-afa3-b4cff8facaee

Chapter 17
Internationalization Through NNES Student Recruitment:
Anticipated Gains and Reported Realities

Anouchka Plumb
https://orcid.org/0000-0003-2895-8141
University of Windsor, Canada

ABSTRACT

It can be difficult to decipher the extent to which Canadian university internationalization efforts have been corralled to actualize mostly through non-native English speaking (NNES) foreign student recruitment. Although international surveys often report that an overwhelming majority of foreign students endorse Canada as a study destination and are satisfied with their Canadian study experience, the voices of students who experience a different reality are often overlooked. This chapter begins with an overview of internationalization values. The author then reviews the ways in which neoliberal ideology reshapes higher education as a good and places NNES foreign students as consumers in competition. Next, the foreign student recruitment is aligned with the internationalization rationales of generating revenue and migrating skills to benefit Canada's national economy. The reported realities of NNES foreign students are shared, followed by questions to springboard dialogue on identifying and mitigating gaps for NNES foreign student university study on Canadian campuses.

INTRODUCTION

The economic benefits gained nationally by Canadian higher education internationalization implemented through foreign student recruitment cannot be denied. At the root of foreign student recruitment at Canadian universities are economic priorities driven by neoliberal ideology (Corradetti, 2011; Horkheimer, 1972; Sherman & Webb, 2005). Canadian higher education institutions have received increased autonomy in setting differential tuition fees propelling them toward securing their position in the transnational education market (Larsen & Vincent-Lancrin, 2002) while reinforcing the position of English-medium, western universities as agents for reproducing relations of power (Kim, 2012). The principles of neoliberalism

DOI: 10.4018/978-1-7998-5030-4.ch017

have legitimized the commodification, commercialization of higher education and the deregulation of differential tuition. Neoliberal forces fuel national economic interests and are expressed in a market-driven narrative of higher education as a sellable good. This supports universities to capitalize on and place foreign student recruitment as a crucial and leading activity demonstrating the inclusion of an international dimension on their campuses.

For foreign students, a Canadian university credential is perceived as, and in some cases is, a major boost to access Canadian employment. University education should not be reduced to training for and entry to the Canadian labour market. However, given the current neoliberal era within which universities operate and that so many foreign students pursue Canadian university education as a first step toward achieving a long-term goal to enter the national labour force, Canadian higher education has become theoretically and pragmatically coordinated with generating revenue and migrating skills' into the Canadian labour landscape. This chapter focuses on neoliberal infiltration in the reshaping of Canadian universities to becoming increasingly more devoted to recruitment than investigating in mechanisms that can help strengthen overall student integration. Neoliberal ideology is tied to economic goals and in turn, frames internationalization implemented through foreign student recruitment; specifically, non-native English speaking (NNES) foreign students. Institution members need to turn their attention inward and toward understanding NNES student experiences on their campuses to begin addressing claims that higher education institutions do not care about the quality of education service provided to international students (Maru, 2018).

Chapter Organization and Design

This chapter is organized by first identifying how three principles of neoliberal ideology: commodification; commercialization; and market deregulation has reworked the higher education model from being a public to a for-profit good. Second, publication from leading national organizations such as the Association of Universities and Colleges Canada (AUCC), the Canadian Bureau for International Education (CBIE) and the government of Canada's Global Affairs, is included to contextualize the role higher education internationalization plays in Canada's international education strategy. In this contextualization, attention is placed on increased higher education institutional dependence on implementing internationalization through foreign student recruitment; lack of metrics to define and track evidence-based markers of quality internationalization; and reported perceptions of foreign students on their Canadian schooling experience. Third, this chapter draws upon research findings highlighting a range of foreign students' experienced challenges.

NEOLIBERAL INFLUENCE – HIGHER EDUCATION COMMODIFICATION

One neoliberal principle at the core of the current international higher education model is the commodification of goods. This principle can be regarded as "a return to primitive individualism" (Merino, Mayper, & Tolleson, 2010, p. 776) by rationalizing "schools as malls [and] students as consumers" (Giroux, 2010, p. 5), purchasing knowledge with the end goal of advancing personal economic gains. All participants in Plumb's (2018) research study held a strong belief that Canadian universities deliver high-quality education. As Participant 9 stated, "I am studying in Canada because it has the highest quality of education" (p. 209). Participants perceived completing higher education in Canadian primarily as a way for professional advancement and enhancing employability. Many participants compared learning in Canada to learning in their home country and noted the greatest differences were: the range of diverse available resources, teaching methods, and career-related opportunities associate with a Canadian degree (Plumb, 2018). Increasing university dependence on unregulated, differential foreign tuition exemplifies the transition from higher education as a public good to a commodified product for sale at uncapped prices. Despite ever-rising tuition for foreign students, increasing numbers of students continue to purchase their seats in academic programs on Canadian campuses; in turn, solidifying the altering relationship between students and higher education institutions from social to commercial (Berg & Seeber, 2016). Plumb's (2018) findings from NNES students' reported perceptions of their Canadian schooling experience revealed most participants held a surprisingly contradictory belief that differential international tuition is "unjustifiable" (p. 223), but still acceptable because it affords for high-quality courses and learning. Most participants perceived that revenue generated from differential tuition was directly reinvested into resources and infrastructure to improve students' overall schooling experience; a piece of the overall product which they purchase. The Canadian international education sector has indeed carved out its place as a leader with "a strong education model ... earning its place in the global community" (Canada's International Education Strategy, 2014, p. 16). Therefore, foreign students' justification and approval of unregulated differential tuition is a result of neoliberal values working as the backbone of "social practice ... that has come to be viewed as natural, normal and necessary; thus, working to ensure that ... these discourses are not questioned nor recognized" (Nolan, 2012, p. 205).

Neoliberal ideology constructs foreign students as consumers of higher education with equal opportunity and ability to invest in skills and knowledge to advance individual productivity, industriousness, and entrepreneurship (Canterbury, 2005; Harvey, 2005). At the same time, neoliberal logic also situates foreign students as competitors racing for access to higher education and positions in the labour market post-graduation. Emphasis on acquiring skills that leverage entrance into the labour force is subsumed under the neoliberal assumption, "the more skills one has, the more productive one becomes" (Brown & Tannock, 2009, p. 378). As one participant, Dale, explained in Plumb's (2018) study: "I think fees a little bit expansive. But it's ok [because] I think the academic skill [plays] an important role in my life in Canada" (p. 223). What Dale is referring to is his belief that his financial investment in the program is justified because the skills he anticipates gaining will be of great benefit. "Creation, production, distribution and consumption" (Harris, 2001, p. 22) of knowledge and creativity is positioned as the source to attain wealth. This notion is further reinforced through the knowledge-based economy rhetoric calling for increased dependence on foreign students with market-driven skills (Stukalina, 2008; The Illuminate Consulting Group, 2009); resulting in claimed urgency to focus on foreign student recruitment and retention (Harris, 2011). However, increasing agreement that higher education credentials alone do not result in employment leaves little promise that Canadian education credentials will result in the same outcome for all foreign students (Grible et al., 2015).

NEOLIBERAL INFLUENCE – HIGHER EDUCATION COMMERCIALIZATION

Intensified competition among Canadian universities is evidenced by accelerated institutional rebranding (Kizilbas, 2011). Canada's international higher education marketing plans have significantly evolved since the days when Canada was described as facing an "identity crisis" (Tibbets, 2008, p. 1) impeding international education growth opportunities. At that time, Global Affairs Canada, previously referred to as the Department of Foreign Affairs and International Trade, laid out the need for a unified international higher education vision in the document, *Canada's Competitive Challenge: International Promotion of Education* (2008). In this regard, higher education commercialization became a crucial precursor to internationalization and gave rise to the original Strategic Mandate Agreement (2017), whereby Canadian universities began to reconstruct and rebrand their institutional identities. The Advisory Panel on Canada's International Education Strategy (IES) also called for a progressive marketing blueprint to ensure Canada grows its market share of the international students ("Canada's International Education," 2014). The 2014 IES report established higher education institutional branding guidelines including (a) developing customized marketing plans for education markets identified as a priority; (b) investing in traditional media and new digital marketing platforms to attract key markets; (c) allocating resources to achieve Canada's international education development objectives.

NEOLIBERAL INFLUENCE – UNREGULATED HIGHER EDUCATION MARKET

Neoliberal ideology stretches capitalism to socio-political and economic realms built upon pervasive complicity with the notion that individual and social well-being at large is best accomplished through unregulated markets generating economic growth (Friedman, 1962; Hayek, 1944; Touraine, 2001). The neoliberal framework positions governments to help create, invest in, promote, and maximize (Harvey, 2007) gains from the international education market through foreign student recruitment. In the context of higher education internationalization, Ministries of International Trade Diversification; Employment, Workforce Development and Labour; and Immigration, Refugees and Citizenship coordinate national economic values, visions and missions to accelerate Canada's international education strategy. The International Education Strategy's approximate $150 million funding commitment ("Building on Success: International Education Strategy (2019-2024)") supports international higher education market expansion and competition. However, ministry role in regulating differential tuition or monitoring the implementation of internationalization goes beyond being uninvolved (Harvey, 2007; Mukherjee, 2003) and is best described as 'getting out of the way.' Neoliberal values are embedded in national economic aims and are reflected in university internationalization actualized through foreign student recruitment by manufacturing consent (Stier, 2004) for maintaining a market-oriented institutional reform. As such, higher education institutions have engaged in a limited review of whether or not their policies, projects and practices support NNES student transition to academics; integrate social capital building opportunities (Bourdieu, 1977) in the institutional life; and reduce disparities between Canadian employment demand narratives and NNES students' reported experiences in accessing employment.

Differential Tuition

High differential tuition has become the norm to generate massive revenue for the Canadian economy (CBIE, 2013) with no guarantee of supports aimed at enhancing NNES students' integration experiences on Canadian university campuses. One critique of higher education internationalization is its characteristic to appear as a "neutral experience within normalizing conceptions of internationalization" (Madge et al., 2009, p. 35). When foreign students of lower socioeconomic backgrounds pay their differential tuition, it creates a perception of equal access to education; furthermore, an "equalization of classes" beyond national borders (Marcuse, 1964, p. 17). The acceptance of differential tuition symbolizes how members of stratified economic classes willingly participate in an economic ideology that may not serve their interests. In this instance, university education internationalization is the maker of "the formal education system [as] a primary mechanism in the perpetuation of socioeconomic inequality" (Edgerton & Roberts, 2014, p. 193; also Bourdieu, 1997). In Beck et al.'s (2013) critical work on internationalization, they address the inequities related specifically to differential tuition:

The inequities reflected in differential tuition fees prompted by universities' efforts to generate revenue from international students in the context of marketization of higher education have concrete impacts on the everyday lives of international students as they strive to gain cultural capital. (p. 88)

Internationalization

The term "internationalization" is commonly understood through broad-strokes institutional missions and policies which direct academic departments, research and student support services to "integrate international and intercultural dimensions" (Knight & de Wit, 1995, p. 336). Abbott (2009) expands the definition of internationalization as a "process of integrating an international, intercultural or global dimension into the purpose, function or delivery of postsecondary education" (p.8). To give detail to and to coordinate the values of internationalization with its implementation, the Canadian Bureau for International Education (CBIE) launched its *Internationalization Statement of Principles for Canadian Educational Institutions* (2015). The *Statement of Principles* outline that internationalization is:

- central to attaining global civic participation, promoting social justice and responsibility;
- in continual pursuit to provide the highest quality learning experience;
- ingrained in the value that international students should be recognized for enriching institutional life and educational experiences of all students;
- inclusive, pervasive and comprehensive, encompassing all aspects of the work of the institution;
- vital to institutions' financial sustainability; however, the financial priorities must not steer internationalization initiatives;
- focused on cross-border and cross-cultural capacity building;
- open to a wide range of community members for engagement.

Since there is no explicit order of importance or weight ascribed to individual principles to benchmark and give insight into a view of what balanced internationalization implementation looks like, higher education institutions are left to their discretion to identify their priorities. On the one hand, the undeniable advantage of this approach is institutional freedom to focus on initiatives such as foreign student recruitment to yield increased revenue. On the other hand, there is no system to explore if higher education institutions are indeed steering internationalization initiatives based mainly on financial priorities, whereby neglecting or even negating other internationalization values.

Recently, Canadian universities have been trying to better plan how internationalization unfolds at their institutions. While over 95% of universities confirmed their strategic plan directly addresses internationalization (AUCC Internationalization Survey, 2014), only 32% in 2006 and 39% in 2014 have implemented measures, tools or procedures to track and assess the quantity and quality of their commitments (AUCC Internationalization Survey, 2014, p. 9); including actions to advance cross-cultural engagement and cultural capital building for foreign students on Canadian campuses. Little remains known about what existing quality assurance results yield and how they have informed NNES foreign student engagement.

National results from the CBIE's international student survey indicated 96% of international students endorse Canada as a study destination and 93% confirm satisfaction with their experience in Canada (CBIE, 2018). These types of student surveys tend to focus disproportionately on what motivates foreign students in choosing Canada as their study destination of choice and on factors which inform their selection of an institution; in essence, critical information that can be used to expand marketing and recruitment campaigns. What tends to be overlooked are the reasons why foreign students on Canadian higher education campuses do not endorse Canada as a study abroad destination or are not satisfied with their Canadian experience. NNES student reported challenges in securing funding for differential tuition, barriers to academic adjustment (Gopal, 2011; Grayson, 2008; Guo & Chase, 2011), social integration (Aune, Hendrickson, & Rosen 2011) and access to Canadian employment (Arthur & Flynn, 2011) reveal disadvantageous realities in need of attention.

Foreign Student Recruitment Serves Internationalization Rationales

The revenue generation and skilled migration internationalization rationales (Larsen & Vincent-Lancrin, 2002) bring to light economic forces driving universities to define and implement internationalization from a recruitment-centric lens. The top five most compelling reasons for promoting and integrating an international dimension (AUCC, 2014) were to:

- Prepare internationally and interculturally competent graduates (84%)
- Build strategic alliances and partnerships with key institutions abroad (49%)
- Promote an internationalized campus (47%)
- Increase the institution's global profile (44%)
- Generate revenue for the institution (43%)

Among all types of internationalization initiatives, international student recruitment continues to reign among the top five institutionalized priorities (AUCC Internationalization Survey, 2014). The Canadian Bureau for International Education's report, *A World of Learning: Canada's Performance and Potential in International Education* (2016), notes that university internationalization is typically pursued through international student recruitment. While over 90% of Canadian institutional leaders claim the primary reason for international student recruitment is to develop an internationalized campus (Association of Universities and Colleges Canada, 2007), approximately 45% report generating revenue is a compelling reason for internationalization (AUCC, 2014). The 2014 AUCC Internationalization Survey, *Canada's Universities in the World*, identified undergraduate student recruitment as the highest priority for 45% of institutions and is identified as one of the top five priorities for 70% of them. International graduate student recruitment is also listed among the top five priorities for 54% of institutions.

Canada's immediate revenue-generating needs are tied to foreign student recruitment and its long-term economic growth depends on the skilled migration rationale. In terms of immediate gains, bringing about revenue from foreign student enrolment in Canadian postsecondary academic programs reinforces international recruitment as a key driver executing a national economic stimulus plan (Foreign Affairs, Trade and Development, 2014). Contributed revenue from foreign student educational expenditures, including differential tuition, accommodation, living expenses and more, grew from $9.3 billion in 2014

(Roslyn Kunin and Associates, 2016), to approximately $15.5 billion in 2017 ("Economic Impact of International Education in Canada – 2017", 2018) and accelerated to $21.6 billion in 2018 ("Building on Success: International Education Strategy (2019- 2024)", 2019). The economic value of international education has encouraged further government investment in international education strategies by allocating $147.9 million between 2019 and 2024 to continue to strengthen the economy ("Building on Success: International Education Strategy (2019- 2024)", 2019).

The success in achieving increased national revenue is based on unregulated differential international tuition and overlooks the question: can foreign students afford their academic program fees? In a study by Houshmand et al. (2014), one participant from India indicated that university administrators "should not expect just the filthy rich people from other countries to come and study here. There are people like me whose parents are spending everything on them just to get them educated" (p. 382). University hyper-internationalization enacted through foreign student recruitment unveils the ongoing commodification of education (Anderson, 2015), inducing competition among international students by forcing them to dish out deposits to secure access to Canadian university schooling. Revenue growth drawn from the influx of foreign students legitimizes rising differential tuition with students paying on average "three to four times that of domestic students" (Anderson, 2015, p. 168). The remodelling of university education is grounded in neoliberal ideology constructing higher education knowledge as a supplied good in high demand; thus, justifying its competitive and unregulated price points.

Unfortunately, foreign student recruitment has become a necessary tool for universities to maintain financial stability. The revenue-generating rationale (Larsen & Vincent-Lancrin, 2002) places greater dependence on revenue produced from international differential tuition than on public subsidy. Continual decrease in provincial funding for post-secondary costs since the 1990s (Canadian Federation of Students, 2012), have forced "cash-strapped university administrators to increasingly turn to tuition fees to cover operating expenses" (Canadian Federation of Students, 2012) and now depend heavily on unregulated differential tuition as a viable revenue source. As an example, the CBC News article, *"Skyrocketing tuition for international students questioned"* (Ireton, 2019), publicized Ontario's 19 universities' growing reliance on unregulated and exponentially increasing international tuition costs. International education is ingrained in contributing to Canada's prosperity (Trilokekar, 2010), functions as a commercial venture (Altbach, 2015) and is the leading business sector ("Building on Success: International Education Strategy: 2019-2024", 2019; Naidoo, 2006). At the centre of internationalization are higher education institutional and national revenue-generating goals (Heller, 2002) that mobilize foreign student recruitment to remain at the forefront of university internationalization activities.

Moreover, the skilled migration rationale situates foreign students as ideal candidates to move into the Canadian labour force (Larsen & Vincent-Lancrin, 2002; "Building on Success: International Education Strategy: 2019-2024", 2019). The general anticipation has been that they would have attained Canadian educational qualifications, demonstrated language proficiency and have immersed themselves in Canadian culture. However, there exists a disconnect between the illusion of available Canadian employment and the unemployment reality for NNES international students' post-university (Calder et al., 2016; Wall et al., 2017). Many foreign students struggle to land gainful Canadian employment after completing their Canadian university education and spending tens of thousands of dollars in differential tuition fees Toman, 2016). Statistics from the Longitudinal Immigration Database (IMDB) also captures the gap between the skilled-migration rationale of foreign students as ideal long-term, permanent residents and the reality that only 38% of 1 373 800 international students who entered Canada between 1980 and 2015 obtained permanent resident status (Akbar & Preston, 2019).

NNES Speaking Students

Foreign student recruitment has traditionally targeted and depended on key source countries such as China, India, and other NNES student demographic markets. With so much attention given to such students and with significant investment in their recruitment through oversees fairs, institutional partnerships targeted school visits, hired student-agents and marketing campaigns (AUCC Internationalization Survey, 2014), it is most appropriate to explore universities' institutional commitment to support NNES students beyond helping them apply to and enrol in academic programs on Canadian campuses. Although many NNES students can barely scrape up sufficient funding to finance their Canadian learning; view themselves as having inadequate English language proficiency; report academic and social adjustment challenges (Gopal, 2011); and experience narrow opportunities to participate in academic relevant Canadian employment after graduation (Arthur & Flynn, 2011), they remain motivated to study in Canada because "an English-medium education ... retains its 'value' in a global HE market" (Waters, 2012, p. 12). NNES international students are acutely aware of the socio-economic and political value of Western credentials along with the advantages that come with the English language as the global lingua franca (Altbach, 2004); in turn, intensifying their willingness to purchase knowledge and skills to propel their individual economic goals. Placing NNES foreign student recruitment for revenue generation at the heart of university internationalization draws institutional focus away from looking into these students' academic transitioning, social integration, and post-schooling employment access.

NNES Students' English Language Skills and Academic Adjustment

NNES students are typically concerned about their English language skills. English barriers can act as major communication obstacles, impede academic adjustment (Guo & Guo, 2017) and serve as a continuous reminder that they cannot express themselves as natives do (Kim, 2012). Reluctance to participate in class discussions leaves NNES students feeling further isolated (Swagler & Ellis, 2003) and linguistically incompetent. These interlinked experiences may unintentionally force NNES students on Canadian campuses to accept their endured fear of communicating in English as valid and normalized experiences. For example, one NNES from Malaysia expressed anxiety: "I have the feeling that my English is not as good as other local students and fear that they won't understand what I mean" (Robertson at al., 2000, p. 7). Also, NNES students are highly aware of how they are responded to. Students' perceptions of their English language ability often derive from how comfortable they feel about using it or from observing how others – native or other non-native English speakers – react to them.

Attention needs to be brought to cases whereby NNES students demonstrate a strong command of English language proficiency, but still view their languages skills as being mediocre. Kim (2012) observed that many international students studying in Western countries begin to "perceive themselves as inferior" (p. 461) as they form a habit of comparing themselves to domestic classmates and possibly to faculty. As another example, 20-year-old Amber from Albania reported feeling uncomfortable answering questions in class because she felt her English "was not good enough" (Plumb, 2018, p. 138). Despite not being able to recall prior negative peer or faculty reactions to her English communication ability, Amber's nervousness and fear to participate in class discussions in English resulted from witnessing unfavourable responses from some native English-speaking classmates toward her Nigerian friend when she spoke in class. Amber explained:

When my friend would talk, I could see the face of other students, especially white students – I think they're Canadian, but I don't know for sure. Anyway, I know that they're laughing at her; you know, you can see them whispering, or they roll their eyes … I don't understand why these people have to do that. (p. 138)

In this example, it is important to highlight that the official language of Nigeria is English and that Nigeria is listed as one of the countries for which university applicants may be exempt from to demonstrate English language proficiency. If the observed behaviours were directed at the Nigerian student because of perceived English language inability, then perhaps it was the Nigerian's native accent that fueled such misperception. As such, "dialectical hierarchies that favour standardized forms of English over non-standard varieties may also serve as barriers for some foreign students who speak English as a first language but do not speak the dialect of preference in their university setting" (Anderson, 2015, p. 178). It is also plausible that responses could have been motivated by the unspoken tension race plays in cross-cultural exchange. Everyday encounters shape the realities of racialized students (Milner, 2007) and can reinforce inequities commonly neutralized in institutional internationalization (Guo & Guo, 2017; Ladson-Billings, 1998, 2005).

Although English language proficiency can be viewed as influencing NNES students' academic adjustment, additional skills and strategies are required for formal academic study. Pre-academic, English for academic purpose (EAP) programs concentrate on developing students' "general academic English register, incorporating a formal, academic style with proficiency in the language use" (Jordan, 2004, p.5). Fox et al.'s (2014) investigation on the impact of EAP support on NNES students revealed that EAP programs were direct, positive and significant contributors to NNES students' academic and social engagement and overall transition to studying at Canadian universities (Fox et al., 2014). In responses to NNES students' common feeling of having no room to tweak communication through trial and error in academic settings, EAP programs create an emotionally safe environment for NNES students to engage in activities which aim to improve English language use; develop new skills such as teamwork, leadership, project management, media literacy; and help build confidence. Plumb (2018) notes that NNES students' self-reported perception of their English language proficiency plays an important role in the types of communication exchange opportunities they act upon and the risks they are willing to take to communicate in English. The more NNES students can experience participating in tasks likely encountered in academic programs, the better prepared they will be to transition and engage.

NNES Students' Social Integration

Despite NNES students' English language communication skills play a role in their cultural adjustment and social integration (Martirosyan et al., 2015), even those who are proficient, experience difficulties in accessing interaction with local students. NNES students who are confident in their English communication abilities face a different but equally substantial challenge – that is, to find opportunities to build localized friendships and networks (Li, 2011). The international students in Guo and Guo's (2017) research study revealed that despite having a strong command of the English language, they still found it challenging to develop friendships with local students. Generalized claims depicting international student presence on campuses as a vehicle for cross-cultural interaction and understanding, and a platform for innovative exchange has gained momentum ("Advisory Panel of Canada's International Education Strategy", 2014); becoming an integral marketing message. However, when it comes to NNES student experiences, the claims go unchecked. Scott's (1998) criticism of the application of internationalization suggested that "it would be a mistake to interpret the pressure to recruit international students … as a reinforcement of internationalism" (p. 125). The success of NNES international students' social integration hinges on meaningful cross-cultural engagement with members of the host society.

Intercultural exchange and relationship-building opportunities between NNES and domestic students are a challenge. Gareis' (2012) findings point out that foreign students repeatedly express great dissatisfaction with not having opportunity to meet, and ultimately foster, friendships with their domestic counterparts (Brown, 2009; Harman, 2005; Myles & Cheng, 2003). Increased focus on failed attempts from NNES students to build relationships with domestic counterparts suggests that students from countries with greater linguistic and cultural differences from the host cultures, tend to turn to their co-nationals which further solidifies "their high identification with the home culture" (Gareis, 2012, p. 321) and limits their "involvement in the new environment" (p. 321). Thus, it is naive to assume that the mere presence of foreign students from global regions on campus is enough to activate meaningful cross-cultural communication on Canadian university campuses. Canadian universities must be committed to going beyond promoting the cultural richness rhetoric associated with the value of foreign students on campuses. Practical applications are needed to infuse cross-cultural engagement in institutional life to support NNES student social integration. According to internationalization values, there should be no instances leaving NNES students frustrated with why they have not built networks with domestic students; or even worse, why they have not had the chance to meet domestic students (Harman, 2005).

A Note on International Cohorts

Culturally segregated academic programs have been replicated across faculty disciplines. For some universities, a quick and easy way to expand internationalization activities is by creating academic programs, commonly referred to as international cohorts, targeting and comprising of NNES students only. This type of program model negates the inherent cross-cultural exchange values of internationalization. Such programs are often described as having been customized to specific demographic markets with limited to no details on student integration and mechanisms to enhance students' Canadian learning experience.

A major factor motivating NNES students to seek academic study in Canada is to enhance their English language proficiency. Many participants in Plumb's (2018) study indicated they felt to have been misled by their agent or interpreted the title 'international cohort' to mean the program was intended for foreign students from a large range of countries including Canada. It is, therefore, unsettling for NNES students to find out they have applied to and enrolled in an academic program with mostly co-nationals and with no interaction with domestic students. Regarding NNES student perception on being in an international cohort program, Dale, one of the participants in Plumb's (2018) study explained: "Basically all Chinese and one or two Indian in the program. I want to make native, Canadian friends" (p. 183). Dale's views were in line with the views of foreign students in another international cohort program (Li & Tierny, 2013), whereby 28 out of the 31 participants wanted to be in classes and to study with Canadian students. Balancing aggressive foreign student enrolment with meeting NNES foreign student expectations and needs is an issue that reflects the "broader marketization of western universities" (Anderson, 2015, p. 169).

International cohorts systemically reproduce social capital, favouring the dominant culture. If higher university internationalization truly aims to incorporate "international, intercultural, and/or global dimensions into the content of the curriculum as well as the learning outcomes" (Leask, 2009, p. 209), this gap indicates a contradiction between internationalization vision and implementation. University administrators need to begin a dialogue around the implications of linguistically or culturally isolating academic programs on NNES students' overall social integration. Despite NNES students' commonly held beliefs that their international cohort program gravely fell below their expectations, and that their participation was merely to generate institutional revenue, none of the participants wanted to discuss this issue with their professor or department head (Plumb, 2018). Instead, they accepted the learning condition as a purchased product with a 'no return' policy. This reflects the "unspoken acquiescence to and default acceptance of the neoliberal status quo" (O'Regan, 2014, p. 537).

Canadian Employment

Canadian employment prospects are scarce for many NNES foreign students planning to transition to the labour market upon graduation. Foreign students are motivated to study in Canada because of the job opportunities they had thought of or "imagined" to exist (Plumb, 2018, p. 2019). Since this is precisely the next step for foreign students as outlined in the skilled migration rationale of internationalization, it is surprising why not more foreign students report high rates of success landing full-time positions within their fields of study. Foreign student worry of never gaining meaningful employment in Canada is in line with Scott et al.'s (2015) findings of gaps between internationalization's skilled migration rationale assumptions and barriers barring foreign students from transitioning to the labour market. The battle for international students to acquire employment exists in both on and off-campus contexts. Off-campus work permits, time extensions to remain in-country to look for employment, and permanent residency paths have been identified as challenges (Plumb, 2018). Other types of challenges stem from the perception of subpar English language ability and the lack of social integration into the host society to understand the nuances of navigating the national employment environment. Foreign student employment anxiety is compounded because they not only need to compete with one another but also with domestic students (Calder et al., 2016). NNES students' English communication challenges perceived in academics also follow them to when they become shortlisted for interviews, directly relating English language proficiency to employability. Two questions not readily brought up when relating to NNES students' English language proficiency to getting hired is – what are employers' perspectives on how they come to define English language proficiency and what aspects of communication do they consider to judge whether or not NNES applicants are linguistically proficient to do the job?

STARTING DIALOGUE FOR COURSES OF ACTION

Each Canadian university is unique in its strengths and challenges they experience in supporting foreign students beyond recruitment. It would be impractical to offer a list of recommendations without investigating each institutional context. As a result, the wide-ranging questions that follow are offered as springboard topics to start a discussion among university institution members, policymakers and researchers on their values regarding aspects impacting how foreign students experience Canadian university schooling:

- Does unmonitored internationalization predominantly through foreign student recruitment excuse Canadian universities from taking responsibility to actively identify gaps between the marketing of Canadian higher education and the experiences of NNES foreign students when it comes to meaningful cross-cultural interactions, social integration, and social capital-building to advance their employment goals?

- How are internationalization activities prioritized in the institution's strategic plan?
- What proportion of internationalization takes shape through each of the seven Internationalization Statement of Principles for Canadian Educational Institutions in each academic faculty?
- What is the relationship between enrollment and internationalization management?
- What types of campus supports (e.g., EAP programs, immigration office, health counselling, career advising, residence) are offered to NNES students?
- How do campus supports identify objectives that directly aim at meeting the needs of NNES students?
- When organizing student support services for NNES students into the categories of (a) pre-arrival, (b) on-campus and (c) post-graduation, which area(s) need to be augmented in either quantity or quality?
- What does collaboration between support services and academic departments look like?
- How are existing campus supports communicated to NNES students?
- How is curriculum internationalization organized within the institution?
- Which internationalization values frame course curriculum objectives?
- How are internationalization values actualized through curriculum internationalization?
- What are the implications of international cohort programs?
- What considerations are required to address the drawback of international cohort programs?
- What markers are used to identify the success of meaningful cross-cultural engagement between NNES and domestic students?
- How can social integration opportunities that empower NNES students be built into their institutional lives?
- Do universities need to play a role in post-graduation employment attainment?
- How does the institution collaborate with community partners to facilitate foreign student transition to the Canadian labour force?
- What do cooperative education experiences look like for NNES foreign students compared to their domestic counterparts? Should differential supports be considered?
- What does access to experiential learning look like for NNES foreign students compared to their domestic counterparts? Should differential supports be considered?
- What is the current scholarship structure for foreign students and to what extent does it offset differential tuition?

CONCLUDING REMARKS

Foreign student recruitment is likely to become further engrained as a significant source contributing to Canada's national economic development. As such, crucial conversations around students' academic transition, social integration and supports to access national employment opportunities merit attention. Foreign student recruitment will also continue to be touted as opening cross-cultural student engagement, collaboration and economic stimulation through the introduction of Canadian trained foreign students to the domestic labour force. However, it is unknown the extent to which policymakers, administrators, academics and foreign students can be confident these will indeed take place. The execution of university internationalization on Canadian campuses need to uphold internationalization values. Viczko and Tascon (2016) describe internationalization as operating within a "disconnected policy landscape" (p.

11) with inherent tensions of little regard to foreign student experiences post-recruitment. Well thought out plans are necessary to identify gaps and implement remedies to better support NNES foreign students studying on Canadian campuses.

REFERENCES

Abbott, A. T. (2009). The general agreement on trade in services (GATS) and education for all (EFA): Conflict of interests? *Educate, 9*(2), 7–17.

Advisory Panel on Canada's International Education Strategy. (2014). *International education: A key driver of Canada's future prosperity* (Final Report) (Cat. No. FR5-64/2012E-PDF). Retrieved from https://www.international.gc.ca/education/assets/pdfs/ies_report_rapport_sei-eng.pdf

Akbar, M., & Preston, B. (2019). *Social characteristics of international students in Ontario and Quebec.* Retrieved from https://crdcn.org/social-characteristics-international-students-ontario-and-quebec

Altbach, P. G. (2004). Globalization and the university: Myths and realities in an unequal world. *Tertiary Education and Management, 10*(1), 3–25. doi:10.1080/13583883.2004.9967114

Anderson, T. (2015). Seeking internationalization: The state of Canadian higher education. *Canadian Journal of Higher Education, 45*(4), 166–187.

Arthur, N., & Flynn, S. (2011). Career development influences of international students who pursue permanent immigration to Canada. *International Journal for Educational and Vocational Guidance, 11*(3), 221–237. doi:10.100710775-011-9212-5

Association of Universities and Colleges of Canada. (2007a). *Internationalizing Canadian campuses: Main themes emerging from the 2007 Scotia-AUCC workshop on excellence in internationalization at Canadian universities.* Retrieved from http://www.aucc.ca/wp-content/uploads/2011/05/scotiabank-internationalization-workshop-2007.pdf

Association of Universities and Colleges of Canada. (2014). *Canada's universities in the world: AUCC internationalization survey.* Retrieved from https://www.univcan.ca/wp-content/uploads/2015/07/internationalization-survey-2014.pdf

Aune, R. K., Hendreickson, B., & Rosen, D. R. (2011). An analysis of friendship networks, social connections, homesickness, and satisfaction levels of international students. *International Journal of Intercultural Journal of Intercultural Relations, 35*, 285–295.

Beck, K., Illieva, R., Pullman, A., & Zhang, O. (2013). New work, old power: Inequities within the labor of internationalization. *On the Horizon, 21*(2), 84–95. doi:10.1108/10748121311322987

Berg, M., & Seeber, B. (2016). *Slow professor: Challenging the culture of speed in the academy.* University of Toronto Press. doi:10.3138/9781442663091

Bourdieu, P. (1977). Cultural reproduction and social reproduction. In J. Karabel & A. Halsey (Eds.), *Power and ideology in education* (pp. 487–511). Oxford University Press.

Brown, L. (2009). A failure of communication on the cross-cultural campus. *Journal of Studies in International Education, 13*(4), 439–454. doi:10.1177/1028315309331913

Brown, P., & Tannock, S. (2009). Education, meritocracy and the global war for talent. *Journal of Education Policy, 24*(4), 377–392. doi:10.1080/02680930802669938

Calder, J. J., Richter, S., Mao, Y., Kovacs Burns, K., Mogale, R. S., & Danko, M. (2016). International students attending Canadian universities: Their experiences with housing, finances, and other issues. *Canadian Journal of Higher Education, 46*(2), 92–110.

Callan, P. (2012, March 8). Ontario tops country in international students. *The Gazette.*

Canada's Performance and Potential in International Education- International Students in Canada 2018. (n.d.). Retrieved from https://cbie.ca/media/facts-and-figures/

Canadian Bureau for International Education. (2015). *Statement of Principles for Canadian Educational Institutions.* Retrieved from https://cbie.ca/wp-content/uploads/2016/06/Internationalization-Principles-for-Canadian-Institutions-EN.pdf

Canadian Bureau for International Education. (2016). A World of Learning: Canada's Performance and Potential in International Education. Canadian Bureau for International Education.

Canadian Federation of Students. (2012). *Funding for post-secondary education.* Retrieved from https://cfs-fcee.ca/wp-content/uploads/sites/2/2013/11/Fact-Sheet-Funding-2013-11-En.pdf

Canterbury, D. C. (2005). *Neoliberal democratization and new authoritarianism.* Ashgate.

Corradetti, C. (2011). The Frankfurt school and critical theory. In *Internet Encyclopedia of Philosophy (IEP).* European Academy and the University of Rome Italy. Retrieved from https://www.iep.utm.edu/frankfur/

Edgerton, J. D., & Roberts, L. W. (2014). Cultural capital or habitus? Bourdieu and beyond in the explanation of enduring educational inequality. *Theory and Research in Education, 12*(2), 193–200. doi:10.1177/1477878514530231

Foreign Affairs, Trade and Development Canada. (2014). *Canada's international education strategy: Harnessing our knowledge advantage to drive innovation and prosperity* (No. FR5-86/2014). Retrieved from https://international.gc.ca/global-markets-marches-mondiaux/assets/pdfs/overview-apercu-eng.pdf

Fox, J., Cheng, L., & Zumbo, B. (2014). Do they make a difference? The impact of English language programs on second language students in Canadian universities. *TESOL Quarterly, 48*(1), 57–85. doi:10.1002/tesq.103

Gareis, E. (2012). Intercultural friendship: Effects of home and host region. *Journal of Intercultural and International Communication, 5*(4), 309–328. doi:10.1080/17513057.2012.691525

Giroux, H. (2010). Public values, higher education and the scourge of neoliberalism: Politics at the limits of the social. *Culture Machine.* Retrieved from https://www.culturemachine.net/index.php/cm/article/view/426/444

Gopal, A. (2011). Internationalization of higher education: Preparing faculty to teach cross-culturally. *International Journal on Teaching and Learning in Higher Education, 23*(3), 373–381.

Government of Canada. (2018). *Economic impact of international education in Canada – 2017.* Retrieved from https://www.international.gc.ca/education/report-rapport/impact-2017/index.aspx?lang=eng

Government of Canada. (2019). *Building on success: International education strategy: 2019-2024.* Retrieved from https://www.international.gc.ca/education/assets/pdfs/ies-sei/Building-on-Success-International-Education-Strategy-2019-2024.pdf

Grayson, J. P. (2008). The experiences and outcomes of domestic and international students at four Canadian universities. *Higher Education Research & Development, 27*(3), 215–230. doi:10.1080/07294360802183788

Guo, S., & Chase, M. (2011). Internationalization of higher education: Integrating international students into Canadian academic environment. *Teaching in Higher Education, 16*(3), 305–318. doi:10.1080/13 562517.2010.546524

Guo, Y., & Guo, S. (2017). Internationalization of Canadian higher education: Discrepancies between policies and international student experiences. *Studies in Higher Education, 45*(5), 851–868. doi:10.1 080/03075079.2017.1293874

Harman, G. (2005). Internationalization of Australian higher education: A critical review of literature and research. In P. Ninnes & M. Hellsten (Eds.), *Internationalizing higher education: Critical explorations of pedagogy and policy* (pp. 119–140). Comparative Education Research Centre. doi:10.1007/1-4020-3784-8_7

Harris, R. (2011). The knowledge-based economy intellectual origins and new economic perspectives. *International Journal of Management Reviews, 3*(1), 21–40. doi:10.1111/1468-2370.00052

Harvey, D. (2005). *A brief history of neoliberalism.* Oxford University Press.

Harvey, D. (2007). Neoliberalism as creative destruction. *A Journal on Integrated Management of Occupational Health and the Environment, 2*(4), 137-154.

Hayek, F. A. (1944). *The road to serfdom.* Routledge.

Heller, D. E. (2002). *Condition of access: Higher education for lower income students.* American Council on Education and Praeger Publishers.

Horkheimer, M. (1972). *Critical theory.* Herder & Herder.

Houshmand, S., Spanierman, L. B., & Tafarodi, R. W. (2014). Excluded and avoided: Racial microaggressions targeting Asian international students in Canada. *Cultural Diversity & Ethnic Minority Psychology, 20*(3), 377–388. doi:10.1037/a0035404 PMID:25045949

Ireton, J. (2019, June 26). Skyrocketing tuition for international students questioned. *CBC News.* Retrieved from https://www.cbc.ca/news/canada/ottawa/analysis-ontario-universities-international-tuition-increases-1.5189755

Jordan, R. (2004). *English for academic purposes.* Cambridge University Press.

Kim, J. (2012). The birth of academic subalterns: How do foreign students embody the global hegemony of American universities? *Journal of Studies in International Education, 16*(5), 455–462. doi:10.1177/1028315311407510

Knight, J. (2003). Updated internationalization definition. *Industry and Higher Education, 33,* 2–3.

Knight, J. (2004). Internationalization remodeled: Definition, approaches, and rationales. *Journal of Studies in International Education, 8*(1), 5–31. doi:10.1177/1028315303260832

Knight, J., & de Wit, H. (1995). Strategies for internationalisation of higher education: Historical and conceptual perspectives. In H. de Wit (Ed.), Strategies for internationalisation of higher education – A comparative study of Australia, Canada, Europe and the USA (pp. 5-29). Amsterdam: European Association for International Education (EAIE).

Ladson-Billings, G. J. (2005). Is the team all right? Diversity and teacher education. *Journal of Teacher Education, 56*(3), 229–234. doi:10.1177/0022487105275917

Larsen, K., & Vincent-Lancrin, S. (2002). International trade in educational services: Good or bad? *Higher Education Management and Policy, 14*(3), 2–45. doi:10.1787/hemp-v14-art18-en

Leask, B. (2013). Internationalizing the curriculum in the disciplines: Imagining new possibilities. *Journal of Studies in International Education, 17*(2), 103–118. doi:10.1177/1028315312475090

Leclaire, R. (2010). Master's Biotechnology Program Target Foreign Students. *The Study Magazine.* Retrieved from http://studymagazine.com/2011/06/28/windsors-masters-biotechnology-program-targets-foreign-students/

Li, C. (2011). Chinese high school graduates' beliefs about English learning. *Canadian Research & Development Center of Sciences and Cultures, 3*(2), 11–18.

Li, X., & Tierney, P. (2013). Internationalization in Canadian higher education: Experiences of international students in a master's program. *Comparative and International Education, 42*(2), 1–16. https://ir.lib.uwo.ca/cie-eci/vol42/iss2/5

Madge, C., Raghuram, P., & Noxolo, P. (2009). Engaged pedagogy and responsibility: A postcolonial analysis of international students. *Geoforum, 10*(1), 34–45. doi:10.1016/j.geoforum.2008.01.008

Marcuse, H. (1964). *One-dimensional man: Studies in the ideology of advanced industrial society.* Retrieved from https://www.marxists.org/reference/archive/marcuse/works/one-dimensional-man/one-dimensional-man.pdf

Martirosyan, N. M., Hwang, E., & Wanjohi, R. (2015). Impact of English proficiency on academic performance of international students. *Journal of International Students, 5*(1), 60–71.

Merino, B. D., Mayper, A. G., & Tolleson, T. D. (2010). Neoliberalism, deregulation and Sarbanes-Oxley: The legitimation of a failed corporate governance model. *Accounting, Auditing & Accountability Journal, 23*(6), 774–792. doi:10.1108/09513571011065871

Mukherjee, A. (2003, March). *Neoliberalism and neoliberal economics.* Social Science, India Point Web Network.

Myles, J., & Cheng, L. (2003). The social and cultural life of non-native English speaking international graduate students at a Canadian university. *Journal of English for Academic Purposes*, 2(3), 247–263. doi:10.1016/S1475-1585(03)00028-6

Naidoo, V. (2006). International education: A tertiary-level industry update. *Journal of Research in International Education*, 5(3), 323–345. doi:10.1177/1475240906069455

Nolan, K. (2012). Dispositions in the field: Viewing mathematics teacher education through the lens of Bourdieu's social field theory. *Educational Studies in Mathematics*, 80(1-2), 201–215. doi:10.100710649-011-9355-9

O'Regan, J. P. (2014). English as a lingua franca: An immanent critique. *Applied Linguistics*, 35(5), 533–552. doi:10.1093/applin/amt045

Plumb, A. (2018). *International students' perceived university schooling experience in the face of internationalization* (Unpublished doctoral dissertation). University of Windsor, ON.

Robertson, M., Line, M., Jones, S., & Thomas, S. (2000). International students, learning environments and perceptions: A case study using the Delphi technique. *Higher Education Research & Development*, 19(1), 89–102. doi:10.1080/07294360050020499

Roslyn Kunin & Associates, Inc. (2016). *Economic impact on international education in Canada- An update final report*. Retrieved from https://www.international.gc.ca/education/report-rapport/impact-2016/index.aspx?lang=eng

Scott, C., Safdar, S., Desai Trilokekar, R., & El Masri, A. (2015). International students as 'ideal immigrants' in Canada: A disconnect between policy makers' assumptions and the lived experiences of international students. *International Education, 43*(3), Article 5.

Scott, P. (1998). *The globalization of higher education*. SHRE and Open University Press.

Sherman, R. R., & Webb, R. B. (2005). *Qualitative research in education: Focus and methods*. Routledge.

Stier, J. (2004). Taking a critical stance toward internationalization ideologies in higher education: Idealism, instrumentalism and educationalism. *Globalisation, Societies and Education*, 2(1), 83–97. doi:10.1080/1476772042000177069

Stukalina, Y. (2008). How to prepare students for productive and satisfying careers in the knowledge-based economy: Creating a more efficient educational environment. *Technological and Economic Development, Baltic Journal on Sustainability, 14*(2), 197-207.

Swagler, M. A., & Ellis, M. V. (2003). Crossing the distance: Adjustment of Taiwanese graduate students in the United States. *Journal of Counseling Psychology*, 50(4), 420–437. doi:10.1037/0022-0167.50.4.420

The Illuminate Consulting Group. (2009). *Department of Foreign Affairs and international Trade: Best practices on managing the delivery of Canadian education marketing*. Retrieved from https://www.international.gc.ca/education/reports-rapports.aspx?lang=eng&view=d

Toman, J. (2016, April 8). Long Odds for International Students to Land a Job. *CBC News*. Retrieved from https://www.cbc.ca/news/canada/windsor/international-students-tuition-jobs-1.3525821

Touraine, A. (2001). *Beyond neoliberalism*. Polity Press.

Trilokekar, R. D. (2010). International education as soft power? The contributions and challenges of Canadian foreign policy to the internationalization of higher education. *Higher Education, 59*(2), 131–147. doi:10.100710734-009-9240-y

Wall, T., Tran, L. T., & Soejatminah, S. (2017). Inequalities and agencies in workplace learning experiences: International student perspectives. *Vocations and Learning, 10*(2), 141–156. doi:10.100712186-016-9167-2

Waters, J. L. (2012). Geographies of international education: Mobilities and the reproduction of social (dis)advantage. *Geography Compass, 6*(2), 123–136. doi:10.1111/j.1749-8198.2011.00473.x

KEY TERMS AND DEFINITIONS

Cultural Capital: Experiences, networks and integration that promote social mobility and may play a role in attaining economic opportunities.

Differential Tuition: Unregulated international tuition fees set by institutions for undergraduate and graduate programs.

Higher Education Commercialization: Transformation of education into a business enterprise model grounded in large investments in institutional branding and marketing.

Higher Education Commodification: Increased institutional competition for students and dependence on private funds.

Internationalization: Incorporating international and intercultural dimensions to facilitate meaningful postsecondary education experiences.

Neoliberalism: An economic and political ideology that supports accelerated competition and market deregulation.

Non-Native English Speaking (NNES): Foreign students whose first language is not English.

Compilation of References

Abase, A. R., & Graves, B. (2008). Academic literacy and plagiarism: Conversations with international graduate students and disciplinary professors. *Journal of English for Academic Purposes*, *7*(4), 221–233. doi:10.1016/j.jeap.2008.10.010

Abbott, A. T. (2009). The general agreement on trade in services (GATS) and education for all (EFA): Conflict of interests? *Educate*, *9*(2), 7–17.

Abbott, A., & Silles, M. (2016). Determinants of international student migration. *World Economy*, *39*(5), 621–635. doi:10.1111/twec.12319

Abubakar, B., Shanka, T., & Muuka, G. (2010). Tertiary education: An investigation of location selection criteria and preferences by international students - The case of two Australian universities. *Journal of Marketing for Higher Education*, *20*(1), 49–68. doi:10.1080/08841241003788052

Adams, T., Banks, M., & Olsen, A. (2011). Benefits of international education: enriching students, enriching communities. In D. Davis & B. Mackintosh (Eds.), *Making a difference: Australian international education* (pp. 9–46). University of New South Wales Press Ltd.

Advisory Panel on Canada's International Education Strategy Final Report. (2013). *International Education: A key driver of Canada's future prosperity*. Retrieved on 4/9/18 from http://www.international.gc.ca/education/report-rapport/strategystrategie/index.aspx?lang=eng

Advisory Panel on Canada's International Education Strategy. (2014). *International education: A key driver of Canada's future prosperity* (Final Report) (Cat. No. FR5-64/2012E-PDF). Retrieved from https://www.international.gc.ca/education/assets/pdfs/ies_report_rapport_sei-eng.pdf

Akbar, M., & Preston, B. (2019). *Social characteristics of international students in Ontario and Quebec*. Retrieved from https://crdcn.org/social-characteristics-international-students-ontario-and-quebec

Alberta Advanced Education and Technology. (2012). *Campus Alberta Planning Resource*. Retrieved from http://eae.alberta.ca/media/299589/capr2012.pdf

Alberts, H. C., & Hazen, H. D. (2005). "There are always two voices…": International Students' Intentions to Stay in the United States or Return to their Home Countries. *International Migration (Geneva, Switzerland)*, *43*(3), 131–154. doi:10.1111/j.1468-2435.2005.00328.x

Alberts, H., & Hazen, H. (2006). Visitors or immigrants: International students in the United States. *Population Space and Place*, *12*(3), 201–216. doi:10.1002/psp.409

Alkharusi, H. (2011). Development and datametric properties of a scale measuring students' perceptions of the classroom assessment environment. *International Journal of Instruction*, *4*, 105–120.

Alkharusi, H. (2013). Canonical correlational models of students' perceptions of assessment tasks, motivational orientations and learning strategies. *International Journal of Instruction, 6*, 21–38.

Alkharusi, H. A., & Al-Hosni, S. (2015). Perceptions of classroom assessment tasks: An interplay of gender, subject area, and grade level. *Cypriot Journal of Educational Sciences, 10*(3), 205–217. doi:10.18844/cjes.v1i1.66

Alkharusi, H., Aldhafri, S., Alnabhani, H., & Alkalbani, M. (2014). Modeling the relationship between perceptions of assessment tasks and classroom assessment environment as a function of gender. *The Asia-Pacific Education Researcher, 23*(1), 93–104. doi:10.100740299-013-0090-0

Allen, M. B. (1993). International students in academic libraries: A user survey. *College & Research Libraries, 54*(4), 323–333. doi:10.5860/crl_54_04_323

Allen, M. J. (2004). *Assessing Academic Programs in Higher Education*. Jossey-Bass.

Almerico, G. M. (2014). Food and identity: Food studies, cultural, and personal identity. *Journal of International Business and Cultural Studies, 8*(1).

Alotaibi, K., & Lordly, D. (2016). A Muslim woman's experience with integration into Canadian culture while completing her graduate nutrition degree: An autoethnographic account. *Journal of Critical Dietetics, 3*(2), 13–22.

Alqudayri, B., & Gounko, T. (2018). Studying in Canada: Experiences of Female Graduate Students from Saudi Arabia. *Journal of International Students, 8*(4), 1736–1747.

Altbach, P. G., & de Wit, H. (2017). Trump and the coming revolution in higher education internationalization. *International Higher Education,* (89), 3-5.

Altbach, P. G. (2004). Globalization and the university: Myths and realities in an unequal world. *Tertiary Education and Management, 10*(1), 3–25. doi:10.1080/13583883.2004.9967114

Altbach, P. G. (2016). *Global perspectives on higher education*. JHU Press.

Altbach, P. G., & Knight, J. (2007). The internationalization of higher education: Motivations and realities. *Journal of Studies in International Education, 11*(3-4), 290–305. doi:10.1177/1028315307303542

Alumran, J. (2008). Learning styles in relation to gender, field of study, and academic achievement for Bahraini University students. *Individual Differences Research, 6*(4), 303–316.

Alyousif, Z., & Mathews, A. E. (2018). Impact of migration on diet, physical activity, and body weight among international students moving from the Gulf Countries to the United States. *Case Rep. J, 2*(7).

Ambrose, S. A., Bridges, M. W., DiPietro, M., Lovett, M. C., & Norman, M. K. (2010). *The Jossey-Bass higher and adult education series. How learning works: Seven research-based principles for smart teaching*. Jossey-Bass.

American Library Association. (2000). *ACRL standards: Information literacy competency standards for higher education*. Retrieved from https://crln.acrl.org/index.php/crlnews/article/view/19242/22395

Ames, C. (1992). Achievement goals and the classroom motivational climate. In D. H. Schunk & J. Meece (Eds.), *Student perceptions in the classroom* (pp. 327–348). Erlbaum.

Amos, S., & Lordly, D. (2014). Picture this: A photovoice study of international students' food experience in Canada. *Canadian Journal of Dietetic Practice and Researc, 75*(2), 59–63. doi:10.3148/75.2.2014.59

Amsberry, D. (2009). Deconstructing plagiarism: International students and textual borrowing practices. *The Reference Librarian, 51*(1), 31–44. doi:10.1080/02763870903362183

Anderson, T. (2015). Seeking internationalization: The state of Canadian higher education. *Canadian Journal of Higher Education, 45*(4), 166–187.

Andrade, M. S. (2006). International students in English-speaking universities. *Journal of Research in International Education, 5*(2), 131–154. doi:10.1177/1475240906065589

Andrews, D. J. (2019). *Advanced writing for Asian graduates in Canada and the United States: A qualitative case study.* Available from Dissertations & Theses @ University of Phoenix. ProQuest Central. ProQuest Dissertations & Theses Global. (2243910750). Retrieved from https://search.proquest.com/docview/2243910750?accountid=35812

Andrews, T. M., Leonard, M. J., Colgrove, C. A., & Kalinowski, S. T. (2011). Active learning not associated with student learning in a random sample of college biology courses. *CBE Life Sciences Education, 10*(4), 394–405. doi:10.1187/cbe.11-07-0061 PMID:22135373

Arbex, D. (2014). *Ninth annual comprehensive student discipline report: 2012-2013.* Retrieved from https://www.uwindsor.ca/secretariat/sites/uwindsor.ca.secretariat/files/apc140410-5.3a_-_comprehensive_student_discipline_report_9th_annual.pdf

Ariza, E. N. (2010). *Not for ESOL teachers: What every classroom needs to know about the linguistically, culturally, and ethnically diverse students* (2nd ed.). Allyn & Bacon.

Arkatova, O. G., Danakin, N. S., & Shavyrina, I. (2015). Enhancing adaptability of foreign students. *Mediterranean Journal of Social Sciences, 6*(6), 276–281.

Arthur, N. (1997). Counseling issues with international students. *Canadian Journal of Counselling, 31*(4), 259–273.

Arthur, N. (2004). *Counselling international students: Clients from around the world.* Plenum Publishers. doi:10.1007/978-1-4419-8919-2

Arthur, N. (2018). Intersectionality and international student identities in Transition. In N. Arthur (Ed.), *Counselling in cultural contexts: Identities and social justice* (pp. 271–292). International and Cultural Psychology. doi:10.1007/978-3-030-00090-5_12

Arthur, N., & Flynn, S. (2011). Career development influences of international students who pursue permanent immigration to Canada. *International Journal for Educational and Vocational Guidance, 11*(3), 221–237. doi:10.100710775-011-9212-5

Association of Atlantic Universities. (2019). *AAU survey of preliminary enrolments.* https://www.atlanticuniversities.ca/statistics/aau-survey-preliminary-enrolments

Association of College and Research Libraries. (2016). *Framework for information literacy for higher education.* Retrieved from http://www.ala.org/acrl/sites/ala.org.acrl/files/content/issues/infolit/Framework_ILHE.pdf

Association of Universities and Colleges of Canada. (2007a). *Internationalizing Canadian campuses: Main themes emerging from the 2007 Scotia-AUCC workshop on excellence in internationalization at Canadian universities.* Retrieved from http://www.aucc.ca/wp-content/uploads/2011/05/scotiabank- internationalization-workshop-2007.pdf

Association of Universities and Colleges of Canada. (2014). *Canada's universities in the world, AUCC international survey 2014.* Ottawa: Association of Universities and Colleges of Canada. Retrieved from https://www.univcan.ca/wp-content/uploads/2015/07/internationalization-survey-2014.pdf

Association of Universities and Colleges of Canada. (2014). *Canada's universities in the world: AUCC internationalization survey.* Retrieved from https://www.univcan.ca/wp-content/uploads/2015/07/internationalization-survey-2014.pdf

Atlantic Colleges Atlantique. (2018). *Fact sheet. The economic value of Atlantic colleges Atlantique.* Author.

Aubrey, R. (1991). International students on campus: A challenge for counselors, medical providers, and clinicians. *Smith College Studies in Social Work, 62*(1), 20–33. doi:10.1080/00377319109516697

Auerbach, A. J., Higgins, M., Brickman, P., & Andrews, P. C. (2018). Teacher knowledge for active-learning instruction: Expert-novice comparison reveals differences. *CBE Life Sciences Education, 17*(12), 1–14. doi:10.1187/cbe.17-07-0149 PMID:29420184

Aune, R. K., Hendreickson, B., & Rosen, D. R. (2011). An analysis of friendship networks, social connections, homesickness, and satisfaction levels of international students. *International Journal of Intercultural Journal of Intercultural Relations, 35*, 285–295.

Azevedo, A., Hurst, D., & Dwyer, R. (2015). Competency-based training program for international students. *International Business Research, 8*(3), 11-28. doi:10.5539/irb.v8n3p11

Badenhorst, C., Moloney, C., Rosales, J., Dyer, J., & Ru, L. (2014). Beyond deficit: Graduate student research writing pedagogies. *Teaching in Higher Education, 20*(1), 1–11. doi:10.1080/13562517.2014.945160

Badke, W. (2002). International students: Information literacy or academic literacy. *Academic Exchange Quarterly, 6*(4), 60–65.

Bai, J. (2016). Perceived support as a predictor of acculturative stress among international students in the United States. *Journal of International Students, 6*(1), 93–106.

Baker, C. A. (2017). *Understanding the study abroad experience for international students from China at the University of Vermont* (Undergraduate thesis). University of Vermont. Retrieved from http://scholarworks.uvm.edu/hcoltheses/132

Baker, S. E., & Edwards, R. (2012). *How many qualitative interviews is enough?* National Centre for Research Methods.

Bakhtin, M. M. (2002). *The dialogic imagination: Four essays* (M. Holquist, Ed., EmersonC.HolquistM., Trans.). University of Texas.

Bakhtin, M. M. (2004). *Speech Genres and other Late Essays (V. W. McGee, Trans.,)* (C. Emerson & M. Holquist, Eds.). University of Texas.

Ball, C., Dice, L., & Bartholomae, D. (1990). Developing discourse in adolescence and adulthood. In R. Beach & S. Hynds (Eds.), *Advances in Discourse Processes, 39.* Ablex.

Bandura, A. (1986). *Social foundations of thought and action: A social cognitive theory.* Prentice-Hall.

Barone, T. E., & Eisner, E. W. (2012). *Arts-based research.* Sage.

Bartlett, J. E., Kotrlik, J. W., & Higgins, C. C. (2001). Organizational research: Determining appropriate sample size in survey research. *Information Technology, Learning and Performance Journal, 19*(1), 43–50.

Bartram, B. (2009). Student support in higher education: Understandings, implications and challenges. *Higher Education Quarterly, 63*(3), 308–314. doi:10.1111/j.1468-2273.2008.00420.x

Basen, I. (2014). *Most university undergraduates now taught by poorly paid part-timers.* Retrieved from https://www.cbc.ca/news/canada/most-university-undergrads-now-taught-by-poorly-paid-part-timers-1.2756024

Battle, C. J. (2004). *The effect of information literacy instruction on library anxiety among international students* (Doctoral dissertation, University of North Texas, Denton, the United States). Retrieved from https://search.proquest.com/docview/305138026?pq-origsite=gscholar

Baynham, M. D., Beck, K., Gordon, A. L., & Miguel, C. S. (1995). Constructing a discourse position: Quoting, referring and attribution in academic writing. In K. Chanock (Ed.), *Integrating the teaching of academic discourse into courses in the disciplines. Proceedings of the conference*. La Trobe University.

Beck, K., Illieva, R., Pullman, A., & Zhang, O. (2013). New work, old power: Inequities within the labor of internationalization. *On the Horizon, 21*(2), 84–95. doi:10.1108/10748121311322987

Beech, S. E. (2019). *The geographies of international student mobility: Spaces, places and decision-making*. Springer Nature Singapore. doi:10.1007/978-981-13-7442-5

Belcher, D. (1994). The apprenticeship approach to advanced academic literacy: Graduate students and their mentors. *English for Specific Purposes, 13*(1), 23–34. doi:10.1016/0889-4906(94)90022-1

Belcher, W. L. (2009). *Writing your journal article in 12 weeks: A guide to academic success*. Sage.

Bennett, R. J., Volet, S. E., & Fozdar, F. E. (2013). "I'd say it's kind of unique in a way" The development of an intercultural student relationship. *Journal of Studies in International Education, 17*(5), 533–553. doi:10.1177/1028315312474937

Berg, B. L. (2007). *Qualitative research methods for the social sciences*. Pearson.

Berg, M., & Seeber, B. (2016). *Slow professor: Challenging the culture of speed in the academy*. University of Toronto Press. doi:10.3138/9781442663091

Berquist, B., Hall, R., Morris-Lange, S., Shields, H., Stern, V., & Tran, L. T. (2019). *Global perspectives on international student employability*. Retrieved from https://www.ieaa.org.au/research/global-employability

Berray, M. (2019). A critical literacy review of the melting pot and salad bowl assimilation and integration theories. *Journal of Ethnic and Cultural Studies, 6*(1), 142–151. doi:10.29333/ejecs/217

Berry, J. W. (2013). Integration as a mode of immigrant acculturation. *US immigration and education: Cultural and policy issues across the lifespan*, 41-58.

Berry, J. W. (1997). Immigration, acculturation, and adaptation. *Applied Psychology, 46*(1), 5–34.

Berry, J. W. (2006). Stress perspectives on acculturation. In D. L. Sam & J. W. Berry (Eds.), *The Cambridge handbook of acculturation psychology* (pp. 43–57). Cambridge University Press. doi:10.1017/CBO9780511489891.007

Bertram, D. M., Poulakis, M., Elsasser, B. S., & Kumar, E. (2014). Social support and acculturation in Chinese international students. *Journal of Multicultural Counseling and Development, 42*(2), 107–124. doi:10.1002/j.2161-1912.2014.00048.x

Bhochhibhoya, A., Dong, Y., & Branscum, P. (2017). Sources of social support among international college students in the United States. *Journal of International Students, 7*(3), 671–686.

Biggs, J. B., & Tang, C. (2011). *Teaching for quality learning at university: What the student does* (4th ed.). Open University Press.

Biggs, J., & Tang, C. (2011). *Teaching for Quality Learning at University* (4th ed.). SRHE & Open University Press.

Birchard, K. (2005). Canada seeks more foreign students. *The Chronicle of Higher Education, 51*(34).

Bista, K. (2012). Silence in teaching and learning: Perspectives of a Nepalese graduate student. *College Teaching, 60*(2), 76–82.

Bjork, R. A., Dunlosky, J., & Kornell, N. (2013). Self-regulated learning: Beliefs, techniques, and illusions. *Annual Review of Psychology, 64*(1), 417–444. doi:10.1146/annurev-psych-113011-143823 PMID:23020639

Black, P., & William, D. (1998). Inside the black box: Raising standards through classroom assessment. *Phi Delta Kappan*, *80*(2), 139–148.

Black, P., & William, D. (2012). Assessment for learning in the classroom. In J. Gardner (Ed.), *Assessment and Learning* (pp. 11–32). SAGE Publications Ltd. doi:10.4135/9781446250808.n2

Bohman, E. (2010). Headed for the heartland: Decision making process of community college bound international students. *Community College Journal of Research and Practice*, *34*(1-2), 64–77. doi:10.1080/10668920903385848

Boice, R. (2000). *Advice for the new faculty member*. Allyn and Bacon.

Bolden, B. (2008). Suds and Stan: Musically enhanced research. *Journal of Creative Arts in Education*, *8*(1). http://www.jcae.ca/08-01/bolden.html

Bolden, B. (2017). Music as method: Musically enhanced narrative inquiry. *International Journal of Education & the Arts*, *18*(9), 1–19.

Bordonaro, K. (2019). Forging multiple pathways: Integrating international students into a Canadian university library. In Y. Luckert & L. T. Inge (Eds.), *The globalized library: American academic libraries and international students, collections, and practices* (pp. 85–97). Association of College & Research Libraries.

Bosher, S., & Bowles, M. (2008). The effects of linguistic modification on ESL students' comprehension of nursing course test items. *Nursing Education Perspectives*, *29*, 165–172. PMID:18575241

Bourdieu, P. (1977). Cultural reproduction and social reproduction. In J. Karabel & A. Halsey (Eds.), *Power and ideology in education* (pp. 487–511). Oxford University Press.

Bourdieu, P., & Passeron, J. C. (1977). *Reproduction in education, society and culture*. Sage.

Boyer, E. L. (1990). *Scholarship reconsidered: Priorities of the professoriate*. Princeton University Press.

Brandenburg, U., & De Wit, H. (2015). The end of internationalization. *International Higher Education*, (62). doi:10.6017/ihe.2011.62.8533

Breault, R., Hackler, R., & Bradley, R. (2012). Seeking rigor in the search for identity: A trioethnography. In J. Norris, R. Sawyer, & D. E. Lund (Eds.), *Duoethnography: Dialogic methods for social, health, and educational research* (pp. 115–136). Routledge.

Breivik, P. S. (2005). 21st century learning and information literacy. *Change*, *37*(2), 21–27. doi:10.3200/CHNG.37.2.21-27

Bresler, L. (2006). Embodied narrative inquiry: A methodology of connection. *Research Studies in Education*, *27*(1), 21–43.

Brewer, M., & Chen, Y. (2007). Where (who) are collectives in collectivism? Toward conceptual clarification of individualism and collectivism. *Psychological Review*, *114*(1), 133–151. doi:10.1037/0033-295X.114.1.133 PMID:17227184

Brigham, S. (2011). Braided stories and bricolaged symbols: Critical reflection and transformative learning theory for teachers. *McGill Journal of Education*, *46*(1), 41–54. doi:10.7202/1005668ar

British Columbia Education Quality Assurance. (2018). *Policy and procedures manual*. Retrieved from https://www2.gov.bc.ca/assets/gov/education/post-secondary-education/institution- resources-administration/eqa/eqa-policy-and-procedures-manual.pdf

Bronfenbrenner, U. (1979). *The ecology of human development: Experiments by nature and design*. Harvard University Press.

Brookfield, S. (2005). *The power of critical theory: Liberating adult learning and teaching* (1st ed.). Jossey-Bass.

Brookfield, S. D. (1995). *Becoming a critically reflective teacher*. Jossey-Bass.

Brookhart, S. M., & Bronowicz, D. L. (2003). I don't like writing: It makes my fingers hurt: Students talk about their classroom assessments. *Assessment in Education: Principles, Policy & Practice, 10*(2), 221–242. doi:10.1080/0969594032000121298

Brown, J. D. (2009). Open-response items in questionnaires. In J. Heigham & R. Croker (Eds.), *Qualitative research in applied linguistics: A practical introduction* (pp. 200–219). Palgrave MacMillan.

Brown, L. (2009). A failure of communication on the cross-cultural campus. *Journal of Studies in International Education, 13*(4), 439–454. doi:10.1177/1028315309331913

Brown, L. I. (2004). Diversity: The challenge for higher education. *Race, Ethnicity and Education, 7*(1), 21–34. doi:10.1080/1361332042000187289

Brown, L., Edwards, J., & Hartwell, H. (2010). A taste of the unfamiliar. Understanding the meanings attached to food by international postgraduate students in England. *Appetite, 54*(1), 202–207. doi:10.1016/j.appet.2009.11.001

Brown, P. A. (2008). A review of the literature on case study research. *The Canadian Journal for New Scholars in Education, 1*(1), 1–13.

Brown, P., & Tannock, S. (2009). Education, meritocracy and the global war for talent. *Journal of Education Policy, 24*(4), 377–392. doi:10.1080/02680930802669938

Bryant, D. (1995). Survival of the interventionist: The personal cost of immersion and social change. *The Interdisciplinary Journal of Study Abroad, 1*, 17–25.

Bucher, K. (2012). The importance of information literacy skills in the middle school curriculum. *The Clearing House: A Journal of Educational Strategies, Issues and Ideas, 73*(4), 217–221. http://www.jstor.org/stable/30189549. doi:10.1080/00098650009600955

Bundy, A. (Ed.). (2004). *Australian and New Zealand information literacy framework: Principles, standards and practice* (2nd ed.). University of South Australia.

Burr, V. (1995). *An introduction to social constructionism*. Routledge. doi:10.4324/9780203299968

Buttaro, L. (2004). Second language acquisition, culture shock, and language stress of adult female Latina students in New York. *Journal of Hispanic Higher Education, 3*(1), 21–49. doi:10.1177/1538192703255525

Butz, N. T., Stupnisky, R. H., Peterson, E. S., & Majerus, M. M. (2014). Self-determined motivation in synchronous hybrid graduate business programs: Contrasting online and on campus students. *Journal of Online Learning and Teaching / MERLOT, 10*(2), 211–227.

Buzzi, O., Grimes, S., & Rolls, A. (2012). Posts of departure: Writing for the discipline in the discipline. *Teaching in Higher Education, 17*(4), 479–484. doi:10.1080/13562517.2012.711932

byrd, d. (2019). Uncovering hegemony in higher education: A critical appraisal of the use of "institutional habitus" in empirical scholarship. *Review of Educational Research, 89*(2), 171-210.

Byrne, E., Brugha, R., & McGarvey, A. (2019). 'A melting pot of cultures'–challenges in social adaptation and interactions amongst international medical students. *BMC Medical Education, 19*(1), 86. doi:10.118612909-019-1514-1

Caffarella, R. S., & Barnett, B. G. (1997). Teaching doctoral students to become scholarly writers: The importance of giving and receiving critiques. *Studies in Higher Education, 25*(1), 38–52. doi:10.1080/030750700116000

Calder, J. J., Richter, S., Mao, Y., Kovacs Burns, K., Mogale, R. S., & Danko, M. (2016). International students attending Canadian universities: Their experiences with housing, finances, and other issues. *Canadian Journal of Higher Education, 46*(2), 92–110.

Callan, P. (2012, March 8). Ontario tops country in international students. *The Gazette.*

Canada's Performance and Potential in International Education- International Students in Canada 2018. (n.d.). Retrieved from https://cbie.ca/media/facts-and-figures/

Canadian Association of University Teachers. (1986). *The CAUT guide to the teaching dossier: Its preparation and use.* Author.

Canadian Bureau for International Education (CBIE). (2018a). *The student's voice: National results of the 2018 CBIE international student survey.* Canadian Bureau for International Education.

Canadian Bureau for International Education (CBIE). (2018b). *International students in Canada.* Canadian Bureau for International Education.

Canadian Bureau for International Education (CBIE). (2019). *Annual report.* Retrieved from https://cbie.ca/who-we-are/annual-report/

Canadian Bureau for International Education. (2015). *Statement of Principles for Canadian Educational Institutions.* Retrieved from https://cbie.ca/wp-content/uploads/2016/06/Internationalization-Principles-for-Canadian-Institutions-EN.pdf

Canadian Bureau for International Education. (2016). A World of Learning: Canada's Performance and Potential in International Education. Canadian Bureau for International Education.

Canadian Bureau for International Education. (2018). *International students in Canada.* Retrieved from https://cbie.ca/wp-content/uploads/2018/09/International-Students-in-Canada-ENG.pdf

Canadian Bureau for International Education. (2018, March 16). *International students surpass 2022 goal.* https://cbie.ca/international-students-surpass-2022-goal/

Canadian Bureau for International Education. (2019). *A world of learning: Canada's performance and potential in international education 2019.* Retrieved from http://cbie.ca/what-we-do/research-publications/research-and-publications/#awol

Canadian Bureau for International Education. (2019). *Annual Report.* Retrieved from https://cbie.ca/wp-content/uploads/2019/11/CBIE-0299---AR-Eng.pdf

Canadian Bureau for International Education. (2019). *Another record year for Canadian international education.* https://cbie.ca/another-record-year-for-canadian-international-education/

Canadian Bureau for International Education. (2019). *International students in Canada.* Retrieved from https://cbie.ca/infographic/

Canadian Bureau for International Education. (2020). *International students in Canada.* Retrieved from https://cbie.ca/infographic/

Canadian Bureau of International Education. (2016). *A world of learning: Canada's performance and potential in international education.* Canadian Bureau of International Education.

Canadian Bureau of International Education. (2016). *A world of learning: Canada's performance and potential in international education.* Retrieved on 19/2/18 from http://net.cbie.ca/download/World-of-Learning-2016-EN.pdf

Canadian Bureau of International Education. (2016). *From permits to permanency: Supporting the international student in status transition*. Retrieved from https://cbie.ca/wp-content/uploads/2016/07/Immigration-RiB.pdf

Canadian Bureau of International Education. (2018). *International students in Canada*. Ottawa: CBIE. Retrieved from https://cbie.ca/wp-content/uploads/2018/09/International-Students-in-Canada-ENG.pdf

Canadian Bureau of International Education. (2018a). *Facts and figures*. Retrieved from https://cbie.ca/media/facts-and-figures/

Canadian Bureau of International Education. (2018b). *International students in Canada*. Retrieved from https://cbie.ca/wp-content/uploads/2018/09/International-Students-in-Canada-ENG.pdf

Canadian Bureau of International Education. (2018c). *The student's voice: National results of the 2018 CBIE international student survey*. Retrieved from https://cbie.ca/wp-content/uploads/2018/08/Student_Voice_Report-ENG.pdf

Canadian Bureau of International Education. (2018d). *A World of Learning: Canada's performance and potential in international education*. Retrieved from https://cbie.ca/wp-content/uploads/2018/04/Infographic-inbound-EN.pdf

Canadian Bureau of International Education. (2019). *International students in Canada: Where do inbound students come from?* Retrieved from https://cbie.ca/infographic/

Canadian Bureau of International Education. (2020). *International students in Canada continue to grow in 2019*. Retrieved from https://cbie.ca/international-students-in-canada-continue-to-grow-in-2019/

Canadian Federation of Students. (2012). *Funding for post-secondary education*. Retrieved from https://cfs-fcee.ca/wp-content/uploads/sites/2/2013/11/Fact-Sheet-Funding-2013-11-En.pdf

Cantarero, L., Espeitx, E., Gil Lacruz, M., & Martín, P. (2013). Human food preferences and cultural identity: The case of Aragón Spain. *International Journal of Psychology*, *48*(5), 881–890. doi:10.1080/00207594.2012.692792

Canterbury, D. C. (2005). *Neoliberal democratization and new authoritarianism*. Ashgate.

Cantwell, B. (2015). Are international students cash cows: Examining the relationship between new international undergraduate enrollments and institutional reviews at public colleges and universities in the US. *Journal of International Students*, *5*(4), 512–525.

Carlson, J. S., & Widaman, K. F. (1988). The effects of study abroad during college on attitudes toward other cultures. *International Journal of Intercultural Relations*, *12*(1), 1–17. doi:10.1016/0147-1767(88)90003-X

Carr, S. C. (2011). A global community psychology of mobility. *Intervención Psicosocial*, *20*(3), 319–325. doi:10.5093/in2011v20n3a8

Carter, A. (2016). Students learning English in Canada: Grounding decisions in evidence and lived experience. *Journal of Professional, Continuing, and Online Education*, *1*(1), 1–14. doi:10.18741/P93W2B

Centre for Applied Special Technology (CAST). (2020). http://www.cast.org/our-work/about-udl.html

Chagnon, J., & Milan, A. (2011). *Population growth: Canada, provinces, and territories, 2010*. Retrieved from https://www.statcan.gc.ca/pub/91-209-x/2011001/article/11508-eng.html

Chambliss, D. F., & Takacs, C. G. (2014). *How college works*. Harvard University Press. doi:10.4159/harvard.9780674726093

Champlin, R. (2019, October 16). *When college students want mental health help but get stuck waiting in line*. Vice Media Group. https://www.vice.com/en_ca/article/evjqwz/college-mental-health-center-wait-times

Chaoimh, E. N., & Sykes, B. (2012). *Mobile talent? The staying intentions of international students in five EU countries.* Retrieved from https://www.svr-migration.de/wp-content/uploads/2014/11/Study_Mobile_Talent_Engl.pdf

Chapman, M. P. (1999). The campus at the millennium: A plea for community and place. *Planning for Higher Education, 2,* 25–31.

Chapman, R. G. (1979). Pricing policy and the college choice process. *Research in Higher Education, 10*(1), 37–57. doi:10.1007/BF00977498

Charles-Toussaint, G. C., & Crowson, H. M. (2010). Prejudice against international students: The role of threat perceptions and authoritarian dispositions in U.S. students. *The Journal of Psychology, 144*(5), 413–428. doi:10.1080/00223 980.2010.496643 PMID:20806848

Charmaz, K. (2003). Qualitative interviewing and grounded theory analysis. In J. A. Holstein & J. F. Gubrium (Eds.), *Inside interviewing: New lenses, new concerns* (pp. 311–330). Sage.

Chavan, M. (2014). Alternative modes of teaching international business: Online experiential learning. In V. Taras & M. Gonzalez-Perez (Eds.), *The handbook of experiential learning in international business* (pp. 202–222). Palgrave Macmillan.

Chen, C. Y. (2010). Graduate students' self-reported perspectives regarding peer feedback and feedback from writing consultants. *Asia Pacific Education Review, 11*(2), 151–158. doi:10.100712564-010-9081-5

Cheng, L., & Fox, J. (2008). Towards a better understanding of academic acculturation: Second language students in Canadian universities. *Canadian Modern Language Review. Canadian Modern Language Review, 65*(2), 307–333. doi:10.3138/cmlr.65.2.307

Cheng, L., Myles, J., & Curtis, A. (2004). Targeting language support for non-native English-speaking graduate students at a Canadian university. *TESL Canada Journal, 21*(2), 50–71. doi:10.18806/tesl.v21i2.174

Cheng, L., Wu, Y., & Liu, X. (2015). Chinese university students' perceptions of assessment tasks and classroom assessment environment. *Language Testing in Asia, 5*(13), 1–17. doi:10.118640468-015-0020-6

Cheng, R., & Erben, A. (2012). Language anxiety: Experiences of Chinese graduate students at US higher institutions. *Journal of Studies in International Education, 16*(5), 477–497. doi:10.1177/1028315311421841

Chen, J. A., Liu, L., Zhao, X., & Yeung, A. S. (2015). Chinese international students: An emerging mental health crisis. *Journal of the American Academy of Child and Adolescent Psychiatry, 54*(11), 879–880. doi:10.1016/j.jaac.2015.06.022 PMID:26506576

Chen, L. (2007). East-Asian students' choice of Canadian graduate schools. *International Journal of Educational Advancement, 7*(3), 271–306. doi:10.1057/palgrave.ijea.2150071

Chen, Y., & Van Ullen, M. K. (2011). Helping international students succeed academically through research process and plagiarism workshops. *College & Research Libraries, 72*(3), 209–235. doi:10.5860/crl-117rl

Cheung, L. (2018). *Understanding imposter phenomenon in graduate students using achievement goal theory.* Unpublished manuscript, Graduate School of Education. Fordham University.

Chiose, S. (2016, Mar. 31). International student work program creating low-wage work force: report. *The Globe and Mail.* Retrieved from https://www.theglobeandmail.com/news/national/international-student-work-program-needs-overhaul-report-says/article29463566/

Chira, S. (2016). *In a class of their own: International students, class identity and education migration in Atlantic Canada* [Doctoral dissertation, Dalhousie University]. DalSpace. http://hdl.handle.net/10222/72176

Chittum, J. R., & Bryant, L. H. (2014). Reviewing to learn: Graduate student participation in the professional peer-review process to improve academic writing skills. *International Journal of Teaching and Learning in Higher Education, 26*(3), 473-484. Retrieved from http://www.isetl.org/ijtlhe/

Choudaha, R., & Schulmann, P. (2014). Bridging the gap: Recruitment and retention to improve student experiences. Washington, DC: NAFSA: Association of International Educators.

Choy, Y., & Alon, Z. (2019). The comprehensive mental health treatment of Chinese international students: A case report. *Journal of College Student Psychotherapy, 33*(1), 47–66. doi:10.1080/87568225.2018.1427513

Chua, A. Y. K. (2014). Expectations, dispositions, and experiences of international graduate students. Handbook of Research on Education and Technology in a Changing Society. doi:10.4018/978-1-4666-6046-5

Cigdem, H. N. (2017). *Former English language learners: A case study of the perceived influence of developmental English programs on academic achievement and retention.* Retrieved from https://search.proquest.com/docview/1896654315

Citizenship and Immigration Canada. (2017). *Economic impact of international education in Canada: 2017 update.* https://www.international.gc.ca/education/report-rapport/impact-2017/index.aspx

Civinini, C. (2018). Canada threatens to overtake UK as top study destination – QS. *PIE News.* https://thepienews.com/news/canada-threatens-to-overtake-uk-as-top-study-destination-qs/

Cleveland, M., Laroche, M., Pons, F., & Kastoun, R. (2009). Acculturation and consumption: Textures of cultural adaptation. *International Journal of Intercultural Relations, 33*(3), 196–212. doi:10.1016/j.ijintrel.2008.12.008

Cleveland, M., & Xu, C. (2019). Multifaceted acculturation in multiethnic settings. *Journal of Business Research, 103*, 250–260. doi:10.1016/j.jbusres.2019.01.051

Coffey, R., & Perry, M. (2013). *The role of education agents in Canada's education systems.* Council of ministers of education, Canada. Retrieved from https://www.cmec.ca/Publications/Lists/Publications/Attachments/326/The-Role-of-Education-Agents-EN.pdf

Colleges and Institutes Canada. (n.d.). *What we do.* Retrieved from https://www.collegesinstitutes.ca/

Connor, U. (2004). Intercultural rhetoric research: Beyond texts. *Journal of English for Academic Purposes, 3*(4), 291–304. doi:10.1016/j.jeap.2004.07.003

Copyleaks. (n.d.). *What is plagiarism?* Retrieved from https://copyleaks.com/education/what-is-plagiarism

Corradetti, C. (2011). The Frankfurt school and critical theory. In *Internet Encyclopedia of Philosophy (IEP).* European Academy and the University of Rome Italy. Retrieved from https://www.iep.utm.edu/frankfur/

Crace, A. (2017). Canada best and worst in IAJN international alumni satisfaction report. *PIE News.* https://thepienews.com/news/canada-best-and-worst-in-iajn-graduate-satisfaction-report/

Crace, A. (2019). Political rhetoric is "substantial barrier" to int'l grad employment – report. *PIE News.* https://thepienews.com/news/politics-employer-barrier-employment/

Cranfield, J. (2012). The changing landscape of the Canadian food market: Ethnicity and the market for ethnic food. *Canadian Journal of Agricultural Economics, 61*(1), 1–13. doi:10.1111/cjag.12000

Creswell, J. W. (2007). *Qualitative inquiry and research design: Choosing among five approaches.* Sage.

Creswell, J. W. (2007). *Qualitative inquiry and research design: Choosing among five traditions* (2nd ed.). Sage.

Creswell, J. W. (2012). *Educational research: Planning, conduction, and evaluating quantitative and qualitative research* (4th ed.). Pearson Education.

Creswell, J. W. (2013). *Qualitative inquiry & research design: choosing among five approaches.* Sage.

Creswell, J. W. (2013). *Qualitative inquiry and research design: Choosing from five approaches.* SAGE Publications.

Cronbach, L. J. (1951). Coefficient alpha and the internal structure of test. *Psychometrika, 16*(3), 297–324. doi:10.1007/BF02310555

Cubillo, J., Sánchez, J., & Cerviño, J. (2006). International students' decision-making process. *International Journal of Educational Management, 20*(2), 101–115. doi:10.1108/09513540610646091

Cudmore, G. (2005). Globalization, internationalization, and the recruitment of international students in higher education, and in the Ontario colleges of applied arts & technology. *Canadian Journal of Higher Education, 35*(1), 37–60.

Dalton, J. C. (1999). The significance of international issues and responsibilities in the contemporary work of student affairs. *New Directions for Student Services, 86*(86), 3–11. doi:10.1002s.8601

Datig, I. (2014). What is a library?: International college students' perceptions of libraries. *Journal of Academic Librarianship, 40*(3–4), 350–356. doi:10.1016/j.acalib.2014.05.001

Davis, B., Fedeli, M., & Coryell, J. E. (2019). International experiences to increase employability for education doctoral students. A comparative study. *New Directions for Adult and Continuing Education, 2019*(163), 147–161. doi:10.1002/ace.20348

Davis, L. (2011). Arresting student plagiarism: Are we investigators or educators? *Business Communication Quarterly, 74*(2), 160–163. doi:10.1177/1080569911404053

De Wit, H. (2019). Dutch cuts to internationalization send the wrong message. *Inside Higher Ed.* https://www.inside-highered.com/blogs/world-view/dutch-cuts-internationalization-send-wrong-message

Deardorff, D. K., Goodman, A. E., Charles, H., & Gee, E. G. (2018). *Leading internationalization: A handbook for international education leaders.* Stylus Publishing.

Debdi, O., Paredes-Velasco, M., & Velázquez-Iturbide, J. Á. (2016). Influence of pedagogic approaches and learning styles on motivation and educational efficiency of computer science students. *IEEE Revista Iberoamericana de Tecnologias del Aprendizaje, 11*(3), 213–218. doi:10.1109/RITA.2016.2590638

Deci, E. L., & Ryan, R. M. (2002). *Handbook of self-determination research.* University Rochester Press.

Del Fabbro, L., Mitchell, C., & Shaw, J. (2015). Learning among nursing faculty: Insights from a participatory action research project about teaching international students. *The Journal of Nursing Education, 54*(3), 153–158. PMID:25693177

Denzin, N. (2011). The politics of evidence. In N. K. Denzin & Y. S. Lincoln (Eds.), *The Sage handbook of qualitative research* (pp. 97–128). Sage.

Denzin, N., & Lincoln, Y. (2011). *The Sage handbook of qualitative research.* Sage.

Desai-Trilokekar, R., Thomson, K., & El Masri, A. (2016). *International students as "ideal" immigrants: Ontario employers' perspective.* Academic Press.

Desai-Trilokekar, R., & El Masri, A. (2016). Canada's international education strategy: Implications of a new policy landscape for synergy between government policy and institutional strategy. *Higher Education Policy, 29*(4), 539–563. doi:10.105741307-016-0017-5

Desai-Trilokekar, R., & Kizilbash, Z. (2013). Imagine: Canada as a leader in international education. How can Canada benefit from the Australian experience? *Canadian Journal of Higher Education, 43*(2), 1–26.

Dhindsa, H., Omar, K., & Waldrip, B. (2007). Upper Secondary Bruneian Science Students' Perceptions of Assessment. *International Journal of Science Education, 29*(10), 1261–1280. doi:10.1080/09500690600991149

Dietrich, J. W., & Olson, C. (2010). In quest of meaningful assessment of international learning: The development and implementation of a student survey and e-portfolio. *The Journal of General Education, 59*(3), 143–158. https://muse.jhu.edu/. doi:10.1353/jge.2010.0015

Dietsche, P., & Lees, J. (2017). *Insight into Canadian post-secondary career service models: Final report.* Retrieved from https://ceric.ca/project/insight-into-canadian-post-secondary-career-service-models/

Dimitrov, N., Dawson, D. L., Olsen, K. C., & Meadows, K. N. (2014). Developing the intercultural competence of graduate students. *Canadian Journal of Higher Education, 44*(3), 86–103. https://www.tru.ca/__.../Nanda_Dimitrov_Developing_Intercultural_Co

Dimitrov, N., & Haque, A. (2016). Intercultural teaching competence: A multidisciplinary model for instructor reflection. *Intercultural Education, 27*(5), 437–456. doi:10.1080/14675986.2016.1240502

Dixon, S. (2018). The relevance of spirituality to cultural identity reconstruction for African-Caribbean immigrant women. In N. Arthur (Ed.), *Counselling in cultural contexts: Identities and social justice* (pp. 249–270). Springer Nature. doi:10.1007/978-3-030-00090-5_11

Doran, L. M. (2017). *A case study of adjunct faculty: Community and collegial support.* Available from Dissertations & Theses @ University of Phoenix; ProQuest Central; ProQuest Dissertations & Theses Global. (2019629158). Retrieved from https://search.proquest.com/docview/2019629158?accountid=35812

Dorman, J. P., & Knightley, W. M. (2006). Development and validation of an instrument to assess secondary school students' perceptions of assessment tasks. *Educational Studies, 32*(1), 47–58. doi:10.1080/03055690500415951

Dreher, A., & Poutvaara, P. (2005). *Student flows and migration: An empirical analysis.* Discussion Paper series. IZA.

Dunlosky, J. (2013). Strengthening the student toolbox: Study strategies to boost learning. *American Educator, 37*(3), 12–21.

Dunlosky, J., Rawson, K., Marsh, E., Nathan, M., & Willingham, D. (2013). Improving students' learning with effective learning techniques: Promising directions from cognitive and educational psychology. *Psychological Science in the Public Interest, 14*(1), 4–58. doi:10.1177/1529100612453266 PMID:26173288

Durkheim, E. (1951). *Suicide: A study in sociology.* Routledge.

Du, X. (2019). International students' daily negotiations in language, culture, and identity in Canadian higher education. In M. T. Kariwo, N. Asadi, & C. E. Bouhali (Eds.), *Interrogating models of diversity within a multicultural environment* (pp. 275–297). Springer International Publishing AG. doi:10.1007/978-3-030-03913-4_14

Dwyer, M., & Peters, C. (2004). The benefits of study abroad. *Transitions Abroad, 27*(5), 56–57.

Eaglestone, R. (2002). *Doing English: A guide for literature students.* Routledge. doi:10.4324/9780203025437

Easley, J., & Tulowitzki, P. (2013). Policy formation of intercultural and globally minded educational leadership preparation. *International Journal of Education, 27*(7), 744–761. doi:10.1108/IJEM-04-2012-0050

Eder, J., Smith, W., & Pitts, R. (2010). Exploring factors influencing student study abroad destination choice. *Journal of Teaching in Travel & Tourism, 10*(3), 232–250. doi:10.1080/15313220.2010.503534

Edgerton, J. D., & Roberts, L. W. (2014). Cultural capital or habitus? Bourdieu and beyond in the explanation of enduring educational inequality. *Theory and Research in Education, 12*(2), 193–200. doi:10.1177/1477878514530231

El Masri, A., Choubak, M., & Litchmore, R. (2015). *The global competition for international students as future immigrants: The role of Ontario universities in translating government policy into institutional practice.* Retrieved from http://www.heqco.ca/SiteCollectionDocuments/Global%20Competition%20for%20IS%20ENG.pdf

El-Khawas, E. (2003). The many dimensions of student diversity. In D. B. S. R. Komives (Ed.), *Students services: A handbook for the profession* (4th ed., pp. 45–62). Jossey-Bass.

Elliot, D., Reid, K., & Baumfield, V. (2016). Beyond the amusement, puzzlement and challenges: An enquiry into international students' academic acculturation. *Studies in Higher Education, 41*(12), 2198–2217. doi:10.1080/030750 79.2015.1029903

Elliott, C. J., & Reynolds, M. (2014). Participative pedagogies, group work and the international classroom: An account of students' and tutors' experiences. *Studies in Higher Education, 39*(2), 307–320. doi:10.1080/03075079.2012.709492

Ellis, R. (2009). Measuring implicit and explicit knowledge of a second language. In R. Ellis, S. Loewen, C. Elder, R. Erlam, J. Philp, & H. Reinders (Eds.), *Implicit and explicit Knowledge in second language learning, testing and teaching* (pp. 31–64). Multilingual Matters. doi:10.21832/9781847691767-004

Eraut, M. (2004). Informal learning in the workplace. *Studies in Continuing Education, 26*(2), 247–273. doi:10.1080/158037042000225245

Eshach, H. (2007). Bridging in-school and out-of-school learning: Formal, non-formal, and informal education. *Journal of Science Education and Technology, 16*(2), 171–190. doi:10.100710956-006-9027-1

Esses, V., Sutter, A., Ortiz, A., Luo, N., Cui, J., & Deacon, L. (2018). *Retaining international students in Canada post-graduation: Understanding the motivations and drivers of the decision to stay.* Retrieved from https://cbie.ca/wp-content/uploads/2018/06/Intl-students-post-graduation-RiB-8-EN-1.pdf

Evering, L. C., & Moorman, G. (2012). Rethinking plagiarism in the Digital Age. *Journal of Adolescent & Adult Literacy, 56*(1), 35–44. doi:10.1002/JAAL.00100

Faiza, O. (2015). *Building rapport between international graduate students and their faculty advisors: Cross cultural mentoring relationships at the University of Guelph* (Unpublished master's thesis). University of Guelph, Guelph, Canada.

Farahbakhsh, J., Hanbazaza, M., Ball, G. D., Farmer, A. P., Maximova, K., & Willows, N. D. (2017). Food insecure student clients of a university-based food bank have compromised health, dietary intake and academic quality. *Nutrition & Dietetics: the Journal of the Dietitians Association of Australia, 74*(1), 67–73. doi:10.1111/1747-0080.12307

Fatemi, G., & Saito, E. (2019). Unintentional plagiarism and academic integrity: The challenges and needs of postgraduate international students in Australia. *Journal of Further and Higher Education*, 1–15. Advance online publication. do i:10.1080/0309877X.2019.1683521

Fei, W. F., Siong, L. K., Kim, L. S., & Yaacob, A. (2012). English use as an identity marker among Malaysian undergraduates. *3L. The Southeast Asian Journal of English Language Studies, 18*(1), 145–155.

Felder, R. M., & Spurlin, J. (2005). Applications reliability and validity of the index of learning styles. *International Journal of Engineering Education, 21*(1), 103–112.

Findlay, A. M., King, R., Smith, F. M., Geddes, A., & Skeldon, R. (2012). World class? An investigation of globalisation, difference and international student mobility. *Transactions of the Institute of British Geographers, 37*(1), 118–131. doi:10.1111/j.1475-5661.2011.00454.x

Firth, C., Maye, D., & Pearson, D. (2011). Developing "community" in community gardens. *Local Environment, 16*(6), 555–568. doi:10.1080/13549839.2011.586025

Fisher, D. L., Waldrip, B. G., & Dorman, J. P. (2005). *Student perceptions of assessment: Development and validation of a questionnaire.* Paper presented at the annual meeting of the American Educational Research Association, Montreal, Canada.

Fisher, D., & Rubenson, K. (1998). *The changing political economy: The private and public lives of Canadian universities. In Universities and Globalization: Critical Perspectives.* Sage Publications Inc.

Flint, T. A. (1992). Parental and planning influences on the formation of student college choice sets. *Research in Higher Education, 33*(6), 689–708. doi:10.1007/BF00992054

Flynn, W. J., & Vredevoogd, J. (2010). The future of learning: 12 views on emerging trends in higher education. *Planning for Higher Education, 38*(2), 4–10.

FoodArch. (2020, March 10). *Our approach: Food Security.* Retrieved from https://foodarc.ca/our-approach-food-security/

Foreign Affairs, Trade and Development Canada. (2014). *Canada's international education strategy: Harnessing our knowledge advantage to drive innovation and prosperity* (No. FR5-86/2014). Retrieved from https://international.gc.ca/global-markets-marches-mondiaux/assets/pdfs/overview-apercu-eng.pdf

Forgie, S. E., Yonge, O., & Luth, R. (2018). Centres for teaching and learning across Canada: What's going on? *The Canadian Journal for the Scholarship of Teaching and Learning, 9*(1), 1–18. doi:10.5206/cjsotl-rcacea.2018.1.9

Foster, K. D., & Stapleton, D. M. (2012). Understanding Chinese students' learning needs in western business classrooms. *International Journal on Teaching and Learning in Higher Education, 24*(3), 301–313.

Foster, M. (2014). Student destination choices in higher education: Exploring attitudes of Brazilian students to study in the United Kingdom. *Journal of Research in International Education, 13*(2), 149–162. doi:10.1177/1475240914541024

Fovet, F. (2019). Not just about disability: Getting traction for UDL implement with International Students. In K. Novak & S. Bracken (Eds.), *Transforming higher education through universal design for learning: An international perspective* (pp. 179–200). Routedge. doi:10.4324/9781351132077-11

Fox, H. (1994). *Listening to the world: Cultural issues in academic writing.* National Council of Teachers in English.

Fox, J., Cheng, L., & Zumbo, B. (2014). Do they make a difference? The impact of English language programs on second language students in Canadian universities. *TESOL Quarterly, 48*(1), 57–85. doi:10.1002/tesq.103

Fox, R., & Ronkowski, S. (1997). Learning styles of political science students. *PS, Political Science & Politics, 30*(4), 732–737. doi:10.1017/S1049096500047363

Freire, P. (2000). Pedagogy of the oppressed (30th anniversary ed.). New York: Continuum.

Freire, P. (2005). Teachers as cultural workers: Letters to those who dare teach (Expanded ed.). Boulder, CO: Westview Press.

Freire, P., & Macedo, D. P. (1987). *Literacy: Reading the word & the world.* Bergin & Garvey.

Frenette, M., Lu, Y., & Chan, W. (2019). *The postsecondary experience and early labour market outcomes of international study permit holders.* Retrieved from https://www150.statcan.gc.ca/n1/en/pub/11f0019m/11f0019m2019019-eng.pdf?st=U-s22c6O

Frey, J., & Fontana, A. (1993). The group interview in social research. In D. L. Morgan (Ed.), *Successful focus groups* (pp. 20–34). Sage. doi:10.4135/9781483349008.n2

Fritz, M. V., Chin, D., & DeMarini, D. (2008). Stressors, anxiety, acculturation and adjustment among international and North American students. *International Journal on Teaching and Learning in Higher Education, 24*(3), 301–313. doi:10.1016/j.ijintrel.2008.01.001

Fu, J. (2018). *The role of two extracurricular programs in international students' informal learning experiences in Atlantic Canada* (Unpublished master's thesis). Mount Saint Vincent University, Halifax, Canada.

Fu, J. (2018). *The role of two extracurricular programs in international students' informal learning experiences in Atlantic Canada* [Master's thesis, Mount Saint Vincent University]. E-commons. http://hdl.handle.net/10587/1932

Gal, A. M. (2020, January 18). The road less travelled to the internationalisation of HE. *University World News, 581*. Retrieved from https://www.universityworldnews.com /post.php?story=2020011308103575

Gale, T., & Parker, S. (2014). Navigating change: A typology of student transition in higher education. *Studies in Higher Education, 39*(5), 734–753. doi:10.1080/03075079.2012.721351

Gallagher, M. (2016). Sound as affect: Difference, power and spatiality. *Emotion, Space and Society, 20*, 42–48. doi:10.1016/j.emospa.2016.02.004

Gallant, K., & Tirone, S. (2017). A 'good life without bells and whistles': a case study of immigrants' wellbeing and leisure and its role in social sustainability in Truro, Nova Scotia. *Leisure/Loisir, 41*(3), 423-442.

Galway, A. D. (2000). *Going global: Ontario colleges of applied arts and technology, international student recruitment and the export of education.* Ontario Institute for Studies in Education, University of Toronto.

Gao, L. (2012). Investigating ESL graduate students' intercultural experiences of academic English writing: A first-person narration of a streamlined qualitative study process. *Qualitative Report, 17*(24), 1–25. http://www.nova.edu/ssss/QR/QR17/gao.pdf

Gao, M. (2012). Classroom assessments in mathematics: High school students' perceptions. *International Journal of Business and Social Science, 3*, 63–68.

Gao, Y. (2019). Experiences of Chinese international doctoral students in Canada who withdrew: A narrative inquiry. *International Journal of Doctoral Studies, 14*(1), 259–276.

Garber, G., Berg, E., & Chester-Fangman, C. (2017). Rethinking plagiarism in information literacy instruction: A case study on cross-campus collaboration in the creation of an online academic honesty video tutorial. In T. Maddison & M. Kumaran (Eds.), *Distributed learning: Pedagogy and technology in online information literacy instruction* (pp. 341–360). Chandos Publishing. doi:10.1016/B978-0-08-100598-9.00019-2

Gareis, E. (2012). Intercultural friendship: Effects of home and host region. *Journal of Intercultural and International Communication, 5*(4), 309–328. doi:10.1080/17513057.2012.691525

Gareis, E., & Jalayer, A. (2018). Contact effects on intercultural friendship between east Asian students and American domestic students. In Y. Ma & M. A. Garcia-Murillo (Eds.), *Understanding international students from Asia in American Universities* (pp. 83–106). Springer International. doi:10.1007/978-3-319-60394-0_5

Gavan, P., Watson, L., & Kenny, N. (2014). Teaching critical reflection to graduate students. *Collected Essays on Learning and Teaching, 7*(1), 56-61. Retrieved from www.gavan.ca/wp-content/uploads/2014/01/Academic-Vitae.pdf

Gerber, B., Marek, E., & Cavallo, A. (2001). Development of an informal learning opportunities assay. *International Journal of Science Education, 23*(6), 569–583. doi:10.1080/09500690116959

Gershon, W. S. (2013). Vibrational affect: Sound theory and practice in qualitative research. *Cultural Studies ↔ Critical Methodologies, 13*(4), 257-262.

Gershon, W. S., & Van Deventer, G. (2013). The story of a poet who beat cancer and became a squeak: A sounded narrative about art, education, and the power of the human spirit. *Journal of Curriculum and Pedagogy, 10*(2), 96–105. doi:10.1080/15505170.2013.782593

Ghazarian, P. G. (2014). Actual vs. ideal attraction: Trends in the mobility of Korean international students. *Journal of International Studies, 4*(1). https://jistudents.org/fall2014vol41/

Giroux, H. (2010). Public values, higher education and the scourge of neoliberalism: Politics at the limits of the social. *Culture Machine*. Retrieved from https://www.culturemachine.net/index.php/cm/article/view/426/444

Glaser, B., & Strauss, A. (1967). *The discovery of grounded theory: Strategies for qualitative research*. Aldine.

Glass, C. R., Kociolek, E., Wongtrirat, R., Lynch, R. J., & Cong, S. (2015). Uneven experiences: The impact of student-faculty interactions on international students' sense of belonging. *Journal of International Students, 5*(4), 353–367.

Gleazer, E. J. (1980). *The community college: Values, vision and vitality*. American Association of Community and Junior Colleges.

Global Affairs Canada. (2014). *Canada's international education strategy*. Retrieved fromhttp://international.gc.ca/global-markets-marches-mondiaux/assets/pdfs/overview-apercu-eng.pdf

Global Affairs Canada. (2018). *Economic impact of international education in Canada –2017 update*. Retrieved on 24/3/18 from http://www.international.gc.ca/education/report- rapport/impact-2017/toc-tdm.aspx?lang=eng

Goodboy, A., Martin, M., & Johnson, Z. (2015). The relationships between workplace bullying by graduate faculty with graduate Students: Burnout and organizational citizenship behaviours. *Communication Research Reports, 32*(3), 272–280. doi:10.1080/08824096.2015.1052904

Gopal, A. (2011). Internationalization of higher education: Preparing faculty to teach cross-culturally. *International Journal on Teaching and Learning in Higher Education, 23*(3), 373–381.

Gopal, A. (2016). Visa and immigration trends: A comparative examination of international student mobility in Canada, Australia, the United Kingdom, and the United States. *Strategic Enrollment Management Quarterly, 4*(3), 130–141. doi:10.1002em3.20091

Gopal, A. (2017). Canada, US and UK: Canada's immigration policies to attract international students. In *Understanding higher education internationalization* (pp. 231–233). Sense Publishers. doi:10.1007/978-94-6351-161-2_50

Government of Alberta. (2019). Budget 2019. Fiscal plan: A plan for jobs and the economy. Edmonton, Canada.

Government of Alberta. (2020). Budget 2020. Fiscal plan: A plan for jobs and the economy. Edmonton, Canada.

Government of Canada. (2012, October 19). *Canadian multiculturalism: An inclusive citizenship*. Retrieved from https://web.archive.org/web/20140312210113/http://www.cic.gc.ca/english/multiculturalism/citizenship.asp

Government of Canada. (2014). *Canada's international education strategy: Harnessing our knowledge advantage to drive innovation and prosperity* (Cat. No.: FR5-86/2014). http://international.gc.ca/global-markets-marchesmondiaux/assets/pdfs/overview-apercu-eng.pdf

Government of Canada. (2014). *Canada's international education strategy: Harnesssing our knowledge advantage to drive innovation and prosperity.* Ottawa, ON: Government of Canada Retrieved from https://international.gc.ca/global-markets-marches-mondiaux/assets/pdfs/overview-apercu-eng.pdf

Government of Canada. (2018). *Economic impact of international education in Canada – 2017.* Retrieved from https://www.international.gc.ca/education/report-rapport/impact-2017/index.aspx?lang=eng

Government of Canada. (2019). *Building on Success: Canada's International Education Strategy (2019-2024).* Ottawa, ON: Government of Canada Retrieved from https://www.international.gc.ca/education/strategy-2019-2024-strategie.aspx?lang=eng

Government of Canada. (2019). *Building on success: International education strategy: 2019-2024.* Retrieved from https://www.international.gc.ca/education/assets/pdfs/ies-sei/Building-on-Success-International-Education-Strategy-2019-2024.pdf

Government of Canada. (2020a). *Immigration and citizenship.* Retrieved from https://www.canada.ca/en/immigration-refugees-citizenship/services/study-canada/work/work- off-campus.html#hours

Government of Canada. (2020b). *Immigration and citizenship.* Retrieved from https://www.canada.ca/en/immigration-refugees-citizenship/news/notices/pgwpp-rules- covid19.html

Grant, T., & Balkissoon, D. (2019, February 6). *Visible minority: Is it time for Canada to scrap the term?* The Globe and Mail. https://www.theglobeandmail.com/canada/article-visible-minority-term-statscan/

Grayson, J. (2011). Cultural capital and academic achievement of first generation domestic and international students in Canadian universities. *British Educational Research Journal, 37*(4), 605–630.

Grayson, J. P. (2008). The experiences and outcomes of domestic and international students at four Canadian universities. *Higher Education Research & Development, 27*(3), 215–230. doi:10.1080/07294360802183788

Green, M. F. (2014). The best in the world: Not in internationalization. *Trends & Insights: For International Education Leaders.* Retrieved from http://www.nafsa.org/Explore_International_Education /Trends/TI/The_Best_in_the_World_Not_in_Internationalization/

Greene, B. A., Miller, R. B., Crowson, H. M., Duke, B. L., & Akey, K. L. (2004). Predicting high school students' cognitive engagement and achievement: Contributions of classroom perceptions and motivation. *Contemporary Educational Psychology, 29*(4), 462–482. doi:10.1016/j.cedpsych.2004.01.006

Greene, M., & Kirby, D. (2012). The impact of tuition fees on access and student migration: Lessons from Canada's Atlantic coast. *Widening Participation and Lifelong Learning: the Journal of the Institute for Access Studies and the European Access Network, 14*(2), 72–90. doi:10.5456/WPLL.14.1.72

Greenleaf, C. L., & Katz, M.-L. (2004). Ever new ways to mean: Authoring pedagogical change in secondary subject-area classrooms. In A. F. Ball & S. W. Freedman (Eds.), *Bakhtinian perspectives on language, literacy, and learning* (pp. 172–202). Cambridge University Press. doi:10.1017/CBO9780511755002.009

Grez, L. D., Valcke, M., & Roozen, I. (2012). How effective are self- and peer assessment of oral presentation skills compared with teachers' assessments? *Active Learning in Higher Education, 13*(2), 129–142. doi:10.1177/1469787412441284

Groen, J., & Kawalilak, C. (2014). *Pathways of adult learning: Professional and education narratives.* Canadian Scholars' Press.

Guest, G., Bunce, A., & Johnson, L. (2006). How many interviews are enough? An experiment with data saturation and variability. *Field Methods, 18*(1), 59–82. doi:10.1177/1525822X05279903

Gulikers, J. T., Bastiaens, T. J., Kirschner, P. A., & Kester, L. (2008). Authenticity is in the eye of the beholder: Student and teacher perceptions of assessment authenticity. *Journal of Vocational Education and Training*, *60*(4), 401–412. doi:10.1080/13636820802591830

Guo, S., & Chase, M. (2011). Internationalization of higher education: Integrating international students into Canadian academic environment. *Teaching in Higher Education*, *16*(3), 305–318. doi:10.1080/13562517.2010.546524

Guo, Y., & Guo, S. (2017). Internationalization of Canadian higher education: Discrepancies between policies and international student experiences. *Studies in Higher Education*, *42*(5), 851–868.

Gu, Q. (2009). Maturity and interculturality: Chinese students' experiences in UK higher education. *European Journal of Education*, *44*(1), 37–52. doi:10.1111/j.1465-3435.2008.01369.x

Gu, Q., Schweisfurth, M., & Day, C. (2010). Learning and growing in a "foreign" context: Intercultural experiences of international students. *Compare: A Journal of Comparative Education*, *40*(1), 7–23. doi:10.1080/03057920903115983

Habib, L., Johannsen, M., & Ogrim, L. (2014). Experiences and challenges of international students in technology-rich learning environments. *Journal of Educational Technology & Society*, *17*(2), 196–206.

Hail, H. C. (2015). Patriotism abroad: Overseas Chinese students' encounters with criticisms of China. *Journal of Studies in International Education*, *19*(4), 311–326. doi:10.1177/1028315314567175

Hanassab, S. (2006). Diversity, international students, and perceived discrimination: Implications for educators and counselors. *Journal of Studies in International Education*, *10*(2), 157–172. doi:10.1177/1028315305283051

Hanbazaza, M., Ball, G. D., Farmer, A. P., Maximova, K., Farahbakhsh, J., & Willows, N. D. (2017). A comparison of characteristics and food insecurity coping strategies between international and domestic postsecondary students using a food bank located on a university campus. *Canadian Journal of Dietetic Practice and Researc*, *78*(4), 208–211. doi:10.3148/cjdpr-2017-012

Han, J. (2012). Information literacy challenges for Chinese PhD students in Australia: A biographical study. *Journal of Information Literacy*, *6*(1), 3–17. doi:10.11645/6.1.1603

Han, X., Han, X., Luo, Q., Jacobs, S., & Jean-Baptiste, M. (2013). Report of a mental health survey among Chinese international students at Yale University. *Journal of American College Health*, *61*(1), 1–8. doi:10.1080/07448481.2012.738267 PMID:23305539

Harman, G. (2005). Internationalization of Australian higher education: A critical review of literature and research. In P. Ninnes & M. Hellsten (Eds.), *Internationalizing higher education: Critical explorations of pedagogy and policy* (pp. 119–140). Comparative Education Research Centre. doi:10.1007/1-4020-3784-8_7

Harrison, H., Birks, M., Franklin, R., & Mills, J. (2017). Case Study Research: Foundations and Methodological Orientations. *Forum Qualitative Social Research*, *18*(1), 19.

Harris, R. (2011). The knowledge-based economy intellectual origins and new economic perspectives. *International Journal of Management Reviews*, *3*(1), 21–40. doi:10.1111/1468-2370.00052

Harumi, S. (2010). Classroom silence: Voices from Japanese EFL learners. *English Language Teaching Journal*, *65*(1), 1–10.

Harvey, D. (2007). Neoliberalism as creative destruction. *A Journal on Integrated Management of Occupational Health and the Environment*, *2*(4), 137-154.

Harvey, D. (2005). *A brief history of neoliberalism*. Oxford University Press.

Harvey, D., Ling, C., & Shehab, R. (2010). Comparison of student's learning style in STEM disciplines. *IIE Annual Conference Proceedings*, 1-6.

Hattangadi, N., Vogel, E., Carroll, L. J., & Côté, P. (2019). "Everybody I know is always hungry... But nobody asks why": University students, food insecurity and mental health. *Sustainability*, *11*(6), 1571. doi:10.3390u11061571

Hawkins, M. R. (2005). Becoming a student: Identity work and academic literacies in early schooling. *TESOL Quarterly*, *39*(1), 59–82. doi:10.2307/3588452

Hawthorne, L. (2010). Two-step migration: Australia's experience. *POLICY, 39*.

Hawthorne, L. (2012). Designer immigrants? International students and two-step migration. In D. K. Deardorff, H. de Wit, J. D. Heyl, & T. Adams (Eds.), *The SAGE handbook of international higher education* (pp. 417–435). SAGE. doi:10.4135/9781452218397.n23

Hawthorne, L., & To, A. (2014). Australian employer response to the study-migration pathway: The quantitative evidence 2007-2011. *International Migration (Geneva, Switzerland)*, *52*(3), 99–115. doi:10.1111/imig.12154

Hayek, F. A. (1944). *The road to serfdom*. Routledge.

Hayes, N., & Introna, L. D. (2005). Cultural values, plagiarism, and fairness: When plagiarism gets in the way of learning. *Ethics & Behavior*, *15*(3), 213–231. doi:10.120715327019eb1503_2

Hayward, L. (2012). Assessment and learning: The learner's perspective. In J. Gardner (Ed.), *Assessment and Learning* (pp. 125–139). SAGE Publications Ltd. doi:10.4135/9781446250808.n8

Hechanova-Alampay, R., Beehr, T. A., Christiansen, N. D., & Van Horn, R. K. (2002). Adjustment and strain among domestic and international student sojourners: A longitudinal study. *School Psychology International*, *23*(4), 458–474. doi:10.1177/0143034302234007

Hegarty, N. (2014). Where we are now – the presence and importance of international students to universities in the United States. *Journal of International Students*, *4*(3). https://jistudents.org/2014-volume-43/

Hegarty, N. (2014). Where we are now-The presence and importance of international students to universities in the United States. *Journal of International Students*, *4*(3), 223–235.

Heller, D. E. (2002). *Condition of access: Higher education for lower income students*. American Council on Education and Praeger Publishers.

Hemsley-Brown, J., & Oplatka, I. (2006). Universities in a competitive global marketplace: A systematic review of the literature on higher education marketing. *International Journal of Public Sector Management*, *19*(4), 316–338. doi:10.1108/09513550610669176

Hendrickson, B., Rosen, D., & Aune, R. (2011). An analysis of friendship networks, social connectedness, homesickness, and satisfaction levels of international students. *International Journal of Intercultural Relations*, *35*(3), 281–295. doi:10.1016/j.ijintrel.2010.08.001

Heng, T. T. (2017). Voices of Chinese international students in USA colleges: 'I want to tell them that ... '. *Studies in Higher Education*, *42*(5), 833–850. doi:10.1080/03075079.2017.1293873

Heng, T. T. (2018). Different is not deficient: Contradicting stereotypes of Chinese international students in US higher education. *Studies in Higher Education*, *43*(1), 22–36. doi:10.1080/03075079.2016.1152466

Henry, F., Dua, E., James, C. E., Kobayashi, A., Li, P., Ramos, H., & Smith, M. S. (2017). *The equity myth: Racialization and indigeneity at Canadian Universities*. UBC Press.

Hentz, P. (2016). Overview of case study research. In M. De Chesnay (Ed.), *Nursing research using case studies: Qualitative designs and methods in nursing* (pp. 1–10). Springer Publishing Company. doi:10.1891/9780826131935.0001

Hernández, R., Fernández, C., & Baptista, P. (2010). *Metodología de la investigación*. McGraw-Hill Interamericana.

Heyward, M. (2002). From international to intercultural: Redefining the international school for a globalized world. *Journal of Research in International Education*, *1*(1), 9–32. doi:10.1177/147524090211002

Hill, K., & McNamara, T. (2012). Developing a comprehensive, empirically based research framework for classroom-based assessment. *Language Testing*, *29*(3), 395–420. doi:10.1177/0265532211428317

Ho, H. J. (2017). *Promoting international college students' academic adjustment from self-determination theory* (Doctoral dissertation). Purdue University. https://docs.lib.purdue.edu/dissertations/AAI10608059/

Hoffman, A. (2012). Performing our world: Affirming cultural diversity through music education. *Music Educators Journal*, *98*(4), 61–65. doi:10.1177/0027432112443262

Hofstede, G. (1997). *Cultures and organizations: Software of the mind*. McGraw-Hill.

Holmes, P. (2006). Problematizing intercultural communication competence in the pluricultural classroom: Chinese students in a New Zealand university. *Language and Intercultural Communication*, *6*(1), 18–34. doi:10.1080/14708470608668906

Horkheimer, M. (1972). *Critical theory*. Herder & Herder.

Hosny, M., & Fatima, S. (2014). Attitude of students towards cheating and plagiarism: University case study. *Journal of Applied Sciences (Faisalabad)*, *14*(8), 748–757. doi:10.3923/jas.2014.748.757

Hossler, D. R., Braxton, J., & Coopersmith, G. (1989). Understanding student college choice. In J. C. Smart (Ed.), *Higher education, handbook of theory and research* (pp. 231–288). Agathon Press.

Hou, F., & Lu, Y. (2017). International students, immigration and earnings growth: The effect of a pre-immigration host-country university education. *IZA Journal of Development and Migration*, *7*(5), 1–24.

Houshmand, S., Spanierman, L., & Tafarodi, R. (2014). Excluded and avoided: Racial microaggressions targeting Asian international students in Canada. *Cultural Diversity & Ethnic Minority Psychology*, *20*(3), 377–388. doi:10.1037/a0035404 PMID:25045949

Howard, R. M., Serviss, T., & Rodrique, K. (2010). Writing from sources, writing from sentences. *Writing & Pedagogy*, *2*(2), 177–192. doi:10.1558/wap.v2i2.177

Howes, D. (2015). *A multiple case study of international undergraduate student choice of Alberta, Canada for post-secondary education* [Doctoral Dissertation. Northcentral University]. Proquest Dissertations Publishing, 3713980.

Huang, J. (2005). Challenges of academic listening in English: Reports by Chinese students. *College Student Journal*, *39*(3), 553–569.

Huang, J., & Brown, K. (2009). Cultural factors affecting Chinese ESL students' academic learning. *Education*, *129*(4), 643–653.

Huang, J., & Cowden, P. (2009). Are Chinese students really quiet, passive and surface learners? A cultural studies perspective. *Canadian and International Education. Education Canadienne et Internationale*, *38*(2), 75–88.

Huang, J., & Klinger, D. A. (2006). Chinese graduate students at North American universities: Learning challenges and coping strategies. *Canadian and International Education. Education Canadienne et Internationale*, *35*(2), 47–61.

Huang, T. (2012). Motivation-orientated teaching model for certification education. *International Education Studies*, *6*(2). Advance online publication. doi:10.5539/ies.v6n2p84

Huang, Y. (2014). Taiwanese graduate students' personal experiences on culturally related language anxiety and adjustment. *Journal of Educational and Developmental Psychology*, *4*(1), 258–271. doi:10.5539/jedp.v4n1p258

Hudzik, J. K. (2014). *Comprehensive internationalization*. Routledge. doi:10.4324/9781315771885

Hu, G., & Lei, J. (2011). Investigating Chinese university students' knowledge of and attitudes toward plagiarism from an integrated perspective. *Language Learning*, *62*(3), 813–850. doi:10.1111/j.1467-9922.2011.00650.x

Hughes, H. (2010). International students' experiences of university libraries and librarians. *Australian Academic and Research Libraries*, *41*(2), 77–89. doi:10.1080/00048623.2010.10721446

Hurabielle, J. (1998). *Canada's public colleges and postsecondary technical institutions' involvement in international education* (Unpublished doctoral dissertation). University of Alberta, Alberta, Canada.

Hyland, K. (2007). Genre pedagogy: Language, literacy, and L2 writing instruction. *Journal of Second Language Writing*, *16*(3), 148–164. doi:10.1016/j.jslw.2007.07.005

Ibrahim, N., & Nambiar, R. (2011). Writing in foreign lands: The case of postgraduate international students and the introductory sections of a project paper. *Procedia: Social and Behavioral Sciences*, *18*, 626–632. doi:10.1016/j.sbspro.2011.05.092

Immigration Refugees and Citizenship Canada. (2018a). *Backgrounder: Study and stay program* [Press release]. Retrieved from https://www.canada.ca/en/atlantic-canada-opportunities/news/2018/07/study-and-stay-program.html

Immigration Refugees and Citizenship Canada. (2018b). *Speaking notes for Ahmed Hussen, Minister of Immigration, Refugees and Citizenship* [Press release]. Retrieved from https://www.canada.ca/en/immigration-refugees-citizenship/news/2018/06/speaking-notes-for-ahmed-hussen-minister-of-immigration-refugees-and-citizenship.html

Immigration, Refugees, and Citizenship Canada. (2019). *Canada: Study permit holders with China as country of citizenship by province/territory of destination, study level and calendar year 1998-2019*. Ottawa, Canada: Immigration, Refugees, and Citizenship Canada.

Ingraham, E., & Peterson, D. L. (2004). Assessing the impact of study abroad on student learning at Michigan State University. *Frontiers: The Interdisciplinary Journal of Study Abroad*, *10*(1), 83–100. doi:10.36366/frontiers.v10i1.134

Institute of International Education (IIE). (2019). *Open door report: Enrollment*. Retrieved from https://www.iie.org/Research-and-Insights/Open-Doors/Data/International-Students/Enrollment

Institute of International Education, Inc. (2020, February 25). *Infographics and data*. Retrieved from https://www.iie.org/en/Research-and-Insights/Project-Atlas/Explore-Data/Canada

Institute of International Education. (2016). *Open doors 2016*. Institute of International Education.

Institute of International Education. (2017). *2017 Project Atlas infographics*. New York: Institute of International Education. Retrieved from https://www.iie.org/Research-and-Insights/Project-Atlas/Explore-Data/Infographics/2017-Project-Atlas-Infographics

Institute of International Education. (2018). *Project atlas: Infographics and data*. Retrieved from https://www.iie.org/Research-and-Insights/Project-Atlas/Explore-Data

Institute of Medicine. (2015). *Transforming health care scheduling and access: Getting to now*. The National Academies Press., doi:10.17226/20220

Interfaith Harmony Halifax. (2020). *Interfaith engagement educational opportunity*. http://ihhalifax.ca/home/interfaith-engagement-program

International Institute for Educational Planning. (2020). *Effective and appropriate pedagogy*. Retrieved from https://learningportal.iiep.unesco.org/en/issue-briefs/improve-learning/teachers-and-pedagogy/effective-and-appropriate-pedagogy

Ippolito, K. (2007). Promoting intercultural learning in a multicultural university: Ideas and realities. *Teaching in Higher Education*, *12*(5-6), 749–763. doi:10.1080/13562510701596356

Ireton, J. (2019, June 26). Skyrocketing tuition for international students questioned. *CBC News*. Retrieved from https://www.cbc.ca/news/canada/ottawa/analysis-ontario-universities-international-tuition-increases-1.5189755

Ishimura, Y., & Bartlett, J. C. (2014). Are librarians equipped to teach international students? A survey of current practices and recommendations for training. *Journal of Academic Librarianship*, *40*(3-4), 313–321. doi:10.1016/j.acalib.2014.04.009

Iwamoto, D. K., & Liu, W. M. (2010). The impact of racial identity, ethnic identity, Asian values, and race related stress on Asian Americans and Asian International college students' psychological well-being. *Journal of Counseling Psychology*, *57*(1), 79–91. doi:10.1037/a0017393 PMID:20396592

Jackson, P. A. (2005). Incoming international students and the library: A survey. *RSR. Reference Services Review*, *33*(2), 197–209. doi:10.1108/00907320510597408

Janghorban, R., Roudsari, R. L., & Taghipour, A. (2014). Skype interviewing: The new generation of online synchronous interview in qualitative research. *International Journal of Qualitative Studies on Health and Well-being*, *9*(1), 24152. doi:10.3402/qhw.v9.24152

Jeong, S. Y. S., Hickey, N., Levett-Jones, T., Pitt, V., Hoffman, K., Norton, C. A., & Ohr, S. O. (2011). Understanding and enhancing the learning experiences of culturally and linguistically diverse nursing students in an Australian bachelor of nursing program. *Nurse Education Today*, *31*(3), 238–244. PMID:21078536

Jiao, Q. G., Onwuegbuzie, A. J., & Lichtenstein, A. A. (1996). Library anxiety: Characteristics of 'at-risk' college students. *Library & Information Science Research*, *18*(2), 151–163. doi:10.1016/S0740-8188(96)90017-1

Jin, L., & Schneider, J. (2019). Faculty views on international students: A survey study. *Journal of International Students*, *9*(1), 84–99.

Johnston, N. (2014). *Understanding the information literacy experiences of EFL students* (Unpublished doctoral dissertation). Queensland University of Technology, Brisbane, Australia.

Johnstone, M., & Lee, E. (2014). Branded: International education and 21st-century Canadian immigration, education policy, and the welfare state. *International Social Work*, *57*(3), 209–221. doi:10.1177/0020872813508572

Johnstone, M., & Lee, E. (2017). Canada and the global rush for international students: Reifying a neo-imperial order of Western dominance in the knowledge economy era. *Critical Sociology*, *43*(7-8), 1063–1078. doi:10.1177/0896920516654554

Jones, E. (2017). Problematising and reimagining the notion of 'international student experience'. *Studies in Higher Education*, *42*(5), 933–943. doi:10.1080/03075079.2017.1293880

Jordan, R. (2004). *English for academic purposes*. Cambridge University Press.

Joshee, R. (2004). Citizenship and multicultural education in Canada: From assimilation to social cohesion. In J. Banks (Ed.), *Diversity and citizenship education: Global perspectives* (pp. 127–156). Jossey-Bass.

Julien, H., & Barker, S. (2009). How high-school students find and evaluate scientific information: A basis for information literacy skills development. *Library & Information Science Research*, *31*(1), 12–17. doi:10.1016/j.lisr.2008.10.008

Kang, D. S. (2014). How international students build a positive relationship with a hosting country: Examination of strategic public, message and channel of national public relations. *International Journal of Intercultural Relations, 43*, 201–214. doi:10.1016/j.ijintrel.2014.08.006

Katem, E. (2018). *Canada is home to nearly half a million international students: An update from the Canadian Bureau of International Education reveals the total number of international students in the country exceeds Canada's 2022 target.* Retrieved on 7/9/19 from https://www.canadastudynews.com/2018/03/19/canada-is-home-to-nearly-half-a- million- international-students/

Kaur, M., & Singh, M. (2015). International graduate students' academic writing practices in Malaysia: Challenges and solutions. *Journal of International Studies, 5*(1), 12–22. https://jistudents.org/

Kayaalp, D. (2014). Educational inclusion/exclusion of Turkish immigrant youth in Vancouver, Canada: A critical analysis. *International Journal of Inclusive Education, 18*(7), 655–668. doi:10.1080/13603116.2013.802031

Kellogg, S. E. (2018). *Competency-based education: Best practices and implication strategies for institutions of higher education.* Retrieved from https://digitalcommons.csp.edu/edd/3

Kennedy, K. (2019a). Post-study work restrictions cost the UK £150 million a year. *PIE News.* https://thepienews.com/news/restrictions-post-study-work-cost-uk-150-million-year-report/

Kennedy, K. (2019b). UK home secretary backs call for post-study work restrictions to be lifted. *PIE News.* https://thepienews.com/news/uk-home-secretary-calls-for-a-lifting-of-psw-restrictions-on-international-students/

Kennedy, K. (2019c). Universities UK warns against 'no-deal' consequences. *PIE News.* https://thepienews.com/news/brexit-briefing-uuk/

Kennedy, K. (2019d). US could have lost US$5.5bn in value from declining market share – NAFSA. *PIE News.* https://thepienews.com/news/international-students-in-us-decline-considered-threat/

Kennedy, K. J. (2007). *Barriers to innovative school practice: A socio-cultural framework for understanding assessment practices in Asia.* Paper presented at the Redesigning Pedagogy: Culture, Understanding and Practice Conference, Nanyang Technological University, Singapore.

Kennedy, P. (2002). Learning cultures and learning styles: Myth-understandings about adult (Hong Kong) Chinese learners. *International Journal of Lifelong Education, 21*(5), 430–445. doi:10.1080/02601370210156745

Khoury, H. A. (2006). *Measuring culture: The development of a multidimensional culture scale.* Graduate Theses and Dissertations. https://scholarcommons.usf.edu/etd/2584

Kim, E. (2012). An alternative theoretical model: Examining psychosocial identity development of international students in the United States. *College Student Journal, 46*(1), 99–113.

Kim, E. (2018). Korean students' acculturation experiences in the U.S. In *Understanding International Students from Asia in American Universities* (pp. 127–147). Springer International Publishing AG. doi:10.1007/978-3-319-60394-0_7

Kim, H. S., & Markus, H. R. (1999). Deviance or uniqueness, harmony or conformity? A cultural analysis. *Journal of Personality and Social Psychology, 77*(4), 785–800. doi:10.1037/0022-3514.77.4.785

Kim, J. (2012). The birth of academic subalterns: How do foreign students embody the global hegemony of American universities? *Journal of Studies in International Education, 16*(5), 455–462. doi:10.1177/1028315311407510

Kim, S. (2006). Academic oral communication needs of East Asian international graduate students in non-science and non-engineering fields. *English for Specific Purposes, 25*(4), 479–489. doi:10.1016/j.esp.2005.10.001

Kim, Y. Y. (2008). Intercultural personhood: Globalisation and a way of being. *International Journal of Intercultural Relations, 32*(4), 359–368. doi:10.1016/j.ijintrel.2008.04.005

Kim, Y. Y. (2017). Identity and intercultural communication. In Y. Y. Kim (Ed.), *The international encyclopedia of intercultural communication* (pp. 1–9)., doi:10.1002/9781118783665.ieicc0999

Kingston, E., & Forland, H. (2008). Bridging the gap in expectations between international students and academic staff. *Journal of Studies in International Education, 12*(2), 204–221. doi:10.1177/1028315307307654

Kirby, D. (2007). Reviewing Canadian post-secondary education: Post-secondary education policy in post-industrial Canada. *Canadian Journal of Educational Administration and Policy, 65*, 1–24.

Kisch, M. (2015). Helping international student navigate career options. *International Educator,* 66-69.

Kislev, E. (2012). Components of intercultural identity: Towards an effective integration policy. *Journal of Intercultural Education, 23*(3), 221–235. doi:10.1080/14675986.2012.699373

Klemencˇicˇ. M. (2015). What is student agency? An ontological exploration in the context of research on student engagement. In M. Klemencˇicˇ., S. Bergan., & R. Primozˇicˇ (Ed.), Student engagement in Europe: Society, higher education and student governance (pp. 11-29). Strasbourg, France: Council of Europe Publishing.

Klemenčič, M. (2017). From student engagement to student agency: Conceptual considerations of European policies on student-centered learning in higher education. *Higher Education Policy, 30*(1), 69–85. doi:10.105741307-016-0034-4

Knight, J., & de Wit, H. (1995). Strategies for internationalisation of higher education: Historical and conceptual perspectives. In H. de Wit (Ed.), Strategies for internationalisation of higher education – A comparative study of Australia, Canada, Europe and the USA (pp. 5-29). Amsterdam: European Association for International Education (EAIE).

Knight, J. (2003). Updated internationalization definition. *Industry and Higher Education, 33*, 2–3.

Knight, J. (2004). Internationalization remodeled: Definition, approaches, and rationales. *Journal of Studies in International Education, 8*(1), 5–31. doi:10.1177/1028315303260832

Knight, J. (2007). Internationalization: Concepts, complexities and challenges. In *International handbook of higher education* (pp. 207–227). Springer.

Knight, J. (2012). Student mobility and internationalization: Trends and tribulations. *Research in Comparative and International Education, 7*(1), 20–33. doi:10.2304/rcie.2012.7.1.20

Knight, J. (2013). The changing landscape of higher education internationalisation – for better or worse? *Perspectives: Policy and Practice in Higher Education, 17*(3), 84–90. doi:10.1080/13603108.2012.753957

Knowles, M. (1980). What is andragogy? In *The modern practice of adult education: From pedagogy to andragogy* (2nd ed., pp. 40–62). Cambridge Books.

Knowlton, M., & Collins, S. B. (2017). Foreign-educated graduate nursing students and plagiarism. *The Journal of Nursing Education, 56*(4), 211–214. doi:10.3928/01484834-20170323-04 PMID:28383744

Kolb, A. Y., & Kolb, D. A. (2005). Learning styles and learning spaces: Enhancing experiential learning in higher education. *Academy of Management Learning & Education, 4*(2), 193–212. doi:10.5465/amle.2005.17268566

Kolb, D. A. (1984). *Experiential learning: Experience as the source of learning and development.* Prentice Hall.

Korpan, C. (2011). *TA professional development in Canada.* https://www.stlhe.ca/wp-content/uploads/2011/05/TA-ProD-in-Canada-Report_July-2011.pdf

Koul, R. B., & Fisher, D. L. (2006). Using student perceptions in development, validation, and application of an assessment questionnaire. In S. Wooltorton & D. Marinova (Eds.), *Sharing wisdom for our future. Environmental education in action: Proceedings of the 2006 Conference of the Australian Association of Environmental Education* (pp. 294–305). Retrieved from http://www.aaee.org.au/docs/2006%20conference/32_Koul_Fisher.pdf

Koul, R., & Fisher, D. (2005). Cultural background and students' perceptions of science classroom learning environment and teacher interpersonal behavior in Jammu, India. *Learning Environments Research, 8*(2), 195–211. doi:10.100710984-005-7252-9

Krol, E. S., & Krol, L. M. (2012). Referencing and citation for graduate students: Gain without pain. *Collected Essays on Learning and Teaching (CELT), 5,* 64-68. Retrieved from http://webcache.googleusercontent.com/search?q=cache:6xVvkn9FwsgJ:celt.uwindsor.ca /ojs/leddy/index.php/CELT/article/view/3403+&cd=1&hl=en&ct=clnk&gl=ca

Krueger, R., & Casey, M. (2009). *Focus groups: A practical guide for applied research* (4th ed.). Sage Publications.

Kulturel-Konak, S., D'Allegro, M. L., & Dickinson, S. (2011). Review of gender differences in learning styles: Suggestions for STEM education. *Contemporary Issues in Education Research, 4*(3), 9–18. doi:10.19030/cier.v4i3.4116

Kuo, B. C. H., & Roysircar, G. (2004). Predictors of acculturation for Chinese adolescent in Canada: Age of arrival, length of stay, social class, and English reading ability. *Journal of Multicultural Counseling and Development, 32*(3), 143–154. doi:10.1002/j.2161-1912.2004.tb00367.x

Kuo, B. C., & Roysircar, G. (2004). Predictors of acculturation for Chinese adolescents in Canada: Age of arrival, length of stay, social class, and English reading ability. *Journal of Multicultural Counseling and Development, 32*(3), 143–154.

Kuo, Y. (2011). Language challenges faced by international graduate students in the United States. *Journal of International Studies, 1*(2), 38–42. http://jistudents.org

Kusek, W. A. (2015). Evaluating the struggles with international students and local community participation. *Journal of International Students, 5*(2), 121–131.

Ladson-Billings, G. J. (2005). Is the team all right? Diversity and teacher education. *Journal of Teacher Education, 56*(3), 229–234. doi:10.1177/0022487105275917

Lambert, D., & Lines, D. (2013). *Understanding assessment: Purposes, perceptions, practice.* Routledge. doi:10.4324/9780203133231

Lam, J. S., Ariffin, A. M., & Ahmad, A. j. (2011). Edutourism: Exploring the push-pull factors in selecting a university. *International Journal of Business & Society, 12*(1), 63–78.

Lampert, L. (2004). Integrating discipline based anti-plagiarism instruction into the information literacy curriculum. *RSR. Reference Services Review, 32*(4), 347–355. doi:10.1108/00907320410569699

Landis, J., & Koch, G. G. (1977). The measurement of observer agreement for categorical data. *Biometrics, 33*(1), 159–174. doi:10.2307/2529310 PMID:843571

Lantolf, J. P. (2000). Introducing sociocultural theory. In J. P. Lantolf (Ed.), *Sociocultural theory and second language learning* (pp. 1–26). Oxford University Press.

Larsen, K., & Vincent-Lancrin, S. (2002). International trade in educational services: Good or bad? *Higher Education Management and Policy, 14*(3), 2–45. doi:10.1787/hemp-v14-art18-en

Lax, J. (2002). Academic writing for international graduate students. *Frontiers in Education, 32*(2), 8–12. doi:10.1109/FIE.2002.1158212

Le Ha, P., & Li, B. (2012). Silence as right, choice, resistance and strategy among Chinese 'Me Generation' students: Implications for pedagogy. *Discourse (Abingdon)*, *35*(2), 233–248. doi:10.1080/01596306.2012.745733

Leask, B. (2013). Internationalizing the curriculum in the disciplines: Imagining new possibilities. *Journal of Studies in International Education*, *17*(2), 103–118. doi:10.1177/1028315312475090

Lechasseur, K. (2014). Critical Race Theory and the meaning of "Community" in district partnerships. *Equity & Excellence in Education*, *47*(3), 305–320. doi:10.1080/10665684.2014.933069

Leclaire, R. (2010). Master's Biotechnology Program Target Foreign Students. *The Study Magazine*. Retrieved from http://studymagazine.com/2011/06/28/windsors-masters-biotechnology-program-targets-foreign-students/

Lee, J. (2015). International student experiences: Neo-racism and discrimination. *International Higher Education*, *2015*(44), 3-5.

Lee, A. (2017). *Teaching interculturally: A framework for integrating disciplinary knowledge and intercultural development*. Stylus Publishers.

Lee, A., Poch, R., O'Brien, M. K., & Solheim, C. (2017). Teaching interculturally: A framework for integrating disciplinary knowledge and intercultural development. *Stylus (Rio de Janeiro)*.

Lee, G. (2009). Speaking up: Six Korean students' oral participation in class discussions in US graduate seminars. *English for Specific Purposes*, *28*, 142–156.

Lee, J. (2014). Experiences of intensive English learners: Motivations, imagined communities, and identities. *English Language Teaching*, *7*(11). Advance online publication. doi:10.5539/elt.v7n11p28

Lee, J., & Ciftci, A. (2014). Asian international students' socio-cultural adaptation: Influence of multicultural personality, assertiveness, academics self-efficacy, and social support. *International Journal of Intercultural Relations*, *38*, 97–105. doi:10.1016/j.ijintrel.2013.08.009

Lee, W. O. (1996). The cultural context for Chinese learners: conceptions of learning in the Confucian tradition. In D. Watkins & J. Biggs (Eds.), *The Chinese learner: Cultural, psychological and contextual influences* (pp. 25–41). The Comparative Education Research Centre, Faculty of Education, University of Hong Kong.

Legusov, O. (2017). The growing reliance of Ontario colleges of applied arts and technology on educational agents for the recruitment of international students. *The College Quarterly*, *20*(1), 1–21.

Lehto, X. Y., Cai, L. A., Fu, X., & Chen, Y. (2014). Intercultural interactions outside the classroom: Narratives on a US campus. *Journal of College Student Development*, *55*(8), 837–853. doi:10.1353/csd.2014.0083

Lei, L. (2020). Returning "home"? Exploring the re-integration experiences of internationally educated Chinese academic returnees. *Emerging Perspectives: Interdisciplinary Graduate Research in Education and Psychology*, *4*(1), 13–18.

Levatino, A. (2015). Transnational higher education and skilled migration: Evidence from Australia. *International Journal of Educational Development*, *40*, 106–116. doi:10.1016/j.ijedudev.2014.11.009

Lewthwaite, M. (1996). A study of international students' perspectives on cross-cultural adaptation. *International Journal for the Advancement of Counseling*, *19*(2), 167–185. doi:10.1007/BF00114787

Li, P. S. (2000). Cultural diversity in Canada: The social construction of racial differences. *Research and Statistics Division: Strategic Issues Series*.

Liang, A., & McQueen, R. J. (1999). Computer assisted adult interactive learning in a multi-cultural environment. *Adult Learning*, *11*(1), 26–29. doi:10.1177/104515959901100108

Li, C. (2011). Chinese high school graduates' beliefs about English learning. *Canadian Research & Development Center of Sciences and Cultures, 3*(2), 11–18.

Li, G., Chen, W., & Duanmu, J. (2010). Determinants of international students' academic performance: A comparison between Chinese and other international students. *Journal of Studies in International Education, 14*(4), 389–405. doi:10.1177/1028315309331490

Li, J. (2012). *Cultural foundations of learning: East and West.* Cambridge University Press. doi:10.1017/CBO9781139028400

Li, M. (2003). Culture and classroom communication: A case study of Asian students in New Zealand language schools. In *NZARE AARE Conference 2003: Educational research, risks, & dilemmas* (pp. 1-19). Auckland, New Zealand: Australian Association for Research in Education.

Li, M. (2015). A case of difficult acculturation: A Chinese student in a New Zealand university. In E. Christopher (Ed.), *International management and intercultural communication* (pp. 41–61). Palgrave Macmillan. doi:10.1007/978-1-137-55325-6_4

Li, M., & Bray, M. (2007). Cross-border flows of students for higher education: Push–pull factors and motivations of mainland Chinese students in Hong Kong and Macau. *Higher Education, 53*(6), 791–818. doi:10.100710734-005-5423-3

Lindgren, R., & McDaniel, R. (2012). Transforming online learning through narrative and student agency. *Journal of Educational Technology & Society, 15*(4), 344–355.

Lin, J.-C. G., & Yi, J. K. (1997). Asian international students' adjustment: Issues and program suggestions. *College Student Journal, 31*(4), 473–479.

Linney, S. (2019). Why your graduate employability matters more than ever. *QS.com.* https://www.qs.com/employability-important-higher-education/

Linn, R. L., & Miller, M. D. (2005). *Measurement and assessment in teaching* (9th ed.). Pearson Prentice Hall.

Lin, S., & Scherz, S. D. (2014). Challenges facing Asian international graduate students in the US: Pedagogical considerations in higher education. *Journal of International Students, 4*(1), 16–33. https://jistudents.org/

Lin, S., & Susan, D. S. (2014). Challenges facing Asian international graduate students in the U.S. *Journal of International Students, 4*(1), 16–33.

Liu, B., & Liu, Q. (2016). Internationalisation of Chinese higher education in the era of globalisation. In S. Guo & Y. Guo (Ed.), Spotlight on China: Chinese education in the globalised world (pp. 85-106). Rotterdam, Netherlands: Sense Publishers.

Liu, S. (2019). *Festivals, Festival foods, and dietary acculturation: A journey of hybridization and Identity Formation for Chinese International Students in Ottawa* (Doctoral dissertation). Carleton University, Ontario, Canada.

Liu, T. (2016). *Learning experience of Chinese international students in Master of Education program at a mid-sized Ontario university* (Unpublished master's thesis). University of Windsor, Windsor, Canada.

Liu, G., & Winn, D. (2009). Chinese graduate students and the Canadian academic library: A user study at the University of Windsor. *Journal of Academic Librarianship, 35*(6), 565–573. doi:10.1016/j.acalib.2009.08.001

Liu, J. (2002). Negotiating silence in American classrooms: Three Chinese cases. *Language and Intercultural Communication, 2*(1), 37–54. doi:10.1080/14708470208668074

Liu, L. (2011). An international graduate student's ESL learning experience beyond the classroom. *TESL Canada Journal,* 77–92.

Liu, M. (2006). Anxiety in Chinese EFL students at different proficiency levels. *System*, *34*(3), 301–316. doi:10.1016/j.system.2006.04.004

Liu, M. (2009). Addressing the mental health problems of Chinese international college students in the United States. *Advances in Social Work*, *10*(1), 69–86. doi:10.18060/164

Livingstone, D. (1999). Exploring the icebergs of adult learning: Findings of the first Canadian survey of informal learning practices. *Canadian Journal for the Study of Adult Education*, *13*(2), 49–72.

Li, X., DiPetta, T., & Woloshyn, V. (2012). Why do Chinese study for a master of education degree in Canada? *Canadian Journal of Education*, *35*(3), 149–163.

Li, X., & Tierney, P. (2013). Internationalization in Canadian higher education: Experiences of international students in a master's program. *Comparative and International Education*, *42*(2), 1–16. https://ir.lib.uwo.ca/cie-eci/vol42/iss2/5

Li, Y. (2004). Learning to live and study in Canada: Stories of four EFL learners from China. *TESL Canada Journal*, *22*(2), 25–43. doi:10.18806/tesl.v22i1.164

Li, Y. (2004). Learning to live and study in Canada: Stories of four EFL learners from China. *TESL Canada*, *22*(2), 25–43.

Logan, S. W. (2016). Where in the world is the writing program: Administering writing in global contexts. *College English*, *78*(3), 290–297. http://www.ncte.org/library/NCTEFiles/Resources/Journals/CE/0783jan2016/CE0783Review.pdf

Lokhande, M. (2016). *Policy Brief des SVR-Forschungsbereichs - Engagiert gewinnt Bessere Berufschancen für internationale Studierende durch Praxiserfahrungen*. Retrieved from http://www.stifterverband.de/study_work/policy_brief_study_and_work_engagiert_gewinnt.pdf

López Turley, R., & Wodtke, G. (2010). College residence and academic performance: Who benefits from living on campus? *Urban Education*, *45*(4), 506–532. doi:10.1177/0042085910372351

López, H. (1994). *Métodos de investigación lingüística*. Ediciones Colegio de España.

Lopez, I. Y., & Bui, N. H. (2014). Acculturation and linguistic factors on international students. self-esteem and language confidence. *Journal of International Students*, *4*(4), 314–329.

López, M. H., Krogstand, J., & Flores, A. (2018). *Most Hispanic parents speak Spanish to their children, but this is less the case in later generations*. Pew Research Center.

Lou, X., & Ma, G. (2012). Comparison of productive vocabulary in Chinese and American advanced English academic writings. *Theory and Practice in Language Studies*, *2*(6), 1153–1159. doi:10.4304/tpls.2.6.1153-1159

Love, K., & Arkoudis, S. (2006). Teachers' stances towards Chinese international students: An Australian case study. *Linguistics and Education*, *17*(3), 258–282. doi:10.1016/j.linged.2006.11.002

Lowe, S. J. (2011). Welcome to Canada? Immigration incentives may not be enough for international students to stay. *Canadian Diversity / Canadian Diversité*, *8*(5), 20-24.

Lu, Y., & Hou, F. (2015). *International students who become permanent residents in Canada*. Insights on Canadian Society (December). Statistics Canada Catalog no. 75-006-X.

Lu, A. (2013). A functional grammar approach to analyzing Asian student's writing. *American Journal of Educational Research*, *1*(2), 49–57. doi:10.12691/education-1-2-3

Lu, C., & Han, W. (2010). Why don't they participate? A self-study of Chinese graduate Students' classroom involvement in North America. *Brock Education*, *20*(1), 80–96. doi:10.26522/brocked.v20i1.147

Lund, J. R. (2004). Plagiarism: A cultural perspective. *Journal of Religious & Theological Information, 6*(3-4), 93–101. doi:10.1300/J112v06n03_08

Macpherson, A. (2011). *The instructional skills workshop as a transformative learning process* [Unpublished doctoral dissertation]. Simon Fraser University.

Madge, C., Raghuram, P., & Noxolo, P. (2009). Engaged pedagogy and responsibility: A postcolonial analysis of international students. *Geoforum, 10*(1), 34–45. doi:10.1016/j.geoforum.2008.01.008

Madgett, P. J., & Belanger, C. (2008). International students: The Canadian experience. *Tertiary Education and Management, 14*(3), 191–207. doi:10.1080/13583880802228182

Madison, D. S. (2012). *Critical ethnography: Method, ethics, and performance.* Sage.

Malcolm, Z. T., & Mendoza, P. (2014). Afro-Caribbean international students' ethnic identity development: Fluidity, intersectionality, agency, and performativity. *Journal of College Student Development, 55*(6), 595–614. doi:10.1353/csd.2014.0053

Marcuse, H. (1964). *One-dimensional man: Studies in the ideology of advanced industrial society.* Retrieved from https://www.marxists.org/reference/archive/marcuse/works/one-dimensional-man/one-dimensional-man.pdf

Maringe, F., & Carter, S. (2007). International students; motivations for studying in UK HE: Insights into the choice and decision making of African students. *International Journal of Educational Management, 21*(6), 459–475. doi:10.1108/09513540710780000

Martirosyan, N. M., Hwang, E., & Wanjohi, R. (2015). Impact of English proficiency on academic performance of international students. *Journal of International Students, 5*(1), 60–71.

Martirosyan, N. M., Hwang, E., & Wanjohi, R. (2015). Impact of English proficiency on performance of international students. *Journal of International Students, 5*(1), 60–71.

Mason, A., & Hickman, J. (2019). Students supporting students on the PhD journey: An evaluation of a mentoring scheme for international doctoral students. *Innovations in Education and Teaching International, 56*(1), 88–98. doi:10.1080/14703297.2017.1392889

Mason, M. (2010). Sample size and saturation in PhD studies using qualitative interviews. In *Forum Qualitative Sozialforschung/Forum: Qualitative. Social Research, 11*(3).

Massing, C., Pente, P., & Kirova, A. (2016). Immigrant parent-child interactional dance duets during shared art-making experiences. *European Early Childhood Education Research Journal, 24*(1), 37–50. doi:10.1080/1350293X.2015.1120518

Mattis, G. (2019). Why is employablity important in higher education? *QS.com.* https://www.qs.com/employability-important-higher-education/

Ma, Y. (2018). Paradigm shift: Learning is a two-way street between American universities and Asian international students. In Y. Ma & M. A. Garcia-Murillo (Eds.), *Understanding international students from Asia in American universities* (pp. 1–11). Springer International Publishing AG. doi:10.1007/978-3-319-60394-0_1

Mazzarol, T., & Soutar, G. N. (2002). "Push-pull" factors influencing international student destination choice. *International Journal of Educational Management, 16*(2), 82–90. doi:10.1108/09513540210418403

McCarthy, E. E., Sen, A. K., & Garrity, B. (2012). Factors that influence Canadian students' choice of higher education institutions in the United States. *Business Education & Accreditation, 4*(2), 85–95.

McDonald, J. T., & Kennedy, S. (2004). Insights into the 'healthy immigrant effect': Health status and health service use of immigrants to Canada. *Social Science & Medicine, 59*(8), 1613–1627. doi:10.1016/j.socscimed.2004.02.004

McFadden, C., Maahs-Fladung, C., & Mallett, W. (2012). Recruiting international students to your campus. [Retrieved from]. *Journal of International Students, 2*(2), 157–167.

McFarlane, A. M. (2015). Internationalization and the role of student affairs professionals: Lessons learned from the international student engagement meeting initiative. *Journal of Student Affairs in Africa, 3*(1), 83–91. doi:10.14426/jsaa.v3i1.94

McFaul, S. (2016). International students' social network: Network mapping to gage friendship formation and student engagement. *Journal of International Students, 6*(1), 1–13.

McGarvey, A., Brugha, R., Conroy, R. M., Clarke, E., & Byrne, E. (2015). International students' experience of a western medical school: A mixed methods study exploring the early years in the context of cultural and social adjustment compared to students from the host country. *BMC Medical Education, 15*(1), 111. doi:10.118612909-015-0394-2

Mcgregor, C. (2012). Art-informed pedagogy: Tools for social transformation. *International Journal of Lifelong Education, 31*(3), 309–324. doi:10.1080/02601370.2012.683612

McKeen, A. (2018, November 1). Majority of Canadian university appointments now precarious gigs. *The Star Vancouver*. Retrieved from https://www.thestar.com/vancouver/2018/11/01/majority-of-canadian-universityappointments-now-precarious-gigs.html

McKenzie, K., Khenti, A., & Vidal, C. (2011). *Cognitive-behavioural therapy for English-speaking people of Caribbean origin: A manual for enhancing the effectiveness of CBT for English-speaking people of Caribbean origin in Canada.* Centre for Addiction and Mental Health.

McKinnon, S. (2013). A mismatch of expectations? An exploration of international students' perceptions of employability skills and work-related learning. In J. Ryan (Ed.), *Cross-cultural teaching and learning for home and international students: Internationalisation of pedagogy and curriculum in higher education* (pp. 211–224). Routledge.

McMartin-Miller, C. (2014). How much feedback is enough: Instructor practices and students' attitudes toward error treatment in second language. *Assessing Writing, 19*, 24–35. doi:10.1016/j.asw.2013.11.003

McMillan, J. A. (2000). Fundamental assessment principles for teachers and school administrators. *Practical Assessment, Research & Evaluation, 7*(8), 89–103. https://PAREonline.net/getvn.asp?v=7&n=8

Medved, D., Franco, A., Gao, X., & Yang, F. (2013). *Challenges in teaching international students: Group separation, language barriers and culture differences.* Genombrottet, Lunds tekniska högskola.

Mehdizadeh, N., & Scott, G. (2005). Adjustment problems of Iranian international students in Scotland. *International Education Journal, 6*(4), 484–493.

Meldrum, L. A., & Willows, N. D. (2006). Food insecurity in university students receiving financial aid. *Canadian Journal of Dietetic Practice and Researc, 67*(1), 43–46. doi:10.3148/67.1.2006.43

Meng, Q., Zhu, C., & Cao, C. (2018). Chinese international students' social connectedness, social and academic adaptation: The mediating role of global competence. *Higher Education, 75*(1), 131–147. doi:10.100710734-017-0129-x

Merino, B. D., Mayper, A. G., & Tolleson, T. D. (2010). Neoliberalism, deregulation and Sarbanes-Oxley: The legitimation of a failed corporate governance model. *Accounting, Auditing & Accountability Journal, 23*(6), 774–792. doi:10.1108/09513571011065871

Merriam, S. B. (2009). *Qualitative research: A guide to design and implementation* (2nd ed.). Jossey-Bass.

Mertler, C. A. (2003). *Preservice versus inservice teachers' assessment literacy: Does classroom experience make a difference?* Paper presented at the meeting of the Mid-Western Educational Research Association, Columbus, OH.

Miles, M. B., & Huberman, M. (1994). *Qualitative Data Analysis: A Sourcebook of New Methods* (2nd ed.). Sage Publications.

Mills, C. W. (1959). *The sociological imagination*. Oxford University Press.

Ministry of Education of China. (2019). *Annual report on the development of Chinese students studying abroad (2018)*. Retrieved January 13, 2020, from http://www.moe.gov.cn/jyb_xwfb/gzdt_gzdt/s5987/201903/t20190327_375704.html

Moglen, D. (2017). International graduate students: Social networks and language use. *Journal of International Students*, 7(1), 22–37. doi:10.32674/jis.v7i1.243

Mohamedbhai, G. (2017, Nov. 3). The changing landscape of private higher education. *Inside Higher Ed*. Retrieved from https://www.universityworldnews.com/post.php?story=2017103110332862

Monroe, J. (2003). Writing and the disciplines - In peer review, Fall 2003, 4-7. *An Association of American Colleges and Universities Publication*. Retrieved from https://www.aacu.org/publications

Montanari, M. (2006). *Food is Culture (Arts and traditions of the table)*. Columbia University Press.

Montgomery, C. (2013). International students and higher education: New perspectives on cultures and communities. *Journal of International Students*, 3(2). https://jistudents.org/

Mori, S. (2010). Addressing the mental health concerns of international students. *Journal of Counseling and Development*, 78(2), 137–144. doi:10.1002/j.1556-6676.2000.tb02571.x

Morita, N. (2000). Discourse socialization through oral classroom activities in a TESL graduate program. *TESOL Quarterly*, 34(2), 279–310. doi:10.2307/3587953

Morris-Lange, S., & Brands, F. (2015). *Train and retain: career support for international students in Canada, Germany, the Netherlands and Sweden*. Retrieved from Berlin: https://www.svr-migration.de/wp-content/uploads/2015/06/study_Train-and-Retain-svr-research-unit-web.pdf

Morson, G. S., & Emerson, C. (1990). *Mikhail Bakhtin: Creation of a prosaics*. Stanford University Press.

Mount Saint Vincent University. (2020). *Quick facts*. https://www.msvu.ca/en/home/aboutus/universityprofile/quickfacts.aspx

Mount Saint Vincent University. (2020a, March 10). *About MSVU*. Retrieved from https://www.msvu.ca/en/home/aboutus/default.aspx

Mount Saint Vincent University. (2020b, March 10). *International*. Retrieved from https://www.msvu.ca/en/home/international/default.aspx

Mukherjee, A. (2003, March). *Neoliberalism and neoliberal economics*. Social Science, India Point Web Network.

Mycek, M. K., Hardison-Moody, A., Bloom, J. D., Bowen, S., & Elliott, S. (2020). Learning to eat the "right" way: Examining nutrition socialization from the perspective of immigrants and refugees. *Food, Culture, & Society*, 23(1), 46–65. doi:10.1080/15528014.2019.1700681

Myers, M. (2009). *Qualitative research in business and management*. Sage Publications.

Myles, J., & Cheng, L. (2003). The social and cultural life of non-native English speaking international graduate students at a Canadian university. *Journal of English for Academic Purposes, 2*(3), 247–263. doi:10.1016/S1475-1585(03)00028-6

Naidoo, V. (2006). International education: A tertiary-level industry update. *Journal of Research in International Education, 5*(3), 323–345. doi:10.1177/1475240906069455

Na, J., Kosinski, M., & Stillwell, D. J. (2015). When a new tool is introduced in different cultural contexts: Individualism-collectivism and social network on Facebook. *Journal of Cross-Cultural Psychology, 46*(3), 355–370. doi:10.1177/0022022114563932

Nakonechny, S. (2019). Suspension of Quebec graduate program leaves international students in limbo. *CBC News.* https://www.cbc.ca/news/canada/montreal/suspension-of-quebec-graduate-program-leaves-international-students-in-limbo-1.5210839

Nardi, P. (2014). *Doing survey research: A guide to quantitative methods* (3rd ed.). Paradigm Publishers.

National Center for Education Statistics (NCES). (2015). *Digest of education statistics: Outcomes of education.* Retrieved from http://nces.ed.gov

Nelson Laird, T. F., Shoup, R., Kuh, G. D., & Schwarz, M. J. (2008). The effects on deep approaches to student learning and college outcomes. *Research in Higher Education, 49*(6), 469–494. doi:10.100711162-008-9088-5

Neuman, L. W. (2014). *Basics of social research: Qualitative and quantitative approaches.* Pearson: Allyn and Bacon.

Ngo, M. N. (2016). Eliminating plagiarism in programming courses through assessment design. *International Journal of Information and Education Technology (IJIET), 6*(11), 873–880. doi:10.7763/IJIET.2016.V6.808

Nguyen, H. M. (2013). Faculty advisors' experiences with international graduate students. *Journal of International Students, 3*(2), 102–116.

Nilsson, P. A., & Ripmeester, N. (2016). International student expectations: Career opportunities and employability. *Journal of International Students, 6*(2), 614–631.

Nilsson, P. A., & Stålnacke, B. M. (2009). Life satisfaction among inbound university students in northern Sweden. *Fennia, 197*(1), 94–107. doi:10.11143/fennia.70337

Njoku, C. P. U. (2015). Information and communication technologies to raise quality of teaching and learning in higher education institutions. *International Journal of Education and Development Using Information and Communication Technology, 11*(1), 122–147. https://www.learntechlib.org/p/151050

Nolan, K. (2012). Dispositions in the field: Viewing mathematics teacher education through the lens of Bourdieu's social field theory. *Educational Studies in Mathematics, 80*(1-2), 201–215. doi:10.100710649-011-9355-9

Norris, J., Sawyer, R., & Lund, D. (2012). *Duoethnography.* Left Coast Press.

Norvaisaite, V., & Ripmeester, N. (2016, Summer). Satisfaction is in success, not in canteen food. *Forum: Member Magazine (EAIE),* 14-16.

Nunan, P. (2006). *An exploration of the long term effects of student exchange experiences* [Paper presentation]. *Australian International Education Conference,* Perth, Australia.

Nunes, S., & Arthur, N. (2013). International students' experiences of integrating into the workforce. *Journal of Employment Counseling, 50*(1), 34–45. doi:10.1002/j.2161-1920.2013.00023.x

O'Regan, J. P. (2014). English as a lingua franca: An immanent critique. *Applied Linguistics*, *35*(5), 533–552. doi:10.1093/applin/amt045

O'Sullivan, M., & Guo, L. (2010). Critical thinking and Chinese international students: An East-West dialogue. *Journal of Contemporary Issues in Education*, *5*(2), 53–73.

Oberg, A., & Wilson, T. (2002). Side by side: Being in research autobiographically. *Educational Insights*. Retrieved from http://ccfi.educ.ubc.ca/publi catio n/insig hts/v07n0 2/contextual explorations/wilso n_oberg/

OECD. (2013). Executive summary. In *Leadership for 21st-century learning*. OECD Publishing. doi:10.1787/9789264205406-

OECD. (2018). *Education at a glance 2018*. OECD Publishing.

Ohta, A. S. (2000). Rethinking interaction in SLA: Developmentally appropriate assistance in the zone of proximal development and the acquisition of L2 grammar. In J. P. Lantolf (Ed.), *Sociocultural theory and second language learning* (pp. 51–78). Oxford University Press.

Ondrusek, A. L. (2012). What the research reveals about graduate students; writing skills: A literature review. *Journal of Education for Library and Information Science*, *53*(3), 176–188. http://www.jstor.org/stable/23249110

Organization for Economic Co-operation and Development (OECD). (2019). *Education at a glance 2019: OECD indicators*. OECD Publishing.

Oropeza, B. A. C., Fitzgibbon, M., & Baron, A. J. Jr. (1991). Managing mental health crises of foreign college students. *Journal of Counseling and Development*, *69*(3), 280–284. doi:10.1002/j.1556-6676.1991.tb01506.x

Oropeza, M. V., Varghese, M. M., & Kanno, Y. (2010). Linguistic minority students in higher education: Using, resisting, and negotiating multiple labels. *Equity & Excellence in Education*, *43*(2), 216–231.

Ortiz, A., Chang, L., & Fang, Y. (2015). International student mobility trends 2015: An economic perspective. *WES Research & Advisory Services*. Retrieved from http://wenr.wes.org /2015/02/international-student-mobility-trends-2015-an-economic-perspective/

Ovie, G. R., & Barrantes, L. (2019). A dialogue of shared discoveries on immigration: A duoethnography of international students in Canada. *Interchange*, *50*(3), 273–291. doi:10.100710780-019-09364-2

Oxford, R. L. (2011). *Teaching and researching language learning strategies*. Pearson Longman.

Packer, S., & Lynch, D. (2013). Perceptions of people in Canada: Canadian-born vs. internationally born postsecondary students' perspectives. *TESL Canada Journal*, *31*(1), 59–85. doi:10.18806/tesl.v31i1.1167

Paige, R. M., & Goode, M. L. (2009). Intercultural competence in international education administration-cultural mentoring: International education professionals and the development of intercultural competence. In D. Deardorff (Ed.), *The SAGE handbook of intercultural competence* (pp. 333–349). SAGE Publications.

Palmer, Y. M. (2016). Student to scholar: Learning experiences of international students. *Journal of International Students*, *6*(1), 216–240. https://jistudents.org/

Paltridge, T., Maysons, S., & Schapper, J. (2012). Covering the gap: Social inclusion, international students and the role of local government. *Australian Universities Review*, *54*(2), 29–39.

Patton, M. Q. (2002). *Qualitative research and evaluation methods* (3rd ed.). Sage.

Peers, I. (1996). *Statistical analysis for education and psychology researchers*. Falmer Press.

Pelling, A. C. (2000). *Cultural shock of international students in Canada* (Unpublished Master's Thesis). University of Lethbridge, Lethbridge, Canada.

Pereira, R. (2020). *An analysis of the use of the on-campus food bank by international graduate students at the University of Guelph* (Unpublished doctoral dissertation). Guelph, Ontario, Canada.

Perkins, R., & Neumayer, E. (2014). Geographies of educational mobilities: Exploring the uneven flows of international students. *The Geographical Journal, 180*(3), 246–259. doi:10.1111/geoj.12045

Peters, B., & Anderson, M. (2017). *Supporting non-native English speakers at the University of Minnesota: A survey of faculty & staff.* University of Minnesota.

Pieterse, J. (2006). Globalization as hybridization. In Media and Cultural Studies (pp. 658-680). Malden, MA: Blackwell.

Plumb, A. (2018). *International students' perceived university schooling experience in the face of internationalization* (Unpublished doctoral dissertation). University of Windsor, ON.

Polkinghorne, D. (2007). Validity issues in narrative research. *Qualitative Inquiry, 13*(4), 471–486. doi:10.1177/1077800406297670

Pollard, V., Hains-Wesson, R., & Young, K. (2018). Creative teaching in STEM. *Teaching in Higher Education, 23*(2), 178–193. doi:10.1080/13562517.2017.1379487

Pollock, A. (2014). *Student employability is a necessity, not a choice.* Retrieved from http://www.labourmobility.com/student-employabilitynecessity-choice

Popadiuk, N. E., & Arthur, N. M. (2004). Counselling international students in Canadian schools. *International Journal for the Advancement of Counseling, 26*(2), 125–145. doi:10.1023/B:ADCO.0000027426.05819.44

Power, L. G. (2009). University students' perceptions of plagiarism. *The Journal of Higher Education, 80*(6), 643–662. doi:10.1080/00221546.2009.11779038

Poyrazli, S., Arbona, C., Bullington, R., & Pisecco, S. (2001). Adjustment issues of Turkish college students studying in the United States. *College Student Journal, 35*(1), 52–62.

Poyrazli, S., & Kavanaugh, P. R. (2006). Marital status, ethnicity, academic achievement, and adjustment strains: The case of graduate international students. *College Student Journal, 40*, 767–780.

Poyrazli, S., & Lopez, M. D. (2007). An exploratory study of perceived discrimination and homesickness: A comparison of international students and American Students. *The Journal of Psychology, 141*(3), 263–280. doi:10.3200/JRLP.141.3.263-280 PMID:17564257

Prieto-Welch, S. L. (2016). International Student Mental Health. *New Directions for Student Services, 156.* Advance online publication. doi:10.1002s.20191

Prince, M. (2004). Does active learning work? A review of the research. *Journal of Engineering Education, 93*(3), 223–231. doi:10.1002/j.2168-9830.2004.tb00809.x

Qi, L. (2015, May 29). US schools expelled 8,000 Chinese students. *The Wall Street Journal.* Retrieved from http://blogs.wsj.com/chinarealtime/2015/05/29/u-s-schools-expelled8000-Chinese-students-for-poor-grades-cheating/tab/comments/

Raby, R. (2000). Globalization of the community college model: Paradox of the local and the global. In N. P. Stramquist & K. Monkman (Eds.), Globalization and education: Integration and contestation across cultures (pp. 149-173). New York, NY: Rowman & Little field Publishers Inc.

Rahimi, M., & Goli, A. (2016). English learning achievement and EFL learner's cheating attitudes and cheating behaviours. *International Education Studies, 9*(2), 81–88. doi:10.5539/ies.v9n2p81

Ramzan, M., Munir, M. A., Siddique, N., & Asif, M. (2012). Awareness about plagiarism amongst university students in Pakistan. *Higher Education, 64*(1), 73–84. doi:10.100710734-011-9481-4

Rao, P. (2017). Learning challenges and preferred pedagogies of international students: A perspective from the United States. *International Journal of Educational Management, 31*(7), 1000–1016. doi:10.1108/IJEM-01-2016-0001

Rawlings, M., & Sue, E. (2013). Preparedness of Chinese students for American culture and communicating in English. *Journal of International Students, 3*(1), 29–40. https://search.proquest.com/docview/1355441919?accountid=458

Razfar, A., & Gutiérrez, K. (2003). Reconceptualizing early childhood literacy: The sociocultural influence. In N. Hall, J. Larson, & J. Marsh (Eds.), *Handbook of early childhood literacy* (pp. 34–47). Sage. doi:10.4135/9781848608207.n4

Reay, D. (1998). "Always knowing" and "never being sure": Familial and institutional habituses and higher education. *Journal of Education Policy, 13*(4), 519–529. doi:10.1080/0268093980130405

Redden, E. (2014). Teaching international students. *Inside Higher Education.* Retrieved from https://www.insidehighered.com/news/2014/12/01/increasing-international-enrollments-faculty-grapple-implications-classroom

Redden, E. (2018). For international students, shifting choices of where to study. *Inside Higher Ed.* https://www.insidehighered.com/news/2018/08/24/international-enrollments-slowing-or-declining-some-top-destination-countries-look

Rempel, H., & Davidson, J. (2008). Providing information literacy instruction to graduate students through literature review workshops. *Issues in Science and Technology Librarianship, 53.* Retrieved from https://pdxscholar.library.pdx.edu/ulib_fac/137/

Richards, E. (2019). *Who are the working women in Canada's top 1%?* Analytical Studies Branch Research Paper Series. Statistics Canada.

Ripmeester, N. (2019a). Employability and Alumni Relations. *Career Professor.* https://careerprofessor.works/employability

Ripmeester, N. (2019b). Essential ingredients for global talent. *LinkedIn.* https://www.linkedin.com/pulse/essential-ingredients-global-talent-nannette-ripmeester/?trackingId=VevkhGQCQcWaJz%2F9av5FGQ%3D%3D

Ripmeester, N. (2019c). *Setting s ail for success: key employability trends & ways to help international students thrive in the workplace.* Paper presented at the 2019 CBIE Atlantic Regional Meeting, Halifax.

Ripmeester, N., & Leese, B. (2018). *What's cooking? A recipe book for employability by Study Queensland.* Retrieved from Queensland: https://www.tiq.qld.gov.au/iet-strategy/wp-content/uploads/2019/06/StudyQld_Cookbook-for-Employability-AW-WEB.pdf

Rise, J., Sheeran, P., & Hukkelberg, S. (2010). The role of self-identity in the theory of planned behavior: A meta-analysis. *Journal of Applied Social Psychology, 40*(5), 1085–1105. doi:10.1111/j.1559-1816.2010.00611.x

Risquez, A., O'Dwyer, M., & Ledwith, A. (2011). Technology enhanced learning and plagiarism in entrepreneurship education. *Education + Training, 53*(8/9), 750–761. doi:10.1108/00400911111185062

Risquez, A., O'Dwyer, M., & Ledwith, A. (2013). 'Thou shalt not plagiarise': From self-reported views to recognition and avoidance of plagiarism. *Assessment & Evaluation in Higher Education, 38*(1), 34–43. doi:10.1080/02602938.2011.596926

Robertson, M., Line, M., Jones, S., & Thomas, S. (2000). International students, learning environments and perceptions: A case study using the Delphi technique. *Higher Education Research & Development, 19*(1), 89–102. doi:10.1080/07294360050020499

Roberts, P., & Dunworth, K. (2012). Staff and student perceptions of support services for international students in higher education: A case study. *Journal of Higher Education Policy and Management, 34*(5), 517–528.

Robinson, O., Somerville, K., & Walsworth, S. (2020). Understanding friendship formation between international and host-national students in a Canadian university. *Journal of International and Intercultural Communication, 13*(1), 49–70. doi:10.1080/17513057.2019.1609067

Robinson-Walke, C. (2011). The imposter syndrome. *Nurse Leader, 9*(4), 12–13. doi:10.1016/j.mnl.2011.05.003

Rosenthal, D. A., Russell, V. J., & Thomson, G. D. (2006). *A growing experience: The health and the well-being of international students at the University of Melbourne.* The University of Melbourne.

Roslyn Kunin & Associates, Inc. (2016). *Economic impact on international education in Canada- An update final report.* Retrieved from https://www.international.gc.ca/education/report-rapport/impact-2016/index.aspx?lang=eng

Roslyn Kunin & Associates, Inc. (2017). *Economic impact of international education in Canada: 2017 update.* Vancouver: RKA, Inc. Retrieved from https://www.international.gc.ca/education/report-rapport/impact-2017/index.aspx?lang=eng

Ross, C., & Dunphy, J. (2007). *Strategies for teaching assistant and international teaching assistant development: Beyond micro teaching.* Jossey-Bass.

Saccone, B. H. (2015). Food choices and eating patterns of international students in the United States: A phenomenological study. *International Public Health Journal, 7*(4), 357.

Sahragard, R., Khajavi, Y., & Abbasian, R. (2016). Field of study, learning styles, and language learning strategies of university students: Are there any relations? *Innovation in Language Learning and Teaching, 10*(3), 255–271. doi:10.1080/17501229.2014.976225

Sam, D. (2006). Acculturation: Conceptual background and core components. In D. Sam & J. Berry (Eds.), *The Cambridge handbook of acculturation psychology* (pp. 11–26). Cambridge University., doi:10.1017/CBO9780511489891.005

Sam, D. L. (2001). Satisfaction with life among international students: An exploratory study. *Social Indicators Research, 53*(3), 315–337. doi:10.1023/A:1007108614571

Samimy, K., Kim, S., Ah Lee, J., & Kasai, M. (2011). A participative inquiry in a TESOL program: Development of three NNES graduate students' legitimate peripheral participation to fuller participation. *Modern Language Journal, 95*(4), 558–574. doi:10.1111/j.1540-4781.2011.01247.x

Samnani, A. K., Boekhorst, J. A., & Harrison, J. A. (2013). The acculturation process: Antecedents, strategies, and outcomes. *Journal of Occupational and Organizational Psychology, 86*(2), 166–183. doi:10.1111/joop.12012

Sandín, M. (2009). Criterios de validez en la investigación cualitativa: De la objetividad a la solidaridad. *Revista de Investigación Educacional, 18*(1), 223–242.

Santos, T. (1988). Professors' reactions to the academic writing of nonnative-speaking students. *TESOL Quarterly, 22*(1), 69–90. doi:10.2307/3587062

Sardiko, L. (2004). *Guidelines on writing a term paper, a bachelor paper, a master paper.* Daugavpils, Latvija: Daugavpils University. Retrieved from https://du.lv/en/

Sawir, E., Marginson, S., Forbes-Mewett, H., Nyland, C., & Ramia, G. (2012). International student security and English language proficiency. *Journal of Studies in International Education, 16*(5), 434–454. doi:10.1177/1028315311435418

Sawyer, R. D., & Norris, J. (2012). Why duoethnography: Thoughts on the dialogues. In J. Norris, R. Sawyer, & D. E. Lund (Eds.), *Duoethnography: Dialogic methods for social, health, and educational research* (pp. 289–306). Routledge. doi:10.1093/acprof:osobl/9780199757404.001.0001

Schaffner, M., Burry-Stock, J. A., Cho, G., Boney, T., & Hamilton, G. (2000). *What do kids think when their teachers grade?* Paper presented at the annual meeting of the American Educational Research Association, New Orleans, LA.

Schein, E. H. (2010). *Organizational culture and leadership* (4th ed.). Jossey-Bass.

Schensual, S. L., Schensual, J. J., & LeCompte, M. D. (1999). *Essentials ethnographic methods observations, interviews, and questionnaires*. Sage.

Schilmann, P., & Choudaha, R. (2014). *International student retention and success: A comparative perspective*. Retrieved from http://wenr.wes.org/2014/09/international student-retention-and-success-a-comparative-perspective/

Schluter, P., Tautolo, E., & Paterson, J. (2011). Acculturation of Pacific mothers in New Zealand over time: Findings from the Pacific Islands Families study. *BMC Public Health, 11*(1), 307. doi:10.1186/1471-2458-11-307

Schmid, M. (2011). *Language attrition*. Cambridge University. doi:10.1017/CBO9780511852046

Schon, D. A. (1986). *Education the reflective practitioner: Toward a new design for teaching and learning in the professions*. Jossey-Bass.

Schroeder. (2011). *Coming in from the margins: Faculty development's emerging organizational development role in institutional change*. Stylus.

Schutz, A., & Richards, M. (2003). International students' experience of graduate study in Canada. *Journal of the International Society for Teacher Education, 7*(1), 56–63.

Schwartz, S. J., Montgomery, M. J., & Briones, E. (2006). The role of identity in acculturation among immigrant people: Theoretical propositions, empirical questions, and applied recommendations. *Human Development, 49*(1), 1–30. doi:10.1159/000090300

Scoggin, D., & Styron, R. (2006). Factors associated with student withdrawals from community college. *The Community College Enterprise, 12*, 111-25. Retrieved from www.schoolcraft.edu/pdfs/cce/12.1.111-124.pdf

Scott, C., Safdar, S., Desai Trilokekar, R., & El Masri, A. (2015). International students as 'ideal immigrants' in Canada: A disconnect between policy makers' assumptions and the lived experiences of international students. *International Education, 43*(3), Article 5.

Scott, P. (1998). *The globalization of higher education*. SHRE and Open University Press.

Scott, W. A., & Scott, R. (1989). *Adaptation of immigrants: Individual differences and determinants*. Pergamon.

Shalka, T. (2017). The impact of mentorship on leadership development outcomes of international students. *Journal of Diversity in Higher Education, 10*(2), 136–148. doi:10.1037/dhe0000016

Shanahan, T., & Jones, G. A. (2007). Shifting roles and approaches: Government coordination of post-secondary education in Canada, 1995-2006. *Higher Education Research & Development, 26*(1), 31–43. Advance online publication. doi:10.1080/07294360601166794

Shan, H., & Walter, P. (2015). Growing everyday multiculturalism. *Adult Education Quarterly, 65*(1), 19–34. doi:10.1177/0741713614549231

Shaw, K. (2014). Internationalization in Australia and Canada: Lessons for the future. *The College Quarterly, 17*(1), 1–17.

Sherman, R. R., & Webb, R. B. (2005). *Qualitative research in education: Focus and methods.* Routledge.

Sherry, M., Thomas, P., & Chui, W. H. (2010). International students: A vulnerable student population. *Higher Education, 60*(1), 33–46. doi:10.100710734-009-9284-z

Shields, C. M. (2007). *Bakhtin primer.* Peter Lang.

Shingler, B. (2019). CAQ's plan to slash immigration levels threatens Quebec economy, business groups say. *CBC News.* https://www.cbc.ca/news/canada/montreal/quebec-immigration-levels-hearings-1.5243632

Siddiq, F., Nethercote, W., Lye, J., & Baroni, J. (2012). The economic impact of international students in Atlantic Canada. *International Advances in Economic Research, 18*(2), 239–240. doi:10.100711294-012-9344-5

Simons, H. (2009). *Case study research in practice.* Sage. doi:10.4135/9781446268322

Singleton-Jackson, J., Lumsden, D. B., & Newson, R. (2009). Johnny still can't write, even if he goes to college: A study of writing proficiency in higher education graduate students. *Current Issues in Education (Tempe, Ariz.), 12*(10). https://cie.asu.edu/ojs/index.php/cieatasu/article/view/45/9

Sit, H. H. W. (2013). Characteristics of Chinese students' learning styles. *International Proceedings of Economics Development and Research, 62*(8), 36–39. doi:10.7763/IPEDR

Smith, C. (2020). International students and their academic experiences: Student satisfaction, student success challenges, and promising teaching practices. In U. Galuee, S. Sharma, & K. Bista (Eds.), *Rethinking education across borders: Emerging issues and critical insights on globally mobile students* (pp. 271–287). Springer., doi:10.1007/978-981-15-2399-1_16

Smith, C., Zhou, G., Potter, M., & Wang, D. (2019). Connecting best practices for teaching linguistically and culturally diverse international students with international student satisfaction and student perceptions of student learning. *Advances in Global Education and Research, 3*, 252–265.

Smith, C., Zhou, G., Potter, M., Wang, D., Pecoraro, M., & Paulino, R. (2019). Variability by individual student characteristics of student satisfaction with promising international student teaching practices. *Literacy Information and Computer Education Journal, 10*(2), 3160–3169. doi:10.20533/licej.2040.2589.2019.0415

Smith, M. W., Wilelm, J. D., & Fredricksen, J. (2013). The common core: New standards, new teaching. *Phi Delta Kappan, 94*(8), 45–48. doi:10.1177/003172171309400811

Smith, R. A., & Khawaja, N. G. (2011). A review of the acculturation experiences of international students. *International Journal of Intercultural Relations, 35*(6), 699–713. doi:10.1016/j.ijintrel.2011.08.004

Soderstrom, N. C., & Bjork, R. A. (2015). Learning versus performance: An integrative review. *Perspectives on Psychological Science, 10*(2), 176–199. doi:10.1177/1745691615569000 PMID:25910388

Soetan, T. O. (2020). Impact of support areas on the perceived academic success of international students in community colleges in Canada. *NAFSA Research Symposium Series*, Vol 4, 161-176.

Song, H., & Buchanan, D. (2019). Engaging English learners and their families: The power of non-fiction text and the participatory approach. *Reading Matrix: An International Online Journal, 19*(1), 47.

Spencer-Oatey, H., Dauber, D., Jing, J., & Lifei, W. (2017). Chinese students' social integration into the university community: Hearing the students' voices. *Higher Education, 74*(5), 739–756. doi:10.100710734-016-0074-0

Spring Institute. (2020). *What's the difference between multicultural, intercultural, and cross-cultural communication?* Retrieved from https://springinstitute.org/whats-difference-multicultural-intercultural-cross-cultural-communication/

Stake, R. E. (1995). *The art of case study research.* Sage.

Starr, K. (2009). Nursing education challenges: Students with English as an additional language. *The Journal of Nursing Education, 48*, 478–487. PMID:19645373

Statistics Canada. (2016). *International students in Canadian universities, 2004/2005 to 2013/2014.* http://www.statcan.gc.ca/pub/81-599-x/81-599-x2016011-eng.pdf

Statistics Canada. (2016). *Visible minority (15), Income statistics (17), Generation status (4), Age (10) and Sex (3) for the population aged 15 years and over in private households of Canada, provinces and territories, census metropolitan areas and census agglomerations, 2016 census – 25% sample data.* Data Tables, 2016 Census.

Statistics Canada. (2018). *Canadian postsecondary enrolments and graduates, 2016/2017.* Ottawa: Statistics Canada. Retrieved from https://www150.statcan.gc.ca/n1/daily-quotidien/181128/dq181128c-eng.htm

Statistics Canada. (2018). *Canadian postsecondary enrolments and graduates, 2016/2017.* Retrieved from https://www150.statcan.gc.ca/n1/daily-quotidien/181128/dq181128c-eng.htm

Statistics Canada. (2019, September 20). *International postsecondary students at school and at work.* Retrieved from https://www150.statcan.gc.ca/n1/en/pub/11-627-m/11-627-m2019070-eng.pdf?st=iDdtQogV

Steele, K. (2010). The changing Canadian PSE landscape. In J. Black (Ed.), *Strategic Enrolment Intelligence.* Retrieved from https://www.academica.ca/strategic-enrolment-intelligence

Ștefan, M. (2019). The human being and socialization through culture. *Memoria Ethnologica, 72/73*, 78–85.

Stier, J. (2004). Taking a critical stance toward internationalization ideologies in higher education: Idealism, instrumentalism and educationalism. *Globalisation, Societies and Education, 2*(1), 83–97. doi:10.1080/1476772042000177069

Stiggins, R. J. (2001). *Student-involved classroom assessment* (3rd ed.). Merrill Prentice Hall.

Stoilescu, D., & McDougall, D. (2010). Starting to publish academic research as a doctoral student. *International Journal of Doctoral Studies, 5*, 79–92. doi:10.28945/1333

Stoller, F., Horn, B., Grabe, W., & Robinson, M. S. (2005). Creating and validating assessment instruments for a discipline-specific writing course: An interdisciplinary approach. *Journal of Applied Linguistics, 2*(1), 75–104. doi:10.1558/japl.v2i1.75

Storm, B. C., Friedman, M. C., Murayama, K., & Bjork, R. A. (2014). On the transfer of prior tests or study events to subsequent study. *Journal of Experimental Psychology. Learning, Memory, and Cognition, 40*(1), 115–124. doi:10.1037/a0034252 PMID:23978234

Stukalina, Y. (2008). How to prepare students for productive and satisfying careers in the knowledge-based economy: Creating a more efficient educational environment. *Technological and Economic Development, Baltic Journal on Sustainability, 14*(2), 197-207.

Sucher, K. P., Kittler, P. G., & Nelms, M. (2016). *Food and culture.* Nelson Education.

Sulikowski, M. M. (2008, Spring). Copy, paste, plagiarize. *Vanderbilt Magazine*. Retrieved from https://news.vanderbilt.edu/vanderbiltmagazine/copy_paste_plagiarize/

Sullivan, C., & Kashubeck-West, S. (2015). The interplay of international students' acculturative stress, social support, and acculturation modes. *Journal of International Students, 5*(1), 1–11.

Sullivan, C., & Kashubeck-West, S. (2015). The Interplay of international students' acculturative stress, social support, and acculturation modes. *Journal of International Students, 5*(1), 1–11.

Sullivan, C., & Kashubeck-West, S. (2015). The interplay of international students' acculturative stress, social support, and acculturation modes. *Journal of International Studies, 5*(1), 1–11. https://jistudents.org/

Sutherland-Smith, W. (2010). Retribution, deterrence, and reform: The dilemmas of plagiarism management in universities. *Journal of Higher Education Policy and Management, 32*(1), 5–16. doi:10.1080/13600800903440519

Swagler, M. A., & Ellis, M. V. (2003). Crossing the distance: Adjustment of Taiwanese graduate students in the United States. *Journal of Counseling Psychology, 50*(4), 420–437. doi:10.1037/0022-0167.50.4.420

Swain, M., Kinnear, P., & Steinman, L. (2015). *Sociocultural theory in second language education: An introduction through narratives*. Multilingual Matters. doi:10.21832/9781783093182

Symonds, Q. (2020). *QS World University Ranking by Subject in Education 2020*. Retrieved from https://www.topuniversities.com/university-rankings/university-subject-rankings/2020/education-training

Szuchman, P. (2012). Imposter syndrome. *Women's Health (London, England), 9*(5), 128.

Tagg, J. (2008). Changing minds in higher education: Students change, so why can't college? *Planning for Higher Education, 37*(1), 15–22.

Tannock, S. (2018). *Educational equality and international students: Justice across borders?* Springer International Publishing AG. doi:10.1007/978-3-319-76381-1

Tatar, S. (2005). Classroom participation by international students: The case of Turkish graduate students. *Journal of Studies in International Education, 9*(4), 337–355. doi:10.1177/1028315305280967

Tavares, V. (2016). *The role of peer interaction and second language learning for ESL students in academic contexts: An extended literature review* (Unpublished Master's thesis). York University, Toronto, Canada.

Tavares, V. (2017). Reflecting on international students' experiences: Strategies that support academic success. *International Journal of Multidisciplinary Perspectives in Higher Education, 2*.

Tavares, V. (2020). *International students in higher education: Language, identity, and experience from a holistic perspective* (Unpublished doctoral dissertation). York University, Toronto, Canada.

Tavares, V. (2019). A review of peer interaction and second language learning for ELL students in academic contexts. *Canadian Journal for New Scholars in Education, 10*(2), 111–119.

Teixeira, J. P., Carraca, V. E., Markland, S., Silva, N. M., & Ryan, M. R. (2012). Exercise, physical activity, and Self-Determination Theory: A systematic review. *The International Journal of Behavioral Nutrition and Physical Activity*, (9), 1–30. PMID:22726453

Telbis, N. M., Helgeson, L., & Kingsbury, C. (2014). International students' confidence and academic success. *Journal of International Students, 4*(4), 330–341.

The Illuminate Consulting Group. (2009). *Department of Foreign Affairs and international Trade: Best practices on managing the delivery of Canadian education marketing.* Retrieved from https://www.international.gc.ca/education/reports-rapports.aspx?lang=eng&view=d

The Ministry of Advanced Education and Technology. (2010). *Advanced education and Technology Business Plan, 2010-2013.* Retrieved from http://www.advancededucation.gov.ab.ca/apps/publications/PublicationItem.asp?ID=912

The Pie News. (2019). *Canada: BC Institutions post $340m surpluses.* Retrieved from https://thepienews.com/news/british-columbia-post-340m-surpluses

Thomas, D. (2006). A general inductive approach for analyzing qualitative evaluation data. *The American Journal of Evaluation, 27*(2), 237–246. doi:10.1177/1098214005283748

Thomas, L. (2002). Student retention in higher education: The role of institutional habitus. *Journal of Education Policy, 17*(4), 423–442. doi:10.1080/02680930210140257

Thomson, C., & Esses, V. M. (2016). Helping the transition: Mentorship to support international students in Canada. *Journal of International Students, 6*(4), 873–886.

Times Higher Education (THE). (2019). *World university rankings 2019.* Retrieved December 1, 2019, from https://www.timeshighereducation.com/world-university-rankings/2019/worldranking#!/page/0/length/25/sort_by/rank/sort_order/asc/cols/stats

Tinto, B. (1993). *Leaving college: Rethinking the causes and cures of student attrition.* University of Chicago Press.

Tolman, S. (2017). The effects of a roommate-pairing program on international student satisfaction and academic success. *Journal of International Students, 7*(3), 522–541.

Toman, J. (2016, April 8). Long Odds for International Students to Land a Job. *CBC News.* Retrieved from https://www.cbc.ca/news/canada/windsor/international-students-tuition-jobs-1.3525821

Tomasello, M. (2019). *Becoming human: A theory of ontogeny.* Harvard. doi:10.4159/9780674988651

Tompson, H. B., & Tompson, G. H. (1996). Confronting diversity issues in the classroom with strategies to improve satisfaction and retention of international students. *Journal of Education for Business, 72*(1), 53–57. doi:10.1080/08832323.1996.10116826

Torkildsen, L. G., & Erickson, G. (2016). 'If they'd written more…'– On students' perceptions of assessment and assessment practices. *Education Inquiry, 7*(2), 27416. doi:10.3402/edui.v7.27416

Torrance, H. (2013). Qualitative research, science, and government: Evidence, criteria, policy, and politics. In N. K. Denzin & Y. S. Lincoln (Eds.), *Collecting and interpreting qualitative materials* (4th ed., pp. 355–380). Sage.

Toughill, K. (2019). Express Entry stalls for student immigrants to Canada. *Polestar Student Immigration News.* https://studentimmigration.ca/express-entry-international-student-canada/

Touraine, A. (2001). *Beyond neoliberalism.* Polity Press.

TRA. (2019). *Employer perceptions of hiring international graduates.* Retrieved from New Zealand Education: https://intellilab.enz.govt.nz/document/583-tra-enz-employer-value-book-pdf?_ga=2.90425946.1569402105.1562193360-1689215942.1528279883

Trainor, L. (2010). The emotional origin of music. *Physics of Life Reviews, 7*(1), 44–45. doi:10.1016/j.plrev.2010.01.010 PMID:20374924

Tran, L. T., & Vu, T. T. P. (2018). "Agency in mobility": Towards a conceptualisation of international student agency in transnational mobility. *Educational Review, 70*(2), 167–187. doi:10.1080/00131911.2017.1293615

Trice, A. (2003). Faculty perceptions of graduate international students: The benefits and challenges. *Journal of Studies in International Education, 7*(4), 379–403.

Trice, A. G. (2004). Mixing it up: International graduate students' social interactions with American students. *Journal of College Student Development, 45*(6), 671–687. doi:10.1353/csd.2004.0074

Trice, A. G. (2007). Faculty Perspectives regarding graduate international students' isolation from host national students. *International Education Journal, 8*(1), 108–117.

Trilokekar, R. D. (2010). International education as soft power? The contributions and challenges of Canadian foreign policy to the internationalization of higher education. *Higher Education, 59*(2), 131–147. doi:10.100710734-009-9240-y

Trilokekar, R. P., & Kizilbash, Z. (2013). IMAGINE: Canada as a leader in international education. How can Canada benefit from the Australian experience? *Canadian Journal of Higher Education, 43*(2), 1–26.

Troia, G. A., & Olinghouse, N. (2013). The common core standards and evidence-based educational practices: The case of writing. *School Psychology Review, 42*(3), 343–357. https://www.researchgate.net/.../258148583_The_Common_Core_State

Tseng, W. C., & Newton, F. B. (2002). International students' strategies for well-being. *College Student Journal, 36*(4), 591–597.

Turner, Y. (2006). Chinese students in a UK business school: Hearing the student voice in reflective teaching and learning practice. *Higher Education Quarterly, 60*(1), 27–51. doi:10.1111/j.1468-2273.2006.00306.x

Tweed, R. G., & Lehman, D. R. (2002). Learning considered within a cultural context: Confucian and Socratic approaches. *The American Psychologist, 57*(2), 89–99. doi:10.1037/0003-066X.57.2.89 PMID:11899565

Uberoi, V. (2016). Legislating multiculturalism and nationhood: the 1988 Canadian Multiculturalism Act. *Canadian Journal of Political Science/Revue canadienne de science politique, 49*(2), 267-287.

United Nations Educational, Scientific and Cultural Organization (UNESCO). (2013). *The international mobility of students in Asia and the Pacific.* UNESCO.

Universities Canada. (2014). *Canada's universities in the world: AUCC internationalization survey.* Ottawa: Universities Canada. Retrieved from https://www.univcan.ca/wp-content/uploads/2015/07/internationalization-survey-2014.pdf

Universities Canada. (2015). *Universities and colleges: Partners in education.* Retrieved on 14/7/18 from https://www.univcan.ca/universities/universities-and-colleges-partners-in education/

University of Idaho. (n.d.). *Information literacy.* Retrieved from https://www.webpages.uidaho.edu/info_literacy/modules/module1/1_0.htm

University of Windsor. (2020a). *English language improvement program (ELIP).* Retrieved from https://www.uwindsor.ca/englishlanguagedevelopment/301/elip

University of Windsor. (2020b). *Master of management.* Retrieved from http://odette.uwindsor.ca/366/master-management

University of Windsor. (2020c). *Overall – 10 year historical.* University of Windsor Office of Institutional Analysis.

Unruh, S. (2015). Struggling international students in the US: Do university faculty know how to help. *Athens Journal of Education, 2*(2), 99–110.

Van Dijk, T. A. (1994). Academic nationalism. *Discourse & Society, 5*(3), 275–276. doi:10.1177/0957926594005003001

Vardi, I. (2012). Developing students' referencing skills: A matter of plagiarism, punishment and morality or of learning to write critically? *Higher Education Research & Development, 31*(6), 921–930. doi:10.1080/07294360.2012.673120

Vasilopoulos, G. (2016). A critical review of international students' adjustment research from a Deleuzian perspective. *Journal of International Students, 6*(1), 283–307.

Vincenti, V. B. (2001). Exploration of the relationship between international experiences and the interdisciplinary work of university faculty. *Journal of Studies in International Studies, 5*(1), 42–63. doi:10.1177/102831530151004

Vincent-Lancrin, S., Urgel, J., Kar, S., & Jacobin, G. (2019). *Measuring innovation in education 2019: What has changed in the classroom?* Paris: Educational Research and Innovation, OECD Publishing. . doi:10.1787/9789264311671-en

Vita, G. D. (2000). Inclusive approaches to effective communication and active participation in the multicultural classroom: An international business management context. *Learning in Higher Education, 1*(2), 168–180. doi:10.1177/1469787400001002006

Vygotsky, L. S. (1978). *Mind in society: The development of higher psychological processes. Cambridge.* Harvard University Press.

Wadhwa, R. (2016). Understanding decision-making and process and destination choice of Indian students. *Higher Education Council, 3*(1), 54–75. doi:10.1177/2347631115610221

Wall, T., Tran, L. T., & Soejatminah, S. (2017). Inequalities and agencies in workplace learning experiences: International student perspectives. *Vocations and Learning, 10*(2), 141–156. doi:10.100712186-016-9167-2

Wang, X. (2009). *Institutional recruitment strategies and international undergraduate student university choice at two Canadian universities* (Doctoral dissertation). University of Toronto. ProQuest Dissertations and Theses database. Retrieved from https://search.proquest.com/docview/375478075?accountid=28180

Wang, V. C. X., & Kreysa, P. (2006). Instructional strategies of distance education instructors in China. *Journal of Educators Online, 3*(1), 1–25. doi:10.9743/JEO.2006.1.4

Wang, Y. (2014). A survey of postgraduates' state of language learning at graduate school, Chinese academy of social science. *Theory and Practice in Language Studies, 4*(1), 160–166. doi:10.4304/tpls.4.1.160-166

Ward, C., & Geeraert, N. (2016). Advancing acculturation theory and research: The acculturation process in its ecological context. *Current Opinion in Psychology, 8*, 98–104.

Wargo, J. M. (2018). Earwitnessing (in)equity: Tracing the intra-active encounters of 'being-in-resonance-with' sound and the social contexts of education. *Educational Studies, 54*(2), 1–14.

Waring, M., & Evans, C. (2015). *Understanding pedagogy: Developing a critical approach to teaching and learning.* Routledge.

Waterfall, B., & Maiter, S. (2003). *Resisting colonization in the academy: From indigenous minoritized standpoints.* Paper presented at the Canadian Critical Race Conference, Vancouver, Canada.

Watering, G., Gijbels, D., Dochy, F., & Rijt, J. (2008). Students' assessment preferences, perceptions of assessment and their relationships to study results. *Higher Education, 56*(6), 645–658. doi:10.100710734-008-9116-6

Waters, J. L. (2012). Geographies of international education: Mobilities and the reproduction of social (dis)advantage. *Geography Compass, 6*(2), 123–136. doi:10.1111/j.1749-8198.2011.00473.x

Webb, A. S., Wong, T. J., & Hubball, H. T. (2013). Professional development for adjunct teaching faculty in a research-intensive university: Engagement in scholarly approaches to teaching and learning. *International Journal of Teaching and Learning in Higher Education, 25*(2), 231-238. Retrieved from http://www.isetl.org/ijtlhe

Webb, R. K. (2015). Teaching English writing for a global context: An examination of NS, ESL, EFL learning strategies that work, *PASAA Journal – Chulalongkorn University Language Institute, 49*, 171-198. Retrieved from http://www.culi.chula.ac.th/publicationsonline/home_p1.php

Weidler, B., Multhaup, K., & Faust, M. (2012). Accountability reduces unconscious plagiarism. *Applied Cognitive Psychology, 26*(4), 626–634. doi:10.1002/acp.2842

Weiss, M. J., Visher, M. G., Weissman, V., & Wathington, H. (2015). The impact of learning community for students in developmental education: A synthesis of findings from randomized trails at six community colleges. *Educational Evaluation and Policy Analysis, 37*(4), 520–541. doi:10.3102/0162373714563307

Wermund, B. (2018, April 23). *Trump blamed as US colleges lure fewer foreign students.* Retrieved from https://www.politico.com/story/2018/04/23/foreign-students-colleges-trump-544717

Williams, J. D. (2014). *Preparing to teach writing: Research, theory and practice.* Routledge. doi:10.4324/9780203082683

Wilson-Forsberg, S. C., Power, P., Kilgour, V., & Darling, S. (2018). From class assignment to friendship: enhancing the intercultural competence of domestic and international students through experiential learning. *Comparative and International Education/Éducation Comparée et Internationale, 47*(1), 3.

Windle, S., Hamilton, B., Zeng, M., & Yang, X. (2008). Negotiating the culture of the academy: Chinese graduate students in Canada. *Comparative and International Education/Éducation Comparée et Internationale, 37*(1), 71-90.

Wintergerst, A., & DeCapua, A. (2001). Exploring the learning styles of Russian-speaking ESL students. *The CATESOL Journal, 13*, 23–46.

Wong, J. K. (2004). Are the learning styles of Asian international students culturally or contextually based? *International Education Journal, 4*(4), 154–166.

Wu, H., Garza, E., & Guzman, N. (2015). International student's challenge and adjustment to college. *Education Research International, 2015*, 1–9. doi:10.1155/2015/202753

Wu, X. (2009). The dynamics of Chinese face mechanisms and classroom behavior: A case study. *Evaluation and Research in Education, 22*(2), 87–105.

Wyatt, J. C. (2000). When to use Web-based surveys. *Journal of the American Medical Informatics Association, 7*, 426–430. PMID:10887170

Xiang, B. (2017). *Classroom engagement and participation among Chinese international graduate students: A case study.* Retrieve from Scholarship at UWindsor. (6028)

Xing, D. (2017). *Exploring academic acculturation experiences of Chinese international students with low oral English proficiency: A musically enhanced narrative inquiry* (Master's thesis). Queen's University, Kingston, Canada. https://qspace.library.queensu.ca/handle/1974/15922

Xing, D. C., & Bolden, B. (2019). Treading on a foreign land: A multiple case study of Chinese international students' academic acculturation experiences. *Student Success, 10*(3), 25–35. doi:10.5204sj.v10i3.1406

Xing, D., Bolden, B., & Hogenkamp, S. (2019). The sound of silence: A musically enhanced narrative inquiry into the academic acculturation experiences of Chinese international students with low oral English proficiency. *Journal of Curriculum and Pedagogy*. Advance online publication. doi:10.1080/15505170.2019.1627616

Xu, L. (2015). Transitional challenges faced by post-secondary international students and approaches for their successful inclusion in classrooms. *International Journal for Leadership in Learning, 1*(3), 1–28.

Xu, Y. J. (2016). Attention to retention: Exploring and addressing the needs of college students in STEM majors. *Journal of Education and Training Studies, 4*(2), 67–76.

Yang, W. (2018). *Investigating academic challenges and coping strategies of Chinese international graduate students in Canadian universities* (Unpublished master's thesis). McGill University, Montreal, Canada.

Yang, X. (2017). *Problems Chinese international students face during academic adaptation in English-speaking higher institutions* (Master thesis). University of Victoria, Canada. Retrieved from https://dspace.library.uvic.ca/handle/1828/8086

Yang, B. (2014). Using non-finites in English academic writing by Chinese EFL students. *English Language Teaching, 7*(2), 42–52. doi:10.5539/elt.v7n2p42

Yang, K., & Chung, S. H. (2015). Key factors for developing a cross-cultural education program. *International Journal of Educational Management, 29*(2), 222–233. doi:10.1108/IJEM-12-2013-0177

Yang, L. (2010). Doing a group presentation: Negotiations and challenges experienced by five Chinese ESL students of commerce at a Canadian university. *Language Teaching Research, 14*(2), 141–160. doi:10.1177/1362168809353872

Yang, R., Noels, K., & Saumure, K. (2006). Multiple routes to cross-cultural adaptation for international students: Mapping the paths between self-construals, English language confidence, and adjustment. *International Journal of Intercultural Relations, 30*(4), 487–506. doi:10.1016/j.ijintrel.2005.11.010

Yan, K., & Berliner, D. C. (2011). Chinese international students in the United States: Demographic trends, motivations, acculturation features and adjustment challenges. *Asia Pacific Education Review, 12*(2), 173–184. doi:10.100712564-010-9117-x

Yates, L., & Thi Quynnh Trang, N. (2012). Beyond a discourse of deficit: The meaning of silence in the international classroom. *The International Education Journal: Comparative Perspectives, 11*(1), 22-34.

Yeh, C. J. (2003). Age, acculturation, cultural adjustment, and mental health symptoms of Chinese, Korean, and Japanese immigrant youths. *Cultural Diversity & Ethnic Minority Psychology, 9*(1), 34. PMID:12647324

Yeh, C. J., & Inose, M. (2003). International students' reported English fluency, social support satisfaction, and social connectedness as predictors of acculturative stress. *Counselling Psychology Quarterly, 16*(1), 15–28. doi:10.1080/0951507031000114058

Yen, W. J., & Stevens, P. (2004). Taiwanese students' perspectives on their educational experiences in the United States. *International Education Journal, 5*(3), 294–307.

Yin, R. K. (2014). *Case study research: Design and methods*. Sage Publications.

Youmans, R. (2011). Does the adoption of plagiarism-detection software in higher education reduce plagiarism? *Studies in Higher Education, 36*(7), 749–761. doi:10.1080/03075079.2010.523457

Yuan, W. (2011). Academic and cultural experiences of Chinese students at an American university: A qualitative study. *Intercultural Communication Studies, 20*(1), 141–157. https://web.uri.edu/iaics/files/11WenliYuan.pdf

Zhang, Z. (2008). *Finding the critical edge: Helping Chinese students achieve optimal development in academic writing* [Unpublished Master Thesis]. Retrieved from The University of Western Ontario, London, ON, Canada.

Zhang, Z., & Beck, K. (2014). I came, but I'm lost: Learning stories of three Chinese international students in Canada. *Comparative and International Education / Éducation Comparée et Internationale, 43*(2), 1-14.

Zhang, J., & Goodson, P. (2011). Acculturation and psychosocial adjustment of Chinese international students: Examining mediation and moderation effects. *International Journal of Intercultural Relations, 35*(5), 614–627. doi:10.1016/j.ijintrel.2010.11.004

Zhang, J., & Goodson, P. (2011). Predictors of international students' psychosocial adjustment to life in the United States: A systematic review. *International Journal of Intercultural Relations, 35*(2), 139–162. doi:10.1016/j.ijintrel.2010.11.011

Zhang, Y. (2015). Intercultural communication competence: Advising international students in a Texas community. *NACADA Journal, 35*(2), 48–59. doi:10.12930/NACADA-15-007

Zhang, Z., & Almani, A. (2018). Information literacy education and plagiarism issues: Inputs from international graduate students. *International Journal of Research in Engineering and Technology, 7*(7), 1–7. doi:10.15623/ijret.2018.0707001

Zhang, Z., & Brunton, M. (2007). Differences in living and learning: Chinese international students in New Zealand. *Journal of Studies in International Education, 11*(2), 124–140. doi:10.1177/1028315306289834

Zhang, Z., & Mi, Y. (2010). Another look at the language difficulties of international students. *Journal of Studies in International Education, 14*(4), 371–387.

Zhang, Z., & Xu, J. (2007). Understanding Chinese international graduate students' adaptation to learning in North America: A cultural perspective. *Higher Education Perspective, 3*(1), 45–59.

Zhang, Z., & Zhang, W. (2013). I am not what you thought I should be: Learning accounts of Chinese international students. *The International Journal of Social Sciences (Islamabad), 3*(6), 576–581. doi:10.7763/IJSSH.2013.V3.306

Zhang, Z., & Zhou, G. (2010). Understanding Chinese international students at a Canadian university: Perspectives, expectations, and experiences. *Canadian and International Education. Education Canadienne et Internationale, 39*(3), 43–58.

Zhang, Z., & Zhou, G. (2010). Understanding Chinese international students at a Canadian university: Perspectives, expectations, and experiences. *Comparative and International Education, 39*(3), 1–16.

Zhao, C.-M., Kuh, G. D., & Carini, R. M. (2005). A comparison of international student and American student engagement in effective educational practices. *The Journal of Higher Education, 76*(2), 209–232. doi:10.1353/jhe.2005.0018

Zhao, J. C., & Mawhinney, T. (2015). Comparison of native Chinese-speaking and native English-speaking engineering students' information literacy challenges. *Journal of Academic Librarianship, 41*(6), 712–724. doi:10.1016/j.acalib.2015.09.010

Zheng, J. (2010). Neoliberal globalization, higher education policies and international student flows: An exploratory case study of Chinese graduate student flows to Canada. *Journal of Alternative Perspectives in the Social Sciences, 2*, 216–244.

Zheng, X., & Berry, J. W. (1991). Psychological adaptation of Chinese sojourners in Canada. *International Journal of Psychology, 26*(4), 451–470. doi:10.1080/00207599108247134

Zhou, G., & Zhang, Z. (2014). A study of the first year international students at a Canadian university: Challenges and experiences with social integration. *Canadian and International Education / Education Canadienne et International, 43*(2), Article 7.

Zhou, G., & Zhang, Z. (2014). A study of the first year international students at a Canadian university: Challenges and experiences with social integration. *Canadian and International Education. Education Canadienne et Internationale, 43*(2), 7.

Zhou, Y., Jindal-Snape, D., Topping, K., & Todman, J. (2008). Theoretical models of culture shock and adaptation in international students in higher education. *Studies in Higher Education, 33*(1), 63–75. doi:10.1080/03075070701794833

Zhu, W., & Flaitz, J. (2005). Using focus group methodology to understand international students' academic language needs: A comparison of perspectives. *Teaching English as a Second or Foreign Language, 8*(4), 1–11. Retrieved from http://tesl-ej.org/ej32/a3.html

Zimmerman, M. (2012). Plagiarism and international students in academic libraries. *New Library World, 113*(5), 290–299. doi:10.1108/03074801211226373

Zimmerman, S. (1995). Perceptions of intercultural communication competence and international student adaptation to an American campus. *Communication Education, 44*(4), 321–335. doi:10.1080/03634529509379022

About the Contributors

Vander Tavares earned a PhD in Applied Linguistics from York University, Toronto, in which he explored the academic, linguistic, and identity-related experiences of multilingual international students in Canada. He is currently an instructor of academic communications skills at Sheridan College, Mississauga. He has extensive experience working with multilingual domestic and international students at the post-secondary level in Canada. His teaching and support experiences have focused on the development of academic language, critical thinking, and research skills in college and university students. In addition to Sheridan College, he has worked with multilingual international students at York University, Brock University, Seneca College, and Saint Mary's University.

* * *

Dawn Andrews, BA/Psych, BSW, MSW, RSW, EDD, is a published author, a professional educator, and has over 25 years counselling experience in social services (i.e., crisis centres, the provincial ministry of health, federally with Veterans Affairs, and an incorporated private practice). Specifically, she has worked extensively with First Nations, multicultural groups, family and children, teens, and adults. Her expertise includes health and human services (e.g., interpersonal communication, business ethics, conflict resolution, human development, prevention, and substance use). Dawn combines practical application and theory to offer individualized feedback focused on students' growth. Her dual-major master's degree focused on administration, not-for-profits, social service management, personnel, social action, career planning and management, and service organizational management. Dr. Andrews' current research focuses on students' experience in international higher education. She is currently completing a book chapter. She is a member of NAFSA Trainer Corp and facilitates workshops at the Annual NAFSA conferences.

Lena Barrantes received her Ph.D. in Educational Research at the University of Calgary. Her current research focuses on analyzing the professional agency of Costa Rican English language instructors in higher education as informed by their rural working contexts on regional campuses and their condition as non-native English speakers.

Benjamin Bolden, music educator and composer, is an associate professor and UNESCO Chair of Arts and Learning at Queen's University, Canada. His research interests include creativity, arts education systems around the world, the learning and teaching of composing, arts-based research, teacher education, teacher knowledge, and teachers' professional learning.

Rohene Bouajram is a passionate proponent of international education and has over a decade of experience in the leadership and delivery of immigration advisory services, international and domestic recruitment, policy evaluation, risk management, program development, intercultural and transition support, crisis intervention and coaching at multiple educational institutions in Canada. Her MA thesis in Intercultural and International Communication focused on the post-graduation experiences of international students; thereby allowing her to compliment her professional work with research. Through her RCIC certification, she also teaches courses on immigration policy and practice. Her excitement for holding space for courageous conversations often leads her to dive headfirst into opportunities to engage ethically and authentically in intercultural settings.

Aylin Çakıroğlu Çevik received her Bachelor's degree from Department of Sociology in Ankara University (Ankara/Turkey) in 2002 and she started her master education in Department of Sociology in Middle East Technical University (METU)(Ankara/Turkey) in the same year. After she received her Master's degree in 2007, she continued her Ph.D. at the same university. In 2011, she had been in University of California, Los Angeles (UCLA) as a visiting scholar and she received her Ph.D. degree from METU in 2015. Dr. Aylin Çakıroğlu Çevik, who worked as a research assistant in the Department of Sociology in METU between 2002 and 2015, has been working as an assistant professor at TED University since 2017. Her research interest includes sociology of education, higher education, quality of life, happiness, aging, methodology and quantitative research methods, social inequality, migration, and gender studies.

Lianne Fisher works with all members of the Brock University instructional community. Her background working as a Learning Strategist in the University and College settings has fostered an understanding of the relationship between teaching, learning, instruction, and content. She is committed to access, inclusion, and diversity. She is an Instructional Skills Workshop (ISW) facilitator and trainer. Her education background includes a BA (Hons.) in Lifespan Development from Simon Fraser University; a MA in Child and Youth Studies (Multidisciplinary Programme); and a Certificate in Women's & Gender Studies. She is currently a PhD student in the Joint Educational Studies program at Brock University.

Sophia Junfang Fu works at the Registrar's Office at Mount Saint Vincent University in Halifax. She came to Canada for Master's study after an eight-year-long career in international education in Beijing, China. By involving herself in various academic activities and volunteer work, Sophia has gained valuable insight into the challenges and obstacles international students face. In her current role, she assists international students in their adaptation to Canadian education and ultimately their integration into society. She is passionate about volunteering, travelling, and international education.

Yue Gu is an international student educator, who has been working in this area for 10 years now. She is interested in research about international education, academic and professional acculturation of immigrants, the relationship between assessment and learning, and socio-economic disparities in academic achievement.

Haojun Guo is a doctoral student in the Faculty of Education, University of Windsor. She is the Graduate Research Assistant for the Reciprocal Learning Program. Her research interests center on childhood bilingualism, translanguaging, foreign language education and cognition development. Her current research interest is in Chinese immigrant children's language development in Canada.

Jennifer Guy is a registered dietitian and full-time faculty member in the Business and Tourism Department at Mount Saint Vincent University (MSVU). Her research interests are in critical food studies, intercultural learning, adult education, and tourism (specifically the food and beverage industry). Jennifer received an IQN Innovation Award, (Citizenship and Immigration Canada) for her work on the MSVU Dietetic Bridging Project. She is a member of the multi-stakeholder group for Internationally Educated Dietitians, as well as a co-faculty advisor for the Inter-cultural Food Bridging Society. Jennifer's doctoral work explores how concepts of adult education are understood and applied in tourism and hospitality programs and industry. She has received a doctoral award from the Social Sciences and Humanities Research Council of Canada.

Darren Howes has his Doctorate in Business Administration from Northcentral University and his Master's in Business Administration from the University of Saskatchewan. Darren has been with MHC since 2002 where he teaches international business, economics and business integration. He has also previously lectured for Athabasca University in the area of international business management and international economics. Darren began his career at MHC as a recruiter before moving into the faculty of business. Along with his teaching, Darren has been the coordinator for the Business Administration program and chair of the department of business. Darren is a faculty advisor for Enactus MHC, an international leadership development program and has also been a faculty advisor for several case competitions including the Alberta Deans of Business Case Competition and the Cor Van Raay Agribusiness Case Competition. Along with tremendous success at these competitions, Darren was awarded a Global Best Award for Community Partnerships from the International Partnership Network in Oslo, Norway in 2016 and in Houston, Texas in 2018.

Xiaoli Jing is a doctoral student at the Department of Integrated Studies in Education in McGill University. Her research interests include the internationalization of education, cross-border education, and international students. She has published over twenty journal articles, book chapters, and newspaper articles in English and Chinese languages. Her journal articles were published on journals including Higher Education, Journal of Higher Education Policy and Management, and International and Comparative Education Review in China.

Gagneet Kaur is an undergraduate international student at the University of Windsor. She participated in this research project as a member of the International Student Learning Community.

Yue Li is currently a MScAHN student at Mount Saint Vincent University (MSVU). During her undergraduate study in dietetics at MSVU she was inspired to explore a non-traditional approach in the field of food and nutrition, including examining the importance of social and cultural factors in population's well-being. Yue is one of the founders of the Inter-Cultural Food Bridging Society, which aims to enhance the learning and living experience of international students and inform cultural competency for all students at MSVU.

Guoying (Grace) Liu is a Systems Librarian and Engineering Liaison Librarian at the University of Windsor. Her research interests include library services for international students, library technology, electronic resources management, and library publishing. Grace is the inaugural Editor-in-Chief of International Journal of Librarianship and the inaugural President of Chinese American Librarians Association Canada Chapter.

Daphne Lordly is a Professor and Chair in the Applied Human Nutrition at Mount Saint Vincent University (MSVU). Her primary research interest area and collaborations are in the area of dietetic education where she seeks to ask new questions and advance practice. She is a co-faculty advisor for the MSVU Inter-cultural Food Bridging Society. Daphne is a Dietitians of Canada Fellow and has received an Honorary Life Membership Award from the Nova Scotia Dietetic Association. She is a recipient of the Recognizing Learning Award for outstanding achievement in the field of prior learning and qualification recognition.

Fabiana Menezes holds a Master of Education in Second Language Acquisition and has been involved in research about culturally and linguistically diverse learners in Canada. Ms. Menezes has been teaching English and Portuguese as additional languages to students from diverse origins and her research interests include social justice, race, class, and gender issues, theories, and applicable equity teaching and learning practices.

Glory Ovie received her PhD in Educational Research from the Werklund School of Education, University of Calgary. She is currently a postdoctoral associate at the University of Calgary. Her research focuses on crises response in postsecondary institutions and the intersection between teaching and learning and mental health and wellbeing of students and faculty.

Karen Pillon is an Associate University Librarian at the Leddy Library, University of Windsor. In previous roles, Karen has worked with international students spearheading initiatives such as the "English Conversation Group" at the Leddy library, and has been a strong advocate of international students through her past role as International Student Liaison.

Anouchka Plumb holds a PhD in Education. Her research interests include higher education internationalization, commodification and commercialization; English for academic purpose pathway program development; learner engagement through technology; international students' postsecondary schooling experiences; international student mental wellness; and learner motivation. Anouchka is the Manager of Language Programs in Continuing Education at the University of Windsor. Anouchka oversees the English for academic purpose pathway program, TESL Canada Standard One and Two teacher education certification programs and a range of community and industry-based language courses.

Michael Potter joined the University of Windsor's Centre for Teaching and Learning (CTL) in 2008, where he is now a Teaching and Learning Specialist. Since joining the CTL he has served as co-creator and coordinator of the University Teaching Certificate (UTC) Program (2009-2017), Chair of the Council of Ontario Educational Developers, Secretary and Vice-President of the Bertrand Russell Society, and in many other capacities for internal and external committees and organizations. He has published a variety of academic and popular works, and is the author of Bertrand Russell's Ethics (2006), co-author of Leading Effective Discussions (2008) and Learning Outcomes Assessment: A Practitioner's Handbook (2015), and co-editor of a special issue of the Canadian Journal for the Scholarship of Teaching and Learning focused on the role of the arts and humanities in SoTL (2015).

Philipp Reichert received his doctorate from the University of Calgary with his dissertation focused on the internationalization higher education and the nexus of government policies, institutional programming and international student career transitions. He received his Masters degree with honours in International Relations from Leiden University in the Netherlands where he was a Nuffic Huygens scholar. Philipp is an experienced international educator with over fifteen year's experience living, studying, and working internationally. Currently, he is the Manager of International Programs and Services at UBC's Okanagan campus, the Co-Chair of the Canadian Bureau for International Education (CBIE) Immigration Advisory Committee and a member of the Central Okanagan Local Immigration Partnership Committee (COLIP). Before joining UBC, he worked at the Rotterdam School of Management at Erasmus University, and the Hague Centre for Strategic Studies. In 2016, he was recognized for his contributions to international education in Canada with the CBIE North Star Award for Emerging Leader in International Education.

Glenn Rideout is Associate Dean, Graduate Studies and Research at the University of Windsor, Canada. He has taught at the University level in both Central and Western Canada. While his research includes topics within Educational Policy and Leadership studies, he is most passionate about humanistic approaches in teaching and learning, both locally and internationally. These domains include Pupil Control Ideologies, Restorative Justice, and experiences of international students in Graduate Studies programs. His funded research and development work have taken him to locations in Africa, Asia, Scandinavia, the US and Canada as a researcher and conference keynote speaker. Dr. Rideout's research has been published in a wide variety of national and international journals such as the Canadian Journal of Education (CSSE), Journal of Educational Administration (Emerald), and Contemporary Justice Review (Taylor and Francis).

Clayton Smith has an Ed.D. from Florida State University. He is an Associate Professor at the University of Windsor in the Faculty of Education where he teaches at both the undergraduate and graduate levels. Over the course of his career, Dr. Smith has amassed significant knowledge and expertise in the areas of enrolment management, internationalization of higher education, and student success.

Taiwo O. Soetan (ORCID-0000-0002-4270-8213) obtained his PhD in Leadership, Higher Education, from the University of North Dakota, Grand Forks, U.S, two masters' degrees in Economics and Economic Management & Policy from the University of Manitoba, Winnipeg, Canada, and Strathclyde Business School, University of Strathclyde, Glasgow, U.K respectively, and his first degree from the University of Ibadan, Nigeria. He is the erstwhile Vice Chairman of the former Canadian Institute of Marketing (CIM), now Canadian Institute of Marketing Management of Ontario (CIMMO). He presently lectures in the Business Administration program at the School of Business, Information Technology & Creative Arts, Red River College, Winnipeg, Canada where he presently conducts his teaching, research, and community service responsibilities.

Deena Wang is International Student Advisor at the University of Windsor. She previously served as Coordinator of International Student Recruitment. Ms. Wang holds two master degrees from York University and Group T – Leuven Institute of Technology, Belgium. She has engaged in various areas of international education including cross-cultural training, recruitment, translations, advising, and has built partnership programs.

398

Deyu (Cindy) Xing is a recent M.Ed. graduate in the Faculty of Education at Queen's University, Canada. She earned both her B.Ec. and B.A. at Beijing Foreign Studies University in China prior to Queen's. Her research interests include foreign language acquisition/education, international students' academic acculturation, and at-risk learners' thriving.

Shijing Xu is Canada Research Chair in International and Intercultural Reciprocal Learning in Education and Professor at the Faculty of Education, University of Windsor. She is the Project Director for a SSHRC Partnership Grant Project, to foster reciprocal learning in teacher education and school education between Canada and China.

Wei Yang graduated from McGill University with a Master's degree of Arts. As a Chinese international student herself, Miss Wei Yang has always been interested in understanding the academic challenges that she encountered as an international student. She believes in order to cope with these academic challenges, it is imperative to have a thorough understanding of the reasons behind these challenges so that corresponding coping strategies can be developed and applied.

Zongyong Yu is the principal of an international school. He has recently received a MEd from the University of Windsor. His research and career interests are focused on international education.

Zuochen Zhang is a Professor at the Faculty of Education, University of Windsor, Canda. His research interests include Action research, e-learning, ICT integration into school curriculum, International education, teacher education, and Teaching English as a Second Language (TESL)/Teaching English as a Foreign Lanauges (TEFL).

George Zhou has a PhD in science education from the University of Alberta. He is a Professor at the Faculty of Education, University of Windsor, Canada. He taught in City University of New York before moving to Windsor. His research covers science education, teacher education, educational technology, and comparative and international education.

Index

A

Academic Acculturation 39, 41-52, 54-57, 59, 61, 104

Academic Challenges 65, 120-125, 127-128, 130-131, 133-134, 136, 171

Academic Contexts 44, 54, 61, 117-118, 244

Academic English 110, 118, 163, 193, 336

Academic Experience 22, 65, 103-104, 107, 190, 200, 205-208, 214, 219

Academic Integrity 222, 224, 230, 240, 242, 244-246, 257, 259, 262

Academic Library 240, 260, 262

Academic Literacy 191, 240, 242, 244-247, 257-258, 262

Academic Success 16, 34, 59, 102, 104, 111, 114, 117, 120, 122, 127, 130, 133, 136, 243, 265-267, 271-273, 276-279, 283-286, 289-290

Academic Writing 7, 111, 128-129, 131, 133, 177-180, 182-185, 188-192, 194, 196, 198-199, 242, 245-246, 262, 287

Acculturation 2-3, 7, 16, 18, 21-25, 27-52, 54-61, 77, 96-97, 99-100, 104-105, 116, 118, 174, 195, 197, 283, 289, 319

Active Learning 66-67, 80, 98, 224, 226-229, 231, 237-238

Advanced Academic Essay Writing 199

Advanced Academic Writing 177-179, 183-185, 189-190, 199

Alberta 26, 288, 292-294, 296-305, 307

Asian 17, 25-26, 37, 46-47, 57-58, 65-66, 78, 98-100, 108, 116, 118, 166, 177, 180, 184-185, 187, 190-191, 195, 199, 238, 274, 288, 295, 342

Assimilation 29, 34-35, 40, 58

Association of Universities and Colleges Canada 329, 333

Authenticity 33, 137, 139-140, 142-143, 146-150, 152, 154

B

Bakhtin 221-222, 226-231, 233-235, 237-239

Bronfenbrenner's Theory of Human Development 266-267, 270, 272, 286, 290

C

Canada 1-5, 9-14, 16-19, 21, 23-27, 30-31, 34-35, 37-39, 41-42, 45, 47-48, 51-60, 63, 68, 77, 81-82, 84-89, 95-96, 98-100, 102-103, 107, 109-111, 113-118, 120-121, 124-125, 127-130, 133-138, 141-142, 144-147, 149-152, 156-165, 167, 169, 171-182, 184, 187, 189, 191-193, 197-198, 201, 204-218, 221, 238, 241, 246, 255, 257-258, 260-261, 265-270, 272-274, 276, 282-284, 286-290, 292-301, 303-306, 308-331, 333-344

Canadian Bureau for International Education (CBIE) 42, 56, 82, 98, 138, 151, 158, 172, 175, 192, 216-217, 293, 304, 317, 327, 329, 332-333, 341

Canadian Experience Class (CEC) 311, 327

Canadian university 25-26, 38, 41-43, 47-48, 52-53, 66, 76, 79, 82, 85, 99-100, 120, 125, 127, 129-130, 132-133, 136-137, 142-144, 147, 149-150, 153, 157, 195, 198, 217, 258, 328-329, 331, 334, 337-338, 344

Career Programming 315, 318, 321

Case Study 37, 39, 59, 86, 99-100, 117, 123-124, 134-136, 160, 176, 187, 191-194, 259, 265, 296, 300-301, 305, 344

Chinese graduate students 86-87, 96, 99, 120, 122-125, 130, 132-134, 137, 139, 142-144, 147, 149-150, 192, 218, 260

Chinese International Student(s) 37, 39, 41, 46-48, 54, 56-60, 79, 81-85, 96, 99-100, 120-121, 129, 133-138, 142, 147, 149-150, 198

Chinese Students 24-25, 31, 39, 49-50, 52-53, 60, 65-66, 81-86, 89-98, 100, 120-122, 124, 127-135, 141, 150, 153, 168, 193, 196, 198, 242-243, 305

Citizenship and Immigration Canada (CIC) 316, 327

Classroom 4, 17, 23, 29-30, 65-66, 71, 74-77, 79, 81-96, 98-101, 103-105, 107-110, 112-117, 121-122, 127-129, 131-133, 137-143, 146-154, 159, 161, 168, 172, 181-182, 184, 189-191, 222-223, 226, 228, 231, 235-236, 241, 246-247, 289, 320

Classroom Assessment 137-143, 146-151, 153-154

Classroom Participation 81-87, 89-90, 93-98, 100-101, 109, 117

Collaboration 5-6, 15, 32, 225, 228, 234, 240, 245-246, 257, 259, 301-302, 309, 339

Community 3, 5-6, 10-11, 15, 23, 26-27, 31, 33, 36-37, 39, 44-47, 52, 54, 60, 64, 76, 85, 96, 102-104, 107-111, 114, 124, 156-157, 159-160, 165, 167-172, 176, 178, 189, 192-193, 197-198, 217, 221-222, 224-225, 228, 230-232, 234-236, 265-270, 272-277, 281, 284, 286-289, 292, 295-296, 298, 303-304, 307, 320-321, 330, 332, 339

Community Integration 156

Congruence With Planned Learning 137, 139-140, 142-143, 149-150, 154

Connection 13-14, 21-27, 30, 33, 35, 40, 46, 56, 68, 107, 129, 139, 316, 322

Coping Strategies 26, 37, 60, 99, 120-123, 125, 130, 132-134, 136, 318

Core Competencies 177-180, 183, 186-187, 189, 199

Cultural Capital 2, 23, 116, 215, 332, 341, 345

Cultural Difference(s) 24, 29, 45, 65, 81-82, 85, 101, 104, 114, 185, 189, 201, 208, 224, 231, 242-244, 337

Cultural Distance 61

Cultural Identity 3, 16, 23-24, 26-32, 34, 36, 40, 161

Curriculum 4, 27, 55, 57, 59, 78, 101, 103, 112, 115, 139, 150, 159, 171, 176-178, 181-183, 185-188, 190, 192, 202, 214, 219, 222-223, 235, 244-245, 257, 260, 268, 337, 339, 343

D

Daphne Lordly 21

Decision-making 33, 56, 179, 197, 292, 294-296, 298, 304, 309, 317

Deep Learning 67, 80

Dialogism 221-222, 226-229, 233, 235, 239

Dialogue 1-2, 4-5, 7, 12, 14-15, 18, 20, 27, 40, 71, 74, 83, 90, 135, 226-229, 235, 328, 337-338

Dietitian 23, 28, 40

Differential Tuition 32, 328-334, 339, 345

Diversity 2, 8, 16-17, 19, 22, 29, 31, 37, 45, 57-58, 60, 63, 65, 71, 75-77, 98, 101-102, 107-108, 113-116, 118, 137, 139-142, 144, 149-150, 154, 170, 172, 216-217, 228, 235-236, 241, 289, 319-320, 325, 342-343

Domestic Student 52, 65, 118, 253-255, 294

Duoenthongraphy 20

Duoethnography 1-2, 4, 12, 15-16, 18-19

E

Effective Teaching 67-68, 221, 223-224, 229

Employability 16, 78, 201, 309-310, 312-315, 318, 321-323, 325-326, 330, 338

English Proficiency 45, 47-48, 51, 55, 59, 61, 83, 125-126, 143, 145, 147, 149, 164, 195, 243, 245, 248, 252, 343

English Speakers of Other Languages (ESOL) 199

Experience 2, 4, 7-9, 15, 21-31, 33-35, 38, 40-41, 43-44, 46-47, 51, 54-56, 59-61, 65-66, 69-70, 73, 75, 81, 83-84, 86-91, 93, 95-98, 101, 103-111, 113, 115, 117, 125, 135, 139, 142, 145, 148, 153, 157, 160, 162, 165-166, 168-172, 174-176, 181, 186, 190, 199, 201-219, 224-229, 231-233, 235, 237, 241-243, 245, 276, 289-290, 296, 298-299, 302-303, 306, 308-314, 316-319, 321, 324, 327-333, 335-338, 344

Experiential Learning 39, 157, 159-161, 172-174, 176, 339

Express Entry (EE) 327

Extracurricular Activity 176

F

Faculty 3, 6, 9, 16, 27, 31, 35, 39, 42, 54, 75-76, 78, 85, 101-107, 109-118, 124, 132-134, 168, 174, 177, 180-185, 188-190, 193, 198, 213, 215, 222-223, 225, 230, 232, 239, 241-242, 245, 247, 253, 257, 270-271, 273, 276, 279, 292, 296, 309, 312, 316, 335, 337, 339, 342

Familial Milieu 219

Focus Group 69, 160-161, 176, 198

Food 2, 7, 13, 21-31, 33-40, 44-45, 50, 158, 168-169, 202, 326

Food Lab Experience (FLE) 27, 40

Food Security 23, 33, 36, 40

Foreign Student 157, 294, 328-335, 337-340

Formal Learning 28, 156-157, 159, 176

G

graduate education 81, 184, 247

H

Higher Education 2, 15, 19, 22, 35, 39, 41-43, 47, 54-55, 57-58, 60, 77-79, 98, 100, 102, 105, 109, 112, 114-117, 120, 133-138, 147, 149-153, 156-158, 164, 167, 171-175, 177-179, 181, 183-185, 187, 189-198, 200-202, 205, 214, 216-218, 222, 225, 230-231, 233, 237-238, 241-244, 247, 257-262, 266-268, 285, 287-290, 293, 295-296, 302-306, 309, 313, 315, 318-319, 322-325, 327-334, 338, 340-345
Higher Education Commercialization 330-331, 345
Higher Education Commodification 329, 345
Higher Educational Institutions (HEIs) 327
Higher Learning 178, 292-296, 298-299, 302-303, 307
Higher Learning Institutions 178, 302-303, 307
Higher-Education 221

I

Identity 2-6, 11-18, 20-37, 40, 57, 108, 111, 117-118, 156, 161, 173-174, 185-186, 199, 204, 238, 330
IELTS 83, 111, 118, 126
Immigration 18, 35-36, 47, 57, 121, 134, 146, 159, 162-163, 171-174, 179-180, 193, 217, 242, 270, 272-273, 276, 282, 286, 294-295, 302, 308-321, 323, 325-327, 331, 334, 339-340
Informal Learning 103, 116, 156-157, 159-161, 168-169, 171-174, 176
Information Literacy 185, 192, 240, 242-248, 252-262
Institutional Milieu 214, 219
instructor 8, 30, 70, 83-87, 89-91, 93-97, 101, 105, 145-147, 182, 195, 223, 225, 227, 229-231, 233, 238, 273, 297
Integration 2-4, 6, 15, 17, 21-23, 25, 27-28, 30-36, 39-40, 45, 60, 67-68, 96, 100, 110, 114, 153, 171-172, 198, 201, 269, 272, 289, 311, 314, 316, 329, 331, 333, 335-339, 345
Interaction 12, 20, 29, 42, 102-106, 114-115, 117, 123, 130, 182, 189, 196, 226, 228, 233-234, 239, 286, 336-337
Intercultural 1-6, 10-12, 14-15, 17, 19-20, 27, 30-32, 34-40, 44-46, 52, 57-60, 64, 78-79, 98-100, 114, 118, 136, 150, 156, 160, 169-173, 175, 177, 184-186, 188-190, 192-193, 225, 228, 236, 238, 241, 257, 260, 272, 288-289, 312, 332, 337, 340-341, 345
Intercultural Connection 40

Intercultural Groups 177
Intercultural Identity 1, 3-5, 11, 14, 17, 20
Intercultural Socialization 1-2, 4-6, 10, 15, 20
International 1-7, 9-11, 14-19, 21-48, 51, 53-61, 63-65, 67-69, 74-86, 88-91, 94, 96-118, 120-123, 129, 133-138, 142-145, 147, 149-153, 156-178, 180-185, 188-208, 212, 214-219, 221-224, 228-229, 233-236, 238, 240-246, 248, 250, 252-255, 257-262, 265-275, 277-290, 292-345
International Cohort 86, 97, 101, 337-339
International Student 11, 14-15, 18, 21-23, 26-27, 31-32, 35, 41-42, 46, 55-56, 58-61, 63-65, 67, 69, 76, 78-79, 81, 85, 96, 102-103, 105-106, 110-111, 114-116, 118, 122-123, 135-136, 142, 144-145, 149, 152, 156-158, 160-161, 163, 165, 168-169, 172-175, 177, 180-181, 185, 190, 196-198, 200-203, 216-218, 233, 241, 245-246, 257, 268, 271, 273, 278, 287-289, 292-298, 302-304, 306, 308-310, 312-315, 321, 323, 325-326, 333, 336, 342, 345
International Student Mobility 41, 56, 61, 173, 175, 196, 201-202, 217
International Students 1-4, 6-7, 9-10, 15, 17-19, 21-24, 26-27, 29-35, 37-48, 51, 53-61, 63-65, 67-69, 74-76, 78-80, 82-86, 91, 94, 96-105, 107-118, 120-121, 123, 129, 133-138, 142, 144-145, 147, 149-150, 153, 156-184, 188-204, 206-208, 212, 214-219, 222, 229, 234-235, 238, 240-246, 248, 250, 252-255, 257-262, 265-275, 277-290, 292-304, 306-327, 329, 331-338, 340-344
International Turkish Students 200, 202, 214
Internationalization 2, 41, 57-58, 60, 65, 116, 120, 136, 138, 152, 178, 181, 183-185, 193, 241, 260-261, 267-268, 287-290, 293, 308-311, 313, 318-325, 328-329, 331-340, 342-345
internationalization of education 120
Internationalization of Higher Education 60, 136, 138, 178, 241, 268, 288, 323, 342, 345
IRCC 308, 310-312, 316, 327

L

Language 7-8, 12-14, 18-19, 22-23, 25, 27, 29-30, 33, 38, 42, 44-46, 48, 54-57, 59-60, 64-66, 76, 78, 81, 83-86, 89, 92-93, 96-99, 101-102, 104-118, 120-121, 124-131, 133, 136, 143, 146, 148, 151-152, 156, 161, 163-164, 178-179, 183-184, 186-189, 192-198, 201-202, 207-208, 211, 214-215, 217, 219, 221-222, 226, 229, 231-238, 240-244, 246-248, 250, 252, 257, 259, 261, 263, 272, 285, 295, 297, 314, 316, 334-338, 341, 345

Language Barrier(s) 29, 38, 46, 64, 81, 83, 97, 101, 130, 250
Learning 5, 7, 11-13, 17, 21-23, 27-36, 38-45, 47, 54-56, 58, 60, 63-69, 71, 73-81, 84, 88-89, 92, 96-100, 103-104, 106-108, 110-112, 114-117, 121-123, 128-135, 138-154, 156-157, 159-162, 164, 166, 168-169, 171-174, 176, 178, 182-184, 186, 188-190, 192-194, 196-198, 202, 206-208, 218, 221-239, 242-245, 257-262, 278, 286-288, 292-296, 298-299, 302-303, 305, 307-308, 311, 323, 330, 332-333, 335, 337-339, 341-345
Learning Preferences. Learning-Centered 63
Librarian 132, 240, 245-246, 257-258
Library Literacy 240, 262
Life Management Skills 101
Linguistic Distance 61

M

Macro-Level Support Area 290
Marketing Post-Secondary Institutions 292
Master 7, 23, 26-27, 59, 68, 81-82, 86, 100, 116-117, 124, 135-136, 162, 173, 179-180, 182-184, 197-199, 205, 217, 224, 246, 248, 261, 266, 343
Membership 2, 5-6, 10, 15, 20, 109, 266
Mental Health 2, 6, 8-9, 16, 18, 20, 22, 25-26, 32, 37, 42, 47, 55-58, 84, 97, 99, 118, 233, 242, 270, 273, 276, 281, 288-289, 312
Meso-Level Support Area 290
Micro-Aggression 85, 101
Micro-Level Support Area 290
Minority Student Group 200
Motivation to Learn 140-141, 149-150, 154
Mount Saint Vincent University 21-22, 38, 116, 156-158, 173-174
Multicultural Food Learning Activity (MFLA) 40
Multiculturalism 22, 33, 37, 39, 102, 107-108, 213, 241, 320
Multilingual 19, 42, 102-115, 118, 181, 193, 199, 228, 234
Multilingualism 102, 107-108
Musically Enhanced Narrative Inquiry 41, 48, 53, 56, 59

N

National Milieu 202, 216, 219
Neoliberalism 120, 328, 341-343, 345
Non-Native English Speaking (NNES) 328-329, 345
Non-native English Speaking Students 328
Non-STEM Students 64, 66-71, 73-77, 80

O

Ontario 26, 37-38, 48, 68, 86, 102-103, 105, 114, 124, 135, 139, 142, 146, 158, 198, 224, 246, 268, 287-288, 320, 324, 334, 340-341
Oral Academic Presentations (OAPs) 83, 101

P

Pastoral 200, 202-204, 208, 211, 215-216, 219
Perceived Academic Success 265-267, 271-273, 276-279, 283-286, 289-290
Permanent Resident (PR) 327
Personal Milieu 215-216, 219
PGWP 308, 311-312, 316-318, 327
PhD students 1-2, 7, 224, 259
Physical Environment 300, 302, 307
Post-Graduation Work Permit (PGWP) 310, 312, 316-317, 327
Postsecondary 18, 22, 37, 39, 63, 65, 68, 73, 76, 80, 117, 136, 241, 260, 288, 314, 324, 332-333, 345
Post-secondary Education 102, 113, 225, 229, 232, 292-294, 296, 298-299, 303, 305-306, 341
Post-Secondary Institutes 307
Professional Development 6, 198, 221-232, 234-236, 238
Promising Teaching Practices 63-69, 74, 76, 78, 80
Psychological Needs 41, 43, 47
Push-Pull 200, 292, 294-295, 303, 305-307
Push-Pull Factors 200, 292, 294-295, 305
Push-Pull Model 295, 303, 307

R

Receiving 26, 38, 111, 128, 138, 143-144, 192, 201-202, 205, 214, 219, 309, 315, 318-319
Reflective Practice 221, 223, 225, 229-230, 232, 234, 236, 239
Resourcing Ideas 188
Retention of International Students 176, 289, 309, 311, 315, 318

S

Saturation 301, 305-307
Scaffolding 7, 26, 178, 189
Self-Determination Theory 41, 43, 57
Sending Country 219
Sense of Autonomy 41, 50, 54
Sense of Competence 41, 44-45, 51, 54
Six Sector Model 307

Social Engagement 44, 336

Social Experience 200, 203, 211-215, 219

Social support 6, 9, 39, 56, 60, 118, 132, 197, 232, 242, 285-286, 288-289

Sociocultural Adjustment 156, 172

Steady-State 199

STEM 63-78, 80, 210, 289, 338

STEM Students 64, 67, 69-71, 73-75, 77, 80

Student Agency 122-123, 130, 133, 135-136

Student Consultation 137, 139-140, 142-144, 149-150, 154

Student Engagement 28, 33, 75-77, 79-80, 135, 198, 231, 288-290, 333, 339

Student Mobility 41, 56, 58, 61, 136, 173, 175, 185, 189, 196, 201-202, 217

Student Perceptions of Learning 63, 67-68, 80

Student Satisfaction 63-69, 71-72, 75-76, 78-80, 289

Student Transition 217, 331, 339

Students' Perceptions 64-65, 67, 69, 75, 77-78, 80, 103-104, 137-143, 147-148, 150-153, 259-260, 300, 335

Study and stay programs 308, 318

Success 6, 8, 10, 16, 26, 34, 39, 43, 59, 65, 78, 102, 104, 111, 114-115, 117, 120, 122, 127, 130, 133, 136, 138, 171, 181, 184, 189, 197, 243, 253, 265-267, 271-273, 276-279, 283-286, 289-290, 310, 313, 316, 324, 326, 331, 334, 337-339, 342

Support Areas 265-267, 269-273, 276-286, 289

T

Teaching 18, 28, 32, 36, 38, 58, 60, 63-81, 84-86, 88-89, 94, 96-97, 100, 102, 104-109, 111-116, 118, 125, 127, 129-130, 132-134, 136-137, 139, 144, 148, 150-151, 153, 164, 167, 173, 178-181, 183-186, 191-199, 208-209, 222-224, 226-239, 241-242, 260, 262, 267, 273, 287-288, 305, 330, 342

Teaching Assistants 69, 112, 114, 144, 208, 221-224, 233-234, 236

Teaching Dossier(s) 225, 229-230, 232, 234, 236-237, 239

Technology 26, 63, 66, 70, 75, 80, 135, 173, 189-190, 192, 196, 216, 237, 243, 259-261, 266, 286-288, 293, 304, 306, 309

TOEFL 83, 111, 118

Transferrable Skills 161, 172

Transparency 137, 139-140, 142-143, 149-150, 154

U

University 1-3, 5, 8-10, 12, 15-16, 18-19, 21-27, 31-34, 37-48, 51-53, 57-60, 63-64, 66, 68, 74, 76-79, 81-83, 85-86, 88, 91, 98-100, 102-110, 112-122, 124-125, 127, 129-130, 132-133, 135-137, 139, 142-144, 146-147, 149-153, 156-160, 162-163, 166-168, 173-178, 180, 190-191, 193-198, 200, 202, 204-211, 213-215, 217-219, 221-226, 229-233, 235-238, 240-242, 246-248, 252-253, 257-261, 266-267, 286-288, 296, 298, 305-306, 317, 321, 327-342, 344

V

Volunteer 15, 20, 157, 160-161, 167-171

Volunteering 10, 157, 160, 171-172

W

Writing Across the Discipline 199

Writing Challenges 184

Writing Within the Discipline 183, 199

Y

Yue Li 21

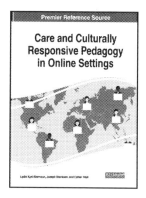
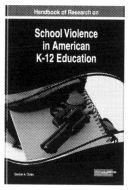

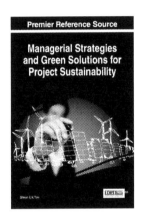

IGI Global Proudly Partners With eContent Pro International

Receive a 25% Discount on all Editorial Services

Editorial Services

IGI Global expects all final manuscripts submitted for publication to be in their final form. This means they must be reviewed, revised, and professionally copy edited prior to their final submission. Not only does this support with accelerating the publication process, but it also ensures that the highest quality scholarly work can be disseminated.

English Language Copy Editing

Let eContent Pro International's expert copy editors perform edits on your manuscript to resolve spelling, punctuaion, grammar, syntax, flow, formatting issues and more.

Scientific and Scholarly Editing

Allow colleagues in your research area to examine the content of your manuscript and provide you with valuable feedback and suggestions before submission.

Figure, Table, Chart & Equation Conversions

Do you have poor quality figures? Do you need visual elements in your manuscript created or converted? A design expert can help!

Translation

Need your documjent translated into English? eContent Pro International's expert translators are fluent in English and more than 40 different languages.

Email: **customerservice@econtentpro.com**   **www.igi-global.com/editorial-service-partners**

Publisher of Peer-Reviewed, Timely, and
Innovative Academic Research Since 1988

IGI Global's Transformative Open Access (OA) Model:
How to Turn Your University Library's Database Acquisitions Into a Source of OA Funding

In response to the OA movement and well in advance of Plan S, IGI Global, early last year, unveiled their OA Fee Waiver (Offset Model) Initiative.

Under this initiative, librarians who invest in IGI Global's InfoSci-Books (5,300+ reference books) and/or InfoSci-Journals (185+ scholarly journals) databases will be able to subsidize their patron's OA article processing charges (APC) when their work is submitted and accepted (after the peer review process) into an IGI Global journal.*

How Does it Work?

1. When a library subscribes or perpetually purchases IGI Global's InfoSci-Databases including InfoSci-Books (5,300+ e-books), InfoSci-Journals (185+ e-journals), and/or their discipline/subject-focused subsets, IGI Global will match the library's investment with a fund of equal value to go toward subsidizing the OA article processing charges (APCs) for their patrons.

   Researchers: Be sure to recommend the InfoSci-Books and InfoSci-Journals to take advantage of this initiative.

2. When a student, faculty, or staff member submits a paper and it is accepted (following the peer review) into one of IGI Global's 185+ scholarly journals, the author will have the option to have their paper published under a traditional publishing model or as OA.

3. When the author chooses to have their paper published under OA, IGI Global will notify them of the OA Fee Waiver (Offset Model) Initiative. If the author decides they would like to take advantage of this initiative, IGI Global will deduct the US$ 1,500 APC from the created fund.

4. This fund will be offered on an annual basis and will renew as the subscription is renewed for each year thereafter. IGI Global will manage the fund and award the APC waivers unless the librarian has a preference as to how the funds should be managed.

Hear From the Experts on This Initiative:

"I'm very happy to have been able to make one of my recent research contributions, 'Visualizing the Social Media Conversations of a National Information Technology Professional Association' featured in the *International Journal of Human Capital and Information Technology Professionals*, freely available along with having access to the valuable resources found within IGI Global's InfoSci-Journals database."

– Prof. Stuart Palmer,
Deakin University, Australia

For More Information, Visit: www.igi-global.com/publish/contributor-resources/open-access or contact IGI Global's Database Team at eresources@igi-global.com.

Printed in the United States
By Bookmasters